THE GOLDEN AGE
OF
PANTOMIME

Joseph Grimaldi to Dan Leno

from THE ERA and other contemporary newspapers

compiled by

JULIA D ATKINSON

Copyright © 2019 Julia D Atkinson

All rights reserved.

ISBN:978-1-9162600-0-9

ISBN-13:1-9162600-0-4

Dedicated to

Berwick Kaler

Veteran pantomime Dame of the Theatre Royal, York

"Me babbies, me bairns!"

ACKNOWLEDGEMENTS

Cover design: Maduranga Sampath of MSN Art Studio.

I would like to thank the British Newspaper Archive for making *The Era*, and many other fascinating vintage newspapers, available online.

The following images are in the public domain in their country of origin and other countries and areas where the copyright term is the author's life plus 100 years or fewer. They are in the public domain in the USA as they were published before 1924:

Joseph Grimaldi by John Cawse (14)
Joseph Grimaldi as Clown (14)
The interior of Sadler's Wells Theatre in 1808 (15)
Grimaldi and a 'vegetable man' (17)
Grimaldi in *Harlequin and Padmanoba* (18)
Melbourn Ellar in *Harlequin and the Swans* (20)
J S Grimaldi (27)
Grimaldi's Farewell to the Stage (32)
Madame Vestris (45)
Sarah Fairbrother (49)
E L Blanchard (64)
Richard Flexmore (67)
Lydia Thompson (70, bottom left cover illustration)
The Aztec Lilliputians (75)
Nelly Power (105)
Jessie, Rosina and Victoria Vokes (121)
Frederick Vokes (124)
Fawdon Vokes (124)
Furneaux Cook (138)
G H Macdermott (142)
Ada Blanche (150)
Katti Lanner (150)
Vesta Tilley in drag (161)
Sarah Lane (175)
Harry Nicholls and Herbert Campbell (179)
Belle Bilton (186)
Marie Lloyd (190)
Little Tich (190)
Dan Leno as Idle Jack (199)
Isa Bowman (202)
Dan Leno and Herbert Campbell (210)
Dan Leno, Johnny Danvers and Herbert Campbell (218)
Dan Leno as Sister Ann (225)
Lord Henry Paget, 5th Marquis of Anglesey (226)
Dan Leno as Mother Goose (229)
The Christmas Pantomime (back cover)

Jack and Jill at Drury Lane (72): Newspaper image © The British Library Board. All rights reserved. With thanks to The British Newspaper Archive.

CONTENTS

Acknowledgements

Introduction

1 – The 1800s: *A Rich Widower of Repulsive Manners*......*13*

2 – The 1810s: *An Enormous Oyster Crossed in Love*......*16*

3 – The 1820s: *A Pair of Indescribables*......*25*

4 – The 1830s: *Terrific Flashes of Blue Ruin*......*36*

5 – The 1840s: *She Lives in a Golden Bowl, and Thinks Herself Handsome*......*48*

6 – The 1850s: *A Pair of Flaming Eyes From the Cupboard*......*61*

7 – The 1860s: *An Ogre of Kleptomaniac Proclivities*......*89*

8 – The 1870s: *A Small Pig in the Soup*......*112*

9 – The 1880s: *Brutally Ill-treating Babies and Old Women*......*147*

10 – The 1890s: *Three Evil Fairies from Liverpool*......*183*

11 – The 1900s: *Frying Pans for Racquets and Potatoes for Balls*......*220*

Index......*235*

About the Author......*241*

INTRODUCTION

PANTOMIME, that quintessentially English form of entertainment, has a surprisingly non-English pedigree. From the late 18th century until approximately a decade after the retirement of the great clown Joseph Grimaldi in 1827, the most important part of any pantomime was the Harlequinade – a madcap whirl of physical comedy and special effects (usually with little or no spoken dialogue) featuring the Italian *commedia dell'arte* characters Harlequin, Columbine, Pantaloon, and Clown. The performers of these roles would have already appeared in the pantomime's opening scene, which typically used a story based on French and German fairy tales, the Arabian Night's Entertainment, English folk tales and nursery rhymes as the basis for a simple plot: the hero and heroine fall in love, the heroine is threatened by her father or guardian with marriage to an unwanted suitor, a supernatural entity in the form of a wizard or evil spirit persecutes the lovers, and a good fairy protects them by transforming the main characters into their Harlequinade equivalents. After a series of trial and tribulations all ends happily, the villains are punished, and a final transformation scene created by increasingly sophisticated stage machinery and scene painting transports the audience to fairyland or some other fantasy world. Gradually the Harlequinade dwindled in importance, pushed into the background as the opening scenes became a showcase for star performers, often recruited from the music hall stage, and the transformation became ever more jaw-droppingly spectacular.

The eighteenth and nineteenth century pantomime was usually the highlight of a double or even triple bill, the first part of which was frequently made almost inaudible by a rowdy audience who were only there to enjoy the panto. Even stranger to modern eyes was the long-standing tradition at Covent Garden and Drury Lane – and some of the minor London theatres – of beginning the Boxing Day performance with a moralising tragedy, usually Nicholas Rowe's *Jane Shore* or George Lillo's *The London Merchant, or the History of George Barnwell*. Pantomimes were also performed at Easter, most notably at York's Theatre Royal, and one-act pantomimes were part of London's theatrical fare throughout the year. It is worth remembering that a visit to the pantomime during this era could involve sitting in an overcrowded, unventilated theatre for well over four hours. No wonder that fights between audience members in the cheapest seats were part of the evening's entertainment...

The reviews in this volume are drawn from newspapers of the day and cover the period between 1806, when Joseph Grimaldi was at the height of his powers, to Dan Leno's final pantomime appearance in 1904. Some of the stories may be unfamiliar to modern audiences but the cross-dressing, topical jokes, comedic catch-phrases, audience participation and special effects (not always going without a hitch on the first night!) will be instantly recognisable. Pantomimes usually opened on or near Boxing Day, but reviews in weekly papers were often not published until at least the first week of the new year – e.g. a production reviewed in 1870 will be found in the 1869 section of this book – and unless otherwise stated they were produced at London theatres.

1
The 1800s
A Rich Widower of Repulsive Manners

1806

Covent Garden
Harlequin and Mother Goose; or, the Golden Egg
AVARO (Mr J Bologna[1], afterwards Pantaloon), the miserly Guardian of Colinette (Miss Searle, afterwards Columbine), breaks a promise he had given Colin (Mr King, afterwards Harlequin), to marry his Ward, in favour of Squire Bugle (Mr Grimaldi[2], afterwards Clown), a rich widower of repulsive manners, as completely disagreeable to the young and sensible Colinette as Colin is, on the contrary, a favourite. The piece opens with preparations for the Squire's marriage with Colinette, which are interrupted by the remonstrances of Colin. During the bustle this occasions, the Beadle and Rustic Parish Officers bring Mother Goose (Mr Simmons) before the Squire as a reputed Witch, and beg she may be punished. The Squire condemns her to the ducking stool. Colin, from the natural humanity of his disposition, opposes the sentence, and warmly espouses the cause of Mother Goose, who escapes from her prosecutors, raises the ghost of the Squire's first wife, and puts an end to the festivity of the intended nuptials. Colin, however, cannot prevail on Avaro to keep his promise, and is giving way to the deepest despair, when Mother Goose, in gratitude for his late interposition in her favour, makes him a present of the Goose so famed in fable for possessing the wonderful ability to lay a Golden Egg every day, with permission to give this curious bird to Avaro in exchange for the hand of Colinette. Avaro receives the Gift with rapture, but instigated by the natural rapacity of his disposition, refuses to give his Ward, unless Colin will consent to open the enchanted animal, in the hope of producing all her wealth at once; Colin refuses, and Colinette entreats for the life of the bird, but Avaro in inexorable; the Squire is again introduced, and about to carry off the lovely prize, when Colin, fearful of losing his betrothed, gives a rash consent to sacrifice the Gift of his Patroness, who indignantly appears, rescues the Bird, and condemns Avaro, Colin, and the Squire to wear the shapes of Pantaloon, Harlequin, and Clown, and wander in mutual contentions for Colinette (who is changed to Columbine), till the Golden Egg, which is cast into the Sea by the Enchantress, shall be again produced by one of the offending parties. The pursuit and alternate passions of the Lady commences and continues through a variety of scenes and situations, interspersed with more than twenty mechanical transformations, which we shall not here anticipate the effect of, by describing. Mother Goose at length relents, commissions a Sea Sprite to restore the Egg, and unites the allianced Lovers in a splendid submarine Pavilion.

Although the story of *Mother Goose* must be pretty familiar to almost every memory, yet we thought proper to give this brief sketch of it, that the leading circumstances out of which such an exuberance of fanciful variety is so happily drawn, may be brought immediately to the recollection. It is scarcely possible to imagine a quicker succession of objects, all differing in appearance, nature, and effect, than this Pantomime exhibits; transformations the most curious and surprising; dances the most ludicrous, grotesque, and graceful; music various and appropriately adapted to almost every scene; scenery and decorations in all their aspects the most beautiful and splendid, more particularly in the first scene, a Village and Sunrise, by Hollogan, and the Entrance into Vauxhall, by Whitmore – every thing combined to render this spectacle the most perfect, in all its accompaniments, in any thing of its kind we have witnessed for some time. Scarcely any of the machinery failed, but all was worked with the greatest ease and dexterity. Bologna and Grimaldi were excellent in Harlequin and Clown; their drollery and feats of dexterity drew down repeated plaudits. […]
Morning Post, 30/12/1806

Joseph Grimaldi by John Cawse

Grimaldi as Clown by George Cruickshank

1809

> ON Thursday night, as Mr Grimaldi, the Clown, was returning from Sadler's Wells to Finchley, he was robbed near Highgate Hill by three footpads, armed with bludgeons, of a £5 Bank note, and other property.
> ***Public Ledger and Daily Advertiser, 19/6/1809***

NEW PANTOMIME
AQUATIC THEATRE, SADLER'S WELLS
Under the Patronage of His Royal Highness, the Duke of CLARENCE.
MONDAY, July 31, and five following Evenings, a Comic Dance, called FUN and PHYSIC. Mr Rees will sing a Comic Song, called "John Bull's Wooden Horses". After which, never before performed, a new Harlequinade, with new Music, Scenery, Dresses, and Decorations, called CASTLES in the AIR, or COLUMBINE COWSLIP. Harlequin Mr Ridgeway, Clown (with Singing) Mr Grimaldi, and Columbine Miss Brown. Scenery – 1. Cottage Farm – 2. Castles in the Air – 3. Harlequin's Chateau – 4. Magic Chamber – 5. Savoy Mountains and Cataract – 6. Ruins of Clifford Castle, Hereford – 7. Twining's Tea Warehouse – 8. Chinese Landscape and Pagoda – 9. Trafalgar House, Strand – 10. Remains of Sudley Castle, Gloucestershire – 11. Gelforth Spouts, Westmoreland – 12. Broad Caricature, or Clown's Ordinary. And (in consequence of the very great curiosity it has excited) the grand Scene of Illuminated Fountains of Real Water, exhibited in the Aquatic Harlequin. In the Pantomime a Grand Glee in honour of the late Lord Nelson. A Burlesque Ghost Duet. To conclude with a *Grand Pas a L'Opera*, by Messrs Grimaldi and Hartland; and Looney's Lamentation for Miss Margery Muggins! to be sung by Mr Grimaldi; also a Quartetto Caricatura, called Cut and Come Again, or the Clown's Ordinary. The Entertainments to conclude with the WILD MAN. The last Scene on Real Water. The whole of the Evening's Performance (Dance excepted) the production of Mr C Dibdin, jun.
   Doors to be opened at Half-past 5, to begin at Half-past 6. Places kept till Half-past 7.
   Boxes 4s. Pit 2s. Gal. 1s. – Places for the Boxes to be taken at the Wells, from 9 to 4. Books of the Songs to be had at the Theatre.
Morning Advertiser, 31/7/1809

The interior of Sadler's Wells Theatre in 1808

NOTES
1 – Joseph 'Jack' Bologna (1775-1846): An Italian-born actor best known for his portrayal of Harlequin, he was also a choreographer and designer of stage machinery. His second wife, dancer Louisa Bristow, was the sister of Joseph Grimaldi's second wife Mary Bristow.
2 – Joseph Grimaldi (1778-1837): The original white-face clown, Grimaldi's acting ability and acrobatic skill made him the greatest pantomime star of his era. He retired in 1823, prematurely aged by years of performing gruelling acrobatic tricks.

2
The 1810s
An Enormous Oyster Crossed in Love

1810

Covent Garden
Harlequin and Asmodeus; or, Cupid on Crutches
WE shall not seriously attempt to analyse the plot of that, which it is not in the powers of human reason to analyse. It may suffice to say, that it was a tissue of pleasantry and absurdity, in which every thing rational was left at an immeasurable distance behind.

It was an annual theatrical sacrifice of Truth and Nature upon the altar of Fiction; but as the sacrifices were merely meant to amuse the tenants of the nursery and the lisping occupants of the boarding-schools, it is not the business of sober criticism to break such butterflies upon the wheels of censure.

The farrago opens with a view of a subterraneous cavern, in which Pillardoc seems to convey a treasure; but this gloom is broken by the interference of Plutus, whose influence is not only felt by Pillardoc, but by every pillager, whether political or civil, within the circle of human agency.

The scene now changes to the study of Pillardoc, who now appears in the character of an alchemyst, where three bottles are exhibited, from one of which the Devil upon two sticks is delivered from confinement, though it is a circumstance of some doubt how a Devil of spirit can be thus incarcerated.

When an engagement hath been duly entered upon between *Le Diable Boiteux* and *Don Cleofas Zumbulo* (afterwards Harlequin), the scene changes to the Prado, by moonlight, where *Don Pedro Alvaro's* house is on fire, and from whence Harlequin rescues *Donna Seraphina* (afterwards Columbine), and from this event, an attachment between the parties arises, and it might be well for human felicity if all attachments could be so well authorised by the course of events.

We are now presented with a view of a Spanish amphitheatre, and a bull-fight, in which two quadrupeds, yclept dogs, eclipse all the other performers.

We then had a view of Cadiz harbour, and then of Shanklin Cline, in the Isle of Wight; then Carisbrook Castle, and then in the bargate of Southampton, where an apothecary lives without practice, which is wonderful, and without knowledge, which is not so.

We had a view of Hanover Square, where Harlequin and Columbine danced a *pas de deux* in the open street, and received so much applause that they repeated the performance with the common consent of the parishioners.

The representation of what they are pleased to call a Spanish Hotel followed this, in which Columbine takes a flying leap to her lover in the interior of a patent lamp.

They presented us then with a view of the Bricklayer's Arms, and a turnpike on the Deptford Road, and, eventually, with a grand launch at Deptford.

We have now a Barber's and Grocer's shop, then a view of Mount Etna, and (as it should be in strict poetical justice) a view of Cupid's Bower, where all the enamoured parties are made happy, and the piece terminates.

This Pantomime is better, generally considered, than they usually are. The incident of boiling the lobster is now too stale for repetition, but the management of the cabbage and its valuable appendages, by Grimaldi, was one of the best tricks that we have seen for many years.

There were but few blunders in this night's performance, which is a compliment to the Machinist; and it was given out for a second representation, amidst the most thundering applause.
Kentish Chronicle, 1/1/1811

1811

Grimaldi and a "vegetable man" in Harlequin and Asmodeus

Lyceum
The White Cat
THE Managers of this Theatre have brought forward a Pantomime called *The White Cat*. It abounds with the particular species of entertainment which is produced by the collision of heads and shins, and the humour of goods and chattels. This mirth of movables, and ingenuity of material substances, is exceedingly diverting. The tricks of the Clown have great novelty, and we think, that with the exception of Grimaldi, he makes more of his faces and the joints of his body than any other performer on the Stage. The Bull in the China Shop, and the Edition of Shakespeare turned into an Elephant, were good contrivances.
Bell's Weekly Messenger, 29/12/1811

Covent Garden
Harlequin and Padmanoba; or, the Golden Fish
FOUNDED on the story of the Golden Fish in the Arabian Tales, the principal novelty in it was the exhibition of a young elephant, bearing the Sultan of Persia from a hunting excursion. As soon as he came on the stage he seemed a little struck with the tumult around him, and on being urged by his driver to come forward, he seemed rather willing to retreat. All efforts, even the application of the goad to his neck, were unavailing to make him stoop for the accommodation of the sovereign of Persia, and he fairly took his Majesty off the stage with him, notwithstanding all that his guards could do to prevent him, who, by the bye, seemed rather shy of encountering such an antagonist.

It would be endless to describe the changes of scenery in this Pantomime, some of which seem the effect of magic; the first is changed by a Genius, from a scene on the side of a river, to one in the celestial regions, twinkling with innumerable stars; and the Comet[1] is seen in all its splendour. After a sheep-shearing, a woolsack is changed, by a touch of Harlequin's wand, into a representation of the Duke of Bedford's statue, in Bloomsbury Square. There is also a good representation of the hoax in Berner's Street[2], with a cry of "room for the Lord Mayor". Grimaldi too has a hit at the Four-in-Hand Club, by rigging a cradle out as a coach; wrapping himself in a couple of blankets for a box-coat, and clapping a wooden trencher on his head for a "bang-up" hat. He was drawn out by a dog harnessed to his vehicle.

Some disapprobation was shown at one part of it; but it was announced for repetition with much applause.
Hampshire Chronicle, 30/12/1811

Grimaldi in Harlequin and Padmanoba

1812

Globe
Harlequin and the Red Dwarf; or, the Adamant Rock
THE Pantomime was called *Harlequin and the Red Dwarf; or, the Adamant Rock*, and is founded on a story in the Three Calendars, in the Arabian Night's Entertainments. In a beautiful scene of a sunset at sea, Prince Cherry's vessel is wrecked on the Rock of Adamant; but a green bird is at hand to assist the Prince (afterwards Harlequin) and instruct him how to gain Princess Fair Star (Columbine), the daughter of the Emperor Longoheadiano. The Prince, with the aid of a magic bow and arrow, speedily dispels the enchantment, and the Princess appears in all the splendour of oriental pomp. He carries her off in a boat to the Emperor, but is refused her hand by the Empress Rondabellyana. This is the most ludicrous scene in the whole pantomime, by the extravagant but whimsical masks worn by the Emperor and Empress, and their respective guards and attendants; the one set being remarkable for their long, and the other for their enormous round faces. Longoheadiano (Norman) is transformed into the pantaloon, and Rondabellyana (Grimaldi) into the clown. The imperial garden is a very beautiful specimen of scenic art. The strictly pantomime part then commences, and the changes run on through Ramsgate Pier, Inn, on the road, the George and Blue Boar, Holborn, the Panharmonicon[3], the Liverpool Museum, the Auction Mart, Bow marketplace, &c, till we come at length to Epping Forest, in which the amusements of the Epping Hunt are to be exhibited.

The stag had been previously led on as an article for Bullocks Museum, covered with large skins, and described as some curious quadruped from Peru, but really to try how that animal felt in his new capacity as an actor previous to the grand business of the hunt; but his performance of the forest scene totally failed, and he disappointed the spectators fully as much as his great forerunner, the elephant, last season. The dogs (said to belong to a certain Baronet, and new County Member) were entirely at fault, and walked about the stage with the most perfect unconcern. We hope that the Managers will take warning from the repeated marks of disapprobation which this exhibition received on Saturday night, and abandon the hideous absurdity on introducing brutes on the stage, for whom nature has done nothing even to render them diverting in such a situation.

One of the changes is the appearance of a little fellow representing Bonaparte, issuing from an Eagle in the Wild Beast Museum, whom the Clown seizes, and pops into the jaws of a tremendous Russian bear, who devours him without ceremony.
London Courier and Evening Gazette, 28/12/1812

Drury Lane
Harlequin and Humpo
HARLEQUIN AND HUMPO is professedly the work of Mr T Dibdin. The pantomime opens with an *expose* of the plot by a fool.

The first display was the procession of the Ambassador of the Dwarfs, to ask in marriage, for the heir apparent, a Princess who had never been permitted to see the day. This procession of little figures, with immense faces and turbans, weighed down with finery, was amusing enough. The interior of the palace, in which the absence of daylight was compensated for by a profusion of tapers and torches, was was extremely showy; the attendants, of course, partook of the character of the place: and all bore some implements which might be termed of "the first necessity" in an establishment, where to let in the sun was to be death to their mistress. Troops of lantern bearers, men capped with enormous extinguishers, dancers with tapers, were not unnatural attendants, and so far the Pantomime had its share of applause; but from this forth, all was dullness and misfortune. The dwarfs wandered backwards and forwards in great innocence and perplexity. The enchantments of the Princess were libels on magic; Harlequin lost the power of his sword; and to all its slaps and citlings [?], the scenery remained inexorable. "Chaos came again"; solid walls walked up and down the stage in the deepest distress – whole houses went astray – pistols and cannons missed fire with "malice prepense"; an antique fountain, spouting volumes of water, pushed its presence into a watchmaker's shop in Cheapside, and stayed there with apparent satisfaction. A plumber's shop, dancing away, was interrupted in the height of its gaiety by a roar from all parts of the theatre, and the whole leaden assemblage of birds and beasts carried off in the arms of the stage servants. Harlequin's customary capers were cut in heaviness of heart; Pantaloon and his friends were kicked in the usual quantity, but even their sufferings and struggles did not tell.

One performer deserved great applause. This was a boy dressed as some savage character. His slight figure was fitted for activity; but his activity absolutely surpassed all that we have ever seen of human distortion. He gave an extraordinary idea of the powers that lie concealed in the human frame. The practice of a few years – for he must still be young – has brought this boy to such command of his limbs, that to walk on his hands or his head, or his back, or his feet, seemed almost equal to him. He ran rapidly round the stage on his hands and feet, with his belly upwards; he bounded from shoulder to shoulder; he sprung from lying flat on the ground with the frightful suppleness of a serpent.

The hissing grew more relentless towards the close; and when the curtain fell, and an attempt was made to give out the pantomime again, the cries of "Off, off," drowned the voice of the delegate upon this occasion.
London Courier and Evening Gazette, 28/12/1812

1813

Covent Garden

Harlequin and the Swans; or, the Bath of Beauty

FEW pantomimes, of late, have even deserved descriptions, except *Mother Goose*, which was made up of a whimsical but intelligible story, and diversified with numerous laughable incidents. *The Bath of Beauty* has rather more of the old character of pantomime than some recent ones; but it is yet a medley, though not a disagreeable one. Harlequin (Bologna), who appears first as a Hermit, receives his magical powers from the Fairy Winifred (Miss Worgman), and is introduced to King Maximo Rotundo (Norman, afterwards Clown), who is distinguished by his obesity, and his courtiers by their noses, as the round bellies and long heads were in the two rival farces of last season. A second Harlequin appears (Ellar)[4], who is commissioned by Glow Glimmer, a fire goblin. After a vast variety of adventures at Bath, Bristol, Cheltenham, Highgate, and London, and many imminent dangers, and ludicrous escapes, in the manner of pantomime, the Hermit Harlequin is finally married to Zoe, the Columbine, through the particular interposition of the Fairy, at the Well of St Winifred.

The tricks and transformations were pretty numerous, and some of them were tolerably amusing. The transforming of the butts, pots, and barrels in the alehouse garden into so many marching soldiers, was a diverting display of Grimaldi's powers. The chopping up of Harlequin in the cauldron, and nailing the separated limbs against the wall, and the restoration of life to the whole body, was very cleverly managed. The performances of the Indian Jugglers were successfully caricatured by Grimaldi appearing to swallow a sword of a most immense size; and his duet with an enormous oyster, supposed to have been "crossed in love", though so ridiculous that it could find its place only in a pantomime, had a certain sort of pleasant absurdity in it, that procured it a good reception.

Some of the scenery is creditable to the artists. In the swan pool, a torrent of real water is introduced which gushes over a painted cascade. The effect would be almost as good without this, which is a much inferior thing to the aquatic exhibition of Sadler's Wells. The view of the Strand Bridge is not well conceived. The scene of the pillar of Europe is showy, and serves to bring forward a procession of both sexes in the military uniforms, and bearing tablets inscribed with the names of the chief heroes, and of the principal battles fought by the European Powers allied against France. This is succeeded by a representation of the Horse Guards, as that edifice was illuminated on the last rejoicings. The whole concludes with the magnificent Temple of Winifred, where Harlequin's wedding takes place, with appropriate dancing and music.
Evening Mail, 29/12/1813

Melbourn Ellar as Harlequin in Harlequin and the Swans

1815

Drury Lane
Harlequin and Fancy; or, the Poet's Last Shilling
THE Author, in the commencement of the plot, accounts for the Theatre having recourse to this species of Entertainment. The ghost of his last shilling appears to him when surrounded by duns, and says that he must give up Tragedy if he means to thrive, and write a Pantomime. And *Fancy* appears, introduces him to *Whim*, who in his turn raise up a strange medley of beasts, birds, &c, to which the stage have of late been so much indebted. *Satire* is indignant at this usurpation, and declares that he will hunt them down, to make room for the display of the genuine Drama. But he is forced to retire, and he tells Whim to

"...enjoy his transient hour,
'Twill quickly pass – then tremble at my power."

    The usual Harlequinade then commences, and is pursued through a variety of laughable incidents, in which the transitions, tricks, and manoeuvres are incessant and most happily imagined. A number of new and well-painted scenes are introduced, and they are generally of scenes familiar to us, such as the Strand Bridge, a Lottery Office, the front of the two Theatres[5], a Masquerade Warehouse, Burlington House, &c. Beside these, the Temple of Dramatic Genius, and the Court of Shakespeare, with which *Satire* regains his triumph, are extremely grand, and do great credit to the respective Artists. The procession of beasts driven by *Satire* from the stage is truly laughable; and the scene after it, representing all our great dramatic poets, had a fine effect. […]
    There are several dances – a Spanish Bolero, a Hornpipe by a child, and a wooden shoe Hornpipe by Pantaloon, which excited much mirth, and was encored. It contains several happy tricks; how to make a man is one of them. The Clown and Pantaloon build up a man of crockery, beginning with his legs and ending with his head, when the figure begins to walk, after which the Clown breaks him in pieces again. The animated pictures in a kitchen are also dextrously contrived, as well as a supper table, which separates and turns into three tables, &c. We have no doubt but that when the scenery, decorations and changes are more perfect than could be looked for on a first exhibition, it will be a popular piece.
Kentish Weekly Post, 29/12/1815

1816

Drury Lane
Harlequin Horner; or, the Christmas Pie
THE first scene opens with a view of the cottage belonging to the family of the Horners; this and the adjacent objects form a most interesting and finely executed landscape. Afterwards there is a view of the inside of the cottage, where a large Christmas pie is served up for the family. An old hag (Miss Tree), who afterwards is transformed into Columbine, comes to implore relief; but is spurned by every body except young Jack Horner (Mr Ridgway). While this is passing a spirit appears in the clouds, surrounded by a brilliant light, representing the sun, descends upon the stage, and, by

supernatural power, turns the old woman into a beautiful young Columbine, Jack Horner into Harlequin, and one of his brothers (Mr Jenkins) into a foppish lover, and the other (Mr May) into a Pantaloon; at the same time a Clown (Mr Paolo) starts up from the midst of the Christmas pie, to the great surprise and delight of the juvenile part of the audience, and then the usual tricks and feats of agility begin.

All these are admirably well executed, and seem to possess a considerable share of meaning, independent of the pleasure with which the various exhibitions of art strike the imagination. One of these excited an uncommon share of surprise and amusement. During a representation of the fair which took place on the river Thames, about three years ago, Harlequin causes the ice to vanish in a moment with a stroke of his wand; he and Columbine get into a boat which appears to sink; immediately after an enormously large fish, moving as if alive, rises up like a balloon, and from its body is suspended a car, in which the two lovers are seated, and they are carried up into the clouds. This exhibition had an admirable effect, and was rapturously applauded.

The following scenes are remarkably well executed: Fair on the Thames, Vauxhall Bridge taken from Cumberland Gardens, New Gas Works, Chemist's Shop, the Admiralty, distant View of London from St James's Park, the British Institution, Interior of ditto, Exterior of a Bazaar, the Hustings in Covent Garden, the Temple Garden, Tumbledown Dick's[6] in the Borough, Country Kitchen. And the concluding scene representing the Temple of Horus and the Garden of the Sun unites an uncommon display of grandeur and brilliancy. The tricks and the metamorphoses, which the lateness of the hour renders it impossible for us to particularize, are for the most part excellent, and on the whole the Pantomime went off with great and deserved *eclat*. [...]
Morning Post, 27/12/1816

Covent Garden
Harlequin and the Sylph of the Oak
[...] IT is founded on the old ballad of *The Blind Beggar of Bethnal Green*, but this of course can only affect the performance in its opening scenes. After the changes take place the customary eccentricities are exhibited, and all traces of the story are lost in the agility of Bologna, and the drollery of Grimaldi.

A good Pantomime should excite laughter and command surprise, and the praise of doing this is certainly due to *Harlequin and the Sylph of the Oak*. [...] Among other pleasantries, Grimaldi is made to take command of a well got up *corps* of giants. They are remarkably well disciplined under his parental care, and become so steady that even the serious accident of their decapitation does not at all put them out of order, and they dress, march, &c, as well with their heads under their arms, as other great men can do with with those appendages to the human frame in the usual situation.

A porter sleeping in a large chair has his seat in a twinkling turned into a large bottle, and he becomes "bottled porter". A milk pail is remarkably prolific, and furnishes in an instant another vessel so like the first, that it is not very easy to distinguish the offspring from the parent pail. A common children's show is converted into Bonaparte's carriage, with its furniture. A telescope becomes an equestrian statue of Lord Wellington; and the bomb in the park[7] rises to be the appropriate record of our triumphs in the Peninsula. To enumerate half of the prodigies of this sort which occur in *Harlequin and the Sylph of the Oak* would fill the remaining columns of our publication, and compel us to pass over two very important personages who last night made their *debut* – a noble Dog, who seems quite enamoured of his profession, and who acted his part, vocal as well as pantomimic, with equal spirit and discretion; and a Monkey from Paris, who dances on the slack rope to admiration. The first mentioned performer was applauded to the skies, and his dying scene was one of the most natural we have ever beheld; the latter was not equally happy, though he is a great curiosity. Some of the personal changes were very good. Harlequin, to elude the vigilance of the Clown, comes on attired as a Turk, with an immense turban on his head. Detected, his head dress falls down, and he in a moment assumes the appearance of an English woman. [...]
Morning Post, 27/12/1816

1817

Drury Lane
Harlequin's Vision; or, the Feast of the Statue
THIS piece has been got up under the direction of Mr Lethbridge, and it affords some evidence of his capability for such compositions. The first scene, which presents a representation of the council chamber of Pluto, was peculiarly brilliant, by far the best, in our opinion, to be found in the piece. It is composed of large arches in the Saxon style, around each of which, as well as up the wings, fire is in motion, and a view of the fiery lake of the infernal regions appears in the rear. Pluto and Proserpine are seated on a throne, with Alecto[8] on the right and Megaera[9] on the left. Pluto summons the Furies; they enter, place themselves on each side of the stage, and sing a chorus. Mercury enters with the Ghost of Don Juan's father, who pleads for his son with Pluto. Pluto promises to forgive Don Juan, but Proserpine at the close of the scene, when the others have made their exit, declares her resolution to assert her empire,

and to have Don Juan as her slave, in despight of Pluto. She employs Mercury as her agent, to excite the vicious propensities and to augment the means of his gratification. Proserpine retires, Mercury waves his caduceus, and a large dark cloud, with fire in motion, rises from below. Mercury ascends in the midst of the fire. The cloud opens, and discovers Don Juan (Mr Hartland) asleep on a couch, with Leporello asleep at his feet. Mercury returns, and touching Don Juan with his caduceus, the latter starts forward, and falling on his knees, vows to love Leonora.

The second scene is occupied with the endeavours of Don Juan to approach Leonora. He kills her father. Elvira is persuaded by Venus, who descends in a car drawn by doves, to assume the garb of Columbine, in order, as the recitation expressed, to save Juan from "dark Proserpine". All the endeavours of Elvira were, however, ineffectual. Don Juan pursues the course, which must be familiar to our readers, from the several shapes his story has been brought forward at the Opera House and the Winter Theatres. But some novelties were introduced on this occasion. Among others, Don Juan was taken in Charon's boat across the River Styx, and instead of being flung into fire upon the stage, he was seized by two Furies, who dragged him, as they threatened, to the domain of Proserpine. This we think an improvement, for the fiery exhibition at all the other representations of this story was certainly not agreeable to good taste. [...]
Morning Chronicle, 27/12/1817

1818

INQUEST – *On Saturday evening an Inquest was taken at the Greyhound, Henrietta Street, Brunswick Square, on the body of Mr W Bristow[10], aged 18 years, of Canton Street, Bloomsbury, whose death was caused by his hanging himself, on Friday morning last. The deceased was brother-in-law to Messrs Bologna and Grimaldi, the Pantomime Performers of Covent Garden Theatre. Mr Page, of Canton Street, Bloomsbury, stated that the deceased was his assistant for three years, for the last two years his health had been much impaired from fits, which frequently attacked him, and in which he remained for a considerable time. On Friday morning the deceased came rather later than usual, and instead of coming into the warehouse he went into the kitchen. The servant went down, and found the door fastened; she gave an alarm, which induced him (witness) to go down, and he called to the deceased, but received no answer. He broke open the door and found the deceased suspended by a piece of cord. He cut him down and sent for a surgeon, who ineffectually tried to bleed him, but life was extinct. He (witness) was of opinion that the symptoms under which the deceased laboured, were greatly increased by deceased's drinking more freely than he formerly did; and was also of opinion that he was in a state of delerium when he committed the act. Verdict – That the deceased destroyed himself, being at the time in a state of temporary derangement.*
Public Ledger and Daily Advertiser, 30/11/1818

Drury Lane
Harlequin and the Dandy Club; or, 1818
THERE is no good broad satire or humour at the expense of that increased and increasing portion of our population, the Dandies, excepting an instance or two where their style of adorning is ridiculed, particularly that of the Dandy-costume of the Clown (Mr Bradbury). [...] Many of the tricks, jokes, changes, &c, were characterized by a bad and gross taste, that was offensive even to our critical friends before alluded to, "the Gods"; such as boring or tapping the Clown in the belly, after taking him out of the water; cutting a Jack-ass in two, each half walking off; a skinned Sheep taken from a Butcher's shop crawling along the stage, &c. The jokes mainly consisted in tripping up, smacking the face, or using the cane or wand across the back. Some of the tricks and changes were well imagined; such as where lighted candles rise up into the sticks after others have been removed by the Clown – where the steps of a ladder drop, leaving the sides, which the Clown converts into stilts, &c. [...]

The pantomime concluded with what its progress would not have led us to expect, "a grand procession of different Nations to the Temple of Peace"; but unhappily this tranquilly disposed ovation took place in the midst of the most terrible and warlike proceedings that we have beheld within the walls of a Theatre since the far-famed O.P. riots[11]. Indeed, "dreadful note of preparation" echoed throughout the House long before the peaceful procession appeared without the Olive Branch; and it was chiefly occasioned by the wild conduct of a M'Naughton, who was seated in one of the dress boxes near the stage. Whether he wanted to make a speech, to criticise the pantomime, or to complain "of the law's delay", we know not; for although he was for a long time "on his legs", using violent action, and still more violent changes of countenance, his performance too was all pantomime. He was hissed and hooted in a terrific manner, but he kept his station; and what was more strange, no officers or persons appeared to remove an individual that thus obnoxiously disturbed the whole House.

But the chief uproar, and the most singular scene of all, was at the end of the Pantomime. Mr Bradbury appeared, and conducted himself as if there were some personal animosity between himself and the Jack in the Box. Mr Bradbury clenched his fist at the unfortunate; then invited him to appear on the stage, to settle the business by single combat, we assume; then "grinned horribly" at the intruder, as if mimicking him; and then turned his back with a good tragic air of contempt upon the Orator, who all the time had busily engaged himself in vociferating and gesticulating to the house. As a sort of garnish to these novel, if not disgraceful, exhibitions, showers of orange peel, divided apples, broken sticks, &c, fell on the poor man, and he in return treated the audience with speechifying, at the same time very forcibly illustrating the oratorical rule that "action, action, action!" is every thing. In the progress of his harangue, he had recourse to a striking illustration of his argument; for imagining that the audience, especially in the pit, wanted intellect not to listen to him quietly, he threw part of the furniture of his own head at them with great vehemence, namely, his hat! […] The orator still persevered in spite of "pelting of the pitiless storms", of the "ear-splitting" yells, and of the rival exhibition on the stage; at length, however, Mr Bradbury retired, but not till he had excited universal regret that he should appear or remain so long on the stage so long after the curtain had dropped.

As the same individual in the box has been guilty of similar conduct in this Theatre, we should imagine that there could not be anything personal in the proceeding; if there were, Mr Bradbury will doubtless adopt means to make it public. But Mc'N persevered for a long time after Mr B had retired, and was greeted with noises and peltings; ultimately he left the box, and then marched up and down Brydges Street, bare-headed, with a crowd hooting at his heels. The House was very full.
Morning Advertiser, 28/12/1818

Covent Garden
Harlequin Munchausen; or, the Fountain of Love
[…] THE piece opens with a view of mountains of snow, with Mount Etna in the distance, the burning lava from which is seen running down the sides, and gradually melting the snow, till a village at the base of the mountain becomes perceptible; the Baron (Mr Simmons) is discovered lying on the ground asleep, and his horse hanging, suspended by the bridle, from the top of the village steeple; he is awoke from his slumber by a chorus of villagers, and releasing his steed from his perilous situation by a shot from his pistol, which divides the bridle, the horse falls to the ground, the Baron mounts him, and rides off in quest of other adventures.

The next scene introduces the audience to the house of Sir Hilario Frosticos, afterwards Pantaloon (Mr Norman), who is about to force his daughter, Columbine (Miss F Dennett), to marry Lord Humpty Dandy, afterwards Clown (Mr Grimaldi). The Baron, however, enters at the window, on horseback, relieves the damsel, and carries her off to the forges of Vulcan, where the lame God is discovered at work forging thunderbolts, and of whom he claims protection for the Lady. Here, however, the Baron proceeding further than he is authorised to do, forces his way into the boudoir of Venus, which is separated from the forges by a brazen door. This freedom enrages the jealous spouse of beautiful goddess, who, however, feels no anger at the intrusion; and to protect the intruder, she, with the help of her son Cupid, transforms Munchausen into Harlequin (Mr Ellar), and sanctions his love for Columbine. At this instant Lord Humpty Dandy and Sir Hilario arrive at the forges, and are by Venus transformed into Clown and Pantaloon.

Here the business of the harlequinade commences, the lovers endeavouring to escape from the father and the Clown, and the latter pursuing them closely; and in the course of this flight and pursuit the parties pass from the earth to the moon, where there is an engagement between the inhabitants of that planet, who carry their heads under their arms, and those of the dog star; the first in defence of the lovers, and the latter siding with their pursuers. From the moon they take a flight to the bottom of the sea, and afterwards escape numerous perils with which they are surrounded in their visits to Constantinople, Dublin, France, a British ship of war, Alexandria, the Pyramids, and lastly, the Fountain of Love, where Hymen, Cupid, and the Graces uniting with Venus in defence of the lovers, their enemies are vanquished, and they are happily united.
Morning Advertiser, 28/12/1818

1819
Drury Lane
Jack and the Bean Stalk; or, Harlequin and the Ogre
THE name tells enough of the story on which it is founded, and gives some idea of the opening scenes. Those which occur before the Ogre makes his appearance, spun out with feeble dialogue, were rather long, and hardly sufficiently relieved by the growth of the Bean Stalk, and the climbing of the representative of Jack's representative (for Miss Povey of course ascends by deputy) to escape the charge of being tedious. But when the real business of the night commenced, all was laughter and tumultuous approbation, and with the exception of one failure, that of a gentleman who played the lower extremities of a cow but indifferently, the whole of the performers were entitled to the highest praise. […]

A patent "Phlebotomizer", which lets the lancet fall like a pole-axe on the patient, is turned into a "Flea-bottomizer" (a Pedagogue with his rod); a "Paramout extractor", which draws teeth with delightful celerity, on a red-hot poker being applied to the sufferer's nose in order to make him recede, manages still to retain its appellation when it becomes a table covered with dice, and other instruments of gaming; and a patent shaving machine, which is to remove the stubble from the chin, by means of steam, when it assumes the form of a Lawyer only becomes a close shaver. One scene, in which a set of tea-things exploded as fireworks, spinning round the table, Pantaloon and the Clown in their chairs all the time they were going off, were prodigiously effective. A good external view of Exeter 'Change is given. The business that takes place in front of it is wound up with a song, which finishes with "Rum to iddity". The two galleries joined in the chorus, and applauded and encored themselves (and Smith incidentally) with admirable grace and modesty. The menagerie is well represented; the wonders it contains are whimsically described; and the final emancipation of the wild beasts from their cages, spreading alarm and confusion among their motley visitors, presented some exquisite groups of Fops and Baboons, and Lionesses and Elephants, with Ladies and their Footmen. A good scene of the New Opening in Piccadilly is given, and the House of the Oilman, that now stands alone, is changed into a correct representation of the County Fire Office.

We have said enough to prove that *Jack and Bean Stalk* is fully competent to charm children from two to six feet high – from two to seventy years old; and with the active Bologna, as Harlequin; the grotesque Southby, as Clown; and the graceful Miss Tree, as Columbine, it cannot fail to have a run.

Morning Post, 28/12/1819

NOTES

1 – The Great Comet of 1811, characterised by its spectacular tail, was at its brightest in the autumn and winter months of the year.

2 – A practical joke perpetrated by Thomas Hook resulted in 54 Berners Street, the home of a Mrs Tottenham, becoming the most famous address in London. Starting at five in the morning on 27th November 1811 and continuing until late that night, the house was besieged by tradesmen, doctors, lawyers, and celebrities including the Lord Mayor of London and the Archbishop of Canterbury, all of whom had been summoned to the house by letters sent by Hook in Mrs Tottenham's name.

3 – A massive mechanical organ capable of imitating other musical instruments and the sound of artillery fire.

4 – Melbourn Ellar: The leading Harlequin of his day.

5 – Between 1737 and 1843 only two London theatres, Covent Garden and Drury Lane, held a royal patent to produce legitimate drama with spoken dialogue. The law was difficult to enforce and widely ignored.

6 – A famous coaching inn in Farnborough, Hampshire. It bore the nickname of Oliver Cromwell's son Richard, who briefly succeeded him.

7 – The Cadiz Memorial, a large cannon abandoned by the French army after the Duke of Wellington's victory at the Battle of Salamanca. The weapon was presented the Spanish government to the Prince Regent and unveiled on his birthday, August 12th 1816. The slang term for such a weapon, a 'bomb' – pronounced 'bum' – was a gift to satirists, given the ample size of the Prince Regent's posterior.

8 – 'Anger', one of the Furies.

9 – 'Jealousy', Alecto's sister.

10 – The brother of Mary Bristow, second wife of Grimaldi, and Louisa Bristow, second wife of Jack Bolgna.

11 – Due to the great expense incurred by the rebuilding of the Covent Garden Theatre, which burned to the ground in 1808, ticket prices were raised. When the new theatre opened on 18th September 1809 rioting broke out during the performance of *Macbeth*, and disorder continued for nine weeks.

3
The 1820s
A Pair of Indescribables

1820

Covent Garden
Harlequin and Friar Bacon; or, the Brazen Head
IT is the legendary and not the true history of the renowned personage whose name is now, not for the first time, united with pantomime, that has supplied the introductory matter on the present occasion. His fame, spread over the Continent, is supposed to have excited the hatred of one Vanderwerst, a German necromancer, who having heard of his formation of a Brazen Head, gifted with universal knowledge, crosses the ocean to destroy his rival and obtain possession of his oracle. All the foresight of the English philosopher is requisite to foil the insidious German. In an unguarded moment – for philosophers are allowed to have their weaknesses – he neglects to attend to the daily responses of his oracle: the charm is broken, the Brazen Head deprived of all its occult and mysterious faculties; and the Spirit that inspired it, to punish the Friar, deprives him of his magic power, and transfers it to Harlequin, transforming certain others of the introductory dramatis personae, who have no claims on that score to notice, into the usual retinue of of the motley hero, Columbine, Lover, Clown, and Pantaloon.

   The pantomimic chase, which is for the recovery of the Brazen Head, then commences with much spirit. As the effect of a pantomime very much depends on the introduction of the reigning follies or extravagant inventions of the day, one of the early scenes is devoted to the ridicule of the rage for quick travelling. A "safety coach" in "five hours from Brighton" is ruined by the competition of a "steam coach" in "one hour"; the passengers, by a sudden explosion, are strewed about the stage, to the infinite diversion of the galleries, whose taste for practical jokes retains its full vigour. The humours of Aldgate Pump, where Grimaldi imbibes gas for water, and suddenly expands to a Falstaff, did not exceed [*sic*] so well; but his incursion into the boudoir of a lady of quality, in the costume of a chimney-sweeper, whose white chairs, toilet, nor even bed, is sacred from his profane touch, renewed the mirth of the upper regions.

   After a few more scenes placed in England, containing little brilliance or novelty, the spectators are suddenly transferred to Wales, and a beautiful view of the scenery surrounding the vale of Llangollen, in the best manner of the Grieves, is enlivened by Welsh peasantry and dancing. Miss E Dennett, who was the Columbine, of course eclipsed the rustics; we have seen her, however, to more advantage in a *pas seul*; the fatigue incident to the character rendered it difficult, perhaps, to give it sufficient energy. The lovers next reach Holyhead, and cross the Channel; and after some very lively scenes among the best we have ever seen in pantomime, exhibiting the eccentricities of an Irish fair, with other peculiarities of the sister island, the search concludes at the Giant's Causeway, where the Brazen Head is recovered and the Friar reinstated in his power.

   The transformations in the pantomime are not numerous; one of the best is the change of the lighthouse at Holyhead into a ship, in which the lovers embark, and cross the channel. It is accompanied with a mechanical contrivance, both new and ingenious, by which the back scene is put in motion, showing a succession of sea views till the vessel anchors in the bay of Dublin.

   Grimaldi, as usual, was the life and spirit of the whole. The dagger soliloquy, from *Macbeth*, given in dumbshow, procured him well-deserved applause. […]
Evening Mail, 27/12/1820

1821

Covent Garden
Harlequin and Mother Bunch; or, the Yellow Dwarf
[…] THE rising of the curtain disclosed a splendid gallery in the Palace of the King of the Gold Mines (Mr Ellar), with his yellow Majesty on the throne of state, surrounded by his Ministers and attendants, and disconsolate for the absence

of intelligence from his beloved Princess Allfair (Miss E Dennett), the daughter of the Queen of Golconda (Mr Barnes), whose hand he has to demand in marriage. At length a message arrives with the consent of the Queen, and urging him to be speedy, in order to prevent her union with the Yellow Dwarf (Mr Grimaldi), to whom she has been promised by Mother Bunch[1]; and his Majesty having bestowed some very uncourteous and forcible tokens of his indignation at the attempts to thwart his royal passion, sallies forth on his nuptial expedition.

The Princess having being inveigled by Mother Bunch to the borders of a sandy desert, where grows an orange tree, enclosing a mystic bower, the residence of the Yellow Dwarf, proceeds to gather some of the fruit from the tree, when she is seized by the Dwarf, who, forcing on to her finger a magic ring with which Mother Bunch has furnished him, thereby becomes master of her person, and carries her into his bower, and from thence to her own chamber in the palace of her mother. Here the King of the Gold Mines appears to demand her hand, and is on the point of being united to her in the nuptial hall, when Mother Bunch enters on her flying car, and prevents it; and the Yellow Dwarf, mounted on a huge tom cat, after a combat with the King, carries off the Princess, and encloses her in a castle of polished steel, whence she is rescued by her royal lover by means of a diamond sword with which Mother Bunch has presented him; but he incautiously throwing the sword on the ground, in the ecstasy of the moment, on beholding his beloved Princess once more, it is seized by the Yellow Dwarf, who is on the point of applying it to the destruction of his rival and reluctant bride at once; when Mother Bunch again interposes, and transforming the King into Harlequin, the Princess Allfair into Columbine, the Queen of Golconda into Pantaloon, the Yellow Dwarf into Clown, and the Captain of the King's bodyguard into a clownish Lackey, attending on Harlequin, condemns them to the customary course of probationary wanderings, and the usual routine of transformations, tricks, and changes of scenery make up the harlequinade; the final union of the content and happy pair being brought about in the palace of the King of the Gold Mines.

A variety of that splendid and beautiful scenery for which this theatre is distinguished was exhibited in the course of the piece; of which the two views of the palace of the King of the Gold Mines, the chamber of the Princess Allfair, the nuptial hall, the castle of polished steel by moonlight, and the garden of the castle, were particularly applauded. Several of the transformations were highly ingenious and diverting; among those particularly noticed were, that of the orange tree into a superb magic bower, which afterwards resumed its original form; a toll-house on Margate Pier into the London *Engineer* steam-packet; a wagon, drawn by two asses, into an elegant carriage with a couple of grey ponies; a barrow of public house pewter-pots into a dinner table, with roast beef and plum-pudding smoking hot; and a basket into a poulterer's stall. One of the most humorous devices of the Clown was the metamorphosis of a bathing tub into a packet-boat, which he contrived with much ingenuity and grotesque effect to rig and provision with a variety of stolen articles, and set sail in her in pursuit of Harlequin.

The performers, Messrs Ellar, Grimaldi senior and junior, Barnes, and Miss E Dennett, acquitted themselves with their accustomed gracefulness, agility, and vivacity. […]
Globe, 27/12/1821

1822

Covent Garden
Harlequin and the Ogress; or, the Sleeping Beauty of the Wood
[…] THE story of the Sleeping Beauty is familiar to almost every juvenile mind. In the present instance but a small portion of the story is preserved, and that portion is only introductory to the Harlequinade.

We are introduced into an Egyptian cavern, where Windlet, Trindlet, and Spindlet are employed, under the direction of the Ogress, in spinning a thread, which being tied round the wrist of the sleeping Princess (an object of jealousy to the Ogress), is to prolong her sleep for another century. The scene then changes to the Enchanted Cedar Grove, where Prince Azoff, and his faithful attendant Abnab, are directed by a fairy sprite unseen, the Fairy Blue Bell, to seek the Princess. The various changes which take place in the form and appearance of the Cedar Grove are beautiful in the extreme, but are totally eclipsed by the succeeding one, which displays to the view of the audience the outside of the Sleeping Beauty's Castle by moonlight. Prince Azoff and his attendants succeed in eluding the vigilance of Grim Grubber, the mischievous guard placed at the entrance of the castle by the Ogress. The Prince and his Squire penetrate to the Chamber of the Sleeping Beauty; the charm is broken, and the Princess awakes. In this scene the artist has exerted his skill most successfully. The ornaments of the room are pink, but in an instant are changed by the aid of the machinist to blue; and that which was an elegant room, containing a splendid bed, becomes in an instant a brilliant audience-chamber, the bed having given place to a magnificent throne.

The Fairy Ogress here appears, and is about to impose new punishments on her victim, but is prevented by the interposition of the more powerful and beneficent sylph Blue Bell, who, to punish the Ogress (Barnes), transforms her into Pantaloon – gives to Grim Gribber (Grimaldi) the form of Clown – bestows on the Prince and Princess (Ellar and Miss Brissak) the characters of Harlequin and Columbine – Abnab (young Grimaldi)[2] becomes Whirligig – and the business of the Harlequinade commences.

All then becomes bustle, confusion, and activity. The scene changes in the twinkling of an eye; one moment the parties are among the pyramids, the next in the harbour of Rosetta; and again, quicker than the wind which blows they are wafted to the happy shores of Britain, and we find them gambolling in front of the Monarch's Palace at Brighton; here Harlequin changes, with a touch of his wand, a fish-stall to a post-chaise and pair, in which himself and mistress are quickly conveyed to London. The Clown, left behind with his patron, Pantaloon, with great ingenuity constructs a carriage out of two velocipedes, a baker's basket, a sign post, and sign board, with various other articles, which fortunately come within his reach, and having completed his vehicle, attaches it to a fish cart, and thus pursues the lovers to London.

A variety of changes follows: Waterloo Bridge, a beautiful scene, changes to Hyde Park and the Statue of Achilles; Achilles and the Park are in an instant changed to Brook Green Fair, the Irish Giant, &c, and these again give way to a most romantic and picturesque representation of a village near London. Pall Mall, the treadmill, Mrs Granger's shop, Piccadilly, and a variety of scenes succeed, till we have Greenwich and the River, as it appeared on the occasion of the Royal Embarkation for Scotland[3], after which is introduced moving panoramic views along the River until the Royal Squadron arrives in Leith Harbour. Upon this portion of the piece the scene-painter has exerted his utmost skill; we are persuaded we are justified in saying the art cannot be carried further; we are imperceptibly carried from meridian day to evening twilight; from twilight to the shade of night. We have then the Moon rising in a cloudless sky; and this succeeded again by the splendour of morning. Gravesend, Sheerness, the Nore, and all the objects along the shore, being represented with the greatest accuracy, and partaking of the character and colouring which the different shades of light prevailing at the time they pass in review before the audience, may be supposed to bestow upon them. The applause which this scene called down was enthusiastic. Harlequin and Columbine are present at the landing of Scotland's royal visitor, and they subsequently experience many changes of fortune, but are subsequently led to happiness by their patroness and protectress, the Fairy Blue Bell, with a splendid view of whose Palace the piece concludes.

The tricks in the piece are numerous, and several of them extremely ingenious, and we never recollect any first night's representation in which the machinery went so free from error. Miss Brissak, who played Columbine, we understand for the first time, performed her task with considerable effect – her figure is, however, too heavy for the heroine of Pantomime.

Public Ledger and Daily Advertiser, 27/12/1822

J S Grimaldi

1823

Drury Lane
Harlequin and the Flying Chest; or, Malek and the Princess Shirine
[…] ON many former occasions we have seen a servant sent on with a broom to clean the stage before the curtain rose, and the gods at Christmas or Easter have never failed to pelt this sweeper so unmercifully that his strength and patience were exhausted before their oranges and apples; and the task has sometimes been very imperfectly performed. Last night, the green baize which had been down for the Tragedy[4] was loosened in the front, and then gradually drawn in

beneath the curtain. This attracted so little notice that the customary compliment from the galleries was omitted altogether.

The title of the new pantomime is Harlequin and the Flying Chest; or, Malek and the Princess Shirine. It is founded by Mr W Barrymore on a Persian tale, and the introductory matter may be gathered from the following epitome of the story:

Lignum Vitae, the great Eastern Machinist, having constructed a Chest that will transport its occupants to any desired place, resigns himself to repose. He is, however, disturbed by the information that the Princess Schirine still pines a solitary prisoner in the Castle of One Hundred Gates, built for her father, the Sultan of Gasua, by the magic arts of the Afrite Niger, who, loving Schirine, had rendered it inaccessible purposely to elude the threat of her Horoscope, that predicted her marriage with a man of ruined fortunes. To thwart these plans, Lignum Vitae directs Malek, the youth designed by the prediction, to enter the Flying Chest, and attempt the liberation of the Princess. The Chest then being stored with various phosphoric and destructive missiles, in case of an encounter, rapidly cleaves the air, and alights on the terrace of the palace, which Malek and his attendant, Querco, enter on the departure of the Sultan and train. Schirine, delighted at the appearance of her lover, is about to escape with him when the alarm is sounded by her Governante, and the Sultan and his Vizier rush in, and bear off the Princess. Malek and Querco enter the Chest, and mount the air, in pursuit of the ravishers, whom they overtake crossing a bridge. Malek, from the Chest, pours down his missiles, which create such confusion that the bridge breaks and precipitates the vanquished into the river. The triumphant Malek then alights, and is bearing away the Princess, when the Afrite Niger appears, and fires the Chest, but Lignum Vitae rising from its centre, extinguishes the flames, and promises the lovers protection.

Niger, causing the Chest to disappear, declares none but its possessor can gain the hand of the Princess; but Lignum Vitae informs them, though hindered by his enemy's spells from disclosing the exact spot of its concealment, he can considerably aid them in their search. He then transforms them into Harlequin and Columbine, whilst Niger changes Sultan and Vizier into Pantaloon and Clown. The usual pantomimical contest then commences, and continues till the Flying Chest being found, the piece terminates with the nuptials of Harlequin and Columbine in the Palace of Zephyr and Flora.

In former years it has so happened that the Pantomimes of this Theatre have been peculiarly unfortunate, and people have sometimes asked "How is it they can never succeed with Pantomime at Drury Lane?" This query will not be in use this season, for Harlequin and the Flying Chest has been eminently and deservedly successful. […] The Flying Chest is a well-managed concern. He must have good eyes who can perceive the means by which it is moved, and while suspended high above the stage, a display of fireworks is given from it. A Cottage is contracted to about a sixteenth of its original size, and subsequently restored to its first dimensions, apparently without any aid but the magic touch. A Stage Coach becomes part of a Lance, and the vehicle thus lost, and in which Pantaloon has taken his seat, is reproduced from a packing case with the important personage thus named looking out of the window. A drum is turned into a very elegant marquee, with seats and a table beneath, and again becomes a drum. Various other changes were effected, which it would be tedious to detail, though it is anything but tedious to witness them.

We cannot do justice to the scenery in the narrow limits which remain to us. The Palace of the Hundred Gates is a most splendid effort; the Boudoir of the Princess is equally superb; and the Bridge scene is good, but the grand triumph of scene-painting is the moving "Diorama". This gives in succession "The quarries at Oreston; the Catwater, and entrance to Hoo; a representation of men of war at anchor in Plymouth Sound; and a general view of Plymouth, with Mount Batten". Nothing could be finer than the effect here introduced. The sombre gloom with which the display begins, though interesting from the first, gives indescribable lustre to the magnificent picture of Plymouth Sound which succeeds, with the exquisite marine paintings which embellish it. No description can do justice to the effect here produced, which called forth the most rapturous acclamation. […]

A great living oddity is presented in one of the scenes. A figure with three heads and six arms appears. Two of the heads and four of the arms, which seem to be the property of a couple of dwarfs, fight the latter figure, which, on raising his head, is immediately knocked down. This is managed by the two arms of a man, being provided each with a head and limbs. The feet are masked to produce the principal or larger figure, which only rises to fall again.

Mr Howell was the Harlequin of the night; Signor Paolo, the Clown; and Mr T Blanchard, the Pantaloon. They all displayed great agility, and the two latter were irresistibly laughable. One of their exploits was to make a roundabout of a ladder, through the spokes of which the head of a third man had been thrust. It went round for some time with great velocity, Paolo been at one end, and Blanchard at the other. They finished by converting it into a seesaw.

A Miss Smith, pupil to Miss Tree, made her first appearance as Columbine. Her dancing was much admired, and she was altogether well received.

Covent Garden
Harlequin and Poor Robin; or, the House that Jack Built

THE tragedy of *Jane Shore* was played, but in what manner, excepting that it was chiefly in dumb show, would puzzle the most acute of critics to pronounce. Previous to the rising of the curtain the jollity of the Gods began to display itself by the usual symptoms of shouting, whistling, fighting, and every kind of uproar. We only observed one novelty in these proceedings. A hat having been thrown into the pit from the gallery, the well known communication was speedily formed, by which such losses are repaired. Instead, however, of being composed of handkerchiefs, it almost wholly consisted of garters. When it reached the bottom, a wicked wag in the pit gave it a sudden jerk, and a weak place was unfortunately discovered near the top. The consequence was that the goddesses occupying the two or three first rows of the gallery were doomed to walk home garterless.

The title of the Pantomime is *Harlequin and Poor Robin*[5]*; or, the House that Jack Built.* The story opens with Jack very busy at building a house which he had to complete upon the following conditions, the same being explained as follows by the author, who has printed and published his work.

By virtue of one of our Forest Charters, if a man do build a dwelling upon common ground, from sunset to sunrise, and inclose a piece of ground, wherein there shall be a tree growing, a beast feeding, a fire kindled, a chimney smoking, and provision in the pot, such dwelling shall be freely held by the builder, any thing herein to the contrary, nevertheless, notwithstanding. – **FOREST LAWS.**

Jack is triumphant, and then demands the hand of Rosebud, the daughter of Gaffer Gander; but a rich squire is preferred as suitor by the old man. The interior of Jack's house is next seen, and the rat comes to eat the malt, is killed by the cat, and puss, in her turn, is worried by the dog – the live dog of Montargis[6]. This part, however, was not well arranged, and should be improved or omitted.

In despair, Jack flies to Poor Robin, the celebrated rival of Francis Moore[7], Physician, to obtain his interest with the stars, &c, in favour of getting him his wife. The hut of Poor Robin commands a most beautifully painted landscape by moonlight, where the Moon makes her way in the Heavens, and passes through an eclipse. Poor Robin takes Jack under his protection, and casts his horoscope. During this operation either Mars or Venus, we cannot precisely say which, had serious fall from the sky down upon the stage, and appeared to lose at least a pint of oil or spirit.

We are next transported to the cottage of Gaffer Gander, and opposite to him lives the "Priest all shaven and shorn", who is thereupon waked by the "cock that crowed in the morn"; and a very gallant sort of strutting Cock it is. There was nothing in the whole Piece at which the audience laughed so heartily. After some difficulty, the Priest makes his appearance, and finding two husbands for one wife, is not long in discovering that the Squire should take precedence of Jack. Poor Robin interferes to forbid the banns, and a general row ensues. Jack has, upon a former occasion, preserved a favourite dove of Venus, and she does him another good turn in his present critical position. Just as Poor Robin has been consigned over to the beadles to be ducked and put in the cage, the whole scene puts on a celestial character of clouds and glory; Iris appears in a magnificent car with her peacocks, and sends little Cupid to put Jack in possession of his bride, and to change the whole set into the characters of Pantomime. Jack and Rosebud (Ellar and Mrs Vedy) are Harlequin and Columbine; the Priest (young Grimaldi) is Clown; and Gaffer and the Squire (Barnes and Ducrow) become Pantaloon and Dandy.

The tricks and bustle which follow in the regular course after this general metamorphose, are for the most part excellent. The first of any note is a scene upon the ice in St James's Park; the stage is covered over with something giving the appearance of ice, and several persons exhibit the new patent skates with great dexterity. There was one in particular who performed some of the most difficult evolutions with a grace and facility we have scarcely ever seen surpassed in the real campaigns of General Frost. An elderly fat Gentleman breaks through, and goes into the water. He is seen struggling at the broken edges for some time, but at last disappears. The officers of the Humane Society being at hand, assistance is afforded, and a most laughable effect is produced by dragging out a figure that distends itself until its altitude is equal to that of the sky.

A series of changes and tricks follows that we have been describing, none of which are particularly remarkable for point, until we come to one of the most admirable and effective ideas that was ever put in practice upon the stage. The chase carries the parties to Vauxhall Gardens, where a balloon is about to start for Paris, and engages to perform the journey in six hours, and to blow steam out of the field. The Clown and Pantaloon take their places, and the ropes are cut; when, to the surprise of the spectators, the balloon appears to be ascending and the house with it, and passing over the country in the direction of the Nore, keeping the river in view as they proceed. The Channel is next seen, with a moonlight view of Calais, and the French coast. The balloon then appears to enter the clouds, and as it subsequently becomes clear of them, the motion is changed to that of descent, and a magnificent view of Paris becomes gradually more distinct until it alights in the garden of the Tuileries. This powerful and astonishing illusion is produced by the scenery moving downwards and upwards, and the admirable manner in which the diminution and increase of the size of objects are preserved by the artist. A file of gendarmerie finding the voyagers arrive without passports, are proceeding to handle them rather roughly, when Harlequin converts the car of the balloon into a steam coach, and they scamper off nearly as fast as they came. There is another very good change from Leadenhall Market to Guildhall with my Lord Mayor's feast. In the midst of the revellers' highest merriment, Gog and Magog[8] descend from their places and scatter the company in dire dismay. The gambols are now soon put to an end by the interference of Robin and Cupid, and the last scene displays the Temple of Iris in a style of magnificence which defies description. [...]

In the acting there was one new feature, which in some respects was a melancholy one. Grimaldi, the Prince of Clowns, was succeeded by his son, in consequence of ill health. A Pantomime without Grimaldi seems only second to *Hamlet* without the Prince of Denmark. Yet the son seemed to feel the honour of his name, and did not let its laurels wither. His limbs and visage seem equally at his command, and there is a great deal of drollery in both; we hope he may acquire the rich comedy of his father by experience. All the other parts were well done by their old representatives, and the efforts of the whole were crowned with complete success.
Morning Post, 27/12/1823

1826

Covent Garden
The Man in the Moon; or, Harlequin Dog Star
[...] THE piece opens with and excellent view, by Stanfield (and which of his views is not excellent?) of Hudson's Bay, with a Dutch whaler bedded in the ice. To this inhospitable region has Speculum Von Dangerfelt (Director of the Joint Stock Travelling Company) been wafted. Dangerfeld (Blanchard) having plenty of time on hand in these dominions of the Ice-King, takes to the study of astronomy, and soon forms an acquaintance with the Man in the Moon, who speedily transports him to the lunarian regions. He there falls in love with the Princess Lunarda, whose espousal with Prince Sirius has already been decided on. A quarrel ensues, which ends by the Man in the Moon transforming Von Dangerfelt into Pantaloon, Greencheese, King of the Moon, and Fromagettina, Queen of the Moon, into a pair of clowns, Prince Sirius into Harlequin (Howell), and the Princess Lunarda (Miss Barnett) into Columbine.

The business then commences, and innumerable are the tricks which the hero of the piebald countenance plays on his pursuers – many of them very clever, and some of them clumsy enough. In the course of the pantomine there are several pleasant hits at some of the prevailing follies of the day. The laxity of the modern boarding-school system is humorously ridiculed in a scene denominated *flirtation*, where the whole of the inmates of a fashionable seminary are, *a la Wakefield*[9], carried away by various officers, civil, military, and naval, to the utter astonishment of the principals, who are themselves ultimately seized upon, the Clown pouncing with ludicrous amorousness upon the most venerable matron of the party. A good laugh is raised at the newly-broached mode of travelling through a cylinder, the air of which has been previously exhausted. The Clown and his friends take their departure for Brighton in the cylinder. They reach their destination almost immediately; but the rapidity of the motion is too powerful for the human frame, and all the passengers are cast into the road broken-limbed. [...]
Evening Mail, 27/12/1826

1827

Drury Lane
Harlequin and Cock Robin; or, the Babes in the Wood
THE first scene disloses "the regions of gloom on the banks of silent waters" (the latter part of the title, by the way, is a misnomer, for the painter has represented his waters as eddying and cascading in all directions, consequently they cannot justly be described as silent). Mr G Smith personates Hypochondria, "Genius of Gloom", and the Genius of Destruction (query – "execution"?) is most appropriately assigned to Mr Sheriff. The last named officer of the fates is denominated Homicide; fortunately, at this gloomy season of the year, he is not accompanied by his kinsman Suicide. However, both he and Hypochondria are provided with a proper number of attendant red devils and blue devils ; the former, Welter, Gore, Clot, and Slaughter – the latter, Croak, Quake, Fidget, and Worrit.

The amiable Genii lay their heads together to destroy Master William and Miss Mary, "the babes", but are opposed in their charitable intents by Innocento, Guardian Genius of Infancy. Sir Roland, "the cruel uncle", to whose guardianship the babes (very surprising babes they are) have been confided by their parents, hires Walter, a carpenter, and Steel, a butcher, to waylay and slaughter the pretty innocents in a wood to which they have betaken themselves for the laudable purpose of gathering blackberries; but the butchers fall out, cast reflections, and subsequently matters of a more solid description, at each other – and the babes, pretty dears, effect their escape from the sword to die (as in the ballad) of starvation. Cock Robin and his assistants now appear with waistcoats as red as those of Bow Street runners, and perform the office of undertakers, covering the children with a leafy tomb, and chanting over their remains the farewell requiem.

The Elysium of Innocence is now opened to our view, and Mr Barnes, who has personated the treacherous guardian, is transformed by the Genius of Infancy into Pantaloon. Walter becomes an active Harlequin in the person of Mr Howell, while Southby and Usher, two frisky clowns, are aided by Miss Ryall, the most graceful of Columbines.

The attractive part of the Pantomime is its scenery. The jokes consist for the most part not in the point or humorous novelty of the tricks, but in the heels of Harlequin, the endurance of Pantaloon, and the roguery of the Clowns. None of the mechanical changes appeared to us to be very new or very striking. There is a hit at gaming houses, but it is clumsy, and several hits at the lawyers, which will scarcely subject their contriver to the dangers of a prosecution for libel. One of the most successful and amusing changes is the somewhat antiquated one of "a house turned out of window", and almost the only point which told with the house was the investiture of a little naked plaster cast of Cupid with a pair of indescribables, under the auspices of the Society for the Suppression of Vice, eastward of Temple Bar. We suppose in the battle of the Geese and Turkeys an allusion to the contest at present carrying on between Greece and the Sublime Porte[10] may have been intended, but it did not appear to be caught by the spectators.
London Courier and Evening Gazette, 27/12/1827

1828

DRURY LANE THEATRE

GRIMALDI sen. had his last theatrical benefit, and made his very last theatrical bow, at this theatre last night. The house was crowded in every part. The entertainments selected for this occasion were – Jonathan in England – a Musical Melange – The Adopted Child – the extravaganza Harlequin Hoax, in which Miss Kelly played Columbine to Mr Harley's Harlequin, and the whole concluded with a "selection of popular scenes from the most approved comic pantomimes". Never was there witnessed such a concatenation of Clowns and Columbines, Harlequins and Pantaloons, as here gathered themselves together to grace the final exit of one who was, for so many years, "the king among 'em all".

He himself performed in only one of the scenes above-mentioned – a barber's shop, from the pantomime called the Magic Fire; in which he played the Clown. To the performance of this part he was led on to the stage, incidentally, by Mr Harley, in the character of Harlequin, in Harlequin Hoax, and he was received with shouts of applause. He was much affected; but, though evidently labouring under great bodily infirmity, he bore up stiffly against it, and went through the scene with so much humour, that the audience laughed as lustily as of old; and they were so delighted with that funny song of his about blue ruin and hot codlings, that there was a very general call for its repetition. He was too much exhausted to obey this call immediately, and eventually he was allowed to retire without repeating it. The other performances then went on, and at their close, he came forward, "divested of his motley", and, "in good set terms", he very feelingly delivered himself thus:

"Ladies and Gentlemen, I appear before you for the last time. I need not assure you of the sad regret with which I say it; but sickness and infirmity have come upon me, and I can no longer wear the motley. Four years ago I jumped my last jump, filch'd my last custard, and ate my last sausage. I cannot describe the pleasure I felt on once more assuming my cap and bells tonight – that dress in which I have so often been made happy in your applause, and as I stripped them off, I fancied that they seemed to cleave to me. I am not so rich a man as I was when I was basking in your favour formerly, for then I had always a fowl in one pocket, and sauce for it in the other. (Laughter and applause.) I thank you for the benevolence which has brought you here, to assist your old and faithful servant in his premature decline. Eight-and-forty years have not yet passed over my head, and I am sinking fast. I now stand worse on my legs than I used to do on my head. (A laugh.) But I suppose I am paying the penalty of the course I pursued all my life; my desire and anxiety to merit your favour has excited me to more exertion than my constitution would bear, and, like vaulting ambition, I have overleap'd myself. Ladies and gentlemen, I must hasten to bid you farewell; but the pain I feel in doing so is assuaged by seeing before me a disproof of the old adage, that favourites have no friends. Ladies and gentlemen, may you and yours ever enjoy the blessing of health is the fervent prayer of Joseph Grimaldi; farewell, farewell." (Here the audience rose and cheered him loudly, with waving of hats, &c.) "Farewell," he continued, "God bless you!"

His son and Mr Harley then advanced, and led him off the stage, from which, we may verily affirm, he retired with "all the honours".
London Evening Standard, 28/6/1828

Grimaldi's Farewell to the Stage by George Cruickshank

Covent Garden
Harlequin and Little Red Riding Hood; or, the Wizard and the Wolf

[…] THE first scene represents the Wizard's cave; a kind of Freischutzian[11] incantation takes place; a son of the Wizard, who is represented by Mr J E Parsloe, is desirous of obtaining the hand of Rose (Miss Egan); he takes the form of a wolf – a strange form, by-the-bye, to obtain favour in a fair lady's eyes – but no matter, it aids the story, and that ought to suffice – pursues her to her grandmother's cottage; but by the kind interference of the Genius of the Rose is prevented from swallowing her up; which, to complete the story, ought certainly to be done. To make a Harlequin for our heroine, it may be as well to mention that a certain Miller has an obstinate apprentice, who, as all dutiful apprentices should, most gloriously belabours his master. In due course of time the usual transformation takes place – the Miller to Pantaloon (Blanchard); the Old Grandmother to Clown (J S Grimaldi); the Miller's apprentice, Harlequin (Ellar); the Wizard's son, Humpo (Parsloe), to Lover, and a nondescript lover he was; Rose to Columbine (Miss Egan).

The pantomime business business then commences, and what it lacks in humour (for we lament to say that the agility, which we confess young Grimaldi possesses, is but a sorry makeshift for the drollery we were wont to see in his father) is made up for in the beauty of the scenery, and the ingenuity of many of the tricks, which worked well, considering it was the first night. There was, we believe, but one that went wrong, and that was where Harlequin is fired from a mortar, and is seen directly in the highest box immediately over the stage – he is afterwards supposed to be over the chandelier – a figure representing him is placed there, but not being taken away in time, he appears at the opposite side of the house at the same time; but it was a trifling mistake, and passed off without any disapprobation. The change of a French diligence (the driver of which is deprived of his boots by the Clown, who caused a hearty laugh by pulling out the wrinkles, when they appeared to measure about seven feet in length) into a steam boat, admirably managed, caused great amusement. A dead hare is converted into a living cat; a guinea fowl into a living grunter whose chief aim seemed to be to make his escape as quick as possible. A variety of other amusing tricks too numerous for detail were highly relished. A most faithful and highly interesting view was given of the opening of St Katherine's Docks, and those who did not obtain a sight of that pleasing spectacle may have their curiosity gratified by seeing this picture. In one of the scenes an attempt was made to ridicule the March of Intellect by introducing the scene of a school, wherein age is to be taught by youth – the young ones flogging the old ones – it struck us as a good idea, but it did not seem to take. Roberts's Moving Panorama of the Grand Russian Army's march from St Petersburg to Constantinople is alone worth going to see the Pantomime for. […]

The audience, considering the season, was most respectable, and to their immortal honour, be it said, the gods had only one fight among them all!!!

Adelphi
Harlequin and the Magic Marrow-bone; or, Taffy was a Welshman
[…] THE story upon which the Pantomime is founded is well known in the nursery among children, though it rather conveys a national failing to which the descendants of St David are no more prone than the descendants of St George; but, however, as it is necessary an audience must have something to laugh at, the simple legend was considered by the Compiler as good stuff to work upon.

We are introduced to the cottage of Grumbo ap Goatsbeard, ap Growley, ap Griffin, afterwards Pantaloon (Mr Sanders) when Llewellyn ap Looby, afterwards Clown (Signor Paolo) comes a-wooing to Taffline, daughter of Grumbo, afterwards Columbine (Miss Barnett), and in his hand he brings a leg of beef as a present to the father, and is received with much favour by him. Shortly afterwards Taffy, afterwards Harlequin (Mr C J Smith) is seen coming over the mountains with a troop of goat-men, alias men mounted on goats, properly caparisoned; and when he arrives at the cottage he orders his troops to storm it, and after a combat, he captures the leg of beef. Pursuit is made after the robber, but he is not at home; in fact, he is gone by command of Goldenray, Sylph of the Sun (Mlle Angelina) to steal a marrow-bone, which if he accomplishes, she promises him wealth and honour. He accordingly sets out, but is encountered by a Cerberus with four eyes and two heads, who guards the bone. He however succeeds in cutting off the head of the trusty guardian, and seizes the bone, which he carries off with triumph. The officers are sent after him, and finding him and his party asleep at Taffy's abode in the blue bog, they recapture the bone and beat it about his head. Goldenray however comes to settle the dispute, and turns the parties into the pantomime characters; and thus the play begins.

The Pantomime is full of bustle and variety, and the tricks and changes are good. The scenery is also excellent. The sunlight saloon of Goldenray is beautifully painted. Among the tricks and changes may be noticed the Royal March of Intellect Institution, in which Professor Brickbat cuts a very prominent figure. Among the candidates for admission as students are a small Sweep with his bag, whom the Clown attacks, and tells him to knock at the door; he knocks, and the Professor comes out bowing; the Sweep says, "I want to learn Greek." The Professor, profoundly bowing, ushers him in. Several others, a Cobbler and a Butcher, equally anxious to be perfected in the classics, present themselves, and are received with similar respect. At length Harlequin, by his magic wand, changes the Institution into a Lunatic Hospital. This, perhaps, was one of the most pointed changes and allusions in the Pantomime.

The Clown gets a harp, and plays and sings "I'd be a butterfly", when Harlequin comes behind and touches him, when a pair of butterfly's wings sprout from his back, and Pantaloon gets an amazingly large hat to catch him under it, as is commonly done by boys – he is caught, but contrives unseen to get away, that is, through the trap-door, and comes in by the side scene, just as Pantaloon is going, as he thinks, to take him from under the hat, and exclaims, "I won't be catched". […]

The overture was composed of Welsh airs, "Ar hyd y Nos", "Of a noble race was Shenkin", &c, and the music which accompanied the action was pleasing.
Public Ledger and Daily Advertiser, 27/12/1828

1829

Drury Lane
Jack in the Box; or, Harlequin and the Princess of the Hidden Island
[…] THE pantomime opens with a view of "The enchanted Grove and Goblins's abode", beautifully painted by Stanfield. Here Peep-ho (Mr Barnes), an enchantress, and the guardian of the adamant box, holds Jack (Mr Richardson) in custody. Jack's crime is that he, having too flippant a tongue, has blabbed the secret of the existence of a "hidden island", where a Princess suffers incarceration, which Princess the destinies have decreed is to be delivered from thralldom by a Chinese knight, assisted by his squire. Heigh-ho (Howell), the Chinese Knight, and Rum-go (J S

Grimaldi), the squire, are represented in "A fairy vision of the Hidden Island" (the excellent work of Stanfield), releasing the imprisoned princess.

They afterwards appear, and realise the vision; Heigh-ho cutting off the hand of Ho-fum, the giant's genius, whose spells have been exerted against Luciana (Miss Ryal), the queen of the Hidden Island. The gigantic figures of Ho-fum, and of his queen Hi-fum, are managed with great skill. Each of them beats Louis, the French giant[12], by a couple of feet; and their grotesque motions caused universal laughter. Their demeanour at a splendid banquet was no less amusing; but here, the Ogre King having taken somewhat too much *aqua vitae*, is placed at the mercy of the cunning Chinese Knight, who fails not to avail himself of the opportunity of securing success to his enterprise. We next behold the adamant box, which encloses Jack, placed near the crater of a burning mountain, and guarded by the enchantress Peep-ho. She, like some of our old watchmen, falls asleep, and is surprised by the Chinese Knight, who seizes her magic wand, and, striking the box with it, Jack is once more restored to liberty. Jack, in return for his deliverance, declares that the knight and the princess shall be united; but, ere that happy event, it is necessary that they should undergo all the trials to which Harlequin and Columbine are usually exposed. [...]

The drama was greatly applauded, and was justly encored. The comic *pas de deux*, by Chikini and Wieland, in the character of the Siamese Youths[13], deserves much praise; it was full of whimsical variety. The scene which follows, where the fishes of "the vasty deep" – crabs and dabs, lobsters and crayfish, turbot and plaice, with a long *et cetera* of piscatory characters – amused themselves with a quadrille, excited much laughter. These scaly travellers were inimitably dressed; a Billingsgate committee could have added nothing to their appearance. The extraordinary activity of the phenomenon, Mynher Von Kleshnig, excited universal astonishment. He appears as a monkey; and in truth his wonderful suppleness of limb and pliancy of body would do honour to any of the simian genus. His limbs appear to be as much under his command as the thoughts of other men are nat theirs. Should he be obliged to emigrate to any of our colonies where monkeys abound, he will be sure, if he succeed not in his ordinary pursuits, to find abundance of hairy friends in the woods. [...]

Covent Garden
Harlequin and Cock Robin; or, Vulcan and Venus
[...] THE story of the pantomime is soon told. Cuddie, a rustic swain, who dwells in the "village of Robin's Nest", is enamoured of Sally, a pretty milkmaid, "whose heart," as Mr Farley prettily says in his official programme of the performance, "Cupid's dart has caused to beat with equal passion" for her faithful admirer and fellow villager. Both are (the gods know why) under the protection of Venus, a sufficient reason for Vulcan, who is bent upon thwarting his wife, becoming their open enemy. Accordingly, the divine blacksmith opposes the union of the lovers; and, to spite them further, resolves upon having Cock Robin, their favourite bird, assassinated. He raises up two rivals to Cuddie: Clout, a mortal professor of the deity's own trade, and Hobnail, his apprentice in the veterinary art: the latter of these being transformed into a sparrow, and provided with a bow and arrow of Cyclopean manufacture, sallies forth to shoot the scarlet-vested bird, and accomplishes his wicked object. Immediately all the inhabitants of the village of Robin's Nest are in uproar, and go into mourning for the deceased, to whose remains the rites of Christian sepulture are paid in the manner so pathetically described in the ballad. Through the instrumentality of Aesop the murderer is discovered, taken into custody, and brought before a court or parliament of birds, over which the Owl presides with the most exemplary judicial gravity. After an impartial trial the Sparrow is condemned to die by the hands of the common hangman. As the sentence of the court is about to be carried into effect, Vulcan rises from his sooty forge for the purpose of protecting the culprit, and Venus descends from her sphere with a contrary intention. After some sharp matrimonial sparring, in which the lady manages to have the last word, Venus transforms Cuddie and Sally into Harlequin (Mr Ellar) and Columbine (Miss Egan), and Clout and the Sparrow (alias Hobnail) become, by desire of Venus, Pantaloon (Mr F Sutton) and Clown (Mr Paolo). [...]

The tricks and transformations can boast of little novelty, and there is not much in them to excite admiration or surprise even amongst the most juvenile of the spectators. One of the best incidents is where the Clown is blown, by an explosion of gunpowder, from a sort of seat in front of "the Spread Eagle" into the wall of the public house, from which he hangs head downwards, at the imminent peril of his neck, to the great joy and astonishment of all the bibs and tuckers in the dress-boxes. Few things are of greater importance to a pantomime than the introduction of smart and sagacious touches at passing topics and events. *Harlequin and Cock Robin* is deficient in this respect – its hits at the times are neither very numerous nor very pungent. There is a transformation of watchmen into constables of the new police[14] – an omnibus – a slight allusion to cheap gin – the Fire King; and these are all, or nearly so. The best piece of mechanism is the star of Venus, but the idea is a century old, and the drollest is the gigantic spider which troubles the repose of the Clown in St Martin's watch-house. In addition to these, we have an elephant that gets drunk upon rum-punch, and then drinks the Thames dry; and a scene of a picture gallery, in which the figures and objects are all in motion.

A great deal of the scenery is unquestionably excellent. "The village of Robin's Nest" is a beautiful snow scene by Grieve; the houses and country appear covered with hoar frost, the trees are laden with icicles, and the water wears its glassy and glistening covering in a way to mimic nature. […] There is some exquisite painting in Robert's diorama of the Polar expedition. It comprehends a succession of paintings, representing the progress of the *Hecla* and *Fury*, in the attempt made by Captain Parry to discover a north-west passage; and some of the most striking scenes in the voyage are portrayed with considerable spirit, and far as we have the means of judging, with fidelity. [...]

Surrey
A Apple Pie; or, Harlequin Alphabet
[…] IT is, in part, founded upon the well-known nursery story of "A was an apple pie, B bit it," &c; a subject not unaptly chosen, considering for whose amusement the pantomime is chiefly introduced at this season. Upon this foundation is raised a regular dramatic plot, in which we have an account of the contest of Prince Sugar-plum, Knight of the Alphabet A, with the Baron of Barley-sugar, Knight of the Alphabet B, for the hand of the beautiful Princess Peppermint-drop, daughter of the Great King of the Island of Sugar-candy. The Prince had prepared, as a nuptial present for his intended bride, an apple pie of almost mountainous dimensions, on which nearly all the cooks of the country had been employed. The Baron seeing the fearful odds which such a gift would raise in favour of his rival, invokes the aid of the members of the alphabet B, whom he arms with huge knives, and they sally forth to demolish the pie. A battle ensues, in which the King and Prince are defeated, and the Baron is about to bear off his fair prize, when the pie opens, a good fairy appears and changes the parties into the usual Pantomimic characters, predicting that after many hardships and escapes, their wanderings should terminate happily in the union of the Prince and Princess in the Palace of Golden Pippins.

It may perhaps be objected by the grown-up lovers of pantomime that this personification of so many nursery dainties is too puerile for their mature years, but it should be observed that the names are likely to be very attractive to the juvenile visitors, and that in its scenery, machinery, tricks, and decorations – in short, in every thing but the names, it is a full-grown pantomime, and as much adapted for grown-up children as any in its class. [...]
London Evening Standard, 28/12/1829

NOTES
1 – In Elizabethan chapbooks Mother Bunch was a fictional inn and brothel keeper associated with bawdy stories and jokes. By the eighteenth century she had evolved into a grandmotherly teller of fairy tales.
2 – J S Grimaldi (1802-1832): The great clown's only son, who enjoyed a brief but moderately successful career in pantomime.
3 – King George IV visited Scotland in August 1822, the first reigning monarch to do so since Charles I in 1633.
4 – *Jane Shore* by Nicholas Rowe.
5 – *Poor Robin's Almanac,* published between 1662 and 1776, was a series of satirical pamphlets.
6 – *The Dog of Montargis, or Murder in the Wood*, was a popular melodrama which existed in many versions during the nineteenth century. The plot tells how a murdered man's dog helps to track down his master's killer.
7 – Francis Moor, the original author and publisher of *Old Moor's Almanac* (still published today).
8 – The legendary giant guardians of London whose statues stand in the Guildhall.
9 – On 7th March 1827 Edward Gibbon Wakefield abducted fifteen-year-old heiress Ellen Turner from her boarding school in Liverpool and married her at Gretna Green.
10 – The central government of the Ottoman Empire.
11 – In the style of Carl Maria von Weber's popular opera *Der Freischütz.*
12 – Louis Frenz, known as 'Monsieur Louis', stood 7' 4'' tall.
13 – Chang and Eng Bunker (1811-1874): Conjoined twins born in Siam but of Chinese ancestry.
14 – Sir Robert Peel founded the Metropolitan Police Service in 1829.

4
The 1830s
Terrific Flashes of Blue Ruin

1830

Adelphi
Grimalkin the Great: or, Harlequin and the King of the Cats
HOWEVER prevalent may be the feeling that the size of the large theatres prevents the intellectual enjoyment of tragedy and comedy, their spacious area and magnificent decorations are in themselves a superb sight, and they add to the enjoyment of operas, whilst they soften the extravagance of melodrama, and are almost indispensable to the effect of pantomimes. In a small theatre, the pasteboard face, the stuffed limbs, the pretense fall, the shambling gait, and mincing steps of pantomime are too palpable to admit of delusions, whilst the tricks are anticipated, and the machinery of the changes is detected. Pantomime, therefore, labours under great disadvantages in a small theatre, but these, like the inherent defects of French tragedy, quicken the invention of the authors and stimulates the exertions of those who have to perform. It is for this reason probably that the Adelphi theatre has, on several occasions, produced pantomimes more full of satire and humour than those brought out by its larger rivals. [...]

The scene opens with a view of a great mousetrap-maker's house, with a conspiracy of the cats to destroy his traps or machinery, because they put them out of employ. Next, Grimalkin, the King of the Cats, offers his daughter in marriage to whoever will cure him of his blindness, and when the successful doctor converts his closed eyes to two most respectable green goggles, he refuses him the reward, declaring that as a King he is absolute and omnipotent, and he asks what is equivalent to "May I not do as I like with my own?" A fairy, however, is the radical reformer who converts Grimalkin, the rat-catcher, the eye-curer, and Grimalkin's daughter to Columbine, Harlequin, the Clown, and Pantaloon, after which they go through the usual scenes of pantomimes, until magic closes the story with the union of Harlequin and Columbine. [...] The biped cats, or Lords in waiting, Ladies of Honour, and Grooms of the Chamber of Grimalkin's Court, showed much of humour in their feline faces. There was a good change of a barrel of oysters into a bowl of punch with drinking glasses, and a good figure of a fat woman without a head, with another made up of musical instruments, and one composed of pots and pans, all three being locomotive, if not animate. We cannot, however, cite the pantomime as one of the most successful of its class.

Covent Garden
Harlequin Pat and Harlequin Bat; or, the Giant's Causeway
[...] WE are hardly able to tell of what the story of this pantomime consists. There used to be a laudable custom of printing little books, containing a kind of shadowy outline of the business of pantomime, by which one was enable sometimes to guess at the "no-meaning" of the performance. This practice has been disused, and the orange women and ourselves are losers by the omission. In the absence, then, of these useful manuals, all that we can tell of the plot of the pantomime is, that it relates to the troubled woes of the renowned Brian Boroimhe, and of his squire, Rhadamisthus O'Mullingar (Mr Power), for Norah and Kathleen, the first of whom is abducted, according to the manner of Ireland, by O'Riork, King of Ulster, and the latter is assailed by an unworthy bag-piper, one Mr McDrone. With the assistance of St Patrick and of the cudgel of O'Mullingar, and of the spells of the Queen of the Fairies, the faithful lovers are preserved from the persecution of their foes, and to reward them for their virtues, O'Mullingar is transformed to Harlequin, his Kathleen (Miss Johnstone) to Columbine, O'Riork (Mr Paolo) to Pantaloon, and the Piper to Clown. [...]

There was not much novelty, nor more ingenuity, in the tricks and transformations, and with the exception of the Pantaloon's body being perforated by a red-hot poker, and his back rubbed with cabbage-leaves, after which he declares he never felt so well in his life before, we do not remember any allusion to the flying follies of the day. [...]
Windsor and Eton Express, 1/1/1831

1831

THE PANTOMIMES

IT is agreed that the Pantomimes are not what they were. The story with which they used to set out, and which formed merely a brief excuse for putting the Harlequinade in motion, now forms a considerable part of the performance; an innovation which we should hail with pleasure, if it were always in good taste, but which is rarely apt to be so, and is followed by a set of tricks and transformations equally stinted and wanting in fancy, and a total departure from the old and genuine Harlequin plot, which consisted in the runaway vivacities of a couple of lovers full of youth and spirits, the eternal hobbling after them of the decrepit Pantaloon, and the broad gluttony, selfishness, and mischief of his servant the Clown, all tending to one point. The Clown retains some of his character still, but the rest has become a mere mass of gratuitous absurdity without object. There is no real action going on. Columbine takes her rest; Harlequin dances at his leisure; the parties, instead of pursuing one another, often join in a mysterious truce; and Pantaloon has become as active as Harlequin, and without any shadow of pretence for not overtaking him. The Clown talks too much, without saying much to the purpose. He does not enter into the true humour of the Clown, which is to be merely sensual and selfish in ordinary, and never to speak, except at some rich and rare interval, when an overwhelming sensation forces the words out of his mouth; better if one word, or a monosyllable. When Grimaldi used to say, "Don't!" to some fellow putting him to a horrible torture; or "Nice!" when eating gingerbread; or "Nice moon!" after sentimentally contemplating the moonlight, the necessity with which he was delivered of his exclamation was made apparent, and contained a world of concentration. Now the sayings are old and iterated, and the occasions gratuitous. [...]

Windsor and Eton Express, 31/12/1831

Drury Lane
Harlequin and Tom Thumb; or, the Seven League Boots

A GOOD subject – a subject of great capabilities, utterly spoiled in the handling. The Ogre is not in the least like an Ogre: his legs are not a quarter big enough, and there is nothing Ogreish in his countenance. Then, as the *Chronicle* critic justly remarks, how preposterously absurd, and out of all keeping – to roast oxen on his spit, when it's known to all the world that his diet was men, princesses, and children! The *Chronicle* is quite right in saying that there should have been a brace of travellers roasting, and a dozen children doing like larks upon one spit. We beg to say that pantomimes are at an end if any compassion or regard for the humanities enters into the head of the author. The genius of pantomime consists in every sort of outrage, robbery, murder, assault, and battery. Why is there no Ogress? There should be one – there is one in the history, and it is shameful to part man and wife, and to defraud the public of the better half of its Ogre. The little Ogres are passably well done; but why have we not the satisfaction of seeing their throats cut – why is it done in a corner? Time was, when we have seen the Clown draw up a whole regiment, and at the word "Dress!" cut off all their heads at one slice of a sabre twenty feet long; and now we can't see the decapitation of seven little Ogres! This is hard. Niggardly management! Penny wise and pound foolish policy! They spend all their money, which should be laid out in slicing off heads and roasting princes and princesses, in pictures, forsooth! A Diorama! What business has a Diorama in a pantomime? [...]

The Examiner, 1/1/1832

1832

FATAL AND MELANCHOLY ACCIDENT AT THE PAVILION THEATRE[1]

ON Wednesday night, shortly after the doors of the gallery were opened, or rather forced open, it was discovered that a youth, of 14 years of age, was trampled to death. An alarm was immediately given, and Thompson and Morgan, the officers in attendance, hastened to the gallery, and carried the youth to the shop of Mr Nicholls, a surgeon in the neighbourhood, who used every means to restore animation, but without effect. The unfortunate deceased, whose name was James Johnson, and who was the son of a silk-weaver, residing in Dunk Street, Spitalfields, it appears was one of those who was near the door when it was first forced open, and being anxious, like most persons, to get to the front of the gallery, was hastening thither, but by some accident he slipped and fell down. The rush being very great at the time, those who followed him in the descent, and the pressure from behind, unavoidably passed over him. Dr Nicholls, on examining the body, expressed it as his opinion that death must have been instantaneous. The body was removed to the Parochial Workhouse, and the parents being very poor people, Mr Farrell, the proprietor, has liberally undertaken to pay every expense attendant on his interment.

Morning Advertiser, 28/12/1832

Queen's Theatre
Harlequin and the Elfin Arrow; or, the Basket-maker and His Brothers

[...] ALBERT TWIST, a young basket-maker, being left in great distress by the loss of his parents, is compelled by his industry alone to support his four younger brothers, and having fallen in love with Ellen, the beautiful daughter of Sir Barnabas Bowstring, the King of the Archers, the lady in secret responds to his passion. Twist is at a loss how to gain her hand, being certain that the father will not allow him to make the slightest advances, and the thought of this drives him nearly to distraction. Barnabas issues a proclamation, stating that in consequence of his love of archery he intends to give his daughter in marriage to him who shall prove the best marksman at the approaching festival, be he rich or poor. This revives the spirit of Albert, and gives him hope of gaining the hand of fair Ellen, but knowing that Sir Hector Ironsides, who is very rich, and the best marksman in the country, is her ardent admirer, he fears his chance will be small, and he throws himself on the ground in despair. King Bluecap, the Elfin Forest King, appears to him, who informs him that, in admiration of his virtues and his worth he is determined to aid him, and invites Albert to follow him to the Golden Glen, where his elfin workmen make him a charmed golden arrow that is sure to hit the centre of whatever it is levelled at. The rocks are split with a convulsion when the little workmen are discovered in their manufactory engaged in all the departments of artisans.

Albert, with the best wishes for his success from the Fairy, disappears, and joins the procession of candidates at the Orange Grove. In the trial of skill, Sir Hector hits within a hair's breadth of the bull's eye. Albert is plunged into despair, but roused by the sight of his beautiful Ellen, he musters courage, makes the essay, and strikes the very centre of the bull's eye. Sir Hector becomes frantic with disappointment, and by tempting tenders of vast sums of gold, induces Sir Barnabas to break his contract, who is, in defiance of entreaty on the part of the maid, and the murmurs of the spectators, about to compel her to accept the hand of the richest suitor. The fairy Bluecap at this crisis appears, and to punish the deceit and avarice of the father, and the villainy of Sir Hector, changes for protection the mutual lovers to Harlequin (Mr C Montgomery) and Columbine (Miss Lee); and the father is transformed to Pantaloon (Mr Law), and Hector to Clown (Mr W Taylor), which forms they are to wear until the golden arrow which he casts into the earth be brought back to him.

Then commences the motley bustle of the Harlequinade, some of the principal features of which are the arrival of Clown and Pantaloon at the top of a house in Soho Square, where the Clown, to check his roving propensities, is locked up in a garret; and, by climbing up one chimney, and descending by another, he regains access to his sweetheart's apartment; but being caught and brought back in the dumps, he goes to bed to shelter himself from the cold of the night. Harlequin causes the garret to disappear, and the Clown's bed to descend to the street, in the midst of a shower of snow. The Clown endeavours to fly from his cheerless situation, but he is prevented by the new police for stopping up the street. An amusing scene takes place here – the boiling of these police at a fishmonger's shop. The Clown, when asked for a fresh-boiled lobster, takes from the pot a policeman, red in colour even to the staff of office. A game of cribbage forms an amusing scene; also the Penny-tentiary which changes to the Halfpenny Hatch. [...]
Morning Advertiser, 28/12/1832

1833

Adelphi
Harlequin and Margery Daw; or, the Saucy Slut and the See-saw
THE idea of this Pantomime is taken from the nursery verses:

See-saw, Margery Daw,
Sold her bed and lay in the straw;
Wasn't she a saucy slut
To sell her bed and lay in the dirt?

To undertake the telling of the story of a Pantomime is as hopeless, and pretty nearly as useless, as if a person were to attempt collecting together the fragments of a half-forgotten dream. So far as we could understand the part introductory to the tumbling, Margery Daw, from excess of benevolence, is soon stripped of all her worldly goods. She appears surrounded by fairies, in the guise of beggars, to all of whom bread bread and other necessities are distributed with an unsparing hand; and, in recompense for her charities, she is assured that she shall through life be fully protected against the visitations of adversity. This assurance is given to her in a scene of great splendour, displaying the mists of midnight hanging over the Shining River, from which issues Wavelet, the Queen of the Stream, attended by the River Fairies, Riplet, Twinkle, Current, Whirlpool, Bubble, and Streamlet, together with River Elves. Margery's farm is seen at sunrise, and Margery herself in the midst of her poultry, enjoying the pleasure of attending to their wants and witnessing their gambols. After a somewhat tedious introduction, in which the usual agency, in which the usual agency of fanciful beings is lavishly employed, the Clowns, Pantaloon, Columbine, and Harlequin are at length evolved from their swathings, and the festive caperings and tumblings of the Pantomime commence.

The principal part of the pantomimic events take place in the well-known Lowther Bazaar, the Civet Cat in the Strand[2], and a gin-shop, got up with all the modern embellishments of paint, glass, and huge gin-vats. Here a great variety of fun, mistake, and misadventure occurs. Butchers and their meat are knocked about; greengrocers overturned; pigs, poultry, carrots, and cabbages fly round in every direction; and all hope of steady, rational shopkeeping seems lost, till the wand of Harlequin sets things to rights again. The gin-shop, in particular, overflows with customers, and much laughter is produced by the Clown, whose painting-brush is busy daubing with black paint the white dresses of all ladies and gentlemen who appear at the bar. After a great deal of carousing the shop disappears in terrific flashes of blue ruin, and frightful goblins are seen flying away with the customers. [...] One of the best of the tricks was a sudden tiger-like bound of the original civet cat, which carried him far over the heads of the folks in the pit, and produced much ludicrous consternation, but he as suddenly flew back, leaving the audience uninjured by his claws. [...]

Some of the scenery was very good. The parts most deserving of notice were the trellised grottoes and glittering gardens of the Queen of the Shining River; a bird's-eye view of London by moonlight from the housetop of Mrs Pentweazle; and the closing scene, the Dazzling Temple of Delight. This is preceded by a fire, from which the inmates of the house are seen escaping in the utmost confusion; policemen, watchmen, and firemen tumbling over one another, and all the fearful disorder of such a scene represented with almost the force and distinctness of reality.

The Clowns were very good; but it is impossible to see our modern performers in that department, and not recollect with regret that Grimaldi has ceased to grin and gambol. The world will never see his like again, at least in the swallowing of sausages. [...]
Morning Post, 27/12/1833

Covent Garden
Old Mother Hubbard and Her Dog; or, Harlequin and Tales of the Nursery
[...] CUPID (Miss Poole), like Apollo and many other famous Deities, for sport descends to earth to visit our celestial globe. He lands upon the island of Flatheads (In-nubibus), governed by King Miximilion Rundytundy O (W H Payne), who, to enrich his wasted treasury, meditates a union with a mine of wealth, in the person of the renowned princess Griffinwinkleblowsabella (Barnes); and for this purpose refuses to give his daughter in marriage to Prince Percinett (Ellar), who, though a prince, is poor. To thwart this union of the King's, Cupid ("the Mischievous Boy" as he is called) assumes various forms; among them is that of the sybil, Old Mother Hubbard (Wieland), who, and her Dog Shock (Master W Mitchinson) are looked upon as a sorceress and her familiar or agent, by all the Islanders of the Flatheads; but, by the power of the God of Love, the King's marriage is prevented, and as a punishment the parties are transformed into the usual harlequinade characters. [...]

The first scene, with the Queen of the Night coursing her way from her "Chamber in the East", succeeded by Morning with Phoebus, driving his four fiery steeds, and terminating with Day, when Venus rises from the sea in an enchanting Coral Bower, was one of the most unique specimens of the painter's art we have ever beheld. The descent of Cupid on his butterfly was extremely well managed, and that surprising little creature, Miss Poole, sang the air "Dear mother, chide me not", with great taste and purity of style.

After the mythological wonders had been disposed of Mr Farley gave us his notions of the Flatheads, and right comical they were. The grand procession of the Princess Griffinwinkleblowsabella (what's in a name) was in admirable keeping, and excited shouts of laughter; Miss Poole, in the next scene of the grand hall in the Palace of Rundytundy O in the disguise of a drummer, sings an air with her usual tact, accompanying herself on the drum in a manner that would inspire jealousy in the breast of any Drum-major. In the interior of Mother Hubbard's dwelling Cupid assumes her form, and shows in *Ombre Chinois* various nursery tales. The most ludicrous incidents of the whole Pantomime, however, are to be found in the sixth scene, where the stage is divided into four parts, the Royal Kitchen, the Parlour, the Counting House, a Garden and Wall. [...]

The only practical hit was at the Temperance Society, a body of the members being changed by the wand of Harlequin into a Society of Pumps; their appearance, with the handles, emblematical of their water-drinking propensities, was exceedingly grotesque. [...]
Public Ledger and Daily Advertiser, 27/12/ 1833

1834

Surrey
Harlequin and Little King Pippin; or, the Golden Crown and Goblin of the Apple
IT is "romantic, satiric, serio-comic, legendary", and moreover is founded upon "ancient records". Little King Pippin (Miss Somerville) is a promising pupil at an academy; some of his schoolfellows propose to rob an orchard, in which they find a magical golden pippin, guarded by a dragon, lineally descended from St George's, which handles the orchard robbers roughly. They are rescued by Little King Pippin, who carries off the golden apple, wherewith he is enabled to release Hesperia (Miss Martin), Queen of the Pixies (Devonshire fairies), from the clutches of an enchanter,

her enemy. The gratitude of this excellent lady is manifested by changing Little King Pippin into Harlequin (personated by Mr R Honner, the director of the pantomime), who has his customary companions, Columbine (Mrs Searle), Clown (Mr Turner), and Pantaloon (Mr Asbury).

There is an abundance of broad fun in the piece, and the scenery is excellent, especially in the last scene, the Royal Palace of Pearmain. A very attractive feature in the evening's amusements was the performance of the Flying Air-diver (Mr Silvester, we believe), who performed a series of "the most extraordinary performances ever exhibited". The house was literally crammed, not a space from which a view of the stage could be obtained being unoccupied.

Adelphi
Oranges and Lemons; or, Harlequin and the Bells of St Clement's
THE prelude to the pantomime is founded on the popular nursery rhymes commencing with the first part of its name. The bells of St Clement's, St Martin's, the Great Bell at Bow, St Giles's, &c, which are personified by the chief characters in the pantomime, have a grand contest as to their respective merits, which in the end turns out to be founded on a love-match between Bellina (Miss Lane), daughter to the Great Bell at Bow, and the Bell of St Giles's. Her father wishes to give his daughter to St Martin's, but she had fixed her mind on the Bell of St Giles's. There is another love-match, in which Goldbell (Miss Griffiths) is the preferred of the Bell of St Stepney. The rival bells are about to come to blows, and all their clappers are going together, when the Fairy Bellwave (Miss Lebatt) interposes, and bids the lovers be of good cheer, for after certain trials, which they must endure for a time, they will be happily united. She then transforms them into the several characters of Harlequin, Columbines (for there were two), Clowns, and Pantaloon, who forthwith commence their accustomed tricks and tumblings, to the great delight of the little holiday folks. […] There were some touches of satire on the new Poor Law Bill and the Chimney Sweepers' Act, that were well enough, but more ought to have been made of the subjects.
Bell's Life in London and Sporting Chronicle, 28/12/1834

1835

Drury Lane
Whittington and His Cat; or, Harlequin Lord Mayor of London
[…] IN the opening scene we have the departure of Captain Cross-the-Line (Henry) for the kingdom of Longobarobonyo, taking with him the "ventures" of the family of Fitzwarren (Yarnold), the London merchant. Poor Dick Whittington (Miss Poole), as in the legend, has nothing to export but an ugly cat, of the complexion commonly called carrotty, but the Captain is not dismayed at the caterwauling, and promises to be a good caterer for the fortune of the persecuted Dick. The latter has fallen in love with Fitzwarren's daughter, Alice (Miss Reekie), and is caught in the act of declaration by Dame Suet (Mr T Matthews), the cook, who drives Dick to such desperation that he runs away from his master's house.

In the meanwhile the vessel arrives at Longobarobonyo, and discharges its cargo. The King and Queen are delighted with the Europeans, and give them a hearty welcome. This scene is exceedingly ludicrous; the masks worn by the whole Court, especially that of the Grand Vizier – which we cannot better describe than to say it was a caricature of H.B.'s caricature of Lord Brougham – excited much merriment. A grand feast is prepared; but as soon as the viands are on the table the rats (we suspect these were meant as a skit upon the Whigs) make their appearance, and, Whig-like, pounce upon all the good things within their reach. Dick's cat, which is upon the spot, attacks the vermin right and left, and soon clears the saloon of the unwelcome visitors. This was cleverly managed. The cat, albeit not so handsome as that most celebrated of all cats, the graceful *Purwootz*, is admirably played by a small dog, who is dressed in the appropriate costume, not omitting a substantial looking tail, right up an end, in American phraseology, and seized the rat, which was alive, in the most feline manner, and quickly sent it to that bourne whence no rats return. Some of the ultra members of the Society for the Prevention of Cruelty to Animals might not have relished this exhibition, and, perhaps, would have *rat*-ed it, but it certainly went of with *eclat*, and was received with shouts of laughter and applause. No *debutant* was ever honoured with a more cordial reception than the representative of the cat; in sooth he proved himself to be extremely well bred.

Rich and rare presents are sent home to Whittington for his fortunate speculation by the King. Dick had, in the intervening space, been at Highgate, where the spot upon which he rested is marked to this day by a stone. The sounds of Bow bells, which to his mind play "Turn again, Whittington, thrice Lord Mayor of London," and the advice of Busy Bee (Miss Marshall), the Genius of London, induce him to return to the metropolis. His beloved Alice is upon the point of being forced to marry Master Addlepate Gobble (W H Payne), when the good fortune of Dick is made known by the kind Captain. Dick is, nevertheless, again subjected to persecution, when the Genius interferes, and transforms him into Harlequin (Ellar), Alice into Columbine, the Cook into Clown, the rejected lover into Harumscarum (another Clown), and his father, Alderman Gobble (Turnour), into Pantaloon. […]

The comic business of the pantomime is sometimes good, but, taking it upon the whole, it is too long, and becomes wearisome. The hit at the omnibus nuisance was not bad. The united efforts of the Conductor, Clowns, and Pantaloon to push into the machine, through the narrow door, a stout lady, were much relished, but the extension of the Mile End omnibus to a mile in length was not so well done as it might have been. The aerial ship "called the Eagle, 160 feet long, 50 feet high, 40 feet wide, manned by a brave, intrepid, dauntless, courageous crew of 17, the first experiment ever made of this new system of aerial navigation," told very well. Its voyage through the clouds, the fear of the Clown that he should be *air sick*, and the approach to the Comet with "such a tale[3]," the falling of a parachute with a monkey in it, and the bursting of the balloon by a shot from a farmer, with the discharge of the crew from the clouds upon the stage, were productive of considerable hilarity. Wieland has a monkey scene, which is rather lengthy, but which has not been excelled even by the renowned Mazurier. Wieland must have studied Landseer, of have been a constant frequenter of the *Jardin des Plantes* in Paris, or of the Zoological Gardens, to have acquired such an accurate imitation of the monkey tribe. The Regent's Park chimpanzee would have been in ecstasies had he been a witness to the scene at the toilette, where the monkey dresses himself as a female, after a model in a dress-maker's showroom. It was laughable in the extreme to hear the monkey playing on the violin the popular airs of the day, with occasional passages and *tours de force*, after the style of Paganini. [...]

Covent Garden
Harlequin Guy Fawkes

[…] THE piece opens with the accustomed preparation of supernatural beings, either clad in radiance and beauty, as Columbine generally is, or in grotesque and ludicrous masquerade. After some tender interviews between young Lord Monteagle and Columbine, Grumblegloom, the Genius of Discontent, is seen descending in a fiery car, for the purpose of exciting to the deed of horror of which Guy Fawkes is to be made the agent. He is attended by his familiar agent, Mischief, and by a host of Blue Devils, Groan, Howl, Mumble, and Growl, and a numerous *cortège* of imps. The Car of Discontent is, of course, a blazing one, surmounted by two fiery dragons. It was hailed with shouts of applause, and the familiar agent, Mischief, flitted through the air at his call with the graceful velocity of a hawk. The fiends are seen busily occupied in preparing powder for Guy, which, being in a state of readiness and deposited under the Parliament House, that worthy personage himself is introduced in triumph seated upon a crazy chair of state, and accompanied as he usually is upon the Fifth of November. He soon enters the cellar, and there begins to make his preparations for blowing up the Houses of Parliament, being furnished with a huge tinder-box capacious enough to boil a round of beef, and with steel and matches in proportion to his box. Lord Monteagle having previously received some dark intimation of the design, and not being able to give it a satisfactory interpretation, proceeds to the house of Sir F Moore, the astrologer, in Palace Yard, to consult him upon the subject. He enters the penetralia of the mighty stargazer, who, with telescope in hand, begins instantly to peruse the Heavens, where he beholds mischief in preparation, mischief of which gunpowder is to be the agent. Upon his suggestion the young Lord descends into the cellars where the powder is deposited, which, being in total darkness, there is a long and laughable game at hide-and-seek between him and Guy. The latter is at length seized, and the mischief thus prevented. The Genius of Discontent once more appears, and, full of wrath at the disappointment, returns, full of threatening and discontent to the Palace of Mischief. Columbine and Pantaloon, Harlequin and Clown, now shuffle off their coils, and the capering, the grimaces, and tumbling commence.

From henceforward to the close the *dramatis personae* are best given in the words of the bill, and they will convey a sufficient idea of what is done: boatmen and fishermen, walkers and talkers, butchers and bakers, and candlestick-makers, playmen and draymen, growers and mowers, silkmen and milkmen. Let a person conceive a representative from each of these occupations and many more, jumbled together and set in motion by various ludicrous incidents, tumbling, thumping, fighting, falling, shoplifting – running away from a mad bull, or gazing at a tame one in the Zoological Gardens – and he will have upon his mind very nearly all the impressions that this or any other pantomime can convey. […]

The tricks and transformations are numerous, and were, for a first display, very successful in the working. The wand of Harlequin and the thiefish propensities of the Clown made very frequent and very laughable use of an archery warehouse, a butcher's shop, and other places of business. Upon one occasion all the joints in the butcher's window are set dancing, and twirl round for a considerable time, to the great amusement of the audience. The Clown not being prevented by this from further persecution, the block disgorges ten or a dozen young butchers, chips off the old block, who assault him valiantly with their knives, and defend the joints from further annoyance. [...]
Morning Post, 28/12/1835

1836

THE CHRISTMAS NOVELTIES

[...] THE class of persons for whose especial entertainment these Christmas pantomimes are produced are the lowest, the vilest. They are also said to be intended for the amusement of children! Gracious Heaven! Can any thinking man justify them upon such a ground? In one night a child may be instructed in more wickedness – in more vice, than the admonitions of parents or the discipline of schools will be able to correct in a year. They learn to laugh at vice and crimes, and wanton brutality to applaud as an excellent jest. They see their fathers and mothers chuckling at the blackguard vagaries of the Clown; and they must think it no sin to imitate the vagaries of so mirth-moving a personage. If they should pilfer, or lie, or break the heads of the servants, who would be to blame? [...] We saw a living cherub in a box at Drury Lane on Tuesday night: she did not laugh when the Clown was pulling about some women and kicking Pantaloon on a part of his person we do not choose to mention, until her father laughed in her face, and the innocent child then laughed also. We could have brained the parent who caused his child to laugh at such a time.

But we saw few children at either house. On Monday we went into that part of the theatre called "the slips" to make ourselves acquainted with the sort of faces that were attracted to the galleries by the "Christmas pantomime", and we shuddered as we looked upon the frightful mass. Imagination can picture nothing of humanity more horrible. There were two seas of living faces, nine-tenths of which bore the unmistakeable marks of ignorance and vice. Of the proceedings of the dirty, drunken and depraved masses, their uproar, and the frequent interference of the police, we abstain from speaking. We will only say that if our theatres cannot be kept open but by pandering to the tastes of such classes of playgoers, it were better they should be shut up altogether.
Bell's New Weekly Messenger, 1/1/1837

1837

THE LATE GRIMALDI – Poor Joe Grimaldi is no more! Who does not remember the name of Joe Grimaldi? Those who are too young to have seen him must have heard of him, and those who are old enough to have seen him can never forget him. Grimaldi was not a mere grinning, face-making clown, whose chief merit consists in the distortion of the human countenance. His performance of the most popular personage in all pantomimic representations was full of those touches which mark the discriminating genius of comedy – in fact, he was a first-rate comic actor, and as such was universally recognised by the public, and even by the critics of his day. But the drop-scene has fallen upon the last of poor Joe's performances, and he is henceforth – as far as this world is concerned – but a thought and a recollection. The deceased Joseph Grimaldi expired on Wednesday night last, at his residence in Southampton Street, Pentonville, in the 57th year of his age. He was formerly, as doubtless many of our readers must know, of Drury Lane, Covent Garden, and Sadler's Wells Theatres; and of the latter, we believe, was formerly, if not of late years, a part proprietor. [...] For the last few months his friends have remarked that he was in the enjoyment of better health and spirits than he had been for some years proceeding. The previous part of the evening on which he died he had spent in the society of a friend, and, after partaking at home of a light supper, he retired with more than his usual cheerfulness to repose – in death.
The Examiner, 4/6/1837

Adelphi
Harlequin Silver Sixpence and the Giant Pennypiece

THE new pantomime at this theatre is called *Harlequin Silver Sixpence and the Giant Pennypiece*[4], and the characters consist of all the current coins of the realm. The first scene exposes to view a copper mine in a certain district, of which, with the limited means supplied by the English alphabet, we shall not attempt the spelling. Here Princess Half-crownia is brought in by Giant Pennypiece, who wishes to marry her to his son; but on her refusing to wed with a man of so base a metal, she is by him deprived of the power of motion. Silver Sixpence, disconsolate at her loss, sets out in search of her, led on by an attendant sprite, Quicksilver, whose nimbleness and brilliant appearance do full justice to his title. Possessed of a magic sword, Silver Sixpence succeeds in penetrating into the castle of his copper rival, and delivers the Princess; but just as he is about to carry her off the Giant enters, and detains the lovers. At this critical moment Fairy Fourpence appears, and, changing Silver Sixpence into Harlequin (Mr Harvey), the Princess into Columbine (Mrs Nailer), the Giant into Pantaloon (Mr Barnes), and his son into Clown (Mr Sanders), the usual bustle and tricks of pantomime commence, and are carried on to the conclusion with spirit. [...] The abode of Fairy Fourpence is very brilliant, and it was rendered dazzling in the extreme by an intense light which was by some means or other thrown upon it.

Drury Lane
Harlequin Jack-a-Lantern; or, the Witch of the Dropping Well
[…] SOME hundred-or-two years ago Sir Palmore (Howell), a Norman knight, with his trusty squire Tristan Snacke (T Matthews), are shipwrecked upon the Yorkshire coast, and take refuge in a lonely castle, where Griselda (Miss Lane), surnamed "the Beauty of the Roman Lock", is confined by the merciless Magician, Aldobrand. Sir Palmore is aided by Mother Shipton, while the Magician Aldobrand is assisted by Will o' the Wisp and his attendant sprites. Sir Palmore is determined to seek his lady love in the castle, and, accompanied by his squire and a powerful friend, in the person of Jack-a-Lantern (Wieland), the attack is made, and Aldobrand's followers yield to the troops of Jack-a-Lantern, who all carry lanterns, and are thus no doubt intended to act as *light* infantry. The sequel may be imagined. Sir Palmore has by his bravery overcome the obstacles presented to his admission to the castle, but worse remains behind, for he has there to contend against the magician's diabolical sorceries and incantations. […]

Two or three scenes are the most laughable it is possible to conceive, particularly a representation of a steeplechase, in which a host of mimic horses, with riders of most motley hue, scour the plain, producing such excitement that a mile-stone is moved to join in it, and actually runs away. The Clown is mounted on a boar, and the whole party finish the chase, which appears to be so amicably conducted as to be intended for a love chase, by rushing into a sort of greenhouse, and smashing the windows, leaving the poor nurseryman nothing but ruin and desolation for his *panes*. [...]
London Courier and Evening Gazette, 27/12/1837

1838

Drury Lane
Jack Frost; or, Goody Hearty
PANTOMIME is as essential to Christmas as plum-pudding, and on Wednesday accordingly Harlequins, Columbines, and Clowns were dished out with Pantaloons at every theatre within the bills of mortality. It is on such a night as this that a theatrical critic ought to be gifted with the powers of ubiquity, or at least endowed with the wand of Harlequin, to enable him to make his appearance for that night only in all the theatres where his labours are required. But to proceed methodically and critically, let us commence with Drury Lane, where the lessee, with the assistance of the old veteran, Reynolds, has served up "Jack Frost" in some of his own ice. For our parts, we think pantomimes should always find their sources in the literature of the juveniles they are meant to entertain; and the most successful pantomimes have always been those founded on those stories familiar to our earliest recollections. The scene naturally opens at the North Pole, to the air of "My lodging is on the cold ground", when *Druda*, the Queen of the Iced Fairies of the North, exerts her magic at the court of the King of Utopia, who being rather roughly treated by his sister, the *Princess Humptia Dumptia* – his subjects, who are tired of her tyranny, entreat their monarch

To marry with a wife as soon as may be,
And bless his subjects with a little ba-by.

The matrimonial decree having gone forth, *Druda* determines to make *Blanche*, one of the daughters of *Dame Hearty*, queen; her ambition, however, clashing with that of her sister-in-law, the court becomes the scene of such uncourtly rows that the fairy is obliged to interfere, and transforms King, Queen, Humptia Dumptia, and Lord Chancellor, into the usual characters of Harlequin, Columbine, Clown, and Pantaloon – and then the true old pantomine begins: –

A piazzo, the corner of Windmill Street, is turned into a peripatetic coffee and treacle shop, when Horsebeans plays the part of the coffee, and Julap the character of treacle, to the manifest injury of sundry intestines which had imbibed them[5]; Windmill Street itself becomes a windmill, and whirls Wieland round on its sails; the mill changes to a flower garden, which is held for nursery-grounds, in consequence of a number of children coming into the world, after the most approved natural history, out of the parsley-bed, and they grow up immediately into full-grown people, through the Clown and Pantaloon depositing them in the hotbed. A doctor and an undertaker's shop then show the natural connection between the two branches of the same profession – the one undertakes to kill, the other to bury. Yates is then exhibited with a Brobdignag Bayadère[6], but it is a failure, from the want of resemblance and form. Van Amburgh's[7] academy for tame beasts likewise met with much disapprobation, which was, however, converted into applause when Harlequin, by the power of his wand, produced the real Simon Pure[8] with his real lions, exhibited in the most effective scene that we have yet witnessed with these animals. After a variety of transformations, there is a capital scene of "Frost Fair" on the Thames, where the acting and bustle give a reality to the scene which is quite delightful. In this scene are introduced Inan and Fanny de Winther, as Zephyr and Flora, who dance on the tight-rope with an agility equal to Gilbert, and and an ease and grace scarcely surpassed by Taglioni or Essler. *Jack Frost's* icicled cavern again summonses the fairies upon the scene, who close the pantomime in the usual manner by a magnificent tableau, which does the greatest credit to Messrs Grieve. The dance of the northern lights, and also of the children, got up by Madame

Soutton, are extremely clever; but the main feature of the pantomime was the first appearance of Wieland as the clown. As Mrs Siddons has spoiled the present generation by the excellence of her Lady Macbeth, so, we fear, has Grimaldi made us too fastidious with regard to his successor. The pantomime is by far too long, and it was rendered longer by the delays of the scenery; so that much disapprobation was evinced, which was increased by the non-appearance of a Nassau balloon, which had been promised. The said balloon was, we understand, quite prepared and inflated; but, being seized with a sudden panic, it collapsed and fainted away, and was not producible.
The Era, 30/12/1838

1839

Drury Lane
Harlequin Jack Sheppard; or, the Blossom of Tyburn Tree
[…] THE pantomime at Drury Lane was preceded by a capital overture, consisting of the best airs from the "Beggars Opera" and "Jack Sheppard"; and the different receptions these met with declared eloquently the predilictions and the taste of the audience. Their applause did not commence till they heard "Jolly Nose", and "Nix my dolly pals, fake away!" but no sooner did the music of these favourite ditties meet their ear than their rapture became uproarious, and a universal encore was the result. Of the pantomime itself, "Harlequin Jack Sheppard, or the Blossom of Tyburn Tree", the introductory part (not the overture), is exceedingly good, and much more amusing than is customary. The tricks are some bad, some good, and some indifferent; and the panorama is super-excellent. One of the most effective changes was that of an entire scene, representing the exterior of the "Queen's Arms", into the "Temple of Charity". This trick, which was a very extensive one, was very dexterously managed, and elicited general applause. Another clever scene exhibited the wreck of the *Royal George*[9] under water, together with a view of the various monsters that inhabit the depths of the ocean. The interior of the Eccaleobion[10], where everything is hatched by steam, with or without notice; the fancy fair in aid of teetotalism, remarkable for the extraordinary feats of Signor Sylvestre and the Scotch military dance by the female rifle brigade. "Puffington's Library" was a remarkable instance of the failure of an entire scene, and the dullness of it might have been fatal to the pantomime, but for the exertions of the "Chiarini family," who, dressed like the Ethiops, the "pearls of the East," performed a dance which not only restored good humour but perfectly delighted the house, and elicited a rapturous encore. Another successful feature of the entertainment was the introduction of a diorama, representing the scenery overland to India, by way of Circassia and Persia. It is beautifully painted by Mr Marshall, and highly gratified the audience, whose nationality was flattered at the close by the capture of Ghuznee. Upon the whole, the pantomime we expect will be much better when we see it again. In many places the conception was much better than the execution, and the jokes hung fire. All we can say at present is, that there is room for improvement, not that we think improvement will be made.

Covent Garden
The Merrie Devil of Edmonton, or the Great Bed of Ware
THE "Merrie Devil of Edmonton, or the Great Bed of Ware", like its rival at Drury Lane, is much more droll at its commencement than afterwards. It is a magnificent work of machinery and painting, and must have cost its fair producer [Madame Vestris] an enormous sum of money. There are two or three capital tricks in the opening, which as a whole, however, is considerably too long. The scene of the *great bed* is the richest in the piece, and at many of the escapades of the *Master of the Horse*, the mirth of the audience grew uproarious; the change from the *bed* to the *throne* (had the machinist any sly meaning in the transformation?) was admirably arranged. *Asbestos* (the Merrie Devil), Gibson, is, of course, necessary in the induction, but he is altogether in the way of the pantomimic characters. His dancing and many (too many) postures are more adroit than pleasing. There were very few hits in what may be termed the business of the pantomime: the liberation of the dogs was too long dwelt upon; and the fitting a fat gentleman with armour for the tournament more elaborate than droll; but the wind-up of the *Eccaleobion*, in which baskets of eggs were changed to babies in cradles, was one of the best touches of the night. Another hit told exceedingly well. A number of policemen rose successively from trap-doors, and put every street-crier in the station-house under the new act, when the prisoners were set free by the conversion of the station-house into a mile-stone, inscribed – "All right, XVI miles from London". The emancipation of the dogs, with the change of the sign of "The Jolly Dogsmeatman" into the "Jolly Dogs", whence issued a number of canine bacchanalians, and the turning of a pile of arms for the Eglington tournament into an umbrella-shop, were likewise very good, although they did not produce the roars elicited by the two incidents first-named. The clown and pantaloon had not much fun depending on themselves, and therefore the parts between the mechanical changes want shortening. The diorama of the Clyde from Glasgow to Eglington, painted by Messrs Grieve, is very beautiful; here and there the red tints are used almost to excess; but in some of the scenes there is a charming life and transparency. Upon the whole, there was never perhaps, with all its faults, a more splendid pantomime; and on Friday and Saturday, as well as the night of its first appearance, the house was crammed to the roof.

Madame Vestris, actress and theatre manager

Adelphi
Harlequin Mother Red-Cap, or Merlin and the Fairy Snowdrop
"Harlequin Mother Red-Cap, or Merlin and the Fairy Snowdrop", is the pantomime at this house, and although the scenes are, of course, of different degrees of merit, there is such infinite variety throughout the whole, that even after some necessary excisions, enough will remain to make a good pantomime. The moving panorama of "Wanderings in Wicklow" is admirable, and the general scenery effective. The tricks, which after all are the main thing, are some good and some bad, but a few of the former class are *very* good. The loves of Prince Albert form the subject of some fun as at Sadler's Wells; but here they have the profanity to introduce not only the "expensive foreign importation from Germany", but the illustrious lady to whom he is consigned. The gentleman, between two and three feet high, comes out of a hamper from the Rhine, and a little lady, of corresponding altitude, starts forth from a sieve of Windsor pears. The whole scene tickled the fancy of the audience hugely, and perhaps there was no louder laughter heard in London, even on pantomime night. We have no room to catalogue the other effective incidents, but we advise our readers to go and judge for themselves – if they can get room.

Sadler's Wells
Harlequin and Old Father Æsop; or, Little Cock Robin and the Children in the Wood
IT is an understood thing that on the night after Christmas nothing but pantomime is suffered to be performed. The actors, indeed, try to get up a play as a commencement, but without avail. The noise in the house drowns their good intentions, and all proceeds in dumb show. This was particularly the case at Sadler's Wells, where the house was crammed to such an extent that many of the audience did not know how to find room for their own limbs, punching their fists into the faces of their friends, and inserting their elbows into the interstices of neighbouring ribs. These little misapplications produced, of course, not a little hubbub; and peace was not restored till the spectators were drawn from thinking of their own inconvenience by the knocks and kicks bestowed upon the personages of the pantomime.

The piece opens with very picturesque scenery, called "the rural retreat of Æsop", in which the water-mill is seen performing its *round* of duty, and the farmer "driving his team a-field". In the fore-ground the lion opens his capacious jaws, erects his terrific mane, and wags his ominous tail; the fox whisks about his brush and "leers with cunning eye"; and the ape chatters with a grimace pleasant to behold. The whole scene is one of animation, and presents a very appropriate introduction to the forest incidents connected with the story of "Cock Robin and the Babes in the Wood". After the introduction of some well executed moveable scenery, the "whereabout" changes to the Terrace of the Golden Dwarfs, surrounding the castle of *Pisarius*. The characters brought on the stage are dressed after the most grotesque fashion. *Pisarius* and his good lady, *Angelica*, are "huge mountains of mummery", with "phignominees" resembling those of the ogres in Guildhall. *Androgus* becomes wickedly enamoured of *Angelica*, and determines upon "dosing" her husband's "gruel", in order to possess himself of her, and then to kidnap the babes, well knowing –

That if those children chanced to die,
As death might soon come on,
The uncle then (none could deny)
Would make their wealth his own!

This murder is at length on the eve of being accomplished, as well as that of the babes, when Æsop interferes, and the "real pantomime" commences; for which the gods were most thankful. The fault is in the length of the introduction, and we have some notion that the impatience of the gods was critically correct. As for the incidents of the pantomime itself, many were exceedingly clever; and one relating to an "expensive foreign curiosity", just imported from Germany, was particularly well received. Out of the box containing this label a young gentleman is conjured, who is well buffetted by the clowns with a German sausage they find in his pocket; and eventually he seeks refuge by bolting through a window into a tavern, called the Queen's Arms. The piece was completely successful.

Queen's
Peter Piper, or Harlequin and the Golden Peck of Pepper

ON Friday evening, after the "Venetian Outlaw" and the "Two Gregories", we witnessed the second performance of "Peter Piper, or Harlequin and the Golden Peck of Pepper". The first two pieces were frequently interrupted by the "gods," who were determined to be pleased only with the comicalities of the Clown and his companions. The introductory part of this most successful harlequinade is exceedingly droll; the dresses and masks of the slaves in the "spicy land of India" are the most grotesque imaginable, and the acting of several performers worthy of much praise. The plot turns upon the rhyme of

Whoever picks a peck of pepper within the hour,
Shall gain a princess from a demon's power.

Now *Columbine* is, of course, the captured princess; imprisoned by *King Niddy Noddy*, afterwards *Pantaloon*, and sought after by the pepper-picking *Peter Piper* (afterwards *Harlequin*) and a slave overseer, subsequently *Clown*. Each amatory candidate receives various assistances and hindrances from diverse active devils and fairies, the subjects either of *King Noddy* or the *Fairy Queen* (Mrs Curling), till at length Messrs Griffith, Fuller, and Linch become *Harlequin*, *Clown*, and *Pantaloon*, and the released princess (Mademoiselle Gooderham) dances forth as *Columbine*. Here the bustle commences; the leaps, tricks and postures are excellent; and some laughable scenes occur on the subject of "Holloway's Ointment", "Fourpenny Postage", "The Female Militia", and the *Eccleobion* (we quote the bill) where a raven's egg produces a young Jim Crow[11], whose song was encored, an honour unsuccessfully attempted for the Clown's "Hot Codlings[12]". The "foreign importation" – Prince Albert – a wooden shoe dance, a *pas seul* by *Columbine*, and Mr James's magnificent Diorama, were the most vociferously applauded. The last closed with the Eglington Tournament, and in the real "passage of arms" in the north, there were, in *our* opinion, few, if any, more deserving the title of Queen of Beauty than the sweet-tempered, ever-smiling Gooderham, the Columbine in this "Harlequin and the Peck of Pepper".
The Era, 29/12/1839

NOTES
1 – The main attraction of the evening was the pantomime *Goosey Goosey Gander; or, Harlequin and the Fairy of My Lady's Chamber*.
2 – The Civet Cat in the Strand was the address of Kendall and Son, perfumers and cabinet makers.
3 – Halley's Comet returned in 1835.
4 – The giant's name may have been inspired by the massive "cartwheel" pennies minted in 1797, some of which were still in circulation in the 1830s.
5 – A reference to the adulteration of food and drink – horsebeans were used as animal fodder and julap, or julep, was an aromatic liquid added to medicines to make them more palatable.
6 – A Hindu temple dancer.
7 – Isaac Van Amburgh, an American lion-tamer.
8 – Slang for "authentic".

9 – The Royal George, a 100-gun warship, sank off the coast of Portsmouth in 1756 and was for many years a hazard to navigation. It was of topical interest in 1839 due to plans to destroy the wreck with gunpowder.
10 – An incubator.
11 – A blackface character created by Thomas D Rice and popularized by his song *Jump Jim Crow* (1828).
12 – A song made famous by Joseph Grimaldi.

5
The 1840s
She Lives in a Golden Bowl, and Thinks Herself Handsome

1841

Covent Garden
The Castle of Otranto; or, Harlequin and the Giant Helmet
THIS celebrated arena for the gambols of Grimaldi was the scene last night of the broadest burlesque and comic humour we ever witnessed at this mirth-stirring season. The new Pantomime is entitled *The Castle of Otranto; or, Harlequin and the Giant Helmet*[1]. It is written by Mr W Bradwell, and produced by Mr W H Payne. The music is by Mr R Hughes, and the scenery by the Messrs Grieve.

The first scene represents the Regions of Romance, where the presiding Spirit (personated by Miss M Glover) invokes the aid of her attendant Spirits to summon, in *propria persona*, the appearance of the Heroes and Heroines of Romance and Chivalry, for a grand procession to the Castle of Otranto, and which is made the vehicle for introducing some very beautiful music and appoptriate airs, adapted to the different countries to which the several entries belong; the scene then changes to the exterior of the Castle of Otranto, "as (so says the play-bill) seen through the medium of romance," and which is so beautifully painted by the Messrs Grieve, as to almost challenge reality; no sooner are they within the castellated walls, than the Spirit of Burlesque determines upon changing the "sublime into the ridiculous", by producing an army of attending Follies to beleaguer those but just within its walls. The business of this scene is the very perfection of burlesque, exhibiting an army composed of such redoubtable heroes as General Bombastes, Don Quixote, and Tom Thumb, who is not only general of his own division, but apparently commander-in-chief; and, although on foot, yet having about him a good supply of horse-flesh in the wicker-basket style; this monster of modern antiquity was ably represented by little Miss Payne, looking a Gulliver among the Brobdingnagians; and on the word being given for "The brave army to kick up a row!" then "fun met fun," and we heard "the din of war" divested of all its terrors, "Fortune having favoured the bold".

We are next shown the interior of the Castle Yard, with the Giant Helmet apparently about seventeen feet high, and into which the usurping Prince of Otranto (Mr Payne) commands an unlucky wight, Mr C J Smith, to be thrust, leaving two of his officers upon guard. The visor then rises and discovers a suitable face for the head that would fit such a helmet, to the no small consternation of those on duty. Then we become interested in the loves of the Lady Isabella and Theodore (Miss Fairbrother[2] and Mr C J Smith, afterwards the Columbine and Harlequin), to escape from the vengeance of the mighty Manfred; but as "the course of true love never did run smooth", the difficulties they have to encounter could never have been surmounted in any part of the world, or at any time, but in London and a Christmas Pantomime. As such the lover of course escapes from beneath the Helmet, and penetrates into the vault of the castle, pursued by the tyrant, who is here informed of some gigantic appearances in the Grand Gallery, and where his progress is stayed by the arms and legs of the Giant Ghost – we say arms and legs, for the body appertaining to limbs of such size could not conveniently stand upright in the pit of Covent Garden Theatre without his head being through the roof.

The next scene introduces the Marquis of Vicenza, Knight of the Gigantic Sabre (Mr Morelli, afterwards Pantaloon) before the castle-gate, with his sword carried by twenty men, to demand the hand of the Lady Isabella. The Page (Master Marshall) having sounded a horn nearly the size of himself, the Warder comes out to know their business, when, after the requisite information having been given by the aid of Scrolls, the party are permitted to enter, when the scene changes to another view of the Castle-yard, with a front view of the Giant Helmet, where the young lady enters, pursued by the tyrant, who is checked in his progress by a voice crying "Forbear!" the which rather astonishes him. A headless gigantic body then rises through the stage, asking, in a voice of thunder, for his head; and, to give additional horror to the scene, a gigantic cock walks on and crows three times, upon which Manfred says – "Why, so being gone I am a man again". The guards bearing the sabre next enter, and unluckily fall beneath its weight. We are here informed, by means of Scrolls, that the "Lady Isabella has hopp'd the twig!" and that "Theodore is the rightful heir of Otranto", who is then blessed by the possession of his lady love, when the Helmet gradually opens and displays a very beautiful piece of mechanism, considering that so many horses and men in armour, the various implements of warfare, with the genius of romance in the centre, should have been contained in so small a space.

Here the transformation takes place, and we have Harlequin, Columbine, Clown, Pantaloon, and his attendant Tiger[3] in all their glory. The comic business commences with a scene called Strawberry Hill, representing a horticultural fete, which affords an opportunity for some capital transformations and tricks; then comes the opening of the Nelson Monument, with a fine view of Trafalgar Square, and the National Gallery; a flag dance arranged by Oscar Byrne is then introduced, and the scene changes to Furnished Lodgings kept by one Mrs Squint.

The best hits in the Pantomime are against the Promenade Concerts and the Penny Post. The former are caricatured in the Temple of the Drama (Old Drury), and the latter at a grocer's shop – a branch post-office – from which the Clown transmits a "sucking pig" in a "scented envelope", upon the seal of which he makes an original impression, by seating himself upon it. The Panorama, by the Messrs Grieve, fully keeps up their high character for pictorial design. St Helena stands out as vividly as nature's self, and the entire series of views from Table Bay to the Bay of Tchusan are painted with a firmness of touch and freedom of pencil which reflects the highest credit on our native school. Vainly may the continental scenic *artistes* attempt to vie with the merest tyro of one of our minor theatres. The whole mounting of the Pantomime, including the dresses, machinery, and mechanical ingenuities, reflect the highest credit on the liberality and vast resources of this our now only national theatre.

Sarah Fairbrother

Adelphi
Harlequin and the Enchanted Fish; or the Geni of the Brazen Bottle
[...] THE "Arabian Nights' Entertainments" has given the subject, and the genius of the adaptor has filled it up with living beings, sufficiently bizarre and grotesque to satisfy even an Eastern imagination, and the imaginative is so merged in the absurd (the very salt of pantomime) that our ideas become transfused into the scene before us, and we become for the time, through our half-belief, participators in the notions of the actors.

We have the poor Fisherman, and the ungrateful Geni, who, because he has been released from a brazen bottle, determines to sacrifice the fisherman for his unintentional kindness, but the artful vendor of the finny tribe gets him into the bottle again, and refuses to release him without a bonus – to wit, some very peculiar *fish* – which he sells, being the Ramadan we suppose, to a podgy Sultan, who had lost his eldest son, and being a huge lover of piscatory delicacies, remarks that he will "think of his son when his dinner is done." He is also sultatory in his moods, and dances the Saraband with his lady cook; this is as it should be, and proves the march of liberal feelings in the Empire of the Soldan. This is somewhat elaborated, and with skill; the fish dancing in the pan with infinite grace, and the Grand Nigger, their master, were presented in a most unexceptionable manner. Wieland is the Clown, and acts with humour, and tumbles with skill; and Ellar, "poor Tom!" the Harlequin of our salad days, danced and cut, and wielded his magic bat with all the spirit that characterised his former efforts. Yates, we laud thee from our innermost heart for thy fine philanthropy, in thus affording a home for an old and talented servant of the public – this alone should crown thy little theatre – and it will. There are some capital hits at the times – "Annuals" 1842 to 1844 changing to four little scions of royalty is really rich – and the joke told well – we fear it may prove expensive – *n'importe*! The Gallic cock and the English game, though excellent, failed only because the wit was perhaps too keen. The opening scene, painted by Telbin, is alone worth a visit; it is exquisite in design, and charming in colour. This young artist stands alone in the scenic art – we miss not Stanfield, of whom he is a worthy successor! At the fall of the curtain Wieland gave out the Pantomime for next week amidst the applause of the audience.

Sadler's Wells
Harlequin and "Poor Richard"; or, Old Father Time and the Almanac Maker
THIS theatre, long famed for the production of pantomimes, has lost none of its energies in the preparations of its Christmas annual for the present season; it has fairly outstripped most of its contemporaries this year, and fully equalled the rest. The novelty of last night is called *Harlequin and "Poor Richard," or, Old Father Time and the Almanac Maker*. It is written by Mr Younge, the facetious inventor of so many of these winter garlands; the opening is excellent; the comic business extremely funny; the scenery, by Cuthbert and Fenton, well designed and beautifully executed; and the costumes and appointments are fanciful and appropriate.

The opening scene represents the abode of Time, in which that respectable personage is discovered, lamenting the great changes which have taken place even in his own person. He is disturbed by the appearance of the Goddess Pleasure, attended by her various Follies, who entreats him to assist her in the formation of a Pantomimic dish. He declines on the score of his present distresses, but summons to her aid his brother Christmas; a very jolly Time indeed, whom he despatches to Earth in search of Poor Richard the Almanac-maker, a poor but honest youth; arrived on *terra firma*, Christmas (Stilt) reaches the dwelling of Poor Richard (Collier), furnishes him with Time's magic hour-glass, and accompanies him to the Castle of the Baroness Rumpelstiltsken (Jefferini), where Mignonetta (F Fentoni), her lovely daughter, receives with more than maiden pride the various suitors for her hand. Sir Grimalkin Ganderguffin (Grammani), the rich and gouty suitor favoured by the Baroness, is now introduced, but is indignantly rejected by the lovely Mignonetta, who, proud of her beauty, will listen to no common tale of love. Poor Richard now determines to try his luck, and boldly, perhaps imprudently, enters the apartments of the lovely fair one.

We are introduced to the lady's *boudoir*, a very excellent scene, where she is discovered attended by her maidens Flirtilda and Vixenella (Richardson and Priorson). She admires her person in the glass, and her example is followed by her maids. Poor Richard now enters, and on being refused, touches with his hour-glass the beauty and her attendants. They are immediately entranced, and Mignonetta on awaking discovers that her nose is longer by an inch; in despair she tears her well curled locks, and finds that they, alas, are grey; she rushes to the glass again and finds her fears are verified; no longer beautiful; she is an ancient venerable maid; she calls her maids, who laugh at her altered looks; she calls attention to their own faces, and upon consulting the glasses they discover that all hopes of obtaining a husband are lost to them forever. The rich and poor lovers now enter. The maiden's pride has fled, and she rushes to the arms of Sir Grimalkin, who, however, being a man of taste, refuses to accept her in an altered state. Poor Richard, however, who has loved more truly, still is willing to accept her hand, which she gives, and Time enters, and changes the various characters.

The comic business consists of hits at Cardigan's Black Bottle[4], the Royal Cheese[5], Prince Albert's Own Regiment, Musard's Concert[6], Railway Murders[7], Temperance Societies, War with China[8], and, the last scene, the Hall of History, painted by Cuthbert, illustrating Britain's various triumphs from the time of Alfred, and ending with a tableaux of the young Princess and Albert and Victoria, is very effective. The Pantomime is carefully produced in every respect; the outlay upon it has been most lavish, and it will, doubtless, have a long and profitable run.

Garrick
The Ocean Queen, and the King of the Ruby Castle
[…] A YOUNG boy (Miss Conquest) is protected by the *Fairy of the Yew Tree Bough* (Miss Raine), who changes him from a poor peasant to the *Knight of the Silver Shield*. He is attended by a fairy follower, and they are to attack the Castle of the Drankenfeles, or Ruby Castle, the King of which (T Blanchard), are attacked by the Knight and his

attendant. They escape the army and approach another portal of the castle, which is strictly guarded by the porter (Elsgood), and after many efforts, they succeed in entering by stratagem, and when they are inside they come to a magic chamber, where a gigantic statue guards the yew-tree bough, which, by aid of the fairy, is given to the *Knight of the Silver Shield*, by means of which they pass through various dangers to the palace of the Ocean Queen, who has been enchained in sleep for 1000 years. The yew-tree bough breaks the spell, they awake, and while the *Knight* and the *Queen* are in dalliance, the dragon of the *King of the Ruby Castle* steals away the protecting bough, and they are in his power. The *Fairy* releases them, and changes the *Queen* to *Columbine*, the *Knight* to *Harlequin*, and the attendant to the imp, *Quicksilver*. The *Fire King* changes the *King of the Ruby Castle* to *Pantaloon*, and the *Porter* to *Clown*. The comic business commences, and many local hits occur in the Pantomime; at last comes a happy termination. T Blanchard as *Pantaloon*, Elsgood as *Clown*, and Miss Rose as *Columbine* were excellent; and Smith was a respectable *Harlequin*. The pantomime was well received, and is got up with great care, and will no doubt be highly successful.

Pavilion
Blue Beard
MOST of our readers are familiar with the tale, but though that was adhered to, it was burlesqued. The piece opens with the demons of *Envy*, *Deceit*, *Revenge*, &c., raising a powerful charm by means of laudanum, copperas, prussic acid, &c, by means of which *Jealousy* appears and foretells the fate of *Fatima*. The scene changes, and we are brought to *Ibrahim's* cottage, where the father and his two daughters, together with *Selim*, come to the usual opening of the piece (only the characters are all grotesque, with large masques and *outre* costumes). Afterwards the story is continued to the Blue Chamber, where a dance of ladies with their heads in their hands takes place; the *Bashaw* returns, discovers the broken key, and condemns the fair *Fatima* to death. The scene of the ramparts succeeds, and as the *Bashaw* is about to slay his victim, *Salim* and his spahis attack the fortress, where *Blue Beard's* party is victorious. At this moment the Fairy, *Sweet Content*, appears, changes *Selim* to *Harlequin*, and *Fatima* and *Irene* to two *Columbines*. *Jealousy* comes on and changes *Blue Beard* to *Clown*, and *Ibrahim* to *Pantaloon*. The pursuit then commences, and we are led through a number of comic scenes and pantomimic adventures, till at last we repose in the Hall of Rubies, and bid "good night" to the harlequinade. The piece is full of good scenery, tricks, and changes, many of the latter most whimsical. There's a hit at the tee-totallers, also at the incident of finding the man in Buckingham Palace[9], with numerous others. [...]
The Era, 3/1/1841

1842

Covent Garden
Guy of Warwick; or, Harlequin and the Dun Cow
THE first scene presents to us a hermit's abode on the banks of the Avon. It is moonlight, and the said pious gentleman is engaged tending a pet owl, and what appeared to us a pair of pelicans. Suddenly some villagers enter, and claim his advice as to how they are to free themselves from the dreadful visitation of a certain Dun Cow. He is touched by their unpleasant situation, and by way of ridding them of their vaccine torment, summons a host of figurantes, gaily bespangled, *selon de regle*; they cut some entrechats, and then to give a finish to the spell, there appears a young lady, rejoicing in the euphonious appelation of Paradisia. Suddenly, on a rock, in luminous Italian characters, is seen "Guy, Earl of Warwick, will return again to Dover." The corps de ballet dance a few steps, expressive of the satisfaction they are supposed to feel, and go off, in a state not to be described.

   It appears that Guy, tired of domestic delight and fatigued with connubial comfort, has been for some time absent fighting the Saracens; he returns in the next scene, fatigued and travel-stained, to his his castle, accompanied by his trusty squire, Tristram. They blow the bugle and Felicia enters, with whom our errant knight tries sundry conclusions. They being not satisfactory, and the gentleman not ultra uxurious, he knocks his better half down, upon which act of gallantry he is carried triumphantly by his vassals into the castle. Our hero is then seen attending to his home duties – sweeping the hall, rocking his baby, and feeding the junior Guys. *En passant*, this portion was deservedly hissed – what it wanted in humour was affluently provided for by grossness.

   He is then waited upon by a deputation of the Warwickshire yeomanry, requesting him to demolish the monster, whose appetite is alone satisfied by feeding on tender maidens and sucking babbies. After some few pros and cons he consents, being bribed with some bags filled with current coin of the realm. He sets off in quest of the fortress of Eskeldered, where the monster Cow is foddered; and after various grievances on the route arrives at the wished-for end of his journey. He is encountered by Colbrand, a lusty giant, who refuses him admission. A combat is fought, and Guy is becoming triumphant when the Cow most cowardly interposes, but ultimately both Giant and Cow are demolished.

   There is a slight episode which had nearly escaped us. Sir Piers and Ethelred, King of the Danes, are rivals for the fair hand of Phœbe, the daughter of Sir Jonas; but the Dane, being a bit of a conjuror, seduces her from her casement, under the disguise of the favoured lover, and she is whisked away on the back of this dreadful Cow. By some means, which we failed to discover, the young lady is set at liberty with the rest of the injured parties. Paradisia then appears, and transforms the fortress into a "Fairy Aviary" – a very beautiful piece of mechanism is here presented of a revolving star – and the Warwick Vase[10], from the centre of which the Fairy Queen transforms the various persons into the usual Harlequinade characters. The dioramic movement of the scenery is clever and effective though not new, the same system being used at the Queen's Theatre in Tottenham Street.

Sibillations and other marks of discontent accompanied the opening, and the fun(!) of the comic portion bordered on the lugubrious. The only scene worthy of remark during the latter portion of the entertainment was a toy-shop, where all the items became animated. The scenery is beautifully painted, and the mechanical portions admirably managed; but these adjuncts, however excellent, go but a very short way to the producing of a good pantomime. The present one is decidedly the least meritorious we have seen for some years at this theatre.
The Era, 2/1/1842

Drury Lane
Harlequin and William Tell; or, the Genius of the Ribstone Pippin
THE real and the ideal tread closely on each other's heels. There are demons and democrats, Britannia and Tell, journeymen imps and British tars, realms of slavery, the "open sea", valleys, lakes, and snowy peaks – all these are placed in a comic cauldron, and produce a strange compound of the domestic-tragico-burlesque.
The scene opens and presents the regions of slavery – implings are forging fetters, and the master demon is blowing the furnace of his wrath by sundry applications of his iron scourge to the shoulders of his workpeople; a sail in sight appears, and the demon seizes a mighty telescope, and exclaims:

But see! A ship, with all her canvas set;
A schooner too – her flag as black as jet;
A slaver too, as I hope to be a lord,
With full five hundred blackamoors aboard.

This is a veritable "Eau de Cologne" to the dingy gentlemen and all rub their palms in evident delight, when their joy is somewhat abated by the appearance of a second vessel, bearing for its figure-head a small Britannia. The demon of slavery faints at the sight – dismay seizes upon them as he exclaims:

Confusion take it! 'Tis a British cruizer!
H.M.'s ship Boxer, Captain Bruizer!

Britannia descends from her station, and a large crew of tiny sailors and marines attack and rout the evil spirits. This was a capital scene, and admirably acted; the bold bearing of the little nauticals, headed by a belligerent boatswain of the very smallest possible dimensions, who proved himself a worthy successor of T P Cooke[11], elicited shouts of approbation. The Genius of Liberty waves her wand, and we are transported to the "Western Indies", where are seen various samples of Jim Crow in a rapid state of emancipation; and next we find ourselves gazing on Tell's cottage and the castle of the tyrant Gessler, and here the bona fide opening of the pantomime commences.

The scenes of the real drama are burlesqued with great humour and kindly spirit. The various incidents of the play are exaggerated, and the effect is most ludicrous. The boy Albert (Hance) is hirsute and carrotty, his parents' pride, playful and petulant, forward and frolicsome; in the flush of youthful recklessness he tumbles into a well, and is saved by his anxious mother. Sarnam (Howell), Gessler's Chancellor of the Exchequer and Collector, enters, attended by his monetary guards, and demands the Income-tax, followed by groaning defaulters, whom he is bearing to the Swiss "Model Prison". Tell (C J Smith) appears – morbid, melancholy, and musing on his country's wrongs, and determined upon a radical reformation. He embraces his wife and infant hope, and sends the boy to prepare the arrows for his toxophilite exercise. The result of his first essay tells well, as he fixes the arrow in his father's rear. Tell is wrathful, and indignantly remarks:

You've missed, you fool! You want a better mark;
I'll make one for you.

He forms a figure to persone Gessler, and "teaches the young idea how to shoot". The mark is missed, but Tell is hit. Melchtal (Stilt) approaches, his head bound up in an immeasurable bandage; the tyrant has cropped his ears; he has carefully carried them to his son-in-law, who patriotically and passionately exclaims, in a poetical triplet:

I can't find words my furious hate to speak,
But had I Gessler before me cheek to cheek,
I'd knock him thus, into the middle of next week.

He summons his friends with the well-known Alpine call of "LA-RI-E-TY!" They swear vengeance against Gessler; they go to rouse the Cantons, when we are introduced to the tyrant's sanctum; he is seen at his toilette; shouts are heard; he presents himself at the casement, and is received with groans and missiles from his liege subjects; he is stricken by a prize turnip, and being, very naturally, disgusted with these striking proofs of popularity, seeks rest from the fatigues of office in the pleasures of the chase; he loses his way amongst the Alpine passes, and is about forming a luncheon for a bear when he is succoured by the boy Albert, and, to evince his gratitude, has him born off to Altorf.

All is merry in the market place. A pole is erected, to which all persons are commanded to bow as to the representative of Gessler; the people humbly bend before it, save Tell, who, in the pride of proper patriotism, contemptuously "takes a sight" at it. The patrician blood is in a boil – the crack archer is surrounded, and the parent is condemned to pop a Ribstone pippin from off the poll of his pride and pet, as the penalty of his disloyalty. A bushel of them are presented to him for selection; the largest is drawn, the tyrant objects and searches for the smallest; this Tell indignantly swallows. A medium pippin is chosen – the boy is fixed – awful stillness reigns around – the father trembles – the hearts of the population audibly beat – the arrow is drawn to the head – it flies through the air – the pippin is transfixed – the boy is saved – Gessler is overthrown – and Switzerland is free! The Genius of the Ribstone Pippin rises, surrounded by the most gorgeous accessories, banishes slavery from the earth, and transforms the *dramatis personae* into the usual pantomimic characters.

There is much merit in this introduction, but it suffered materially from its great length; upon condensation it will act faster, and a correspondent benefit will be gained. Mr C J Smith, as William Tell, was excellent. The parent and patriot were happily mingled. The comic business, as it is technically termed, lacked fun, the great essential. […] There are hits at the times. "Hydropathy", "Music for the Million", the arrival of the greatest English singer, and the change to the interior of the new Teetotal Temperance Music Hall, with its myriads of animated tea-kettles, are very good. The best scene, however, is the kitchen at the Blossoms Inn; there is intention, and, if we may use the expression in speaking of pantomime, it is legitimate. Mr T Mathews is the Clown, and worthily wears the mantle bequeathed by the great Grimaldi; there is the same quiet enjoyment – the same twinkling of the eye, which tells of the anticipated theft – the same reckless and almost child-like chuckle at mischief contemplated, or mischief achieved.

Marylebone
Mother Bunch

THE opening is a very good idea, and full of effect and business. Mother Bunch, the last of the pantomimic race, is discovered lamenting over the tombs of the pantomimes, and by her spells the dead are raised, and Mothers Hubbard, Goose, Shipton, Red Cap, &c., are for a short time restored to life. These old witches concert together, amd resolve to treat the public with a representation of one more pantomime before the race becomes wholly extinct. The witches fix upon Little Jack to play Harlequin, and commence building a theatre in which the pantomime shall be played. Accordingly, they build the Marylebone Theatre; but, as their work progresses, a demon troop use many artifices to destroy it, which are frustrated by Prosperity, the Fairy Queen, and her court. The threatre is built, the consent of the audience is asked, and then the characters are transformed and the pantomime commences.

What follows is full of humorous tricks, and presents a series of grotesque situations and animated incidents. Monsieur Buck is a very lively clown, imitating rather closely T Mathews. The "Arab Wonders" perform their clever feats, and and are well-deserving of the applause which they receive. Prior to the pantomime a series of dissolving views are exhibited, which, for brilliancy and effect, are not inferior to any we have seen. *Mother Bunch* is likely to live as long as any of her contemporaries, and we have no doubt will at her decease be much regretted by the thousands she has delighted.

Pavilion
The Little Boy Blue; or, the King of the Gold Mine

THE story runs thus: – The Demon of Discord having made Avaro, a miser (Johnson), the father of Primrose, afterwards Columbine (Mrs Gibson), rich – upon the condition that when she arrives at a certain age she shall be his victim – is enraged upon finding she loves and is beloved by Little Boy Blue (Mr Lufkin), and determines upon his destruction by means of gold; he is, however, thwarted in his plans by Heartsease, Queen of Fairy Land (Mrs Yates), who determines to protect him. On his way to visit his lover he is met by the Demon of Discord, who darkens the air, and on the light returning he discovers in his path a bar of gold. Overjoyed at thus suddenly becoming rich, he is about to proceed to the cottage of the father of Primrose, and give him the gold to let him marry her, when he is met by the Fairy Queen, Heartsease, in the garb of a beggar, desiring alms. He gives her all he is possessed of, and in return she informs him, whenever he is in trouble, to call upon her. Little Boy Blue then goes to the cottage of Primrose, and meets with her. Her father, who comes out, sees them together, and parts them. The Demon of Discord then enters and reminds Avaro of his promise, this being the time agreed on, and asks him if he will give him more gold; he assents, and the Miser gives Primrose to him, who is carried off to his palace, followed by the Boy Blue.

The next scene discovers the Hall of Discord. The Demon of Discord enters with Primrose, followed by her father Avaro, who reminds the demon of his promise of gold; he informs him that all is gold about him, and to take all he likes. Little Boy Blue then enters in pursuit of Primrose, who flies to him for protection. The Demon, enraged at this, determines to sacrifice them together, and is about to kill them when Little Boy Blue calls upon the Fairy, who enters, and changes the characters to Harlequin, Columbine, Clown, and Pantaloon. The harlequinade and comic business embrace the most popular hits at the present events, and were excellently supported by the various performers. Singing for the Million, the laughing gas, and the Frankfurt case[12], elicited much laughter. A diorama of the embarkation of Her Majesty for Scotland was well painted.
The Era, 1/1/1843

1843

AN UNREHEARSED INCIDENT IN A PANTOMIME
ON Wednesday evening last the following singular and ludicrous circumstance occurred at the Olympic Theatre. During the performance of the pantomime of "Harlequin and Old Cocker", one of the attendants upon Dame Interest in the early part of the pantomime has to be pursued by Multiplication, and as this pursuit was being carried on, the attendant, unable clearly to distinguish through his mask the path he was taking, slipped from the stage into the orchestra, where, falling upon the drum, the parchment covering gave way with his weight, and he suddenly disappeared from the sight of the audience. The audience seemed to consider this occurrence as one of the most amusing incidents in the evening's performance, and the laughter occasioned by it was almost unbounded when the fact was discovered that the poor victim of pantomime frolic had got so wedged in his mask and other characteristic encumbrances that his extrication from the drum, as it then stood in the orchestra, was a matter of utter impossibility. In this dilemma, the drum and its occupant were hoisted on the stage, when, with considerable difficulty, the unlucky attendant was literally shaken out, without having, as it afterward appeared, sustained the slightest injury from the occurrence. The performance of the pantomime was then resumed.
The Era, 29/1/1843

Marylebone
The Singing Mouse; or, the Giant, the Talking Cat, and the Amazonian Queen
THE Giant, having determined upon making a sumptuous meal upon a young damsel, whom he held captive, if she would not wed him, the Amazonian Queen and her aeriel attendants determine to frustrate his purpose by strategem or war, and enlist to their assistance the Singing Mouse. The fair prisoner's lover is now met with, who joins the fairy train on their adventure to the Giant's Castle. The Giant, hearing of the design of the Amazonian Queen, consults the prophetic skill of Old Dame Trot, who lends him her Wonderful Cat. Towser, however, on encountering the mouse, becomes enamoured of his musical abilities, and the ferocity of nature yields to the charms of music. The mouse, unperceived, threads his way to the prison-room of the fair captive, and effects her liberation by gnawing her hempen bonds. The Amazonian Queen now banishes the Giant and his masked retinue to the regions of Imagination, and transforms the emancipated damsel and her lover, with the Singing Mouse and the Wonderful Cat, into the primary agents of pantomime.

The plot, though simple, was interestingly told and pleasantly enlivened by the volatile performance of Miss Martin as the Amazonian Queen. The bustling changes which followed, though not marked by any originality, by the cleverness of the Clown (M Buck) and Pantaloon (Mr Millburne) were got through to the delight of the audience, who testified their approbation in deafening applause.
The Era, 31/12/1843

1844

Birmingham Theatre, Birmingham
The Dragon of Wantley; or, Harlequin Knight, and the Fire King of the Burning Isle
THE pantomime at the Birmingham Theatre has been very well received. This year it is taken from an ancient ballad, well known in domestic history as "St George and the Dragon". It is written expressly for the company by Mr J Ridgeway, late of Drury Lane, and presented under the title of "The Dragon of Wantley: or, Harlequin Knight, and the Fire King of the Burning Isle".

The piece opens with a chorus of fiends in the vaulted chamber of gigantic Cyclops, the abode of *Fire-fiend-blazeaway* (Mr Barton), who soon makes his appearance and awaits the arrival of *Devilskin* (Master Holmes), his attendant Sprite, who has been sent upon the mission of capturing *Resplendina* (Miss Conway), Fairy Queen of the Sun, strongly opposed to the demon king. His majesty proposes marriage to her, but is rejected, and decrees that she shall be cast into the haunted well of Wantley Abbey, which is guarded by a dragon.

The second scene presents the Guildhall of Wantley, where *Sir Roger* (Mr G Cooke), the mayor, is petitioned to find out some means or other to get rid of the *Dragon* (Mr Allen), which infests the place, and creates such terror throughout. While the "learned functionary of the law" and the deputation are discussing the mode of destroying the monster, the latter is heard without; all are seized with fright, and the mayor's daughter, *Mauxelinda* (Mrs J Ridgeway), desperately in love with the hero of the play, is carried off by him. *Goggles* (Mr Jones), the mayor's thin clerk, suggests immediate destruction of the scaly monarch, and while formidable preparations are being made for that purpose, the hero, *Mr Moore* (Mr J Ridgeway), of Moore Hall, arrives, having rescued *Mauxelinda* from her perilous situation.

The daughter of the worshipful chief magistrate then expresses her deep gratitude, and, with the deputation, prevails upon *Mr Moore* to fight and destroy the winged serpent; he consents, and the third scene finds him at the well in which the fairy queen is confined. It is guarded by "two masculine specimens of the feline race, endowed with speech and long tails", and known as *Tibby-spit-fire* (Mr Bullock) and *Tom-catch-a-rat* (Mr Atkins). The pest of the neighbourhood appears, heavily laden with eatables and drinkables stolen from different larders; *Moore* is at first alarmed, but at last encounters and overcomes him. The spell is now broken; the *Dragon* descends to the regions of the *Fire King*, and the scene is immediately changed to the Cloud Palace of the Fairy of the Sun, and magnificent temples, with revolving pillars of the attendant sprites of *Resplendina* – the good genius. The Queen is discovered on her throne, in a brilliant star of diamonds and rubies. Good and evil spirits are still at variance; however, an entire new face is soon put upon affairs, and an instantaneous transformation to the harlequinade follows – *Moore* and *Mauxelinda* become *Harlequin* and *Columbine*, and *Tibby-spit-fire* and *Tom-catch-a-rat*, *Clown* and *Pantaloon*. Now commences the various adventure of the motley heroes and heroine of the pantomimic scene. We need not enter further into an analysis of the piece; suffice it to say that the several tricks were very amusing indeed, and the house was kept in a regular fit of laughter for the remainder of the evening by the many excellent jokes cracked by *Clown* and *Pantaloon*; and the several beautiful dances introduced by *Harlequin* and *Columbine* (among which we particularly noticed the Parisian Polka, El Tripoli Tripola, and the new Jockey Dance), were exceedingly interesting and pleasing. [...]
The Era, 5/1/1845

1847

Princess's
Old Father Time; or Harlequin and the Four Seasons
[...] THE mechanical effects in this pantomime are more elaborate than can be imagined. Time's daughters, Spring, Summer, and Autumn, and his son, Winter, appear before him an an allegorical tableaux, after which the Abode of Time disappears, and discovers the Banks of the Blue Moselle. Spring reigns in all her verdant beauty for a time, when the fruits and flowers of Summer bud forth, and the scene, by magical effect, is transformed to a beautiful Bower of Love, the Dwelling of Summer. In this scene the foliage expands and discovers Philip the Falconer, and the Summer season, "The Last Rose of Summer", leads to Autumn; all disappears and produces a Vineyard on the Rhine, with the Feast of the Vine, Dance of the Vine Dressers, and all the effects of a bountiful vintage. Autumn is intruded on by the approach of Winter on his Throne of Glittering Icicles. The whole of the characters are transfixed by stern Winter, and a fourth grand mechanical change of scene takes place to the Chateau d'Hiver, Winter's Palace.

Here the introduction ends, and the characters are changed to Harlequin, Columbine, Sprite, Clown, and Pantaloon. There are a variety of tricks and transformations, amongst which the following are the most prominent: – The Disappearance of the Bathing Machines, leaving all the bathers up to their chins in water; the Market Place, with all its commodities, changing to an Eating House. This is a most elaborate, yet a most perfect, transformation. There are a variety of other tricks in this pantomime, which are equally effective. The pantomime is written and invented by the celebrated composer and author, George Herbert Rodwell.

Marylebone
Eyes, Nose, and Mouth; or, Harlequin Prince Perfect and the Birth of Beauty
THE Pantomime opens in the Cavern of the Prince of Ugliness, amid accumulated horrors, hideous toads, and distorted imps of every size and shape. His Majesty shortly appears from a wonderfully constructed cobweb car, and informs his subjects of the unpleasant state of things in general, and of Ugliness in particular, who is on the eve of being attacked by the federal powers of Beauty, Verri Pretti, and Sunbeam; and, in case of defeat, his (Ugliness's) empire sinks to none at all. One trial has to prove the fact, and Prince Perfect, who is out in search of a wife, is to be the object of their manoevering. A fantastic creature called Fright is ordered to insinuate himself into the Prince's service and councils, by which means they hope to unite him to a perfect fright in lieu of the matchless being the Queen of Beauty is endeavouring to gain for him. The Queen is served by a beautiful spirit named Sunbeam, and the spell commences.

Prince Perfect, in a vision, beholds the Princess Paragon reposing in the Isle of Beauty, and becoming on the instant deeply enamoured, resolves to travel in search of her. Ambassadors arrive with portraits of various incomparables, from which he is expected to make choice of a bride; but poor Perfect's thoughts, being solely occupied with the "bright excellence of his vision", he is disgusted with them, and, conducted by Fright and attended by his faithful valet Scrimble Scramble, proceeds on his journey, via the Empire of Eyes, the Nation of Noses, and the Monarchy of

Mouths. Amongst the Eyes he encounters a troop of Amazons, who, finding that all their self commendations move not the Prince, endeavour to repel his further advance by a variety of warlike manoeuvres, but are defeated through the instrumentality of Sunbeam, who makes them appear in their proper characters. Perfect, grateful for his delivery, travels on until he reaches the Nation of Noses, still attended by Scrimble Scramble, who, between love for his master and horror at what he is doomed to witness, and the annoyance he experiences from the demon Fright, is in an "awful fix". The Prince is courted by Pugnose, Snubnose, and other nasal charmers, but he still remains faithful to the "fond object of his dream," and determines to dismiss his attendant Fright, whose treachery here begins to manifest itself openly. The Prince is not to be baffled, Scrimble Scramble plucks up courage, and he and his master at last reach the great Mouth itself. Ugliness and Beauty encounter each other in *propria persona*, a few words ensue, and the transformation commences.

In the course of the harlequinade several very clever and palpable hits are made at the ruling topics of the day; and, with Howell for Harlequin, the "great Tom"[13] for Clown, and Bradwell's tricks, we may rest assured that tact in adaptation and skill in execution will not be lacking.

Victoria
The World of Wonders; or, Harlequin Caxton and the Origin of Printing
THE first scene is the abode of Stupidity, whose slaves are forging the fetters of Ignorance and Superstition. Stupidity finds his designs frustrated by the appearance of Intelligence, who dissipates the clouds of darkness, and transports the visitors to the realms of Intelligence, where the Arts and Sciences are discovered surrounded by their attributes. We are then introduced to the dominion of the Press, embodying the newspaper and periodical literature of the day. Then there is a view of Caxton's house in the Almonry at Westminster, with a distant prospect of the village of Charing. The ancient pastimes – a game of skill in throwing the quoit takes place, "the fayre ladye", Rosabelle, being the prize in view. We then have the interior of Caxton's house, who, in company with his coadjutor, Wynkin de Worde, go to sleep. Truth appears from the bottom of a well and favours them with a prophecy, and an allegorical tableau of the progress of printing.

Lambeth Marsh, in the Olden Time, is the next scene, where the lovers are in trouble, but are saved by fairy intervention; the last scene of the opening being the Temple of Typographia, with the display of the glories of the printer's art, all the different styles of letter, as Pica, Brevier, Minion, &c, being personified. The transformation then takes place – Harlequin, M. Lupino; Pantaloon, Mr Morelli; Columbine, Mlle Zitelli; Clown, Paul Herring; and Sprite, Signor Molino. A great variety of comic scenes ensue, every circumstance of note coming in for a hit.

Strand
The Man in the Moon; or, the World of Waggery
[…] THE principal features turn upon the adventures of Young England in his attempts to force a passage to the moon. He applies to the Goddess of Night (Nox), and, by aid of an electric telegraph to the upper regions, gets invited to the realms of King Lunardi. The Green Cheese monarch is at the time in great despair from the loss of his only daughter, the Princess Twinkle, who had been stolen or decoyed away to the dominions of King Dog Star. Young England, of course, becomes the champion of the fair princess, and ultimately restores her to the arms of her loving parents. Much fun and equivoke originate in the world of waggery.

Young England, who is said to be the pride of Europe, although always in a merry key, consults Nox about the propriety of hiring a villa in the country of Moonshine. Nox, herself a wag, observes that as the moon is made of green cheese, it would be advisable to advertise for a house on the Rhine. A controversy ensues as to which of the London newspapers should be the possessor of the affiche. Nox recommends that Venus herself should take it to the *Star*, or that Atlas should bear it to the *Globe*, or that Phictor should take it to the *Sun*, and Young England, disliking the female sex, recommends the *Mail*; but, ultimately, Bacchus, being a friend to the Tap Tub, is allowed to take it to the *Morning Advertiser*. These preliminaries settled, Young England takes to the atmospheric line, and invades the territories of the inimicable Dog Star, who is vanquished in mortal combat, and, by the usual license of the season, becomes Pantaloon; the Princess Twinkle is changed into Columbine; Young England, the original party-coloured hero, into Harlequin, and King Lunardi throws off his kingly garb and becomes Clown. The business of Pantomime then commences, and we congratulate Mr Cooper in securing one of the best (if not *the* best) Columbines on the stage, Mlle Louise Blanche.
The Era, 26/12/1847

Royal Lyceum
The Golden Branch
[…] THE story here adapted is the fairy tale "Le Rameau d'Or", by the Countess d'Anois, who wrote "The Sleeping Beauty" and "The White Cat". From such productions Mr Planche carefully extracts the purer metal, retaining something more than the glitter, and rejecting the dross. […] Here is the main thread of the story: –

The first scene displays the Spirit Vaults and Private Still in the Enchanter's Castle, in which the magical juices are extracted by Humguffin, an enchanter (Mr F Matthews), Mandragora, his sister (Mrs Macnamara), and Blueruino, an illicit spirit (Mr H Marshall). By means of their distillations they have thrown a fair young princess, Benignanta (Miss Gougenheim), into a nap of two hundred years' duration, and an equally handsome Prince, her lover, has been turned into an Eagle, who, with a Golden Branch – the magic charm which is to break the spell – "bides his time" with the mournful patience peculiar to birds in distress. Pastorella, a fairy of the new school (Miss Marshall), knocks at the Enchanter's door at the moment Humguffin is preparing to be "off to town on a little bit of a spree", and to the tune of "It's no use knocking at the door".

Two hundred years having elapsed, introduces us to the King of all the Browns, who is tyrant of the Silly Islands (Mr H Hall), and a monarch of great potency in affairs of the state matrimonial. Prince Humpy (Miss Kathleen Fitzwilliam), an ugly and deformed scion of the regal house of Brown, refuses to marry the Princess Dumpy (Miss Howard), the only daughter of King Stumpy. The young lady has the misfortune to be born without legs, and with a face as plain as the ugly nose on young Brown's frightful face. She lives in a golden bowl, and thinks herself handsome. Prompted by her waiting-maid Suivanta (Madame Vestris[14]), the Princess is determined not to throw herself away upon such an ugly brute as her supposed love. Indeed there is no love lost between the exceedingly ordinary pair; and the upshot of the whole is, that King Brown, exasperated at the overthrow of his scheme, immures the Prince in the round tower of his castle, and tells the women to go to some other place not quite so cool. By the aid of an illuminated manuscript, in the first page of which is a living facsimile of Prince Humpy and of the lady of whom he is enamoured, the key to the difficulty is discovered, and the young Prince makes his way to the "Turquoise Chamber", where the Queen of Arcadia (Miss Gougenheim) lies entranced. The spell is broken, and the Queen, to reward the deformed Prince, transforms him into a handsome Corydon. The scene that follows is one of the most tasteful, fairylike compositions ever seen on any stage. It represents the "Bowers of Arcadia", with groups of figures artistically arranged. A "Fête al Frisko" occurs, in which the following dances are exhibited: – Pas de deux, *á la* Watteau, by Mr Gilbert and Miss Ballin; pas de ditto, *á la* Catchafairy, by Mr and Miss Marshall, and an Arcadian mazurka, polka and pastoral galoppade.

The second act discloses the transformenus of the unhappy eagle into Transimenus (Miss Fairbrother), and Arcadian Prince, and that of Princess Dumpy into the handsome Phillis. Tityrus, the former attendant upon Prince Humpy, is represented by Mr Harley, who is as much in love with Amaryllis, the former Suivanta, as his master is with Phillis. The "pastoral landscape in Arcadia" is a gem in scene painting, and does great credit to the artists. Some clever dancing is exhibited by the Arcadians, and Miss Fairbrother and Miss Howard dance a "Transatlantic medley pas de deux". The "Spirit Vaults" again appear, as in the first scene, and Phillis and Corydon are once more in the power of the Enchanter, who, in revenge for having broken his spells, turns them into a cricket and grasshopper. The concluding scene represents the "Golden Gardens and Fairy Tree", and the cricket and grasshopper, who are seen in the hollow of the tree, are released by the fairy, who divides the trunk asunder, and changes them to their natural shapes. The whole closes with a grand and magnificent tableaux.

The whole of this extravanganza is represented in a succession of exquisite tableaux, several of which are pictures perfectly resembling the works of Watteau. Mr Planche, in portraying Arcadia, has strictly adhered to the style and notions of our ancestors, who not only sung the charms of pastoral life, but imitated it in silks and satins, and illustrated it on paper, on canvas, and in china. We have shepherds and shepherdesses, dressed exactly to pattern, and grouped precisely after pictures that we have seen; the faultless manner in which all this is contrived is truly remarkable. One of the dances, for instance, is made up by a party of ladies so exquisitely attired, after the fashion to which we allude, that every couple (and they are all picked ballet dancers), make a Corydon and Chloe, upon whom "no expense has been spared" to make the resemblances perfect. In this dance there is a novelty in the way of using a rose wreath. This is attached to the top of each crook; the dance proceeds, with the flowers raised aloft, and swinging and turning into graceful festoons, without entanglement or derangement to the bearers – a very pretty effect. The dancing is, indeed, all characteristic and excellently performed, and we never remember to have seen a *corps de ballet* better drilled or better looking. Of course the pastorelle, the minuet, and the gavotte are introduced. Mr Gilbert and Miss Ballin performed a *pas de deux*, so do Mr and Miss Marshall. The abilities of these ladies and gentlemen are well known to the world. While alluding to the dancing, we must mention that occasion is taken for displaying the charming person and finished style of Miss Fairbrother. This lady appears as a prince, and no fairy creation could look more gracefully captivating and regally lovely. In a dance with Miss Howard, she renders that which is essentially common, elegant and polished; as her twinkling and tiny feet tread lively steps to a popular measure, we admit that it is the manner of doing a thing which makes it vulgar or otherwise.

These performances are enhanced by the scenery which surrounds them, and all this, too, is chaste, elegant and highly finished, elaborate in execution, and splendid in effect, but softened down and "tempered into beauty". It is impossible to describe in a few words the artistic merit of many of the scenes. That which ends the first act is the most gorgeous exhibition imaginable, a very temple of flowers, designed, one would think, by an architectural Flora, and executed by magic hands; and this is so delicate withal, that its brilliancy is like moon rays, and its tints resemble those of the rainbow; there is nothing gaudy in the whole production, although everything belonging to it is rich. More credit falls upon Messrs Sloman and Beverley than upon any other gentlemen of their profession who have this year employed themselves in scenic composition.

The fair manageress takes a prominent part in the piece, which bears proof throughout of her superior tact and control. She shines forth a star in her own hemisphere, and the manner in which a song to the tune of "Cherry Ripe" is encored, is evidence of the satisfaction which her presence creates among her audience. [...]

Among the men-folk, Mr Hall is worthy of mention. He is the veriest King Brown that ever reigned, and in his mock heroics, his imitations of Charles Kean and William Macready, are very striking. Nor must the redoubtable Frank Matthews be forgotten. He is a veritable Humguffin, with a voice more refreshing than ever; and the renowned Harley too, at whom people are in such a hurry to laugh that they will not wait until he tries to make them do so – he is a rustic swain to the minutest touch, and so deeply is he embued with a pastoral spirit, that he sings and dances, marking the precise time with his voice and feet, so as to create roars of admiration.

And thus we may, did our space permit, give a passing word of commendation to every actor and actress in "The Golden Branch". That our praise in not unmerited may be seen by the throng that collect round the doors, and the crowded state of the house. This is, as we have said, the piece of the season – everybody who has seen it subscribes to the fact, and the public at large have discovered it – a fortunate circumstance for the successful and deserving Management of the Royal Lyceum.

This production is included as a typical example of burlesque, a year-round entertainment very similar to pantomime but without the Harlequinade characters.
The Era, 2/1/1848

1848

Surrey
Harlequin Lord Lovel; or, Lady Nancy Bell and the Fairies of the Silver Oak
THE forthcoming Pantomime at this theatre is written by Francesco Frost, and is entitled *Harlequin Lord Lovel; or, Lady Nancy Bell and the Fairies of the Silver Oak*, the plot of which, as will readily be surmised, is founded upon the ballad of the "Mistletoe Bough".[15]

The first scene, the Druids' Haunt by Moonlight, with a Druidical Chant and Invocation, to the air of "Stoney Batter!"[16] will be found amply explanatory of the details of a row that is supposed to have taken place among them and one Baron Allaflam, upon whose domains, at Stonehenge, they have thought proper to make a settlement, meeting his legal notice to quit with a war cry of "Freedom and Stonehenge!" and then resolving to be revenged upon him for his tyranny by setting fire to the forest, and further causing the death of the Baron's daughter, who is about to be married to Lord Lovel. By the timely intervention, however, of the Fairy of the Oak, the forest is saved from destruction, in addition to which a plan is laid to thwart the deadly design of the malignant Druids against Lady Nancy Bell, Lord Lovel's betrothed, whose death is to result from – now mark this, ladies, and beware! – the evil effects of a kiss under a mistletoe bough, on which the Druids cast a potent spell for the maiden's destruction. The fatality thus intended is to be brought about on the very day of her nuptials, and, accordingly, after the grand banquet which Lord Lovel's father-in-law gives in honour of the occasion, the bride, becoming "weary of dancing", proposes to vary the evening's amusements with a game at hide and seek, which is agreed to, and then comes the incident of the Old Oak Chest, and Lady Nancy Bell's supposed imprisonment therein. It eventually turns out, however, that, although according to the natural course of events nothing could have saved the damsel from suffocation, she is, in reality, just as much alive as ever, and makes her appearance under the protection of the Fairies in a sort of *tableau vivant*, intended to illustrate an "Apotheosis of the Oak", which is the last scene of the Pantomime opening.

Then comes the broader practical fun, duly intermingled with pantomime tricks and transformations, most of which, we are informed, will be found to possess considerable novelty. The scenery, by Mr Jones of the Theatre Royal, Drury Lane, is unusually splendid, the properties got up regardless of expense, and the Pantomime altogether has been well-managed in every department. The Clown is the unrivalled Tom Matthews, who, by the way, sings a capital song with the Great Sea Serpent; Harlequin, Duelin; and Columbine, Mlle Theodore. The theatre has been entirely redecorated, and, indeed, almost entirely reconstructed.

Victoria
The Land of Light; or, Harlequin Gas and the Four Elements, Earth, Air, Fire, and Water
THE opening scene is the Retreat of the Fairies in the Goblin Coal Mine, 5,000 miles below the surface of the Earth, whither they have been driven by the triumphant power of Science. The second scene is the Lustrous Land of Light (Bude Light[17], Gas, Camphine[18], and every other kind of light). A wager is here made between Science and the Fairies, that the powers of the former shall outdo those of Fiction; and the objects of trial are, as usual, the two lovers, between

whom there is a rivalry for the hand of a certain maiden, Science, with her attendant sprite, Gas, taking one side, and Oberon, King of Fairy Land, the other. The contest accordingly commences, involving the unhappy lovers in most extraordinary reverses, which are at last ended by Science proving victorious, and then, in the excitement of her triumph, volunteering to treat all her friends present with a Pantomime, which she immediately commences by the usual transformations into Harlequin, Columbine, &c.

The scenery, this year, appears by the bills to be got up on a scale of extraordinary greatness, one of the depictions being nothing less than the "Great Globe itself". In short, between such rival powers as we are here introduced to, what extraordinary doings may we not expect? Tricks and transformations, truly marvellous, with incidents of a like nature; and, we believe, we may add that, in these respects, the Victoria playbills are seldom found to hold out expectations which are not realized almost to the letter. The Pantomimists are Messrs Buck, Lupino, White, and Madame Zitella. The scenery is painted by Mr Mildenhall.

On the pantomime's opening night, 26th December, two boys were killed when the handrail of the staircase leading to the gallery gave way under the crush of people pushing to reach their seats.
The Era, 24/12/1848

1849

Standard

Harlequin and the Magic Teapot; or, Chi-Ki Ski-Hi, King of the Golden Pagodas

IN the opening we are introduced to Old Christmas in his Halls of Revelry, with the Head of Knowledge, with his attendants Mirth, Good Humour, Rhyme, Punch, and Old Pantomime (grown grey in the service). Mercury Walker (the postman) arrives with a letter from the Manager, who requires a subject for his Pantomime. Pantomime is exhausted in ideas. The Genius of Invention taps the Head of Knowledge – the mouth expands and shows a tableau of a Poor Needlewoman eating her Christmas dinner, a herring. The next tableau shows the Shirt Seller's Christmas dinner. He is shown surrounded by every luxury. (The condition of the poor shirt makers has been aptly hit.) The Shirt Seller has also a large grocery establishment, and is in love with the Needlewoman, and they agree to send her to China, and dismiss Mercury with the subject.

We next find Hyson Souchong (the ci-divant Shirt Seller) with his servants preparing to pay a visit to the Needlewoman, whom he is in love with, and after much fun and comicality he departs. Lucy Miggins (the Needlewoman, Miss Eliza Terry) is mourning over past events, when she is interrupted by the arrival of Souchong. He attempts to carry her off by force, but her band of needle-women rush to the rescue, and they carry the day at the needle's point. She is about to swallow (sloeleaf) poison, when the Mother O'Steam appears in her magic teapot, and informs her that it is her destiny to wed the Prince of China, and thither she transports her. Determined not to be foiled, Souchong consults his friend, the Wizard Sloeleaf, and his agent, Bad Conscience. The Wizard suggests an aerial trip with the brave Lieut. Gale, and a capital effect here takes place of the ascension of the Royal Cremorne Balloon from the Gardens. We now find Lucy travelling through the misty air, and Mother O'Steam calls upon her Fays, who appear with some hundreds of lights to guide her on her way.

We now arrive at China, and are presented with a magnificent scene of the Hall of a Hundred Pillars. Prince Yellow Ochre (Mr Saunders) is in great grief, being about to be forced into marriage with the Emperor's daughter, to the regret of the Mother Queen Foofoo-foozlefat (Mr G Herbert). The Prince and Lucy (who he has seen in his dreams) meet, and as usual with "love at first sight", vow to part no more, and they depart to meet the bridal procession, which takes place in the Temple of the Golden Pagodas. Souchong arrives, and claims Lucy; the Emperor aids his suit, and Lieutenant Gale (the Game Cock) is requested to prepare his balloon to convey the hapless Lucy back, but Mother O'Steam opportunely arrives and transforms the lovers into Harlequin and Columbine. Our friend the Wizard, however, is not to be done, and in return he changes the Emperor and Souchong into a pair of clowns, and the doting Mother into Pantaloon.

The comic business is excellent. Particular mention may be made of a Central Californian Railway, which changes to a view of the "Diggings", &c, a Coal Shed, which is transmogrified into the Coal Exchange, and an extensive and excellently painted view of the Procession on the River. A Dance of Coalheavers, executed by twelve little children, here takes place, which will no doubt tell capitally. The greatest effect, however, will be the Interior of a Coffee-House, which is converted into two streets, with upward of twenty shops lighted with real gas. The Pantomimists are strong – Messrs Doughty and Buck are the clowns; Mr Saunders, Harlequin; Mr Bird, Pantaloon; Miss Pauline, Columbine; and the Messrs Andrews, Sprites. The scenery, dresses, and appointments are of a very gorgeous character. The Pantomime is full of excellent tricks, and embraces upwards of twenty-four new and elaborate scenes. A great hit may confidently be expected.
The Era, 23/12/1849

NOTES

1 – Horace Walpole's *The Castle of Otranto*, upon which the pantomime plot was loosely based, is widely regarded as the first Gothic novel.

2 – Sarah Fairbrother (1816-1890): A burlesque and pantomime actress best remembered for her marriage to Prince George, Duke of Cambridge (1819-1904), a cousin of Queen Victoria. As the marriage took place without the Queen's consent, Fairbrother was known simply as Mrs Fitzgeorge and their children were not granted titles.

3 – A liveried groom or carriage servant.

4 – In May 1840 James Thomas Brudenell, seventh Earl of Cardigan and commander of the 11th Hussars, illegally ordered the arrest of a Captain Reynolds for placing wine on the mess-table in a black bottle rather than a decanter. Shortly afterwards Brudenell mistook another Captain Reynolds for the culprit and had him arrested for impertinence. The incident was reported in the *Morning Chronicle*, and Brudenell challenged the author of the article, Captain Harvey Tuckett, to a duel. Although Tuckett was wounded Brudenell was acquitted on a technicality.

5 – One of the wedding presents received by Queen Victoria and Prince Albert was a wheel of cheese weighing 1,000 pounds.

6 – Philippe Musard (1792-1859): A French composer known as the "Lord of Quadrilles and Galops", he gave a series of concerts at Drury Lane Theatre in October 1840.

7 – On 10th December 1840 John Green was murdered whilst working on the construction of the Edinburgh and Glasgow Railway.

8 – The First Opium War, also known as the Anglo-Chinese War (1839-1842).

9 – Edward Jones (1824-1893), who broke into Buckingham Palace three times between 1838 and 1841.

10 – An enormous Roman marble vase owned by the Earls of Warwick. In 1841 several newspapers reported that the greenhouse at Warwick Castle built to house the vase was now in a state of decay.

11 – Thomas Potter Cooke (1786-1864): An actor particularly associated with nautical roles.

12 – A reference to a court case in which nineteen-year-old Alice Lowe was charged with stealing jewellery from her employer, Lord Frankfort. It was implied that Lowe was Lord Frankfort's mistress.

13 – The actor Thomas Matthews.

14 – Lucia Elizabeth Vestris (1797-1856): An actress, opera singer and manager of several theatres.

15 – The legend of a bride who plays hide-and-seek at her wedding and hides in a chest, only to become trapped and not discovered until her body has been reduced to a skeleton, is associated with several old houses. A song on the subject by T H Bayley and Sir Henry Bishop, written in the 1830s, become a well-known Christmas carol.

16 – *The Rakes of Stoney Batter* is an Irish folk song.

17 – A brilliant oil lamp first used to light the House of Commons in 1839.

18 – A trade name for purified spirit of turpentine.

6
The 1850s
A Pair of Flaming Eyes From the Cupboard

1850

City of London
Knife, Fork, and Spoon; or, Harlequin's Breakfast, Dinner, Tea, and Supper

THE acknowledged house of call for legitimate pantomime has prepared for its patrons one of the most ingenious, whimsical, and truly laughable concoctions that has ever emanated from the fertile brains of Mr Nelson Lee. When submitting the programme to our readers, they will be enabled to judge of its perfect originality. The title is not exactly in everybody's mouth, but near to it, *viz, Knife, Fork, and Spoon; or, Harlequin's Breakfast, Dinner, Tea, and Supper*. The opening scene represents a Grand Hall of Knives, Forks, and Spoons.

PLATE THE FIRST: – The Cooks are preparing for a Banquet of Fun. The dishes, smoking hot, arrive in rapid succession, the Clerk of the Kitchen taking Notes. Bub and Grub make their appearance with the intelligence that the City Aldermen have been out to Peck and Booze. Whitebait and Champagne have had free liberty. This causes a sudden consternation, knowing that each Alderman will have to pay his share. The matter is soon settled by the timely arrival of M. Soyer, who soon works a reform in the kitchen. He states to his cooks that the Fairy Queen, Plenty, intends to start the Four Meals as a subject for the Christmas Sports. Bub is despatched to Guildhall. Grub he takes with him to work out the idea of the Fairy Queen. This brings us to

PLATE THE SECOND: – The Golden Grove of Prosperity, the supposed abode of Plenty, the Fairy Queen. Roundabout has been going her rounds, bringing together the Fairy Court by a special mandate from the Queen. A Dance of Revelry here takes place, at the conclusion of which a sudden storm bursts forth on Fairy Land. The Fays instantly obtain their Fairy Umbrellas and sing a chorus to the clouds, which has the desired effect, the sun shedding his rays in great splendour, when the Fairy Queen, Plenty, makes her appearance to the great joy and delight of the Fairy Court. Plenty tells them a pretty little story, in which she states it to be her intention to protect Sterling Pantomime, informing them of the subject she has chosen, viz., the Four Meals. The Fairies readily promise their assistance. A special mandate is forwarded to M. Soyer to be in readiness to dish up the idea. Here the Fairy Court takes their departure, bringing us to

PLATE THE THIRD: – Grand Council Chamber, Guildhall: here all is confusion worse confounded, the City Aldermen have lost their Breakfast and Dinner. A council is held. Swordbearer is called to render assistance to prevent a famine among the Corporation; an oath is taken, and he is invested with power and intrusted with the infantry. He departs for the east, there to take command of the troops. They each propose to take different roads in search of the scoundrel Dinner, who it appears has bolted with Breakfast. This determination brings us to

PLATE THE FOURTH: – Public Dining Rooms, on the Land of Good Cheer. N B Queen Mab's House of Call. The bell denotes the arrival of Dinner, who is attended by his bride, Miss Rosy Breakfast – they instantly enter the rooms to refresh. Swordbearer and his troop of Beef-eaters make their appearance. He being possessed of magic power, changes the Dinner Rooms to Supper Rooms. This brings home Supper, who finding Dinner within his abode is highly indignant, and drives him out – an arrest is about to take place. Dinner calls Fish, Flesh, and Fowl to his aid. A conflict ensues, which is joined by Swordbearer and his troop. Dinner is eventually compelled to yield, and taken prisoner. He exclaims

The Reading Sauce will become my bail.

Swordbearer replies,

If we have any of your sauce, you shall go to Reading Gaol,
The silent system will soon cook your goose.

Away with the runaway – resistance is of little use.

Dinner is instantly taken off, bringing us to

PLATE THE FIFTH: – A most original scene, Tea Cottage, Gunpowder Row. Here Dame Hyson is lamenting the loss of her Breakfast through not being up in time. The Aldermen not being able to obtain their Dinner have come to the Dame to get a strong cup of tea, when to their horror they discover the tea caddy has been taken away by Breakfast. Great fear is entertained for the Corporation. The three resolve to find this Dinner out or perish in the attempt, which places before us

PLATE THE SIXTH: – Starvation Hall. Here Spiderlimb, Skillagalee, Narrowaist, and Pineaway, four Sprites, amuse themselves by singing a chorus; after which Dinner is brough on a prisoner, with a padlock on his mouth; he is in sad distress, but takes courage and calls on the Fairy Queen, Plenty, who bursts through his prison walls and releases him, despatching the true lover to her palace. The Queen exclaims,

In a land of freedom, starvation must not be,
My power soon will set the lovers free.

The power of the Fairy Queen brings us instantly to

PLATE THE SEVENTH: – Grand Halls of Plenty, where a grand procession of Breakfast, Dinner, Tea, and Supper takes place, which is followed by the lovers, who are pursued by the Dames Tea and Supper. The Queen settles the hash by stating –

Dinner will suit Breakfast to a T,
Her future fate now rests with me,
Doctors say, and I'm inclined to think they're right,
Supper can be dispensed with any night.

Here a general transformation takes place; the characters being placed in a saucepan, and cooked into a "Dish of all Sorts", *viz* – Harlequin, Columbine, Clown, Pantaloon, Sprites, and Lover, forming a strength unequalled. The Clown, Mr G Perry, of great provincial celebrity. Among the comic scenes will be found: – the New Industrial Exhibition, introducing great wonders; Wolf, Fox, and Lamb; J Ellis, clothier, Aldgate; Barrett's Dining Room, High Hill Ferry; Mechi's Razor Dêpot; Parker's Hat Warehouse, Shoreditch, &c.

Standard

Harlequin Buttercups and Daisies; or, Great A, Little B, the Cat's in the Cupboard and She Can't See

AT the commencement Gorgona (Mr Nelson), the gnome, is informed by Quasimar, his principal attendant (Mr H Lewis), of the Love Alderman Great A (Mr Gates) has for Columba (Miss Eliza Terry), daughter of Bouncing B, the Beadle (Mr G Herbert), in which love he is likely to be thwarted, the young lady preferring Little A, an artist (Mr H Saunders), in whom she had found a young fellow "just suited to her mind". The gnome, who is a lover of mischief, directs Quasimar to mar their loves, and he, in obedience and to aid his designs better, assumes the form of a cat.

We are now transported to the field of wild flowers, where the buttercups and daisies are blooming in the meadows. Here Daisymead, the fairy queen (who is a patron of merit), is informed of the danger that threatens the little artist A, and promises protection; she summonses her fairy train, and her elfin band appear peeping from the flowers, whilst others are borne to her presence from pearl-like cars floating down the Silver Lake. Upwards of fifty children form the elfin court, which, from their costly attire and brilliancy of scene, will prove very striking. The usual promise is given to the queen, and we next arrive at the garret of Little A, the artist.

Columba the fair and the artist meet – their *tete-a-tete* is broken by the arrival of the Alderman Great A, who possesses, amongst other advantages (query), a family of twelve sons who inherit the family caste of countenance, *viz*, a certain obliquity of vision, usually denominated squint-eyed. This settles the question with Columba, who indignantly spurns his offer, and the cat coming in opportunely, attacks and drives her suitor and his family away. They return, however, and destroy the artist's pictures, rejoiced to think that their mischief is unknown, for "the cat's in the cupboard and she can't see", but a pair of flaming eyes from the cupboard convinces them that the cat can see, and they fly in dismay.

The lovers having fled, fall again into the power of Gorgona in the Haunted Dell of the Golden Rock, from which innumerable demon faces meet the gaze of the unfortunate fugitives, but by the magic touch of the fairy Daisymead, the hideous forms are replaced by those of her fairy elves – a capital and very elaborate mechanical effect. The cat at length is caught in the silver web of Destiny, and the transformations take place in the Glittering Bowers of Buttercups and Daisies.

Mr H Saunders is the Harlequin, Buck and Doughty the Clowns, M. Silvani the Sprite (from the Princess's Theatre), and Pantaloon Mr Bird; Columbine, Mlle Pauline, and Harlequina, Mrs Buck. The pantomimic cast is thus very strong. The scenery is, throughout, very beautiful and novel. Nor have passing events being lost sight of by the manager; Barclay and Perkins's Brewery – the exterior of the Crystal Palace – a registered lodging house – a review of the police (the police being sustained by children) – a moving Panorama of the principal shops in Shoreditch, and, above all, a triumphal arch created in celebration of her most Gracious Majesty, which is instantaneously illuminated with upwards of 3,000 jets of gas, are deserving of particular mention. There are no less than forty scenes in this Pantomime, and a great run is anticipated.
The Era, 22/12/1850

1851

Surrey
The King of the Golden Seas; or, Harlequin Prince Bluecap and the Three Kingdoms, Animal, Vegetable, and Mineral

THE subjects for pantomime becoming every year less numerous, and the stock of fairy tales now exhibiting some unequivocal symptoms of being utterly exhausted, Mr E L Blanchard has gone to more recondite sources for his plot, and a certain apocryphal Persian fabulist, Hafiz Al Fun, is said in the bills to have furnished the legend on which he has built the present Christmas comicality of THE KING OF THE GOLDEN SEAS; OR, HARLEQUIN PRINCE BLUECAP AND THE THREE KINGDOMS, ANIMAL, VEGETABLE, AND MINERAL.

The opening, which is rather more in the burlesque style than usual, being prodigally provided with political puns and popular parodies, commences in the Land of Barli Shoogs, where the Fairy Trifla, Sovereign of all the sweets, announces her intention of aiding the Prince Bluecap to obtain the hand of a certain Princess Sacharrina, with whom he has been for some time smitten.

The principal fairy, Bonbon, being intrusted with the execution of this mission, the scene changes to a magnificent view of the Golden City and the Islands of Shoogar Candi, where the Emperor Alicampagne, attended by his gold nobles, soon after makes his appearance, and insists upon the marriage of his daughter Saccharina with the Great Grimguffin, King of the Ugli Isles, who comes to establish his claim. Prince Bluecap, however, interferes at this crisis, and after some difficulty gets the consent of the Emperor to wed his daughter, on condition that he shall set forth at once and procure three treasures, each to be respectively obtained from the Animal, the Vegetable, and the Mineral Kingdoms.

Aided by his fairy protector, the Prince first passes, by a panoramic process, through the Animal Kingdom, where he meets with a fine dog, a real Skye terrier, who is pronounced by the Fairy Queen to be the greatest treasure he can have, possessing the most remarkable virtues and the most astounding sagacity. He is congratulating himself on having secured so servicable a canine companion when when the revengeful Grimguffin waylays him, and a capital travestie takes place of those daring encounters between the biped and quadruped combatants which, in the dog-days of the drama, used to elicit such uproarious applause.

We are next introduced the the Castle of King Cauliflower in the Vegetable Kingdom, where we find a population of real vegetarians, the figures being made up exclusively of familiar esculents. In this very novel scene a grand review of the troops takes place for the amusement of Prince Bluecap, and the second treasure required is procured by the dog from King Cauliflower's, whence a magical spade is taken, having the desirable property of turning up gold whenever it is struck in the earth.

Hence, a descent is made to the Mineral Kingdom, where Prince Bluecap discovers the third treasure, Gold, and the Emperor, obliviously unmindful of his promise, is going to retract his engagement, when, through the agency of the dog, a grand magical transformation takes place and the cavern changes to a brilliant Temple, with an allegorical representation of the Hive of a Thousand Sweets, one of the most extraordinary effects ever witnessed on this side of the Thames. Here the usual pantomimic *metamorphosis* takes place, the Prince becoming Harlequin; the Princess Saccharina, Columbine, Miss Cushnie; the Great Grimguffin, Pantaloon, Signor Bradbury; and the King Cauliflower, Clown, M. Buck. The dog, played by M. Deani, is transformed to a Sprite, and the comic business commences, which this year is more opulent than usual in smart, pungent hits at the times, and elaborate mechanical effects. A scene of the "Great Bed in the Austrian Department of the Exhibition[1]" is full of novel effects, and there is not a passing subject but has received its appropriate pointed illustration.

The scenery by Mr Callcott is very beautiful and exhibits much originality in design, whilst the general getting up of the Pantomime displays a liberality on the part of the management which is almost suggestive of a subterranean communication existing between St George's Fields and the Gold Regions of Australia. Mr Shepherd has been indefatiguable in securing the completeness of every department, and a long run may be anticipated.

E L Blanchard

Marylebone
Sir John Barleycorn; or, Harlequin Champagne and the Fairies of the Hop and the Vine
SIR JOHN BARLEYCORN; OR, HARLEQUIN CHAMPAGNE AND THE FAIRIES OF THE HOP AND THE VINE, is the title of the XXX Comic Pantomime to be produced at this theatre; the author, called in the bills "A Licensed Wit", being well known under his popular pseudonym of Francisco Frost. The novelty of the idea is very well carried out by the grotesque embodiment of all the beverages familiar to the lovers of social enjoyment, and a perfect allegory is sustained throughout.

The opening scene is the Great Brewery of Pantomime, where the concoction takes place, under the superintendence of the Genius of Fun. The centre of the vat opens, and discovers the well known picture of Sir John Barleycorn with a foaming tankard of ale in his hand, on which Fun exclaims:

Hail, glorious John, old England's fame and boast!
This is the stuff that Britons prize the most;
Be this our subject – real old English ale!
Who sees that head will never find it's stale!

Corkscrew, the original Cove of Cork, is now summoned, and we hear Sir John being desirous to ally himself to the fair Light-Heart, who has already been sought-after by Champagne. Proceeding from his residence in the in the Valley of Richingrain, Barleycorn goes with his attendants, Pale Ale and Extra Stout, to the abode of Old Port in the Wood, the guardian of the fair Ladye Light-Heart. Here a contest takes place between the Knight of the Hop and the Knight of the Vine, ending in an elopement of Champagne with Light-Heart, who is conveyed to the Castle of Champagne on the banks of the Rhine. Sir John, with a formidable battery of soda water bottles, storms the Castle; and Corkscrew, insinuating his body through the wall, opens the gates to the Barleycorn Barrel Army. The fugitives take refuge in the wine vaults of the Castle, and finally a truce is granted, on the condition that the Hop and the Vine shall unite in their endeavours to cheer the hearts of mankind.

The transformation now takes place, Light-Heart becoming Columbine (Miss Adelaide Malcolm), Champagne, Harlequin (M. Veroni), Old Port, Pantaloon (Paul Kellar), and Sir John Barleycorn, Clown, personated by the unrivalled Tom Mathews. The Harlequinade embraces a comic panorama of all the events of the past year, and the innovation of the Bloomer Costume[2] is humorously touched upon by the Clown in a facetious duet that he sings with a pair of breeches.

The scenery, by Mr Mildenhall, is of a very striking character; and the procession of the Champagne Army, who are composed of inverted wine glasses and foil-tipped bottles, and having cigars for spears, constitute a very animated and unhackneyed introduction. The aim of the management seems to have been to combine the grotesque with the real in their treatment of the subject; and there is no doubt that the success of the Marylebone Pantomime will warrant the enormous outlay to which the Lessee has gone in its production.
The Era, 21/12/1851

1852

Marylebone
Undine, the Spirit of Water; or, Harlequin Teetotum and the Chinese Cup and Sorceror

THE first scene represents the abode of Undine, who, unlike the heroine of the German romance, seems to have a large family connexion, the spirits so agreeably blended with water in this instance being a host of captivating young ladies in blue muslin, and with an appropriate variety of coral emblems. Rippel, her sprite in attendance, is commanded to attend her to the Court of the Emperor Congou, who desires, as the personification of tea, to enter into an alliance with the genius of the New River.

We are, therefore, next introduced to the "City of Cougou", with the Cougou army under the direction of the Emperor, facetiously represented by heads and bodies fashioned out of cups, saucers, milk jugs, and the other appurtenances of the tea table. Here we find Miss Sue-Chong, who is beloved by Young Hyson, of the Green Tea faction, and discover that the Emperor, her father, being opposed to the union, has excited the disapprobation of Undine in consequence. The regiment of Spoons, to whom the Emperor confides the care of his daughter, next make their appearance, and the Emperor goes off to fight King Coffee, who threatens to invade his dominions, and who has another enemy in Chicory, a traitor in the camp, who wants to usurp his throne. Young Hyson, in the meantime, has eloped with Sue-Chong to the "Land of Lump Sugar", a sort of neutral ground for both parties. Here the fairies of the Sugar-loaf territory lend their aid.

The palace of King Coffee next reveals to us the Monarch of Mocha gloomily pondering over his position, his pleasant looking attendants, Muffin and Crumpet, being equally as perplexed as himself. Suddenly a war-cry is heard, the Tea party rush in, and King Coffee is compelled to fly. He goes to the borders of his dominions, where we find the Milky Lake and Island of Cream presenting a picturesque appearance. Hearing that a magic cup, belonging to the Chinese sorceror Hanki Panki, will grant to its possessor every wish, the lovers hasten to obtain it. Nearly successful, they are pursued, when the intervention of Undine causes the scene to be changed to the wondrous World of Waters, where revolving water-wheels, lucid waterfalls, and sparkling fairy fountains give a due significance to the title.

Congou is changed to Clown (Rochez), Young Hyson becomes Harlequin (Mr Harvey), and Sue-Chong Columbine (Mrs Harvey), whilst Coffee and Rippel furnish respectively the Pantaloon and Sprite. The comic business is replete with tricks, funny and practicable, of every description; and, altogether, the Marylebone will have nothing to fear from the competition of any of its rivals.

Queen's
The King of the Carbuncles; or, Harlequin Prince Peerless and the Enchanted Beauty of the Diamond Castle

THE opening scene introduces us to the Hall of Snowball, a cave of frosted silver spars, when the Spirit of the Happy New Year enters, and calls on Bleak December, who appears in the centre of a gigantic snowball. After some slight disagreement between the Old Year and the New about the approaching festivities of Christmas time, the Happy New Year brings from a Magic Jest Book four Sprites, Wit, Fun, Mirth, and Jollity, and instructs them to form a Pantomime – racy, rich, and new. They consent, and depart on their mission, while December and the New Year join hands, and promise to act together.

A flying Pavilion then descends from the clouds, from which Stargleam, a Fairy, alights, and, after calling on the Fays, changes the scene to the Moonlit Lake of Silver Waters and Island of the Starry Spirits. The Fairy Queen, Silver Sceptre, appears on the lake, drawn in her car by swans. She calls a Council of the Fairies, informing them that the Princess Rubylight, daughter of the King of the Carbuncles, has been seized by Koh-i-Noor, the King of the Diamond Mines, and imprisoned in his glittering castle, from which captivity, by the aid of a young Prince, she intends to free her.

The Fairies promise to assist her plans, and depart to the Moving Grove of Magic Blue Bells, when a talisman is given to the Fairy Stargleam to deliver to the Prince, on which errand she departs, while the scene passes away and discovers a grand and extensive view of the City of Jewels and Palace of the King of the Carbuncles, who enters with his procession of Golden Guards, and issues a proclamation inviting all Princes to aid in rescuing his daughter from the Diamond King, her hand to be the reward of the successful Champion. Prince Gold arrives with his brilliant train, and is accepted; Prince Silver follows, and is also accepted; Prince Copper, the Princess's lover, then appears, but is rejected, on account of his poverty and mean appearance. The Princes depart, when Stargleam arrives, changes Prince Copper to Prince Peerless, and gives him the talisman to protect him on his journey. After numerous adventures in the Fantastic Forest and Weird Wood, they arrive before the steel gates of the Diamond Fortress. Prince Peerless, by the aid of the Fairy's charm, enters through the keyhole. Gold and Silver, however, get into a row with the two porters, Short Stumps and Long Body, and a terrible fight ensues, in which the porters lose their noses. Prince Peerless then gains the Magic Corridor of the Brazen Hand, and, seizing the ring from off its finger, breaks the charm.

The Fairies appear, and the scene instantaneously changes to the Diamond Dome in the Palace of Gems, with the Princess Rubylight on her enchanted couch – a scene of unparalleled splendour. The Demon is defeated, the transformation takes place, and the Harlequinade commences. The Electric Ball in the Strand, the Emigration to Australia, Uncle Tom's Cabin, the Militia, &c, are all hit off with great humour.

Messrs Grey and Felix Palmieri are the Clowns; Williams and Crosby the Pantaloons; Mr G Teague the Harlequin; Miss Julia Weston the Columbine; and Mlle Annete the Harlequina.

Adelphi
Nell Gwynn; or, Harlequin and the Merrie Monarch and the Orange Girl
THIS is the first Pantomime played for some years at this favourite house. It will be looked forward to with pleasure by the lovers of that kind of entertainment, the more particularly as the immortal Flexmore is to appear as Clown. The management have judiciously selected Mr Nelson Lee for the author, whose experience and talent cannot be disputed. The subject chosen is most happy, being *Nell Gwynn; or, Harlequin and the Merrie Monarch and the Orange Girl.*

The curtain rises, presenting to view the Interior of the Cave of Slander, or the Magic Halls of Malice and Hatred. Stab-i'-the-Dark and Backbiter are discovered, one feeding the ravenous dragons with fire, the other watering a neglected stinging nettle. The Chief informs his Sprites he lives in fear from one "Nell Gwynn". Hatred states she is protected by the Fairy Queen, Charity. The Chief, Scorpino, instantly proposes that Nell Gwynn shall be stabbed by Slander. Hatred agrees, and further remarks that King Charley, surnamed Rowley, has taken a great liking for this orange girl, at which he is enraged.

We are suddenly wafted to the Temple of Charity, in the Land of Benevolence. The Fairy Queen immediately informs the Court that she had been selected to frame a Pantomime, exclaiming –

Charity to keep her position the favour of the town must win,
So what think you, sisters, of poor "Nell Gwynn?"

She waves her wand, when a miniature model of Chelsea Hospital rises, from which a number of living Marionette Chelsea pensioners march out. This incident will be doubly interesting from recent events. After some pleasing evolutions they march to their duty.

We are here presented with the Royal Picture Gallery of Court Beauties at Whitehall. King Charles, surnamed Rowley, arrives, attended by his courtiers and his favourite dogs. After his toilet is attended to, the King appears languid – tired of the frivolity of the Court. Rochester observing it exclaims –

Name but your wish, your Majesty, let your free thoughts appear.

The King replies –

My Nelly must sell no more oranges or ginger beer.

Rochester promises to use his influence to obtain for his Majesty an interview with the charming Nell. He proposes to his Majesty to disguise themselves as sailors, to avoid discovery by the Court. Meanwhile the King amuses himself with his favourite puppy. Rochester soon returns with two dresses, which they immediately put on, and start direct for the King's Theatre.

This presents to view His Majesty's Theatre, which at that period stood on the same site as the Theatre Royal Drury Lane (it was the first theatre, as the present is the fourth; it was opened on April 8th, 1663, when Nell was thirteen years old). It is supposed to be about the time of opening the doors; visitors arrive – link boys and bill men are very busy – a sedan arrives containing Mr Pepys, Mrs Pepys, and the children Pepys, going to the Pantomime on the first night – Nell Gwynn makes her appearance with apples, oranges, and ginger beer – Pepys is struck with her beauty – Rochester introduces her to the King – she consents to visit him at Whitehall – she throws her oranges, &c, away, and departs with Rochester.

We are next introduced to the well-known tavern. The King and Rochester, still in disguise, arrive with Nell. Supper is ordered, at the finish of which a dance is proposed, when old Captain Cupp, the landlord, demands payment of his bill. The King here discovers the loss of his purse, which has been taken by his puppy, and, to prevent discovery, gives his watch. The old Captain, suspecting it stolen, bolts them in. The King lowers Nell from the window, following himself, falling through a skylight.

We now arrive at the Tulip Gardens at Whitehall, with view of the Thames in 1676, supposed to be in the morning of laying the foundation stone of Chelsea Hospital. Nell and his Majesty arrive in their State Barge, attended by the ladies of the Court, who are envious of the success of Nell. The Captain makes his appearance with the watch, but is horror-struck. At this moment the Finger of Scorn rises, and points to Nell, when the State Barge changes to a Fairy Car, containing Charity. Scorn sinks instantly. The Queen, to protect the lovers, changes the King to Harlequin, Nell to

Columbine. Here Scandal rises, and changes Rochester to witty Clown, Captain Cupp to Pantaloon. She presents the bat with this charge: –

For every wound Charity will find a salve;
Remember the King's words, "Don't let poor Nelly starve."

The usual fun here commences. Mr Nelson Lee's budget having opened shows the whims and follies of the day, with food enough for Flexmore to revel in. No expense is spared in the production of this Pantomime, and from the above programme our readers will see it is a work of some talent, and with a cast of characters unequalled in London.
The Era, 26/12/1852

Richard Flexmore

Princess's
Harlequin Cherry and Fair Star; or, the Green Bird, the Dancing Waters, and the Singing Silver Tree

[…] ONE never expects a plot in a Pantomime – that, indeed, would too much distract the attention. Still, it is necessary that we must quit the general for the particular, and describe briefly the incidents of the Pantomime under notice. Alseren is an amiable King of Cyprus, blessed with a large – a remarkably large – family, the most prominent of whom is the eldest son, the Prince Cheribil. The King has also a niece, the Princess Fair Star, and it is to woo and win this damsel that Prince Cheribil's energies are mainly devoted. The Princess herself appears nothing loth; but there exists a horrid geni, one Djinn Sling (of American birth, we presume), who has a hatred of all good things, and who interposes between the Prince and his bride. Man against demon of course stands no chance, and the diabolical spirit would have it all his own way but for the intervention of Everiweriana, the good Queen of the Peris, whose special mission it is to protect the young lady in question. But the Princess is a wilful being. The Peri having saved her from a passing danger, places her in her own retreat in "the realms of illusion".

This is a description of paradise, and here the Princess may disport herself as she pleases, and do as she pleases, all but one thing. There are two vases in the retreat, and these she must not touch. True child of Mother Eve, how is it to be expected that she can refrain from doing the very thing that she is forbidden? She touches the vases, and immediately the power of Djinn Sling over her is restored. Still, the Peri has one resource – the transformation – which at once takes place in a scene of superb splendour, which may be described as the very perfection of scenic and decorative art, the Peri Palace of Peacocks. Prince Cheribil (Mr F Cooke) then becomes Harlequin, in the person of Mr Cormack; Princess Fair Star, hitherto anything but an impersonation of her name (Mr Daly), becomes a lovely and most attractive Columbine (Miss Carlotta Leclerq); Djinn Sling (Mr Rolleston) is transformed into Clown (Mr Huline); and Topak-al-Widdi (Mr H Saker), in the introduction Master of Horse to the Prince, a famous make-up of Widdicomb, is converted into Pantaloon (Mr Paulo).

The fun of the harlequinade then commences, and right-down rollicking fun it is. Though the "hits", as they are termed, at the events of the day, are spare, the fun is abundant, and the changes are of a most gigantic character. In one scene, a windmill, with sails in full motion, miller's house, granaries, &c, changes instantaneously, with one touch of

Harlequin's wand, to the interior of the League Bakery – not a vestige of the mill remains; but here are myriads of bakers, in their night-caps and complete costumes, working away in the production of the staff of life. How Clown interferes in all these scenes – how he gets into the blazing oven, and comes out again, like a Salamander, without a scorch; how he cuts off policemen's heads, and poor Pantaloon's feet, and all the rest of it, it boots not now to tell. […] Miss Leclerq, as we have already intimated, was a charming Columbine; and by the judicious arrangement, now becoming general, of not allowing those in the harlequinade to perform in the introduction, they are enabled to maintain their vigour and freshness until the last scene of their arduous performance.

Nor must we omit one word on behalf of the *corps de ballet*. A more efficient or lovely *corps* we never saw in any theatre. Their dressings and groupings were most tasteful; and whilst their dancing was all that could be desired, there was nothing that could offend the most fastidious.

All honour to Mr Charles Kean for the strictness with which he avoids the slightest approach to indelicate and meretricious displays!

Royal Park Theatre, Liverpool
Ye Siege of Leverpole; or, Harlequin and Prince Rupert and ye Fayre Mayde of Toxteth

WE subjoin the following notice from a contemporary: – "This theatre on Monday evening was densely crowded from pit to ceiling by an audience who had evidently met there to be pleased. The new local Pantomime, entitled *Ye Siege of Leverpole; or, Harlequin and Prince Rupert and ye Fayre Mayde of Toxteth* was evidently the attraction. This Christmas piece met with the most perfect success, which it well merited, for the opening, written by Mr C Millward of this town, is far above the average of such productions, and full of capital hits at political and local affairs. The puns are numerous and new, and the whole dialogue full of happy hits and smart allusions.

There are, as usual, a pair of lovers who get into a variety of troubles, and are aided and made happy by good-natured fairies. Prince Rupert is again visible to the eyes of our townsmen, and the puritanical roundheads – the 'bogies' of the piece – are thrashed by him in right royal style. His Highness is personated with due dignity by Signor H Boleno – the Clown of clowns – whose dress, ornamented with the arms of Liverpool, is singularly novel and effective. The masks and properties are amusingly eccentric, and the whole piece put upon the stage in a style of the utmost completeness. The scenery is very fine, and painted with evident care. We are presented with views of the Regions of Toffee, the Royalist Encampment at Everton, a Lonely Dell in the Dingle, the Ancient Park of Toxteth and the Banks of the Mersey by Moonlight, Panoramic View of the Cheshire Side in 1644, the Castle of Liverpool, Hall of Precious Stones, and the Submarine Grotto of the Naiads. The latter are very dazzling and beautiful scenes. Of the harlequinade we can only say that being got up by Signor Boleno, it was full of fun. […] The music is very pretty and appropriate, but its effect was marred by the inefficiency of the orchestra.
The Era, 2/1/1853

1853

National Standard
Plum Pudding and Roast Beef; or, Harlequin Nine Pins and the Card King of the Island of Games

IN the opening we are introduced to a view of Card Castle and the City of Topsy Turvey, near the Park of Roast Beef. Here we find, as in some other regions, folly engaged leading her votaries on by means of card, dice, dominoes, and other games. Roast Beef wishes to negotiate a marriage between his son, Young Holly, and Margery, Plum Pudding's daughter, which is somewhat interrupted by the appearance, "a la Amina"[3], of fair Margery herself, who is strongly attached to susceptibility, sentiment, and sleepwalking. Their happiness is interrupted by the inopportune arrival of King Poodle, of the Island of Games, who has himself been smitten by the damsel's charms, and is attended by a grand retinue of followers and guards, representing an almost innumerable number of games, and amid which figure conspicuously dice-boxes, dominoes, the fifty-two cards, skittles, nine-pins, racquets, &c, &c., all represented by living persons, of whom, it is said, upwards of 150 are engaged. The ingenuity and novelty of all this reflects very great credit upon Mr John Douglass, by whom the whole has been designed.

In the scene of the Golden Palms of Butterflies and Grasshoppers, the favourite retreat of the fairies, we behold the Fairy Fete of Flowers, introducing upwards of fifty children, who appear to have been trained with great skill and dexterity. In another scene, which is of astonishing extent, and called the Fairy Encampment of the Emperor of all the Rushes, at the foot of the White Mountains, on the borders of the Black Sea, with a distant view of Card Castle, Dominoe Tower, and Dice-box Hall, in the Gardens of Enchantment, we behold a truly brilliant display of fairy troops (infantry in more senses than one), aided by the singular presence of the north and south winds, which are resolved to blow everybody good, except the bad.

Then follows the Diamond Club Room, in Card Castle – a scene of great novelty; and immediately afterwards we find ourselves introduced to the Giant Kitchen of Nine Pins, where we discover poor Margery reduced to great distress by the unlawful proceedings of King Poodle, and bewailing her imprisoned fate. Then follows the superb arrival of the

Fairy Court, and, after a few more hits, and smart ones too, upon the times and the games most in vogue, the usual transformation is effected in a novel and striking manner.

The abode of the fairies is presented, and this unclosing displays a beautiful metaphorical picture of the Nine Muses, in frames of gold, with Faith, Hope, and Charity, encircled by Cupids, and surrounded with the almost numberless host of brilliantly dressed Fairies. Harlequin is represented by Mr Charles Reeves, recently of Glasgow; Dandy Lover (an old idea well restored), Mr Dolphin; Pantaloon, Mr E Bird; Clown, Mr Buck; Sprites, by the Burdett Family; Columbine, Mlle Leoni (her first appearance); and Harlequina, Mrs Buck. The great scene of the pantomime appears to be that entitled "Jack of all Trades", in which about 200 mechanical figures, all in action, represent almost every description of business in active operation.
The Era, 25/12/1853

Haymarket
Harlequin and the Three Bears; or, Little Silverhair and the Fairies
THE first pantomime ever produced at this theatre was brought out on Monday evening, and entitled *Harlequin and the Three Bears; or, Little Silverhair and the Fairies*; and is founded upon Southey's well-remembered nursery story, and adapted for the Christmas revelry at the Haymarket by the manager, Mr Buckstone. […] There was an excellent house, and the performances of the evening were carried out in a manner evidently gratifying to the company, the only drawback being the extremely late hour at which the pantomime was brought to a conclusion. The story of the latter is thus sketched in "the bill of the play:" –

"Little Silverhair, while playing in the forest, hearing some strange music in the distance, follows the sound till she finds herself among the fairies, who feast her with dainties, and with whom she sports and dances till the dawn of morning. The cause of this kindness on the part of the fairies is owing to the term of their existence being at an end if they fail to procure as a guest during their last midnight hour some young and good girl.

Little Silverhair having become this guest, and the means of prolonging the lives of the fairies for another century, returns home quite changed in her nature, and with a strange disposition to touch and to meddle with everything she sees. The squire of the place, in which she resides with her mother, courts her with presents, and she snatches them from him. Her lover returns home from sea, and offers to share his prize-money with her, but she snatches it all out of his hand, and again runs into the forest, where the first thing she sees is the house of the Three Bears, who have gone out for a walk while the hot porridge, which they have prepared for breakfast, gets cool.

Little Silverhair enters this house, and, seeing three porridge pots with porridge all hot in them, tastes every one, and empties the last. Then she sits in the three chairs belonging to the three bears till she sits the bottom of one of them out. Then, falling sleepy through being with the fairies all night, she goes upstairs to find a bed to lie down upon, when she sees three beds; she lies down upon all of them, and falls fast asleep upon one. Then home come the three bears. They find the porridge has been tasted and one of the pots emptied; they find the chairs have been meddled with, and one of them with the bottom broke through; they then search for the intruder, and find her fast asleep in the bed. 'Somebody has been lying on the bed', exclaims the smallest of the bears, 'and here she is!' Silverhair then wakes up in a fright, and, seeing the bears, endeavours to escape from them; but they catch her, and, being about to cut off her head, she begs a boon, which is that they will give her a hammer and a long nail before she dies. The simple bears agree to this, when she immediately nails all their three tails to the floor, and is about to escape by the window when the bears break away from their fastenings and again pursue her; but the Queen of Fairies now, being her friend, suddenly appears, and as Silverhair has been followed to the house by her mother, her lover, the Squire, and his man, the Fairy, after thinking the matter over, changes the little girl's lover to Harlequin, the little girl herself to a beautiful Columbine, the Squire into Pantaloon, and his man into Clown, so that after a time Silverhair may recover her natural position, be married to her lover, and live happily ever after."

The principal scene in the introduction was the Ruined Abbey by Moonlight, which changed to the Lotus Lake and Waterfalls, and was quite a triumph of technical skill, it being difficult which to admire most, the gay grouping of the waterlily nymphs, the scenic *chef d'oeuvre* of Mr W Calcott, or the cleverness with which the startling and pleasing change was effected. The Fairy Ballet was much admired, and then came the representation of the Interior of the Bears' House, after Little Silverhair (Miss Lydia Thompson) has evinced her prying propensity in tasting the porridge. […]

The harlequinade is full of humorous entertainment, and apt allusion to most of the striking events of the year – the Camp at Chobham[4], the Strike of the Cabmen[5], the Poultry mania[6], &c. The Haunted Chamber scene was remarkably good, where the Clown is alarmed by seeing the ghost of himself, and this was much applauded, likewise the performance of the large tom cat. The dancing of the ladies throughout the pantomime was highly attractive, and told wonderfully towards the success of the entertainment. The Fantasia, *a la* Paganini, by the Clown ought not to be omitted, and it was so cleverly introduced that an encore was called for. The last scene was one of the most splendid efforts at pictorial grouping ever witnessed, *viz*, Spithead, with four-and-twenty jolly tars all of a row, and the Queen of England in her yacht, the *Fairy*, leading the British fleet out to sea.

Lydia Thompson

Royal Grecian Saloon
Harlequin Charity Brat; or, the Magic Christmas Piece
AFTER the appearance of *Violette le Grande* on Monday evening, the Christmas annual, in all its comic novelty, was commenced, entitled *Harlequin Charity Brat, or, the Magic Christmas Piece*, written by Mr T H Webb, and produced under the direction of Mr R Phillips. The plot is meagre, but worked out in many gladdening and humorous effects, with the novel construction and mechanical arrangements of Mr Smithers.

Jack Industry, a charity boy in a village school, under the sanction of Lord Cockagee, is, on account of his persevering habits, beaten by his schoolmates, and his new Christmas piece – his long-cherished masterpiece of writing – is also quite spoiled by them. In this dilemma, appears his guardian angel, Goody Bluemantle, who promises him the means of gratifying his revenge. Scenes of Constantinople and the Dublin Exhibition follow, and Jack has his Christmas piece restored to him, which, having passed through fairy hands, secures him ever afterwards against the machinations of both sprite and ogre.

The second scene represents the interior of Giant Scrunchbone's Castle; and the third, the interior of Plumtree Cottage, where Jack details to Mother Bunch his delight at having for his piece obtained five shillings, which he designs for his sweetheart, Rosebud, her daughter. The latter has been decoyed into the Giant's Castle. Jack invokes (by his piece) fairy aid to restore the Plumtree Rose, which is accomplished by the death of Scrunchbones; and in the final scene of the Palace of Golden Palms and Rubies, with all the fairies, the queen renders the lovers happy, and thus causes the transformation, and the comic business begins. Mr H Power and Mr and M. Richarde are the Harlequins; Mlle Julie, Columbine; Mr T Roberts, Pantaloon; Mr Edwin Blanchard, as Clown; Mr Plimmieri, as Sprite; and Miss Simmonds, as Harlequina. The exertions of these parties were much approved of, and the whole terminated by an allegorical tableau of Neptune and Britannia, acknowledging the naval supremacy of Old England.
The Era, 1/1/1854

1854

Drury Lane
Jack and Jill; or, Harlequin King Mustard and the Four-and-Twenty Blackbirds Baked in a Pie
[…] WHO does not remember the ancient legend that sets forth how:

......up the lofty hill,
Paced the twin heroes, Jack and Jill;
On trudged the Gemini to reach the rail
That shields the well's top from the expectant pail,

When ah! Jack falls, and rolling in the rear,
Jill feels the attraction of his kindred sphere;
Head over heels begins his toppling track,
Throws sympathetic somersets with Jack,
And at the mountain's base bobs plump against him, whack!

This latter catastrophe is, however, averted, and in what way will be seen by our brief sketch of the plot, which seems as if it must be taken as an allegory of the culinary art. The Halls of Hypochondria in the Dark Domains of Dullness show us, among other blue devils, Fog, Drizzle, Quarter-Day, Taxes, Spleen, and Indigestion, busily concocting an extra dose of melancholy for the million, to the delight of their their chief, Miss Ann Thropy, who enters, riding on her favourite nightmare. The approach of Good Humour (Miss Arden) in her Christmas car, however, puts these azure diabolicals to immediate flight; and as the season is suggestive of gastronomic indulgences, she invokes the shades of Mrs Glasse[7], Dr Kitchener[8], Ude[9], Mrs Rundell[10], and the rest of our peptic preceptors, to furnish a good receipt to make a Christmas dish. The reflective Mrs Glasse (Miss Collins) responds to the summons, and emerging from the leaves of "Soyer's Shilling Cookery Book"[11], she thus proceeds, after her ancient admonition to "first catch your hare", to give the required instructions thus: –

First take your tale, which tale is better old,
Then roll it out till you that tale unfold;
Season it well with what will suit the taste,
And keep it stirring – but don't cook in haste –
Served up in the best style, before your friends then put it,
And after some eight weeks have passed, then cut it!

After the selection has been made of the subjects, to Mrs Glasse is confided the concoction, and we are then introduced to Jill's Cottage and Enchanted Kitchen Garden, on the Borders of Fairyland. Here Jack, who is beloved by Jill, attempts, with her assistance, to fill the bucket at the well, when, possibly, as an illustration of the disadvantages of not leaving well alone, the brickwork is accidentally disturbed and discloses the last will of the father of Jill, in which there is this important injunction: –

Jill must not a husband take
Till she a pie can bake and make.

As Jill confesses to an utter ignorance of the art of cookery, this condition would be fatal to her hopes did not Mrs Glasse come to her rescue, and, animating the fruit trees first, make her acquainted with the mystery of Preserves. These are personified by some forty fair and fascinating young ladies, who, led by Marmalade (Miss Kate Warrington), proceed to manifest their attractions in a grand ballet, where Miss Therese and Miss Annie Cushnie appear as the principal dancers.

In the next scene, by the same agency, all the various kitchen requisites become likewise instinct with life, and personally explain their several uses. The kettle sings a song and introduces the saucepan, who, taking off his lid to the lady, makes a profound bow.

With this remarkable retinue Jill next goes to the court of King Mustard, who lives in Cruet Castle, in the Tablecloth Territory. The king here makes her acquainted with the royal family of the Peppers, the Empress Vinegar, the Princess Sweet Oil, and the other inhabitants of this continent of condiments. The Army of Zests, composed of grotesque embodiments of the most esteemed relishes in vogue, is next passed under inspection, and Jill, progressing in her culinary career, is next taken to the abode of Chutnee, Chief of the Pickles, where the Pickles, previously prepared by Vinegar, treacherously mislead her, and cause her to lose her way in the Labyrinth of Salt. At this crisis Jack, however, instructed by the Preserves, has upset his pail on the hill above, and the water, penetrating the salt mine, causes the stalactite saline columns to dissolve, and reveal the memorable Blackbird Pie, duly completed with the Emerald Temple of Salad, where the sweets and sours are happily commingled.

Here, amidst some novel effects in the way of gorgeous splendour, the transformation takes place. [...] Some of the scenes, instead of presenting mere flat surfaces, are positively built out, and two gigantic heads of celery used as wings are marvellous in their approximation to nature. The last grand national *tableau*, with its stirring patriotic appeals, its brilliant temple and revolving columns, with the "Allied Army Quadrilles", led by Julien the younger, will prove an electric climax to what is anticipated to be a great hit.

Jack and Jill at Drury Lane

Astley's
Gulliver's Travels Through Liliput, Horse Island, and Brobdignag; or, Harlequin Britannia
THE allegory is admirably conceived. The Liliputians are the Turks, the Emperor Blefescu is Nicholas, and Gulliver the English and French combined.

The curtain rises, commencing in the clouds; the four winds, East, West, North, and South, are anxiously waiting to know what *blow* will be sent to Earth this year, when their monarch, Old Boreas, despatches his four winds to get up a storm. Here the clouds disperse, presenting to our view the crystallised grot of the Queen Britannia; the fairy Joy is on the look-out. A whistle is here heard, and a car sails on, containing the Queen of the Deep, Britannia, who is exceedingly liberal, ordering a banquet, giving a ball, and relating her intention of foiling Old Boreas, and protecting Young Gulliver.

A vision is seen of a vessel becoming a wreck, and Gulliver swimming for his life, when we finds ourselves on the Island of Lilliput. The little Turks are marching to relieve guard, and find him on the coast. Then come on the Forts of Lilliput with a distant view of the Emperor's stronghold – a sort of Sebastapol in miniature. Gulliver is discovered fast asleep, tied down with thread. Suddenly the man-mountain (Gulliver) awakes, striking terror to the heart of the noble Lillipitians. Gulliver proffers friendship, which is most willingly accepted. Having so strong a force the Sultan relates the treachery of the Emperor, who wishes to claim a portion of his land. Here the Emperor Blefescu appears. Gulliver, who seems to have the strength of England and France, walks into the water, fastens a line to his fleet, and draws the ships from the harbour in the midst of the rejoicing.

We pass on to the Island of Honyhuhums and the Royal Mews, where the horses rule the roast. The jahoos are beasts of burthen, and the horses sitting at the banqueting table. A friendly conversation takes place between Gulliver and the horses. His departure scene brings out Mr William Cooke's admirable skill as a horse trainer.

At the Island of Brobdignag the Giant arrives with his victims. Gulliver follows their track to the strong room of the Giant's Castle, and frees the prisoners. To make all secure he cuts the Giant's head off. This brings to aid the Fairy, who instantly starts them on the Land of Pantomime. The portfolio of fun is now opened, giving hits at the localities of the time. Bennett's Clock Tower[12], London Bridge, introduces some knock-down work – the illuminated clock tower is brought down – the baby show[13] – (the prize baby, an immense affair) – all ending at a National *fete*.

City of London
Birds, Beasts, and Fishes; or, Harlequin Natural History
THE opening scene of this one presents the Signs of the Zodiac, introducing the subject, Birds, Beasts, and Fishes, out on parole. In the midst of their debate Dame Nature arrives as a most welcome visitor, and inquires what each has seen as they journeyed on their way? The Bird exclaims –

I saw from above treachery at work,
A Russian bear was worrying a Turk.[14]

The Beast –

Saw deserving objects driven from the workhouse door,
For no other offence than being poor.

The Fish –

Saw some ships sunk while anchoring quietly in the bay.

Nature promises –

For such treachery they shall dearly pay.

Gold Fish explains the treachery of the Bear. Truth informs Gold Fish that Goldfinch, the Prince of Fairy Land, has resolved to assist their cause, having despatched his commands to King Lion, who will join with the French Eagle, and at once quell this revolt. At this information Nature instantly exclaims –

Birds depart to air, beasts to earth, and fishes to the sea,
'Tis merry Christmas time, you all may wander free.

They immediately take their departure, sending us at once to Feather Island, a very Paradise of Fairy Land by Sunlight, and a variegated Picture of Delight, with the singing of the fairy birds. Ladybird is late to meet the Prince, in consequence of having stopped out late with a party at Cremorne. The Prince, resolved to punish her, desires her instantly to fly away home, stating that her house is on fire, and her children at home. Attention is called to the note of the Skylark, who descends on earth, and joins the fairy throng. Here a festive dance is introduced with a Feast of Flowers. Some dissatisfaction is now expressed by Jenny Wren –

As all the public houses must close at ten.

She is cheered up by the following information: –

Remember this, my fays, 'tis a positive fact,
We all are bona fide travellers, in the meaning of the act.[15]

The Prince aids Dame Nature, and the Fairy, Truth, for which purpose they depart for the Grand Marine Palace of King Lion, witnessing the arrival of Jackall, the Lion's provider, with his tray of shins of beef. The Prince is received with due honours, the staff being composed of English and French officers, and are welcomed by his Majesty. The Guards receive him with a roar. This pleases his Majesty. Here the mandate from Fairy Land arrives, disclosing the treachery of the Bear. This brings us to the Crystallized Grot, the abode of old Cock Salmon. Troutina, daughter of the Salmon, appears by a trout-stream, pursued by the Bear, who, by a trick, gets her from the Grot, and is in the act of carrying her off, but is prevented by the unexpected appearance of the British Lion.

This brings to our aid the Fairy Prince, who starts them on the land of Pantomime. He becomes Harlequin; Troutina, Columbine; King Lion, Clown; Cock Salmon, Pantaloon; and the Bear, Sprite. Here Mr Nelson Lee's comic budget commences, introducing the popular hits of the day, amongst which Bennett's Clock Tower, Grossmith's Bouquet[16], Roses and Moses come in for a share. The Blue House makes true-blue jokes, and the whole ending in the Zoological Gardens. Parents and guardians can pat their youngsters on the head, and take them to see the City Pantomime, if only to improve them in natural history. The clowns engaged are Mr Paul Herring and Mr R Stilt, so that this theatre will be well able to cope with others in this respect.

Pavilion
Jack and Jill; or, Harlequin and the Four Leaved Shamrock
IT commences with the distillery of King Alcohol, where demon distillers are making one hundred puncheons of whisky for the Emperor Nicholas. The king is informed that they can get no water from the pond, that Jack and Jill take it all away. He vows revenge – calls on the elfins to thwart and punish them for their audacity. Hibernia, the Fairy Queen, resolves to save Jack and Jill from the malice of their enemies; she calls to her aid Clericaun, her faithful fay, and despatches him to earth on his mission.

Next appears the cottage of Farmer Stubble, the dame and farmer being in altercation about Jill and her lover Jack. The farmer threatens to turn them out, but Clericaun promises to aid them, on condition they will be good. The beadle, the Irish esquire, and Proofstick, the exciseman, appear as suitors to Jill; she despises them all but her faithful Jack, who is sent to the Devil's Pond, and Jill is taken by the demons. Jack escapes, and finds the magic Shamrock in the fairy dell. Jack then seeks the abode of Queen Hibernia, wandering into the Hall of Peacocks and Silver Pillars (in which are executed groupings by fifty ladies and children, a grand ballet, and appearance of Hibernia in a fairy car formed of peacocks). The Queen enjoins Jack to seek Jill in the abode of King Alcohol. All depart to the abode of Alcohol, who is preparing to celebrate his marriage with Jill, but is interrupted by Jack. Alcohol is about to strike Jack, when he uses the shamrock; he strikes the King, and a mechanical change takes place, bringing us to the stalactite retreat of Queen Hibernia, followed by the transformation – Jack and Jill to Harlequin and Columbine; farmer and beadle to Pantaloons; squire and exciseman to Clowns, &c.

Britannia, Hoxton
Egypt 3,000 Years Ago; or, Queen Cleopatra – a Dream in the Crystal Palace
THE curtain rises on a model of the tomb of Abou Simbel, in the Egyptian Court, with its four colossal statues of King Rameses II sitting in front of the temple. A "rout" of Egyptian characters enter, chaunt an invocation, and the broad-limbed giants become animated. A great magician informs them of his intent to furnish the slumbering manageress (Mrs S Lane) with a plot for her Christmas Pantomime.

The good king Cambyses has, it seems, a wicked son named Rhadamanthus, who, being intimate with the Evil One (Nicholas, subauditur[17]), has evil designs on a youthful Princess named Polyanthus (the juvenile vocalist and actress, Miss Clara St Casso). To frustrate their machinations, the Magician transforms Mrs S Lane into a similitude of the renowned Queen Cleopatra, and invests her with a portion of his necromantic power and a baton of formidable efficiency. The Princess being carried off by the Prince, all opposition thereunto notwithstanding, Queen Cleopatra follows to the rescue, dares every obstacle, incurs every danger, braves mummies that rise out of the earth, scorns grim demons that rise out of cabinets, despises stone statues that roll their eyes and yawn most portentously, dares frightful apparitions, and, notwithstanding a treacherous memory that lets slip a cabalistic word at the critical moment, perseveres till she discovers the dungeon in which the Princess is confined, and holds at bay the Infernal Powers who wish her destruction.

Having rescued the royal dove from her cave, the triumphant Cleopatra suffers a terrible reverse, becomes the sport of adverse powers, and, being offered a choice of deaths (graciously including the agreeable alternatives of roasting, boiling, or stewing), with a fearful array of gridirons, frying-pans, and monster boilers, is obliged to succumb; and the only friend of the poor Princess is marched off in a lugubrious plight to the place of execution. Encouraged by the downfall of their opponent, the Principalities of darkness rush anew to the attack. After a variety of adventures they are once more foiled by the good Magician, who, in the nick of time, baulks the Furies, and restores Queen Cleopatra to vitality and power.

Here the metempsychosian change takes place, the Prince is transformed into Harlequin (Mr W Smith); and, as a penance, is condemned to follow a tattling Egyptian waiting-maid, who is changed to Columbine (Mlle Celeste Stephan); the youthful Princess is metamorphosed to Harlequina (Miss C Borrow); Old Nick is transformed to tottering Pantaloon (Mr W H Newham); the sorrowing King to merry Clown (M. Louis); and all are destined to run the usual race of cross purposes during the bustling incongruities of the comic scenes. It will be seen that this list of pantomimists includes considerable talent; indeed, Mlle Celeste Stephan is a first-rate opera dancer.

Of Mr John Gray, the artist, it is scarcely possible to speak too highly. The most striking of his scenes are, perhaps, the second, called "The magnificent Pavilion of Queen Cleopatra in the Garden of Cedars"; the fourth, entitled "The Banks of the Nile and Entrance to the Port of Pharoah Rameses"; the seventh, styled "The Illuminated Grotto, looking into the Silver Lake"; and the last scene of all, "The Temple of Memnon", which is surpassingly beautiful.

To any of the frequenters of the Britannia it would be sufficient to say that Mrs S Lane acts in the opening; but, lest there should be any playgoers in the far west who have not yet visited this popular place of amusement, we venture to add that Mrs S Lane as a soubrette had few equals, and as a singing chambermaid, will bear comparison with any of our first class actresses. Among other attractions, the opening introduces that highly talented young lady, Miss Clara St Casso. Though extremely juvenile and petite in form, she is graceful in action and a giant in intellect, is also most singularly gifted with a genius for acting, and possesses a magnificent singing and acting voice, with rare musical acquirements. But when, to all these *bon bons*, it is added that the far-famed Aztec Lilliputians[18], those marvellous freaks of nature, are engaged, and will appear at a morning performance every day during the holiday week, and again in the evening, it seems impossible to predict anything but brilliant houses and a treasury overflowing to reward the the enterprising proprietor, Mr S Lane.
The Era, 24/12/1854

The Aztec Lilliputians

Haymarket
Little Bo-peep; or, Harlequin and the Girl Who Lost Her Sheep
[...] THE first part of the Pantomime, or rather the prelude to the real Pantomime, is founded on the well-known nursery rhyme of

Little Bo-peep who lost her sheep,
And can't tell where to find them.

The part of Bo-peep, who is a pretty Arcadian shepherdess placed in charge of a small flock of sheep, is played by Miss Lydia Thompson; Colin, her lover, is another shepherd, represented by Miss Harvey; and the fairy Pastorella (godmother to Bo-peep) is intrusted to the keeping of Miss Fanny Wright, whilst a troupe of wolves, rejoicing in the gentle cognomens of Scruncher, Gnasher, Crasher, Howler, Prowler, &c, are played by a number of juvenile bipeds, transformed for the occasion into quadrupeds. The dialogue is attributed to Buckstone himself, and his peculiar talent for droll and striking positions is nowhere better seen than in the manner in which the wolves are represented. Each little urchin carries a carbine, and all have wolves' heads. They are attired in satin breeches, their stockings gartered, and hairy brigand jackets, the tail of the jacket being formed by the tail of the wolf.

The incidents of the piece are soon told. Little Bo-peep, although a very good girl in other respects, is addicted to one fault, that of going to sleep in the day-time, when she ought to be keeping a keen eye upon her sheep. The captain of the wolves, observing this little foible, resolves to steal her sheep in revenge for having been rejected as a lover by Bo-peep, who prefers Colin. He accordingly carries his wicked intentions into effect, cuts off the tails of the unoffending sheep, and hangs them up to dry on the branches of a tree. The theft is performed whilst Bo-peep is asleep, and dreaming a wonderful dream, in which her godmother, the fairy, shows her a striking picture of industry and idleness, which she thus forcibly illustrates: – Two young girls rise from the earth, bearing a strong resemblance to Bo-peep. One is neatly arrayed in the garb of a milkmaid, with a milkpail on her head, short petticoats, shoes and buckles, rosy-cheeked and smiling; in her hand she holds forth a large purse, and on her milkpail is seen the word "Industry". The other girl who rises is in rags, very pale, barefooted, her hair in disorder, her pockets turned inside out, and on a placard hanging round her neck appears the ominous word "Idleness". Bo-peep awakes from her dream, and soon discovers that her sheep have been stolen – a discovery which is speedily confirmed by the sight of the tails of the unfortunate animals dangling from the branches of the tree. Bo-peep, however, by bribing a cowherd, to whom the care of the sheep has been intrusted by the wolves, contrives to get them all back – tails and all. She then assembles a number of friendly shepherdesses, who sit down with needles and thread, and very gravely go through the ceremony of sewing on the tails of the sheep. Soon after this extraordinary restoration Bo-peep herself is carried off by the wolves, and both herself and Colin are made prisoners.

Virtue and innocence having thus got themselves into a "fix," the transformation follows. The fairies appear, and Colin is converted into Harlequin (M. Chapino); Bo-peep into Columbine (Miss Mary Brown); the Captain of the Wolves into Pantaloon (Mr W A Barnes); and the Cowherd into Clown (Mr Appleby). The Pantomime then fairly begins with all its uproarious fun and merriment. Many of the changes and transformations occasioned by the magic wand of Harlequin are really effective and well performed, and some of the principal events of the day are made to play a part in the succession of drolleries. The Crystal Palace, the New Beer Act, the Smoke Prevention Bill, and the Baby Show, all come in for a share of attention. A bust of Sir Joseph Paxton is struck by the magic wand, and suddenly a view opens of the Crystal Palace in all its bright sunshine of glory, the bust being converted into a green garden box inscribed "Paxton's laurels" – a graceful compliment. A somewhat novel feature is introduced in the disposal of Harlequin, who is summarily seized on by Clown and Pantaloon, and, to all appearance, is actually cut and chopped into pieces on a kitchen dresser. The murderers then proceed to roll out a gigantic paste into which are thrust the mangled remains of Harlequin, which are thus transferred to a huge kettle and boiled into a pudding. On proceeding to cut up this dainty dish, up jumps Harlequin safe and sound out of the pudding to the great amusement of all who witnessed the clever trick.

The whole of the Pantomime, including the prelude, was admirably put upon the stage, and although, in hackneyed phrase, we cannot refrain from saying that evidently "no expense had been spared", many of the scenes were really beautiful as works of art; and the dresses were fantastically rich, elaborate, and appropriate. Amongst the scenes, the grove of golden laburnums – called by the French "showers of gold" – in which Bo-peep's dream takes place, and the fairy conservatory of Pastorella, are truly magnificent, and worthy of a higher style of representation than the Pantomime which they adorned. […]

On the whole the Pantomime was, as it deserved to be, and will be for some weeks to come, well received, by a house which, though crowded, yet lacked that large attendance of the juvenile community – of schoolboys and misses – which one expects to see at a Christmas Pantomime. This arose, no doubt, from the unwillingness to expose these tender plants to the uproar which frequently prevails on Boxing Night. Hundreds of bright, merry, and laughing faces have since supplied the void. The piece was not deficient in a certain air of morality and useful teaching, and although the morning performance probably diminishes somewhat from the attendance of the youthful portion of society in the evening, we strongly recommend that our little friends now recreating in London should not lose the opportunity which Mr Buckstone affords them of seeing a first-class Pantomime.

Princess's
Harlequin and Blue Beard, the Great Bashaw; or, the Good Fairy Triumphant Over the Demon of Discord
[…] IT is modelled after the fashion of the real old English Pantomimes. The introduction is written in a dashing, off-hand style – the doggerel rhythm flows merrily and cheerily along, and one is only surprised to find this old nursery tale of "Blue Beard" "done" into so agreeable a verse, and dressed altogether in so new and delightful a guise. The Harlequinade rests upon the exertions of the original characters, Clown, Pantaloon, Harlequin, and Columbine; and with the excellent materials which are provided for them, no adventitious aid is required from sprites, or marvellous dogs, or any other extraneous source. The performances of this quartette are replete with fun, life, grace, and vigour; and there is no coarseness of expression or vulgarity of action to mar the rich enjoyment which a pure young mind may experience at witnessing their drolleries.

It is, of course, unnecessary to go into the plot of the simple story of Blue Beard, but we may briefly explain how it is made the fitting subject of Pantomime, and how virtue is so persecuted, and innocence so injured, as to render the transformation which precludes the harlequinade a matter of absolute necessity. Blue Beard is, as we all know, a ruffian of so deep a dye – so hideous, so relentless, and so furious, that he has absolutely attracted the admiration and assistance of the demon Rustifusti, who views in him, as it is supposed, something of an *alter ego*. Scene one discloses to us the winter quarters and last stronghold of this ferocious demon. He is surrounded by his imps in most impish garb, and, in something of a Macbeth-like scene, they are engaged in stirring up the cauldron of discord. Whilst thus pursuing the congenial task, Blue Beard's ambassador arrives, with a missive from his imperious master. Sooth to say, great Blue Beard is in a quandary. He meditates taking to his arms the youthful Fatima; but the experience which he has had of twenty-one previous wives does "give him pause," and before entering once again upon the sea of wedded life he seeks the counsel of his sage friend and coadjutor Rustifusti. Now Rustifusti is no admirer of the sex, for though he had had but one, he had been unable, demon though he was, to manage her, and he hesitates therefore to advise, but summons to his aid all the principal old witches in the neighbourhood to consult with him. These old ladies are dressed in the most approved style of witchdom, and we should not have been greatly surprised had each mounted the stick which she carried, and started off at a rapid pace through the air. To the leader of the band, Rustifusti imprudently intrusts the charge of his magic wand. Deprived of this symbol of strength, our demon is powerless; and lo! in an instant, a marvellous transformation. Away fly red cloaks, masks, and sticks – the Winter Quarters of the Demon vanish, and in their places we have the Enchanted Gardens and Summer Residence of the Good Fairy, with Preciosa herself before us, arrayed in dazzling brightness, and surrounded by a bevy of as lovely Fairies as it was ever our lot to witness.

Scene three introduces us to the Kitchen in Blue Beard's Castle, where great preparations are going on for the wedding breakfast. Cooking by steam is carried out here to its fullest extent, and two handles indicate the mode for turning it "on" or "off". By mistake, Blue Beard turns on the steam, already at too high a pressure, and a frightful mishap ensues. The whole breakfast and every thing in the room are blown, to use an expressive Hibernicism, to "smithereens", and all is thrown into the wildest confusion. From this we are carried to a Turkish village, with Ibrahim's Cottage; and here, in something of a Romeo and Juliet style, Selim addresses young Fatima at the balcony. They are interrupted in their intended flight by the arrival of Blue Beard, preceded by his guards of honour, military bands, and other attendants. This is a magnificently mock-heroic procession, and the rich variety of the masks and dresses almost surpasses conception. A frightful encounter takes place between Blue Beard and Selim, in which the former eventually prevails, and, as the result of which, he succeeds in carrying off Fatima. Then follows the fatal Blue Chamber, and the catastrophe is speedily accomplished. Scene seven, however, intervenes, and the good fairy interposes in the Illuminated Temple of Concord, which is one of the most brilliant and gorgeous effects we have ever witnessed. […]

Here, of course, the transformation ensues, Selim, before played by Mr Saker, becoming Harlequin in the person of Mr Cormack; Blue Beard, once Mr Rolleston, Clown, in the shape of M. Huline; Ibrahim, Mr Paolo, Pantaloon; and Fatima, originally represented by Mr Daly, Columbine, now intrusted to Miss Desborough.

Our notice has already extended to unwonted length, and yet there is much more to say, which stern necessity, however, warns us must be left unsaid. The bathing-beach at Brighton is one of the most admirable things ever introduced in a Pantomime; but if that be so, what can be said of the view of the Crystal Palace, at Sydenham; Spithead, from South Sea Common; the quarter-deck of the Royal Albert; and the final national allegorical tableau? We have exhausted our vocabulary of praise; and it is scarcely necessary that we should urge every reader of these pages, who has it in his power, to get a sight of this marvellously excellent Pantomime. The quarter-deck of the Royal Albert, with its tiny crew of some fifty or sixty children, trained with a perfection almost beyond belief – the startlingly-novel and charming dance of "La Flotte" – the illuminated Temple of Concord before referred to – and the concluding tableau, would amply repay the most penuriously disposed person for the outlay which he must incur in treating his family to the Princess's.

The truth is, that when Mr Kean undertakes anything of this sort he puts his heart and soul into it; he does it with vigour and determination; and he carries such perfection into the most minute details, that nothing can be left for the most fastidious to desire. It only remains to add that the scenery has been painted by the artists of the establishment Messrs W Gordon and F Lloyds, and that the acting of every one concerned, from the terrific Rustifusti (Mr F Cooke) to the tiniest powder monkey on board the Royal Albert; or, from the pretty, clever, little Kate Terry (as Preciosa, the good fairy) to Mr Rolleston (the great Abomelique, surnamed Blue Beard); or, again, from Mr Daly's broad, but not coarse, Fatima, and Mr Saker's amusing Selim, to the irresistible ladies of the *corps de ballet* and the nameless little urchins who enacted the imps – all was perfect.
The Era, 31/12/1854

1855

Drury Lane
Hey Diddle Diddle; or, Harlequin King Nonsense and the Seven Ages of Man
[…] THE first scene is the Region of Nursery Rhymes, a portion of the domains of King Nonsense, and here round the cradle of Infancy are gathered the well-known nursery heroes, Jack Sprat, Simple Simon, Humpty Dumpty, Little Jack Horner, and others of the same fraternity. King Nonsense, who declares himself to be their illustrious progenitor, comes

to look after the fruits of his invention, when Common Sense arrives, and, after some amusing badinage as to the effect of their respective dealings with mankind, offers to form a royal alliance in the production of a Pantomime. An obstacle appears in the form of Routine, accompanied by his inseparable friend Red Tape, but he is speedily dismissed to Noodledom by Common Sense, and a proposal to work out the life of man from the cradle is agreed upon.

Accordingly the next scene, representing the village of Prettiwell-cum-Thankye, introduces us to Young Hopeful creeping like snail to the village school. Here, under the scholastic control of a certain pedagogue, hight Dr Birch, are seen collected a band of merry urchins whose faces undergo an unwonted elongation over their lessons. Hobbedyhoy, a mischievous schoolmate, is the dunce of the establishment, and leads Young Hopeful through a remarkable series of adventures and misadventures. All the incidents of a schoolboy's life, from the truant-playing and the first falling in love with a pretty face at the Young Ladies' Establishment opposite, to the plum cake brought from home by the village carrier and the interview with the weekly bun-woman, are wrought out in amusing detail, and a game at cricket played by the roguish Hobbedyhoy and his companion results in precipitating the Dominie into a pond, and enabling him and Young Hopeful to run away in the confusion.

We next find Young Hopeful, who is the hero of the opening, becoming the lover, and writing the memorable sonnet which in this instance is addressed to Rosa, the ward of a certain Justice of the Peace, who lives in the Manor House adjacent. The Justice, however, steps in to interfere with the progress of this attachment, and Young Hopeful enlists as a soldier, to which he is partly urged by despair and partly by a desire to become by promotion a more desirable suitor. In the Old Abbey Ruins, where the lovers meet, the Spirit of Love comes to their assistance, and in the Bower of Beauty reveals to them the fascination of bright eyes and beauteous forms, through the medium of a grand ballet, in which Miss Rosina Wright prominently figures. The Justice Hall is afterwards shown, and a strong allusion to the case of the Essex labourers, who were so severely sentenced for going to see a review, is given as one of the "modern instances" of the judicial wisdom of the "Great Unpaid".

Finally, the lovers elope, and take refuge in the Ruined Cottage of Old Age, when one of Mr Beverley's great scenic transformations takes place. The wintry aspect of utter desolation melts away into a gorgeous fairy region, typical of the Realms of Perpetual Spring, and here the Pantomime characters receive their customary merry mission. […]

Haymarket
The Butterfly's Ball and the Grasshopper's Feast; or, Harlequin and the Genius of Spring
[…] WE here find that a fair Butterfly, Lady Silverwings, who is in love with and betrothed to the Grasshopper, has given rise to a jealous feeling of revenge on the part of the Wasp, a rejected suitor, and who, in the first scene, waits upon Belladonna, the poison-witch, to obtain a draught of deadly nightshade, wherewith he may destroy, at one fell swoop, not only the lady and her lover, but all the friends she has invited to the ball and feast, given in celebration of the nuptials. The poison is supplied, but the insidious plot is overheard by Brightray, Genius of Spring, who hastens to the Garden of the Butterflies, and there promises protection to the light-winged race. Silverwings and her lover are, however, interrupted in a very pleasant *tete-a-tete* by the wicked Wasp and the sanguinary Spider, who are only discomfited by the activity and bravery of the gallant Grasshopper.

On his way to the feast, for which he had received a card of admission, the Wasp looks in at the Kitchen of the Lady Silverwings for the purpose of administering the fatal concoction that he had obtained and poisoning the dishes that are being prepared for the banquet. The cook, seeing a wasp upon the premises, makes sundry vain efforts to catch him, but his escape is only purchased by the loss of his phial, which he breaks during the conflict he has with the *chef de cuisine*.

The trumpeter Gadfly now summons the guests, and we see a procession of all the insects passing on until the scene of revelry is reached, which is a beautiful green lawn overshadowed by the spreading branches of a mighty oak. The nuptial banquet is literally going as "merry as a marriage bell", when the Wasp and his objectionable friend the Spider intrude upon the festive throng. Finding that he has lost the poison, the witch still determines the mischievous intents shall not be frustrated, and changing the beautiful summer landscape into a cheerless winter one, the insects become suddenly torpid, and pass into a state of hibernation.

Brightray, the good friend of the Butterflies, sends forth, however, at this critical juncture, one of her brightest and most genial rays, and warming up under its reviving influence, the insects revive, the scene becomes one of glittering sunshine, and whilst the Grasshopper and Butterfly are changed into Harlequin and Columbine, (Mr Milano and Miss Mary Brown), the Wasp and Spider are transformed, by the opposing power, into their tormentors, Clown and Pantaloon (Mr Appleby and Mr Mackay), when, of course, the Pantomime chase commences, and continues until the lovers again meet in the Bower of Bliss, and where they promise to carry out the indefinite notion of domestic enjoyment, known as living happy ever afterwards. The Harlequinade, which has been supplied by Mr William Dorrington, abounds in social and political allusions to the prominent events of the passing year, and the Grasshoppers' Feast seems very likely to be one of the best stage banquets served up at this peculiarly festive season.

Princess's Theatre
The Maid and the Magpie
WE have the benevolent fairy, Paradisa, who rules in the Island of Birds, and her mortal enemy, the wicked magician Hankey Pankey, who exercises sway over the Island of Beasts. The one is the protector, the other the persecutor, of Annette, who is no other than our old friend, the Maid of Palaiseau. She has lost her favourite magpie, and purchases another from from Hankey Pankey, disguised as Benjamin, the Jew pedlar. This malicious substitute is a deserter from the ranks of Queen Paradisa, for which he has been drummed out of her service, and condemned to be shot, but the chosen guard who execute the sentence are bad marksmen, and suffer him to escape without injury. He then arrives in the Kingdom of Hankey Pankey, to whom he offers his aid in working vengeance on Paradisa's godchild, Annette. The mischief then goes on rapidly, as in the original story. The magpie steals the ladle, for which theft his innocent mistress is tried, found guilty, and ordered for execution. The missing ladle is discovered at the critical moment, and the fairy steps in, as good fairies always do, exactly when they are wanted, to punish the guilty and reward the innocent.

The usual probation of the Harlequinade is imposed on Annette, her lover, and her persecutors, and all parties are finally reconciled in a fairy temple in the realms of Queen Paradisa. In the course of the Harlequinade, the interior of the Princess's Theatre is exhibited, with a juvenile version of the celebrated banquet scene in *King Henry VIII*, represented by a whole army of children, carefully trained under the instruction of that experienced tactician, Oscar Byrne. The leading Pantomimists are: – Harlequin, Mr Cormack; Clown, Mr Huline; Pantaloon, Mr Paolo; and Columbine, Miss Phoebe Beale.

Sadler's Wells
Harlequin and Puss in Boots; or, All the World and His Wife, and the Ogre of Rats' Castle
THE opening commences in the Retreat of All the World and his Wife, who are bewailing, with the smaller circles of the great world, the embarrassments that attend their respective spheres. Novelty and Mirth are, however, found to be yet in existence, and by their agency we are transported to the Land of Fable, where the subject of Puss in Boots is chosen for pantomimical representation. The mill and the memorable legacy to Jocelyn, the miller's son, will then show the peculiarities and eccentricities of the booted Grimalkin to amusing advantage. The original story is closely followed, and the achievements of Puss in Boots are made to furnish some highly laughable situations.

King Log, the Emperor of the Woodenheads, not having any appetite, his daughter, the Princess Gloriana, goes in search of game wherewith to provide some savoury morsel, but would fail utterly in her filial mission did not the ingenious Puss come to the rescue, and snare for Royalty a plentiful supply of hares, rabbits, pheasants, and partridges, which which he departs to the Palace of King Log as presents from Jocelyn, whom the cat has created, without a patent from the Herald's College, the most noble the Marquis of Carabas. Being called upon to show his estate, the tact of Puss is again called into requisition, and the King is told that all the land and corn-fields that he can see belong to the Marquis. Ocular proof being deemed essential, the cat leads King Log through the corn-fields, having previously given the threatening injunction to the reapers, and here the invasion of some long-whiskered Muscovite rats among the corn gives Puss an opportunity of displaying his physical prowess. The ogre of Rats' Castle appears to take revenge for this destruction of his followers, and carries off a couple of reapers under his arm to serve for his evening repast. He is pursued by the valiant Puss, who vanquishes his Rat Guard in detail after a tremendously comic conflict, and then takes possession of Rats' Castle, where, having persuaded the Ogre to transform himself into a mouse, he gobbles up the universal gobbler, and receives the king and his train as visitors to the castle of the Marquis. Jocelyn becomes Harlequin (Mr Charles Fenton), the Princess, Columbine (Miss Caroline Parkes); King Log, Pantaloon (Mr Naylor); and Puss in Boots played throughout the opening by the clever girl who made such a sensation here as Puck, in the *Midsummer Night's Dream*, Miss Rosa Edouin, is transformed to Clown (Mr Nicolo Deulin). The Harlequinade is spoken of as full of points, and the scenery by Mr F Fenton is extremely beautiful.
The Era, 23/12/1855

Covent Garden
Ye Belle Alliance; or, Harlequin Good Humour and Ye Field of the Cloth of Gold
[...] THE opening scene, of the Caverns of the Gnome Brittanicus, in Subterrananussia, is very good. The so-called Dioramas are not what could be wished. The third scene, representing the Deck of "The Great Harry", four-decker, of 128 guns (the first English line-of-battle ship, it is said), as she was lying alongside the quay at Dover, and the Embarkation of Henry the Eighth, was very effective and complete. Here we are introduced to his Majesty King Harry the Eighth, who comes on board with Cardinal Wolsey and a numerous suite. To Mr Harry Pearson the part of Bluff King Hal was assigned, and he certainly did all that could be done to sustain an admirable burlesque. His conduct while on board the vessel, especially during the storm; his humorous demeanour when first he shook hands with the monarch

of France and embraced him; and his subsequent amorous pursuit of a fair village maiden, almost convulsed the audience. Mr Pearson we are confident must be a man of genuine humour.

The Abode of the Fairy Queen in the Golden Groves of Good Humour was a gorgeous display of artistic work, but there was some delay in completing the tableau. Here the "general transformation" took place, and the business of the Pantomime began in good earnest. The Harlequin of Mr C Brown is a display of graceful dancing; the Pantaloon of Mr W A Barnes, and the Columbine of Miss Emma Horne were all most creditably performed. Flexmore, as the Clown, may be said to be the leading character in the Harlequinade department. The moment the business begins, he displays his aptitude for his position, and his versatile genius. He reminds us of old Joe Grimaldi, for while he is always alive to that which is strictly within his province, he at the same time has "his eyes about him" to detect any momentary mishap in the machinery, &c, for executing the tricks. Among other efforts which created quite a furore in the audience, we may particularise his burlesque "grand equestrian feats" on two children's wooden horses. We could scarcely persuade ourselves we were not in the arena at Astley's. The costume, the movement of the body, keeping time with the supposed action of the horses, the jumping over the garter, and the jump through the hoop, were admirably grotesque, and yet singularly correct as to the performance he imitated. Then, again, his dancing throughout was all that could be wished. He threw genuine humour into each of the metamorphoses he acted.

Among other laughable scenes is one of Adulteration Buildings, Turmeric Row, Red Lead Square, where there are some smart hits at the malpractices of certain tradesmen. Rap Street, Spirit Square, Apartments to Let, afforded much amusement. The Clown knocks at the door of a large mansion, and at the magic wave of Harlequin's wand, the windows are closed by shutters on each of which is a knocker which "raps" with amazing rapidity, and creates a perfect din.

The change from the Wizard's Laboratory (a scene the object of which we could not divine) to the New Castle at Balmoral was very cleverly managed, though, for the instant, some persons were alarmed, believing that the scene itself was falling. The change is so contrived that on the machinery falling to the ground there is the representation of corn fields, with Balmoral Castle in the distance. The scene is very appropriately enlivened by the presence of many bonnie Scotch lads and lasses, who, with characteristic zeal, execute several highland reels. Here Flexmore again delighted with a *pas seul*.

Some clever changes were made from a Filter Manufactory, Pickford's Parcel Warehouse, &c. The purifying of Old Father Thames was a very laughable process. The Pantomime closed with "the Apotheosis of Ye Belle Alliance", designed by M. Guerin, England and France mourners at one altar, victors on one throne. The Coronation of the Coronals of Valour, by the Genius of Victory. The affair was thus described in the bills, and the *tableau* elicited very hearty cheers from every part of the theatre.

We must repeat our hope that those who have the responsibility of conducting this Pantomime will apply the pruning hook with a judicious hand. If this be done, there can be no doubt that the Pantomime will receive from the public that large amount of favour to which it is fairly entitled. Aided by the exertions of Mr Harry Pearson, and the activity, judgement, and humour of Flexmore, we can scarcely imagine any Pantomime could fail. We believe that this has been produced at an immense outlay, as the *tableau* representing the royal *corteges* of Francis the First and Harry the Eighth alone would indicate; and the same remark applies to the scene of the Golden Groves of Good Humour. Mr Anderson has entered on a large speculation, and we hope that his treasury will be well garnished by the receipts arising from the presence of audiences as overflowing as that which graced the theatre on "Boxing Night".

Standard
A Merry Christmas; or, Harlequin King Candle and Princess Prettydear, of Taper Land
OF all gas-artists Mr John Douglass is about the most successful. Gas seems the agent to "marshal" him the way which he should go. He worships it. Within the theatre, without the theatre, gas reigns. Stars, dramatic and operatic, appearing at this theatre, are emblazoned to the world with gas. In pantomimic productions Mr Douglass has been most happy with his gas scenes. The Fleet Well by Night, at his bidding, becomes an arcade brilliantly lit with gas. […] The public have already had from him some most beautiful gas scenes, but, to our opinion, none so beautifully, so tastefully arranged, as in his new Pantomime of A MERRY CHRISTMAS; OR, HARLEQUIN KING CANDLE AND PRINCESS PRETTYDEAR, OF TAPER LAND. The opening of the Harlequinade is also, as far as language can do it, another proof of Mr Douglass's desire to have light, for he here lights up satirically men's actions and motives, without fear or favour. Royalty does not escape, for he tells his audience that we want better qualifications for field marshals than men who rear cochin-chinas and fatten beasts for cattle shows. The opening, which is well-written, abounds in allusions to the events passing and past, all of which told amusingly with the audience.

The plot is of the usual character of all Pantomime openings. Two young and virtuous lovers are pursued by those the very reverse. Such lovers are Prince Taper and Princess Prettydear. Prince Taper is son to King Candle, whilst King Extinguisher – Candle's bitter enemy – is the parent of Prettydear. The parents, of course, oppose the match. The lovers

are protected by Queen Crystaline, who finally, when both are in the Demon Coal Hole, appears and changes the dreary abode into the great scene of the evening, the Hall of Prisms, which is one entire blaze of gas jets carried in borders, of horseshoe form, from the stage up to the extreme height, each border diminishing, and thereby giving the notion of an immense depth, at the extreme end of which are numbers of gas stars and pillars, and one large revolving gas star in motion before them. All the space of the wings, not occupied with gas, is thickly studded with jewels, thereby reflecting the gas lights in countless numbers. In various groups are children, as fairies, dressed in white and silver gauze. This, when lit with coloured fires, presents an appearance of indescribable beauty, and was the signal for one entire call for Mr Douglass. […] The Pantomime passed off most pleasingly, and notwithstanding it plays above three hours, it never once flagged.
The Era, 30/12/1855

1856

Princess's
Aladdin

VIRTUOUS and bold, Aladdin, decidedly, is no longer. We regret to state that he is a most unwilling son and a most outrageous coward. We are far from sure that the enchanter did not endeavour to put him to his right use, in making him a catspaw wherewith to obtain the jewels as big as chestnuts and the other riches of the cavern. It is impossible to retain any respect for a young Chinese tailor who beats his mother in defiance, not only of Chinese law, but of the ordinary arrangements of society.

But we must explain. In the opening of Mr Kean's new Pantomime we are introduced to the cell of the magician Abanazer. Like most clever men, this personage allows his household to go on in the most irregular fashion, while he is meditating on higher matters. We should not say much of his books, and instruments, and all the rest of his magic tools, being treated in the most irreverent manner by his domestics, but the way in which a tabby cat, one of the handsomest we ever saw, conducts himself in the philosopher's chair, upsetting everything and scratching everybody in sheer mirth, is not to be passed without notice. The Magician, however, contrives to pursue his studies, and by the aid of his familiars, especially a demon on a fiery dragon, obtains information as to the cave and the treasures for which he is worldly enough to sigh, instead of waiting till some Chinese Kenyon leaves him a legacy.

He visits the house of Aladdin, whose mother is a sort of female Moses, and is of the tailoring persuasion. She is an estimable woman, but excitable, and irons her apprentices with a hot goose, or cuts off their noses with the shears, if they neglect their duty. With these deductions for temper – and we all have our little tempers – nothing can be said against Widow Ching. Aladdin, a pleasing young tailor, devotes himself to painting the portrait of the Princess Royal of China, instead of minding the business, and propensity occasions a few fights between him and his parent. She demolishes his picture, and he blackens her face with his pigments; but they seem to be on a tolerably good understanding, and Aladdin might have sobered into respectability but for the magician's arrival. A series of fictions fail in convincing Mrs Ching that the Wizard is her brother-in-law, but two purses of money are more successful, and a little *diablerie*, which clothes her and her son gorgeously, and provides them a splendid repast, completes the business. Aladdin is seduced to the wood, and after recovering from the trifling accident of a stone of some tons' weight falling upon him, and though disgustingly as terrified, becomes, as in the story, the possessor of the lamp, having previously insisted on his uncle's handing over the ring.

Meanwhile great scandal goes on in the Palace. The Princess comes to take her bath. A very ugly grand vizier, who has obtained his own consent to marry her, insists on intruding upon the chaste mysteries of the bath-room. […] The Princess stands – no nonsense, and as the enamoured Actaeon *will* come in, he gets exceedingly well wopped, and finally soused in the bath, just then at "water boils". Aladdin, escaped from the cavern, has come to the rescue, and subsequently, on the Princess once more falling into her persecutor's hands, kills him, as far as cutting him down, chopping him up, dancing over him, and generally maltreating him can effect the purpose, and then claims the lady. Her haughty yet grateful father assents, providing the lover can supply her with a palace fit for her. What is the good of a genius if he cannot perform a trifle like that. Down comes the loveliest palace in the world, with translucent columns and interminable vistas of light and loveliness, and – out comes Miss Laura Collins in exquisite attire, and pronounces the words which turn the drama into Pantomime.

This Pantomime is characterised by the elegance which marks all the productions at this theatre. It is not a vehicle for riotous fun, nor for incessant allusions to topics of the day, but it is as refined a production as it is possible to render this class of spectacle, and there is a constant supply of merriment throughout. The scenery is extremely beautiful, and one grand effect – the appearance of the Genie in revolving rings of coloured jewellery – is as chastely magnificent as anything we have ever seen. This, combined with the Fairy Palace scene, forms a termination whose refulgence will send home thousands of Hans Christian Anderson's young English friends to dream of realized glories like those he has described to them. Next to this, the best effect is a capital skating scene, which delighted the audience, in which a tremendously fat swell, after performing all kinds of evolutions, and overthrowing scores of smaller folks, goes through a hole in the ice, and the Humane Society's drags dive after him in vain. Pantomime Park is another very elegant scene, and is got up with as much care as if it were the "set" of a comedy of fashionable life. Indeed, throughout the whole spectacle, evanescent as the effects are to be, the proverbial finish of the Princess's Theatre is invariably bestowed upon them.

Mr Huline's graceful Harlequin, Mr Cormack's lithe and indefatigable Clown, and Mr Paolo's lissome Pantaloon have been too often recognised to require more than mention, the names of these favourite artistes sufficing to indicate the class of performance. Miss Caroline Adams, the Columbine, looked and danced as prettily as could be desired, which is saying a good deal considering how much prettiness we are accustomed to see at this house. In the introduction, Mr Saker's Aladdin was full of comic humour and agility, and Mr F Cooke was a most picturesque Magician. We must not omit to add (although we could have borne the omission of the interlude itself), that M. Deserais' troupe of dogs and monkeys are introduced towards the end of the Pantomime. One of the dogs, a brown one, who takes astounding leaps with evident enjoyment, is really a feature in the evening's entertainment; but the monkeys have yet to study their profession. [...]
The Era, 28/12/1856

1857

Haymarket
The Sleeping Beauty in the Wood
[...] THE opening scene is the Abode of the Fairy Spiteful (Mr Clark), where she is discovered frizzling on a gridiron or warming pan, to which she has been condemned for some former indiscretion for fifty years. The term is on the point of expiry when the piece opens, consequently she is about to be let loose upon the world again to play her antics, to the annoyance of all right-minded persons who unhappily might be brought within her influences. Her term of frizzling having expired, she summons her familiars around her, and on learning that the king's daughter is about to be christened, and that a grand banquet is to be given in honour of the event, to which all the good fairies have been invited, she determines to go herself without an invitation, and she sets out for that purpose.

The second scene is the Royal Nursery, where we are introduced to three celebrated characters, known as Mrs Gamp, Betsy Prig, and the shadowy Mrs Harris[19]. These interesting females have charge of the infant Princess, who is on the lap of one of them. The parents of the royal juvenile visit it in the nursery, and the royal father, in his energy and anxiety to embrace the precious infant, falls upon it with the whole weight of his body, thereby apparently knocking the life out of his offspring. Everybody, of course, is in consternation, but Mrs Gamp, happily, has resort to the bellows, and by its agency infuses an animating flatus into the royal infant, which has the effect of making it as well as ever.

The next scene is that of the Samphire Cliffs on the Coast of Fairyland, and a very pleasing scene it is, in which a novel and most pleasing effect is introduced. It is that of the waves breaking upon the sandy shore – that almost imperceptible ebbing and flowing of the tidal wave, when the sea appears, at a short distance to the eye, to be perfectly calm and motionless. This was a charming effect. In this scene is a grand ballet of the fairy godmothers, led on by Miss Fanny Wright.

The next scene is a procession of all sorts, sizes, and descriptions of pantomimic characters to the banquet in honour of the christening of the Princess. At the end of this procession the bad fairy Venoma appears, and intimates that she'll be amongst them at the coming banquet.

Then we have the Banquetting Hall of the Silver Columns, which really looks all gold. From its massive appearance, and the richness of the banquetting service, we must assume that the Kingdom of Spindledom in which this scene is laid is very prolific of gold fields. Before the guests have settled themselves to the repast the bad Fairy makes her appearance, and there and then foretells that the baby will, when she grows up, prick her finger with a spindle and die of the wound. The Fairy Brighteyes, however, says she shall not die, but simply sleep for a century, and then wake to marry a beautiful prince. Venoma, thus foiled in part of her malevolent plan, determines to have some malicious pleasure on the spot, and so sets all the viands dancing in the air out of the reach of the guests. Then follow the scenes as foretold by the two fairies.

A lapse of sixteen years introduces us to the Princess grown up, and, of course, with a will of her own. She meets with an old woman with a spindle; she determines, of course, because it is forbidden, to possess it; pricks her finger; goes off into her century of slumber; is awakened therefrom by the promised Prince, and this brings us to the Transformation Scene, in which the entire resources of the establishment have manifestly been expended. It is gorgeousness itself. It is designated the Golden Groves and Amaranthine Arcades of the Seven Fairies. The stage appears to be a mass of gigantic Golden Feathers, and as these gradually rise they disclose the fairies reposing in tropical flowers, each flower bud at the end of its stem containing the form of the fairy. In the midst of these magical bouquets on a pedestal are the chiefs of the fairies. This scene called down thunders of applause, and Mr Buckstone led on Mr William Callcott to receive the felicitations of the audience.

After this came the harlequinade, which opened with a truthful scene of the New Harbour at Dover, with the arrival of the Calais mail boat. The passengers land from the boat, and amongst them is a gentleman apparently suffering excrutiatingly from the agonies of gout. An examination of his gouty and bandaged leg, however, takes place, and then it is discovered that his gout arises from a plethora of contraband articles which he had concealed in the bandages on his legs. Next appears a drilling machine, through whose agency a band of raw recruits are instantaneously converted into trained soldiers of the line. The remainder of the scenes are of the ordinary rattling description, in which a practical ascent of Mont Blanc, *a la* Mr Albert Smith, is made by the Clown; and the whole winds up with a Baronial Hall, with Christmas in the Olden Time, with jesters, yule log, hobby horses, &c.

The house was crowded in every part, and amongst the occupants of the boxes we observed many members of some of our highest aristocratic families.

Princess's
Harlequin White Cat; or, the Princess Blancheflower and Her Fairy Godmothers
WE must aver that a more decorous audience could scarcely be found than that which occupied the upper region of the Princess's this eventful evening. We are enabled to record the important statistical fact that pugilism was at a discount, only *three* encounters having occurred during the evening. It is not to be expected, however, that the opportunities afforded by the orchestra for obbligato accompaniments should be neglected, and the skill of various whistlers was exhibited, and particularly distinguished in the pathetic melody of "Old Dog Tray".

So much for the *et ceteras*, now for the Pantomime. It appears that Mr J M Morton – anxious to inculcate the aesthetic lesson that it is desirable if you invite one member, it is both duty and policy to invite the whole of a family – has chosen the fairy story of *The White Cat* as the foundation. He has reared upon that basis a succession of circumstances, and brought under mortal ken a number of personages who could not be met with out of fairy land or its substitute, the theatre, and we are consequently introduced to the heroine – the Princess Blancheflower (the white cat), personated in the first instance by Master R Hodson, and to her parent, King Simplesimon 232rd.

When the time for the christening arrives we become acquainted with the very desirable people yclept the Fairies Golden Star, Topaz, and Rosebud, who officiate as godmothers to the infant princess, and endow the young lady with no end of virtues and witcheries. The Fairy Dragonetta, the fourth of the fairy group, had *not* received the invitation to the ceremony, but came an unbidden and unwelcome guest, and nullified, like the spiteful fairy she is, all the good gifts lavished, and condemns the royal infant to assume the form of a white cat,

Until some prince in love with her shall fall,
And ask her paw in marriage,
Whiskers, tail, and all.

How the Princess is relieved from the spell thrown over her by the wicked fairy by the loss of her head and tail, our young readers know; and we, therefore, hasten to say that the youth destined to perform this kind office is one of the three nephews of King Downinthemoutho, King of the Oh! Oh! Islands, to wit, Prince Broadogrinno, who, in following his favourite sport – stimulated thereto by his uncle's offer to abdicate in favour of that nephew who can bring him the largest pearl and a lovely Princess, who for sixteen years no mortal eye has seen, falls overboard, and finds himself in the Kingdom of the Fishes. He there saves the life of King Salmon (Mr F Cooke), and makes love to Queen Carp, and in return for his amenities and services, he is presented with the enormous pearl required, and is once more placed on *terra firma* by the express engine Flying Fish.

The youth, guided by destiny, finds himself in the neighbourhood of Cat Castle, and eventually in the presence of the White Cat herself (Miss Kate Terry), appropriately attended by Tortoiseshell Toms and Tabbies. This scene is very beautiful, and reflects great credit on the artist, Mr F Lloyd.

We then return to the court of King Downinthemoutho, who is congratulating himself on the apparent ill success of his nephews in the performance of the tasks assigned, when they arrive, one after the other, with pearls of various sizes and beauties according to taste. Broadogrinno has, however, been most befriended by fortune, and, as matters have by this time approached a climax, it becomes necessary for the Fairy Dragonetta to reappear, and the transformation commences.

This scene, also by Mr F Lloyd, is called the Fairy Christmas Tree, and is unquestionably most gorgeous, the tree being, of course, the receptacle for a galaxy of beauty, the display of which, by the rising of the branches, was the signal for unanimous applause.

The Harlequinade, which followed, was not remarkable for novelty, very few new tricks having been introduced – a toy shop, with all the toys in motion, being, perhaps, one of the most completely successful. The prevailing fashion of extensive dresses for ladies, with Mr Punch's peg-top suits to match for gentlemen, of course came in for a share of caricature, and the introduction of waist-holders, to enable gentlemen to dance with be-crinolined ladies, caused a

general laugh. There were no political allusions in the piece that told with the audience, and much dissatisfaction was occasionally expressed at the failure of the tricks. The Harlequin was Mr Cormack, and Pantaloon M. Paolo. Mr Huline was the Clown, and Miss C Adams Columbine. The graceful dancing of the lady, seconded by Mr Cormack, elicited frequent bursts of applause, and a Hop Garden, with a characteristic dance "La Garlandaise," met with much favour from the audience. Upon the whole, the Pantomime was successful, but the enthusiasm was not general at the close.
The Era, 27/12/1857

1858

Sadler's Wells

Harlequin and Old Izaac Walton; or, Tom Moore of Fleet Street, the Silver Trout, and the Seven Sisters of Tottenham

GOOD Old Izaak Walton could have little imagined, when he indulged in the pleasant pastime he loved so much, on the banks of the River Lea, that some couple of centuries afterwards his name would be the great attraction to the noisy crowds of Boxing-night. Yet so it evidently will be, for Mr Greenwood, whose judgement and skill in this difficult branch of dramatic art have so often been manifested, has made him the hero of his new Christmas piece, entitled HARLEQUIN AND OLD IZAAC WALTON; OR, TOM MOORE OF FLEET STREET, THE SILVER TROUT, AND THE SEVEN SISTERS OF TOTTENHAM.

As an appropriate prelude to the grander movement to follow, the Muddy Mountains of Old Father Thames will form the first scene, and exhibit our noble river of his being so bad that he had not been able to rest one minute in his bed. The great physician, Dr Board-of-Works, comes to prescribe for him, and though he admits the cure is only to be accomplished through a heavy drain on the other's resources, thinks it is to be ultimately accomplished.

Thames is tired, however, of the doctors and his own untidy state, and determines to consult his fairer tributary, the gentle River Lea, to whom he pays a visit in a charming spot, to be recognised as the Peerless Pool of the Water Nymphs. The Lea is, however, herself in sad distress through finding her finny population gradually diminished by the incursive rod and line of that persevering piscator, Old Izaac. The entrance of a chub and a barbel, with other fishes, in mourning for the loss of their scaly progeny, rouses her indignation still further, and the New River Head is appealed to as an oracle to give a hint to stop the marauder. He suggests that if Izaac could be got to marry, he would soon leave off angling, and the Fair Mayde of Tottenham, known to the readers of "Walton's Complete Angler" as Maude, the Milkmaid, is to be thrown in his way to complete the spell.

We are next to have an authentic view of old Izaac's dwelling in Fleet Street, and the old picturesque shop where he carried on his business as a hosier. Tom Moore, of Fleet Street, who will be remembered by those well versed in the lore of ancient story books as being a scapegrace who kept a remarkable jackdaw, turns out to have been the apprentice of Izaac, and he turns out, moreover, at six o'clock in the morning to take down the shutters of his master's shop. Maude, the milkmaid, comes round with the morning milk, and Tom is smitten by her charms, but the mischief of the Jackdaw and the appearance of the Hosier, who has not the patience of Socrates, puts a stop to their tender protestations. Izaac loves the maiden himself, and after a variety of incidents illustrative of his business and the sport which he makes his peculiar pleasure, he resolves to go to Tottenham farm, make a solemn proposal for her hand, and go a-fishing.

A beautiful series of dioramic scenes will conduct the audience through the green lanes and bridle roads of suburban London as existing two hundred years ago to the pastoral banks of the Lea, their refreshment on the way, "whilst a smoking shower passes off," being taken, of course, at that memorable hedge ale-house where that delicious compound was concocted said to altogether "too good for any but us anglers."

Arrived at the farm on the banks of the river Izaac can no longer restrain himself from hooking a fine trout, but finding it when caught too large to be conveniently stowed away, he seeks aid from the homestead, when the seven sisters – Maude, the milkmaid; Esther, the eldest; Phoebe, the plump; Dorcas, the dirty; Prudence, the prim; Lucy, the lazy; and Sally, the stout, vie with each other to render him assistance. The manifest preference displayed for the youngest and prettiest, however, excites their subsequent wrath and indignation; and when Tom and Maude are known to be affianced, the eldest sister only accedes to their union on the condition of the former accomplishing apparently two impossible tasks, recovering a bracelet from the bottom of the river, and obtaining a rook's nest that grows on the slender branch of a very high poplar. The trout that he has rescued from the hook of Izaac and his ever faithful Jackdaw enable him to execute both tasks; but the amazed six sisters, who despise the pretty and amiable seventh, won't hear of anybody being married before themselves, and the bargain being repudiated, Tom would be cheated out of his reward did not the Aquatic Fairy of the Lea come to his aid, change the six unscrupulous sisters of Tottenham into trees, and receive the seventh in her Palace of Pearl in the Realms of Crystal.

Here Maude becomes Columbine (Miss Caroline Parkes), Tom Moore, Harlequin (Mr C Fenton); the Elder Sister, Clown (Nicolo Duelm); and Old Izaac, Pantaloon (Mr Naylor); whilst the trout and the jackdaw are metamorphosed into a pair of sprites. [...]

Standard
Queen Anne's Farthing and the Three Kingdoms of Copper, Silver, and Gold; or, Harlequin Old King Counterfeit and the Good Fairy of the Royal Mint

THE story turns upon King Knowledgebox and Queen Allpowerful having called together their Court for the purpose of choosing a husband for their daughter the Princess. Two unexpected difficulties occur: in the first place all the nobles put forth their individual claims for the hand of the Princess; in the second, the Princess has selected a future lover in the person of Sir Mighty. Like most parents, the King sees with very different eyes to those of his daughter, and decrees her to remain single until, as the price of her hand, a Queen Anne's farthing is produced. Dame Nature very naturally seeks the aid of the Fairy Queen in the cause of the lovers, and Truth is appointed to aid Sir Mighty in his search for the much-valued coin.

The farthing is in the custody of King Counterfeit, and an expedition is undertaken to Brummagem Castle in search of it, but as the road lies through the three kingdoms of Copper, Silver, and Gold, difficulties beset them on their way, which eventually are overcome by the defeat of the Demon Cant. Having gained his end, Sir Mighty returns to claim the hand of the Princess. Counterfeit follows, confusion, of course, ensues, and then comes the Transformation Scene.

The opening scene, the Grand Audience Chamber of King Knowledgebox, with all the world at one view; the Ballet Scene of Glittering Fountains; and elaborate moving panorama, leading to Brummagem Palace, where a novel effect is produced by the introduction of living coins of every description, will be found very attractive. In the comic scenes will be especially noticed a mechanical change from a bill-posting station to the New Chelsea Bridge illuminated. The Harlequin is Mr W Smith; Columbine, Miss Annie Cushnie; Pantaloon, Martin; and Clown by the renowned Tom Matthews.

The Era, 26/12/1858

Royal Grecian
Guy Faux; or, the Amazon Queen and Her Sea-girt Isles

[…] THE first scene striking us as most novel was the Hall of History, where the different kings of this country, from the commencement down to the era of the Gunpowder Plot, are summoned by Old Christmas. The masks were all exceedingly good, representations of the traditional likenesses of the different kings, excepting that of Richard the Second, which was most unmistakeably a likeness of Mr Charles Kean, and so recognised by the audience, amidst great laughter and most good-natured, hearty cheering. The different styles of costume were also truthfully adhered to, and the group which the monarchs formed was a most effective though richly comic historical group.

The next scenic effect was the Seaweed Home of Aqua Regia, where the Amazon troupe of fairies assemble and go through a very beautifully arranged and tastefully executed series of dances, poses, and military manoeuvres, each dancer armed with a sword, lance, and shield. Here the Spanish conspirator Guido is raised, and sent to earth upon his mission. The character of Guy was undertaken by Mr G Conquest, whose make-up and impersonation of the flabby rag Guy we see carried about the streets on a chair was richly humorous, as was also a parody, which he sang to a popular nigger melody.

Once upon the earth a very nicely painted scene of King James's Bedchamber, with the royal babies in a cradle, attended by the nurse Alice, Miss Amelie Conquest. In the room a mechanical bed through which Guy comes to kill the King created much amusement. We then have the exterior of the conspirator Percy's Coal Shed and Oyster Shop, and an announcement that he will commence business upon the 5th of November. We also learn that he has his coals by the Eastern Counties Railway, and his cellars are beneath the House of Commons; and that he intends having powder in lieu of coals.

Then come the Vaults, which change to the Gold Lace Boudoir and Fairy Jewelled Chamber of the Fairy Aqua Regia – a scene which for dazzling beauty and effect may be equalled but not surpassed. It consists of richly ornamented pillars, profusely hung with gold lace and jewels; draperies rise, and discover jewelled caskets and recesses; fairies ascend through the stage, supported upon their gold rods, whilst from the draperies above others descend, and at the conclusion the whole of the Pantomime characters ascend from a trap in the centre, without going through the usual transformation. […] The comic business is very good, and amongst other changes was one from a tea shop and fort in China to a British man-of-war; and another where a huge potato changes to a butchers, bakers, and candlestick makers. The whole winds up with a beautiful painting of Her Majesty's recent visit to Cherbourg, with the fleet dressed out for the occasion. […]

Theatre Royal, Halifax
May and December; or, Harlequin June and His Magic Tune

FOR the first time in our recollection we have had, literally, a Christmas Pantomime, all its predecessors having being got up at Bradford, and brought here afterwards. The Pantomime is entitled *May and December; or, Harlequin June and his Magic Tune*. The plot of the opening is simple and apparent, and the libretto smart and telling, and free from vulgarity.

It commences in the Hall of Mildew, where the plot that May and December should marry is concocted by the Fairy Blight (Miss Glanville), and changes into the abode of Time in the Dazzling Halls of Light, when Old Time (Mr Frank Saymour) resolves to aid the youthful lovers May and June, and summons the Fairy Graciosa (Miss Graham) to his assistance, who calls on the seasons, an admirable series of *Tableaux Vivants*, to aid her to protect Young May. Old Time now presents June with his Golden Fiddle, at whose magic notes all who hear dance till he commands them to stop.

The next scene is the home of Young May, with the village green decked out for the festivities on the occasion of December's marriage, which, however, is frustrated by the appearance of June with his Golden Fiddle, who sets the old folk dancing to such a quick step that old December vows to relinquish all claim to the hand of Young May, provided June will have pity and *cut* their capers. In this scene is also introduced a pretty and graceful sheaf dance by a bevy of young girls, and the characteristic Maypole Dance by the villagers, both of which were much admired. After the union of the young lovers the transformation takes place near the Silver Lake in Dreamland, a piece of beautiful artistic effect by Mr George Wilson. [...]
The Era, 2/1/1859

1859

Drury Lane
Jack and the Beanstalk; or, Harlequin Leap-Year and the Merry Pranks of the Good Little People
THE allegorical introduction raises us to the elevation of forty-five miles above the earth's surface, where the atmosphere is penetrated by the chief almanac concocters, anxious to discover the kind of weather likely to befall in the year ensuing. The Weather (Miss Mason) herself appears in due course, and finding that a Pantomime is among the essentials for the winter season, introduces each month in the year, attended by the principal days, appropriately embodied, to give their illustrative aid to its development. The subject being selected, every scene thenceforward takes place in a distinct month, which affords an advantageous opportunity for scenic contrasts.

January reveals to us the snowy fields of Devonshire, where Jack's cottage is presumed to be situated, and the appropriate pastimes of the season are shown in a bustling episode of rustic schoolboy life. Jack (Mr Templeton) is found to have been brought up by Goody Greyshoes (Mr Tom Matthews) in ignorance of his real birth, and to have cultivated a tender attachment with Rose (Madame Boleno), his supposed sister. The disclosure is made that Jack was found in a bundle, which we afterwards learn was dropped by that terrible giant, Fee-Fo-Fum, when he conveyed away Jack's father, Prince Caradoc, to his castle, some years before the story begins. Goody is in pecuniary difficulties, and a seizure for three quarters' rent is threatened, but she disposes of the intruders in a way that, however satisfactory to the audience, can hardly be recommended for the imitation of householders in arrears. February presents us with the grotto of the Pixies, the Pixies being the West of England name for the "good little people", or fairies, who are always so ready to assist the deserving. Jack is taken under their patronage, and a Pixy (Miss Grace Darley) is commissioned to go in the disguise of a farmer to give the magic bean in exchange for a calf. Here takes place the grand ballet, and we are then shown a Breezy Heath in March, where the memorable bargain is made, and the peculiarities of that boisterous month are strikingly exhibited. April is illustrated by Jack's Garden, where the bean is industriously cultivated by hundreds of little Pixies, and at last, under their treatment, rises to a height which Jack gradually attains to ultimately find himself in May before the gates of the Giant's castle. Here he rescues the imprisoned fairies, decapitates the gormandizing giant, and after performing feats of valour only to be heard of in connection with legendary heroes, he is ultimately rewarded in triumph by the good Fairy Prism (Miss Helen Howard) in her Floral Home with all the floricultural show of June to grace the climax. This brilliant transformation scene is followed by comic business that continues the illustration of the months with July, a Hot Day at the Seaside; August, a Hot Day in Town; September, a Sporting Day in the Country; October, a Lively Day in the Hop Season; and November, a Foggy Day in London, whilst December crowns the year with the genial good humour of Old Father Christmas in his Halls of Good Cheer. [...]

Princess's
Jack the Giant Killer; or, Harlequin King Arthur and the Knights of the Round Table
THE first scene is in Jack's Cottage, where, according to the legend, an old beggar woman arrives and is treated with marked contempt by Jack's Mama, and with amiable attention by Jack. She is, of course, a Fairy in disguise, and soon discovers herself as Queen Bee (Miss Rose Leclerq[20]), the Protector of all Industrious Children, changing the scene almost immediately to the Queen Bee's Haunt and Home of Perpetual Sweets, where she awakens her bees, who perform a ballet. This scene is one of great beauty – unique in its construction and appointment. The innumerable groups of Fairy Hives, nestling amidst clusters of gorgeous foliage, and embowered by a lattice work of exotic creepers, and heightened by the artistic groupings of the Busy Bees attendant on their gentle Queen, approximates very

closely the human ideal of fairy perfection. The chief features in this fanciful Terpsichorean creation are the indescribably fantastic Mons. Espinosa, who, as a simple rustic, is inducted, as if by enchantment, into the mysteries of the dance by the fascinating Mlle Marietta Rosetta, a lady from the La Scala, equally brilliant in her art, and certainly a lady of first-class pretensions as a *premiere danseuse*. Jack (Miss Louse Keeley) is soon introduced to his protectress's favourite subjects no less than the much-coveted sweetmeats of our childhood, and presents him with a sword of sharpness, shoes of swiftness, and a cap of knowledge, with which she despatches him to try his luck at exterminating the giants infesting the neighbourhood of his home.

In the next scene, the interior of the Good King Arthur Tavern, we find Sybil (Miss Laidlow) despatching her two little brothers to school, and on her retiring, we are introduced to the Giant Gorgibuster (Mr J G Shore), the youngest of the three giants in question. He haunts the tavern containing Sybil, on whom he is particularly sweet, and having planted his two big brothers round the corner, intimates his intention of carrying off his love in the middle of the forthcoming wedding festivities, and for a while retires. Then enter the wedding folks, celebrating with good cheers and good cheer the union of a particularly virtuous peasant and peasantess. In the midst of their enjoyment the King is announced, and King Arthur (Mr Saker) and his redoubtable Knights appear on the scene. He is, however, condescending, and ordering out the Round Table, proceeds to enjoy the sports. Suddenly a shriek is heard, all is confusion and terror, when the landlord (Mr Paolo) rushes in and announces the appalling fact that the Giant has eloped with his child. The King immediately offers knighthood on the spot to anyone bold enough to follow and fight the depredator; but the knights do not seem to relish the notion, and the poor Boniface is in an agony for his daughter's safety, when Jack arrives and immediately undertakes to search out and encounter the dreaded Giant. The King knights him, and he starts on his way amidst the cheers of the populace generally.

We then follow the Giant, and find him carrying his lovely burden to his home, closely followed by the avenging Jack in his seven-leagued shoes, and we come to the interior of the Giant's house. We here find a nervous valet of Gorgibuster's, called Tremoloso (Mr F Cathcart), complaining of the way in which he is treated, and of the impossibility of his carrying out his matrimonial intentions regarding Cook (Mr J W Collier). Their love passages are interrupted by the arrival of "master" with his fair charge. Supper is ordered and brought on, but the meal is interrupted by the arrival of a young pilgrim, no less than Jack in disguise, who is made particularly welcome, for his host perceives that he is young, and plump; and little knowing what kind of guest he is harbouring, he offers him the best his house can afford, of course with ulterior views of a cannibalistic nature.

Bed time arrives, and Jack goes through the "business", so well-known to children of all ages, with a chair, placing it in the bed, and hiding himself to watch the proceedings of his enemy. The Giant takes down his club, and soon reduces, as he thinks, his guest to a pulp, after which he exhibits some Macbeth-like qualms, but eventually sleeps as if nothing were on his mind. All four prisoners are then in a fair way to escape, when, as ill-luck will have it, the Giant wakes. A combat ensues, in which Jack is eventually victorious, the Giant dying very hard indeed, with no signs of repentance, but with the hope that his big brothers, Cormoran and Blunderbone, will avenge him. They appear in the next scene to be driving all before them, and Jack, whose shoes would enable him to escape himself with ease, cannot make up his mind to leave Tremoloso and his enamoured Cook to their fate. The Giants seize, and are about to despatch them, when the Queen Bee rises with her satellites (who settle upon the legs of the Giants, almost maddening them, and finally reducing them to submission), and changes the scene to a very beautiful Transformation Scene entitled the Barley Sugar Retreat, or a Good Boy's Bower of Bliss.

There is, we believe, a freshness about the comic business likely to render it more than usually acceptable. The humorous Mr Forrest (his first appearance here) exhibits, as Clown, his varied accomplishments on stilts, the violin, &c. Our agile favourites, Mr Cormack, Mr Paolo, and Miss Caroline Adams, are, as Harlequin, Pantaloon, and Columbine, the admirable supporters of the merry harlequinade. The great gun of the latter consists of a highly elaborated rifle dance by a corps of ladies in full costume most elegantly appointed in every particular.

The Era, 25/12/1859

NOTES
1 – This huge, elaborately carved bed draped with rich red curtains was described as being more suitable for the lying in state of a corpse than as an item of furniture.
2 – Temperance advocate and womens' rights pioneer Amelia Bloomer (1818-1894) popularized, but did not invent, this alternative to the restrictive clothing of the day. It consisted of a short skirt worn over a pair of Turkish-style wide trousers gathered at the ankle.
3 – Amina, the heroine of Rossini's opera *La Sonnambula*, sleepwalks into her lover's bedroom.
4 – In 1853 the camp at Chobham was the site of the first military manoeuvres held since the Napoleonic Wars.

5 – The cabmen of London went on strike in protest against a new law which set fares at sixpence a mile, twopence less than had been customary.

6 – A craze for keeping poultry, particularly exotic breeds such as Cochin China chickens, was sparked by Elizabeth Watts, a poultry maid from Hampstead. The hobby increased in popularity when Queen Victoria founded her Home Farm at Windsor.

7 – Hannah Glasse's first cookery book, *The Art of Cookery Made Plain and Easy*, was first published in 1747 and remained in print well into the 19th century.

8 – Dr William Kitchiner (1775-1827): Author of the bestselling *The Cook's Oracle*.

9 – Louis Eustache Ude: Author of *The French Cook*.

10 – Maria Rundell (1745-1828): Author of *A New System of Domestic Cookery*.

11 – A book by the French chef Alexis Soyer (1810-1858), published in 1854.

12 – The clock above Sir John Bennett's watch and jewellery shop was famous for its automaton figures of Gog and Magog, who rang chimes every fifteen minutes.

13 – The National Baby Convention, held in Springfield, Ohio.

14 – A reference to the Crimean War.

15 – "Bona fide travellers" were those more than three miles away from home who could legally buy alcoholic drinks at pubs or hotels during hours when they were closed to locals.

16 – A perfume made by Grossmith of London.

17 – Perhaps an indication that the character was made up or costumed to resemble the deeply unpopular Nicholas I, Emperor of Russia.

18 – Aztec Lilliputians: Maximo and Bartola, a Salvadorean brother and sister suffering from microcephaly.

19 – Mrs Gamp and Betsy Prig are characters in Charles Dickens' *Martin Chuzzlewit*; Mrs Harris is Mrs Gamp's imaginary friend.

20 – Rose Leclerq (1843-1899): An actress best remembered for creating the role of Lady Bracknell in Oscar Wilde's *The Importance of Being Earnest*.

7
The 1860s
An Ogre of Kleptomaniac Proclivities

1860

> THEATRICAL DISPUTE – COURT OF COMMON PLEAS, THURSDAY
> FALSE IMPRISONMENT – MOON V TOWERS – *This was an action for an assault and false imprisonment, to which the defendant pleaded not guilty. The case was tried before Mr Justice Williams on the 19th April last.*
>
> *It appeared at the trial that the plaintiff was the property-master, and the defendant was the proprietor, of the Victoria Theatre, and on last Boxing Night the Pantomime of* Harlequin King Pippin; or, the Enchanted Chicken, *was produced, in which appeared several gigantic chickens with fireworks issuing from their mouths against the Clown, Pantaloon, and all the performers, frightening the whole of them off the stage and remaining sole occupants of the enchanted hills and valleys, and still belching forth volleys of fireworks, to the extreme delight of the admiring audience, when a quantity of blue and other fires appeared, and the enchanted chickens are carried off in a volume of smoke. These fireworks it was the duty of the plaintiff to purchase, which he did, and took receipts for the amounts so expended by him. As the Pantomime did not take so well as was expected, it was determined that a new piece should be added to it, in which also fireworks were introduced, which greatly increased the expenses of the theatre, and he was discharged by the defendant for having expended too much money. The defendant's son, who was the treasurer of the theatre, afterwards went to the plaintiff's house with a policeman, and gave him in charge for defrauding the defendant, his father. He was taken before the magistrate at the Southwark Police Court, when he was remanded for a week, and upon the further hearing of the case, the magistrates discharged him.*
>
> *The defence was, that the defendant never authorised his son to give the plaintiff in charge, and after hearing the evidence, the jury returned a verdict for the plaintiff – damages, £20.*
>
> *Subsequently a rule* nisi *was obtained by Mr Hawkins, Q C, on the part of the defendant, calling upon the plaintiff to show why the verdict should not be set aside, and a new trial had, on the ground that the verdict was against the weight of evidence.*
>
> *After hearing the arguments of the learned counsel on both sides, their lordships said they were of the opinion that the son had not the authority of the defendant to give the plaintiff into custody; therefore, the defendant could not be made liable, and the judgement would be for the defendant.*
> The Era, 27/5/1860

Haymarket
Queen Ladybird; or, Harlequin and the House on Fire

[…] THE piece opens in the Cell of Aphis, King of the Green Flies, where a conspiracy is hatched by the said King (Mr Coe) and his lieutenant, Greengoggle (Mr R Carroll) to waylay and assassinate the Queen Ladybird (Miss Weekes), as she is about to visit Prince April (Miss Fanny Wright) in order to arrange for his nuptials with the Princess Three-spots (Miss Louise Leclerq), whose hand Aphis has vainly sought in marriage. The conspirators are dispersed for the time by an April shower, which, passing away, displays an April day in the country, a piece of Watteau scene painting which brings down, as it deserved, the unanimous applause of the audience. Here the Queen is attacked, but, luckily, Prince April arrives in time to save her, and conduct her to his Allegorical Palace. The Queen having retired for the night, Princess Three-spots arrives and invites the Prince to a grand ball, which she and her thirty sisters propose to give in the absence of their natural parent, having first duly placed the ten juvenile brothers to bed, where we next see the said juveniles engaged in a grand bolstering match, during which Aphis and Greengoggle arrive to carry out their plans for firing the house, and are duly bolstered.

Passing through the Leafy Recess in the Ladybird Bower and the Gossamer Approach, we arrive at the Honeysuckle Bower of Queen Ladybird, where the young Ladybirds have a grand merrymaking and Ballet, in which the Princess Three-spots takes the lead; and certainly a prettier or more enticing Ladybird than Miss Louise Leclerq it would be difficult to find between Tyburn Arch and Aldgate Pump. But, if every cloud has a silver lining, all pleasures have their alloy, and the merrymaking is brought to an abrupt termination by the incendiary efforts of Aphis and his myrmidons, who fire the house.

In the meantime, the Queen is prevented from sleeping by bodings of evil likely to befall her forty darlings, a number which she accounts for by having been repeatedly married; and, viewing the distant conflagration, is reminded by voices in the air to return home, as her children are alone – which, in fact, they are not – as Prince April is with them, and, by his power, brings down a pelting storm to assist in putting out the fire, at which we see the engines and fire-escapes in full activity. Now it is that the Fairies appear on the scene, viz., she of the Rose, she of the Honeysuckle, and she of the Hops, personated by three young ladies: Miss Hendrade, Miss Addington, and Miss Coleman, who, as good Fairies always do, take the virtuous under their protection, and determine on the destruction of Aphis and his Lieutenant, restoring Prince April to the arms of his beloved, and her forty children to those of Queen Ladybird.

Here comes the grand scene of the piece, Queen Ladybird's New Palace, with its glassy retreats, silver fountains, dancing jets, and running streams of real water; and anything more magnificent was never put upon the stage, and would of itself be sufficient to stamp the success of the piece – the playing of the light upon the gorgeous dresses of the pillars of living beauty, and the falling of the water forming a *coup l'oeil* not easy to describe. Here the grand Transformation takes place, when Prince April becomes Harlequin (Mr Arthur Leclerq); Aphis, Pantaloon (Herr Cole); Greengoggle, Clown (Mr Charles Leclerq); and the Princess Three-spots, Columbine (the charming Fanny Wright).

Having assumed their respective characters, and the Clown having duly announced that "Here we are again!" the scene changes to the front of the County Fire Office, where all the fun of the fair begins, and an excellent waltz is introduced by the Harlequin and Columbine. We next see the White Horse Cellar, Piccadilly, "as it used to was", rather than as it is, and a hurdy-gurdy *pas à la Suisse* is given by Mr Arthur Leclerq and his sister Louise, which is sure to become popular from its eccentricity and the energy with which it is performed – and the scene of other days changes to the platform of the Great Western Railway, with a train ready to start, a most excellent and truthful picture of things as they are. We next find ourselves at the entrance to Rotten Row, Hyde Park, where a great meeting of equestrians and pedestrians takes place, to petition respectively for and opposing the new ride which drew down so much opposition last year from those whom it could not by any possibility affect. Next we are introduced to Kensington Gardens, with its new terrace, fountains, walks, &c, where a very novel and excellent dance of muffs and whips is introduced by "the equestrian and pedestrian ladies of the ballet," which was immensely applauded.

The Genius of Pantomime next wafts us to the Broadway, New York, a beautiful scene, and the announcement that the *Great Eastern*[1] has arrived, and may be seen for one dollar, having no effect in drawing the money from Cousin Jonathan, the price is at once reduced to one cent. Here, also, we see a number of darkies, on pleasure bent; and the Fairy of the Rose again appears, and informs Harlequin and Columbine that their pilgrimage of trouble is run, and that they may now be united in the bonds of holy matrimony, and live happily hereafter – i.e., until the following evening, when, by the permission of the audience, they may pass through the same pilgrimage for their own behoof, the entertainment of a generous public, and the filling of the manager's pockets. But before they conclude their labours, the said Fairy introduces them to the Capitol at Washington, with the reception of the Prince of Wales by the President of the United States, concluding with the playing of "God Save the Queen" and "Yankee Doodle". […]

There are various tricks and transformations; which, if not all particularly new, are always welcome, the best being the production from the Clown's *Multum in Parvo*[2] (an ordinary-sized chest, not quite so large as that of M. Nadolsky[3]) not only of a complete suite of drawing-room furniture, chandelier included, but the dinner table duly laid for a party of twenty or thirty; these by far outstripping the ingenious foreigner to whom we have just alluded. Then we have hats converted into pork pies from which appear live pigs; Volunteers who turn out incipient Wellingtons; England's best defence, the Armstrong gun[4]; and many other hits at passing topics. On the first night King Frost interfered with the grand scene by taking the water under his own charge, without asking the permission of the manager, and the machinery was most reluctant to work; but, now that all the difficulties incipient to the first representation of a Pantomime, which are looked for as naturally as the Pantomime itself, have been overcome, there cannot be found within the sound of Bow bells a better or merrier entertainment, or a Pantomime which is destined to have a longer run; it being an excellent specimen of the powers of Mr Buckstone in this department of dramatic literature. […]
The Era, 30/12/1860

1861

Princess's
Whittington and His Cat; or, Harlequin King Kollywobbel

WE had an instructive friend with us, and he would talk. "You are aware," he said, "that there was a Sir Richard Whittington, a citizen and mercer of London, who served the office of Lord Mayor three times, the last in 1419. The marvellous stories connected with his name are wholly without truth, but his munificent charities are little known and seldom praised. He founded – " but luckily our instructive friend was stopped here by a crinoline that would go by to her place, and utterly swallowed him up, besides hurting his knees awfully. When he emerged from the eclipse, and had done using objectionable words against women, he resumed – "As for the Cat, that is an Oriental invention. Sir William Gore Ouseley says that in the tenth century a widow's son, called Keis, embarked for India with a cat, his sole property. He fortunately arrived at a time when – " Again came a providential deliverance, and up went the curtain.

Mr Byron has treated the Nursery Story with much simplicity, and has thereby shown that he understands how a Pantomime should be worked. The action is, as it ought to be, perfectly comprehensible to the eye, for the Pantomime is for the million, and the art of appreciating an involved plot or elaborate writing is an acquired taste, by no means general. He has scattered a good deal of smartness over the introduction – in fact, we should doubt Mr Byron could write dully, even on the currency question, but his aim has been to make the audience recognise their old friends, and their old emotions, through the amiable distortion of masks and extravagant action.

So we have old Fitzwarren (Mr Raymond), who is a puffing tradesman, and Dick Whittington (Miss Maria Harris), the prettiest and most dainty 'prentice, and Alice (Miss Pauline Leclerq), much attached to Dick, and the Cook (Mr Hastings), a victim to a policeman of the period (Mr Moreland), and the Cat (Master John Haslem). We incline to think the evil 'prentice, Billy Badlot (Mr Garden) to be an interpolation; but there were, no doubt, evil 'prentices in the fifteenth century, and one of them may have had black hair and a turn-up nose.

The adventures of Whittington we should be ashamed to insult our readers by recapitulating, but the way they are made available for Pantomime is this: – The Cat is "Robin Goodfellow" (Dr Charles Mackay[5] having no further use for him), and he attends Dick in his wanderings, and scratches his enemies a good deal. But when the Cat has to do her work at the Court of King Kollywobbol (Mr R Cathcart), her brief victory over two rats gives the Princess Popsiwopsi (Miss Rose Leclerq) to Richard; but the Rat King (Mr Collett) is too mighty for Puss, and sends in an army of rats, like those who eat the Bishop in Southey's poem, and the adventurers are defeated, and the Cat faints away like a lady. Then the lovely Genius of Good Humour (Miss H Howard), who does excellent justice all through, comes to the rescue, revives the Cat, overthrows the wicked generally, and brings on the Transformation. Miss Helen Howard looks charming, and delivers her pretty speeches in the most captivating manner.

But the story is not the strongest part of the pantomime. It has been got up at lavish cost, and in the most gorgeous manner, in order to attract not only the regular lovers of such things, but the London that does not care much about the pasteboard epigrams and tumbling, but likes elegant Spectacle and the Ballet. In these respects the Princess's Pantomime is one of the richest we ever saw. The Second Scene – a Rose Bower (real perfume sent over the house) – is exquisitely painted, and the beautifully dressed young ladies (the Princess's is famed for the personal graces of its danseuses) execute some charming dancing. The procession, in which the Princess is brought on, is a magnificent Oriental pageant, which, were the laughable masks and exaggerated weapons cut away, would be a worthy adjunct to what we hope never to see – the revival of an Oriental Play of high art. The view of Old London from Highgate is admirably painted, and so are several other scenes. The beautiful Ballet of Bayaderes in the Banquet Hall (excellently painted by Mr Cuthbert) is as good a thing as ever was done; one part, in which a silver ball is shot by each lady from one of her bouquets to the other, and back – it seems a small thing to mention, but the sparkling effect is singularly novel.

But the grand effort is, of course, reserved for the Silver Glade – the Transformation Scene – and it would be unfair to describe it minutely. It is one vast mass of graceful form, rich colour, and vivid brilliancy, and the charming faces of the glittering ladies, who glide about in all sorts of possible and impossible ways, and the enchantment, and then the coloured fires, which bring up new beauties, finally sends the spectator into a pleasant bewilderment of admiration. No wonder that Mr Gates, the painter, was called for, and brought in by Mr Harris, amid a storm of applause.

The other "feature" in the Pantomime is the marvellous little fellow, John Haslem. He is a pupil of Gabriel Ravel. As a pretty little semi-clad Bacchus, he won all the ladies' hearts; then, as a Cat, he enchanted the children; and then, as a Leotard, he did Trapeze feats which made the men say, "By Jove". Add some smart dancing, and we are not sure that we have catalogued half his accomplishments. He is a treasure to the Manager.

For the Harlequinade, we may say that it is up to the usual mark, and when the multitudinous arrangements of a Pantomime, little known of by the impatient, have got into complete order, and a few of the less effective "hits" have been eliminated (we could have written "cut out", but polysyllables imply a polite education), this part of the performance will be entirely satisfactory to those who enjoy the Italian comedy. […]   ***The Era, 29/12/1861***

1862

> ON Friday evening week two Pantomimic accidents occurred – one at Drury Lane Theatre and the other at the Victoria Theatre, which fortunately, however, were not fatal. At Drury Lane, Mr Huline, the Clown, in firing a pistol at the Pantaloon, Mr Tanner, misdirected it, and unfortunately wounded the lean and slippered gentleman above the eye and on the cheek, but not seriously. At the Victoria Theatre, behind the scenes, there was an escape of gas, and considering the extent of the explosion, it is a perfect miracle that the whole edifice was not enveloped in flames.
> *The Era, 5/1/1862*

> ### Fracas on the Stage of the Victoria Theatre
> Samuel Lockyer, an active-looking man, described on the charge-sheet as an actor, was brought on Monday before Mr Burcham at the Southwark Police Court, by Herrington, the officer of the Victoria Theatre, charged with committing a violent and unprovoked assault on Mr Isaac Cohen on the stage of the above theatre.
>
> Mr Cohen, whose right jaw was much swollen, said that he was Stage Director of the Victoria Theatre, and the prisoner was engaged as the Sprite in the Pantomime. On Saturday night, during the first scene of the comic business, the prisoner had to go through a kind of drawing-room entertainment with his two sons, who were very young. In the course of their tumbling and jumping the defendant performed in such a clumsy manner that the audience hissed them off the stage. Witness was at that time attending to his duties on the stage, when he saw the defendant knocking one of the lads about in an unmerciful manner, and dragging him up some stairs. Witness thought it his duty to interfere for the protection of the lad, and, while he was endeavouring to get the latter away, the defendant struck him such a tremendous blow on the right jaw that he firmly believed that it was broken.
>
> Mr Burcham asked whether he knocked him down? – Witness replied that he fell against a wall, and was stunned for some moments.
>
> In answer to the charge, the defendant said he was extremely sorry for what had occurred, and was willing to make an ample apology to Mr Cohen.
>
> Mr Burcham observed that he supposed it was necessary that he should be perfectly steady when he went through that hazardous performance with his sons.
>
> Mr Cohen said that it was, and his being under the influence of liquor endangered their lives and limbs. Not only that, but the audience were disappointed.
>
> Mr Burcham said that the conduct of the defendant was very bad indeed. The performance of itself was extremely hazardous, and required a great deal of hard training before before they could accomplish those feats; therefore, his lads ought not to be treated in such a brutal way. Mr Cohen had acted kindly in going to the protection of one of them, and then he was attacked, and his jaw nearly broken. Defendant must pay a penalty of 40s for the assault on Mr Cohen, or go to prison for fourteen days.
>
> The prisoner paid the fine.
> *The Era, 26/1/1862*

Covent Garden
Harlequin Beauty and the Beast; or, the Gnome Queen and the Good Fairy

[…] THE first scene is the boudoir of Brutina, the Gnome Queen, who has tried all her charms on the unsusceptible heart of a captive prince. He will have nothing to say to her, though she calls in the aid of the Court coiffeur, modiste, and enameller, and finally brings to her aid the attractions of an allegorical ballet, in which the Prince is successively, but not successfully, tempted by wine, youth, and beauty. Encouraged at the callousness of the youth, she changes him to a beast. A good fairy, whose power is equal to the Gnome Queen's, makes a stipulation with her that, should any maiden be found to declare a passion for the transmogrified Prince, he is to instantaneously assume his original form.

Squire Tiddlywinks and his man-servant, Muddlehead, are returning home in the family gig, when a terribly high wind drives them into an enchanted wood, in which the trees do all sorts of strange things, and in which the belated travellers eventually come across the palace of the beast. Entering this magic domicile, they are entertained most sumptuously by fairy attendants, who cut up magical legs of mutton and draw enchanted champagne corks, and treat them generally with extreme hospitality. The squire, having promised his three daughters a present each, plucks a rose for his youngest child, Beauty, and is immediately seized by the outraged beast, whose horticultural feelings appear of as sensitive a nature as those of the head gardener at Hampton Court. The squire is about to lose his life, when he makes a pathetic appeal, and the Beast lets him go home on a promise to return with Beauty. The Squire brings his charming child back with him, and the Beast falls in love with her and detains her, permitting the parent to return to his suburban villa. All his attentions, however, are bootless. Beauty adores her father, and refuses to be comforted by the inevitable grand ballet which is popularly supposed to have a soothing effect upon heart-broken heroines.

When she sees in a vision her father utterly broken-down with grief, she implores the Beast to let her go, and she is allowed to return to alleviate the Squire's sufferings, although the Beast says he shall be utterly distraught and miserable without her. The return of his child restores the Squire to reason, for since her leaving him he has become a maniac and a prey to a troupe of variously thinking physicians, and they all start off to the Beast's palace. They are too late, however; the Gnome Queen, afraid that her scheme may fail, has poisoned him, and the poor Beast is discovered dead, to the extreme agony of Beauty. In her wretchedness she exclaims that, were he alive, she would love and wed him; and the Beast immediately vanishes, the original Prince appearing in his place, to the extreme delight of everybody concerned, with the exception of the Gnome Queen, who retires to the sulphurous seclusion of her own palace. […]

Theatre Royal, Westminster (Astley's)
Lady Bird; or, Harlequin Lord Dundreary
THIS will be the first return made for thirty years to the old style of pantomime, the story of the opening being told by action, except when the fairies assert their powers of loquacity.

The first scene represents a Farmhouse on the estate of Lord Dundreary[6], in Norfolk. James, his lordship's footman, is in love with Buttercup, the daughter of Farmer Barleycorn, and about to lead his bride to the altar. To the assembled rustics James displays his muscular powers amidst immense applause. In the middle of his triumph the landlord is announced, and enters with his fop friend. Dundreary is smitten with Buttercup; she rejects him, but eventually rank and wealth prevail over calves and plush. James in despair is set aside. His lordship goes to embrace the bride when he sees a Ladybird on her dress; disgusted with the insect he is about to brush it off when Buttercup interposes to protect the lucky little creeper; James also officiously interposes, receives the indignity of a kick from his master; insult is now added to injury, and James, throwing off his livery, shows fight. His lordship is persuaded to give him a lesson, and undertakes to do it; a ring is formed, and a fight, after the Mace and King[7] style, is gone through, ending in the discomfiture of the nobleman.

Buttercup, however, is carried off, and James is left disconsolate and alone with the Ladybird whose life he fought for and saved. After various futile efforts at suicide the Ladybird changes into a fairy and offers him her protection against his master. Here Goldiva, the Fairy of Riches, steps in, and declares her resolve to protect Dundreary. The fairies exchange challenges and disappear. Quickly we are brought to a Moonlight Fairy Dell, in which Lady Bird invokes her subjects; all the insect tribe appear; bees, hornets, beetles, wasps, dragonflies, and gnats come buzzing to her call. She marshals them, and they go out to attack Lord Dundreary in his Castle of Fopsall on his bridal night. Now we are introduced to this noble residence and his lordship's bedroom. Here, as may be expected, Dundreary's toilet is assailed by insects and troubles of every kind; he tumbles from one misery to another until he is driven frantic. James, as a garotter, is constantly following him throughout.

At the height of his miseries, his guardian fairy, Goldiva, rescues him by changing his chamber to a Fairy Palace, in which the characters are severally transformed into Clown, Harlequin, Columbine, and Pantaloon. Messrs Huline and Duprex, Miss Annie Cushnie, and Mr Sylvester then engage in comic business as it is called, during which we have a Fishmonger's Shop in the Haymarket, New Lambeth Bridge, and the Machinery Annexe of the Great Exhibition. The last scene will be what is usually called the Transformation Scene. […]

The lighting of the auditorium will also be on an entirely new principle, the reserved seats will be kept all the evening, and a most desirable arrangement is that the performances will invariably conclude at eleven through the season, so that visitors may catch their trains for the suburbs at the Waterloo Station and elsewhere.

Pavilion
King Sillyninny, Who Sold His Wife For Half a Guinea; or, Harlequin and the Enchanted Princess
PRINCESS SCRUMPTIOUS having excited the anger of a wicked Magician, is transformed into a state of ugliness, causing everyone about her to go dancing mad whenever she laughs, the spell being decreed to remain in force until a charmed half-guinea, which has been thrown into the moor, shall have been discovered and broken in twain. The Fairy Queen, pitying the condition of the Princess, sends one of her court to obtain possession of the magic talisman, but as he returns with it he is waylaid by two myrmidons of her demon foe, and the charmed half-guinea taken from him, when Robin Redbreast, hearing cries of distress, attacks the imps, and is left in sole possession of the charmed coin, which he afterwards speculates in the purchase of King Sillyninny's wife, that monarch having disposed of his better-half by public auction.

The purchase money is no other than the charmed half-guinea, which, after a variety of adventures, falls into the hands of the Fairy Queen, who also causes the Princess to be rescued by Robin from the tower where she has been confined by the King and Demon till she can regain the coin. The half-guinea broke in twain, the Princess resumes her natural form, but as her union with Robin is opposed by the Demon, the Fairy Queen decrees the usual pantomime transformation as a set off. The Grove of Golden Acorns, with the ascension of Phoebus in her glittering car, is the scene in which the ballet takes place. The Transformation scene will represent the Bower of Enchanted Ferns. The pantomime company will be composed of Mr J Rickards, as Clown; Felix Safferini, as Pantaloon; Miss Clara King, as Columbine; and M. Lavigne, as Harlequin. Sprites by the Brothers Costello.

City of London
Harlequin Sing a Song of Sixpence; or, Pocket Full of Rye, Four and Twenty Blackbirds Baked in a Pie
THE first scene is the Fungi Cave, where the wicked Fairy, Ergotina, is opposing Cereale, the guardian of corn. The Golden Rye Field shows us the rustic Chickabiddy endeavouring to find a lucky sixpence he has lost. Rescuing a blackbird from a trap he finds he has gained the good opinion of Cereale, who restores him his lucky sixpence and makes him a prince. He is presented to the Queen with a pocket full of rye, and entrusted with a magic charm to foil the fairy Ergotina, who has caused a sudden blight, but the charm prevails and we see the Harvest Home of the Fairy Queen, where a brilliant ballet takes place.

We meet Prince Chickabiddy anon at the Counting House of the King Love-and-Money, where the monarch is engaged in financial matters, whilst the Queen is eating bread and honey. The Prince makes love to the daughter, the fair Preciosa, but a conflict ensues with the King's guards, and when Preciosa is sent to gather honey in the Cherry Orchard, Honeysuckle Grove, they meet again but to part. The King determines to exterminate the whole race of blackbirds, when twenty-four blackbirds make their appearance. The King fires, when the whole are brought down by a single shot, and they are borne off in triumph to the Royal Kitchen, where the cooks are rolling out the paste. They depart to cover up the pie; the Prince, who is on the watch, follows to perfect his part of the charm by placing in the pie a pocket full of rye, and we next find ourselves in the Banquet Chamber. The King, Queen, and Princess enter, attended by the Chamberlain; when the pie is opened the blackbirds all begin to sing. The Garden and Drying Ground of the Palace shows us Preciosa, attended by Moplul, the Laundry Maid, busy hanging out the clothes, when suddenly a blackbird arrives and "pops off her nose". An immediate flight takes place to Wildbriar Heath, and the lovers are pursued by the King and his guards, but the Fairy Queen arrives and transports them to the Lake of Water Lillies.

Drury Lane
Little Goody Two Shoes; or, Harlequin and Cock Robin
THE heroine of the well-known story, personated by that clever actress and *danseuse*, Miss Lydia Thompson[8], has taken upon herself the education of the poor children of the neighbourhood, and at her village school we first meet with her endeavouring to teach the young idea how to shoot under those circumstances which peculiarly conduce to comicality of situation. Pecuniary difficulties form a barrier to her marriage with Little Boy Blue (Miss Ellen Howard), a shepherd swain, who is her faithful lover; and she has a terribly refractory pupil in one Tommy Green (Mr George Weston), who has attempted to drown her favourite cat in the well after the manner referred to in the ancient nursery legend, and who is the very reverse in disposition of the good-natured Johnny Stout (Mr Joe Robins), who has extricated the feline pet. Little Goody's harsh landlord, Sir Timothy Gripe (Mr Tom Matthews), having no sympathy with her disinterested labours on behalf of the juvenile population of the village, appears as a suitor for her hand, and, being rejected, turns her out of the cottage, so that she is compelled to make the neighbouring wood the scene of her educational experiments. Here, making a couch of a bank of wild flowers, she passes the night, and in a dream she assumes the form of Forget-me-not, whilst the animated wild flowers rush forth to welcome her arrival amongst them, when one of Mr Oscar Byrne's ingeniously-arranged ballets takes place.

The wicked Tommy Green has invoked the Spirit of Envy, and has urged the destruction of Little Goody's favourite pet, Robin, which is to be done through the agency of a malicious Cock Sparrow. Then we have the Dawning of the First of May and the Celebration of a Village Carnival, which introduces all the rustic sports and pastimes formerly in vogue among us. Goody Two Shoes is crowned Queen of the May, and Little Boy Blue, who has been assisted by their guardian, Good Nature (Miss Kate Saxon), has made money enough to discharge her liabilities for rent, so that the end of her trials seems to be near; but the terrible tragic event, which has been lyrically immortalised, is impending. The cruel Sparrow, urged by Envy, discharges the fatal arrow at poor Robin; but the perpetrator of the dark deed is suddenly denounced by a host of unexpected witnesses, and all is brought to a happy and, of course, a splendid climax.

The harlequinade, which is full of pantomimic drollery, is supported by Mr Harry Boleno and Mr Charles Lauri, as Clowns; Mr Cormack and Mr St Maine are the Harlequins; Messrs Tanner and Deulin Johnson, the Pantaloons; and Madame Boleno and Miss Gunniss are the Columbines. The mechanical changes are very extensive, and an enormous expense has been gone to in order to secure the effectiveness of every department.
The Era, 21/12/1862

The Surrey
Mother Goose; or, the Queen of Hearts and the Wonderful Tarts

THE opening is full of true pantomime humour, without attempting the higher walk of burlesque, the puns of which are scarcely ever heard, and not understood when they are. This production is full of pure pantomimic fun, which can be seen, and not mistaken.

The first scene, Mother Goose's Cottage covered with snow and the adjacent country, was a most perfect illusion of a snow scene, more especially the cottage door, where the snow appears on the porch, and also the snow image made by the boys' snow-balling. The next one is the Trysting-place of the Fays, which opens and comes to a rising sun occupying the whole of the back of the stage, from which Phoebus appears, and here the ballet takes place by the nymphs. This scene alone was enough to save the production; but the Card Palace of the Queen of Hearts, with all the Court Cards, surpassed that one, the dresses, properties, and masks being most beautiful; and a grand *cotillion*, danced by the whole of the characters, had a most picturesque effect. Following this was the Warder's Porch and Tennis Court of the Palace, a beautiful piece of architectural painting. Then came what was termed Bluebelle's Boudoir in the Old Hill, a prettily painted scene, which preceded the Transformation one, and any description that can be given of it on paper must of necessity be too faint to do justice to its beauties, but we will attempt a description.

The scene last alluded to gradually, in the darkness which prevails, fades from the view, and the first thing that is seen, as if it were growing out of the mist, is a bunch of ferns, occupying about half the centre of the stage, and on each side are two nymphs, but very faintly seen, emerging apparently from the leaves by which they are surrounded, and upon them is thrown, by some means, a very softened lavender-coloured light, which at first but barely shows their features, and is concentrated to a very small circle upon them. This gradually spreads, and the leaves from which they seem to be rising open like a fan from the centre, gradually move round in a semi-circular form, and from the centre rise bunches of flowers, from which nymphs emerge. With this the light gradually increases, and a golden hue over the whole scene takes the place of the light that was at first but faintly seen, and this continues, the lime-light intermingling with it until the scene closes. Whilst this is going on the wings gradually become animated with fays, having shown themselves to be perforated ferns. Various other branches of flowers then rise, until the entire stage, both in height and width, is filled to the extreme back. The whole is lit by innumerable jets of gas, the extreme glare being softened by having to show through the gauzes upon which the scenery is painted. These gauzes being spangled, and the dresses of the fays being some of them scarlet and the others emerald green covered with lace, thickly spangled, the effect, when the light is fully at play upon it, is beyond description.

During the whole of the Transformation, which lasted a considerable time, a beautiful piece of music, by the leader, Mr Isaacson, arranged from one of the old but well-known piano serenatas, added materially to the scene, which positively seemed to electrify the audience, and the result was a unanimous call for the worthy Lessee, and also the scene-painter, who came on hand in hand.

The comic business then commenced, and the fun ran furious and fast. The London Bridge Railway Station, Bathing at Ramsgate, where there are two bathing machines, which the Clown and Pantaloon take possession of, and, as a matter of course, send the sexes into the machines indiscriminately. Screams are heard, the sky darkens, and a shower of mackerel falls, and being taken possession of by the Clown and the others on the stage, a grand pelt winds up the scene. The next a pair of flats, with Lodgings to Let for Uneducational Lodgers, has some severe cuts at the Guards. For instance, courting servants is called garrison duty. The scene was full of hits, and and created the greatest amounts of laughter.

The concluding scene then followed, and this also was a grand scene, the principal features being fairies draped about with flowers, and illuminated with various coloured fires. This also obtained for the Lessee, Mr Shepherd, another unanimous call, to which he responded.

The parts in the opening were too well played by all parties for us to particularise each individully. The principal ones were, however, by Miss Julia St George, who is a great acquisition to this company; Mr Thomas Thorne, Miss Elizabeth Webster, Miss Lydia Foote, and Miss Johnson. The arrangement of the ballets reflects the highest credit on Miss Clara Morgan. The pantomimists are Mr Hildebrandt, who is not unknown to our London audiences, and is now so much improved that he may rank amongst the first Clowns of his class; Rowella, the Harlequin; and the Misses Morgan, the Columbines. The music, by Mr Isaacson, was exceedingly beautiful, and the scenery reflects the highest credit on the long list of artists named in the bills.

The Princess's
Prince Riquet with the Tuft; or, Harlequin and Mother Shipton

[…] WHEN the curtain rose it disclosed a very fanciful and beautifully-painted scene, the Dropping Well of Knaresborough and the Abode of Old Mother Shipton, by Moonlight. Here some two dozen birch brooms are very cleverly made to dance to good time, when suddenly Mother Shipton (Mr Cockrill) makes her appearance and puts an end to the dancing. This is no sooner done than Mother Bunch (Miss Florence Gray) appears, and reminds Mother Shipton of a certain wager that had been made as to which would obtain an admirer first, the Princess Amouretta (Miss Hudspeth) who is silly but very handsome, or Prince Riquet (Mr Charles Seyton), an exceedingly ugly and deformed man. The wager still being unsettled, they resolve to go and satisfy themselves, an accordingly mount a broomstick, and by a very clever contrivance ride through the air.

The scene then changes to Mushroom Marsh on a Misty Morning. Here they make their descent in the midst of mushrooms. This, perhaps, is one of the more novel scenes that was ever put on a stage. There are some seventy or eighty enormous mushrooms, the chief fungus being Miss Hart, which gradually expand, and opening, disclose reclining in each mushroom a demon dressed in red, with silver helmet and battle-axe, the effect of which is considerably enhanced by a strong green light being thrown upon the figures. When the mushrooms fully expand, the demons simultaneously rise, and beginning to dance, are interrupted by the appearance of Mother Shipton, when they fall upon their knees in three circles, producing a novel and effective tableau, which drew forth a burst of applause.

By the magic influence of Mother Bunch, the scene gradually dissolves, and after a minute we find ourselves gazing on one of Mr Beverley's exquisite realisations of a fairies' haunt in the Lake of the Water Lilies, where a ballet takes place by the attendant Gossamers, the Water Lily (Miss Alice Lee) and the Gossamer Geni (Miss Annie Collinson) being the principal *danseuses*, who performed a series of *pas* in a manner that deservedly solicited the warm acknowledgment of the audience. We are next conducted to the Presence Chamber in the King's Palace, and for the first time Rumbustical, surnamed the Rampageous, King of Little Brittany (Mr G Belmore), and the father of Princess Amouretta, makes us acquainted with his desire to get his handsome daughter married, and arranges to receive suitors for her hand. After interrogating and dismissing some of his attendants, he calls for his daughter, and tells her to prepare to receive her suitors. Prince Mannikin (Mr Moreland), Gogmagog (Mr Collett), and Prince Riquet with the Tuft (Mr Charles Seyton), here have an interview, and the two former retire. This scene was very amusing and funny, especially the acting of Mr Belmore and Mr Seyton, who sang a duet. We next come to the Bright Home of the Gossamer Fairy, the grand Transformation Scene, and we think without exception, a more beautiful scene of Fairyland could not be imagined. [...]
The Era, 28/12/1862

1863

Princess's
Harlequin and Little Tommy Tucker; or, the Little Old Woman Who Lived in a Shoe and Had so Many Children She Didn't Know What To Do
TOM TUCKER (Miss Helen Howard) is shown to be the son of the old Dame with the troublesomely numerous family, to whose support he largely contributes by his talents. The well-known Taffy, who, on excellent authority, we know "was a Welshman," and is here besides shown to be an ogre of kleptomaniac proclivities, steals the marrow-bone from the old lady's habitation with as much coolness as he has already stolen the perverse Princess Mary, "quite contrary," the daughter of Old King Cole (Mr Charles Seyton). Attended by Chanticleer, a marvellous specimen of sagacious poultry, Tom proceeds to the ogre's abode, and obtains an interview with the fair prisoner, who is, however, turned by Taffy, in consequence of her obstinacy, into stone, and thus becomes the Fair Lady of Banbury Cross. It is found that music only can break the Spell, and Old King Cole and his "sons of Harmony" try to re-animate her much after the fashion indicated in the popular song, but Tom Tucker, a skilful violinist, is the successful performer, and he obtains the Princess accordingly for his reward.

Then follows Mr Lloyd's gorgeous Transformation Scene, which will convert the stage of the Theatre into a lake of real water, and develops some extraordinary effects. The Harlequinade is an illustrated Pasquinade, satirically showing the follies and absurdities of the past year, and will be supported by Mr Arthur Leclerq as Harlequin, Mr Charles Leclerq, Mr Huline and Master Huline as two Clowns and a half, Mr Naylor as Pantaloon, and Miss Caroline Adams as Columbine. [...]

Sadler's Wells
The Prince of the Peaceful Islands; or, Harlequin, the Magic Pearl, the Centaur, and the Fairy Amazon
THE scene is laid in the kingdom of the Peaceful Islands, ruled over by King Covetous (Mr W D Gresham), who is possessed of two sons, Prince Humpty, a hunchback (Mr George Fisher), and Prince Exquisite, a youth of tender years (Miss Minnie Davis). The King, wishing Humpty to sign away his succession in favour of his brother, the hunchback has, as he supposes, Exquisite secretly made away with, but he is only left in a wood by the ruffians. Here he is found by an eagle (Mr A Baildon), and conveyed to its nest, but is rescued by some shepherds, who appropriate him as a sacrifice to a Centaur (Mr T B Bennett), to whom they are bound every year to furnish a child. He is, however, saved by means of the Fairy Queen (Miss Mandlebert), who overcomes the Centaur, and delivers Prince Exquisite into the hands of Agricolo (Mr A Daniel) to rear, and who is no other than King Sublime, the late monarch of the Peaceful Islands,

who has been deposed by King Covetous, and is forced to seek safety in flight, afterwards adopting the life of a shepherd.

In the meantime his youngest daughter, the Princess Peerless (Miss Eliza Hamilton), who fell into a lake when a child, and was transformed into an oyster pearl by the Fairy Queen, is restored to life through the instrumentality of Prince Humpty, who falls in love with her; but his suit being rejected, she is doomed to confinement for life, but is again set free by means of the Fairy Queen, and, disguised as a shepherdess, seeks out the hut of Agricolo, her father, where she arrives, and falls in love with Prince Exquisite. But Agricolo, not thinking him a fit match for his daughter, has him carried while asleep into a dense wood, where, however, he is found by the Princess, through the aid of the Fairy Queen, who presents her with a ball of magic twine, which, by fastening to his dress, leads her to his hiding place. Here they are very nearly discovered by Prince Humpty and his retainers, who happen to be out hunting, but are saved by the timely interference of the Fairy Queen changing them into two toads, who attack and disperse Prince Humpty and his followers. On their road they fall in with Agricolo, and, deeming his inquiries respecting the Princess Peerless, whom he is seeking, somewhat suspicious, he is conveyed by them before King Covetous, when he is recognised as King Sublime, and only saved from death by the arrival of the Princess Peerless and Prince Exquisite, in whom King Covetous discovers his long-lost son.

The arrival of the Fairy Queen further explains matters, and results in the Transformation. The scenery, representing the Eagle Peak by Moonlight, Arcadian Retreat (Ballet scene), the Valley of Fountains, and the Transformation Scene is exquisitely painted; the ingenious and unusually splendid effects in the latter are by Mr Charles S James, the artist. The music, selected, arranged, and composed by Mr B Isaacson [...]

Pavilion
Dick Whittington and His Wonderful Cat; or, Harlequin Humpty Dumpty and the House of Content in the Realms of Happiness
THE first scene is the Interior of Guildhall (by midnight), with the guardian geniuses of the City, Gog (Mr George) and Magog (Mr Henderson), busy in solemn thought. A procession of tiny watchmen enter, and with their quaint dresses and various coloured lanterns go their rounds, singing their Christmas carol. The hour of twelve is sounded, and Christmas (Mr F H Henry) rises in his car of state. He inquires of Gog and Magog the doings of the year, and some dialogue, with hits on the various topics of the day, ensue. The illuminated window becomes an elegant Fairy Temple, and the joyous Queen Content (Mrs H Lindon) in a song congratulates Christmas, and promises her assistance in anything he may undertake. The Cat (Miss J Lindon) springs up, and implores Christmas to give *him* a chance. All is arranged, when Humpty Dumpty (Miss A Lindon), a wicked little demon, bursts from his favourite egg, and informs them he will frustrate all their plans.

The Fairy Volunteers are summoned, a general scene of excitement ensues, and in the confusion we are taken to the large Drapery Establishment of Master Fitzwarren, in the Chepe. Here we meet Tommy, or Tomaso the Terrible (Mr F Bousfield), a mischief-making apprentice, and Dick (Miss E Ellington), who arrives in London fatigued and footsore. Dick's Sleeping Apartment shows us Humpty Dumpty meditating mischief. The envious Tommy attempts to murder Dick, who is, however, saved by the Cat, and they fly. Tommy is turned out of the house in disgrace, and then Highgate Hill, with London in the distance, shows Dick and his faithful Cat still persecuted. Whittington, fatigued, sinks exhausted, an invisible chorus of the well-known words, "Turn again, Whittington, Lord Mayor of London", is heard, Dick and the Cat fall asleep, and we are taken by the Fairy Queen Content to the Realms of Happiness. Dick's dress is transformed, and he is despatched to win his love, attended by his Cat. A ballet *divertissement* concludes the scene. Next we have the King's Palace, where Henry (Mr G Hamilton) is seen amongst his courtiers. Tommy is now a servant to the King, and introduces his guests, among them Alice (Miss M Campbell), and her Father and Mother (Messrs Saville and Lindon). Tommy claims the hand of Alice. Dick appears and forbids it. The banquet is spread. The palace is suddenly swarmed with rats, who are quickly destroyed by the faithful Cat. The King knights Dick Whittington, and all repair to the Chepe and Dancing-green, where we find Tommy and his myrmidons in ambush. The various adventures and escapades of Whittington follow; he falls into the power of Humpty Dumpty, is released by Christmas and Content. The Transformation Scene comes next; artist, Mr Charles Quick. [...]

The Grecian
Robinson Crusoe; or, Harlequin and His Man Friday, and the Magic Pearl
THE first scene opens in the Wild Waste of Weeds, where Jack o' Lantern rises and cons over the events of the past year, when the Eagle rises and drops from the Tavern Top with a message from Mr Conquest, asking for a subject for a Pantomime. Jack invokes the aid of the Weeds; they change to Demons, and then change to the title of the Pantomime. Second scene shows Crusoe (Miss Victor) on board ship, the crew all indulging in yarns and hornpipes, when they are attacked by Bullyhumpseybar (Mr H Grant), Chief of the Black Indians, with his tribe, and Crusoe is pitched overboard. Scene third – Under the Sea. The Fairy Mother learns from the Book of Fate that her daughter, Pearl of the

Sea (Miss L Conquest), must ascend on to earth and pass through the trials and temptations of the mortal world; her mother gives her a magic pearl to protect her from all harm, and most of all from the goddess Love. This pearl also gives the magic power to all who may possess it. Boreas is to be sent with her as a protector. They are about to depart when they discover Crusoe sinking to the bottom. He revives, and becomes desperately enamoured of Pearl, but she does not reciprocate the feeling, and they are parted. Scene fourth – The Crystal Ball, and by the means of which we have a further peep into the history of Robinson Crusoe. Scene fifth – A View of the Desert Isle, with Crusoe and his Dog, Cat, and Goat; sees the footsteps of a human being; is about to track them, when he meets again with Pearl; she escapes from him by the aid of Boreas. The Black Tribe and their Chief have just returned from their war with the Red Tribe; they bring in their prisoners, amongst whom is Friday (Mr G Conquest); they tell him to prepare to be eaten. His sweetheart, Indiana (Mrs G Conquest), is also a prisoner, and is the daughter of Rummyphiz, Chief of the Red Tribe (Mr Manning). Scene sixth shows the Black Tribe at their picnic, Friday about to be roasted, when Crusoe enters and rescues him. The Red Tribe then arrive with their chief; they are in pursuit of the blacks, to recover their people who have been taken prisoners. Scene seventh – the exterior of the hut, where the Black Chief meets Pearl, and falls in love with her. She escapes him. Friday then overhears them concocting a plot attack the hut, and he makes preparations for their reception. Scene eighth – Interior of the hut. The Red Chief gets dreadfully inebriated and goes to bed in a tub. Crusoe then gets the magic pearl from Pearl. Here a desperate encounter takes place for the possession of the pearl, but it at last remains in the possession of Friday. Pearl having lost her magic power, immediately becomes mortal. The Black Tribe then attack the hut, but all escape safely till the next scene, when Pearl and the Red Chief are taken prisoners and carried off. Crusoe and Friday go in pursuit. The next scene discovers them all bound to trees. Friday and Crusoe release them. The Black Chief is again about to pounce upon his prey when Friday, by the aid of the magic pearl, makes them all disappear. Black Chief gets the magic pearl, and commands them to return. They do so. They are immediately secured and tied back to back, and are about to be burnt when the Spirit of Pantomime (Miss J Conquest) rises, and introduces them to the Transformation Scene, designed and painted by Mr C Smithers. […] The Pantomime is, as usual, the production of Mr H Spry and Mr George Conquest.

Drury Lane
Sindbad the Sailor; or, the Great Roc of the Diamond Valley and the Seven Wonders of the World
[…] THE Great Pyramid of Egypt opens the Pantomime, showing Cheops (Mr Neville) and his attendant Mummies in trepidation at the approach of Young England (Miss Rose LeClerq), who is bound on a journey of discovery. The Spirit of the Nile (Miss Cicely Nott[9]), whose long-cherished secret is thus likely to be found out, applies to the ancient founder of the Pyramids to devise means to arrest his progress. The Seven Wonders of the World are summoned, and the Spirit of the Past appears; but they fail to divert Young England from his purpose, and the conundrums of the Sphynx are answered by him with such defiant readiness that neither the propounder of enigmas nor the vocal Memnon can stay his onward march. He explores the mysteries of the Mountains of the Moon, and drinks from the very source of the Nile, which places him in possession of a power over all the genii of the East, who appear before him and own his supremacy in a grand ballet, which takes place in this scene.

The seaport of Bassorah, on the Persian Gulf, next shows Sindbad starting on *his* voyage of discovery. Sindbad (Miss Lizzie Wilmore), in company with Ali Ben Rumfiz (Mr Tom Matthews), a Turkish merchant, embarks and arrives in due course in the Court of the Indian King, El 'Eb-Nee (Mr Fitzjames), where he is fascinated by the Princess Ivora (Miss Coventry). He seeks in the Valley of Diamonds a present worthy her acceptance, and here he meets with the adventure which is so closely linked with his name, being borne from the earth by a stupendous bird called the Roc, which takes him to the Island of Pigmies, where he gets into still greater danger. The encounter with the Old Man of the Sea (Master Percy Roselle[10]) follows, and he is captured by the Pigmies and conveyed to their basaltic city.

At the moment when the dwarfs seek to dispose of their victim the Fairy of the Diamond is appealed to, and Mr William Beverley's great Transformation Scene follows. The Harlequinade includes Mr Harry Boleno and Mr C Lauri, as Clowns; Mr J Morris and Mr Barnes, as Pantaloons; Mr Cormack and Mr Saddle, as Harlequins; and Madame Boleno and the Misses Gunniss, as Columbines, so that a strong double pantomimic company is formed. […]

City of London
Harlequin Black Beard; or, Dame Trot and Her Comical Cat
A RUINED Abbey by Moonlight is the first scene. It is filled by bats and owls, who only then can wander forth. Stab-i'-the-Dark and Gloom are sharpening pikes on a magic grindstone to be ready for the enemies of Night. The other sprites are rejoicing when the Demon Chief, Black Night, rises in his emblematic car of state. He is enraged at the attempt to stop night-houses, by which he will be deprived of his victims, so is resolved to foil their plans of happiness. He calls Mischief to his aid, entrusting him with a talisman and a packet to convey to Black Beard, the noted Pirate Chief.

This takes us to the Cottage by the Sea. He we have Jack Trueheart, a poor fisher lad, who cannot catch enough fish to make up his rent. Old Grey Russet, his cruel landlord, threatens him with prison if it is not forthcoming. The Fairy Queen Sunlight appears before Jack in the disguise of a beggar. He relieves her and gains her fairy aid.

Next is the Fairies' Haunt in a Woody Dell, where a most novel effect is introduced, sunset, moonlight, and sunrise being shown by a novel electric light called the Iris Light, which brings before us the Fairy Queen, Sunlight, who holds a cabinet council, relating to her Faye the treachery of Night, who protects the Pirate Black Beard, sending him instructions to carry off Sweet Patty of the Mill, depriving young Jack Trueheart of his only love. The Fairies promise their aid to secure for Jack his bride, and after a Fairy Festival we get on board the Pirate's lugger. Here the sprite Mischief, true to his orders, arrives and presents his talisman.

This brings us to the Mill on the Floss. Here we see Humphery with his Flail and Dorothy Draggletail, with the Millers and the Miller. Sweet Patty arrives, who is pestered and followed by old Grey Russet. Jack makes his appearance, but is ordered off by her cruel parent. The Pirate Black Beard, to secure his prize, calls on Jack Frost, and changes the summer-bloom to frost and snow. Patty is seized and carried off.

A Stalactite Cavern presents Patty as a prisoner, left to consider the offer of Black Beard. Jack, by the aid of Dame Trot's cat, finds a passage through the wall. He promises to return in danger's hour. The Pirate makes his appearance and takes her to his castle. On the road a storm causes them to rest at Dame Trot's cottage. Here Mischief is seen in two places at once or nearly so. After a sharp fight the Pirate departs with his intended bride.

We are now at Black Beard's Castle, situated in a wild, romantic spot. Presents arrive for the bride, and so does Jack and his favourite cat, who release Sweet Patty. The lovers fly to a stagnant pool. Their flight is intercepted by Black Beard, which brings to their aid the Fairy Queen, Sunlight, who changes the gloomy scene to the Prismatic Home of Sunlight, by Mr Beaumont; the mechanical arrangements by Mr J Berkett. The comic scenes follow: – Road to a Country Market, the Grand Tournament, High Street, Wapping; Mrs Lirriper's Lodgings[11], in which the Ghost Effects will be seen, duly registered. Mr Nelson Lee has this season taken good care of himself. The Pantomimists at the City are Harlequin and Columbine, Mr and Mrs Lupino; Clown, Mr Matthews; Pantaloon, Mr Morelli; Sprites, the Brothers French and Matthews' children.

The Victoria
Giselle; or, the Phantom Night Dancers
THE grand Christmas Pantomime at this establishment (which had undergone such a wondrous reformation under its present Managers), is from the German story of "Giselle; or, the Phantom Night Dancers", and is adapted to its present form by Messrs Osmond and F Fenton, and allows the latter gentleman great scope for the display of his well-known scenic effects, and having such a co-operator as Mr Frampton in the ballet arrangements, groupings, comic business, &c, we can safely predict that it will rank with any Theatre in London, no expense, we are assured, having being spared on its production. It is interspersed with songs, duets, &c, from all the popular operas of the day, and is full of wit and humour.

The following is a synopsis of the scenes and incidents: – Scene the First represents a Demonic Divorce Court, and introduces the Demons Discord and Jealousy, also Hymen and Cupid, the Gods of Love and Marriage (Miss Farren and Miss Elise). Giselle (Miss Harland) and her lover Hilarion, a young huntsman (Miss M Daly), are passed through the fiery ordeal, and Love, for a time, proves triumphant over Jealousy and Discord. A pretty ballet is introduced, and the scene changes to Hymen's Sylvan Home. The Wili Queen appears, and tells Cupid that she will, by aid of the Demon Discord, snatch Giselle from his protection, and make her fall a victim to the Wilis' mystic dance. Hymen vows to protect her, and the scene changes to Old Dame Bertha's Cottage. Here we meet with the Dame, and Peterkin, her son (Mr G Yarnold), who, by his pranks and ill conduct, proves neither a beautiful nor dutiful boy. The Prince, Princess, and Burgomaster (Mr T Howard) arrive, and announce the annual *fete* is to take place, and the prize will be bestowed on the best dancer. Giselle determines to try her Terpsichorean powers, goes to the *fete*, and wins the prize, through the influence of the Wili Queen. The success makes her discard her lover, Hilarion, for a Mysterious Stranger. Night comes on. Hilarion, after his grief for the loss of his fickle fair one, falls asleep in the cottage. Peterkin enters, and discovers who the Mysterious Stranger is, when, by the power of Discord, he also is charmed into an uneasy slumber, and annoyed by strange visitors. Wilis enter and bear away Giselle. Hilarion and Peterkin awake at this moment, and follow to the Fairy Lake and Abode of the Wilis. Giselle, now a Wili, entices Hilarion into the water. Peterkin, alarmed at the appearances of the Wilis, falls into the water. All are now seen at the "bottom of the lake". Various adventures take place, and eventually, by the joint power of Cupid and Hymen, all are made happy. [...]
The Era, 20/12/1863

FIVE THOUSAND PANTOMIME POSTERS Now Ready. Large Assortment of various Grotesque Designs. A separate Picture for every Pantomime. Thus Managers will not be inconvenienced by any other Theatre using the same

> *Pictorial. Sizes from one sheet Double Crown to any size. One Hundred Comic Pictures, Two Feet and a Half by Three Feet Four Inches for One Pound. P.O.O. to Chief Office, GEORGE WARD and COMPANY, Designers, Lithographers, Engravers, and Printers, 3, Snow Hill, London.*
> **The Era, 27/12/1863**

The Grecian
Punch and Judy; or, Harlequin Prince Valiant, Shallabalah; or, the Good Little Fairy of the Wood
THE plot turns upon the life of Punch and Judy, with various alterations to adapt the subject to a burlesque pantomime. The first scene opens in the Land of Toys, where King Holiday pays a visit to Jack-in-the-Box, and consults with him for a present to his friends of Earth. After recommending all the various toys in their turn, they at last hit upon the idea of Punch in the form of a Pantomime. The Good Little Fairy of the Wood (Miss I Conquest) rises and tells them that a Pantomime without a loving Prince and Princess would be sad, she therefore promises to find the requisite personages to complete the work.

    The next scene brings us to the Caves of Despair, where Spleen, Spite, and Ill-Nature are conspiring for the overthrow of Punch. They send a demon on earth to track him, and lead and tempt him to all sin and wickedness. Scene third shows the Stalactite Caves, where Princess Rosebud (Miss L Conquest) has strayed to while out hunting with her father. A panoramic effect takes place which brings us to the magnificent scene of the Groves of the Golden Banyans, where the ballet takes place. The next scene is the Enchanted Forest, where King Nervous (Mr Jackman) has lost his way. He is threatened on all sides by wild animals, when Shallabalah (Mr H Grant), a Gnome King, rises and promises to rescue him if he will sign a document. The King does so. Scene sixth brings us to the Home of Punch and Judy, Judy (Mr J Manning) busy washing baby, &c. Punch (Mr George Conquest) reels home very tipsy, followed by Toby[12]. Here all the acknowledged business of the street show takes place, ending, as usual, with the murder of Judy. Punch, overcome with remorse, falls on the floor, when the scene changes to a monster balloon, and carries Punch off to an unknown country in the map of Europe. Scene Seven, Lake Lonely by Moonlight, shows the King's two nephews conspiring to prevent Prince Valiant's (Miss Victor) return to court. The balloon is seen in the distance to take fire and fall into the lake below. Punch is seen struggling in the waters, and at last reaches land exhausted. Prince Valiant returns and discovers the body of Punch, and calls a doctor. Here again the show business takes place, and the scene ends by vows of eternal friendship between Punch and Valiant, who promises to take him to Court.

    To the Court of King Nervous Valiant returns, and claims the hand of Rosebud. The marriage ceremony takes place, when Shallabalah enters and claims the fulfilment of the King's contract, for having saved him when in the Enchanted Forest. He claims the hand of Rosebud. Valiant opposes him; but in spite of all, Shallabalah carries her off by force, and places her for safety in his Cottage *orné*[13]. Punch and Valiant come to rescue her. Punch rings at the door with the well-known sheep bell. The black servant sends him away, but Punch perseveres, and, after the show business, attempts to get in at the windows, and, after hanging on gutters, tumbling backwards out of second-floor windows, falling through roofs and down wells, succeeds at last in releasing the lady, when at that moment Shallabalah returns, and Punch is compelled to beat a hasty retreat, leaving Prince Valiant and Rosebud in his power.

    The next scene forms an immense Punch and Judy Show, where the beadle comes to arrest him for wife-murder. The usual show business again takes place, ending by Punch getting Shallabalah in a line, and leaving him hanging. The Fairy at last arrives, and takes us to the Transformation Scene, designed and painted by Mr Messenger. The Clown is Harry Wright; Harlequin, W Ozmund; Pantaloon, Mr Power; Columbine, by Miss Dewberry; and Sprites, by the Brothers Leopold.
The Era, 25/12/1864

1865

City of London
King Flame and Queen Pearlydrop; or, Harlequin Simple Simon
THE Interior of a Volcano is the abode of King Flame, who is attended by Havoc, Destruction, Fury, and Slaughter. He summons Red War to assist in the council, and they proceed to plot how they can overthrow the Water Queen. A red-hot ball is sent to earth to waste and destroy the happy Village, and all the Fiends of Fire depart to fulfil the wishes of King Flame.

    In the Cottage of Old Collywobble, the market gardener, we meet Simple Simon. Miss Beauty, Old Collywobble's daughter, appears on the scene, and, in answer to Simple Simon's declaration of love, tells him his suit is hopeless; but, seeing Young Constant coming, shows by her manner that she is not without a sweetheart. Young Constant, however, soon undeceives her by informing her that he is devoted to a water nymph, and that he must respectfully decline the honour of an alliance with his master's daughter. For this he is dismissed and thrown upon the world. Simple Simon now turns round upon Beauty, and joins the fortunes of Young Constant as a faithful squire. Queen Pearlydrop has the power of assuming the shape of a fish, and in this guise was once saved by Constant when fishing in the sea. As a reward for his kindness she resolves to introduce him to her daughter Pearl, knowing at the same time he had beheld her face while sitting near the sea-shore. The offer is eagerly accepted by Constant, who takes a tremendous header, followed by his faithful squire, Simple Simon.

We are now below the waves, and discover that the water nymph, Pearl, is also beloved by a sea monster named Naughtylus, who is assisted in every bad scheme by Shark, Neptune's lawyer, and Hip Periwinkle, which latter personage is in the habit of drilling his Periwinkle Guards with a very large pin. The arrival of Constant fills the breast of Naughtylus with jealousy. Seeing that Queen Pearlydrop favours the suit of Young Constant, he immediately resolves to rebel against her authority, secure the treasures of the ocean, and become King. The bottom of the deep blue sea, with caves illuminated for a grand aquatic *fête*, shows us the Fishing Basket Trick, when the sports are suddenly interrupted by the appearance of the Great Eastern steamship, paying out the cable above (moment of great suspense). The cable breaks, and sinks to the bottom. The Queen Pearlydrop orders it to be taken care of till called for. (The shareholders of the Atlantic Cable should visit the City of London Theatre to mark the precise spot.) Naughtylus now proclaims his passion for Pearl, but is defeated by the Water Nymphs, who rush to the assistance of their Queen, and foil the plotters.

Young Constant and Pearl are sent to earth, and a Palace built by tiny fairy hands. King Flame burns it down. Another is instantly erected by the power of the Fairy Queen, and as "true love never did run smooth," Constant and Pearl are secured by Naughtylus. Pearl is borne away to the Coral Caves, Young Constant confined in a dismal place called Shark's Alley, between the hills of Silver Sand. They are both rescued by the faithful squire, Simple Simon. Thus Queen Pearlydrop is triumphant over her enemies, and the lovers united. Simple Simon resolves to remain below the sea, and marry Anne Chovy, daughter of John Dory. Now, by a magical power known only in Pantomimes, everybody is transported to the grand Transformation Scene, which report says is one of the most novel ever beheld.
The Era, 24/12/1865

> *A FEARFUL scene occurred at the Lyceum Theatre, Sunderland, on Thursday night, during the performance of the Pantomime* Robin Hood. *A gutta-percha tube connecting the wing lights became detached, and the gas escaping, ignited, and a loud explosion took place, the flames shooting up to the top of the stage. A rush was made to the door by the audience, who thought the Theatre was on fire, but they were stopped by seeing Miss Louisa Ricardo[14], who was engaged as Columbine Watteau, rush on to the stage enveloped in flames. She had been standing amongst a group collected at the wing, waiting her turn to go on, when the flames caught her muslin skirt. She shrieked and rushed on in the middle of the scene, where her father was playing as Clown, but was thrown down by one of the stage carpenters. Mr Bell, the Lessee, rushed from his private box, and his top coat was pulled off and wrapped round the poor girl and the flames were beaten out. A number of the audience clambered from the pit to the stage while the fearful scene was going on, but they ultimately resumed their seats, and the performance proceeded.*
>
> *Miss Ricardo was removed home and attended to by medical men, and on Friday morning no dangerous results were apprehended, though she was sadly burnt about the arms and chest. She died, however, at two o'clock in the afternoon from her injuries and the shock to her system. Her father was so much burned in endeavoring to put out the fire that he will be unable to resume his profession for some time.*
> *The Era, 31/12/1865*

1866

Marylebone
Ding-Dong-Bell, Pussy's in the Well; or, Harlequin Who Killed Cock Robin?

JOHNNY GREEN and Johnny Stout are rivals in the affections of Princess Lovelie, daughter of King Jollydayne and Queen Honiswete, the rulers of the Land of Happygoluckie. Stout, enraged to find that his foe is the favoured suitor, sends an ambassador to the Witch of Stonehenge, demanding her interference and help. She immediately summonses Grimalkin, the Demon Cat, and, telling him to take the magic fiddle, bids him lure from the Palace Cock Robin, who is the Princess's fairy protector. Here we have illustrated the story of "Who Killed Cock Robin?"

Armed with this assistance, Stout betakes himself to the Palace of King Jollydayne. The King is counting his enormous wealth, and the Queen is eating bread and honey, and all is ease and happiness; no sooner, however, is Johnny Green chosen by the Princess as her future lord than Stout arrives at the Palace, at the head of an armed band, and vows vengeance.

Guided by Little Boy Blue, Johnny Green pays a visit to the house of Ba Ba Black Sheep, and obtains from him the magic cap made of magic wool. With this gift he repairs to the Court of the Fairy Queen, who advises him how to act, bids him instantly to return to the Princess, and, above all, to bear manfully whatever trials may come upon him.

He arrives at the City of Happygoluckie to find that Stout has declared war against Jollydayne, and and succeeded in carrying off the Princess. In his despair he encounters Grimalkin, who has just caused the death of Cock Robin. Green seizes the Cat and throws him into a ruined well, after which he starts in search of the Princess. Grimalkin is extricated by Johnny Stout, who, in his rage, suddenly changes Summer to Winter, producing a very beautiful pictorial effect. Jollydayne has fallen from his prosperous state, his subjects rebel, war is disastrous to him, and his daughter lost. His trials, however, though severe, are not of long duration. Green discovers Lovelie in Stout's castle.

The parties are re-united, the good made happy, and the guilty punished by the Fairy, who introduces them to the Grand Mythological Transformation Scene, which consists of six tableaux. First, the Prismatic Abode of the Goddess, which is illuminated by the Hues of the Rainbow; second, the Bower of Pomona; changing to third, the Garden of Hupunus, with the Golden Fruit; fifth, the Flight of the Ariel Synopus; sixth, the Flight of Dani, in Torrents of Molten Gold. This grand triumph of science and art will bring into operation the whole resources of this mammoth stage, and is the production of Mr William Beaumont, the artist of the Theatre, who has also designed and executed, with numerous assistants, the whole of the scenery. Mr J Arnold Cave sustains a principal part in the Opening, as usual. The Harlequinade will introduce a double company of Pantomimists.
The Era, 23/12/1866

Theatre Royal, Manchester
The Fair One with the Golden Locks
THE story relates how the Fair One (Mr E Righton) falls desperately in love with Zephyr (Mrs Bickerstaff), who has been sent to obtain her hand for his master, King Blubberoso (Mr W Templeton). The Fair One declares that he can only win her who recovers for her a ring she lost while bathing; slay a giant who seeks her hand; and obtain a bottle of magic water that can confer the gift of beauty, from a dell inhabited by a fiery dragon. All these risks Zephyr performs by the aid of Queen Carp (Miss Le Batt), who restores the ring, and of a Crow and Owl, the first of which picks out the Giant's eyes, thus enabling Zephyr to fulfil the second requirement, while the Owl procures the beauty-water during Zephyr's contest with the Dragon, in which he is victorious. The Fair One, however, flatly refuses to wed King Blubberoso, and the latter, hoping to propitiate her by improving his personal appearance, drinks her hair dye under the impression that it is the beauty-water. The effect is, of course, most unlooked for, and the miserable King at length sanctions the union of the Fair One with Zephyr.

The present Pantomime is decidedly the best that has been presented at this house for a considerable period. Novel and appropriate costumes adorn the representatives of Pounds, Shillings, Pence, Brass, Copper, Steel, &c. The Giant is a wonderful creature, standing about five yards high, and the Dragon is still more wonderful, flapping its large and scaly wings, and vomiting forth fire in a most terrible manner. A pretty scene, painted by Mr Bickerstaff, and entitled the Coral of the Deep, introduces an admirable *ballet divertissement*, supported by Miss Fanny Brown as the Fairy Mariner, and a judiciously selected *corps de ballet*. The Dragon's Den in the Dripping Dell is a most cleverly constructed scene, real water being exhibited, falling over a mossy arch into the Den. But adequate terms of praise can scarcely be found for the Transformation Scene, painted by Mr Roberts. It is called the Pearl of the Ocean, and discloses a nymph standing erect upon a glittering silver globe, while around are others gracefully reclining in tastefully coloured shells; at the last, the Fairy Corallina (Miss May Holt) completes the group by emerging to view in the foreground. When the final light has been shed over all, the scene is one of the most dazzling splendour. [...]
The Era, 30/12/1866

PIETRO CARLE, the Great Clown, who has won for himself such wondrous renown. This year LIVERPOOL is his location, where, in the minds of the public, he has caused a sensation. He can Dance, Sing, and Act, likewise play on a Trumpet, and, in his Hornpipe on Pattens, doesn't he stump it? His dresses are new, and best patterns made, which entirely throws all the rest in the shade; but he does not believe in that work they call spangling, 'cause when they're sent to the wash they get spoilt in the mangling; but with that famed Pantaloon, W Butler, by his side, in Pantomimical Freaks, competition's defied. – (Signed) – PIETRO CARLE, Clown, Royal Colosseum Theatre, Liverpool.
The Era, 30/12/1866

1867

PRESENTATION TO A DONKEY – On Monday last Mr W H Payne, the pantomimist, presented to the Fore and Hind Legs of his Donkey two handsome Silver Medals, for their strict attention to his training and instruction. The medals were manufactured by Messrs Loewenstark and Sons, Masonic Jewellers, of Garrick Street, and bore the following inscription: – "Presented by W H Payne, of the Theatre Royal, Covent Garden, to Master William Allcroft and Master John Mapstone in remembrance of his donkey, Ali Baba, *1866 and 1867." They were received by the Legs with kicks of delight and rapture.*
The Era, 20/1/1867

> *PANTOMIME TRICKS – The Best Trick to introduce is the Bowls of Water and Gold Fish from an Empty Scarf, and Bowls of Liquid Fire, which, upon being touched, burst into a volume of flame. Price, large size, 7s each; small, 5s; of A TAYLOR, Magical Apparatus Maker, Seven Sisters' Cottage, Holloway, London, N.* **The Era, 10/11/1867**

Covent Garden
The Babes in the Wood; or, Harlequin Robin Hood and His Merry Men

HOW the legends are dovetailed may be understood by an intimation that the Cruel Uncle of the pathetic Norfolk tale is now known as the Baron (Mr Payne), who has care of the Two Babes, Milendo (Mr Fred Payne) and Primroshilina (Mr J Clarke), who devote themselves to the destruction of his china, glass, furniture, and perishable property. Maid Marian (Miss Maria Harris), their nurse, does her best to defend them, but in vain, and affairs are brought to a crisis by the arrival of a telegram from Black Diamond, the Coal King (Mr Lingham), recommending the Baron to summon his Villain, and get him to "spifficate" the children in the wood. The purport of this message is caught by Maid Marian, who, threatening to call in the assistance of Robin Hood, is thrown into a dungeon by order of the Baron. Freed from the nurse he sends for his creature, the Villain (Mr Stoyle); a bargain is struck, the children are fetched, and overcome, notwithstanding the Villain's unprepossessing appearance, by the attraction of some sugar sticks, and induced to accompany him for a walk in the wood.

Robin Hood (Miss Amy Sheridan), with Little John (Miss M Marshall), Will Scarlett (Miss Nelly Harris), and the Merry Men, happen that same day to be holding a picnic in the deepest part of the forest. In the midst of this entertainment Marian arrives, having escaped from the Castle, and announces the terrible danger that is hanging over the babes. One and all determine to capture the Baron without delay, and breaking up their picnic, depart in search of him.

The Villain reaches a secluded spot with the children, and is about to despatch them, when their tears move him, and he abandons his guilty design. The Baron, however, who has been suspecting something wrong, and watching, intervenes, when a fight ensues, in which the Villain is worsted, and the defenceless babes are left to their fate. Making up their bed of leaves, they are about to terminate their career in the usual manner, when Brilliantina appears and sends the robins to their assistance. Instead of burying the birds arouse them, and at length come in such numbers that the babes are struck with the idea of taking them home to attack their uncle. For this purpose they drill them, and all of them march off towards the castle.

The Baron has in the meantime been caught by some of the merry men, and "ducked" in a neighbouring stream, while the Villain, who has patched himself up with sticking plaster, has promised to reform his ways. The Baron goes to bed with a severe cold. Here he is tortured by his nephew, his conscience, and the cat, and is at length aroused by the news that the castle is attacked. Eager for the fray, he puts on his armour, flies to the battlements, where a desperate struggle of all concerned ensues, leading to the mutual intervention of Black Diamond and Brilliantina, and a final adjournment to the Transformation. Great reliance is placed on the effect of the ballet and the picturesque groups in the Forest Scene.

Grecian
Harlequin Ric Rac, the Giant of the Mountains, and the Goblin Gift and the Kingdoms Three; or, the Good Fairy and the Pretty Princess

MR GEORGE CONQUEST, of course, plays the principal character, and without him, indeed, the chief glory of the Grecian Pantomime would be wanting.

We could tell how a quarrel arises between Fairy Will-o'-the-Wisp (Miss Martineau) and the Mushroom King Fungus about possession of a Goblin Gift, which gives power over all things, and how the Fairy triumphs. We shall, however, only hint at present that in the Curious Court of King Chafer there is much bewailing over the loss of the entire female population, the Princess Butterfly, his own niece, being the only lady left in the land. All the rest have served as a meal for the formidable Ric Rac, the Giant, and the Giant is, of course, Mr George Conquest. We shall tell hereafter how through the Three Kingdoms, Animal, Vegetable, and Mineral, the Giant passes in various forms. From being nine feet high he suddenly becomes King Turnip, only two feet high; next he becomes a monkey, and carries off the Princess, Mr George Conquest performing in one of those marvellous combats for which he is so renowned a series of extraordinary acrobatic and gymnastic feats. In the mineral kingdom of Tom Tiddler's Ground the Transformation Scene of the World of Wealth takes place, showing how money is made, earned, and lost, finishing with the speculation of Fairy Land. […]

The Era, 22/12/1867

Drury Lane
Faw, Fee, Fo, Fum; or, Harlequin Jack the Giant Killer
[…] THERE is never anything coarse in Mr Blanchard's Pantomimes. He always writes for ladies and gentlemen, big and little, and he has the true man's faith, that these are to be found in the gallery, as well as the boxes. Notwithstanding the fog, when the curtain rose upon FAW, FEE, FO, FUM; OR, HARLEQUIN JACK THE GIANT KILLER, on Boxing Night, the Theatre was crammed from roof to ceiling. There was "not room to put a pin in", as the saying is.

The first scene presents us with the Giant's Causeway by Moonlight, where we find the Leprechauns, or Irish Fairymen, searching for the four-leaved shamrock, which is to be a talisman for the ills, not of Ireland alone, but of the whole world. While thus engaged, and before the shamrock is found, they are scared by the appearance of a number of terrible Giants, who hold a meeting and resolve *nem. com.* that nothing but evil shall have sway in the land.

The two opposing primary elements of Pantomime, Good and Evil, are now fairly at work, and we come to the Golden Garden of the Peerless Pool, an exceedingly rich and beautiful scene in Mr Beverley's happiest style. Here are congregated the Fruit Fairies, a bevy of pretty girls, holding in their hands cornucopiæ, over-brimming with luscious fruits of all kinds. To them appear Fata Morgana, the Scotch Brownie, the Irish Banshee, &c., who, with the Fairies, form a league to resist the machinations of the wicked Giants; and after a song, charmingly sung by Miss Poole, in the character of Ondine, and a very clever and graceful dance by the Fairies, a hundred strong, the Water Spirit proceeds on her mission to find a champion worthy of the common cause.

This transports us to a Fishing Village on the Cornish Coast (a really artistic bit of painting), where Jack (Mr Irving) comes on the scene, flying his kite. The village is visited by the Duke of Cornwall (Mr Moreland) – not at this period Prince of Wales – and his pretty daughter, Adelgitha (Miss Edith Stuart). While the Cornish fish wives are entertaining his Grace with a characteristic dance the roar of the Giants is heard, and presently Cormorant is seen coming over the sea, which fearful apparition causes a general skedaddle. Jack, however, inspired by Ondine, and love of the Duke's daughter, undertakes the tackle the Giants, and at once proceeds to do so. Knowing Cormorant's weakness, he fishes for him with a hook baited with a leg of mutton, and catches him.

After this, taking the road to St Ives, he encounters and slays Blunderbore, and, at last, growing more and more audacious with success, attacks the castle of the most terrible of all the Giants, the three-headed Faw Fee Fo Fum. The pretty daughter of the Duke of Cornwall has fallen into the hands of this monster, and Jack is determined to deliver her. There being little chance for force against such odds, he uses stratagem, and, getting the Giant in bed, he knocks him on the head, or rather on his three heads, with his club.

The scene now changes to the Ruins of the Giants' Castle, which, the four-leaved shamrock having been found, dissolves into the Fairy Boudoir, where Jack's gift is presented and all are made happy. The Fairy Boudoir, which forms the Transformation Scene, surpasses all Mr Beverley's previous efforts at this house. It recalled to the recollections of many of the audience the brightest days of the Lyceum under Madame Vestris. The whole staged is draped in lace, with pendants of pearls, a golden temple rising at the back, supporting, or being supported, by living female caryatides, in garments of gold, glittering all over with diamonds. The effect of this was really charming – a scene of bewildering beauty, which fairly drove the audience wild with delight. There were calls for "Beverley!" before the scene was half developed, and they never ceased until the gifted artist appeared upon the stage to bow again and again his acknowledgements.

All the parts in the opening were capitally played. Mr Joseph Irving, as Jack, delighted the audience with some very clever and characteristic dancing. Miss Poole, as Ondine, charmed their ears with singing far above the usual Pantomime standard; and Master Percy Roselle, as Pigwiggin, looked as juvenile and roguish as ever. […]

The Harlequinade – the comic business, as it is emphatically called by those concerned in it – is distinguished by several decidedly novel features. The inventors, Mr Harry Boleno and J Cormack, obey Shakespeare's injunctions to the letter, holding the mirror up to nature, and, if not exactly showing vice and virtue their own images and features, most certainly exhibiting the very age and body of the time, its form and presence. The follies of the day are fired at on the wing, and hit with unerring aim. The leading social events of the year are passed under review by Field-Marshal Harlequin, and we have practical allusions to the grievances of the cabmen, to the high price of meat, and some sly hits at that new growth of trade competition, the Licensed Victuallers' Tea Association. One of the most striking scenes in the Harlequinade is a miniature picture of life in Paris, where every type of French character is represented by a little boy or girl, concluding with a review of French troops by the Emperor, the Empress, and the Prince Imperial in miniature. This really charming scene reflects great credit upon the inventor, Mr Cormack. Another capital scene represents a Russian forest, where snow-balling and skating take place. The performance of Madame Fredrika and Mr Elliott, "the champion skaters of the world," was exceedingly graceful, and gave great delight to the audience. The flambeaux dance was also very effective; but the scene which will give the liveliest satisfaction to the juveniles, and put a distinguishing mark upon the comic business of the Drury Lane Pantomime of 1867, will be, we predict, the miniature representation of life in Paris. [...]

Percy Roselle

Prince's Theatre, Manchester
Gulliver's Travels; or, Harlequin Billy Taylor and the Good Spirit of Energy

THE original story is pretty closely adhered to, though several new characters are introduced, the principal of whom are the Demons Ignorance (Mr W Banks) and Sloth (Mr P Rae), and the Good Spirits Energy (Miss Kate Leigh) and Knowledge (Miss Ada Travers). The strife between these opposite powers commences in the first scene, the Home of Sloth, where the Vices are seen at work forging fetters for the human race. War to the knife is declared, and the fortunes of the mariner Gulliver are to be the immediate bone of contention. Ignorance boasting much of his strength, while Sloth places great confidence in the power of *vis inertiæ*. The Birthplace of Energy is the next scene. Here ensues the Ballet of the Bright Ideas and Happy Thoughts, the brightest of the former being most adequately represented by Miss Lillie Davis (the *premiere danseuse*), and the happiest of the latter with considerable vivacity by Miss Frances St Maine. After the ballet, which is tastefully designed and prettily executed, we come to Gulliver's House, where Mrs Gulliver (Mr J B Dale) is discovered making preparations for her husband's intended voyage. Here enter Gulliver (Mr J Chester), the Captain (Mr J Rogerson), Jenny, Gulliver's daughter (Miss Jenny Taylor), Billy Taylor, her lover (Miss Mary Townley), and Lord Bateman (Miss Maggie Brennan), who, instead of going, as he intended, strange countries for to see, stays behind to make love to Jenny. The next scene is on board ship. The crew, who are most picturesquely attired, dance a hornpipe, and the ship afterwards founders in a storm, which is very effectively represented.

A most beautiful landscape picture next discloses Gulliver in Lilliput, fast bound to the earth, according to tradition, and we there have the first view of the great feature of the Pantomime, the Lilliputian Army. Tinymite, the Emperor (Miss Nelly Smith), and Dear Little Sing, the Empress (Miss Alice St Maine) enter in a magnificent stage coach, drawn by miniature white horses, and at the Emperor's command Gulliver is conveyed from the spot by an infinitesimal railway. We are then shown the Courtyard of the Royal Palace, with the sea in the background, a truly charming scene. Here, however, Gulliver's troubles begin, for the Emperor, suspecting his consort of a *penchant* for his monster ally, taxes her with it. However, in honour of Gulliver, he orders a grand review of his entire forces. A series of difficult manoeuvres are executed with remarkable precision, for his army of Lilliput actually boasts a squadron of horse, who canter briskly round the square. The Emperor and Empress also manifest their joy by a dance. (Miss Nelly Smith, who played in *The Fast Family* at the Adelphi some time ago, is certain to add greatly to her reputation as a child actress by this last impersonation.) Gulliver and Billy Taylor arrive at home again in time to preserve Jenny from a forced marriage with Lord Bateman. Gulliver's travels terminate in Brobdignag, where two enormous Giants are discovered, and from whose power he is rescued by Knowledge and Energy.

Then ensues the Transformation Scene – Energy changing Billy Taylor to Harlequin, and Jenny to Columbine, while Ignorance transposes Gulliver to Clown, and Mrs G to Pantaloon. The Transformation Scene opens with a dark cavern of stalactites, from each column of which emerges a Fairy. The ground becomes glorious with golden verdure, the dark columns fade away, and are replaced by glittering shrubs, each bearing a graceful and ethereal looking being, a fountain rises in the background from a lake and casts a rainbow arch over all, while a winged seraph descends floating through the air, and, the lights then being thrown on, a scene of exquisite and radiant beauty is revealed. The deafening applause in this scene brought on Mr Haynes, and also Mr Walford Grieve, the latter gentleman having also had several times previously to bow his acknowledgements, all the scenery in the Opening being the work of Messrs T and Walford Grieve. [...]
The Era, 29/12/1867

1868

FATAL ACCIDENT AT A THEATRE – *A sad and fatal accident has occurred at the Theatre Royal, Leicester. It seems, from the evidence adduced at the inquest, held on Tuesday evening before the Coroner, Mr J Gregory, that on Saturday night at the Theatre, which is now under the Management of Mr G H Ashton, was extremely full, and that the deceased, Henry Payne, a youth about twelve years of age, at his own request, accompanied his father into the gallery for the purpose of witnessing the performance of the Pantomime,* Little Red Riding Hood. *In the course of the entertainment, owing to the crowded state of the gallery, the deceased and about thirty others were let into the "side slips" adjoining, and while there, looking over the front on to the stage, it would seem that some mischievous youths succeeded in carrying unperceived into the gallery, from the lobby, a large and heavy door for the purpose of making a platform from which to obtain a better view of the performance, but which overpowered them and fell with considerable force on to the back of the deceased, crushing him severely against the front of the gallery, and causing him to sustain severe internal injuries, from which he died on Tuesday. The Jury returned a verdict of "Accidental death", and Mr Ashton promised to secure the door, and to pay the funeral expenses of the unfortunate youth.*
The Era, 26/1/1868

LITTLE RED RIDING HOOD'S FAREWELL TO HER JUVENILE FRIENDS
"Good-bye, dears, and thank you very much for your kind visits to me. The cruel Wolf tried very hard to entrap me, but my dear Jack Horner has given him so severe a lesson that I am sure he will not trouble us any more. Froggy (poor, silly Froggy) has gone back to his Mother, and, safe below in the depths of the Green Pond, he promises ne'er again to go a-wooing without her consent; indeed, I hear he has joined the Bulrush Volunteers (uniform, a bright yellow, turned up with green). I and Jack are to be married as soon as the buttercups and daisies come in, and as Granny has left me her rose-covered cottage – dear Jack will be able to farm the land there in peace and contentment – we hope to be happy all the rest of our lives. Jacky says I must never leave off my cloak, for he loves it as part of myself; so you see, although I shall soon become his bride, I shall always be
  Yours truly, dears, with many thanks,
    "LITTLE RED RIDING HOOD"
"P.S. – Wolf has just written to say that he is very sorry he ate dear Grandmother, but I don't think I can ever forgive him, for all we have found of the poor, dear old lady has been her spectacles."
The Era, 16/2/1868

The Surrey
Jack and Jill and the Sleeping Beauty; or, Harlequin Humpty Dumpty

WE are first introduced to Toadstool Bog in the Haunted Swamp, a capitally set scene, with some enormous specimens of the fungi growing in the centre, surrounded by numbers of smaller toadstools, each competing with the other for evanescent ugliness; and here it is we make the acquaintance of all sorts of characters, good, bad, and indifferent, and learn that the time for awakening the Sleeping Beauty has come, and accordingly Prince Sunbeam (Miss Elizabeth Webster) – than whom a better Prince never trod the boards – having determined to search out the Sleeping Beauty, enters upon the scene, and a desperate combat ensues between him and Phosphoresco (Mr Sylvan), the Goblin Sprite of the Toadstool Swamp. Oceana (Miss Florence Gerald), the Spirit of the Waves, watching over Sunbeam's fortunes, invokes the aid of the Glimmery (Miss Ellen Leonard), who at once comes to Prince Sunbeam's aid, and, releasing him from the power of Phosphoresco, tells him where he may find the Sleeping Beauty.

We next make the acquaintance of the old woman of the shoe (Mr Howard) and Prince Humpty Dumpty (Mr Harry Crouste), the latter of whom as a *protege* of the old woman of the shoe seeks the abode of the Sleeping Beauty. Some capital Pantomime ensues, and the old woman coming the virago too strongly Humpty Dumpty rebels against the thraldom, and in a mock heroic attitude exclaims –

Old woman just you draw it mild,
I'm now a nice young man and not a child.

A hint which the old woman takes in good part, and tells him how to find the Sleeping Beauty, but Glimmery and Prince Sunbeam go off in a balloon to the popular air of "Up in a Balloon, Boys", the chorus of which was taken up by the whole house and sung with immense gusto, and are landed near the glistening waters of the Silver Valley – another splendidly painted set scene, which produced an unanimous call for Mr Albert Callcott, the artist, where floods of silver water spring from rock to rock, and are lost in dazzling spray.

A capitally arranged ballet follows, the principal dancers being the Sisters Duvalli, new to the London stage, but who are destined to become great favourites, every *pas* and *pose* being full of life and grace, and eliciting most deserved applause. The grouping of the ballet ladies in this scene is deserving of especial praise, and says much for the good taste of Mr Chapino, the ballet master.

We next come to the Sleeping Apartment of Prince Drowsy Wowsy, where Princess Diamond Eyes (Miss Alice Dodd) is aroused by Prince Sunbeam. A capitally arranged duet, admirably sung, ensues, as a matter of course, and, being well sung, was, as a matter of course, encored.

In the next scene we have the Hill which Jack and Jill went up to fetch a pail of water, and on the slope of the hill a gigantic shoe, the residence of the old woman who "had so many children she didn't know what to do" – not the only woman we fear who has been similarly circumstanced. The scene is brimful of fun and comicality, and kept the audience in a continual state of laughter from beginning to end. The escapade of Jack (Mr Walter Searle) and Jill (Mr Mat Robson) going up the hill was amusingly played out. Then the host of children were fed from a gigantic basin, and duly slapped and packed off to bed, to the great glee of the younger portion of the audience, who literally screamed with delight as one after another of the old woman's children were dispatched.

After very many dangers and escapes we are shown the Witches' Common and Bull Rush Glen, where the artist seems to have exhausted his powers in producing ugliness as a fitting type of witchcraft. Here we have some capital singing and dancing by Prince Sunbeam, Princess Diamond Eyes, King Rough-and-Tough (Mr C Jones), Jack, and Jill.

Then followed the Grand Transformation Scene. Up to this point – save for the hitches inseparable from a first performance – all had gone on admirably, and the audience were excessively delighted and in high good humour, as indeed they should have been, considering the excellent fare set before them; but here some of the complex machinery got out of gear, and the Transformation Scene, which consists of a series of elaborate changes, each beautifully worked, could not be unfolded so quickly as it will be hereafter. The first part of the scene shows a draped palace, shrouded in golden clouds, which gradually disperse and show a silver and gold landscape, sparkling with the rarest gems. Then comes another change, and we have Pomona's Court and Throne in the Garden of Hesperides, a beautiful temple of gold and silver tissue, supported by charming female figures, with silver and gold drapery, with innumerable Fairies floating in mid-air. It was here the sad hitch occurred, provoking alike to artist, manager, and audience. The machinery would not work, and the top of the temple, after several trials, went up some ten feet, and gave a slight glimpse of the splendours behind, and then suddenly came down, provoking a slight scream from the ladies, and a storm of disapprobation from those sharp and inconsiderate critics, the "gods". It was here Mr Shepherd made his appearance before the footlights, and, in apologetic and excited tones, said:–

"Ladies and Gentlemen: – You are not more put out than I am. It is simply impossible that any one of you can feel, however disappointed you may be – I say it is impossible that any one in this vast assembly can be more hurt and more disappointed than I am at this moment. Everything that long experience could suggest has been done, and I looked to this Transformation Scene as a crowning effort, and I am disappointed. I say I am disappointed, because I am sure you would have been delighted with it, and I am disappointed because I do not like to have to make apologies for shortcomings. Whatever shortcomings there maybe elsewhere, we are not used to them, and we do not expect them, at the Surrey. (Loud cheers.) I thank you for those cheers, and I can assure you if it had been within my power to prevent it this should not have happened (hear, hear), but unfortunately one of our ropes broke, and it is impossible for us to rectify it just now. I venture to think, however, that judging from what you have seen, you will be convinced that no expense has been spared to contribute to your pleasurable enjoyment, and that you will kindly excuse the unfolding of the remainder of this scene."

Mr Shepherd made his bow, and retired amid a volley of applause, and the Harlequinade commenced. With Harry Crouste as Clown, Mr Gellini as Pantaloon, Mr Sylvain as Harlequin, and the Misses Duvalli as Columbine and Harlequina, need we say it was all that could be desired. In one of the scenes there are exhibited a number of magical trees, introduced by Mr J Bland, which would put to shame any modern wizard; and, upon the whole, despite the hitch we have above recorded, we think Mr Shepherd is to be congratulated upon having presented a Pantomime which will be a great success and have a long run.

The Victoria
Bluff King Hal; or, Herne the Hunter and the Miller's Daughter of the River Dee

[...] THE first scene, representing a portion on Windsor Forest as seen by moonlight, though of a somewhat sombre character, was a more elaborate picture than opening scenes sometimes are. Here a company of Demons, bearing lighted torches, engage in dancing and singing while awaiting the arrival of their master, Mammon (Mr Howard Russell). Chief among the leading Sprites are World o' Money (Mr J Baker), Graspyetin (Mr Maynard), and Antler (Mr Fletcher). Mammon rises through the ground, borne up by a kind of Dragon, which flaps its huge wings now and then, as such creatures are wont to to. While holding a conference with his attendants about choosing a subject for a Pantomime, Herne the Hunter (Miss Emma Mowbray) is named as being likely to furnish an excellent one, and that personage is immediately summoned forth from the mystic oak in which he abides. Partly in speech and partly in song the wizard sportsman bids them all lend their aid, and promises plenty of life and fun.

Whereupon the scene changes to Glittering Stalactite Caverns in the Palace of Silverstream (Miss Emily Forde). This beautiful scene, like the previous one, is the work of Mr T Evans. A troupe of Nymphs assemble here, and a ballet *divertissement* takes place, in which the most prominent parts are taken by the Sisters Duvernay. These young ladies are very light and graceful dancers, and their active and airy tripping to and fro excited great applause. Silverstream comes on in a silver car, drawn by six silver swans, which are strikingly natural in shape. The Queen of the Fays makes a speech on the topics of the day, and her friend Pearly Drop (Miss Annie Wells) puts in a few words occasionally. Their speaking is interrupted by the sudden intrusion of Herne, who forthwith proceeds to speak his mind very plainly about the evils of the times.

The third scene is the Chamber of Anne Boleyn (Mr Fred Wright), where the Queen and her nurse and child are introduced. Scene four, which, with the one immediately preceding it, has been painted by Mr W F Robson, is a very neat and bright picture of the exterior of the Palace of King Hal (Mr Cave). Soldiers, bearing arms and banners, and musicians and pages, appear here, and, under the direction of the Grand Chamberlain, Baron Doembrown (Mr J Bradshaw), sing and dance, and then arrange themselves in order to receive their imperious Monarch. Mr A Cave, as King Hal, was both a magnificent and amusing individual. He was very corpulent and fiery looking, and was splendidly dressed. His singing was admirable, and much laughter was occasioned by some tiny trumpeters playing squeaking instruments while the whole group paraded, as their burly master warbled "Shout, boys, shout, keep advancing." After a comic quarrel between the King and Anne, of whom he has grown weary, Herne comes to the aid of the changeful, amorous Hal, and promises to assist him in his attempts to win the affections of the daughter of the Miller of Dee.

The view of the mill and the adjacent country, which now becomes the scene of action, is exceedingly picturesque and good, and so much delighted the spectators that they insisted on Mr Robson, by whom it was executed, coming forward to be cheered. Old Mic (Mr M Roberts), the miller, and his wife, Dame Grumblegrizzle (Mr Charles Cooper), have two very robust and not handsome daughters, named Stuttina (Mr G Carter) and Woppinda (Mr Johns), besides Pretty Little Blossom (Miss Florence Farren), who is loved by Young Lively (Miss Jessie Francis). The introduction of the masculine romps to the King, and the rough reception which he gives them, were very laughable incidents. Blossom is hurried off to Windsor and Anne Boleyn is to be executed, but, by the timely interference of Herne, Hal's wicked schemes are frustrated, and the victims are in the end saved from all further molestation. To console himself, Old Harry sings a patter song about his predilections, which was written expressly for Mr Cave by H S Leigh, Esq, and a lively break-down, by all the principal characters, prepares the way for the Transformation Scene, which is a highly artistic and beautiful production.

Drooping Ferns, in an Elfin Dell, are first seen, and these, on being withdrawn, reveal an elegant boudoir or pavilion, formed of what look like lace curtains. To this succeeds a very brilliant and beautiful representation of a region of roses, and this spectacle is followed by the final one, which presents a view of the realm of jewels, which is gorgeous in the extreme. This scene comprises three three vast vases in the centre, containing charming looking girls who represent jewels. Others are placed on each side of the stage and in front. To crown all a magnificent car, in which two lovely creatures are reclining, descends and hangs in mid-air, and the completed scene is most resplendent. Mr Robson, the designer and painter of it, was loudly called for, and he and Mr Marchant, who was also invited to come forth, came on accompanied by Mr Cave, and they were all three cheered most enthusiastically. [...]

The closing scenes exhibited an advertising station, the shops of a baker and butcher, the Old Lion inn, which changed into a railway station, a hairdresser's, and a pretty view of the Home of Pantomime forms the finale. [...]

The Era, 27/12/1868

1869

Covent Garden
The Yellow Dwarf; or, Harlequin Cupid, and the King of the Gold Mines

[...] IN the first scene the Yellow Dwarf (Mr J D Stoyle) carouses with a company of quaintly masked followers, and drinks to the health of all the vicious gnomes who inhabit the subterranean regions of the earth. The scene represents a huge cavern with sharp buttresses of rock in every direction, and the whole very suggestive of a volcanic origin. This roomy apartment is lighted by lamps of various colours, which have an appropriately weird effect against the dark background. Messrs Dayes and Caney are the painters of this picturesque scene. The Desert Fairy, Siroccatina (Mr W H Payne), the Dwarf's godmother, and a withered dame of the Meg Merrilies type, bewails her faded appearance, and, like very many matrons of the upper world, determines to make herself beautiful forever. A Pantomime introduction without a Bogie would not be sufficiently orthodox, and a terrific-looking individual of that name is played by "Herr Grimm". Bogie holds both the Dwarf and his antique godmamma in subjection. The small yellow man is condemned to marry at four and twenty hours' notice, and Siroccatina agrees to further his matrimonial views.

From gloom to summer brightness, and the flowery "Bureau de Cupidon", is a transition rapidly made. Miss Maria Harris, as Cupid, is in supreme command here, and appears in a charming costume of rose-coloured silk. She wears the neatest pair of white wings, and has at her beck and call a few smaller editions of herself. Cupid has a mission, and that is to turn the wayward heart of the wilful little Princess Allfair (Miss Nelly Power[15]) from dolls, toffey, and toys, to a passion more worthy of young womanhood. The God of Love leaves his Bower (painted by Mr Hawes Craven), and sets his plot on foot in the Gardens of the Palace, an admirably executed scene by W Telbin, Jr. Mr Aynsley Cook appears as King Kammomile the Kantankerous, a monarch of the properly boisterous, violent, and energetic kind. Mrs Aynsley Cook plays his far from submissive Queen. Miss Nelly Power's reception was highly flattering, and her exquisite costume became her to perfection. The little Princess is not condemned to what old-fashioned people used to call "long frocks". On the contrary, her movements are unimpeded, and pale blue satin assimilates well with a fair complexion.

In this scene a number of suitors are introduced to Kammomile's royal court and daughter, but with a pretty petulance she continues to amuse herself with nursery toys, brought by Twitterino (Mr F Payne), her favourite page, a retainer of extraordinary personal activity and grotesque appearance. Twitterino has a head as smooth as a pumpkin, and a style of locomotion entirely his own. He dances on and off with the most sublime contempt for the etiquette of the Palace, and is devoted to his young mistress, who forgives all his mistakes but one, namely, that of eating a basket of cakes, and thus placing her in the power of the Dwarf. The first who makes his appeal is Prince Ching-A-Ring-Ching (Miss Craven), who does not even patronise "pigeon English", but talks Byronic Chinese. The Prince of Pearl Island (Miss Love) tries his fortune, but with no success, though in the matter of personal appearance he is exceptionally charming. The Great Little Mogul (Miss A Cook) and the Persian Prince (Miss Lee) follow suit. The next potentate announced is Prince Pet (Miss Nelly Harris), a dainty little exquisite, magnificently costumed, and quite irresistible to ordinary mortals. The Princess is, however, a creature of an uncommon order, and difficult to please. The right man at last enters the Halls of Kammomile, and Dulcimer, King of the Gold Mines (Miss Julia Mathews), aided by the prettily mischievous Cupid, subjugates the lovely Princess. Dulcimer, as becomes a Prince with so musical a name, can sing, and proves the fact to the satisfaction of the audience in a vocal address to the whole assembly in the Palace Gardens. The unsuccessful suitors have very little to say or do. When they stand in a group the effect of the costumes is extremely brilliant. At the end of the scene Miss Power and Mr F Payne gave an admirable burlesque dance. On Monday night it was encored by acclamation. The ball thus being opened, nothing remains but the usual struggle between the rival lovers.

The Abode of the Desert Fairy (the work of Hawes Craven) is a moonlight scene of remarkable power. The stage represents the mouth of a ravine, the sides formed of steep rocks, and from the end the moon shining down the pass. This set is a fine specimen of one kind of stage effect, which is heightened by the appearance of a number of enormous antediluvian animals. These are wonderfully well managed. Mr W H Payne is always amusing when making his toilette, and the venerable Siroccatina puts on an extensive chignon and rouges herself into a most diverting assumption of youth and beauty.

Twitterino's fair mistress disappears in the trunk of a tree with the Dwarf, and he falls insensible only to wake in the Haunt of the Houris (Hawes Craven), a region of loveliness, animal and vegetable, that has its effects upon the page. The elderly Siroccatina, by a process of enchantment, takes the place of a Houri, who has fascinated poor Twitterino. He sinks into a state of bewilderment in this Garden of the Hesperides, where banks of flowers and wide-leaved plants rise up to meet hanging gardens and tendrils, that droop over the mouths of grottoes. The whole stage forms a vista of blossoms and fairy-like vegetation, and the tone of colour is beautifully graduated. The ballet ladies wear white dresses relieved with a simple festoon of dark coloured but glittering leaves, and the effect of these comparatively simple dresses against the stronger background is charming.

The Royal Gardens (Dayes and Caney) are invaded by a troop of the Dwarf Guards, and a better set of masks than these could not be seen on any stage. A detachment of Amazons range themselves on either side the avenue through which the marriage procession enters. In a short time the stage becomes filled with minstrels, guards, and attendants, forming one of those brilliant pictures for which Covent Garden is famous. Dancing girls enter to slow and dreamy music from the orchestra, and Twitterino carries a wedding favour as big as a tambourine. Dulcimer subsequently laments the abduction of his Allfair in a medley song, commencing with a pretty melody from Offenbach's *Perichole*. This was delightfully sung by Miss Julia Mathews.

The ninth scene – the Steel Castle – by W Telbin, is a point of surpassing interest in the spectacle. No more striking piece of glowing loveliness than this has ever been seen on any stage; and for some minutes on Monday night the applause continued in unabated volume. The audience seemed altogether taken by surprise, and vehemently called for the artist, who, however, did not respond. To the right the Steel Castle of the Dwarf is seen perched on a rock that rises from a lake stretching into the far distance, bounded by towering mountains bathed in the soft light of sunset. Two gigantic palms in the foreground show clear against the sky, and on the whole of this grand *tableau* rests a soft, mellow glow that greatly assists the poetical effect. The watch-dog of the castle, a mailed quadruped, is cut in halves by Twitterino, and this little passage of arms the audience were very anxious to see over again. Here occurs a dance of Steel Fairies with metallic wings on their heads, armour plate hanging over the hip, and skirts that might be taken for chain mail. To these enter a number of rosy Cupids, carrying silver bows, dressed in pink dresses, and wearing gilded boots. The entrance of this charming band from the realm of the loves is a thing to see. They fascinate the fairies, and no wonder, and by this means assistance reaches the pretty little Princess, immured in the steel dungeon. Miss Nelly Power here has a vocal solo, and when she had finished it on Monday night a something that looked like a young Christmas tree was thrown on the stage. Miss Power was recalled to sing the song again, when she picked up the curious production and threw it off at the wing. This seemed to give offence to some part of the audience, so she fetched the precious gift back, and, with a deprecatory gesture, showed the audience what it was – an enormous artificial rose, and no kind of compliment. Miss Nelly Power was, to all appearance, victimised in the matter, and had the sympathies of the best part of the audience entirely with her.

A circumstance of the kind described is very likely to interfere with the pleasure and enjoyment of everyone, but it was not so in this case. Princess Allfair being rescued by Dulcimer and Cupid, there is very little else to do than to effect the usual reconciliation between the good and bad Spirits, who may have been at variance for two hours, more or less. This is soon done by the Genius of Pantomime, and the way is then made clear for what is always considered the crowning glory of Christmas time – the Transformation Scene, from which the Harlequinade start on their mission of practical joking, working wondrous mechanical changes, and sending the old and young people home in a good humour.

Mr Julian Hicks is the artist to whom this responsible duty has been entrusted. The Roses of Fairyland in the Home of the Sweet Briar Fays describes the scene in the book of words, and such a subject allows unlimited scope for artistic fancy. A net-work of roses, gently ascending, discovers, through a net-work of golden briars, the forms of the reclining "Fays". The whole stage represents a bower of roses, and the Fairies appear as it were to rest on these masses of blossoms. Venus, from her Home among the Roses, gave the commission to the Pantomimists, namely, Mr F Payne as Harlequin, Mlle D'Esta as Columbine, Mr Harry Payne as Clown, and Mr Paolo as Pantaloon.

The first scene in the Harlequinade, which, according to custom at this Theatre, is refreshingly short, is the Thames Embankment (W Telbin), showing part of Westminster Bridge, the steamboat pier, and the Houses of Parliament. Mr Harry Payne is by no means a silent Clown – in fact, few Clowns are, nowadays. An allusion he made to the prohibited game of skittles was received with a roar of approbation from by the gallery folk, and their ecstasy was increased by his asking the question, "When are they going to do away with billiards?" The Police Force is always fair game, and the Chief Commissioner's marvellous stroke of wisdom is a chance few privileged satirists would let slip. A bonbon distribution to the occupants of the stalls takes place under Mr H Payne's immediate superintendence; and the Thames Embankment, being a good place for public meetings, one in which all kinds of momentous questions are to be discussed, is held. The Clown takes the chair, and the chair takes him higher than he desires, for he is at last mounted up many feet above the level of the stage. The unhappy "Bobby" pursues him, but of course comes to ignominious grief. One of those mysterious and elegantly got-up boxes peculiar to the Pantomime season is produced, and inside is a pretty little girl of about three years, who goes through the dumb-bell exercise with great determination. The Crystal Palace, a very effective scene by Messrs Dayes and Caney, brings forward the subject of bicycles. Several performers thereupon, including two ladies, a clever boy, and some adult male *artistes*, go through various evolutions, and after the "Bicycle Leger" comes the "Jockey's Revel", by a select few of the ballet, in the smartest of sporting costumes. The Crystal Palace Grounds and the Ancient Order of Foresters are always closely associated, and a neatly-devised dance of Robin Hood and Maid Marian is given. A scene – Cornhill (by Mr Cuthbert) – completes the Harlequinade, and the traditional "business" is quite safe in the hands of such a troupe as that engaged at Covent Garden. […]

The Era, 27/12/1868

Nelly Power

NOTES

1 – The largest ship of its day, designed by Isambard Kingdom Brunel and of all-iron construction.
2 – "Much in a little".
3 – Nadolsky was the presenter of an illusion in which large objects, including items of furniture, were taken out of a small cabinet.
4 – Designed by Sir William Armstrong, this type of rifled breech-loading field and heavy gun was used extensively by the British Army in the Second Opium War.
5 – *Robin Goodfellow* was a short-lived journal founded by Charles Mackay (1814-1889), author of *Extraordinary Popular Delusions and the Madness of Crowds.*
6 – A dim-witted aristocratic character in Tom Taylor's play *Our American Cousin.*
7 – In 1862 boxer Jem Mace defeated Tom King in a brutal (and illegal) 41-round fight for the English heavyweight championship.
8 – Lydia Thompson (1838-1908): A popular pantomime and burlesque actress credited with introducing burlesque to America in 1868.
9 – Cicely Nott (1832-1900): The mother of pantomime star Ada Blanche and aunt of actress Dame Cicely Courtneidge (1893-1980).
10 – Percy Roselle (1856-?): A dwarf actor famous for playing child roles in pantomime. He was the brother of Amy Roselle, an accomplished actress who never achieved star status and died with her husband in a murder-suicide pact in 1895.
11 – *Mrs Lirriper's Lodgings* was a short story by Charles Dickens.
12 – Punch's dog.
13 – A fanciful cottage, often thatched, used as a summerhouse or garden embellishment by the wealthy.
14 – Louisa Ricardo was only twelve years old – many dancers and bit-players in pantomime were children.
15 – Nelly Power is best remembered for her song *The Boy I Love is up in the Gallery.*

8
The 1870s
A Small Pig in the Soup

1870

The Surrey
Harlequin St George and the Dragon; or, Old Father Time and the Seven Champions of Christendom

[…] THE Opening is written by Mr W R Osman, and abounds in smart allusions to the social events of the day. The first scene is the Abode of Old Father Time, "the oldest inhabitant of the globe", being played by Mr C F Marshall. Invention (Miss Lizzie Collier), a dainty little person in short skirts, breaks in upon the old gentleman's reveries, and shows him a few little vanities of modern times, such as the Great Eastern, the electric telegraph, and an express train. Luna (Miss Clara Morgan), a very charming and benignant divinity, assists in the preliminary discussion, and, the question of the Pantomime being amicably settled, the audience are at once taken to the Cave of Kalaba, the Enchantress of the Woods.

Miss Nelly Kemp's remarkably handsome face and figure and regal style of beauty invest this small character with an interest which, under other circumstances, it would hardly possess. Kalaba has enclosed six of the Christian Champions in statues, and is desperately in love with St George (Miss Millie de Vere). With most unaccountable obtuseness he refuses to return her passion, and robs her of her magic wand. The Champions are liberated, and come down the stage in a perfect blaze of magnificent costumes. Miss Louisa Collier appears as St Patrick of Ireland, Miss Davis as St Andrew of Scotland, Miss Robina Bellingham as St David of Wales, Miss Davis (whose speciality is singing) as St Denis of France, Miss C Shelly as St James of Spain, and Miss Marie de Grey as St Anthony of Italy. The ballet scene, by Mr Albert Callcott, is a fanciful and artistic composition. […] The grouping is good, and the termination of this Terpsichorean revel is exceedingly brilliant, for the seven Champions, in their gorgeous dresses, join in a "Can-Can" illustration of the gay Mabille[1]. The effect of the bright-coloured dresses among the white ones worn by the corps de ballet is very striking.

From the more ethereal regions of Fairyland a transition is made to the Palace of King Ptolemy (Mr H Rignold), a monarch blessed with two daughters, Una (Miss Ellen Leigh) and Stormosa (Mr John Murray). Ptolemy himself is rather energetic, not to say violent in manner, but Stormosa is a termagant of the most appalling kind. This character is played with great vivacity by Mr Murray, who appears as a girl of the period, with a mighty chignon, a short dress, and blue boots. Stormosa knocks the Royal guards off their feet, and keeps her papa and sister in a state of terror. Una is altogether an amiable contrast, and is very prettily acted by Miss Leigh. St George, of course, falls in love with her and she with him, Stormosa being obliged eventually to content herself with St Patrick of Ireland. Ahmider, the Prince of Morocco (Mr W H Harvey) comes to Ptolemy's palace as a Christy Minstrel, and is attended by a Nigger bodyguard, armed with the familiar banjo. These Nigger masks are very good, and throughout the Pantomime this important department of the grotesque has been well attended to. With one or more Niggers present a break-down becomes inevitable, and this is a form of amusement the Surrey public delight in.

St George, the brave and indomitable little Champion of England, undertakes to kill the Dragon, and as an earnest of his prowess, presents Ptolemy with the head of a crocodile that much disturbs the comfort of the Royal Court. This "property", fashioned by Mr Lloyds, is a good specimen of the class of work. The Brazen Pillar of Memphis, and Magic Seven Dials in the Valley of the Nile, is the scene of various exploits of the Champions, and here the fair Princess Una is spirited away by that grand Egyptian Kalaba, and is shut up in the brazen pillar. St George is surprised, confounded, and disgusted, but is not disconsolate. He is promised the assistance of his knightly friends, and sets off for the Dragon's haunt, into which Una has passed by the medium of the brazen pillar.

The Dragon's Cave is a capital scene, and the mythical animal himself is an admirable specimen of make-up, from his hideous head to his cloven feet. A better stage monster than this we have not seen in a long time. Before this *tableau* is discovered we should mention that St Denis, the pattern of gallantry, has extricated Eglantine (Miss Marie Paterson) from imprisonment in the trunk of a tree. In due time the fight between the Dragon and St George comes off in the cavern, and the monster, finding his tail very much in the way, amputates it without hesitation. The roar of laughter that follows this action may be well imagined. We may here take the the opportunity of giving Miss Millie de Vere her just due for her exceedingly intelligent, earnest, and most painstaking performance of St George. There is in her acting a downright intention and thorough devotion to the business of the stage, and Miss Millie de Vere never for one moment forgets that she is there to amuse the public and not herself. In a word, she knows her business and attends to it, instead of staring about the house and holding *sotto voce* conversations with those near her, as some burlesque actresses do. St George is in her hands just the brisk, active, and indomitable personage the author intended, and a better performance of its kind no-one could expect to see.

In the Crypt of the Black Castle and Cavern of the Seven Lamps, Stormosa and St George, armed with immense bull's-eye lanterns, encounter each other; and here the whole of the characters meet preparatory to the development of the Transformation Scene, entitled the Golden Corridor of the Temple of Ismalia, in the Glittering Glades and Gardens of Gladness. This is a triumph for the artist, Mr Albert Callcott. Though magnificent in the full sense of the word, the scene is simple in idea. From a bed of branching palms rises an avenue of pillars, in which Fairies stand like statues round a column. The centre of the stage is occupied by a temple refulgent with gems, and guarded by more Fairies. Over this *tableau* female figures are suspended, and the great area of the Surrey stage, crowded with glittering objects, is lighted up with the indispensable coloured fires. On the night we visited the Theatre this crowning glory was received with vehement applause. [...]

In the first scene [of the Harlequinade] the Clown produces much laughter by unceremoniously pushing his friend the Pantaloon into a Post Office letter-box, and afterwards serves ordinary passers-by in the same way. There is a Furnished Apartments scene, and this always implies a great amount of practical fun. Among other trials he has to put up with, the Clown is annoyed by a monstrous flea, and the whole scene is keenly relished. [...]
The Era, 2/1/1870

1871

Theatre Royal, Manchester
Dick Whittington and His Treasure of a Cat

[...] THE history of Dick Whittington, as related in the legends of the nursery, is pretty faithfully adhered to, but allied to it in the plot of this Pantomime is the story of the Yellow Dwarf, the two narratives being closely interwoven. It would seem that the personage just named, and who receives from the author the appellation of Gambogia (Mr Dampier), has conceived a passion for the Princess Brighteyes (Miss Jenny Taylor), daughter of Veri Hi Kokilaurum, Emperor of Morocco (Mr Barsby). His suit not being successful he seeks the aid of Huglioalstik (Mr C Cooper), a wizard, whose eyrie is situated "somewhere near Van Demon's Land", and who combines a high regard for the Rat tribe with a perfectly consistent aversion to the feline race. He grants his aid to Gambogia, on condition that a cat is never to be allowed within the precincts of the latter's Castle. The Dwarf then demands the Princess from her papa, and being refused summons his army of huge-headed followers, and after a conflict with a corps of beauteous Amazons attached to the Emperor's court, succeeds in carrying her off.

Dick Whittington (Miss Emmie d'Este), who after going through his usual adventures, hearing the bells predict his future greatness, making love to his master's daughter, and going to sea to make his fortune, is shipwrecked by the Wizard's arts, but reaches land on a raft, together with Captain Jack Bower (Miss Evah Hamilton) and his Cat. At the Court of the Emperor Puss puts to flight the legions of rats who make the monarch's existence a burden, and the Captain wins the regard of the Princess.

After she has been carried off, Dick and the Captain, accompanied by the Cat and the Emperor and his Court, set out in pursuit, and arrive at the Enchanted Castle, the threshold of which is guarded by a huge dog. The Captain valiantly severs the monster in halves, and the Cat, entering the Castle, breaks the charm by which the Dwarf maintains his power, and is himself changed into a rat. The Princess is of course delivered to be united to the gallant Captain, and Dick, loaded with riches, returns with his redoubtable Cat to his native land.

Here he discovers that his old master has been reduced to poverty, and has gone no one knows whither. His elevation to the dignity of Lord Mayor does not reconcile Dick to the loss of the lovely Alice (Miss Zerbini), who remains constant, and rejects the attentions of Bobby Neverswets (Mr H Taylor), Dick's former fellow 'prentice. She is likewise exposed to the rude commands of Gambogia, who has been transformed to a glaringly yellow policeman, and who orders her to "move on" "keep the peace". These injunctions are also addressed to Dick, who opportunely arrives, and who upon declaring his rank inflicts a final and crushing blow to the hapless Dwarf.

The reunion of the lovers being thus accomplished, undeniable proof of Dick's greatness is afforded by a representation of the Lord Mayor's Show. This pageant is the hit of the opening. The guilds and city companies are in the procession with their various banners and devices; Gog and Magog, tremendous beings some twelve feet high, appear; knights in armour, morris dancers, emblematic groups representing the seasons, the four quarters of the globe, and Britannia; the Lord Mayor's Coach and his numerous retinue, heralds, marshals, trumpeters – all are comprised in the procession, the rear of which is brought up by the ubiquitous Cat bestriding a bicycle, which Pussy's clever representative – the little fellow known as Young America – manages with surprising skill. […]

Covent Garden
The Sleeping Beauty; or, Harlequin and the Spiteful Fairy
OF the thousand and one legends of Fairyland that tempt that tempt the fancy and imagination of the pantomimic author at merry Christmas time we know of none more inviting than that of THE SLEEPING BEAUTY, and certainly there is no Theatre where the history of that remarkable damsel could be told with greater effect than at Covent Garden. Of course, the Sleeping Beauty is a Princess. Nothing short of royalty ever satisfies the craving of the juvenile mind for ideal magnificence, and even then it is a royalty unfettered by the narrow limitations of modern thrones.

The royalty of the young idea is something possessing endless power and universal splendour, so that when we are introduced, at the Opening of the Pantomime, to a regal christening, the richness of the banquet is taken for granted by our young friends in boxes and stalls. The Princess Dollfondella (Miss Nelly Smith), the infant heiress of King Dunderhead (Mr C J Smith) and his Queen, Fiveandfortina (Mrs Aynsley Cook) is about to cast unwonted responsibility upon her godfather, Baron Sponsorwitz (Mr Aynsley Cook), and her Fairy godmothers, chief of whom is Hygenia (Miss Marie Leslie). A number of distinguished guests are invited to take pot-luck with the royal host and hostess, and the Baron does not forget the customary knife, fork, mug, and spoon. The Fairy godmothers also come and endow the infant Princess with all those virtues and talents which elevate royal heirs and heiresses, and make them so conspicuous as examples to inferior mortals. But one important invitation has been neglected – that of the Spiteful Fairy, Maligna (Miss Julia Mathews), who, like some rich but crusty old bachelor uncle who must be conciliated, or poor relative who won't take offence, soon joins the party, and proves an element of discord. In a car, appropriately drawn by dragons, the Spiteful Fairy drives up to the Palace, making herself much more free than welcome. Maligna has, however, one redeeming quality. Instead of pouring forth her invectives in choice Billingsgate, she utters her maledictions musically, and prognosticates that the Princess will come to an untimely end through a wound from a spindle. But there is still a refuge for threatened Princesses where mortal afflictions count for nothing, and Hygenia conveys Dollfondella to Fairyland.

The wars of the Red and White Roses were mild in comparison with the tremendous feud that now commences between these rival enchantresses for command of the destinies of the Princess. Hygenia ultimately, when her *protegée* is fourteen years of age, seeks a husband for her in the person of Sir I O Hugh de Basinghall (Mr W H Payne), who with his lean and hungry squire, Chevy Chase (Mr Fred. Payne) are in a lamentable condition of impecuniosity, dunned by creditors who will not take "No!" for an answer, and worried, in addition, by the Housekeeper (Mr Taylor). Hygenia visits them, and promises Sir I O Hugh the hand of the Princess, only he will have to wait seven years ere the happy event can take place.

We are then introduced to the Valley of a Thousand Streams, a haunt of almost magical beauty, where a host of Sylphs and Fays indulge in a fairy revel as enchanting as it is appropriate to the scene. Maligna, however, still pursues the Princess, and tempts her in chase of a butterfly beyond the boundaries of Fairyland. Here she falls in with the royal hunting party, but would probably have failed to recognise her parents but for the presence of their pet dog (Master John Secchi). Once more installed in the royal nursery, Dollfondella is in greater peril than ever, for Maligna, disguised as an old woman spinning, wounds her with the spindle; but Hygenia once more comes to the rescue, and consigns the Princess to a sleep of one hundred years, to be awakened only by the kiss of her lover. In order to get over this difficulty Hygenia consults Father Time (Mr Marshall), who kindly consents to leap over a century to oblige a lady, but how to deal with Sir I O Hugh is the next difficulty. That chivalrous knight has become so decrepit during his hundred years sleep that he is no longer a suitable match for a Sleeping, much less for a waking, Beauty; but Hygenia kindly gives him an armlet, which restores his youth, and with his faithful squire Sir I O Hugh reaches the Impenetrable Forest with which Maligna has surrounded the Palace of his lady-love.

This is one of the most effective and remarkable scenes ever placed upon any stage. Encountered first by an army of frogs, leaping and croaking in every corner of the enchanted wood, the knight and his squire have scarcely driven off these enemies ere the very trees themselves assume goblin shapes. Every gnarled trunk is transformed into a weird and fantastic demon, and the skeleton branches wave their arms as if in defiance of the adventurous lover. Strange fires dance before his eyes, and stranger noises ring in his ears, when he remembers the armlet. Happy thought! The horrors of the enchanted forest disappear instantly, and through an opening in the distance is seen in the moonlight the castle of the adored one. Once more the knight presses onward assured of victory. In vain do bolts and bars, fiendish elves, and even the Spiteful Fairy herself, stand in his way. He penetrates the Castle, and peeps into the Chamber of the Sleeping Beauty. Then comes the kiss, the awakening, the last struggle against the power of Maligna; then victory, and the

Home of the Enchanted Bells, a Transformation Scene seldom equalled, and not surpassed by any Transformation Scene in our remembrance.

The Harlequinade begins, and we dash at once from the sublime to the ridiculous, and find ourselves, in the company of the Harlequin (Mr Fred Payne), Columbine (Mlle Vitocq), Harlequina (Mlle Hoffmann), Pantaloon (Mr Paolo), and Clown (Mr Harry Payne), at One Tree Hill, Greenwich. The fun of the fair is carried on merrily with a variety of hits at the popular follies, fancies, and fashions of the day, one of the illusions, received with immense merriment, being pointedly delivered at the Chancellor of the Exchequer, who, with Mrs Lowe, sat in the stalls, and laughed as heartily as anybody at the joke raised at his own expense.

The scene changes to an Uncomfortable Attic, where Clown and Pantaloon go to bed in happy ignorance that they will wake next morning in a Pine Forest in the Steppes of Russia. This was a charming scene, the tall pines, the wintry branches, and dull, frosty sky being painted in a manner which proves the artist, Mr H Cuthbert, to have uncommon abilities in depicting landscape. Some amusing incidents keep up the interest of this scene. Groups of Russian peasantry snowball each other with much spirit, and slide down the slope of a pine-clad ridge with great velocity, while Clown and Pantaloon are doing their best to avoid the embraces of a black and white bear who show a disposition to fraternise with them not at all inviting. The scene concludes with a Russian Revel, danced by eighty ladies of the corps de ballet, and then we are introduced to a National School, which gives an opportunity for some droll satire against the new school boards. Little boys, with "shining morning faces", creep so unwillingly to school that the teachers are compelled to drag them thither by main force, and Clown, whose system of school teaching evidently belongs to a past generation, administers the birch pretty freely. Sundry tricks and changes, introducing us to a Music Shop, with suggestions as to a forthcoming Royal Marriage[2], and a tartan plaid with a sketch of a bridecake in the centre, lead us to the last scene that winds up this eventful history, and we find ourselves once more for a brief space in Fairyland, the next transformation being the darkness and nipping atmosphere of the frosty street. [...]

The Surrey
My Son Jack; or, Harlequin Mother Goose and the Gaping, Wide-Mouthed, Waddling Frog
THE name of the Surrey is so closely associated with pantomime triumphs that its Christmas novelty is always eagerly anticipated even by the more aristocratic sight-seers whom nothing else would tempt to a Theatre south of the Thames. [...] Boxing Night at the Surrey can only be outrivalled in the enthusiasm it excites by by Boxing Night at "Old Drury", each being important items in the festivals of the pleasure-seekers of the North and South of the Thames respectively. The crowds which besieged the doors of the Surrey long before the time announced opening rendered the Blackfriars Road almost impassible. No sooner, however, did the time arrive than the rush for seats became like the rush of a mighty river, and money-takers, check-takers, box-keepers, and other attendants, were overwhelmed and bewildered by the surging overflow. Every seat soon had its occupant, the philosophical axiom that "two bodies cannot occupy the same space at the same time" being set aside for the occasion. In spite of danger the "gods" perched themselves on pillar and on post, and some hundreds must have entered the building who neither saw nor heard anything of the proceedings from first to last. [...]

During the long, and, we supposed, unavoidable delay which occurred after the farce with which the performance commenced the unanimity between the "gods" was something wonderful. First they whistled, then screamed, then hooted, then stamped, then whistled again, then a lull. But the lull was for an instant only. Like a well-trained choir of stentors, and as if in obedience to the *baton* of some, to us, invisible conductor, they in unison struck up a chorus in praise of "Old Mother Gum", and "Shout Hurrah for Old Mother Gum" was given again and again in a style which would have delighted the heart of that doubtless estimable lady had she been present. Wearied by these exertions refreshment was now the order of the night, and the bottles and baskets and their mysterious contents which we saw produced, and eagerly consumed, did as much credit to the appetites of the gentlemen without coats as their singing and shouting did to their strength of lungs.

The delay, however, at length came to an end, and good humour was reflected in every countenance as the curtain rose upon the "Grand Christmas Pantomime" entitled MY SON JACK; OR, HARLEQUIN MOTHER GOOSE AND THE GAPING, WIDE-MOUTHED, WADDLING FROG, produced under the direction of Messrs E T Smith and T H Friend. To describe the plot of this gigantic production, in which we fear to say how many nursery tales are combined, is somewhat difficult. But for the sake of the juveniles, in whose interest, of course, all Pantomimes are written, we will attempt the task.

The rising of the curtain revealed the Abode of Old Mother Shipton (Mr Dudley) in Motherland. That a preparation is going on for a Christmas feast we learn from a blazing cauldron, and from the good things put into the pot. But the proverbial slip 'twixt the *cup* and the lip is likewise applicable to the dish, and the repast, to which we find old Mother Hubbard (Mr J Marshall) and her Dog, Dame Trot and her Cat, Dame Durden, Mother Bunch (Mr Clements), Mother Redcap (Mr Wood), and other folk to childhood memory dear, have been invited, is upset by the arrival of the Demon of Discord (Mr H Butler), and his attendant, Mischief (Mr J Gardener), with a band composed of War, Despair, and other Demons too horrible to be tolerated at this festive season. Peace (Miss C Shelley), however, comes to the rescue with her faithful followers, Harmony and Plenty (Misses Claire and Clark).

By her magic wand we are next introduced to the Flowery Meads of Peace, a simple but charming scene, with a pretty lake view in the distance. This pleasant spot is soon filled by its fair inhabitants, represented by one hundred ladies of the corps de ballet, bearing wreaths of roses. The dances which followed were, we regret to say, not unattended by mishap, M. Dewine, whose skill as a dancer we have frequently had occasion to notice, catching his foot in some projecting part of the stage, and sustaining a sprain, which disabled him, at least for that performance. Mlle Clavelle, the *premier danseuse*, proved herself an accomplished dancer, and was loudly applauded.

In the next scene we are taken to Frog-dom, where Master Rowley (Percy Roselle) holds sway supreme. Rowley is an aspirant for the hand of Alice (Miss Anne Thirwall), daughter of Squire Hedgeanddish (Mr R Williams), but has a rival in his suit in the hero of the piece, My Son Jack (Miss Caroline Parkes), who is, of course, the offspring of Old Mother Goose (Mr G Yarnold). Inspired with jealousy by the demon Mischief, Rowley conspires with Booby, the Squire's son (Mr R Sweetman), to ruin Jack. In front of Mother Goose's Cottage, a pretty rustic picture, admirably arranged, we find Jack lamenting the absence of his mother, as lamentation can be illustrated by a song and a vigorous hornpipe, the latter being the first thing insisted on by the noisy "gods". His mother's return, accompanied by her Goose, is followed by the arrival of the Squire and his lady (Mr H Marshall), to demand his rent, the inability to pay which is to work Jack's ruin. Turned out of his house and home, even the Goose being seized, Jack's good genius comes to his aid in the person of Mother Shipton, who, we should have explained, has descended from beyond the moon in a basket.

From her Jack learns the auriferous powers of the Goose, and we then arrive at a Country Fair, where "merry-go-rounds", ginger nuts, Punch and Judy, thimble-riggers, and the usual festivities abound. This affords an opportunity for the introduction of M. Raslas, the "Man-Monkey", and of Etherton's performing dogs, the latter causing roars of laughter and thunders of applause in a novel and clever performance. Jack soon recovers his Goose. Booby gets completely "unrigged" at thimble-rig, and meets with no better luck at skittles, to which he is challenged by Rowley. Jack, with the proceeds of the golden egg, appears in gay attire, but is still rejected as a son-in-law by the haughty Squire.

We have next the appearance of the good Fairy, who magically brings to our view the Exhibition of 1871, before which takes place the most animated scene of the piece in a grand procession and ballet of all nations. Headed by the Lilliputian band – capital players upon wind instruments – come trooping representatives of every nation under the sun, bearing their distinctive banners, and attired in their national costume. The mingled mass of various colour, and the almost innumerable personages engaged in the procession, had a curious but pleasing effect; and a hornpipe, in which Britain's representatives displayed their skill, was greeted with uproarious cheering. For the gratification of the little folk we may at once disclose that this is *not* the Transformation Scene. A Surrey Pantomime must have more glorious surprises than one; and this was one of them.

Another suitor to Alice turns up at the Squire's mansion in Captain Rock (Mr J Everard), who orders Jack to be seized and carried away to sea, but again he is rescued by the good Fairy, who speedily sets our curiosity at rest, and discloses the grand Transformation, the Nativity of Venus. We shall not attempt to describe what is simply indescribable, but must content ourselves by saying that the blaze of brilliancy and beauty revealed to the spectator certainly equals if it does not surpass anything produced here in bygone years. [...]

The Harlequinade is well supported, and includes Harry Boleno, Clown; Tom Lovell, Pantaloon; Fred White, Harlequin; E Howard, Columbine. There are two scenes, the first representing the London Road Market by Morning, Noon, and Night, and the second the Terminus Hotel Kitchen. Both are capital sets, and in each the fun is of the genuine sort, some capital tricks accompanying the practical jokes in which Clown and Pantaloon indulge. And here we may, in all good humour, advise Harry Boleno to confine his practical joking to the stage. To pelt the audience with "dummy" 56lb weights is not funny, and might lead to retaliation of a more realistic nature. *Verbum sapienti*. In the "Kitchen" some really laughable proceedings take place, and the audience laughed as only a transpontine audience can laugh as Clown first decapitates an inoffensive policeman, and afterwards experimentalises upon the head. Another hornpipe – making about the twentieth which the gallery had demanded – was given by the Harlequin, and every one was charmed by the good looks and animated but graceful dancing of Miss Howard, as Columbine. The final scene of the Home of the Fairies formed a gorgeous conclusion to the gigantic and merry Surrey Pantomime of Christmas, 1870. [...]

The Era, 1/1/1871

"WHITTINGTON AND HIS CAT", at the Theatre Royal, Bradford, appears to have created a furore, *hundreds being turned away on many occasions, but on Saturday last the excitement reached a climax somewhat alarming. Nearly two*

> *hours before the time for opening many hundreds were clamouring at the "extra doors," which were opened very early; still the multitudes increased as train after train arrived from surrounding towns (one train alone consisting of twenty-six carriages). This continued until the band was heard by those struggling outside, who then became furious, and with a sudden rush burst open the other doors, only to find the place crammed, while those outside vented their rage by smashing the windows. It was only on the Manager's haranguing them that they could be dispersed.*
> The Era, 29/1/1871

1871

Astley's
Lady Godiva; or, St George and the Dragon

GOODANDPRETTI, Queen of the Fairy Realm of Awfullijolliland, having shown some slight disregard of punctuality, is rebuked by her Court. She explains that her fault was caused by the unexpected arrival of intelligence from earth that Leofric, Earl of Mercia and Coventry, and his wife, the lovely Godiva, have adopted a foundling as their son and heir; and further informs her interested hearers that they are all invited to the christening. As they are starting they overhear a conversation between the sorceress Kalyba and her familiar Hankipantrix, in which she commands him to accompany her to Coventry for the purpose of carrying off the child.

The three following scenes are laid in that ancient city and its suburbs. Leofric, having imposed more taxes than the citizens can pay, the latter are reduced to a condition of pauperism. To induce her stern lord to remit some portion of these imposts the Countess Godiva consents to ride through the city at noon "without a stitch upon her". Leofric issues a proclamation ordering the citizens to keep to their houses during Godiva's ride. The patriotic Countess performs her promise with scrupulous adherence to the prescribed terms, and the city is relieved from its fiscal burdens. But a prying tailor, one Tom Slyford, has been detected by Godiva in the act of peeping at her, and he is accordingly denounced by her to the infuriated populace, who drag him from his shop, and hand him over to King Edward, who attempts, ineffectually, to administer personal chastisement to the tailor. Godiva then undertakes the punishment of Peeping Tom, and is eminently successful in demonstrating the true significance of women's rights. Tom, having been knocked out of time by the vigorous and scientific Countess, is seized by the citizens, immersed in a horsetrough, and finally pumped upon. During the hubbub Kalyba enters, and carries off the infant heir, who has been christened St George. A reward is offered for the recovery of the stolen child, but has no effect beyond inducing a peasant and his wife, further urged on by the now revengeful Tom, to endeavour to foist a female infant of their own upon the now heirless earl as the real St George. The imposter is, however, easily detected.

A lapse of twenty years occurs, and we find Kalyba watching the sleeping St George, who, although arrived at manhood, has slept through the long interval. Having an impressionable temperament, the Sorceress has fallen deeply in love with the unconscious youth, who now wakes, and on being close pressed to admit Kalyba's merits, moral and personal, proves a very indifferent critic. Kalyba does not resent the youth's coldness, but at his solicitation, or rather demand, provides him with a squire, a fellow named Pickaback, and introduces him to the remaining six champions. Rendered unsuspicious by the warmth of her love for St George, the Sorceress, to humour him, lends him her magic wand, the power of which he immediately tests by enclosing Kalyba in a rock.

He then rides off with his companion champions in search of adventures, and arrives at Cairo, which, as well as the entire surrounding country, has been nearly depopulated by a most voracious dragon. Dismissing the champions to various parts of the Paynim world, St George undertakes the deliverance of Egypt from its terrible ravager, and at the farewell dinner given by the Khedive, in his harem, in honour of his daughter, the Princess Sabra, who has been selected by the Dragon for his next *piece de resistance*, he, in the presence of Kalyba, an uninvited guest, throws down the gauntlet and defies the monster.

The gallant youth, with his timid squire, proceeds to the Dragon's haunt, and the Dragon, summoned by the Sorceress, appears, and a deadly combat ensues. St George is nearly conquered, but the Dragon, who is as amorous as he is voracious, happening to catch sight of Sabra, forgets the peril he is in and makes mute declaration of love. St George immediately takes advantage of his opponent's blunder, and administers the *coup de grace*. He is, however, now attacked by a whole army of dragons, and with the greatest difficulty succeeds in vanquishing them. Thoroughly exhausted he falls to the earth, amidst the exultant gesticulations of the Sorceress, and the despairing cries of Sabra and the faithful Pickaback. Goodandpretti here proves that she can be of immense assistance to the "cause of truth and justice", and adjourns the action to the next scene, which is that of the Transformation. Miss Amy Sheridan will represent Lady Godiva, and Miss Marie Henderson, St George. Miss Cicely Nott and Miss Rose Mayne are also engaged.

Grecian
Zig-Zag the Crooked; or, Harlequin, the White Cat, the King, and the Pretty Princess

SCENE the first shows us the Cave of the Passions, where Demonio (Miss Denvil) learns that Prince Stoutheart is creating a monster to terrify all his rivals to the Princess's hand. Demonio immediately makes his way to the quarry, where he calls on Froggy (Master G Conquest) and bids him give him timely notice of the completion of the monster. The Prince Stoutheart (Miss M A Victor) arrives, followed by his servant, Quiveryquake (Mr John Manning). The monster now becomes animated, and, from his extraordinary form and movements, the Prince christens him Zig-Zag the Crooked (Mr G Conquest). Demonio instils the various passions in his mind.

The Princess Beauteous (Miss M Barrie) meets her lover, the Prince, and Zig-Zag seeing her, the passion Love fills his breast, and the lovers depart, the Prince somewhat sorry for having created a slave who, he thinks, may one day become his master. Demonio tells Zig-Zag that he shall go to court and bid for the Princess's hand; that he shall have magic power, and a faithful attendant in Froggy.

In scene three we see the Palace of King Locash (Mr Harry Lynn), who is attended by his Minister of State, Penniwise (Mr Jackson), and Headmuck (Mr W G Ross). He receives the various Princes, who bid for his daughter's hand. Prince Pettite (Miss Acton Burton), like the rest, is refused by the Princess, who has determined to wed none but Prince Stoutheart. Zig-Zag arrives in great splendour, but terrifies the whole Court; he gives the Princess three magic eggs. Possessing these she has but to wish, and her wish will be fulfilled. She immediately wishes for her father's consent to her marriage with her lover, and wishes Zig-Zag gone, who, in revenge, seizes the remaining egg, and carries the Princess off on his Winged Frog. All are filled with dismay.

Zig-Zag, to obtain her love, takes her to the Land of Fruit and Flowers, and transforms himself to a Pineapple. An incidental ballet takes place here. He then introduces her to Fairy Rosebud (Miss Lizzie Conquest), to whom she tells her woes, and she, touched by her distress, calls her true love. Zig-Zag instantly appears, tall and well-formed. Still she refuses him; and Zig, finding Stoutheart, instantly withers the flowers, and calls on Jack Frost (Mr Willimore) and John Snow (Mr Malcolm), who transform all to ice.

Zig-Zag then changes the Princess to a Cat, and conveys her to Cat Castle, where her parent and lovers learn the only way to transform her is to cut off her head and tail and and burn them within twenty-four hours, or by that time she dies. They do this, but Zig-Zag arriving at that moment, seizes head and tail, leaving all in distress. The Fairy Rosebud tells them to follow him to the Haunt of Reptiles. Here a fight takes place, still leaving the victory with Zig-Zag.

The characters now arrive at the Hall of Time, where a device is tried to postpone the evil hour, but in vain. Zig-Zag destroys them upon the stroke of the hour, but the life of the Princess is saved by the arrival of the Fairy Queen, who, as usual, sets matters right.
The Era, 24/12/1871

Theatre Royal, Manchester
The Children in the Wood

THE author, Mr J Strachen, has grafted some of the fairy characters in *A Midsummer Night's Dream* on the familiar nursery tale, and taken the usual licence allowed to Pantomimic historians in his treatment of the narrative so dear to childhood. The cruel uncle is the wicked Baron Graball (Mr Dampier), and the opening scene takes place in his library, whose voluminous contents are a curious commentary on the tastes of its owner. Here a number of imps are interrupted in their goblin gambols by Puck (Miss Tilly Wright), who summonses a grand cat show, which is attended by numerous pussies. The cat show is scarcely concluded when the Baron appears, very hungry and very angry, for the goblins have stolen his breakfast.

The Baron has turned a covetous eye upon the inheritance of his wards, William and Jane (Miss Lily Lee and Miss Josephine), "The Children in the Wood", and meditates their destruction. The Baroness (Mrs Bickerstaff) urges him to the deed much as Lady Macbeth incites her husband to the murder of Duncan. He summonses his "henchman", Roberto (Mr Harry Taylor), and confides to him the sanguinary task. What between his dread of the Baron, his own squeamishness, and his amatory difficulties with Marianne, the nursemaid (Miss Jenny Taylor), Roberto has rather an unhappy time of it.

We are next introduced to the Nursery, where the Babes are contending with a cross-grained governess (Mr Goating) and their cousin Arthur (Mr F Barsby), a spiteful and malicious urchin of the diminutive height of about five feet ten inches in his stockings. They, however, find a friend in Walter, the good gardener (Miss Emily Thorne), who is permitted to accompany them on their pretended journey. Roberto now appears, bristling with numerous swords and daggers, and with the conventional aspect of a villain of the deepest dye.

We next see the Bower of the Bonnie Bells, a lovely Fairy landscape, bathed in sunlight, with a beautiful lake glimmering through a row of palm trees. Here Oberon (Miss Laura Joyce), Titania (Miss Romanelli), and Puck confer on the best means of rescuing the Babes from their impending peril. They are joined by Prince Tantivy (Miss Eva

Hamilton) and his sister the Princess Diana (Miss Dot Robins), who are out on a hunting expedition, and who undertake the rescue of the orphans. To the Prince Oberon gives a magic sword and bugle, and then entertains his visitors with a Fairy ballet. A very pretty effect is produced when the tambourines borne by each Fairy change suddenly to bouquets. In this scene also Mlle Roze and M. Ajax dance a *pas de deux*. The lady is extremely nimble and graceful, and Monsieur, whose dancing is of a comic character, is clever and diverting.

The locale now changes to the Enchanted Wood, whither Roberto has led the guileless Babes in order to complete his wicked enterprise. Walter, however, interferes, and dares the villain to mortal combat. They fight, and Roberto receives a number of dreadful wounds, any one of which would have suffered to despatch a ruffian of less obstinate vitality. He, however, makes his escape, whilst Walter, believing him dead, goes in search of the children, who have during the combat wandered away. Night comes on, and the Babes lie down to sleep, and are visited by a flock of compassionate robins, who under Puck's guidance protect them from the cold with a coverlet of leaves.

Soon after the Prince and Princess make their appearance, and now the Enchanted Wood begins to justify its title. The trees assume hideous faces, with red and gleaming eyes; they become possessed of locomotive power, and move across the stage, tossing their huge arms about as if in search of prey. One ugly old tree has the audacity to wink at the pretty Princess, and others assume a hostile demeanour towards Tantivy. The magic sword, however, does the Prince good service, and enables him to put his foes to the rout, including one Skrattel (Mr Kellino), an evil spirit who shoots up and down vampire traps for the purpose of attacking or eluding him.

Tantivy and his friends now arrive before the Baron's Castle, and demand its surrender and the restoration of the persecuted Babes. The Sheriff, Sir Hubert de Konkey (Mr Clifford Cooper), who is the Baron's guest, inquires with judicial calmness if the Prince is the Claimant, and other jocular references are made to the Tichborne[3] *cause celebre*. The Sheriff then proposes to read the Riot Act, but Tantivy, having sounded his bugle three times, brings to his aid a host of warlike robins and steel-clad Fairies, who carry the Castle by storm. Walter, who has proposed to, and been accepted by the Princess, appears with the Babes, who are awarded their rights by Oberon and his Fairy Court, to the discomfiture of the Baron and the advent of the Grand Transformation Scene.

Language is inadequate to describe the transcendent beauties of this lovely production, which is the work of Mr Charles Brew, and is entitled the Nativity of Venus. Its first phase reveals the God of Day in the disc of the setting sun, whose rays spread out and illuminate the whole of the heavens. Jupiter descends on the pinions of his golden eagle, and counsels Apollo to retire. This being done, Jove declares he will create a being whose influence shall soften and elevate the rugged hearts of man, and descends into the ocean, in the bed of which giant marine plants are seen, from which emerge numerous lovely figures, till at length an anemone opens, and Venus herself is disclosed, the loveliest of all. She gradually ascends to the surface of the ocean, where she is met by a shower of roses, and, the lights being turned on the scene presents a tableau of indescribable beauty. [...]

Drury Lane
Tom Thumb the Great; or, Harlequin King Arthur and the Knights of the Round Table
[…] THIS is emphatically a Pantomime for children – the children so loved by the author (Mr E L Blanchard), who crowd about him at Christmas-time, and rifle his pockets for all the good things he has hoarded up for them. It flows over with loving-kindness and that particular delicate and pure fancy which suits the innocence of childhood, and is so esteemed by those of a larger growth who would imitate childhood's simplicity. "Let the great world spin for even down the ringing grooves of change." Elsewhere the purely comic business may be sacrificed for the glitter of pure extravaganza, and the entertainment may be overladen with costly magnificence; but here, at old Drury, combined with most welcome glitter are found the very effects which children most love.

How the little ones will chatter about the great Dolls' House in action! An original and charming effect; and then for months to come we shall hear nothing but descriptions of how the old Cow swallowed the Boy – how he was picked off a stile by a Brobdignagian Crow – how he was tumbled into the gaping mouth of Giant Blunderbore, returned into a convenient moat, and finally taken to King Arthur's Court in a monstrous Salmon. Add to these effects the mischievous schoolboys who bully old Gaffer and Goody, the frequent dances and songs, and, finally, the superb pantomimic art of the Vokes Family[4], possessing such a smile and a mirth-inducing manner, that, under its influence, a hermit would dance the "Cure", and we have at once a Pantomime which can have no rival.

The prologue or induction to the Pantomime is in the highest degree fanciful and ingenious. The dolls, at twelve o'clock, when their tormentors are in bed, discuss the horror of their position, and determine, as a mild revenge for the meltings, wrenchings, arm-pullings, and batterings they have endured, to make the children dream of the Pantomime they will see, and that happy hour when the Theatre will be visited, and the dolls left in peace. This scene is enacted entirely by children, and extremely clever children they are, dressed up in pretty imitation of every imaginable style of doll. Miss Amalia, who represents Dollalolla, Queen of Lowther Arcade[5], speaks her lines with delighted emphasis, and promises to be a valuable little actress. This pretty child is ably assisted by her companion dolls, who bear a look of marked intelligence. The interior of the dolls' house is capitally managed. The front of the house removes in the orthodox fashion, and then the three floors of a dolls' house are discovered with living dolls. In the bed-room the children are making beds and tidying up. In the parlour the dolls are receiving company. In the kitchen the cooks are at work with the dinner. The realism of this picture made the children shriek with delight.

The Pantomime proper commences with the Garden of Dainty Devices, a celebrated Dresden China Scene, which will soon be the talk of all London. A picture so elegant and refined as this has seldom been seen or attempted. The whole stage represents a drawing-room ornament of Dresden china, and the blues, yellows, purples, violets, greens, and ambers of the shepherds and shepherdesses, the golden cages, the baskets of flowers, when heightened by the lime-light, form a picture of surpassing beauty. A little maiden in our immediate vicinity covered her face with her hands and whispered to her papa that it was too beautiful to look at. But the gorgeous effect of the scene does not end with the mere scene. Miss Sylvia Hodson as La Faye, the Enchantress, summons Poetry (Miss Amy Fellowes), Painting (Miss Hasting), Dancing (Miss Nelson), and two more Fairies (Miss Burt and Miss Carry Morgan), and together they discuss the Pantomime subject, listening meanwhile to Music (Miss Russell), who sings one of Mr Blanchard's lyrics, "The Magic of Music", to a taking air, specially composed by Mr W C Levey. Then comes a superb Watteau ballet, the very perfection of taste, led by Mlle Marie Gillet, a most graceful *danseuse*. The scene changes all too soon, and hides a spectacle of perfect beauty.

We next find ourselves in the atmosphere of comic business at the Cottage of Gaffer Thumb (Mr H Naylor) and Goody (Mr Francis). The mischievous boys tease the old people, and are rewarded justly with spanks from the red-hot poker, and the couple are just complaining of the misery of having no children when in comes Merlin, the Enchanter, played by the favourite actor, Mr Brittain Wright, to grant their desire. Tom Thumb (Master John Manley) is born mysteriously, tumbles into the batter-pudding, and is carried off by the tinker prior to the triumphant entry of King Arthur (Mr F Vokes) and his rollicking court. They are preceded by Gybe Dagonet, the Court fool (Mr Fawdon Vokes), as active as ever, and their approach is the signal for a perfect hurricane of applause. In comes Sir Tristan (Miss Victoria), all purple and gold, a Knight so beautiful that ladies would faint at the sight of him, with a springy step and a laughing air which makes merry the atmosphere he breathes. In comes Sir Caradoc (Miss Rosina Vokes), all silver armour and apple blossom, the liveliest, merriest knight of all the Round Table, whose every step is a suggestion of fun, and whose smile is deadly in its effect. [...] Then the fun commences in real earnest. King Arthur in his yellow wig has a knack of putting his leg over everyone's head, Miss Victoria is for ever singing and showing her inimitable art, Miss Rosina is the very soul of fascination, while Miss Jessie (Sir Lionel), Miss Coveney (Sir Lancelot), and Mr Brittain Wright complete the merry party. They are in search of the lovely child; but alas! The child has been carried off in the pudding by the tinker.

Still laughing over the whimsicalities of the Vokes Family, we see the scene change to a country landscape, and here is danced an old English dance with pipe and timbrel, or rather timbrel and triangle. The dance, invented by the indefatigable Mr John Cormack, is singularly effective, and it was loudly cheered. Following on we see the swallowing of Tom Thumb by the Cow singularly well managed, and his fate with the Giant. So perfect are these illusions, and so cleverly managed the changes between the real Tom and the doll, that the audience is inclined to shriek when Mr Hurly Burly, the hideous giant, vomits the boy into the Moat of the Castle.

On we go again to another scene dedicated to the Vokes Family. This is the making of the wonderful pie by King Arthur in his own kitchen, accompanied by constant songs and innumerable dances by his inimitable knights. The appearance of the Princess Guinevere (Miss Alice Hamilton) stops the enthusiasm of the King regarding his matrimonial prospects, and Tom Thumb, though rescued like Jonah from the belly of a fish, takes arms against the invincible Arthur and beats down the guard of his knights.

An Encampment by Moonlight of General Tom Thumb's Lilliputian Army is then shown, and the Captain of the Guard (Master H Collard) sings a parody on "Oh, let me like a soldier fall" with such capital effect and with such musician-like tones that he is encored with a will. The upshot of the struggle between Tom Thumb and King Arthur may be easily guessed, and, having added that Merlin, madded by the art of the "wily Vivien" (Miss Marie Courtenay), and possibly charmed by her singing of a parody on "Il Segreto", becomes young again, and all difficulties having been surmounted, there is nothing to do but to take us to "Fairy Land, reflected in the light of Fancy's ever-changing colours".

This is of course the Transformation Scene, and is one of singular beauty. Picture a bouquet of revolving flowers, each cup filled with gold and silver Fairies, tinted now with the golden glare of the sun, now with the silver rays of the moon, now with the ruby glory of the sunset, now with the pale greenish tint of a midnight landscape, and you may have some idea of the beauty of Mr Beverly's Transformation Scene. [...]

We still enter our protest against the omission of the Pantomime formula at the actual Transformation, which Mr Blanchard has forgotten for two years. However, in come Messrs F Evans and W H Harvey, two capital and popular Clowns; Messrs Willie Harvey and Fawdon Vokes, most active Harlequins; Messrs Paul Herring and J Morris,

Pantaloons, who thoroughly know their business; and for Columbines, Misses Jessie and Rosina Vokes, for the sake of whose dancing the audience would consent to remain in the Theatre long past midnight. The only exception that could possibly be taken to the Harlequinade is that some of the scenes are a trifle lengthy. Possibly some of the artists in the Harlequinade forget that the audience has been sitting, laughing, and looking ever since seven o'clock, and that efforts should be made to insure rapidity, smartness, and a constant succession of incident in the Harlequinade. For instance, the scene called Furnished Apartments in Belgravia is a trifle too long, not as regards the merit of the business, but considering what has gone before. A Trip Waltz, danced by Miss Jessie and Mr F Vokes, could certainly not be dispensed with.

As is the custom nowadays, the Harlequinade introduces entertainments most varied and original, and may be separated distinctly from the Pantomime proper. On this occasion we have a performance by the Almonte troupe of very clever tumblers; Mr Harry White in a capital stilt dance; Mr Powell, who introduces his performing Cats, as well as a Pony and a Monkey; an imitation of Birds and Beasts (very clever) by Mr B Sloman and his daughter; a skipping rope dance (much applauded) by Miss Leslie, and a pretty jockey dance by thirty children. The points, however, which will probably be best remembered in the Pantomime are the trick of the animated furniture in the Belgravia Scene; the dancing of the "Dolly Varden Polka" – a charming effect – to the original music of Mr W C Levey; and a miniature representation of Frith's "Derby Day[6]", which fairly astonished the house on account of the completeness of representation. [...]
The Era, 31/12/1871

Jessie, Rosina and Victoria Vokes

1872

PAUPER CHILDREN AND PANTOMIMES
AT a meeting of the Industrial Schools Committee of Kirkdale, on Tuesday, last the following extraordinary conversation took place: – "Mr Hagger (the Clerk) said that an invitation had been received from Mr De Freece, the Lessee of the Theatre Royal, Liverpool, inviting the children of the schools to the Theatre to witness a performance of the Pantomime. A Member – Another Pantomime? Another Member – It would seem almost like a conspiracy. Mr

> *Stubbs said this was one of the results he foresaw, and one of the reasons why he opposed the children being allowed to go to the Circus. He did not object to the Circus, but he saw that it would be opening the door for the children going to other more objectionable places, and would have the effect of exciting the feelings and disturbing the minds of the poor children. Mr Aitken – It is not opening the door; the door has been opened all along until Mr Stubbs shut it. They have been to see Pantomimes before. Mr Stubbs – The more the pity. Mr Aitken – You should have seen how they enjoyed themselves. Mr Hagger – It is due to this gentleman who had been kind enough to send the invitation to give him some answer. The Chairman – We have given them one treat. Why should we thrust more treats upon them? Mr Chapman was not opposed to the children being allowed to go and see the Pantomime, but he did not think it was necessary they should go to so many places. Mr Guilliam – It would only be unsettling the minds of the children to send them to one place of this kind and then to another. Mr Chapman moved that in the present instance Mr De Freece's invitation be respectfully declined. Mr Aitken seconded this, which was agreed to.*
> *The Era, 28/2/1872*

Drury Lane
The Children in the Wood; or, Harlequin Queen Mab and the World of Dreams
[…] A WIZARD, necromancer, or supernatural being of some kind generally has the first word in Pantomime. This time it is Doctor Dee (Mr J Johnstone), alchemist, astrologer, fortune-teller, and impostor of the period of James the First. He is discovered stirring an unholy compound, which gives out flames of various colours, and scattered around him are the properties of his trade, such as the books inscribed with magic characters, and the miraculous crystal globe in which Dr Dee's interesting patients saw their future. The great man is visited by Geoffrey Nimble Legs (Mr Walter Vokes), running footman to Sir Roland (Mr Frederick Vokes), the cruel uncle of the nursery story. The manservant does not belie his name. His activity is wonderful, and his terror of Dr Dee is expressed in admirable action by this member of the Vokes family. Geoffrey gives the astrologer a letter from his master, who wishes to know how long his little nephew and niece will live. The stars answer to the effect that the babes will enjoy perpetual youth, and Geoffrey is dismissed.

The new Licensing Act is too good a subject for a satirist to lose sight of, and Mr Blanchard treats this new form of petty tyranny playfully, but incisively. Dr Dee is visited by a number of tavern signs, such as the Cat and Bagpipes, the Cock and Bottle, and the Spotted Dog, Mother Redcap (Miss Alma) being the pretty mouthpiece of the whole party. She enumerates the restrictions now put upon long-suffering Englishmen, and very much astonishes Dr Dee, whose ideas of the liberty of the subject are not in accordance with those of our beloved rulers. This closes the first scene.

The second is full of bustling life and fun, and practical facetiousness of the true pantomimic kind. At Magpie Hall reside the boy and girl, Master Willie (Miss Victoria Vokes), and Miss Mary (Miss Rosina Vokes), under the care of a nursery governess, Mistress Winifred (Miss Jessie Vokes). The "babes" object to studies of any kind, burst into tears and lamentations on the slightest provocation, and sedulously cultivate all the little airs and graces permitted to people of their tender years. Their disposition is sportive, swinging and skipping-rope exercises being the delight of charming Miss Mary, and leap-frog being the favourite diversion of Master Willie. Sir Roland visits his nephew and niece at Magpie Hall. A bad temper and a good appetite are the characteristics of this "wicked uncle". Mr Frederick Vokes personates the fiery nobleman with a quaintness and originality most amusing. He is capitally made up, with a bald head and a moustache that bristles up whenever his fits of rage are coming on. Sir Roland's temper is sorely tried at Magpie Hall. In the first place his servant Geoffrey insists upon turning the back of a mirror towards him when he wishes to do his hair. Again, when Sir Roland sits down to dinner he finds a small pig in the soup, and various other things happen for which the servants are belaboured with ladles, knives, and forks, according to the good old-fashioned plan. Children are a special horror of the wicked uncle, who is furious when he reads the message from Dr Dee, and immediately begins to think about making arrangements for their final disappearance. Sir Roland takes the lead in a general dance, throws his long legs over the heads of nephew and niece, and goes through a variety of contortions suggesting the absence of bones in his physical construction, and the probability of his extremities being jerked into the pit. The eccentricity of this member of the Vokes family of dancers and the grace and finish of the others are in pleasant contrast. The dance was encored, and will, we imagine, be redemanded every night.

Master Willie and Miss Mary are then supposed to sleep and enter the dominions of Queen Mab (Miss Violet Cameron). Here, under the beneficial rule of the Fairies the children dream of Little Red Riding Hood, Aladdin, Blue Beard, Cinderella, and the Four-and-twenty Blackbirds, who burst into song from the depths of a pie. Mr Beverly calls his pretty scene "The Ivory Gate of Dreams", and has so managed that distant objects shall be seen through a light film of gauze, supposed to represent a screen of gossamer web. The dream of the children is illustrated by groups, which appear to float through the air. Miss Cameron is only a child, but is clever beyond her years. The little lady comes down to the front and speaks her words with a distinctness and elocutionary force not always attained by actresses of long experience. This child's earnestness in her work might be imitated by many burlesque actresses who seem to think they are on the stage to amuse themselves rather than the public. Queen Mab is accompanied by Sonnambula (Miss Russell), Morphea (Miss Alice Hamilton), Somnola (Miss Kathleen Ryan), Fantasy (Miss Florence D'Arcy), Whimsy (Miss Miller), and Shadowina (Miss Lizzie Grosvenor). Sonnambula is vocally inclined, and Miss Russell's fine voice and cultivated style are very effectively exhibited in a gracefully-written song, *a la valse*, composed by Mr W C Levey. The solo is called "Beautiful Dreams". Mr John Cormack's ballet "A Gossamer Dream" is pretty and fanciful, and the grouping of the ladies, as they form various combinations with thin scarfs, is exceedingly effective. Miss Temple and Miss Mowbray, as solo *danseuses*, enhance the attraction of this scene, and the dresses are remarkably chaste.

The scene then changes to Sir Roland's breakfast room. He is mentally disturbed, and is plotting the deaths of the "babes". Walter, the Woodman (Miss Harriet Coveney), a dapper young man, and a courageous, appears to fall in with Sir Roland's views as to the extinction of the "babes". The chosen instrument is Rufus the Ruffian (Mr Brittain Wright), a bandit of the old Coburg[7] and Richardson's Show[8] pattern. He carries no end of cold steel in the form of knives and pistols, and his appearance is as villainous as a Pantomime mask and make-up can render it. Mr B Wright sang, danced, and acted to the satisfaction of the audience; and we must pay a deserved tribute to the bright and clever actress Miss Harriet Coveney, as Walter, the Woodman, who takes the children's part, but cannot prevent their being left to die in the wood. Willie and Mary's mischievous tricks are all over when they see the formidable creature who is to take them on a journey. Poor little Mary refuses to be conciliated, and the acting of the Misses Victoria and Rosina Vokes in the scene of the departure is especially good. Before they leave Magpie Hall the children set free their pet bird and squirrel, and this bears upon what follows in the forest scene.

The "skirts of the wood" are soon reached, and a party of boys, habited as hunters, sing in unison the old Bohemian melody known here as "Unfurl the Gypsy's Tent". One of the prettiest effects we have ever seen in Pantomime occurs in the scene of the Foxglove Dell. The notion may be old or may be new – in either case it is graceful in the extreme, and would be advantageously worked out at greater length. When entering the forest the children are supposed to hear the melody "The harp in the air", and to think of dreamland. The Fairies are watching over them, and each flower opens to show a girl's face, which disappears when the flowers close.

The Depths of the Wood is the title of one of the most elaborate scenes in the Opening of the Pantomime. Huge trunks of trees in position at the back of the stage have their uses, and the gloom of the forest is suggested with the force to be expected from an artist of Mr Beverly's skill. Walter, the woodman, turns aside the dagger intended for little Mary, and saves her life and that of her brother. Rufus decamps, and the "babes" are left to cry themselves to sleep on a green mound. The stage is then unoccupied, until a squirrel cautiously peers forth from one of the tree trunks. Another follows, and in a little time they swarm among the branches, leap to the ground, and and surround the children. The squirrels make way for a whole flock of forest birds, also the very good friends of the ill-treated brother and sister. These cover them with leaves as shelter from the cold, and the squirrels bring nuts to save them from perishing of hunger. […]

Rufus calls upon Sir Roland for his fee, and presents his account for payment. The depraved noble offers to fight Rufus for the amount, and vanquishes him in a broad-sword combat on the melodramatic model. Willie and Mary appear, none the worse for their temporary seclusion in the forest, and Sir Roland expresses contrition for past offences.

Mr Beverly, who was enthusiastically called forward when the Transformation was fully developed, has chosen "Queen Mab's Car" as his subject. This choice gives excuse for any venture into the domain of the fantastic and imaginative. The idea sought to be embodied is pretty in itself. At the back of the stage, supposed to represent a lake, is the fairy car of Queen Mab. The whole structure advances towards the footlights, and in front of it are some milk-white doves moving their wings, and guided by Fairies. These birds are held by blue streamers, and from the topmost height of the stage hang long fibres of gold and silver. The central groups of Fairies and the surrounding figures brought into the design have a very rich and brilliant, but singularly refined effect, and the whole Transformation may be described as a pretty idea, worked out in the best possible taste.

As usual at Drury Lane, where the comic business is a great consideration, a double company of pantomimists is engaged. The two Harlequins are Messrs Walter Vokes and Willie Harvey; the Columbines are Miss Jessie Vokes and Miss Lizzie Grosvenor; the Harlequina is Miss Rosina Vokes; the two Clowns are Messrs F Evans and W H Harvey; and the Pantaloons are Paul Herring and J Morris. A group of artists more perfect in their several departments could not be found, and, in no spirit of slight to the rest, we may specially praise Mr F Evans as one of the Clowns. [...]

Frederick Vokes

Fawdon Vokes

Grecian
Nix, the Demon Dwarf; or, Harlequin, the Seven Charmed Bullets, the Fairy, the Fiend, and the Will-o'-the-Wisp
TAKING *Der Freischutz* as a foundation, the authors have built up a Christmas entertainment as thoroughly calculated to please the holiday public as any we have seen.

The incidents upon which Weber's famous opera were written serve admirably for Pantomime. Consequently we follow the fortunes of the handsome young lover who gets into the clutches of the Demon Huntsman with the keenest interest, increased tenfold when a gigantic head waddles upon the stage representing Nix, the Demon Dwarf, whose aid has been solicited to assist the Demon Huntsman in his conquest of the hero.

The various scenes in which King Cockalorum (Mr H Lyne) figures, and especially the rifle match, where that remarkable monarch proposes to bestow the hand of the Princess Duxidearie (Miss Lizzie Beaumont), his daughter, on the best shot, caused infinite amusement and not a little astonishment when Nix, the dwarf, who has been concealed behind the target, is shot, and by a startling mechanical change is suddenly transformed from the monstrous grotesque shape in which he had hitherto appeared to a sprightly fiend, far more mischievous than ever, who instead of aiding the Demon Hunter, determines to possess Duxidearie himself. It would fill a volume to relate all the schemes of this ubiquitous fiend, who is here, there, and everywhere in a moment, now fighting a phantom combat, where at every stroke of his opponent's sword he disappears into the bowels of the earth – now flying through a trap and alighting upon some frail support in mid-air – now leaping from a tall rock or terrible precipice upon his foe – now transforming at a word a brilliant saloon to a magical forest, where fairy forms are couched under every tree, where rippling fountains gleam in the silvery moonlight, and all that is beautiful and fairylike tempts the unconscious lovers to wander in its deceitful bowers. We need hardly say that Mr George Conquest is the magician who performs all these wonders, and to his extraordinary talent the greatest effects of the Opening are due.

The Transformation Scene at the Grecian is of unequalled beauty, change after change revealing to the delighted audience new features of form and colour, and eventually becoming elaborated into one gorgeous blaze of bewildering splendour, in which all the resources of the scene-painter, the carpenter, the machinist, and composer, with the entire array of pretty faces presided over by Mrs Conquest, are called into requisition, and the enchanted audience shout until they are hoarse the approbation of the result achieved.

Nor is the Transformation Scene the only good effect of the Pantomime. A scene called the Skeleton's Haunt, reproducing on an immense scale the effects familiar in *Der Freischutz*, is introduced, only at the Grecian we have twenty times the number of weird phantom shapes with, among other things, a self-acting skeleton, who does the drollest things imaginable, administering a right-hander his bony fist, bestowing a kick upon royalty with his fleshless foot, opening and shutting his cavernous mouth, and smoking a cigar besides. In this scene there are skeletons of strange beasts, birds, and fishes, such as Noah might have been familiar with before the Deluge. Altogether, the

Skeleton's Haunt and the phantom fight which takes place there, may be set down as one of the most fantastic and novel scenes ever witnessed.

Another pretty effect is the Enchanted Wood, a charming rustic landscape, painted upon a transparent canvas, illuminated from behind the scene, and a series of dissolving views are thrown upon it from time to time, terminating with a group of magnified insects, &c, which caused as much surprise to the "gods" as to how they came there as good old King George manifested respecting the apple dumpling. So much to the taste of the Olympians was the scene that they encored it at once, and it was repeated to gratify them. […]

When we come to the Harlequinade we find a host of things to commend. Little Levite as Clown to begin with, who danced so gaily and played such merry pranks that he became a tremendous favourite in five minutes – and his popularity increased until all he did was greeted with thunders of applause. Scarcely less successful was Pantaloon in the hands of Mr Reuben Inch – a good Pantaloon every inch of him. Mr Ozmond was a clever Harlequin, hardly light enough for the lofty leaps, but admirable in his attitudes and his dancing. The Columbines were Misses Gerrish and Squib. The latter name sounds quaint for a Columbine, but we quote from the bill. Anyhow, Squibs or Rockets, "nothing could go off" better than the performance of the ladies.

What shall we say of the comic business? Shall we tell how Clown and Pantaloon caused a terrible confusion on Margate sands by tumbling into the sea, and when a crowd rushes to their rescue they suddenly leave their hold on a rope that is hauling them ashore and allow their preservers to fall backward? Shall we describe how the Clown sets up as a Dentist and pulls out a gentleman's tooth nearly a foot long? Or how he transforms a flower pot into a modern bonnet? Or how a pack of magic cards are played which decide some important questions of the day? Or how Clown and Pantaloon set up an electric battery which turns everybody to shakers, and causes the Policeman who arrests them to shake most of all? […]

Only the Pantomime was given on Christmas Eve, and that alone occupied from seven o'clock until midnight, at which time the curtain fell upon a success which had been proved beyond question.
The Era, 29/12/1872

1873

IN the Harlequinade of the Pantomime at the Theatre Royal, Bradford, Mr E Laurie (the Clown), has introduced a trick which is worthy of remark. We all know that in Harlequinade the poor policeman as a rule gets more kicks than halfpence. In this case the Clown seizes a huge knife and cuts off one of the legs of the "active and intelligent" officer. The amputated leg remains stationary on the stage until its owner, with the single leg he has left, commences to dance a hornpipe. A fellow feeling at once induces the amputated limb to follow suit, the effect, of course, being comical in the extreme. The mystery is explained when we state that Mr Laurie is assisted in this trick by M. Pierrot, the famous one-legged dancer.
The Era, 9/2/1873

Princess's
Little Puss in Boots; or, Harlequin the Cruel Ogre and the Miller's Son
[…] THE overture to a Pantomime is no unimportant matter, and Mr Barnard has composed an excellent one on the most popular melodies of the day, which were accompanied by the Olympians with their usual gusto.

The curtain then rises on the Lower House of Cat's Parliament. The Cats are assembled, and their different faces and their expressions of assent and dissent in the voices peculiar to the feline race caused much merriment. The cats are indignant at the cruel treatment they receive at the hands of man, and Felino, Secretary of War (Miss Lewis), proposes that hostilities be at once commenced against the human race. This is opposed by the leader of the house, and the debate growing decidedly unparliamentary, Minette, the Fairy Queen of Catland (Miss Everard) rises to order, and proposes that one of the cats should render such service to some mortal as to secure better recognition of their merits for the future. Puss (Miss Fanny Heath) volunteers; his services are accepted; he is endowed with human form, and departs on his errand as Puss in Boots. The scene ends most effectively with a song and dance to the popular air of "The Magic Circle".

The second scene is the Interior of Muggin's Mill, where we find Bloco (Mr Tye), and Duffero (Mr Quentin), the late Miller's nephews, and Ferret, a Notary (Mr Lloyd). To them enters Jocoso, the Miller's youngest nephew, and the Cat, which is the only thing he has inherited. Being left alone, he receives a visit from the Fairy, who changes the Cat into the Puss of the first scene, who invites his master to set forth at once in search of fortune to the Court of King Kokahoopo.

The next scene is that monarch's Palace, which commences with the entry and evolutions of a number of Ashantee warriors, made up with some of the most comical and grotesque masks we have ever seen. Minette appears to watch over the fortunes of her friend, and sings a very pretty and poetical song, "How nice to be a fairy", which was encored. We next make acquaintance with the King (Mr Egan), a terrible monarch indeed, even for a Pantomime one; his lovely daughter Opaline (Miss Lloyd), her attendant, Blanc de Perles (Miss Villiers), the Lord Chamberlain (Mr Bruton), and chief Cook (Mr Bush). The King is in great trouble because there is no game for dinner, but the Royal mind is relieved by the appearance of Puss with a present of partridges. Jocoso is then, by Puss's artfulness, supplied with a handsome suit from the King's wardrobe, and introduced as the Marquis of Carabas. He and the Princess fall in love at first sight, and the King accepts an invitation to spend a month with him at his Castle.

Then arises the question of how the Castle is to be procured, and in the next scene Puss and Minette agree to storm the Steel Castle of the Ogre, an ancient enemy of the feline race, being a descendant of one Care, who is notorious for having killed a cat. This same Castle is a good scene, and here there is a grand review of Amazons in brilliant dresses, admirably arranged by Mr Milano, and greeted with much applause. The Ogre (Mr C H Fenton) is a most awful person, but very funny withal. He is evidently, as we suppose Ogres generally were, a *bon-vivant*, and, to judge by his guards, an admirer of female beauty, and probably too gallant to eat the fair sex. Puss calls upon the Ogre to turn out of his property, and on his refusal the army of Cats storm the Castle, and after a terrific combat between them and the Ogre's guards, the Cats are triumphant. Puss is now obliged to resume his original shape, but at the request of Jocoso Minette consents that he shall retain his human form, and all ends happily, with the union of Jocoso and the Princess in prospect, and a chorus to a remarkably pretty air.

Surrey
Jack and the Beanstalk, and See-Saw Margery Daw; or, Harlequin Man in the Moon and the Love Birds of Fairyland
[…] AFTER the National Anthem by the band, a medley overture on popular airs was played with great spirit, and the curtain rose on the den of the Demon Butcher. Here we see Marrowbone, the King of Low Spirits and evil genius of the piece (Mr G Cullen) his journeyman, Sheepanasti (Mr W E Cuthbert), with their friends, Taxation, Adulteration (a party of the name of Simpson), Licensing Act, Old King Coal, Discord, and Railway Signal, who chuckle over their respective successes in causing unhappiness during the past year. They are interrupted by the appearance of Benevolentia (Miss Florence Dodd) and her attendants, Ruby and Rainbow (Miss Leoni Chesterfield and Miss Bessy Lee). These good Fairies have resolved to protect the hero of the Pantomime, and the Evil Spirits naturally desire to thwart their benevolent intentions.

The scene now changes to the Exterior of the Widow's House and Dairy, an exceedingly pretty set scene, which elicited a well-deserved call for the artist. Here we are introduced to Jack's mother (Mr James Fawn), who had a hearty reception. The old lady is a cow-keeper in reduced circumstances, which may be some excuse for the daring infringement of the new Act, to which the pump standing opposite her house is a strong temptation. The Act is apparently in force, as two officials, described as Lachrymose Lactometers (Messrs G Russell and Mr E James) appear, and test the milk in the old dame's cans, and are treated by her in a way which suggests that she had but little respect for the dignity of the law.

Her son Jack (Miss Nelly Power) now appears, and is warmly greeted by the audience, and, after an effective duet, mama leaves young hopeful to sell their only cow. The Demon Butcher offers to become a purchaser; the cow is led forth for inspection, and a very fine cow it is. We can safely assert that there was none like it at the Agricultural Hall this year, and that it would be sure to carry off the first prize at any cattle show in the world. Jack and the Butcher having come to terms, celebrate their bargain in a song and dance, and the cow, *mirabile dictu*, takes her part in the breakdown, and does it very well. This was very funny and caused much laughter. The Butcher having departed with the Cow, Jack shows the bag of gold to his proud parent, but to their dismay the coins have all turned to beans. The old lady is very angry, banishes her son from home, and will not listen to the intercession of his sweetheart, Margery Daw (Miss Marie Stuart). Poor Jack is left alone, and falls asleep. A group of little Fairies appear to watch over him, and by the spells of the kind Fairy Benevolentia the beans, which were thrown away in disgust, grow up at once, and form the beanstalk which reaches to Fairyland. She also tells Jack in his sleep that her friends the Love Bird Fairies are shut up in their cage in Fairyland, and can only be released by a mortal.

Jack wakes up, and climbs the beanstalk, and the scene changes to the Regions of the Moon, where he makes the acquaintance of the Man in the Moon, aptly described in the bill as "a fine bright chap" (Miss Nelly Moon), and is introduced to the Morning Star (Miss Lizzie Mordaunt), the Evening Star (Miss Rose Mandeville), the Southern Star (Miss Jane Rayner), and Night (Miss Elliott). The clouds now disperse, and show the cage of the Love Birds, a most beautiful fairy scene, which gained another summons for the artist and for Mr Holland. Here Jack meets with the King and Queen of the Love Birds (Miss Adina Thornhill and Miss Marie Patterson) and their attendants (Miss Katie Liston and Miss Clara Martin), and from these he receives some fairy gifts in return for his services. The admirable ballet in this scene is worthy of Mr Milano's reputation, the dances by the three sisters Elliott and the solo dance by one of them are perfectly charming, and the grouping and evolutions of the Fairies bearing silver feathers produce a most brilliant and harmonious effect, greeted with loud and prolonged applause, and a call for the popular ballet-master.

We are now taken to the Kitchen of the Giant Grumble Grin, a clever grotesque scene. The Giant (Mr E D Lyons, a gentleman of really gigantic stature), goes to sleep after his dinner, and Jack, his mother, who has come in search of him, and the Giant's Page Liveliboi (Mr W B Fair) carry off the hen which lays golden eggs.

We next meet with them in the Baronial Hall of Sir Roger de Coverley (Mr H Hemmings), where Christmas is being kept in the good old style, and among the guests are Jack and his mother, who have become rich by means of the golden eggs. The Man in the Moon is also on a visit to Earth. A capital representation is here given of a Christmas merrymaking in the olden time. The mummers, Father Christmas, Merry Andrew, Friar Tuck, Robin Hood, Maid Marian, and other characters too numerous to mention crowd the stage, and at last a good old country dance brings the scene to a merry and effective conclusion.

Jack's troubles now appear to be over, but he has a rival, one Robin (Miss Nelly Herbert), who, rejected by Margery, seeks aid from the Demon, and carries her off to the Castle of Malignant Spirits; but this is stormed by Jack and his friends, and after an exciting battle, the lady is rescued, and the Demon and his ally, the Ogre, are defeated, and all ends happily in a magnificent scene, which is fairly entitled a Glorious Transformation. This has both artistic merit and novelty in design, as well as gorgeous brilliancy, and forms a worthy culmination to a most excellent and elaborate Pantomime Opening.

As only one scene of the Harlequinade was represented, and as we were informed that this was incomplete, we must postpone our notice of it to another occasion. Mr Holland assured the audience that it would all be complete on Boxing Day; and we have no doubt from the names of the artists engaged in it that it will be worthy of the rest of the entertainment.

To return to the Opening. In such charming young ladies as Miss Nelly Power and Miss Nelly Moon Mr Holland has undoubtedly had more than one *(N)elli*ment of success to begin with; both of them sang, danced, and acted admirably, and all the other ladies whom we have named were satisfactory in their respective characters. Mr James Fawn's impersonations of female character are well known over the water, and on this occasion he could scarcely have disappointed any of his admirers. We would, however, suggest that his make-up would be improved by the sacrifice of his moustache. [...]
The Era, 28/12/1873

1874

ALL lovers of Pantomime are by this time aware that Mr Rice in his magnificent and amusing Pantomime Little Red Riding Hood *at Covent Garden has introduced a number of real sheep, which nightly excite the admiration and enthusiasm of all the little people whose good fortune it is to be present. On the occasion of the recent visit of their Royal Highnesses the Prince and Princess of Wales and family the said sheep were introduced to the Royal box, much to the delight of the Royal children, whose expressed sympathy on account of the fate which they imagined would await the "muttons" when the Pantomime had run its course led to an offer of purchase by his Royal Highness, an offer, however, which was respectfully declined, Mr Rice being in no hurry to sacrifice his pets.*

AMONG the "tricks" likely to live long in the memory of those who witness it, and introduced into the capital Pantomime which nightly delights crowded audiences at the Surrey Theatre, is the sudden transformation at the touch of Harlequin's wand of a huge tree into the head of Mr W Holland, "the people's caterer", on whose world-renowned moustache a couple of acrobats perform a series of feats which astonish all beholders. The "trick" is as amusing as it is novel, and never fails to elicit loud laughter and applause.
The Era, 18/1/1874

Surrey
The Forty Thieves and the Court Barber; or, Harlequin and the Five Tiny Pigs, the Sad Little Prigs, and the Fairies of the Laburnum Lake
[...] SCENE the first is called the Witches' Rookery, the abode of Alabad (Miss Florence Arden), an evil spirit, but, as frequently happens in Pantomime, of very comely appearance. Alabad bears a family likeness to our old friend Mephistopheles, and his familiars are the Witch of Endor (Mr G Reeves), and the Fat Woman of Brentford. Alabad's opponent in his lawless design is Titania (Miss Celine Wallace), who is attended by Puck, a tricksey spirit (Miss Kate Russell).

Not long after the rise of the curtain a pretty rural landscape is disclosed, with cottages and the usual adjuncts all complete. This is a very lifelike scene, so far as inanimate nature is concerned. The inhabitants of the favoured region are all literally pig-headed. Five young porkers and their parents, with long ears and snouts, go through various facetious performances, and in this situation the talents of Mr T Elliott as Old Mother Pig, Turtle Jones as their eldest son, and others of the Elliott family as little pigs, are employed with great advantage to the life and bustle of the scene.

The pig colony is disturbed by the entrance of Alley Barber, who strikes a bargain for a finely grown donkey, which they take back to Bagdad.

Their servant Morgiana (Mlle Annetta Scasi) is much given to vocalisation, and her singing is fortunately something of a counteracting influence to the extremely dolorous complainings of Cogia (Mr H Nichols), the long-suffering Alley's wife. In this scene Mlle Scasi sings a ballad, "My Lonely Cottage Home", composed by the conductor, Mr Sydney Davis. One of Alabad's *protegès* is Abdallah (Miss Nellie Moon), the handsome and dashing young Captain of the Forty Thieves, who attempts to carry of Morgiana, but is foiled by Ganem.

The Bagdad family are left in peace, and we are taken to the Haunt of the Fairies of the Laburnum Lake, a really beautiful scene, painted, we presume, by Mr Grieve. It is an extensive and picturesque "set", and the effect of the sun-tinted mountains on the opposite side of the lake is remarkably good. The foreground is taken up with foliage, flowers, and rocks of the usual fantastic form peculiar to fairyland, and Titania holds chief command over the revels. Alabad sows discord between the bee and butterfly fairies, but the enmity between these graceful partisans does not appear to be very strong. The introduction of children in a ballet is not generally followed by good results. In this case, the groupings and general action are much improved thereby. The ballet is full of pretty notions and effects devised by M. Espinosa, and with one or two repetitions will be a thing to see. Simplicity and good taste are observable in the dresses, and the black and gold costumes of the bees contrast well with the plain white of the butterflies. […]

In the next scene, representing the shaving shop of Alley Barber, Cassim, his brother, calls, and threatens to sell him up for the rent of his house. Alley and Ganem are next seen in the "wood near Bagdad", accompanied by the much-beloved donkey (a good example of stage contrivance, by the way), and pursue their new trade of wood-cutting. Suddenly they hear a trumpet signal, and that tells them the forty thieves are on the march to their cave. They enter, fully armed, and Alley and Ganem keep watch from a convenient tree they have climbed. Abdallah, in a splendid dress, is attended by his subordinate officers, Hassan (Miss Rose Mandeville), Assad (Miss Lizzie Mordaunt), Ahmed (Miss Walsingham), and Feriz (Miss Beaumont). All these ladies are magnificently costumed, and form a remarkably brilliant group.

The mysterious door into the cave opens and shuts, and the thieves disperse, leaving the way clear for any enterprising individual to enter. The cave is left in charge of Hasserac (Mr W B Fair) and Muley (Mr G Reeves), a black slave. Cassim finds his way to the interior of the cave, of vast extent, and full of plunder. This is one of the great scenes of the Pantomime, and is particularly clever, both in drawing and in colour. Cassim is pounced upon in a state of inebriety, and an instantaneous court-martial of the forty thieves condemns him to death. The thieves here go through the evolutions to which we have already alluded. They are by no means simple, but include changes of position and formation that would take some time in the learning. Armour is extensively used in these handsome dresses, and a powerful light thrown upon it produces an effect positively dazzling. Armour is always an expensive article for the stage, and there is no stint of it in this scene.

Morgiana's vengeance on the forty thieves, who come to wreak their vengeance on her master, soon follows. Before she pours the boiling oil, or to speak literally, the hot water, into the jars, she bursts into song. This time it is the "Scasi Waltz", composed expressly for her by Amy Weddle. Miss Weddle will, perhaps, do better next time. Mlle Scasi has a very forcible style of singing. She was vehemently applauded, and had to repeat the solo.

The Transformation follow hard upon the retribution awarded to the thieves, and is a grand specimen of its kind. Through successive changes it progresses until the whole area of the stage shows a mass of recumbent and partially recumbent figures. Fairies rise slowly upwards, and at the back are small temples each enclosing a draped figure. The effect of the richly-coloured dresses is very grand, and this Bower of Queen Titania, as it is called, is a stage picture of rare beauty. An accident occurred to one of the ballet. Some part of her dress ignited, but was extinguished immediately, and without occasioning any delay in the working of the scene. […]

The Grecian

Snip-Snap-Snorum; or, Harlequin Birds, Beasts, and Fishes

[…] THERE is a certain fascinating Princess, Sweetlips (Miss Lizzie Conquest), whose lips and whose hand are sought by all the world in general, and by Herbert the Hunter (Miss Annie Delamonte), and and Prince Violet (Miss Millie Cook) in particular. Her father, King Furibon, the Furious, changes his bitter foe, Demonio, by turns into a Bird, a Monkey, and an Oyster, being himself transformed before the story is completed, from a King to a Lackey, and becoming, in consequence, the subject of kicks innumerable. And here we pause to remark that the idea of a French comedy produced in Paris some eighteen months since has been very ingeniously worked out, and gives rise to some of the most amusing episodes in the production. The valet of Prince Violet – by name Quake – is a kind of human talisman. Slap him in the face and wish, and the wish is granted. After three wishes the locale of the extraordinary charm is changed, and ere it finds a seat

Just in the place where honour's lodged.

Poor Quake suffers much, but the King, when he has changed places with him, suffers more; for, being mistaken for the charm-bearing lackey, he is kicked from pillar to post, and is fain to seek refuge even in the Mangrove Swamp, where, by the aid of Daddy Longlegs, he succeeds in capturing his foe Demonio, now bearing the form of a monkey, and to pave the way for felicity all round.

We skim thus lightly over the story because more important matters claim our attention. And first among these is the marvellous versatility displayed by Mr George Conquest. The wonders he has worked in previous years; the curious forms he has taken, ranging from an animated oak tree to a being all head, we have duly recorded in these columns. Now he has fresh mysteries in store. When we first catch a glimpse of him in the Devil's Pool, he bears the form of a bird. But what a bird! Perhaps it may be most aptly described as having the appearance of an ornithological giraffe; endowed with speech; something of a philosopher; susceptible of the tender passion; and with marvellous capacities in the way of yawning, sleeping, and winking its left eye. And then the monkey! Never was monkey like him seen upon the stage. Not only in those entomological hunts in which monkeys delight, but in every movement was this one most natural. His tail was eloquent of fun; his teeth cracked jokes as well as nuts; the art of "how to scratch" was illustrated in a style so graphic as to have made glad the bosom of a Scotchman; and his agility was on a par with that of the prehensile-tailed denizens of tropical forests.

And this agility reminds us that we have not yet alluded to the Phantom Flight in the Mangrove Swamp. In previous years we have described its various details, and it only remains to be said that now, as then, the Conquests, *pere et fils*, shoot upwards like rockets, shoot downward like meteors, appear and disappear with lightning-like speed, dart hither and thither in fashion quite bewildering, and, in fact, become living embodiments of perpetual motion. [...]

Mr Herbert Campbell[9] as Furibon the Furious, and Mr Arthur Williams as Quake, not only sang well and danced well, but contributed no small share of the fun. There is the scene in the King's Bed Chamber, for instance, where the two worthies who have changed their identities, as explained above, quarrel for possession of the bed and over the time-honoured maxim which says – "Last in bed puts out the light". The King's Bed Chamber boasts a light which won't be put out, or rather which, being put out, puts itself in again, and here the laughter of the spectators is loud and long. [...]

And even now we have not told of the merry music and the incessant fun of the third scene – the King's Palace, Vestibule, and Grand Staircase; a scene which comes before us literally in the twinkling of an eye. Nor have we described the wonderful procession of Birds, Beasts, and Fishes, embracing "specimens" which range from an elephant to an owl; from a lion to a lobster; nor have we spoken of the prowess and beauty of a brilliantly-clad Amazonian Army; nor of the dazzling delights of the Transformation Scene entitled the Floral Home of the Queen Bee. We merely throw out the hint that in these will be discovered fresh sources of attraction, fresh aids to holiday enjoyment. [...]
The Era, 27/12/1874

Sanger's Amphitheatre
Aladdin and the Wonderful Lamp; or, Harlequin and the Forty Thieves and the Flying Horses of Lambeth
DIFFICULT, indeed, would be the task of him who strove to tell circumstantially the entire plot and incidents of a production in which no less than three Eastern tales are placed under consideration. Something must, however, be said, or we shall fail to give an idea of the lavish wealth of pantomime materials placed before the public. There are Spirits of Earth, of Air, of Fire, and Water summoned to a council as to the subject of the Pantomime, and the result of the discussion is a reference to the "Arabian Nights", when the adventures of Aladdin at once turn uppermost. [...] In the Opening we find representatives of every clime under the sun clad in appropriate costume, thus brilliantly leading up to the actual story of Aladdin's fortunes and misfortunes.

The Widow Twankay (Mr Mat Robson) is first seen at the washing-tub, consoling herself with an occasional sip from a teapot which she carries in her pocket, and which contains a liquid so emphatically reflected upon the Widow's nose that it *must* be something stronger than Bohea. Widow Twankey, as Mr Mat Robson delineates her, is strong of wind and limb, but it is to the pleasure and profit of Aladdin's mamma to call herself a "poor weak woman", even when, with resolute fist, she floors the tax-inspector and topples over the pretended uncle who beguiles Aladdin (Miss Florrie Seaman). The widow is uncommonly funny, and the life and soul of the comic portion. Mr Mat Robson must also be complimented upon the possession of no slight ability as a vocalist. His command of the falsetto was not only very droll, but was also worthy of praise from a musical standard. [...]

The Pantomime will be remembered by all who have seen it as the most gorgeous spectacle ever presented at this Theatre. One scene alone ought to tempt all London to the "Surrey side". This is the Grand Carnival, which takes place after the ascent of Aladdin's flying Palace. The procession employs seven hundred persons, and the enormous stage is filled to its extreme limits. All the details of Eastern splendour are carried out with the utmost brilliancy. There is a herd of trained elephants, eleven in number, with their attendants arrayed in every colour of the rainbow; camels, dromedaries, oxen, &c; fifty knights "armed in complete steel" flank the stage, and move in picturesque contrast to an army of Amazons occupying the front rank. Hundreds of children carrying banners, and decked out in all the fantastic gorgeousness of Eastern costume, circle round these groups, and with flags and streamers add to the glittering procession; and upon a raised terrace in the far distance the spectator is dazzled by figures in shining armour elevated high above the surrounding groups, and attracting the eye by their elegance and statuesque attitudes. Over all this wonderful assemblage floods of light, emulating Eastern sunshine, fall with bewildering effect.

Everything that finished art, good arrangement, and refined taste could suggest could suggest has been brought to bear upon this unique spectacle. We have only a single hint to give, and that is to the musical conductor, who would do well, we think, to introduce another march (say Mayerbeer's "Coronation March") as a relief to the ear whilst this astonishing procession is passing. [...]
The Era, 3/1/1875

1875

WE should very much like to know on what grounds poor orphan children of City schools ought to be debarred from seeing a Pantomime. At a meeting of the Common Council, on Monday, Mr Medwin gravely inquired whether it was true that the children attending the orphan schools had received permission to see the Pantomime at the Surrey Theatre. Of course, the question was greeted with derisive laughter by the more rational members of the Council; but Mr Medwin had not done with them yet, and requested the Committee "to consider carefully the evil consequences of taking children to such places." At this point our philosopher was again interrupted by renewed laughter, and and was finally "shut up" by Mr Ashby, the Chairman, who told this bigoted noodle that it was by the express desire of the Lord Mayor that the children were to be taken to a morning performance, and they acquiesced with the wishes of his Lordship. Mr Medwin must be a jovial and genial spirit truly, to grudge these poor children a few hours' harmless enjoyment of stage fairyland and the humours of Clown and Pantaloon. What have they to cheer them, poor creatures? They are orphans. Their very food and clothing depend upon the bounty of others, and they must, in most cases, look forward to a career of toil. There are unhappily too many of the Medwin school of philosophy who would shut out from the young, and especially if the young are poor also, every glimpse of a more cheerful and genial existence, so that they may become mere plodding machines, to do the rough work of the world, and to make life a little easier for the Medwins.
The Era, 14/2/1875

The Grecian
Harlequin Spitz-Spitze, the Spider Crab; or, the Sprite of Spitzbergen

[…] WE may remark, by the way, that scarcely anything connected with the first night was more extraordinary than the eagerness with which the audience sought to have a glimpse of the new production. People have been accustomed to all sorts of odd fancies at the Grecian for some years past. The Demon Head that *walked upon its whiskers* has not been forgotten yet, and many a mile away from the City Road it is still talked of. But we question if Mr George Conquest has not taken upon himself a more difficult task than ever in the latest effort of his facile fancy. He has quitted the realms of the supernatural for the natural and realistic, and now gives us his idea of a Spider Crab of monstrous size, which, if he could only learn the art of remaining an indefinite period under water, would certainly cause the Westminster Aquarium to become the eighth wonder of the world. But Mr Conquest is satisfied for the time in turning the stage of the Grecian into an imaginary aquarium, and there displays his intimate acquaintance with the habits of those interesting marine creatures.

At a very early period of the Pantomime we find Terra (Mr Donne), with Boreas (Miss Matthews), Salamader (Mr George Conquest Junior), Triton (Miss Inch), and others, discussing the preliminaries of the Pantomime, and making that complication of the affairs of mortals and immortals without which the reign of Pantomime must soon come to an end. We have just a pleasant hint of Byron in the person of Miss Dot Robins, superbly arrayed, and looking extremely pretty as Conrad, the Corsair. We are not aware that he was cast ashore upon the "Iron Islands", but the bills tell us so, and who at Christmas time would be so bold as to question the latitude and longitude of a pantomimic island as stated in the log – we mean the playbill? So on we go merrily with Conrad, the Corsair, finding him delightful company; the same being said with equal reason of Miss Amy Forrest, who not only impersonates Prince Pauvret admirably, but whose singing is really exquisite, and gains applause and encores of the most enthusiastic description. Contrasted with these fascinating young ladies we have an extremely comic personage, a youthful King, "Sillikin the Sixtieth", a specimen of monarchy, which Mr Herbert Campbell makes very amusing indeed, with a dress like a schoolboy, a very red head, and a face smeared with jam and treacle.

After a fantastic introduction of the subject of the Pantomime, wherein we have hints of the Monster Crab, that remarkable creature actually appears in the second scene. Strange to say, this monster of the deep is a fiend, and, what is more, a fiend in love with a young damsel, having the pretty name of Pearlina, and this Pearlina, moreover, being represented most agreeably by Miss Lizzie Conquest we can all the better understand the rage of the Spider Crab when his ladylove says, like Hamlet, "Thou com'st to me in such a questionable shape that I'll have nothing to do with you in the shape of a husband." But the Crab finds somebody to take pity upon him, and is eventually hauled out of his deep sea cave, and set at liberty to pursue poor Pearlina with his attentions.

But ere this monster puts on the guise of mortality we must describe him – a task easier to propose than to accomplish. However, let out readers who have *not* been to the Grecian – they will soon be in the minority – suppose a crab so large that his claws extend from one side of the stage to the other – further let them fancy that the curious dark spots seen upon the body of a spider crab are transformed into flaming eyes – that a lurid light plays from and around the figure, and seems to exaggerate its huge proportions. Beyond this, let them fancy a mouth that gives little indications of the crab having a taste for lollipops, but is rather employed in grinding up little fish to make dainty morsels to gratify its voracious appetite. Then remember this is not a mere unwieldy pasteboard property to raise a laugh by its very absurdity. It is really an exact copy of the crab itself, a little idealised to be sure. But the most significant thing about this crabshell is *that Mr George Conquest is inside it*. When we have said that we have said all, for nothing can exceed the facility and freedom with which this many handed and fancifully minded comedian manipulates the secret springs of his wonderful contrivance. Weird, grotesque, original, and eccentric as the whole affair is, there is yet a strange fascination about it, and while it is on the stage we cannot take our eyes from it.

But this is only one of a score of extraordinary changes that take place in the course of the Pantomime. In another scene Mr Conquest, in the course of his pursuit of the persecuted Pearlina, transforms himself to a hermit, and executioner, a conjuror, a dwarf, and a tiny little manikin more resembling a marionette figure than anything human. All these difficult feats are accomplished without the slightest hitch or blunder of any kind. […]

Alexandra Palace
Harlequin Yellow Dwarf; or, the King of the Gold Mines
GREAT was the disappointment when, on reaching Muswell Hill on Tuesday week, it was found that not only was the Pantomime postponed, but that Mr Conquest was disabled. A medical certificate respecting the cause of this mishap to the prince of pantomimists stated that Mr Conquest had "twisted his spine". This intelligence not only caused disappointment, but alarm. Happily two days' rest so completely restored Mr Conquest's powers that he was enabled to appear on Friday, 24th *ult*, when the Pantomime was most successfully produced; and, if we were to judge by the extraordinary feats he performed on that day, we should recommend all performers who follow in his path to get a "twist in the spine".

The Pantomime prepared for the Alexandra Palace is called *Harlequin Yellow Dwarf; or, the King of the Gold Mines*, the Brothers Grinn being the authors. So neatly and well is the story told that our old friend appears to great advantage with a pantomimic face. The Pantomime opens with a Silver Hall of Icicles in Jack Frost's Winter Palace, which, by a very slight exercise of the imaginative powers, we may fancy somewhere near the North Pole, especially as a good imitation of the aurora borealis is produced by means of artificial lights. Here the Shortest Day (Miss K Smith) has an interview with Father Time and Good Cheer (Miss Inch), Jack Frost (Mr Fredericks) making his own comments upon the proceedings, which end in a Pantomime being proposed. Meanwhile, as an earnest that even in the realms of Jack Frost some amusement could be found, the Brother Guida have enlivened the Arctic scene with some very clever skating.

But enough of icebergs for the present. We see them melt into the Golden Temples of Indian Fairyland, a scene by Mr William Brew and Henry Nedmé, one of the most brilliant pantomimic achievements we have witnessed this season. This Indian scene is really one of the most exquisite spectacles ever placed upon the stage; and not only is it remarkable for scenic effects, but the brilliant ballet introduced brings upon the stage such a host of gaily dressed and animated groups that we very much doubt whether the real Indian spectacles the Prince of Wales has witnessed would not look tame and dull by comparison with that of the Alexandra. Elephants and other animals, covered with gay trappings, attended by slaves fancifully costumed, and carrying banners with all sorts of quaint and picturesque devices, occupy the background, while in the centre of the picture there is a splendid ballet. […]

Allusions to the Royal visit, to the Suez Canal, and other topics of the day, are warmly taken up by the audience, and soon the actual story of the Yellow Dwarf begins. We see the Orange Grove and Withered Tree, where lurks the mysterious Dwarf, in what guise it is as yet difficult to conjecture, for Mr Conquest is a man of many moods. He may be an eagle, a boa constrictor, a creature all head and no body, or a headless monster, with eyes in his stomach, for aught we can tell as present. But Miss Carry Nelson comes as King of the Golden Mines, very brilliantly arrayed, and Miss Dot Robins as Princess Allfair is indeed a heroine that might tempt any young Prince to brave many dangers to win her. Miss Dot Robins was dressed in exquisite style, and her entire rendering of the character was very pleasing. The Yellow Dwarf has of course his attendant sprites, and these are represented by the Jackley Brothers.

But now a mysterious movement takes place in the Enchanted Grove. What have we seen yet? Nothing but orange trees and dense tropical foliage. Hark! What is that that shakes the withered tree? The wind, perhaps. No; the fantastic motions have a life of their own, which no passing breeze could have bestowed. It moves; it uplifts its weird and twisted arms, and from one ghastly knotted excrescence there issues a hollow and supernatural tone, and we see the gleam of unearthly eyes. Well may the Princess Allfair start when, with a chuckle of self-satisfaction, the enormous tree folds its skeleton arms, shakes its fantastic head, and coolly steps off its roots for the purpose of making the young lady an offer of marriage. The tree is not a tree, as our readers have already guessed, but Mr George Conquest, and we are greatly pleased to find that the tree can bend its spine most politely to the lady, who, however, is by no means fascinated with the proposition, which, the tree perceiving, changes with electrical rapidity into an owl. So sudden and complete is the transformation that the audience are breathless with astonishment. But the Princess sees the owl before her, his "fiery eyes burning into her bosom's core". The owl is a wise bird, and perceives that the Princess is not fascinated yet, whereupon he changes as suddenly as before, and at last appears before us as the venerable Yellow Dwarf. But how Mr Conquest's body is compressed in that space is a mystery we do not pretend to solve. Perhaps the "twisting of the spine" was not a misfortune after all, but a necessary means of accomplishing what would otherwise be an impossible feat; and how he manages to skip across the stage "and yet no footing seen" is another puzzle for the million which will add to the excitement of the Alexandra Pantomime another feature of the deepest interest.

The Dwarf claims his bride, and the scene changes to the Reception Hall of King Marmalade's Palace, another splendid scene, where the Dwarf appears and performs some novel conjuring feats. But King Marmalade has destined his daughter for King of the Gold Mines, and he is in despair at the appearance of the Dwarf.

A laughable finale in imitation of grand opera ends the scene, and we find ourselves next in front of the Steel Palace of the Yellow Dwarf, where the King of the Gold Mines comes in hopes of recovering his bride. Mr George Conquest Jr lends his aid as Magnet, a Sprite, and Miss A Forrest as the Desert Fairy does good service not only in protecting the lovers, but in singing admirably. The Sprite, enlisted in the service of King Marmalade, starts in pursuit of the Demon Dwarf, and then comes the most exciting scene in the Introduction, the Great Phantom Fight in the Cobweb Cave and Spider's Glen. The pantomimic powers of Mr George Conquest and his son are in this scene brought into full play in a series of most exciting incidents. It is a game of hide and seek on a most gigantic scale, for no sooner does the Dwarf disappear through one magical trap than we see him bounding through another, literally flying through the air from the footlights to the highest part of the stage, and in one marvellous leap we see him shot into the air and then out of sight, as if the new eighty-one ton Woolwich Infant had been employed in the operation. […]

Prince of Wales's Theatre, Birmingham
Gulliver's Travels; or, Harlequin Prince Rover, and the Princess Tricksey-Wicksey
DAVY Jones's Locker, with which the piece opens, is supposed to be the resting-place of departed salts, and is here represented as a Submarine Elysium, round which the little fishes disport themselves gaily. The scene changes to the Floral Home of the Fairies, one of the prettiest scenes of the whole production. Gulliver's daughter Dolly (Miss L Short) is the heroine of piece, and she appears here requesting to be transformed into a Fairy, in order to circumvent her rivals and secure the affections of Prince Rover (Miss Katie Nott), who is of a somewhat inconstant disposition. A ballet follows, in which Miss Ettie Morris, as the Fairy Queen, and Madame Emilie Stevens play a conspicuous part. The dances are carefully and picturesquely arranged, and the dancers are dressed in an elegant and tasteful manner. At Gulliver's lodgings we find his two assistants, perfect pantomimic imps, personated by the Brothers Stevens, who by their contortions and agile movements impart a vast deal of fun into the performance. In a subsequent scene – the Enchanted Home of Drugs and Drachms – the two contrive to play no end of mischievous and fantastic tricks, and to shelter themselves from the results of vagaries they purloin a magic book from their master's limited but mysterious collection. As soon as they begin to pore over their cabalistic contents they are alarmed by flashes of lightning, and manifest their fright by the most ludicrous capers, showing the brothers in some of their most daring and amusing genuflexions.

Gulliver is not seen again until we find him among the Liliputians. The scene is here very striking and effective. It represents the Great Market Place at Liliput. The streets are made up of long avenues of diminutive domiciles of quaint construction. In the distance is the parish church, making altogether a complete and effective picture. Business in the Market Place is very active; the little folk are buying and selling, and standing apart in gossiping groups. They are very prettily dressed, and evidently carefully trained. To these is Gulliver brought in, striding like a Colossus among pigmies. The contrast between the prisoner and his captors was very grotesque, and elicited roars of laughter. Additional excitement is caused by the arrival of the little Emperor and Empress, and the interest is increased when the occupants of the shops and market standings come forward, and join in the festive dance. The Empress becomes enamoured of the gigantic Gulliver, and, much to the annoyance of her Imperial spouse, expresses an intention of kissing him, and a ladder is brought for the purpose.

The next scene represents the Garden and Palace in the Flying Island of Ski-hi, and the next great achievement is the Hall of Point Lace in the Palace of Laputa. This production of Mr Butts, the artist to whom the whole of the scenery has been intrusted, was received with repeated cheering. The Hall, which occupies the whole capacity of the stage, is occupied by a double ballet, splendidly dressed, and with each dancer provided with cymbals, which are clashed together, marking time with the music. These were followed by successive companies of Liliputian bands, some with drums and some with bells, to the sonorous and tintinnabulary accompaniments of which they sing alternately warlike and homely songs. For the training of these children (180 in number) and for the proficiency to which they have attained in their movements and in music credit is due jointly to Mr Walter Raynham and the leader of the orchestra.

The translation of Gulliver to Brobdignagian territory brings a laughable contrast to the scenes just quitted, and much amusement is derived from one incident, in which two of the huge inhabitants place their baby in the care of Gulliver, who finds the infant a trifle heavier and bigger than himself. [...]
The Era, 2/1/1876

1876

ON the 22nd inst, at the Thames Police Court, a poor-looking man named Jameson was charged with driving five sheep along a public thoroughfare at illegal hours. David Markham, a constable, 139 K, said he was on duty in the Commercial Road when he saw the defendant driving five sheep at prohibited hours. The defendant said he was engaged to take the sheep out for exercise. They performed at the Pavilion Theatre in the Pantomime Little Bo-Peep has Lost her Sheep*. 'Little Bo-Peep' was marked on one side of their backs and 'the Pavilion' on the other. He had no idea he was doing wrong in giving them a little recreation after their performance, or else he should not have brought them out. Mr Paget said the defendant must find some other place to exercise Bo-Peep's sheep, and must not drive them up and down the road. He was inclined to think it was an advertisement for the Pantomime. He should not impose any penalty in the present case, but the defendant would have to pay the cost of the summons.*
The Era, 30/1/1876

Covent Garden
Robinson Crusoe

[…] MR MCARDLE has conjured up a Robinson Crusoe of his own, and his career differs very widely and very comically from that of Defoe's hero. We shall be pardoned for telling as briefly as possible the story which he has "evolved from the depths of his inner consciousness". It opens in the house of Crusoe (Mr G Thorne), whose shrew of a wife (Mr J W Wallace) relinquishes her multifarious duties to her daughter Kate (Miss Lizzie Russell) and her son Jim (Miss Nellie Bouverie), a street Arab, while she goes to find her husband, who has been carousing. During her absence a gallant young lieutenant, Tom Trunnion (Miss Pauline Markham) brings a message, and, seeing Kate, falls in love with her, but, being surprised by the return of Mrs Crusoe and Robinson, hides in the clock, whose hands betray the irregularity of the proceedings. The delinquent is soon "bowled out", and is only saved from immediate punishment by being ordered on board by Captain Scuttle (Mr Furneaux Cook[10]), who persuades Robinson to go also.

Scene second reveals a quay at Southwark, with a view of the Tower. The sailor lads, after disporting themselves Terpsichoreally, take farewell of their lasses, and the old and crippled sailors bid them adieu in chorus. The apprentices arrive, and drill in a wonderful manner, and after they have gone on board Kate comes to take farewell of her brother, and is induced by the Lieutenant to accompany him as a "stowaway". Crusoe is followed by his wife and family, whose appeals are in vain, the matron in despair taking a "header" into the river.

The ship now begins to move; the King's procession, rowed towards the Tower, comes in sight; the joy bells ring, flags are waved, the yards are manned, the sailors swarm up the rigging, and we pass on to the third scene, "between docks". A shark is seen following the vessel, and is caught and opened, the wonders it contains numbering Mrs Crusoe. The storm increases, and all hurry to the boats. We are now shown the stormy ocean, with its dioramic effects, the gradual abatement of the tempest, followed by sunrise and a distant view of the wreck on an island, from a cone where neriads disport themselves in "grand ballet" fashion.

The next scene is a view of the island after a supposed lapse of a year or more, and here Robinson Crusoe discovers a footprint on the sands, which so astonishes him that he leaves the sea chest he is dragging home from the wreck and conceals himself. Some savages enter, open the chest, and make free with its contents; but King Hokeepokee (Mr Augustus Glover) pounces on them, and orders one of them to immediate execution. As the prisoner is about to be slain a shot is heard, and they fly, leaving the victim in the hands of Crusoe, who christens him Friday.

We are now shown the Interior of Crusoe's Hut, where his dog, goat, and parrot keep him company, Friday and his father (Saturday) receiving sundry lessons at the hands of their master. After some of the very broadest Pantomime fun all retire to rest; but suspicious heads peer over the palisades. The savages are in search of Friday. A fight takes place, and the invaders are defeated, although carrying off Friday's father.

We now come to the Friendly Islands, where the Captain, Lieutenant, and many of the sailors wander disconsolately as "peculiar people", hoping to reach the wreck on Crusoe's distant shore.

The next scene is one of Telbin's most beautiful sets. It is a Mountain *Gorge*, where the natives retire to *feast*. A rocky path descends the ravine, over which runs a cascade of real water. Here the various tribes assemble. The dragon carriage brings on the King, and there comes from another part of the Island the tribe of a neighbouring Queen. Her gorgeous procession has scarcely arrived when swarms of savages of all tribes come down the mountain bringing plunder from the ship. Then takes place the "King's Custom". Amid dances, marches, choruses, &c, a victim is to be slain, but when again a shot is heard all stand dismayed. Crusoe's dog seizes the executioner, and Friday's father is saved.

Presently Mrs C, who imagines herself a widow, and whose attentions to Captain Scuttle have been rejected, is found by Friday and his father, who endeavour to capture her. Robinson, having found the Savage Queen fainting from alarm, resolves that she shall share his home. The King in turn encounters Mrs C and resolves to make her his squaw, but Crusoe's old love returning at the unexpected sight of his wife, he makes an exchange, preferring the old shrew to the new cannibal.

With Tom and Kate, happy in mutual love, and the announcement of the arrival of a ship, we come to the Transformation, St Valentine's Temple, a stage picture equal to, if not surpassing, and of Mr Telbin's former achievements. We wish we could adequately describe it. But the feat is an impossibility. One peep at its thousand and one glories will be found worth a whole volume of words, and even then the spectator will find that he is able to carry away only a confused but remarkably pleasant idea of a magnificent temple with its portals surmounted by a star which is dazzling to look upon; of a sky of ethereal blue, twinkling with a million stars; of arches resplendent with precious stones relieved by fairy foliage opening out and revealing gracefully posed nymphs rising here, descending there, and helping to fill up the wondrous picture. Decidedly, St Valentine's Temple should be seen by all who love the beautiful.

Other scenes, likely to live in the memories of those who visit Covent Garden during the present holiday season, are the Storm at Midnight; the Ravine and Gorge, where the grand procession of natives takes place; and the View of Constantinople from the Garden of the English Consulate, copied by Mr Telbin from a picture painted on the spot by his late father. The dioramic effects in the first-named are wonderfully realistic, and we may remark that it leads up to the grand ballet, which, as usual here, is remarkably complete and effective, both the dances and the groupings of a host of comely *ballerines* with branches of coral and glittering shells being worthy of the warmest commendation. By the way, the bills inform us that the "thousands of pounds' worth of coral used in this scene" are lent by a certain importer, whose name is also given. We think we might be tempted – that is, if we were in the back row of the ballet – to break off just a little bit for private use. We hope in saying this we shall not be accused of suggesting a felony. The second scene alluded to is strikingly picturesque, and if ever we should be called upon to assist at a feast of "long pig" – we believe that is the correct term for roast missionary – we hope the surroundings will be as pleasant as they are here while the "King's Custom" is being celebrated. […]

In the Harlequinade Mr Ted Lauri, "the little lump of fun", is the Clown, and his drolleries furnish abundant cause for laughter. Mr Clown as the agent for an insurance office "sounding" a would-be insurer, and looking at his interior by the aid of a corkscrew, is one of the funniest fellows we have seen for some time. […] In the course of the Harlequinade Mr Doughty introduces his cleverly trained dogs, and in the closing scene the spectators are startled by the clever and daring doings of Messrs Veillon and Selbini, who, as bicyclists, accomplish feats certainly never equalled upon that vehicle. […]

Drury Lane
The Forty Thieves

[…] FACT it is that Old Drury presented a magnificent spectacle on Boxing Night. Fact it is that the vast audience was a most orderly one. Fact also it is that for once in a way the gallery was on the best of terms with the pit, and that its occupants kept their orange peel for home consumption. Fact also it is that the worthy individual who for some years past has in shirt sleeves conducted the "gods" through their choruses was absent from his post. But what of that? There were as many stentors present as on any former occasion, and no sooner did Herr Karl Meyder and his magnificent orchestra give them an opportunity by commencing the overture than forth there went a mighty sound, in which all the popular airs of the day appeared to be curiously intermingled. […]

The curtain is up, and we are all waiting eagerly to give the world-famed members of the Vokes Family they must have been conscious during their travels was in store for them on their return. The scene is the Market Place in Bagdad, where the traders are busy disposing of their wares, and where the idle are amused by snake charmers and conjurors, who, of course, indulge in a little practical satire at the expense of a certain "Spiritualist" who has recently made himself notorious. "The Forty", bearing their numbers unblushingly, are mixing with the crowd on the look-out for unconsidered trifles, and the first cheer goes forth for their Captain, Abdallah, who appears in the person of Miss Jessie Vokes, a charming thief, who steals – not *steels* – our hearts and our admiration. Mr Fred Vokes happens to be Ali Baba, a dealer in shoes as well as a cutter of sticks; and, as his saucy son Ganem is personated by Miss Rosina Vokes, we need hardly say that an enthusiastic reception is in store for them; Miss Victoria Vokes tripping on very soon afterwards to share in the kindly welcome in the character of Morgiana. Nor was Mr Walter Vokes as Hassarac, the robber lieutenant, "left out in the cold". When we have made the acquaintance of the rich and haughty Cassim Baba (Mr F W Irish) and of his warm-tempered spouse Cogia (Miss Harriet Coveney) we can proceed very rapidly with the old familiar story.

We can visit the Divan of the Genii, and enjoy the pleasure of an introduction to Eureka (Miss Clara Jecks), who will not only sing to us very sweetly and prettily in her beautiful home, but will bring Morgiana in her dreams to enjoy the wonders she has at command, and will permit us to see how her tastefully attired companions can dance, and how, by the aid of fans and feathers, and flowers magically produced, they can realise the poet's idea of a "garden of girls". This, of course, is the grand ballet, and in it Mlle Bossi greatly distinguishes herself, and secures a volley of cheers.

And now to the Date Tree Grove, where some of the most enjoyable of fun is set before us. Ali Baba, Ganem, and Mokanna, the immortal donkey, are on their way to the wood. The donkey before setting out had evidently made up his mind that he *wouldn't*, and here, with his companions, he indulges in antics which on Boxing Night kept the spectators in a roar. This donkey can wink his eye as well as kick up his heels; can solve the problem long ago propounded by Lord Dundreary, *viz*, how to waggle your left ear; can talk, and – *mirabile dictu!* – can sing. Somebody who speaks of the donkey as the only real burlesque on animated nature extant, compares his voice to a steam whistle troubled with bronchitis. Such a comparison is a libel on Mokanna, who joins in the "Two Obadiahs" with manifest gusto, and beats time with his tail. Presently he takes it into his asinine head to dance, and up he goes on his hind legs, presenting a picture perfectly irresistible to mortals gifted with the risible faculty. This donkey before the Pantomime season is over is sure to become the pet of all who see and hear him, and is certain, in the words of dear old "Punch", to

Make childhood's clear laughters
Ring up to the rafters.

In the next scene, the Enchanted Cavern in the Depths of the Forest, the fun is furnished chiefly by the comic terror of Ali Baba, who, having possessed himself of the treasures hidden by the Forty Thieves, fears discovery, and Ali Baba, literally "up a tree", is a person to be seen and immoderately laughed at, little Ganem doing his best to scare him out of his wits by his false alarms. Need we tell how Cogia, desirous of sharing the spoils, is captured, and executed on the spot? How Abdallah, by strategem, seeks revenge? How Morgiana outwits him and "settles the hash" of his comrades with boiling oil, causing them in more senses than one to *turn up their toes*? How the loves of the lady and Ganem are crowned? How even through the skilful needlework of Morgiana the cut-up Cassim is revivified? Is not all this written in nursery lore? When we reach the glorious Transformation Scene, the beauties of which words would but faintly describe, we are conscious that we have renewed pleasurable acquaintance with an old friend clothed in the newest and most fanciful of dresses by Mr Blanchard, and we are quite ready to accept his moral:

Thus years to come this tale will teach our youth,
Naught can contend with Fortitude and Truth.

[...] We shall not be far wrong in saying that even the terrible downpour of sleet and rain which greeted the Boxing Night visitors on the departure failed to spoil the enjoyment of the Drury Lane Pantomime prepared to merrily usher in the year of grace, 1877.
The Era, 31/12/1876

1877

ON Tuesday evening, as the Pantomime of Sinbad the Sailor *was progressing at Her Majesty's Opera House, Aberdeen, great cause for alarm was created by the rear quarters of the "elephant," which accompanies the pseudo Prince of Wales on his Indian tour, taking fire, possibly from some of the side-wing jets in passing on to the stage. The house was crowded to repletion, and many instinctively jumped up in the middle of the pit and stalls ready to make for the door, while not a few rushed down stairs on the first appearance of the flames, without waiting to see whether there was sufficient cause for their retreat. The "legs" of the "elephant" – represented by two supers – threw down the body, and and the burning parts were soon extinguished. Had a panic ensued, disastrous consequences could not have been prevented, notwithstanding the excellent arrangements which exist at this house for the suppression of fire. With the Brooklyn calamity[11] still fresh in their minds, the fear of the audience was, doubtless, intensified, and it was very bad taste on behalf of one of the company on the stage at the time to cry "Fire." The mishap, slight though it was, is only another instance of the great necessity which exists for every reasonable and continued precaution being taken against the dreaded enemy.*
The Era, 7/1/1877

The Standard
The Enchanted Prince; or, Harlequin Beauty and the Bears
[…] WE may as well say at once that the bears alluded to among all classes of those who are delighted with stage glories, for in what is called the Festival of the Bears we get a scene which is characterised as much by its novelty as its beauty. […]

Conjure up, then, in your imagination the vast stage of the house under notice transformed into "Palace Gardens". And what gardens they are! They boast "gorgeous arcades and poetic bowers". From golden boughs hang golden cages. The only living things that meet the eye when we first catch a glimpse of the scene are peacocks, whose plumage is in keeping with the beauties of the place. So much at home are they here, so pleasant is the spot, that presently there is some difficulty in inducing them to leave it, and, as the services of a fearless monkey had to be requisitioned for the purpose, not a little amusement was the result on the occasion of the initial performance.

It is not for long that they have the stage to themselves, for from a nook seemingly far distant come tripping troops of white-coated bears, pleasant to look upon and full of grace. About 150 members of the *corps de ballet* are called upon to assume a bearish character without the bearish clumsiness. The dress, except for the headgear, is very much like that made familiar to sight-seers by Miss Lydia Thompson in the famous burlesque of *Robinson Crusoe*, and as the groupings have been remarkably well arranged the effect may be better imagined than described. A number of the "bears", selected presumably for their symmetry of person, their grace of action, and their superior skill, take their stand upon an outspread baize (the colour of which affords a pleasing contrast to their dress), and, armed with clubs, posture in fashion which presents to the spectator a series of pictures effectively illustrative of "Chiefs in Council", "Peace or War", "Trial by Battle", &c. Presently the bears have an alphabetical fit, and, armed with all the letters from A to Z, they by skilful combinations contrive to test the political feeling of the audience in fashion which would be instructive to some of our rulers. When the bears had put together the word "Germany" the spectators hissed; when "Osman Pasha"[12] and "Plevna"[13] were put into alphabetical order they cheered lustily; and when the word "Czar" came to the front there went forth a howl of execration. […]

The other scene to which we should like to call attention, and which is calculated to create a sensation from a spectacular point of view, is called the Charming of the Serpent. It takes place in the Python's Haunt, a marvellously clever bit of rock painting, reflecting high credit on Mr Richard Douglass, the artist, who also is responsibe for the many other scenic beauties of the production. Some scores of charmers – serpent charmers – fill the stage, their dark dresses being relieved in fashion, which is made more effective by a clever use of the lime-light. […]

Drury Lane
The White Cat
[…] MR E L BLANCHARD is not long in introducing us to Queen Mytymama (Miss Harriet Coveney); to the Princess Blanchette (Mrs F Vokes), to King Colorado (Mr H Moreland), to Prince Natty (Miss Victoria Vokes), to Prince Nectar (Miss Jessie Vokes), to Prince Tremor (Mr Fred Vokes), to Psycho the Golden Dwarf (Mr Walter Vokes), and these in return take but a very short time to convince us that their humorous and saltatory powers have not diminished a jot since they last trod the boards in Pantomime here.

When in very pretty fashion has been illustrated "a coming of age in the golden time", when the birthday festival had been interrupted by a wicked fairy, and poor Blanchette has been condemned to take the form of a White Cat, then we arrive at a remarkably attractive scene bearing the romantic title of Lake of the Water Lilies and Fairy Grove by Moonlight, which must be pronounce one of Mr William Beverly's very best efforts. It is close to this lake that there occurs the new grand ballet bearing the mysterious title "FBC", the numerous *coryphees* being headed by the well-known *premiere danseuse* Mlle Pitteri, who secured by the grace of her movements some of the loudest applause heard during the evening. The dances and groupings by the members of the corps de ballet reflected the continued skill of Mr John Cormack, who has contrived a marvellous coup l'oeuil for the termination of the saltatory revels, the mirrors carried by the dancers suddenly taking the forms of blazing suns, and producing an effect which may not inaptly, we hope, be compared to that of an unexpected and brilliant display of fireworks.

In the Pathway through the Wood of Enchantment, to which we follow the three Princes, we get some of the principal fun of the Opening. "Night came suddenly on," says the story, "and with it a violent storm of thunder, lightning, and rain; while, to add to their perplexity, they lost their path, and could find no way out of the forest." now, under such circumstances, imagine, if you can, dear reader, the terrible and yet comical state of nervousness into which Prince Tremor would be thrown. Imagine also Prince Natty the Neat and Prince Nectar the Nimble seizing every opportunity to add to the terror of the nervous one, with Mr Walter Vokes as the Gnome King bringing all sorts of occult arts into practice to fright him from his propriety, and then you will get just a small idea of the laughable nature of the scene. The great hit is made in a comical pas de trois, in which the ladies and Mr Fred Vokes astonish and delight the lookers-on by the nimbleness of their legs and the airiness of their feet; while their faces and bodies are concealed beneath a huge umbrella. This dance had to be repeated, in accordance with the unanimous desire of the audience, expressed in enthusiastic applause.

And now further fun is in store at the Cats' School of Cookery. This is a capital scene, full of life, bustle, and mirth-moving antics. The assembly of Cats is marvellous to look upon. They are of all sizes and all colours, and they are very busy preparing a dinner for somebody. There are blazing fires, looking remarkably comfortable on a cold night, and the basting that is going on would make the mouth of an epicure water. There is a sudden incursion and excursion of rats, and the instantaneous change on the part of the Cats from a perpendicular to a horizontal position proves very effective and very diverting. Mr Fred Vokes and a very lively pussy contrive any amount of practical fun, and the spirit of this scene is never allowed to flag.

Very telling, too, is the next scene, the Mother of Pearl Pavilion in Cats' Castle. Here the cats prove musical. The White Cat sings a parody on "Nancy Lee", with a "Mol-row" substituted for a "Yo-ho!", and a pussy, rejoicing in the name of Signor Harditty, conducts a full band of cats, who contrive to furnish music much more pleasant than that generally supplied by the feline race.

And now we are rapidly approaching the end, for when the White Cat has been by the loss of her head brought back to her original form as the Princess, when she has accepted the hand and heart of her princely suitor, and when she has joined the wanderers and the Gnome King in one of those extraordinary dances which have made the Vokes Family famous, then we get a peep at a charming scene called the Tangled Brake, which presently opens and reveals to our astonished gaze all the glories of the Transformation, illustrative of the Bridal Gifts of the Fairies and Distribution of the Wedding Cake, the development of the multifarious beauties of this scene eliciting general manifestations of delight. […]

The Harlequinade, which as usual here is a double one, is particularly calculated to afford enjoyment to the little folks. Mr C Lauri as Clown is at the head of a company of pantomimists, which includes Mr F Sims as Harlequin, Mr H Lauri as Pantaloon in Court costume, Miss Fanny Lauri as Columbine, and Master C Lauri, a young gentleman who appears to be equal to any emergency, and to be running over with comicality. Some of the tricks introduced in a scene representative of a mansion which is to be let and a florist's are exceedingly good. The illustration of how to make and sell umbrellas caused great hilarity, notwithstanding the fact that it presented Mr Clown as a very great rogue indeed. The Clown, at the end, desires to take the vacant mansion, but, by a wave of Harlequin's wand, the interior being brought before his notice, he discovers that it is crowded with cradles and babies. The Clown rushes off in horror, and the spectators indulge in a hearty roar. Mr Evans (Clown) also has any number of ingenious tricks at his command, a ladder which cannot be mounted and a pair of steps which have a habit of running away from the feet that would touch them, being worthy of notice. Mr Evans also causes some excitement by the introduction of a "box of foreign toys", from which he brings in succession capital effigies of the Czar, the Sultan, and the Prime Minister. […]

Covent Garden
Puss in Boots
[…] THE first scene of *Puss in Boots* opens in an old Mill, where we learn that the Miller's will has been read with but sorry results to his supposed offspring Fondalin (Miss Alice Cook), who, in company with the faithful Puss (Mr R Henry), goes forth to seek his fortune. This scene also introduces several of the characters who afterwards figure in the Pantomime – Mealymouth (Mr Ford); Spiderlimb (Mr Henry Raynor), a lawyer; and Flora (Miss Lee), a village coquette. The first scene is essentially introductory, and we do not get much pantomimic spirit out of it.

The second scene is the exterior of the Mill, where a scene of rustic enjoyment affords an opportunity for a host of performers, the chief effect being a skipping rope dance, which, on the first night, evidently showed that further rehearsing would have improved it. […] Fondalin comes to take a farewell of the rustics, and something like poetical justice takes place in the fall of a huge millstone, which "knocks into a cocked hat", as the Americans say, the ugly and ill-conditioned brother of the hero, Branbruiser (Mr Wylsone).

The third scene is a chamber in the mansion of Baron Blue Bubble (Mr Furneaux Cook), whose services were of considerable value to the Pantomime vocally and dramatically. A song in this scene for Mr Cook, with the refrain "She said it was Eau-de-Cologne", was well received. Some long dialogues introduce us to further incidents of the story, and to the fact that the giant Fee-fro-fum demands that the Baron's daughter Mignionetta (Miss F Champneys) shall marry Rover the Reckless (Miss Ethel McAlpine). But the Baron's sister Spindelotta (Miss Kate Kearney), a spinster who is not very particular as to what gentleman she accepts if only somebody will come forward, is willing to take the place of Mignionetta. But that young lady orders the family coach, and sets off herself, and the discovery is made that the supposed Miller's son is heir to the Marquis of Carabas, whose castle has been captured by the Giant. The Baron, delighted, orders the family coach onward, and the Nigger footman Pongo (Mr C Raynor), a very diverting Christy Minstrel indeed, gets up on the box; also Lightfoot (Mr Levite), a page modelled upon the pattern of the immortal fat boy in "Pickwick". But the drive is interrupted by a storm, and the appearance of a swarm of fairy figures from an enchanted pool, of course, leading to the introduction of a grand ballet, in which Signora Cavalazzi and Miss Tessy Guaniss, as the principal dancers, successfully disport themselves, and win no little applause.

There is a scene called the Druid's Oak, where Elves carry away the disconsolate heroine and bring her to Carabas Castle, which is the sixth scene. Some fun is made by Mr Levite, as the fat boy, dancing until the Banting process is outdone, and the tricks outside the Castle were much applauded. The "Cats' Duet", introduced by the Tyrolese Minstrels, and since heard frequently in the Music Halls, caused much amusement. The idea of a comic serenade originated by Offenbach is here grotesquely caricatured. With cymbals, trombone, trumpet, and big drum a serenade is performed that would wake the dead.

The seventh scene is in Carabas Castle, where we behold probably the biggest giant that was ever seen upon the stage. His proportions are so enormous that he occupies nearly the whole of the scene. He is indeed fearfully and wonderfully constructed. His eyes glare fiercely, and when under the influence of wrath or pleasure the Giant's hair stands on end like "quills upon the fretful porcupine". He has a mouth capable of taking in a sirloin, teeth like steam hammers, and the ferocious twirl of his moustache has never been equalled by any "swell" officer in the Guards. In a corner of the chamber we see the Baron's daughter suspended in a cage. In response to Fondalin's defiance, the Giant changes himself to a lion and then to a mouse, and thus serves as a dainty meal for Puss in Boots.

The result is that the Castle disappears and the Giant's Salt Cellar and Glaciarum is shown. Three hundred of the Giant's female victims frozen in this gloomy abode once more return to life. This will probably be considered the great scene of the entire Pantomime, but on the first night it was imperfectly exhibited, and Mr Rice, evidently conscious that the display fell short of his former triumphs, came forward and addressed the audience, explaining that, owing to the unfortunate railway accident he met with, he had been unable to devote that attention and care to the Pantomime which on previous occasions led to such successful results, and he craved an indulgence, which was accorded with the generosity always forthcoming from a Boxing Night audience. [..]
The Era, 30/12/1877

Furneaux Cook

1878

The Gaiety
Jack the Giant Killer

[…] HOW the famous old legend is treated may soon be told. With the rising of the curtain we are introduced to Jack's 'Umble Roof, where we see the gallant little fellow waking up from a pleasant dream in which we suppose has been foreshadowed some of the doughty deeds which are to immortalise his name and make him prominent among all the heroes of nursery lore and beloved and admired by all little people in after ages. It is Queen Progress (Miss Hazel) who invests Jack (Miss Jenny Hill[14]) with the sword and his cap, which is to make him invisible, and his boots, which are to work wonders in enabling him to pursue his gigantic foes; and in the second scene we find him making the acquaintance of King Arthur (Mr Squire) and his Knights, some represented by pretty Gaiety girls and some by gentlemen who have gone in for something almost alarming in the way of nasal development. It is in this scene, too, that we are introduced to the Giant (Mr H M Clifford), who begins by singing "I'm so dizzy", and ends by running off with Sybil (Miss Wadman), the maid of the inn. When we have looked on with pleasure at "a right merry old English gambol", we pass rapidly on to the Glowworm's Dell, stopping only meanwhile to note how curious a method a Giant adopts when he wants to serenade his lady-love. What takes place in the scene we have mentioned we shall describe further on. The fifth scene gives us a peep and something more at the interior of the Giant's Kitchen, and we find some amusement in taking stock of his culinary arrangements. The remaining scenes include a Landscape, a Rocky Pass, with introduced preparations for the death, decapitation, and burial of the Giant, and a Corridor in King Arthur's Palace, where the gallant little champion is created an Earl, decorated with the Order of the Garter, and is further rewarded for his gallant and daring deeds.

Our first attention must be given to what undoubtedly will soon become the talk of the town. We allude to the "Flying Dance" introduced in "The Glowworms' Dell in the Haunted Forest", which forms the fourth scene. The flying dancer is a pretty little lady named Mlle Aenea, who may be pronounced the embodiment of all that is graceful. Mlle Aenea makes he first appearance upon a rustic bridge which spans the dell. She is some twenty feet up above the other occupants of the stage, and very picturesque does she look. Suddenly we are startled by seeing her step from her bridge to the stage. The action seems so natural it is accomplished before we have time to think or to wonder how it is done. And then this little lady dances. She seems almost to dance upon nothing – so light and airy and fanciful are all her movements. Poised upon the tips of her toes she looks positively bewitching, and we are fairly entranced when, taken in hand by her companion, "the Benighted Peasant", she darts upward and alights – as naturally and as quietly as a bird upon a bough – upon the shoulder of the gentleman who has impelled her – or has seemed to – in her flight. Later on we see Mlle Aenea again upon the bridge. The bridge suddenly parts in twain. Down she comes again, light and graceful as before, to provide further cause for wonder and further excuse for acclamation. She takes her leave of the spectators in a sort of Lulu leap, darting upwards from the footlights to the "flies", and coming back again only to receive the enthusiastic applause of the delighted beholders. We repeat that the Flying Dance should be the talk of London, and we are sure that our readers who see it will be grateful to us for having called their attention to it.

The Transformation Scene is described in the programme as the Golden Gates of Progress, and very tasteful and pretty it is, particularly when, being fully developed, we get a glimpse of Atlas, bearing upon his shoulders a globe which dazzles one to look at, with the handsomest of Mercuries surmounting. […]

In the Harlequinade the big hit was made by Lieutenant Walter Cole, whose ventriloquial business created great astonishment, and whose comical figures, with comical sayings put into their mouths, provoked many a shout of laughter. There was the old gentleman with the red "beak", to chaff his master; the old lady and the little one to sing; the Quaker, to drone and to drawl; the black boy in buttons, to indulge in cachinnatory peals; and, finally, the man on the roof, to take up the refrain of a song, and to prove the artist's power of throwing his voice here, there, and everywhere. Mr Hector worked hard as the indispensable Policeman, and showed that it is possible for a member of the force not only to stand on his head, but to spin on it. […]

Drury Lane
Cinderella; or, Harlequin and the Fairy Slipper
[…] SOMEBODY has very recently been putting forth the theory in somewhat dogmatic fashion that Cinderella's slippers after all were not of glass, but of satin. Mr Blanchard says they were of glass. He sticks to the belief of his and our days of childhood, and that ought to settle the matter at once.

When the curtain rises he introduces us to a Mountain Pass and Woody Glen in the Black Forest by Sunset, a capital picture, reflecting great credit on Mr William Beverly, whose wonderful skill, as in years gone by, has been requisitioned for the supply of the scenery. Here we begin with the most mirth-provoking fun found in the trepidation exhibited by the Baron Pumpernickel (Mr Fred Vokes) and his trusty servant, Kobold (Mr Fawdon Vokes), in presence of any number of wild boars. They are the most wonderful stage boars we have ever seen, and, unlike most stage bores, they tire us not in the least. Indeed, they make us laugh most heartily, for the order of things is reversed, and instead of the Baron hunting the boars, the boars actually hunt him, and run off with his luncheon. Hungry as he is he is glad to scrape acquaintance with Prince Amabel (Miss Jessie Vokes), who comes that way in search of sport, and who presently joins the whole party in a pleasant game of "Nap". We do not mean to insinuate that gambling goes on. Nothing of the sort. Everybody goes to sleep, and the Prince in his dream sees, as we see out of our dreams, the face of the beautiful Cinderella (Miss Victoria Vokes). That vision dispels his drowsiness. He must find the owner of the face he has seen. He determines to give a ball, and at once issues orders for the invitation of all his subjects and their relations, thus suggesting a Christmas family party – which, like Christmas family parties generally, is sure to end in a squabble.

The second scene affords us a peep, and something more than a peep, at the Glass Factory of the Fairy Slipper in the Basaltic Valley. The basaltic columns look remarkably picturesque; the glass goblins are remarkably busy, but what most delights our eyes comes to the fore in the persons of the dwellers in this wonderful region, no fewer than one hundred coryphees, headed by the graceful Mlle Gosselin, treating us to what is very properly described as a grand prismatic ballet.

We pass on now to the Gardens of the Baron's Chateau, and presently come face to face with the heroine of the story. But what meaneth this? Cinderella of old has become Cinderella the new. She has evidently put the cinders, which help to give her a name, into the dust-bin, and has "cleaned herself" for the occasion. She is the prettiest, and the sauciest, and the smartest, and the most mischievous Cinderella that ever stepped upon the stage in Christmas Pantomime. And shall we, therefore, quarrel with Miss Victoria Vokes, who is Cinderella's representative? Perish the thought! […] The one sister, let it be remembered, is fair headed; the other is dark. Now mark how Cinderella indulges in a little mild revenge. Called upon to "do" the hair of the fair one she appends the black pig-tail which belongs to the other, reversing the process when it comes to the other, reversing the process when it comes to the turn of the dark one to be "done" – that is, got ready for the ball.

For, while we have been laughing with Cinderella the invitation has arrived from the Prince, and the Baron has been indulging in a few preparatory "steps", and has suffered, consequently, a few twinges of the gout. Our heroine, of course, is to be left behind – for Mr Blanchard is orthodox if Cinderella is not. Her sisters triumph over her, and then to them she sings a pretty song, set to tuneful music by Julia Woolf. But her boast avails not at the moment, and when, after some laughable business connected with the toilet of the invited ones, she is left with the kitchen fire and the chairs and brooms only for company we imagine Cinderella's cup of bitterness to be full. Not at first does she discover this. She is light of heart and nimble of feet. She will have "The Lancers" all to herself, and the broom and the mop shall be her "partners". No sooner said than done. She even affects to take her wooden partner to refreshment. The gaiety is, however, but forced. Poor Cinderella's tears *will* fill her eyes and *will* run over, and *will* wet her cheeks, and down she sinks sobbing at the thought of her desolation and her disappointment. "What!" we hear the reader exclaim – "tears, or the suggestion of tears in a Pantomime?" Yes, dear reader; and let us remove your surprise by reminding you that the author of twenty-nine Drury Lane "annuals" aims at poetry as well as puns, and that fun is made the more acceptable by occasional contrast with feeling. Mr Blanchard has furnished here an opportunity of which Miss Victoria Vokes makes the most. A Boxing Night audience at Drury Lane stopped roaring for a moment because its sympathies had been touched. It appreciated the buoyant fun of the actress, but it appreciated still more more this one little bit of nature, and awarded the lady with a hearty outburst of applause.

Not long does Cinderella mourn. By the aid of the Fairy Iris she is soon gaily and richly attired, and a wonderful gilt coach drawn by wonderful "property" horses carries her away to the Illuminated Ballroom in the Palace of the Prince – a room where everything and everybody is resplendent, even to the moon which at the full casts its rays through the open windows upon the dancers. How Cinderella is admired by the Prince; how she excites the jealousy of her sisters; how Papa joins them in wonder at her likeness to the little drudge they think they have left at home; how with the clock ticking twelve she hurries away; how she leaves her glass slipper behind her – (on Thursday it went flying at the head of the "second fiddle" in the orchestra) – and how subsequently that slipper, being found to fit her, helps her to the hand and fortune of the handsome Prince Amabel need not be told, for is it not all written in the story books?

When Cinderella and the Baron, and the Prince, and the Page have indulged in a "grand *pas fantastique*", and have repeated it in accordance with the strongly expressed desire of the delighted onlookers, the Transformation Scene is revealed. It is called "The Assemblage of the Hours", and is credited very properly with "*striking* effects". We shall not attempt to describe the indescribable. […]

In the Harlequinade there is as usual here a double set of pantomimists. Mr Charles Lauri, supported by Messrs H Lauri, F Sims, and Miss Fanny Lauri, start in scenes representative of a Police Station and a Restaurant, the fun being of the order known as fast and furious. There is introduced an "Italian" organ grinder, who, on being stripped of his outer garments, turns out to be a "wild Irishman", his instrument being suddenly, and, we may say wittily, transformed into a jar labelled "Italian *sauce*". Great fun, too, is made out of the process of taking in wines and spirits – not into the mouth, but into the restaurant cellar. But in winter weather, and particularly such weather as we have had lately, Mr Lauri should take care that his horses are "roughed". Through neglect of this precaution a valuable animal, which must have cost the property master any amount of trouble, came to grief on top of the footlights on Boxing Night, and had its coat singed. Happily the creature was of a quiet disposition, or Karl Meyder might have had his brains knocked out. […]

Covent Garden
Jack and the Beanstalk; or, Harlequin and the Seven Champions as We've Christened 'Em
[…] THE story opens in the Home of Father Time Junior (Mr G Vokes), where that gentleman discusses the story to be chosen for this year's Pantomime with Quicksilver (Miss Lizzie Coote). The scene then changes to the Model Dairy Farm of Jack's Mother, who is ominously named the Widow Simpson (Mr Herbert Campbell). Mrs Simpson is hard up, in spite of her adulterating propensities, partly to be accounted for by another propensity which is suggested by her song in which her son is urged to –

Run with the bottle, Jacky dear,
Mother's taken awfully queer.

The Widow's dog Punch (Master Lauri) comes to take part in the dance which follows, and attempts to satisfy the cravings which he shares with his unfortunate household by stealing some of the dubious compound his mistress dispenses as milk, a feat that induces his being chased round the stage and leads to Thomas, the Page (Mr G H Macdermott), tumbling over him. Jack (Miss Fannie Leslie) enters upon this scene of confusion, and after a concerted piece expressive of their impecuniosity, it is decided that Jack shall sell the cow, and after a trio to the tune of "The merry chink, chink", Jack and Thomas go off with the animal to make the bargain, which results in their bringing back to the Widow, who is beset with duns, only a hatful of beans. The irate lady beats them both for their pains, and after she has gone within doors throws the beans out of the window in very natural indignation.

The stage darkens and Quicksilver, rising from a trap, summons imps (Messrs Waite, Anderson, Richarde, and Elvin) to help him, and under his magic wand the beans germinate and the beanstalk rises, its blossoms being bright with transparent lights; it may also be mentioned that eyes in the masks of the attendant monsters are also illuminated in a very effective and ingenious manner. The beanstalk fully grown, and the supernatural people gone, Jack returns and prepares to climb the quickly growing vegetable, followed by his mother and Thomas.

Then, as the stalk descends, the beautiful scene that has furnished the stage goes down likewise, only to display a still more charming one, the Home of the Lily of the Valley, in which that elegant flower bears a very conspicuous place, and droops at each wing until the eye loses it in the distance of the background, where it still forms the artist's subject. Jack climbs to this abode of the Fairy Queen (Miss K Paradise), and there receives from her majesty the injunction to kill the neighbouring Giant. The former departs upon his mission, and then intervenes in the action a grand ballet, in which the gold bodices and silver skirts and wreaths of the dancers, who hold snowdrop sprays in their hands, which they wave with the most graceful effect during their performance, would claim an enthusiasm of admiration were not that emotion demanded by far greater wonders later in the Pantomime.

The story is resumed, and we find Jack outside the gates of the Giant's Castle, where he is soon joined by his mother, Thomas, and Punch. In answer to Jack's knock at the portal, demons come out; but, influenced by the magic sword that Jack has received from the Fairy Queen, they attack each other, and are put into the bag which Thomas carries with him. Then the audience are shown some specimens of the Giant's belongings, such as the Giant's nursemaid, the Giant's soldier, the Giant's milkman, and the Giant's shoemaker, all contrived in most clever manner, and having heads with faces excellently modelled, and we must not forget the Giant babies. Meanwhile Punch gives the agreed-upon "Bow-wow" as the signal that the coast is clear, and Thomas, who has stolen the Giant's hen with golden egg laying proclivities, and Jack, who has rescued the Princess Pansie (Miss C Jecks), daughter of King Pippin (Mr E J George), hurry off, accompanied by the Widow and Quicksilver, the latter having brought the young hero a telegram from King Pippin, calling him to Court in recognition of his service to the Princess, which shows that the King was more far-sighted than some monarchs are.

A capitally rendered parody of "Emancipation Day", by Misses Leslie and Jecks, and Messrs Macdermott and Campbell, brought the scene to a close; and then the audience witnessed a spectacular display such as, we believe, not one of them had ever looked upon before. In the Grand Palace of King Pippin the stage exhibited its dimensions to its fullest extent. The scene consisted of light columns, which sustained arches of carved wood, which formed the ceiling; towards the back, left, and right, broad staircases led the way to a large, handsome balcony or gallery; while the back centre of the stage was open to allow entrance for the vast concourse of ballet ladies that were soon to strike the spectators with wonder and delight. First came an artistic band of wind instruments, the performers being dressed in blue and gold, and playing as they marched. These were followed by ballet ladies in green and silver, with point skirts; then excellent property hippopotami, attached to triumphal cars, in which classically-draped ladies stood, were led on by their keepers, with expressive faces and heads of a large size, followed by girls in white bodices, with zig-zag stripes of green; to them succeeded others dressed in purple and white, who gave place to those dressed in light blue and silver armour, to be in turn pursued by others clad in red, after whom were led buffaloes guided by their sable attendants. Then came ladies with dresses of yellow striped with brown, and wearing gold armour; then some with drab bodices and puffed shirts, then with lavender and blue, then with white striped with orange; to these succeeded Giants, ladies with the bodice black and skirt yellow; others with light and dark blue, scarlet and gold, white and mauve, one leg of the tights being striped and one plain white; heralds with silver tunics, cooks bearing a capital property wedding cake, giant groomsman and bridesmaids, ballet ladies dressed completely in silver, all with the most suitable head-dresses, some wearing helmets; and ever and again this pageant of loveliness was interrupted by property zebras, or lions, or reindeer, who joined the procession with the triumphal cars we have already described. So the charming crowd came on in all the bewildering sheen of sparkle and light; meanwhile the band had marched up the staircase and had taken their places in the balcony, there to play alternately with the musicians in the orchestra, and at times to combine with them. [...]

We next find the Giant dead, and he is of such dimensions that his length is more than the width of the stage. To make this bulk appear still greater, he is represented surrounded by children. A juvenile soldier walks, as sentinel, to and fro his chest, a juvenile special artist sits on the toe of his boot to sketch him, a juvenile Jack (Miss K Barry) sings the Bullfighter's Song from *Carmen* in commemoration of his death, and juvenile villagers dance and drink in delight of it. This scene was one of the prettiest and most entertaining of the Pantomime, and reflected alike credit on Miss Katie Barry, the children concerned, and those who had the training of them.

After a somewhat stale toilet scene between King Pippin and his Chamberlain (Mr Tully Louis) the outcome of the plot arrives. Jack is knighted and made happy with the Princess; Thomas has to put up with Mrs Simpson, and in the natural order of events the Transformation Scene takes place. First of all, framed by frost-glittering walls, the stage shows female figures draped in red, and standing on large chaplets of laurel to the right and left of the scene, while a *figurante* is lowered from the flies midway between them and the stage; then the scene changes to borders of golden flowers, the red-draped figures are drawn up, displaying below them groups of three under each, while from the flies descend semi-circular frames, some with the arch at the top and the others with it underneath, on which the *figurantes* are placed, the back of the stage being filled with a bevy of girls posed under lace festoons. [...]

The Harlequinade is especially notable for a clever painting of the Derby Day, in which a ballet of female jockeys occurs. The comic business is fairly good. The joke in the Cracker Bonbon, My Symphony in Yellow, and the chase of Clown by the Policeman through the Chest that suddenly becomes all doors, were the best features of the comic business, which is by Mr H Payne. We recommend our readers to lose no time in going to Covent Garden.
The Era, 29/12/1878

G H Macdermott

1879

The Grecian
Harlequin Rokoko, the Rock Fiend; or, Kingdoms Three, the Toad and the Tree
[...] THE first scene is Toadstool Valley, where King Toad (Miss Alice Denvil) reigns supreme. The young Prince Generous (Miss Marie Loftus[15]) is hunting in the neighbouring forest, and falls in love with Princess Beauty (Miss Lilian Adair), the daughter of King Muddler (Mr Henry Parker). Fearing rivals, he employs his talent as a sculptor to carve a grotesque figure upon a rock in the shape of a toad, which strange figure is by magic means endowed with life, and is, in fact, no other than Rokoko (Mr George Conquest). The conception and elaboration of this scene is novel and ingenious, and has not been surpassed by anything Mr Conquest has achieved.

When we first see Rokoko, he is crouching on the rock like a hideous sculptured toad of gigantic size. It is difficult to believe that this hideous form can be human. It might be one of those monstrous toads of which naturalists tell us – shut up in some cavern far beneath the surface of the earth, or imprisoned in solid rock, until some convulsion of nature or some effort of man sets the weird creature free. Mr Conquest was made up so as to hide every vestige of the human form divine, and was a study of the most original kind, and nothing could be more artistic in the way of pantomimic effect than the manner in which, when the toad comes to life, the performer gradually shows, by fantastic movements and attitudes, the first indications of feeling, sensation, and vitality. The monster toad shakes his gigantic head gently, opens his monstrous glittering eyes, slowly puts forth his grotesque feet, and appears to give a spasmodic shudder through his frame, as if shaking off with a tremendous effort the sleep of centuries and blindly struggling to accommodate himself to new conditions of existence. With a clutch and a quiver, as if at some imaginary support to aid it in descending the rock, the strange creature at length crawls to the centre of the stage amidst the deafening plaudits of the spectators. There is no common art, no common skill on the part of a performer who can produce such an effect as this. The impersonation, if such we may call it, is striking in the extreme, and displays a close observation of nature combined with pantomimic talent of the most original kind.

But to the story. Rokoko having been created as the slave of the young prince, no sooner acquires the power to move, speak, and act like mortals than he also becomes possessed of other attributes of humanity, and one of the first to get him into trouble is the tender passion. The sight of the beautiful Princess, beloved by his young master, inspires him with an intense desire to possess her, and this rivalry is naturally the grand motive of the plot, to which all other matters are secondary. Rokoko is so full of fiendish impulses that great efforts are made by all to mar his evil influences and to curb his propensities, and for a time King Toad succeeds in doing so by changing the monster into a turnip. But not until other transformations have been effected, one in particular being exceedingly well done. This was a sudden change from the Goblin Gorge, where Rokoko is first seen, to the splendid Palace of King Muddler. The change was absolutely instantaneous. All the gloomy surroundings of the Goblin Gorge disappear in an instant, and are replaced by columns and arches, fountains and statues, a very clever and well-managed transformation.

Rokoko does not find himself quite comfortable as a turnip, and as he still possesses power for mischief he changes the Royal Palace into a gigantic cucumber-frame, and all the courtiers, guards, and Royal servants into vegetables, while the beautiful Princess he imprisons in the cucumber-frame as a dainty morsel for himself. Her lover eventually finds her, and they escape only to be again confronted with the fiendish Rokoko in another shape. He has changed to a tree and stands in a deep glen, a wild, withered, blasted tree, but still with some resemblance to a human form, for his leafless limbs move like human arms, and the roots serve as feet. Seeing the lovers he threatens vengeance, but he has to sustain a contest with the insect world, and this enables Mr Henry Emden to present one of the most graceful scenes in the Pantomime, the Insect Haunt in Fairyland. Mr Emden was called for and greatly applauded when this charming scene was revealed.

Following the fortunes of Rokoko we discover that his power is on the wane, and King Moth (Miss Minnie Inch), using his skill on behalf of the lovers, transforms the monster to his original shape, an incident which leads to the Transformation Scene. […]

One most laughable incident is where Rokoko's letter is received in the King's Palace. First the Princess glances at it, swoons, and falls and drops it upon the floor. It is taken up and read by one and another of the courtiers, and always with the same result, until a whole swarm of them are scattered about the Palace floor, while the astonished gazers are still ignorant of the contents of the letter. Such a scene could hardly fail to set the house in a roar. […]

Drury Lane
Blue Beard
[…] THE familiar story of *Blue Beard* will render our readers prepared to hear that the lovely sisters Fatima and Anne have a needy parent, but on the present occasion it is a *male* one. When the curtain rises he is being dunned by his creditors, in the form of his labourers, headed by Rustifusti, foreman of the farm (Mr J A Shaw), for be it explained that Ibrahim, the male parent in question (Mr Fred Law), suffers from agricultural difficulties, which even in these days can be appreciated, the Albanian village of Kommixongortoo not being exempt from such bucolic epidemics. He in vain tries to conciliate his people with mild words; he pleads –

I am not rich – these empty pockets show it you;
But Ibrahim, though poor, is just – I'll owe it you,

and sings a song telling them to "chalk it up", but without any good result. The people become more resentful, and threaten physical force, when Fatima (Miss Victoria Vokes) comes to the rescue, and, with the aid of a rolling pin and her numerous suitors, induces them to wait until tomorrow. Ibrahim urges Fatima to give her hand to their landlord, Blue Beard, to whom he owes three years' rent, but she refers to the Turk's six wives, and her suitors speak of his dealings with the Demon, and explain the manner in which he became a widower. Fatima silences her lovers, and declares her devotion to Selim, the Sailor (Miss Jessie Vokes); and at that moment Ollapodrida (Mr Will Simpson) announces the coming of Blue Beard (Mr Fred Vokes), who arrives preceded by a grand procession, and followed by Shacabac, his factotum (Mr Fawdon Vokes). In a concerted piece, in which the Great Bashaw sings his own March and receives the adulation of the populace, Blue Beard urges Fatima to accept him as a husband, but she affirms herself true to her mariner. She exclaims –

I love that sailor, gone on distant tracks.
Oh, Selim, Selim –

– Yes, I will, with whacks,

is Blue Beard's aside speech. The father and Blue Beard invent a falsehood about Selim having been wrecked; but Sister Anne (Mrs Fred Vokes), accompanied by her lover, Ali Sloper (Miss Bessie Sansom), brings in a present from Selim and a letter informing Fatima that he will be home that night. Thus perplexed, Blue Beard resolves to use the magic spell commanded by the words 'Hey, Cockalorum', to rouse the demons of the storm, and, getting on their mules, he and Shacabac take their departure. But Jack-a-Lantern, the good Goblin (Miss Cora de Lisle), appears and announces his intention of thwarting the Bashaw's evil measures.

The scene ends with a capital parody on "That's what puzzles the Quaker", and we next find Blue Beard and his factotum in a small boat which they can neither manage. The Wicked Demon, Kee-Div (Mr Romaine), is summoned, and a storm is sent. Selim's vessel is seen to approach and to be wrecked upon the rocks, and Selim is found battling with the waves, and then threatened with the great sea-serpent, but is saved from his peril by Fatima and party, who come to his aid in a lifeboat.

The next scene takes us to a caravanserai on the coast, where Selim is reposing after his fatigues. Blue Beard propounds a wonderful remedy, putting in poison unseen by others. He then asks for Fatima, and tries to carry her off, but Selim defends her, when Blue Beard, repeating the magic words, causes the other *dramatis personae* to disappear, and left alone with Fatima he bears her to the Cave of Mystery, gets her entangled in the Silver Web, places a ring upon her finger, and as he bestows a kiss upon the insensible girl the stage is filled with Sylphs, and a grand ballet of Fascination is performed. Meanwhile Ibrahim and Selim seek Fatima, finding her at last as Blue Beard's bride, and the Bashaw bears her away.

We are then carried to Blue Beard's Castle, whither in time Selim follows his lady love, and then learning that she is married leaves her. Then comes the familiar incident of the Blue Room, the impending fate of Fatima, and and her rescue by Selim and his sailors, assisted by Shacabac; and, with the threatening chorus of Blue Beard's headless wives, and his plea for pardon, the humorous and witty Opening reaches its conclusion.

It must be stated that the Management has made every possible use of these very capital materials – scenery, dresses, every detail of elegance and costliness have been supplied with unstinting liberality. The opening ballet, with the girls dressed in red and green, was a sign of the taste to be supplied afterwards. The advent of Blue Beard soon after with his colossal Black Guards, preceded by female soldiers in yellow tunics and brightly spangled tights, the big property elephant upon which the Bashaw sits when he makes his entrance, not to speak of the smaller one, which is really an important help to the fun of the piece, was but an instalment of what was soon to be paid in full.

The ballet that occurs after the entanglement of Fatima in the Silver Web reached the climax of display of profuse elegance. The ballet ladies dressed in pink bodices and net skirts, with silver lace, danced before a scene of variegated flowers, festoons of blossoms descending from the flies. The second dance with hoops, from which hung fringe and bells, was most elegant in its effect.

The other principal scene of spectacular display is in the Ottoman Pavilion, in front of a scenic representation of Moorish character, in which the stage was filled with ladies of every description; black attendants, with long feather faces, jostled giant guards, one or two of the masks of which were capital; female soldiers in black and gold were were followed by others in amber, and to these succeeded some in red, while the dancers in this scene were attired in longish skirts hung with white beads.

The Transformation that begins in the region of ice, in which a human face is fancifully designed, breaks away displaying a Robin perched upon a horizontal bough, a figurante reclining at each side of this charming picture; this in turn opens when we see brightly dressed female forms on each side interspersed with branches bearing golden bell-shaped blossoms, the centre at the back showing ladies in front of a large Chaplet of Wheatears, which opens also to disclose fresh forms of loveliness, while from the flies descend, some solitary, others in a group, numerous figurantes, making a picture of beauty that the lusty plaudits of the crowded audience could not pay in full. […]

Covent Garden
Sindbad the Sailor

[…] SCENE one shows us the Web of Witchery, with Aphrophora, the Fairy Fiend (Miss Annie Stuart), amongst the Spiders she has subdued. Wishing to check all adventurous spirits and to stay the march of progress, she objects to Sindbad undertaking his voyages of discovery, and, hearing that he is about to start upon one of his expeditions from Bagdad, departs in her fairy chariot in order to prevent him. Her plotting is, however, overheard by Cupid (Miss Marie Williams), who is reclining among the roses, and who flies on the wings of love to foil her plans.

In scene two we see the Port of Bagdad, with the good ship Battledore preparing for her voyage. The Captain, Mustapha Jenks (Mr G H Macdermott), has a daughter, Zelica (Miss Annie Rose), who, being enamoured of Sindbad (Miss Fanny Leslie), resolves to follow him on his adventures. In this scene we are also introduced to Ali Ben-bolt, otherwise Buccaneering Billy (Mr Herbert Campbell), a pirate of tender years; Rahat Lakom, the Captain's wife (Mr Arthur Williams), several Midshipmen represented by Mesdames Emily Duncan, Julia Vokins, D Ernstone, Nora Davis, Grace Otway, Clara Fisher, &c, and a wonderful Monkey, played by Master C Lauri, all of whom accompany Sindbad on his voyage, which the Fairy Fiend arrives too late to prevent.

Scene three represents the Battledore very much at sea; and in scene four, through the combination of Thunder, Lightning, Wind, and Rain, who are summoned to the aid of the Fairy, the good ship sinks on the oyster reef "twenty thousand leagues under the sea". Here Cupid turns up to the rescue with a diving bell. In this scene we are treated to a chorus by "real natives", and a ballet of sea nymphs, headed by Mlle Columbier.

Scene five takes us to the Cuddy on board *HMS Bib*, on which the whole party have sought refuge. After a wonderful exhibition of cookery on the part of Rahat and Billy, Cupid guides the vessel to scene six, the Big Roc's Nest, where the Man of the Sea (Miss Jenny Rogers), faithful to the story, nearly brings Sindbad to grief. Roc ultimately flies off with Sindbad and the Captain to the Diamond Valley, which we see in scene seven. Here we view a grand procession of the King and Queen of the Valley of Diamonds. In scene eight, which shows us the head of the modern Memnon on the borders of the scientific frontier, we hear the oracle consulted by Sindbad and his friends, who are now anxious to return. The irrepressible Fairy Fiend endeavours once more to accomplish their destruction, but is prevented by Cupid, who wafts everybody through the clouds to the grand Transformation of a Christmas Card. […]

When the curtain went up the spectators found their interest at once entangled in that "web of witchery" mentioned above, and from that moment until the Transformation they were not able to get it clear again. Why, the very flies that would not walk into the spider's parlour were worth a journey to see as marvels of the skill of the property maker, and surely nothing was ever seen like that "fly" chariot, drawn by flies and bearing off the Fairy Fiend, who at the outset proposes to do all the mischief, making way for saucy Cupid. The grand ballet is prettily arranged, the dancers, who carry coral branches, going through their task in pleasing fashion. The fun in the Cuddy on board the *Bib* is fast and furious, thanks mainly to the doings of the ubiquitous Monkey, whose mischievous propensities are not to be curbed even by a pistol shot and a carving knife. The great Roc and the little Roc are birds that are sure to delight all little people, and to set them wondering whether after all the wisdom of the poet the feathered ones really do "in their nests agree", for they appear to chatter incessantly. The great Roc is a splendid fellow, and he takes his flight with his victims in his claws in a way that makes us open our eyes very wide indeed.

This, however, is the Roc upon which the Covent Garden Pantomime will *not* split, for it introduces us in the Diamond Valley to a scene so dazzling, so brilliant, and so beautiful that it would be impossible for words to adequately describe it. We might tell of the crystal steps which span its centre; of the jewelled stalactites that droop in all directions; of the seemingly countless array of bejewelled Amazons that come marching past; beauties fair and beauties dusky; some bearing lamps; some carrying burnished weapons of war, and all arrayed with exquisite taste and elegance. […]

Certainly one of the biggest hits of the performance was made by Master C Lauri as Pongo. So active and comical a stage monkey has not often been seen. This monkey's escape from shipwreck, and the means whereby that escape is effected, is about as clever and comical a bit of business as has ever been executed, and while it was in progress every spectator was screaming with delight. Later on, in the Cuddy scene, Master Lauri distinguished himself by running up a rope stretched perpendicularly from the stage to the flies, by taking headers through traps and property frying pans, and by a number of antics of an exceedingly droll description, and denoting extraordinary gymnastic skill. [...]
The Era, 28/12/1879

NOTES
1 – The can-can was supposedly first performed at the Bal Mabille, an open-air dancing venue in Paris.
2 – A reference to Princess Louise's wedding to the Marquis of Lorne, which took place in March 1871.

3 – In 1866 Thomas Castro, an Australian butcher, attempted to pass himself off as Roger Tichborne, heir to an English baronetcy, who was thought to have been lost at sea in 1854. He managed to convince Tichborne's mother but not the English courts.

4 – Siblings Fred (1846-1888), Jessie (1851-1884), Victoria (1853-1894), and Rosina Vokes (1854-1894), together with their American partner Fawdon Vokes (1844-1904) – real name Walter Fawdon – were pantomime and music hall stars for many years.

5 – Lowther Arcade was famous for its toy shops.

6 – This iconic painting by William Powell Frith, first exhibited at the Royal Academy in 1858, was so popular that a barrier had to be installed to protect the work from its crowds of admirers.

7 – The Royal Coburg Theatre, now the Old Vic, was for many years strongly associated with melodrama.

8 – Richardson's Show was a travelling fairground theatre offering programmes of melodrama and burlesque.

9 – Herbert Campbell (1844-1904): An actor, music hall star, and regular cast member in the Drury Lane pantomimes.

10 – Furneaux Cook (1839-1903): An actor and opera singer best remembered for his Gilbert and Sullivan roles.

11 – On December 6th 1876 a fire at the Brooklyn Theatre in New York killed at least 278 people.

12 – Osman Pasha (c1762-c1860): An Ottoman naval commander bearing the title *Patrona* (Vice Admiral).

13 – The Siege of Plevna (or Pleven) took place between July and December 1877. It was a decisive battle in the Russo-Turkish War.

14 – Jenny Hill (1848-1896): Known as "the Queen of the Halls", she one of the greatest music hall stars of the Victorian era.

15 – Marie Loftus (1857-1940): An actress best known for her performances in burlesque, which earned her the title "the Sarah Bernhardt of the Halls".

9
The 1880s
Brutally Ill-treating Babies and Old Women

1880

> *ON Tuesday night, during the performance of the Pantomime of* The Sleeping Beauty, *at the Holte Theatre, Birmingham, a singular fatality occurred. The stage is illuminated by an electric light. The wires which transmit the electric current runs along the passage leading to the orchestra. Attached to these wires are two brass connections, which are placed underneath the stage. Between eight and nine o'clock the members of the band left the orchestra for a short time. Mr Augustine Bierdermann (or Mr Bruno, as he was professionally known), the euphonium player, as he went out placed his hands upon the connections, presumably to try the effects of an electric shock. Unhappily, as the lights were out, the full force of the current was in the wires. The result was that immediately Bruno's hand touched the wires he fell back insensible and unable to move. He was lifted up by some of his colleagues, but before medical aid could be procured he expired. For a time the occurrence was kept from the audience, but when it became known it caused much sensation, and great sympathy was expressed. Bruno, who was an Italian, was much respected. The Coroner's inquiry was opened on Wednesday, but was adjourned after evidence of identification had been taken.*
> **The Era, 25/1/1880**

The Surrey
Hop o' My Thumb; or, Harlequin No-Body, Some-Body, Busy-Body, and the Wicked Ogre with the Seven League Boots
[…] THE scene opens in No-Body's Land, where Myth, Nought, Nil, Nonentity, and other nobodies, after asserting in chorus that they care for nobody, begin to discuss affairs in general, when they are joined by King No-Body (Mr George Conquest Jr) and his familiar Sixanait[1] (Mr J H Rowan), the demon lawyer. King No-Body is a wonderful personage, all head and legs; but what a head! With flowing locks, and with a face that seems to have life itself, and to be capable of expressing the emotions of the mind. Eyes, eyebrows, mouth, tongue, jaw, suit the action to the word, and give a strange and weird vitality to this incorporeal presence, if we may so express ourselves. Sixanait is dressed in black, the tail of his respectable coat of broadcloth developing itself into the caudal adornment of the serpent, while the legal fee which his name suggests is inscribed on the back and front of this devil of a lawyer. The King suggests that nobody hates good children, and, including Hop o' my Thumb in the number, Sixanait resolves to work his ruin, but the Fairy Busy-Body, attended by her Lieutenant Some-Body, appears, and tells the malignant King and his familiar that she will protect Hop from their malice, and, with a chorus and dance, in which latter Miss Grace Hamilton and Miss Grace Mainstone especially distinguish themselves, the scene changes to the Village of Bizziebeedom, where a Harvest Festival is in progress, the rustic characters being represented by children. […]

The story may now be said fairly to commence. The stage being clear, the Dame (Mr Frank Wood) enters to bewail her poverty, although, for all her tears, an empty bottle ominously suggests that her grief is dry. Of course, in such a situation, she is bound to sing a parody on "What I've suffered", at the conclusion of which her husband, Gaffer Noodle (Mr Fred Hughes) returns from his pursuit – begging – with five of his six sons. He complains that Charity Organisation has spoilt his occupation, and his wife suggests that they should get rid of three of their children by deserting them in the wood. This plot is overheard by Hop o' my Thumb (Master Charlie Adeson), who, coming from the pump where he had been concealed, reveals to the audience his intention of thwarting it by dropping crumbs on their way, so that he may thus have a clue by which to find his road out of the forest, his song to the tune of "Sweeter than jam" being enthusiastically encored. The departure of the impecunious family is for the moment interrupted by the arrival of King Kockahoop (Mr W S Parkes), who comes accompanied by his courtiers, charming young fellows, whose elegant costumes in amber, red, mauve, and green satin were shown to the best advantage by Misses G

Campbell, R Evered, L Quintin, P de Walski, M Lowry, and N Vernon. The Herald has already announced the King's trouble in having had his daughter, the Princess Prettyeyes (Miss Katie James), stolen by the Giant Ogre-if-erus (Mr George Conquest Jr), and we must think that in ordinary life such a season was not the one for a father to listen to a band of music, but as it was Tyler's Silver one, and discoursed charming melodies, the audience was delighted with it, whatever the King might have been. But harmony must be crushed, for troubles accumulate, the peasants rush in exclaiming that the Ogre has devoured a whole town, and the King in vain appeals to his people to go and slay the monster. The hope of having the Princess for a bride induces Prince Perfect (Miss Maud Beverley), accompanied by his squire Lollipop (Miss Queen Mab) and Prince Chic (Miss Kate Newton) to volunteer in so dangerous a cause.

With a chorus and dance in which Miss Kate Newton was particularly successful, the scene changes to the skirts of the Woodland. Jem and Eye (the Brothers Wems), the twins, the Ogre's servants, bear in the Princess, and at the recommendation of Sixanait they carry her off to their master, a lively quartet enabling Miss Katie James to show that grief does not prevent her singing and dancing capitally.

Meanwhile the Princes go in search of the Ogre, the Dame and Gaffer desert their children, and Hop is attacked by a raven brought to him by Sixanait. The little hero overcomes his assailant, and is introduced by the Fairy Busy-Body to Amphitrite's Coral Isle of Beauty, a charming scene of coral and shells, with rocks in the distance, and with branches of coral for borders, thus framing in the stage and lending beauty to the elegant ballet invented and arranged by Mr Paul Valentine, whose Terpsichorean contribution is worthy of Mr J Keith's scenic one. In front of this picture *coryphees* enter; some are dressed in blue silk with silver fringe and bear coral branches, some carry scallop shells which they open for the concluding *tableau* with artistic effect; and a more graceful or better ballet troupe it would be difficult to find. […]

To return to the story, we next find Prince Perfect on the road to Ogre Land, where Miss Maud Beverley lightens the way by singing "Hearts beat true". He is joined by his squire, and they seek consolation in their arduous journey by singing a duet to the tune of "Raspberry tart in a little poke bonnet". Prince Chic follows on the same road, and, having relieved Fairy Some-Body disguised as an old woman, in true nursery tale style, is rewarded by the assistance of those serving-men who aided Fortunio in years gone by.

We then come to the Ogre's Bedchamber, in which Jem and Eye go through a scene that recalled the old Payne family of the past. The Dame and the Princess seem to be equally destined to be married to the Ogre; indeed, the former already commences her care of her future step-children, the Ogre's babies, although from the eccentric habit these children in necessarily long clothes have of wearing boxing-gloves and of using them, her future can hardly be considered a bright one. Her own offspring led by Hop enter by the window, and, taking off the crowns from the Ogre's children who are in one bed, Hop and his brothers occupy the other. Thus deceived the Giant kills his own children, and in his attempt to prevent the escape of the Princess and Prince Chic, who, with his servants, has come to the Giant's Castle, is overcome by the little villagers summoned to his aid by Hop o' my Thumb. But, although baulked, the Ogre is not yet beaten, and after the Princess has been restored to her father by Hop, Sixanait brings a challenge from the Giant which is accepted by Hop, and the latter's triumph is achieved in a combat parodying that in *The Corsican Brothers*. […]

The defeat of the Ogre leads to the union of the Princess with Prince Chic, and of course to the Grand Transformation Scene, in which Mr Holland once more displays his enterprising liberality, and Mr G H Prodgers shows his artistic and inventive powers. When the golden-hued canvas is removed rich variegated ground pieces are displayed, between which appear coryphees handsomely dressed in blue and crimson material, profusely trimmed with silver; at the back rises a pedestal supporting three figurantes in yellow satin tunics sustaining a single figure similarly attired; at each side of the stage ladies are drawn up, bearing, in recumbent positions, baskets of flowers; and within the two rows rise female figures with like burdens, standing upon slight silver columns elevated to a considerable height; making, with the aid of blue-belled wing decorations and a laced background, a very charming tableau, which was warmly applauded. […]

Drury Lane
Mother Goose and the Enchanted Beauty
[…] MR BLANCHARD has been the friend of little children since he was himself a child, and for nearly thirty years he has at Christmas time ministered to their holiday pleasures here. He asks them now to accompany him, first to take a peep at the World by Night, and to listen to a chorus of witches, and to be introduced to such old acquaintances as Mother Hubbard (Miss de Vere), Gammer Gurton (Miss Howard), Dame Trot (Miss Ridgeway) and Mother Shipton (Miss Agnes Hewitt), who seem to possess the power to bring about rejuvenescence, becoming "young and pretty" just when they will, and tantalising the old in front by indulging in the interrogatory reflection, "Wouldn't some people like to find this secret out?" […]

Mother Goose (Little Addie Blanche) comes upon us now by surprise, for she springs from an egg and begins to tell of an invitation to a royal christening, and to remind the invited ones that a present will be expected from each. This affords excuse for a visit to Lowther Arcade with its Noah's Ark and ballet of toys, arranged by Mr John d'Auban, and its dancing dolls represented by the tiny pupils of the National Training School for Dancing, and arranged by Madame Kattie Lanner[2]. This, although carried out by such little people, is undoubtedly one of the big features of the Pantomime, and is certain to please all who see it.

Now we get a remarkable sudden change, for Mother Goose's Model Farm is transformed with lighting-like rapidity into the Illuminated Palace of the King (Mr Mark Kinghorn), and all eyes take in with delight the view of the grand entry of the Court returning from the Royal baby's christening. The presents already referred to are brought in, and endow the recipient with beauty, grace, fancy, fun, imagination, "and all the charms best suited to her station". The general joy, as usual, is marred by the appearance of a wicked sorceress, this time called Maligna (Miss Louisa Payne), who foretells that on arriving at the age of twenty Bella, the Princess, shall die through wounding her hand with a spindle, Mother Goose stepping at once to the front to announce her intention to protect the child. How to keep spindles out of the country is now the King's most anxious thought, and he issues this command, which we may quote as illustrative of the humour which pervades the dialogue:

What can't be shan't be! Guards, for twenty years
See that no spindle in this land appears!
Proclaim throughout my fleet from stem to starn
No sailor is allowed to spin a yarn!
And anyone to spindle-shanks seen dwindling,
That instant shall be taken up for spindling!

Time is now called in to make the world twenty years older, and we get to the Royal Nursery, a capital scene, which will be the joy of every little boy and girl who sees it. The walls are just as the walls of every nursery should be if we had our way, for every panel tells a nursery tale. [...]

The next scene shows us the Battlements of the Castle. The Princess (Miss Ada Blanche[3]) has made her escape from the parental apron-string, and fancies she is going to enjoy the delights of fresh air, fresh faces, strolls about the parks, balls, operas, parties, plays, and, most of all, some nice young man to talk to; but she pricks her finger with Maligna's spindle, and has to sleep one hundred years, the King, Queen, and courtiers desiring to share her slumbers, and getting their desires gratified.

The Flight of Time is illustrated by the next scene, the hours, days, weeks, months, and years being marked by a clock with a living pendulum. Here takes place what is described as the Grand Ballet of Stars, the dancers, in glittering array and with spear-crowned heads, being led by Mlle Palladino (a nimble and graceful *premiere danseuse*), Miss Clara Fisher, and Miss Marian d'Auban.

The hundred years soon pass for us, and we are at once introduced to Prince Florizel's Picture Gallery, where we make the acquaintance of a set of smart young cadets and their tutor, Dr Syntax (Mr Arthur Roberts), who coaches them in a new song called "Strictly Proper". Prince Florizel (Miss Kate Santley) now invites them to accompany him in search of the beautiful Bella, and we are transported to the Valley of a Thousand Charms, peopled with shepherds and shepherdesses, the majority of whom are about the age of five years. The Prince introduces his "fellahs" in a "La-di-da" chorus, and then having declared in song that they are "All on the Job", a start is made to the castle where Beauty sleeps. On their way in the Enchanted Wood they encounter a number of owls that look very much like judges. Then there is "a lion in the path", and a very wonderfully made lion it is. In the Courtyard of the Castle, which they presently reach, takes place an exciting "Fight of Demons", headed by Mr William Waite, and some hard knocks are aimed at that wonderful griffin which stands so defiantly on top of the Temple Bar Memorial. We have got to the scene with Prince Florizel by a journey through some lovely country, beautifully represented in a panorama painted by Mr Telbin.

And the end? Well, everybody will guess it. And, so having listened to the King, the Prince, and the Courtiers, in their capacity as wandering minstrels, and having laughed over a droll duet, in which Dr Syntax and a country bumpkin named Yokel take part, we pass at once to the grand Transformation called Love's Fountain. This is a fountain from which spring Cupids without number, armed with their bows and arrows, and prepared to make us love them. It is a scene of dazzling beauty, and on the opening night called forth a tempest of applause. [...]

In the Harlequinade there are four scenes. The first represents a Railway Station, where Messrs Fred Evans and Rowella provide an abundance of fun by brutally ill-treating babies and old women; by frightening nursemaids; by dodging the police – there is a capital policeman here; by actually forcing the company of a sweep upon a smartly-attired wedding party; and by making a kind of football of a fat gentleman in a check suit, divertingly represented by Mr Ross. Then in a Cool Retreat we get some good comic skating and a most mirth-provoking burlesque of the duel scene in *The Corsican Brothers*[4], the weapons being carrots. So funny was this made by the Clowns named that an elderly gentleman, seated very near the footlights, was seized with a fit of uncontrollable hilarity, and made us slightly anxious for his safety.

In a street scene, subsequently, was enacted some capital pantomime by children, and, as a finale, there was what is called a "Grand Reflected Statue Ballet". The front of the stage is filled with coryphees representing statues. At the extreme rear is reflected, or seems to be reflected, the entire auditorium of the Theatre, every dancer appearing to have her double exactly imitating her movements. Some who were present on Monday evening would have it that the stage was divided by a huge mirror; others that a simple gauze cut off a second section of the ballet, trained in precisely the same movements as those practised by the first. Here, then, is a puzzle to be solved, and it will doubtless furnish an additional incentive to a visit to Old Drury during the run of *Mother Goose*, which is sure to secure a long lease of popularity. […]

Ada Blanche as Robinson Crusoe

Choreographer and former dancer Katti Lanner

Covent Garden
Valentine and Orson; or, Harlequin and the Magic Shield
[…] WHEN Carl Meyder takes his seat and lifts his baton to give the signal for preparation to the magnificent orchestra there is general excitement, which, of course, is increased when the lifting of the curtain reveals the Tartarean Forge in the Realms of Sorcery, with the Green Knight (Mr F Barsby) concocting wicked plots and making audacious puns just as coolly as though he were engaged in business the innocence of which could not be disputed. But excitement waxes stronger still when everybody's eyes are feasted with a true, full, and beautiful view of Cupid's Home in Watteau Land, where takes place the Grand Fairy Watteau Ballet, which is sure to command the admiration of all those whose privilege it is to see it. […] We want to look as long and as eagerly as possible at this wondrously choice spectacle. There in the background are the rocks and the dancing waters, and nearer to us are the dwellers in this lovely spot in their Dresden china dresses – that is the only possible way of describing them – and we can see at a glance that these picturesquely clad beings are anxious to abandon their pretty posings to show that they are alive, and to set their feet twinkling to the merry music which continues to issue from the orchestra, and to set the heads of the listeners wagging

in time. Indeed, when King Pippin's Castle comes down from above, and rises from beneath, to shut out the charming scene, something like regret is felt, notwithstanding that the said Castle has beauties of its own.

We have here to listen to those naughty boys Haufrey (Miss Gertrude Wynne) and Henry (Miss Amy Fanchette). They are singing a parody of "Nancy fancied a soldier", and we wonder much that such nice-looking and evidently clever youths can be so wicked as to conspire against so brave a hero as Valentine (Miss Victoria Vokes). Our admiration, however, is soon wanted for the marvellously-made masks worn by the soldiers and attendants of King Pippin (Mr J G Taylor), and by the country folk, who come rushing in to tell of the doings of the Wild Man of the Woods. We have to listen to the hunting song and chorus from *Der Freischutz*; to a parody on "Over the Garden Wall"; and to another, "You're always sure to fetch 'em with a w'st, w'st, w'st", which seems to indicate that his Gracious Majesty King Pippin, who sings it, must at some time have enjoyed the acquaintance of "the great Macdermott".

And now laughter loud and long arises, for the scene is changed to the Royal Stables, and something very comical in the way of horseflesh is introduced. One noble, but somewhat fiery steed, is harnessed to the dog cart which is to carry Valentine and the faithful Hugo (Mr Fawdon Vokes) to the New Forest, in search of Orson, and a second is placed in a stall to undergo the process of grooming. This second horse, on Boxing Night, attracted everybody's attention and excited everybody's laughter. Never was known such a wonderful animal. He had a back that described a semicircle and an eye that seemed to be very much awake, and to take in the whole house at a glance. And when we say "take in", we have not the slightest desire to insinuate that the horse or his eye was an impostor, for though they belonged to the order known as "properties", and relied for their intelligent movements on human means, they both afforded most welcome diversion. Our readers who see the Covent Garden Pantomime must look out for that horse.

Valentine and Hugo have made ready for their journey, and to Mr William Beverly we are greatly indebted for the opportunity to see the route they take – their road running by rocks and vineyards, in striking contrast with the desert waste which succeeds, and which is made more desolate by the black clouds which are being driven by the tempest that is raging. The travellers have presently to pass some wonderfully gnarled tree trunks, a roaring waterfall, a verdant wood, and a beautiful lake, bearing on its bosom water-lilies in abundance, and with its waters glittering in the light of the moon. Mr Beverly's panorama on the the first night did not work quite smoothly, but none, we imagine, will be found to question its artistic merits.

And now we have arrived at the New Forest. Here, indeed, is provided a treat for the boys and girls who are home for the holidays, for the forest swarms with pretty little bears. There are bears black and bears brown, and they are all so gentle and well-behaved that they deserve to be hugged as well as to hug. Some remarkably droll business ensues with the coming of Valentine and Hugo upon the scene, and roars of merriment were heard as there went on a chase between the travellers and Orson (Mr Fred Vokes) and the Little Bear (Master C Lauri), the cub fed by the wild man, and attached to him, as the author puts it, by a kind of cub-board love. The merriment becomes still greater when the orchestra strikes up some familiar ghost music, and Valentine is seen stripping off his coat and breaking his sword in twain, to imitate somebody who here shall be nameless, to challenge Orson to mortal combat, and so to frighten him as to cause him to exclaim – "this is *un-nerving*". The result of the fight will readily be guessed; but Valentine and Hugo cannot lead their captives away until they have joined them in a "characteristic dance".

Then suddenly the New Forest disappears as though by magic, and there is revealed a remarkable scene, showing the Hall of Chivalry, with its noble staircases and galleries, in King Pippin's Palace. His Majesty had resolved to do high honour to Valentine, but first persuades him to put the captive cub through sundry "tricks", thus affording Master Lauri an opportunity for the display of his extraordinary agility. Now look out for the grand triumphal procession, one of those imposing and brilliant and bewildering spectacles only possible upon a large stage, and only obtainable by a vast expenditure. In the beauty and variety of the dresses, in the curious make and shape of the banners, borne by innumerable people, who come marching across the galleries and down the staircases already alluded to, the eyes of the spectators seem to find ever-recurring delight, to be renewed when a troupe of Folly dancers come tripping through the arcades formed by spears and flags, and renewed again in the glorious grouping, filling the entire stage at the end.

But why waste words in a vain attempt to describe the indescribable? To be appreciated this grand Triumphal Procession must be seen; as, too, must the Transformation, which is now not far off, and which is illustrative of "Valentine's Valentine". It is very easy to describe the laced envelope, which contains this Valentine, and which brings something choice for the little ones, as we may tell by its superscription:

This message comes from Fairyland,
To children great and small;
We wish a Merry Christmas, and
A Happy New Year to all.

We forgive the poetical sins of this because of the kindly feeling which inspired it. It is not so easy to describe what is inside and is presently disclosed. We might fill another column by writing of fruits and flowers on either side; of fairies reclining gracefully as it were on the borders of the valentine; of fairies rising from somewhere to dazzle us by their beauty and the beauty of their surroundings; of more fairies descending from somewhere else and hanging, as it were, in golden chains. [...]

Mr Fred Vokes was not introduced until the fifth scene, but then he proceeded to make up for lost time, his triumph being complete when Orson, the wild man, was discovered transformed into a swell of the first water. Mr Fawdon Vokes as Hugo was untiring in his endeavours to add to the fun, and there was much laughter when he was found in the panoramic display running his hardest to keep up with Valentine's property horse. [...] Some of the loudest applause heard during the initial performance fell to Master C Lauri, and that very properly. His activity was simply marvellous, and when, in King Pippin's Palace, this "little Bear" proceeded to hang on by his toe nails to a suspended pole, to extend his body horizontally with only this slender support, and to execute other astounding gymnastic and acrobatic feats, the admiration of the spectators knew no bounds. [...]

All but the children will object that the Harlequinade is too protracted; but, as the enjoyment of the juveniles is the first thing to be considered at Christmas-time, we would not have its proportions in any way curtailed. Mr Harry Payne appears as Clown appears in the first two scenes, representing respectively Nowhere Street, with various shops, and Mrs Suds' Steam Laundry, and his jokes – practical and otherwise – will be found a cure for the unwelcome malady known as the "blues". There is a realistic representation of a butter shop, which we may recommend to notice. Mr Harry Payne has some rare fun here, and the very walls of the house seemed to shake with laugher as a very naughty boy put him, in his character as butter-shop keeper, in a terrible rage by flinging a lump of mud right into the middle of a half-tub of "best Dorset". [...]
The Era, 1/1/1881

1881

AN extraordinary scene was witnessed in the Leicester Theatre Royal on the 14th inst, just before the close of the performance of the Pantomime of Cinderella. *In the second gallery, it appears, a woman had attracted some attention by her strange conduct, but nothing very remarkable happened until she was seen to throw her muff over the front of the gallery on to the floor of the Theatre. This attracted general attention, and, to the alarm of the house, the woman was seen attempting to jump clear of the gallery herself. She caught against the brass railings, and, amid the shrieks of the audience, she fell over and landed with a heavy sound on the reserved stalls in the first gallery below. It was exceedingly fortunate that she did not clear the reserved gallery, or she must have been killed on the spot, and in all probability seriously injured those on whom she must have fallen. The reserved seats on which she fell were luckily vacant. When picked up she was found to be seriously injured. It is stated that she was under the influence of drink, and was suffering from delirium tremens.*
The Era, 15/1/1881

THERE is a certain class of idiots that infests stage doors to worry actresses with silly attentions. To this class must belong the individual who has been recently haunting the Crystal Palace, and who the other day left at the stage door of the Theatre the following original epistle for a certain pretty and clever actress, who is engaged in the Pantomime. Here is the precious document: –

"Norwood. – Please do not be cross at my taking the liberty of writing to you, dear Miss ------. I have been wanting to for ever so long, but could never make up my mind. You are so awfully lovely, and I have fallen in love with you. Don't laugh, please. It is quite true, and very silly of me, I know. We go to the Pantomime nearly every day, but scarcely ever look at any one but you. If you are not cross at my writing this, will you please throw two carrots at your mother (you know who I mean) in the scene where you find yourself at home? Do please. Ever yours, SILLY. *PS. – You have seen me before with my sister, near the stage door."*
The Era, 29/1/1881

The Britannia
The Enchanted Dove; or, the Princess, the Poodle, and the Sorceress
[...] THE chief incidents are these: Jean, a young peasant and poultry farmer, has a pet dove, which is really a princess under enchantment. This princess was beloved by Amouroso (Mr E Newbound), a magician; but his wife, Jealoustina (Mrs S Lane), who is a sorceress, discovering his passion, transformed the princess into the above-named bird. There is a meeting of witches, who do their utmost to prevent her happiness in the future. Amouroso succeeds in buying the dove from the sister of Jean, and immediately restores her to her original form, proposes his love, and bears her off to the Palace and Gardens of a Thousand Pleasures. Jealoustina, his wife, in the character of an old gypsy, arrives, and tells the fortunes of the various characters present. The magician gives Rosebloom, the Dove (Miss Emily Adams), some magic bon-bons, and, to escape his importunities, she snaps one – a magic car appears – and she escapes. In this

scene a grand Oriental ballet takes place, in which Mlles Luna and Stella dance admirably. A large *corps de ballet*, well trained, enhances the effect.

Two princes, Jolliboy (Miss Mariette Nash) and Merryheart (Miss Rose Randall), on their travels meet with the Princess and Lizette (Miss Julia Lewis), and by flirting excite the jealousy of Jean; they also meet with Pompey (Mr G Lewis), who was under enchantment as a poodle dog, but released at the same time as Rosebloom, and is now Captain of the Sultan's Guard. The Princess, in the flying car, lands safely near a village inn, where the sorceress is playing waitress and King Kurious (Mr G B Bigwood), bewitched by her arts, is landlord. The lovers all meet here and are very jolly, when Amouroso appears and bears the Princess away to the Steel Castle. The sorceress, at the head of her troops, attack and storm the Castle, rescuing the Princess and Lizette from captivity. Fortunate for humanity would it be if all sieges were conducted in future like that in which Mrs Lane appears as the leader of the forlorn hope. Instead of cannons and bombshells, only vegetables are employed, and, after a cyclone of carrots, a cataract of turnips, and a typhoon of cabbages, the stern defenders of the Steel Castle are compelled to yield.

We next see the Palace of King Kurious, where the princes, tired of wandering, return home and present their friends at court. Amouroso appears as an old man, and tells them that, to learn who are the parents of Rosebloom, she must consult the Oracle of the River. She goes at night to do so, and again falls into his clutches; but Jealoustina and the good fairy appearing at the right moment he is finally defeated, and promises to be a good boy in future, and devote himself to his wife. Rosebloom is discovered to be the daughter of King Kurious.

After some lively comic business and a dance, which was so congenial to the taste of the Hoxtonians that it had to be repeated no less than four times, the stage grew dark and the first glimpses are obtained of the grand transformation scene. It is called "The Glittering Bower of Amaranthe in the Realms of Radiance". […]

Although fairy scenes and fantastic effects are largely introduced in the opening there is no lack of pantomime fun. One of the most amusing was a skit on the Salvation Army, and the drolleries of the Brothers Wemms as a couple of comic valets pleased the audience as much as anything seen or heard in the pantomime. […] Mr Bigwood had one of those eccentric parts in which he revels. As King Kurious he was indeed a Kuriosity, especially when the Convivial Monarch is brought home to the Palace gates by some irreverent street boys, who, finding him royally "tight", suppose him to be a "guy", and carry him until the Royal Chamberlain discovers him after a magnificent reward of twopence halfpence has been offered for the missing monarch. Is this intended for a satire upon the King of Bavaria? He, like King Kurious, frequently leaves the palace and says nothing to nobody until there is a hue and cry, when King Ludwig comes quietly back and discreetly holds his tongue as to where he has been wandering. King Kurious does not mind confessing that he has been making a night of it. […]

The Surrey
Mother Bunch and the Man with the Hunch; or, the Reeds, the Weeds, the Priest, the Swell, the Gipsy Girl, and the Big Dumb Bell
[…] THE curtain rises before a Weedy Waste in Surrey, where Mothers Bunch (Miss Blanche Fenmore), Shipton (Mr J G Wilton), Goose (Miss Fanny Matthews), and Hubbard (Mr Dale) are engaged discussing the subject for the Surrey pantomime, Mother Goose suggesting that they shall consult the Red Elves in the matter. Then comes the first bit of ingenuity; the boys who personate the Elves repeat in chorus the various nursery rhymes, with which pantomime writers are but all too familiar, and, turning round at the conclusion, the single letters on each boy's back make up the name of the subject, Bo-Peep, Oranges and Lemons, Jack and Jill, and the like. But Mother Bunch declares that they all are worn threadbare and won't have any of them, when Novelty (Miss Lily Barry) appears, and, calling up her library, places it at the disposal of the assembled maternities. As she calls over the books the juvenile representatives of their principal personages step from the case and salute the audience. […]

Esmeralda (Miss Lizzie Beaumont) is selected for the heroine of the pantomime, and, with Mother Bunch for her friend, and Mother Shipton for her foe, the Gipsy Girl starts on her career, and the scene changes to an old street in Paris with the exterior of the residence of Count Collywobbles (Mr H M Edmunds) and his three handsome daughters, before which a dance of male and female peasants in sabots is executed in a characteristic manner, the stamping on the ground in their wooden shoes being done in capital time, and the blue dresses of the girls appareled as men contrasting effectively with the brown skirts of their partners.

The stage clear, Count Collywobbles returns home in a cab drawn by a most obstinate property horse driven by Cabby OOO, who certainly did not waste his money when he bought a whip. This scene, indeed, is the very spirit of pantomime, and kept the house in a roar while it lasted. Mr Edmunds as the Count, Mr B Albert as Cabby, and Mr W Albert as Jeames, the Count's servant, exhibited that combination of spirit and fun with which we used to associate the Payne Family years ago. Cabby beats his horse with his whip, the Count applies his umbrella for the chastisement of Cabby, who retaliates with his whip, upon which the Count drags him right through the front window, he himself quitting the vehicle by the back of it. Indeed, such an excellent "trick" cab is it that there seems a means of egress at every part except the roof, which is occupied by the Count's luggage, especially by a large trunk. To see Jeames and Cabby take that trunk off the cab, to remark how its weight makes its removal altogether hopeless until suddenly it jerks forward and capsizes the unhappy Jehu on to the back of his horse to the discomfiture of that animal, and not to roar with laughter, in defiance of all social propriety, would be utterly impossible. Then, the box being got down, it is as difficult of locomotion as ever, and Cabby pushes and Jeames drags in vain, until at last the Count undertakes to carry the trunk into his house himself. With the assistance of the Count's daughters they manage to raise the thing onto his shoulders, when he is crushed by the weight. As the box resumes its place on the ground, his lordship having been forced through the bottom of the trunk, however, his family turn the key in its lock and set their parent free. […]

Downey Cardo (Miss Lizzie Beamont), the gipsy king, accompanied by Esmeralda and her goat (Master Leonard Lauraine), and followed by the populace, enter. The goat, who is spoken of by Downey as "the perfect cheese", and by his mistress as "an excellent butter", hardly deserves all the compliments he receives. The gipsy is entertaining the crowd when Claude Frollico (Mr G H MacDermott[5]) appears, and, oblivious of his calling, pays court to Esmeralda, which she cannot be said to encourage. By the way, what a costume Mr Macdermott assumed! The ballet girl whose dress was said to begin too late and leave off too soon was nothing in the latter respect compared to Frollico's. A monk's robe tied at the waist by a thick rope, suggestive of personal discipline, and going no farther than under half a yard below it, is, to say the least, unique in ecclesiastical vestments. Snubbed by the gipsy, and threatened by her brother, who leave him after they have sung "I say, copper, come and see me righted", he is joined by Squashimodus (Mr Cruikshanks), the hunchback bellringer, who is being hunted by the boys.

It is a singular coincidence that the ill-grown personage should be enacted by Mr Cruikshanks, but it is no less certain that the impersonation could hardly be improved. There was a breadth and strength in the assumption that at times raised it above its associations and surroundings; makeup, voice, manner, all were in excellent keeping, and entitled the actor to the applause awarded to him. Squashimodus learns that his love for Esmeralda has a rival in Claude, and with a duet, "You're quite a John Bull", and the tossing in a blanket of Collywobbles, who is mistaken for the hunchback, the scene closes.

We are now brought to Sir Guy de Faux (Mr James Albert), whose son, Captain Phoebus (Miss Marie Loftus), is engaged to the Count's daughter, Fleur de Lys (Miss Vinny Edmunds), who does not love him, and would hand him over to either of her sisters, whilst Phoebus is in love with Esmeralda. The interview that now occurs between the latter two is surprised by Fleur de Lys, who renounces her claim upon Phoebus, acknowledging her passion for Ernesto, prettily acted by Miss H Claremont. A quartette, and a dance by Miss H Claremont, Miss Marie Loftus, and Miss V Edmunds, very neatly performed, clear the stage for Claude and the Hunchback, who come on resolved to follow Esmeralda and carry her off.

The Frogs' Pool and Gipsy Encampment of the next scene, showing the gipsies reclining about the stage, a most picturesque *tableau*, presented a characteristic tambourine dance of the Romany people, the precision of time and position, as well as the simultaneousness with which the tambourines were struck by the dancers, showing very careful preparation and rehearsal. […]

The Night Picnic – Collywobbles, his daughters, Sir Guy, and Jeames, with the talk about ghosts and the phantom table cloth – was another excruciating scene of pantomime fun, although it would gain by compression, which will have doubtless been effected by this time. Collywobbles's assertion to his daughter, who, by the aid of the already alarming table cloth, pretends to be the ghost of her grandfather, that he never could afford a ghost, was very humorous; and the triple short sword combat between the Count, Sir Guy, and Jeames, a most adroit performance, brought the interlude to a successful end.

Mother Bunch bears Esmeralda to her floral home, where, amidst festoons of roses, before banks studded with margarets, the background being of water and mountains, and with a summer-house rising from a promontory, a most elegant ballet is represented. The *danseuses*, dressed in white with bright green leaves, which depended from the waist, and decked with silver spangles, their heads ornamented with flowers, once more displayed their careful training as to their positions on the stage, their most brilliant effect being that with the Chinese umbrellas, which upon being lowered in the *tableau*, showed clusters of roses, violets, sunflowers, &c. Once more Madame Sidonie appeared and, with her dances on one foot, on the tips of her toes, with her *tours de force*, and when she revolved upon some blossoms, commanded the audience's applause.

Passing over the next scene, in which Ernesto and Fleur de Lys seek Claude's study for him to marry them, we come to the Palace of a Thousand Delights, in which Captain Phoebus surprises his father by refusing Fleur de Lys, and announcing that the Princess Esmeralda is his chosen bride, an arrangement that is spoilt by Mother Shipton asserting that she is only a gipsy; the statement from Downey Cardo, that she is a Princess born, being baulked by Mother Shipton's saying that until bells shall cease to sound she shall only be known as a gipsy girl. This scene is especially noticable by the parade of warriors, glitteringly attired, and by the appearance of the juvenile embodiments of sports and games represented by cards, dice, draughts, lawn-tennis, cricket, trap, bat and ball, dominoes, battledore and shuttlecock, and cribbage-boards.

Mother Bunch by means of her Elfin crew gets some dumb-bells cast, then comes the end. Claude stabs Squashimodus with a dozen daggers, is himself arrested, and Downey Cardo, thanks to the dumb-bells, no longer silenced by Mother Shipton, reveals the fact that Esmeralda is the Princess Charming. Phoebus and she are united, and the Transformation comes, where, from gilded foliage falling in festoons, the scenery sinks and a grand centre of jewels appears, while from the flies hangs a pendant of precious stones, behind which is spread a fan which sinks and rises to exhibit fresh beauties again and again; a second fan being drawn down upon which handsome *figurantes* are discovered, clothed in gold, silver, and in white cambric, standing upon silver battlemented terraces supported by silver pillars; the Transformation being accompanied by the orchestra, first in Gounod's "Meditation on Bach's Fugue", and finally by the "Wedding March". […]

Drury Lane
Robinson Crusoe

[…] AS in duty bound, we begin at the beginning, with spirits that are "moony" and otherwise, and then pass on to things that are mundane in the picturesque neighbourhood of Primrose Farm Dairy, and the Jolly Sailors' Tavern. Mrs Crusoe (Mr Arthur Roberts) is the owner of "Ye Too Intensely Utter Dairy", and from this description painted over the door it is readily guessed that she is a victim of the aesthetic rage. As is the mistress so are the maids, as we find directly when they come out, looking very pretty in their quaintly built bonnets to feed the chickens. The maids coming from the dairy are met by some very jolly and smartly dressed sailor boys from the tavern across the road, and by general consent some pretty singing is indulged in. Robinson (Miss Fanny Leslie), who is to be the hero of the piece, has fallen desperately in love with Polly Lovage (Miss Amalia), the pretty daughter of the innkeeper. So, too, has Will Atkins (Mr Harry Nicholls), "the bold bad man" of the story, who contrives presently to lure all the young people in whom we are interested, and some of the old ones, on board his ship lying in "the Port of London".

On the spacious deck, which forms the third scene, we make the acquaintance of some very Liliputian sailors, all capitally dressed, and all equal, at least, to the sailor's first duty, of being able to dance a hornpipe. Some of these Jack Tars, we should say, stand about two feet and a half in height, and have attained the mature age of about four years. The spectators were delighted with these little people, as well they might be, and their dance had to be repeated, in compliance with an irresistible demand.

And now the good ship, that has so bad a captain, sets sail, and we have our eyes feasted with a beautifully painted and ingeniously contrived panorama showing both sides of the Thames. As the sea is approached the vessel begins to rock, and, when fairly in the open, the heaving billows, the dark thunder clouds, the flashing lightning, seems to predict disaster, and to enter, as it were, conspiracy with wicked Will Atkins.

It is all very realistic, and very exciting, and we get quite a sense of relief when, by the aid of some lovely sirens, we are permitted to go with the wreck to "the bottom of the deep blue sea", to be spectators of what is called the Ballet of Silver Fishes. It takes place among the coral branches and other curious and beautiful things that lie "full fathoms five", and it fairly dazzles us by its brilliancy, the effect here being greatly enhanced by the use of the new patent lime-light apparatus, manufactured for the pantomime by Messrs Allan and Co, of Cardiff. Next we pass to the Sea Shore of the Uninhabited Island, and find that Robinson Crusoe has not only been saved, but has made himself possessor of a very intelligent and sharp-witted Cockatoo (Mr Harry Jackson).

We listen to Robinson's patriotic song, and then we are taken back to the Jolly Sailors' Tavern, where, in Polly's Bedchamber, some fun is supplied and provokes hearty merriment, and where Mrs Crusoe and Mr Lovage (Mr James Fawn) indulge in a topical duet that is encored some half-dozen times. Polly, sleeping, sees in a vision what has happened to her beloved Robinson, and, with Mrs Crusoe and her papa, determines to go to his rescue, Will Adams, who has escaped drowning, artfully proposing that they shall take ship with him; that if they find Crusoe Polly shall marry him, and that if their search is unsuccessful, he, Will Atkins, shall claim her hand.

The eighth scene shows us Crusoe's Island, and it is here that takes place that grand Indian ballet which is likely to become the talk of the town. Curious looking people arrive upon all sorts of animals, including elephants, alligators, ostriches, turtles, and giraffes. The stage is very soon crowded by a glittering throng, and the eye becomes fairly dazed and the brain bewildered in the attempt to take in all the wondrous paraphernalia of this marvellous spectacle, which denotes unstinted outlay, and which speaks volumes for the taste and fancy of Mr Alfred Thompson, who designed the dresses and properties. Preparations are here made for roasting and eating Friday (Mr Charles Lauri Jr), but Robinson comes to his assistance and he is able to escape.

After some exceedingly comical business in Crusoe's Cave, the adventurers start for home, and introduce us to London in the Last Century, a quaint and splendidly built up scene. While children dance with delight, and the inhabitants crowding the balconies cheer, there come marching in the representatives of a host of trades and professions. First of all are the heralds, then the soldiers, and then in turn night-watchmen with their lanterns, clockmakers encased in their clocks, sweeps stuck fast in chimney-pots, bootmakers in big boots that are spurred, and that are accompanied by a mighty shoe, tailors riding on geese, barbers tied up in their shaving-brushes, but contriving to carry their poles, hatters in hats, umbrella-makers in umbrellas, carpenters bearing mallets, candlestick-makers, to show that they are not to be extinguished, even by the electric light; watermen, jewellers, grocers, goldsmiths, silversmiths, millers with sacks of flour, fishmongers, butchers, poulterers, spectacle-makers, and brewers, looking rubicund and jolly as befits their calling.

Soon after this we arrive at the Transformation; not, however, before Robinson Crusoe and Polly Lovage have joined hands, and put Will Atkins hopelessly out of court. The Transformation is called the Wedding Cake. [...] This wedding cake is, of course, that of Robinson and Polly. They stand high up on the top of it, and we hear Crusoe saying, in the author's witty words:

For many years the problem still will be,
How many boys has Crusoe sent to sea!
As each of these became some famous man,
Send to see Crusoe – every one you can.
The Era, 31/12/1881

1882

THE POLICE AND THE PANTOMIME
ON Monday, January 23rd, proceedings against Mr Charles Hemingway, described as of Dawes Street, were reopened in the Borough Court, Town Hall, Bolton. The charge against defendant was that he did permit to be used words and expressions offensive to public decency...[...] On the 14th inst the police visited the Temple Opera House, not quite on their own motion, but a complaint had been lodged as to what was said, and they went for the purpose of taking notes. [...]

Detective-inspector Ormrod was the first witness called. He said – On Saturday night, the 14th of this month, I went into Majilton's Opera House. A pantomime* was going on.

Mr Hall (prosecuting) – Did you hear any of the performers say anything?

Witness – I heard Princess Prettypet (Miss Louisa Crecy). Mrs Majilton here came forward, and was identified as "Miss Crecy". Princess Prettypet said:

There is a young gent
Sits down there,
It is a perfect riddle;
He has been to see us every night,
And he fancies her in the middle.

Mr Hall: – People should understand that this is not a day performance of the pantomime.
Witness – She also said:

If I tickle you and you tickle me,
And we both tickle one another:
But if I tickle you and you don't tickle me,
I'll go home and tell my mother.

One of the men, Baron Boosey (Mr A Rivers), sang a song and whistled at the end of the verse. At the end of the verse he mentioned something about the old crinolines, and he added "You could almost see the darlings' ------," and then he whistled. [...]

Mr Wharton (defending) – Will you swear that the words were not "He parts his hair in the middle?"
The witness did not seem willing to answer the question with a direct negative or affirmative, and it was only after some fencing between him and the barrister that he said he could not swear those words were not the words used.

Mr Wharton – Now, in this whistling song of Baron Boosey's there is whistling in every verse? – Yes.

How many verses did he sing? – He has only sung two since. That about the "darlings' ------ has been omitted, and the tickling has not been mentioned since.

Well, I'll read it to you:

With the skin-tight fitting dresses,
Girls had better draw the line,
For they show us quite too much

> Of the human form divine.
> But their dear old crinolines
> Were quite as bad as these;
> For when they used to wear them
> In a strong and roguish breeze,
> They were blown about until
> You almost saw the darlings' ------
>
> *...and then, you know, he whistled. The word ending the line before was "breeze," so instead of using a word which rhymed he whistled. Didn't he? – He did.*
>   *Well, can you tell me a single word that would rhyme with "breeze" that would be in any way indecent, except "knees?" – I cannot say that I can.*
>   *Detective Howcroft, the next witness called, corroborated Ormrod's statements.*
>   *At the conclusion of Detective Howcroft's evidence, the magistrates retired, and, after an absence of about a quarter of an hour's duration, they returned into court.*
>   *The Mayor then said – I may say, gentlemen, that the magistrates have been out to consider the case; and we have come to the unanimous conclusion that that the prosecution has failed in establishing the case, and we dismiss it.*
>   *Mr Wharton – Of course it is not necessary at all to say a single word about the case. I can only say I was instructed to go into the whole thing upon its merits, and we have ample evidence to show that there is not the slightest thing to offend anyone.*
>   *The court was then cleared.*
> *Cinderella.
> *The Era, 28/1/1882*

Theatre Royal, York
Robinson Crusoe

WHEN all that remains of the pantomimes, in the vast majority of towns, is the pleasant memory which this popular form of Christmas entertainment has left, the York playgoers are on the tiptoe of expectation as to the good things which the Easter annual will contain; and, judging from the large audience which assembled on Saturday last, and the still larger one on Monday, it is very evident that at York the Easter pantomime is not going out of fashion, and also that *Robinson Crusoe* will prove a great success.

The first scene is Davy Jones's Locker, where the redoubtable Davy (Mr W H Templeton), Hurricanos (Mr A G Clinton), Torpedo (Mr Gilbert Fenny), and Will o' the Wisp (Miss Emily Spiller) are seen plotting against the comfort of everyone in general and Crusoe in particular. A hurried visit from the fairy Oceana (Miss Theresa Stirling), concerning the subject of the pantomime, causes a temporary interruption, and, the choice falling upon *Robinson Crusoe*, the scene ends with the Good Fairy's promise to protect the hero against the designs of Will o' the Wisp, who is commissioned to wreak all manner of vengeance on his devoted head.

Scene two, the Port of Hull, opens with a grand nautical ballet by the Sister Belton and *troupe*, after which Polly Pert (Miss Susie Montague), Jack Mainbrace (Miss Lucy Weston), Crusoe (Miss Grace Huntley), Will Arthur (Mr George Capel), and Mrs Crusoe (Mr Victor Stevens) are introduced in quick succession. Atkins loves Polly, who of course exercises her good taste, and prefers Crusoe; and to be revenged the villain puts the brokers in possession of the Dame's humble abode. The old lady's goods and chattels, consisting of

Six water-butts, two mouse-traps, one dead rat,
One tabby teapot, and a china cat,

are not worth much, and Jack Mainbrace, a rejected suitor for Polly's hand, promptly settles the claim. Atkins tries to induce the Dame to send Crusoe to sea, and take a trip with him herself, intending in their absence to secure Polly. The Dame replies:

But then the ocean is so awful damp,
The very thought of it gives me the cramp.
I love the briny when it's very cross;
I love to see it playing pitch and toss;
I love to see it leaping to the skies;
I love it when to dive us deep it tries;
I love to hear the winds and waves contending;
I love to hear their voices with the thunder blending;

I love to see the surging foam upon it;
I love it, but you'll never catch me on it.

Not to be baffled, Atkins calls on the press-gang, who seize Crusoe, his mother, and friends, and convey them to the cabin of the *Lively Polly*, scene third. Then follow more promises of protection from Oceana, and vice versa from Will o' the Wisp, and after some amusing business, a first-rate realisation of storm and wreck of the ship is given, which reflects the highest credit on Mr Stevens' stage management. The dismasted hull is seen drifting and tossing about in all directions, until it finally disappears beneath the waves, leaving the crew struggling in the storm-tossed water.

Scene fifth, a Rocky Coast, on which the ship has gone to pieces, brings us to the home of the cannibals, where King Krunchimunchi (Mr Hal Forde) and his Prime Minister (Mr L T Dawson) are found lamenting the absence of white man from the royal larder, when the Dame wanders on in a very dilapidated condition, and after mourning her sad state as follows:

Well, this is nice! Chuck'd on a barren coast,
If caught by Niggers me they'll quickly roast;
I've to a mummy on the rocks been beaten
With naught to eat, expecting to be eaten.
What shall I do? These Nigs I can't abear 'em,
I'd wash their clothes – but here they never wear 'em.
I've mashed one black, and me he tried to follow;
He wore a scarf pin, and a paper collar.
Where is my boy? To find him I have tried;
I fear he, like that good young man, has died,

gives vent to her feelings in song concerning that same young man, and is immediately claimed by Krunchimunchi as his squaw.

The action is now transferred to the interior of the Island of Delight – a splendid set – where, after Oceana and Will o' the Wisp have had further contention as to the fate in store for Crusoe, Friday (Mr Fred Cairns) is pursued and captured by the cannibals; but, escaping, he claims and receives the protection of Crusoe. The Dame, who has escaped from Krunchimunchi, and Will Atkins then turn up, in the guise of street mendicants, and converse thus:

DAME:
Tuppence a day, to find myself a dinner,
It ain't no wonder as I'm getting thinner;
Me and my partner begs from all we sees,
All we sees we wants; all we wants we sieze.
ATKINS:
Kind Christian friends, so far from home we've come
Please to assist the starving deaf and dumb;
I lost my speech when I was six weeks old,
My mother pawned it, so at least I'm told.
Chuck us a copper or we'll starve; 'od rabbit it,
I quite forgot the island's uninhabited,

and then sing a ditty dealing with local events. They meet Polly and Jack, and are congratulating themselves on their luck when they are recaptured by his dusky majesty, the drop falling on an effective tableau. This cloth is a very picturesque representation of the Jungle, and the action being briskly carried onward, Crusoe's hut is reached, where a lot of fun is obtained through the medium of Friday and the various animals, much to the delight of the juvenile portion of the audience. The climax is, however, drawing near, and after Crusoe has rescued his sweetheart and conquered the cannibals, all depart for England, the concluding scene being a capital view of York's famous cathedral, in which all ends happily. [...]

The Standard
Little Red Riding Hood; or, Harlequin Boy Blue, Miss Muffit, the Wolf, and the Bears
[...] THE first scene is a kind of Pandemonium, very lurid, wild, and picturesque, with groups of weird figures flashing and glittering in a vast subterranean hall supported by giant columns. This fanciful scene, lighted by tripods emitting flame, made a good opening scene; and here is plotted the scheme which is to thwart the proceedings of those innocent mortals, Little Boy Blue (Miss Alice Aynsley Cook), Miss Muffit (Miss Marie Williams), and Little Red Riding Hood

(Miss Louise Neville). By means of demonic letter-boxes the ruler of the supernatural realm receives communications from the upper world; but, while rejoicing in the prospect of ensnaring the youthful hero and heroines, King Christmas (Miss Blanche Newton) takes them under his protection, and the scene suddenly changes to the region of perpetual winter, where Queen Crystal (Miss Lucy Millais) holds sovereign sway.

In this scene is introduced a very pretty ballet of icicles, and the gambols of winter are specially illustrated by the rolling of an immense snowball, greatly to the delight of the younger portion of the audience, who have had no chance of such an amusement this year. The rolling of the snowball is cleverly managed, for when it is first seen it is not much bigger than a cricket-ball; but, as one good turn deserves another, the fairies twirl it until it grows to a monstrous size.

The next scene is Blunder Castle, an antique fortress standing in the middle of mountain scenery. Here Baron Blunder (Mr Edward Sass) is seen agitated by an unholy passion for Little Miss Muffit, who lives close at hand. The Baron is a very peculiar specimen of a medieval lord. He has invented a code of signals to save him all trouble of giving orders to his servants. A flag is hung outside the castle walls, and according to its colour the servants are to bring the Baron's dinner, his newspaper, his boots, his shaving water, or night-cap. No matter what he may require, a flag is supposed to indicate his wishes; and, of course, being a pantomime Baron, he never gets what he wants. Even his passion for Miss Muffit is thwarted by Little Boy Blue, who, when the Baron serenades the fair one with a trombone very much out of tune, gives him a sound thrashing.

But the Baron is also terribly plagued with his hopeful son Timothy (Mr John Barnum), who in frilled trousers, short jacket, and turned-down collar, is extremely forward in his admiration of the fair sex, for he never sees a pretty girl without attempting to kiss her. In fact, he is so fast that he is always ahead of his papa in such matters. There are, in fact, "heaps of trouble on the old man's mind", as he is the parent of two extremely plain daughters, who worry him perpetually to get husbands for them.

At this juncture a great sensation is made owing to the proclamation of a reward for the capture of a terrible wolf (Mr Fred Shepherd), and the Baron, fired with martial glory, determines, like Queen Victoria, to hold a review of his household brigade. But the Baron's household brigade is not by any means of a military character. His "infantry" consists of a long line of perambulators, each containing a couple of squalling babies. His "guards" are policemen taken from their beat. His "sappers and miners" are the Shoeblack Brigade. His "artillery" consists of housemaids and scullery-maids armed with the implements of their occupation, and his "lancers" are footmen. With these motley regiments a brilliant show is made, and, when the Baron calls for three cheers, even the babies in the perambulators respond.

Red Riding Hood has been expelled from the castle owing to the cruelty of the Baron's daughters, but Timothy, the booby son, has fallen in love with her, greatly to the disgust of his father, who still pursues Little Miss Muffit, and finds her in the kitchen, where the opportunity for pantomime "business" is made the most of by all who take part in the scene. The ugly daughters seeking to hinder the Baron are disposed of, one being put in the clock case, which is turned upside down, revealing the feet of the maiden sticking up in the air; while the other daughter, whose rotundity is her great difficulty in life, gets into the copper, but is speedily roasted out. [...]

Little Red Riding Hood meets her foes in the glades of the forest, and the wolf follows her home and imitates her old grandmother, but again Little Boy Blue comes at the right moment, and gives the wolf such a drubbing that he is glad to howl for mercy.

Here is seems as if the story was upon the point of winding up, but suddenly the scene changes to Pleasure's Paradise, a showy and brilliant effect being produced by a grand spectacular ballet of a very magnificent character entitled the Gnomes of Folly. The stage is completely filled with the representatives of Folly in cap and bells. Beautiful dresses, in almost every variety of colour, blend with exquisite effect, and the evolutions of the dancers proved how careful their training had been. The groups were cleverly arranged, and the concluding tableau, in which all the prominent figures are suddenly decorated with wreaths of flame, and carry wands which are also illuminated in a similar manner, may be chronicled as a triumph, for not a few of the country cousins who witnessed it must have been puzzled to know how the pretty and novel effect was produced.

Once more Little Red Riding Hood is in trouble, having by accident got into the clutches of three young bears, but she is speedily rescued, and now we approach the grand transformation scene, and Little Boy Blue gains the reward for killing the wolf, and also the hand of Little Miss Muffit, although the wolf appears again in a ghostly representation of his former self, and is pardoned for his crime, as holiday audiences expect everybody to be forgiven before the curtain rises upon the transformation scene, which is entitled Under the Moonbeams on a Midsummer Night.

The scene is introduced by a legend pleasantly told by Miss Blanche Newton, and while the various changes take place, Miss Lucy Millais, who has a charming contralto voice, sings appropriate vocal music. This is a good idea, as it interests the audience while watching the gradual unfolding of the scene. The transformation is of a gorgeous kind, and in form and colour could hardly be more graceful and picturesque. The rapid and instantaneous changes of light upon the scene and the elegant groups of figures which gave life and animation to the ethereal effects evoked most emphatic demonstrations from the audience. […]

Drury Lane
Sindbad the Sailor

[…] WHAT audience would not be good-tempered on the evening of Boxing Day? But it had its patience and its temper sorely tried before the advent of the transformation scene in *Sindbad the Sailor*. Into the reasons for the hitches, and the delays, and the confusion which cropped up in many of the scenes, and that caused some to be altogether cut out, we do not think it necessary to inquire. It is proverbial that mistakes will arise even in the best regulated companies, and we are sure that no one could have more regretted those of Tuesday evening than the hard-working and energetic lessee, whose annoyance must have been intensified when he found that the impatient ones in front would not listen to his explanation, and in the mishaps that arose sought and found opportunity to revenge themselves for a fancied wrong which came of the voluntary sacrifice of the trifling extra sum, which had enabled them to get shelter from the drizzle by an earlier admission than had been promised. Playgoers in general, and pantomime lovers in particular, are not ungenerous; and we are sure that many who were present at Drury Lane at the initial introduction of *Sindbad* will, on reflection, be sorry for the hisses and the howls they sent forth in the direction of the stage whenever a wait or an accident occurred. […]

But the reader is doubtless by this time anxious to know something of the character of the work that has here been provided for their holiday delectation, and we begin with the beginning, without, however, undertaking to tell in detail of all the beautiful things that are to be seen between the introduction of the Cave of the Old Man of the Sea and of the Rose Queen's Bower and that Grand Transformation which is appropriately called Christmas, which brings to light the very largest and the very handsomest "Father Christmas" yet born, and which reflects such great credit on the artistic skills of Mr H Emden.

The prelude over, we at once were brought into contact with that fun for the provision of which all the world knows every pantomime is intended. We are taken into the Courtyard of Kybosh Pasha's House, and we made acquaintance with the most comical, and certainly the sleepiest, fat boy we have ever encountered. His eyes told a wonderful tale of enjoyment first and drowsiness afterwards as he listened to a certain Ali's singing of "The Winkle and the Whale", which brought into relief the droll humour of Mr Arthur Roberts, who was dressed in a nautical costume and a bald head that have only to be seen to be laughed at. Mr Roberts was presently joined by Mr James Fawn as Koolinari, female cook to Kybosh, who is represented by Mr Harry Jackson; by Mr Herbert Campbell as Kabob, the young Khedive on his travels; by Mr John D'Auban as the young Khedive's papa, with the most nimble of nimble legs, and by Uglimugli, the destined wife of the young Khedive, represented by Mr A Estcourt.

But what of Sindbad the Sailor? Well, we have been looking through Mr Blanchard's book, and we find that it is as replete with wit and poetry and fancy as in any time during the past thirty years, but although Sindbad is not dropped altogether – being here in the attractive person of Miss Nelly Power – his story is, and nobody appears to trouble very much about it.

We pass on to a very effective picture of an Egyptian port and slave market, stopping though on the way to hear Sindbad sing of "Tiddy-fol-lol". In the scene alluded to occurs a really charming Persian ballet, in which Mlle Zanfretti most distinguishes herself, and provokes acclamation. Here, too, a famous and marvellously clever poodle (Mr Charles Lauri Jr) is put through his paces prior to his sale by auction with other goods and chattels, and then with some good pantomime effects, which should be very attractive when they get into full working order, we go "over the sea, over the sea", and are greatly amused when the agile doggy falls overboard, and has to swim for life. We presently get an introduction to a gigantic whale, whose back forms a playground for the poodle, and that is able when necessary to shut up his tail after the manner of a telescope.

The fifth scene brings us to the Bridal Bower, where the Rose Queen and the Diamond Prince – Mlles Luna and Stella – fairly delight us by the beauty of their appearance and the grace and delicacy of their movements. The place is peopled with dainty lords and ladies, most exquisitely attired, and we think we could look for an hour at least upon the minuet ballet, which had been arranged by Mr John D'Auban, and which very properly calls forth vociferous applause.

In scene the sixth, the Garden of the Old Khedive's Palace, with the drilling of the Pigmy Guard, we find reason to admire some wonderful properties, and the artistic skill which has been brought to bear by Signor Briosche, and then comes a dance of dolls; or perhaps we should say *with* dolls. This ballet, executed entirely by children, made the great hit of the evening, and is sure to prove one of the most attractive and most successful features of the pantomime. The dancers go through some most delightfully expressive pantomime in the way of caressing and smacking their dolls, and herein is provided a sight that is likely to make the hearts of many little people beat more quickly with joy and sympathy.

The flight of the Roc with Sindbad comes soon afterwards, and is very effectively worked, and then we hear a certain Diamond Princess exclaim –

Now, be instructed as a view appears
Of England's history through a thousand years.

And we polish our glasses or open wider our eyes in order to get the full benefit of that grand historical procession which has been talked about so much, and upon which the Drury Lane lessee has spent so much money in his resolve to surpass all previous pantomime glories. The kings and queens of England from the time of William the Conqueror come trooping in, and with them come illustrations of incidents in their respective reigns [...] to the House of Hanover, which brings with it a review of the British troops from Egypt, and Sindbad the Sailor, actually, by some magic process, is transformed to Britannia, who "never, never, never" will have her subjects slaves, and who sings patriotic songs.

Mr Fred Storey won some deserved applause by the elasticity of his legs. Mr Charles Lauri, too, as the Poodle, won plenty of favour, so natural were his movements, the spectators becoming greatly excited when this poodle, escaping from his keepers, went at a gallop right round the front of the house, by the ledge of the first circle, and the supports of the second, making a pretence of falling into the pit when mid-way upon his journey. Mr Harry Jackson's honours came of his wonderfully realistic impersonation of the first Napoleon. [...] Miss Annie Rose brought considerable chic to bear in the part of Zaidee, and Miss Vesta Tilley[6], in her male impersonation and song, seemed to be generally admired. All the ill-temper and dissatisfaction of Boxing Night – that is, of the latter part of Boxing Night – have now disappeared, and *Sindbad the Sailor* is certain to prove remunerative.

Vesta Tilley in drag

The Surrey
Puss in Boots, the Ogre, the Miller, and King of the Rats; or, the Pretty Princess and Queen of Cats
[...] WHEN the curtain rises we find Bristleback (Mr Ramsey) and Sharpfangs (Mr Lindsey), with their king, Ratifero (Miss Lizzie Claremont), discussing with other rats the aggression of cats, and of Tom (Willie Edmunds, whom we are to know as Puss in Boots), most particularly. Tom is driving them from the miller's, where they obtain good forage,

and something must be done to get rid of him. The cat queen, Felina (Miss Hariett Claremont), comes in with a flag of truce, and proposes that cats and rats shall alike leave the neighbourhood, but this Ratifero will by no means agree to, and the two enemies part company with mutual defiance.

Then, the prologue being over, the story begins. With a bright background, whose golden hues suggest the promise of a rich harvest, and built by the side of a broad stream, whose swift waters turn the big wheel that grinds the corn, stands the mill of the deceased gentleman who was presumably known as the Miller of the Dee. Opposite this picturesque and profitable establishment a bridge spans the river, whilst high up in the air on top of a pole rests a dove-cote. The scene is pleasant to the eye and suggests peace and affluence; but, unluckily for the Widow Oatmeal, familiarly known as Jack's mother, as well as for Jack himself, so much prosperity is not to be theirs.

When we are introduced to the Widow she has been in that condition a year, and, in accordance with the eccentric provision of her late husband, has been kept in ignorance of the manner of the disposal of his effects up to that day. The more or less lamented Mr Oatmeal having been dead a twelvemonth, the time has arrived when his brother Grindoff (Mr H M Edmunds), assisted by the village lawyer, Red-tape, and the latter's clerk, Copy-o-Writ (the Clayton Twins), has to read the last will and testament of the deceased miller. Pending this exciting ceremony the bereaved lady, who is well experienced in matrimony, may pass the time agreeably in singing of a previously enjoyed domestic happiness. The Marquis of Carabas (Mr Victor Stevens), very appropriately styled Glumpo, attracts the lady's attention; but as he is up to his eyes in debt, and is on the look out for a rich wife that he may mend his own fortunes, he does not offer Mrs Oatmeal much encouragement, except in the small way of singing an aesthetic duet with her.

Grindoff and his sons, Hodge (Mr James Albert) and Willie (Miss Vinnie Edmunds), with his legal advisers, come to read the will of the former's brother. The property goes to Grindoff, Mrs Oatmeal has the broomstick, which she used to give her lord in happier days, and poor Jack (Miss Sara Beryl) only has the Cat. Even the latter legacy is jeopardised for the hero by the evil intelligence of Ratifero, who suggests to Grindoff that he shall pitch him in the stream. The miller might certainly be annoyed by the way in which Tom throws down the tea service and knocks over the table, but it was too much to drown him for it; indeed, it was too much for the miller. The chase of Puss, which occurred in the attempt to put him in the Dee, was something to see.

We now follow the fortune of Jack, who, left by his mother, seeks consolation in singing of a darling and a daisy, supplemented by a dance, which deservedly obtained for Miss Sara Beryl the compliment of a bouquet. Felina comes to him, and, conferring the power of speech and a pair of top-boots upon Puss, tells Jack the Cat will be his best friend. Glumpo joins Jack; the former is on his way to King Doughnutt's dominions, hoping to espouse the king's daughter, Princess Brilliantine (Miss Carmen Barker), but remains to sing a duet with Jack about going far away in the morning.

Meanwhile the king (Mr Charles Cruikshank) arrives with his daughter and court, especially with his giant page Tiny. This youth, who is about twelve feet high, and with corresponding bulk, is one of young Mr Conquest's marvellous giants. His mask – so well arranged that the mouth moves naturally with the utterance of the words, which sound clear and distinct, whilst the forehead is creased and the practicable eyes close themselves in slumber and wink with mischief – is only equalled by his wonderful legs, which can perform a step dance or cross themselves in careless naturalness as if they were the actor's natural limbs. We may, while we are talking large, refer to the Ogre of a later scene, whose fierce optics and hungry tongue, as he licks his lips in cannibal anticipation, quite bear out the blood-curdling, &c, qualities accorded him in the programme.

To return to Jack, we may explain that, with the advice of Puss, he throws off his peasant dress and pretends to be drowning while bathing. Puss, who has presented the king with a couple of rabbits in the name of his master as the Marquis of Carabas, having obtained a card belonging to the real lord, is invited to the palace with Jack, who is rescued from drowning and brought on in the Princess's sedan chair. When the stage is clear the Widow enters, taking her tipsy brother-in-law, Grindoff, home in a wheel-barrow. The lady's rough usage of the tipsy miller, their duet "I know that you love me", and Grindoff's drunken dance, were excellent.

We are next carried to the King's Palace, the Court of the Alhambra, an amplification of that shown at Sydenham. [...] The unfortunate Glumpo in vain tries to obtain an audience of the king, who believes him an impostor, Jack having taken the former's name and title. Pertine (Miss Alice Spry) announces Jack as the Marquis, and, looking prettier even than in her first dress, Miss Beryl enters attired as a nobleman. All the village attends the king's reception, including the Widow wearing a ballet length dress of mauve and yellow, with a wide straw hat trimmed with yellow silk and flowers, and with mauve stockings, one of the best feminine assumptions by an actor that we have seen. All recognise Jack, and Glumpo claims the title he bears; yet, thanks to the king's deafness and Puss's help, our hero pulls through, and is accepted by the king for his future son-in-law. But Ratifero arrives from the Ogre with a message that unless his ogreship weds the Princess Brilliantine he has sworn to devour the king and his court. As the intimation comes at the same moment that the rats have eaten the entire banquet provided by the king, war is declared against the rodent race, and, with a patriotic chorus, "Shoulder to shoulder", joined in by the crowd of soldiers that fill the stage, the scene closes.

We next see the main deck of the *SS Catapult*, on its way to Rat Island. Glumpo is there as artist correspondent, showing a sketch of the embarkation; on which the Widow asks "Embrocation?" but Glumpo explains "You don't rub this in; you rub it out." All goes well, until Ratifero summons two of his evil spirits and orders them, whilst the people sleep, to gnaw holes in the ship, so as to sink her. The scene that ensued was even more spirited than that of chasing the Cat, which we have already mentioned. The sprites were represented by most agile acrobats; vaulting through everything, shooting straight up in the air, sinking rapidly through the stage and darting up just as suddenly by the vampire traps, the expert pair seemed ubiquitous.

The sprites overcome, we went below "'tween decks", where sea sickness and the dispute about berths afforded a conveniently elastic carpenter's scene, and kept the house in a roar. Indeed, to see the Widow get into her carpet bag, from motives of diffidence, and not to laugh would be simply impossible.

The vocal medley that brilliantly concluded the boisterous fun mentioned was followed by the Fern Valley, in which the rival monarchs of the unseen world once more defy each other; and then, after a capital drum solo, the soldiers of Rat Island are attacked by the Grenadiers, Highlanders, and Naval Brigade of old England, and, of course, are defeated in a capital stage contest.

Meanwhile, King Doughnutt, with his lovely daughter, Dolly, the royal dairymaid, and Pertine are brought bound to the Ogre's Castle by the treacherous Tiny, to be devoured by the monster; but Jack and Puss arrive in time to save them. Jack persuades the Ogre, who is also a magician, to change himself into a mouse, when Puss kills him, and, thus, all the bad people punished and the good Queen Felina victorious, there is nothing more to do than to bring the dramatis personae together, which is accomplished in a comprehensive scene, and then ring up the transformation, which is entitled the Fairy Home of the Anemones.

The mounting of the pantomime displays all the liberality of the present management; but the most prominent exhibition of it is found in the procession in the King's Palace. First came the royal guards, and to those succeeded the Seven Champions of Christendom, each knight with his company of supporters, who crossed and recrossed the stage and terraces with dazzling effect, whilst, as they came down to the footlights, the several knights and their followers sang some national song or chorus suitable to the country to which they belonged. Then succeeded lads dressed as Grenadier Guards, Highlanders, and members of the Naval Brigade, until the stage could hold no more. We may refer to the able rifle and bayonet manoeuvres of the British troops, and also to the most admirable contest afterwards on Rat Island, to show the careful and excellent stage-management that has been brought to the work. […]
The Era, 30/12/1882

DURING the rehearsal of the pantomime Robinson Crusoe *at the Plymouth Theatre, on the 22nd inst, a funny incident occurred. The water surveyor, unknown to the manager or those inside the theatre, was trying the "service," and unwittingly turned on a wrong tap, which caused the "water curtain," which was created after the last fire at the theatre, to suddenly pour down a torrent on the stage just in front of the orchestra. The band beat a hasty retreat over the barrier into the pit stalls, while the actors and actresses, who were rehearsing, flew in all directions, one lady doing a very clever "header" into one of the private boxes. The damage exceeded £50.*
The Era, 30/12/1882

1883

A SERIOUS accident occurred on the 16th ult at Plymouth Theatre, where the pantomime of Robinson Crusoe *was being performed. In one scene a camel is introduced, and the keeper, William White, having in the course of the performance struck the camel across the legs while it was attempting to rise, the camel suddenly knelt on him, and remained in this position until another of the supernumeraries came to White's rescue. It was then found that, besides having sustained other serious injuries, his thigh was broken. He was at once removed to the hospital.*
The Era, 3/3/1883

The Britannia
Queen Dodo; or, Harlequin Babilo and the Three Wonders

[…] THE Valley of Mushrooms, a very capital scene, and not by any means of the obscure and gloomy kind which used to be thought the orthodox way to begin a pantomime, is the haunt of Scratchcat, the Red Witch (Mr Mark Mills), who every year has to do an act of benevolence to some member of humanity as a set-off for her malice during the rest of the twelvemonth. Cupid (Miss Alice Harvey) brings to her for this purpose Babilo (Miss Alice Rogers), a young prince, who is someway kept out of his rights by King Krakpot the First (Mr Fred Lay), a monarch with a mania for School Boards and a disregard of the sterner necessities of life. Scratchcat is about to hand Babilo a silver coin when Rhino, the Silver King (Mr E Newbound), enters and stops him. Babilo is told of his regal claims, but Rhino avers that he will not be able to enforce them until he has previously executed three tasks. To restore life to a statue; this is the

Princess Merryheart (Miss Lily Wilford), whom Rhino has turned to stone for rejecting his addresses; to wake up a dead city, and to make everybody speak the truth.

Then the scene changes to the City of Highkulchar, where King Krakpot and his gifted son, Tiddy-fol-lol (Mr G H Chirgwin[7]), reside. Tiddy comes on with baggy yellow trousers, all buttoned over a blue jacket; he has a wide collar and a large muffin cap, and wheels a hoop with one hand whilst the other holds his schoolbag and slate. He sings of his misfortunes "The very first day I was born", and complains of too much teaching and too little food; indeed, it is the general complaint of Court and People. The King and Dr Tolu (Mr G Lewis) enter, and the latter puts the young Prince through a medical examination, feeling his pulse at the ankle, and looking at three or four inches of his tongue, which the royal youth contrives to put out for his scientific inspection. For Tiddy and his unseen brothers, Krakpot has advertised for a governess, who arrives in the person of Vere de Vere, the entrance of Mrs S Lane in that character being marked by a most enthusiastic greeting on the part of the audience. But the fault is not to be corrected by a governess at four pounds a year. Dodo, the Cook (Mr Edward Granville), reports an empty larder, and Krakpot and Tiddy go off to lunch at a restaurant, leaving everybody else to feed the mind. In his absence De Vere, Dodo, and Tolu disparage his Majesty, singing of his being "an awfully ramparty, rather a scamparty, lend-us-a-quid sort of fellow". The result is that when the King and Tiddy return the former has been dethroned, and the crown is put up by lottery. Dodo comes from hanging out the clothes on a line and draws the crown, Babilo's claim being rejected on account of his unfulfilled tasks, and with a medley, in which Tiddy sings "She's drawn the lucky number", the scene concludes.

We are next taken to the Cave of Silence, possibly so called because the unfortunate Princess Merryheart is imprisoned in the ice there, as well as having been changed into a statue. Rhino, his creature Goldeneye (Madame San Martino Campobello), and the burglar-proof policeman Funnifiz (Mr E Drayton) keeps watch over the cave. But Babilo contrives to intoxicate Funnifiz and restores life to Merryheart by kissing her; when the two go through a duet, "Kiss me darling, kiss me honey", which is followed by a well-executed dance. Merryheart returns to her pedestal, and the new Queen coming to the cave for a picnic, attended by her instructress, De Vere, and Tolu, Babilo makes Merryheart go through a series of attitudes, which are explained by Prince Tiddy, who enters with his father, dressed as street minstrels, and in a very famished condition. The first was described as "Mrs Weldon[8] demanding Woman's Rights", the next "Innocence asking if *Town Talk* is a Sunday paper for girls", and after Red Riding Hood and Bo-Peep, the final *pose plastique* was Britannia mourning at the condition of the poor in London.

These specimens of *tableaux vivants* were particularly well received, and, Goldeneye having in vain tried to seduce Babilo from the Princess, the action is carried to the Garden of Coins, a scene in which coins form a conspicuous feature. A small circular Temple at the back of the stage is hung about with them, coins swing from the flies, are painted on the sky-pieces, and their gilt counterfeits glitter at the wings. The ladies of the ballet have countless numbers of such representatives of value, and may be said to dance to a pretty tune. […]

Rhino determines that Babilo shall not reach the dead city, but Cupid descends in a balloon, and carries off the Prince and Princess. Meanwhile Queen Dodo prepares to go to see with her court, which includes the ex-King, who as an Admiralty official wears a uniform of which the epaulets are pieces of cannon, whilst his son's are a couple of ships. In the scene a vast quantity of fun is crammed, for it includes a short-sword engagement, several boxing encounters, numerous songs, a capital dance, especially as regards Mr G H Chirgwin and Mr Fred Lay's very comic share of it, and concludes with the balloon ascent.

We are next taken on board the yacht, when a very charming chorus is given by the characters in their – well, yes, in their *robes de nuit* – with candlesticks in their hands, when they musically bid each other "Good night". But before this Jossero (Mr G B Bigwood), Dodo's neglected husband, has drilled his numerous family, Dodo has fallen overboard to be rescued by a life-belt, and Prince Tiddy has performed very cleverly on the bagpipes. Rhino, who is on the yacht disguised as the pilot, on being pressed by Tiddy to confess who he is, takes off his beard, and with the assistance of a baby, &c, appears as Mr Augustus Harris in the last Drury Lane drama. Rhino dooms the ship to destruction, but the occupants manage to reach the Dead City by getting into casks, whilst Babilo and his Princess arrive there in a balloon.

Babilo brings back life to the city, and, finally, by means of a magic chair, supplied by Cupid, which compels its occupants to speak the truth, the Prince performs his third "wonder", and gains his kingdom, Dodo being very glad to give up her crown and go back to the Kitchen. […]

The transformation scene is one attraction which demands our notice. In the centre and at the sides of the stage clusters of jewel-decked plants are grouped; from the flies descend festoons of lace, in front of which hangs rich crystal-like fringe. All this changes its tints from time to time under the influence of the coloured rays thrown upon it. Then, slowly, *figurantes*, which have been half visible between the leaves, rise at different altitudes, until the whole stage is a scene of female beauty and floral brilliancy. […]

Drury Lane
Cinderella

[…] THE opening scene is a very pretty one, illustrative of Baron Fillettoville's Manor House and Courtyard. The Baron (Mr Harry Parker) is about to be married to the mother of the ugly and selfish and spiteful Blondina (Mr Harry Nicholls) and Brunetta (Mr Herbert Campbell), and already, in spite of the festivities that are being prepared, in spite of the ringing bells and cheering villagers in their quaint and picturesque costumes, we guess that there are hard times in store for the Baron's only daughter Cinderella (Miss Kate Vaughan[9]), and very soon afterwards our guessing is confirmed, for she is consigned to the kitchen to keep company with black beetles and other nasty things, and is given to understand very clearly that she will have to be the drudge of the household.

Under these circumstances, nobody who knows anything of fairy ways will be surprised to learn that Scintilla, the Fairy Godmother (Miss Kate Sullivan), calls all her fays together in a beautiful moonlit glen, and bids them protect Cinderella against all harm, and defeat every one of the projects of her arch enemy, whose name is Ignoramus (Mr George Lupino). The fays are so delighted with their mission that they dance in the moonlight, the rustling of the leafy garlands they wear making a pleasant accompaniment to the music provided from the orchestra in front of them. […] But a more striking effect was to come. With the break of day and the rising of the sun "the horn of the hunter is heard on the hill", and very soon, the fays having fled, hill and dale are covered with huntsmen, whose scarlet coats and black hats stand out well against the green of the overhanging boughs, and help to complete a picture which is full of colour and full of animation, and which again brings together the hands of the spectators in appreciative acclamation. Before we are allowed to leave this glen we are witnesses of a pretty love scene between Prince Pastorelle (Miss Minnie Mario) and our heroine, who has come out to gather sticks, and we know what the end will be. The course of true love is not going to "run smooth", but it will come right by-and-by.

Love affects different people in different ways. It causes the Prince to become a member of the Junior Johnnies' Club, the Junior Johnnies being mashers who are very extravagant but very tasteful in the matter of dress, as we find when, without the process of election, we are introduced to their set.

Now we hear that the King (Mr Reuben Inch) proposes to give a ball, and the old, old story goes on until we find poor Cinderella, left behind and dreaming in her dreary kitchen, awakened by the Fairy Godmother, who provides her with everything necessary, even to the glass slippers brought through the air by the swift-winged Electra, the Spirit of Light (Mlle Aenea).

After witnessing the humorous adventures of the Baron, the Baroness (Miss M A Victor), and the two ugly sisters on the way to the Palace – depicted in a well-painted panorama by Emden – we are taken to the Illuminated Garden of the Palace – a grand scene by W R Beverley, occupying the whole of the stage. Here the preparations for the ball are on a magnificent scale, and here is provided the great feature of the pantomime. It is called a Grand Procession of fairy and nursery stories. Some of us who have grown old and critical may be inclined to say that there is something too much of this; but children will vote it delightful, and will clap their hands with glee as they make the acquaintance of the heroes and heroines, the bad people and the good they have hitherto known only through the medium of their story books. [...]

The Surrey
Jack and Jill; or, the House that Jack Built After the Water was Spilt

[…] AFTER the usual plotting, this time at the Well of Truth, we are taken to the Harbour of Somewhere and Dame Durden's Cottage, and make the acquaintance of that lady (Mr Frank Wood) partial to "blue ruin"; of Bhadlotte (Mr G Conquest Jr), a mysterious stranger engaged for the time being in the pawnbroking line; of Jill (Miss Kate James), upon whom he has some designs; of King Cashless (Mr C Cruikshank) and his Minister (Mr James Albert), anxious to raise the wind upon a flat iron, seemingly their only earthly possession; and of the dashing Prince Crammer (Miss H Claremont), who means to take advantage of the information afforded by Jill respecting some magic acorns to be found by the Demon Oak in the Golden Glade, which is not far off.

A comical company also comes along by the steamboat *Masher Queen*, Jack (Miss Lottie Harcourt) being the most handsome and the most popular among the arrivals. Captain Cuttle (Mr H M Edmunds), crew, and passengers being landed, the first-named sings a wonderful song of adventure, and the others, with "Right you are, old skipper", endorse every one of his fibbing assertions, the audience following suit by redemanding the song and by loudly applauding the accompanying dance. A comical addition to the crowd is Paul Jones De Vanderdecken (Mr V Stevens) – a pirate of the penny plain and twopence coloured and blood and thunder and "once on board the lugger" order. Everybody, referring to the magic acorns, cries "The secret's mine – I shall be there." Indeed, in their own words, they mean to be "on the job", preparing for the business with more songs, choruses, and dances, and with an indescribable scene of bustle and fun, in which the Captain, the Prime Minister, and Pongo from the Congo (a monkey – Willie Edmunds) are engaged, the spectators fairly screaming with merriment.

Now to the demon oak, Paul Jones being first in the field – that is in the wood – so sing with reference to a gin-drinking wife of the long ago "I'll never look upon her like again". He also declares his love for Aquarina (Miss Ada Vinetta), the daughter of the King, and Jack has to come along to rescue her from his clutches. Here then are the "Sailor and his Lass", and together they will look for the magic acorns. The Demon Oak when found is a demon all over – all alive with fearful horns and fearful eyes, and fearful arms and hands, his locomotive privileges, though, being limited to one hour each night. This is one of the "properties" suggestive of the name of Conquest, and it is worthy to take rank with the wonderful things that have gone before it, and that have come of the inventive genius of the owner of that name. The wood demon makes love to Jill, and frightens her into acquiescence with his proposals. He is none other than Bhadlotte in one of his curious disguises. Aquarina gets the acorns, and divides them with Ben Backstay (Miss Vinney Edmunds), the first lieutenant, who wishes to be a silver king; with Captain Cuttle, who wishes to be King Carrot; and with the Prime Minister, who wishes to be a monkey like Pongo.

We are taken now to the Silver Palace, a very gorgeous scene by Mr Gwilt Jolly, where a fête is given in honour of Aquarina, who receives deputations from the vegetable and mineral kingdoms. Here we have some wonderfully realistic properties, reflecting much credit on Mr T Major. All the vegetables seemed only to require boiling to be fit for the table, with the exception of the celery, which we fancy could have been spared the ordeal of the pot and would have been toothsome. The representatives of the minerals, gold, silver, copper, sapphires, rubies, emeralds, and diamonds, formed as brilliant a throng as have ever been seen in pantomime on the Surrey stage. Some dazzling and marvellous effects were produced by the aid of the lime-light, and applause did not cease until Mr George Conquest had made his appearance at the footlights. Now the King's daughter is promised to Jack only if he will get water from the top of the famous hill to cure the fibbing tongue of Prince Crammer, and this is thought to be a good opportunity for the Fairy of the Well (Miss Kate Lovett) to provide a stirring chorus with "Steady, boys, shoulder to shoulder", and for Mr Harry Lynch to introduce his comical donkey, Shotover, to sing "Whoa, Jerusalem", to excite more laughter and to prove his skill as a clog dancer, and for Miss Kate James to sing very sweetly "Wait till the clouds roll by", with an unseen chorus.

Next we pass to the Hill, another beautiful scene. Up go Jack and Jill, and down they tumble so as not to do outrage to history as it has been written for the nursery. Jack tries again, though, and succeeds in getting the pail of water. Then he claims the Princess, and is ordered to build a house by the next day. So come we to "the House that Jack Built", the Fairy of the Well calling Dot (Master Babo), the chief of the Pigmies, to his assistance. The busy bustle in connection with the building of this house is sure to delight all the little people who see the Surrey pantomime. Bhadlotte sets fire to the house, and then in pantomime we get a melodramatic *Streets of London* sensation, the spectators applauding lustily with the arrival of the Pigmy Fire Brigade.

In the ninth scene, "The Roadside Inn", we are treated to some rare fun, and for some twenty minutes the spectators are kept in a high state of hilarity by the antics of Pongo and the sufferings of his victims, Captain Cuttle and the Prime Minister. Bhadlotte is still plotting, and in the next scene we get a fearful phantom fight, in which traps and trapezes are brought into use.

In the end of course Jack is made happy with the hand of the Princess, the defeat of Bhadlotte is completed, and we pass on to the transformation scene, representing the Four Seasons, and painted by Mr Gwilt Jolly, for whom it is a veritable triumph. [...]
The Era, 29/12/1883

1884

THAT a pantomime should ever become capable of being recommended as a vehicle for lessons in elocution would seem to be impossible of belief, yet a better illustration of the value of tone and emphasis could hardly be afforded than the topical duet so amusingly rendered by Mr Harry Nicholls and Mr Herbert Campbell as the two elderly sisters in the Drury Lane comic annual of Cinderella. *In about a dozen verses these acting vocalists show that fifty different significations may be imparted to such a simple phrase as "I beg your pardon." With a slight change of facial expression and a little alteration of emphasis, the words convey on each repetition quite a different meaning, and the varying inflexions of tone are worth studying by all who would wish to master the full capability of the human voice in the expression of a particular thought.*
The Era, 5/1/1884

IN the representation of Whittington and His Cat *at the Theatre, Winter Gardens, Southport, Mr Herbert Budd, assistant stage-manager, who plays the old merchant, recently met with a heavy fall in a tussle with the Cat (Master Frederick Liebert), and with great difficulty succeeded in going through his remaining scene. This endeavour aggravated the injury, which, at first thought to be a severe sprain, turned out to be the fracture of a small bone of one leg, and the patient was put both in splints and in bed. The Sunday intervened, but on the Monday night Mr Budd, nothing daunted, chartered a cab to the theatre, and had himself dressed with his leg made up as an immense gouty*

> *package, and then and since has nightly played the part upon a pair of crutches. It is needless to see that this display of pluck met with a hearty reception from the audience, and his novel reading of the part has turned into quite a success.*
> **The Era, 12/1/1884**

Elephant and Castle
A Frog He Would a-Wooing Go; or, Harlequin, Sleeping Beauty, and the Demons of the Mystic Pool

[…] THE pantomime is quite in the old-fashioned style, and is all the more likely to please in consequence. It opens in the Abode of King Envy (Mr Charles Lerigo) in the Realms of Spite, and the monarch declares that everything is "going to the bad", whereupon is attendant demons rejoice greatly, and express their delight in a fantastic dance. These disagreeable personages, are, however, soon confronted by the Fairy Kindheart (Miss Birdie Irving), and it is clear throughout the opening there will be perpetual war between these opposing leaders.

The second scene is the Palace of King Timido the Tremulous (Mr George Belmore), a monarch as spiritless as his name; but he has a spouse, Queen Furioso the Forcible (Mr Frank Hinde), who, although she declares herself to be as "gentle as a lamb", rules her husband with unflinching energy. This royal couple have a fair daughter, the Princess Lovelinessa (Miss Emma Victor), and to this rare and radiant maiden comes many suitors, whose attentions might lead to matrimony if it were not for a dark secret and a mysterious rival. The secret is the possession of a magic gem, which if lost will bring ruin and despair to the heroine, and the dreaded rival is no other than King Frog the First (Mr George Skinner), the mystic reptile "who would a-wooing go", and whose endeavours to win the beautiful Princess and to possess the magic diadem keep all the good fairies in a constant state of activity to thwart his evil designs.

It will be seen that there are ample materials for pantomime fun and fancy in these incidents, and the opportunities are not lost. Excellent effects are introduced, and such scenes as the Castle of King Frog, the Coral Chamber and Reception Grotto of the Good Fairy, and especially the Village of Toys in the Kingdom of Teetotum, will delight the patrons of the theatre. The Village of Toys is as quaint, novel, and amusing as anything of the kind produced during the present season. There is a toy castle, all sorts of toy houses, a toy windmill, and, in the course of the scene, the stage is filled with toy figures, all working in the most eccentric manner. A group appear first as military heroes, and then, turning their backs, suddenly become jolly jack tars and dance a hornpipe. Through all the Froggy Monarch pursues the fair heroine. There is a grand reception at the Palace of King Timido, which serves to introduce a host of popular personages. The Commander of the Egyptian Campaign, Mr Gladstone, Mr Bradlaugh, Lord Randolph Churchill, and a host of others, including Mrs Weldon, are brought forward to win the applause and laughter of the audience. […] After many adventures Prince Radiant, represented by Miss Laura Sedgewick, succeeds in supplanting the Froggy rival, and all ends happily in the grand transformation scene, which is designed by Mr Robert Burriss, and is entitled May's Bridal Day. […]

The Marylebone
Beauty and the Beast

[…] A FEW words will suffice to show the course of the story as it has been worked out by Mr Denny, whose task has been cleverly accomplished. The Demon Mephistophili (Miss Annie Merton) changes Prince Amour (Miss Lauraine) into the Beast (Mr Allan Morris). Amaranthe (Miss Cecile Stanhope), a Fairy Queen, becomes the guardian of the transformed Prince, and decrees that if Beauty (Miss Violet Hunt) will consent to love the Beast, the Prince shall be restored to his original form and condition. After diverse adventures and mishaps, the desired consummation is attained.

The pantomime opens less gloomily than has been customary with such productions. Scene the first represents Stonehenge by Moonlight. Here the evil spirits, headed by Mephistophili, assemble and plan mischief; but, though the chief demon as he enters utters the exclamations "Ha! Ha! Ho! Ho! Fe! Faw! And fi! Fo! Fum!" he is by no means formidable. Among the attendants of Mephistophili are maidens who carry torches in their hands and dance in a lively manner round their master as he makes an incantation after the fashion of the witches in *Macbeth*.

The second scene brings us to the Baronial Hall of the Baron Von Tartiscum, and introduces the Baron (Mr Harry Moss), his daughters Cranberry (Mr Fred Mitchell), Bilberry (Mr Cyril Courtny), and Beauty, who has already been referred to, and Whirligiggle (Mr J G Wilton), the Baron's servant. Here, too, we make acquaintance with Lord Random Dasher (Miss Henrietta Mitchell), and Sir Evergreen Masher (Miss Connie Forrest), who are suitors for the hand of Beauty, and with Trimtop (Miss Lalor Shiel), a lively, saucy fellow of the tiger species. Much laughter is caused by the plain daughters trying to captivate the swells who have come to seek their sister. The Baron, being in financial difficulties, goes abroad to seek his fortune, and soon finds his way to the Realms of Eternal Snow and Ice in company with Whirligiggle, Dasher, and Masher. Amaranth, the Fairy Queen, appears to help them, and the scene changes to the Groves of Oranges and Lemons in the Beast's Garden. In this scene, which is a brilliant one, a grand fairy ballet takes place. […] Scenes five and six represent the Exterior of the Baron's Hall and the Wine Cellars in the

Beast's Palace, in the latter of which a comic ballet, arranged by Mr Wallie Decopa, and supported by himself and members of his troupe, takes place. The seventh scene depicts a Grand Saloon in the Beast's Palace. Scene eight, the Baron's Hall. Scene nine is a very beautiful one called Beauty's Garden. Here the Beast, whose palace the garden adjoins, introduces his retinue, and entertains his guest. Numerous pretty pages, guards with huge heads and grotesque faces, and a band of richly dressed Amazons appear here. The last named dance, execute evolutions, and attitudinise in gladiatorial style in a way which excites very warm applause. At length the Beast is changed into the Prince and the performance of the opening terminates with a lively medley finale founded on popular airs of the day.

Then follows the transformation scene, which is as splendid as it is elaborate. It comprises many changes, and partakes chiefly of a floral character. Living figures are effectively introduced, and last of all is seen a chariot containing goddesses, far in the rear and high over all. [...]

The Era, 27/12/1884

Theatre Royal, Bradford
Little Red Riding Hood and Her Sister Bo-Peep

[...] THE popular nursery story is considerably elaborated, and the opening is in nine scenes. Scene one introduces us to the Den of the wicked Wolf, Lupus (Mr Arthur Fenwicke), who is holding a conversation with Lupina, his spouse (Mr Fred Burton), as to the requisite change necessary in his diet, when Reynard the Fox (Mr Harry Cane) enters, and to save his own carcase he promises to provide Little Red Riding Hood, or, as she is called, Rosa (Miss Cissy Burton), as a dainty relish. By the aid of a sprite, Fire-fly (Miss Eugenie Forbes), Lupus beholds a vision of Rosa, and a compact is entered into with Reynard for her delivery to the Wolf.

Scene two, a charming piece of work, is the Village of Once Upon a Time. Here rustic revelry takes place, and in the midst of a very animated scene Bo-Peep (Miss Lottie Collins[10]) appears with her flock of real sheep. She relates a very horrid dream of danger to her pets, and, after a cleverly executed and original dance, she starts for a stroll in the meadows, and the Baron Blustrum (Mr Harry Martell) appears. He at once falls in love with Flora, a village coquette (Miss Florrie Dudley). Roland, her affianced (Miss Bronner Herbert), resents the Baron's familiarities, and a quarrel ensues. Dame Durden (Mr George Power) comes upon the scene.

Some humorous business follows, and we are taken to the Tangled Wood, scene three, where Reynard encounters Rosa, but he is foiled in his intentions by the Baron and his two huntsmen, Tantivy and Yoicks (the Harvey Brothers). The two latter disagree and a laughable combat takes place, and we find ourselves at the Lily Dell, a very beautiful conception, with a real waterfall. A fairy ballet is here seen, Miss Topsy Elliott, a very clever and graceful *premiere danseuse*, eliciting applause.

Rosa appears to gather herbs for her sick granny, and is protected by Benevolentine, the Fairy Queen (Miss Marie Jay). Reynard, being again foiled, is swallowed by a huge Fiery Dragon (a very wonderful animal); but the monster can't digest him, and he is freed again. Bo-peep, coming on the scene in search of her lost sheep, finds their tails only (Reynard having cut them off), and hies away to find her flock, and stitch their tails on again. The Wolf appears, and is bearing away Rosa, when he is encountered by Marmion (Miss Eugenie Jonghmans), a young warrior home from the wars, and Rosa is rescued.

We are now at the Castle Gates. Dame Durden, her son Billy (Mr J H Danvers), and the Parish Beadle (Mr Robert Templeton) are in pursuit of the Fox, whose tail Roland has cut off and presented to the Baron. Bo-Peep enters, the Baron sees her, and bears her off within his stronghold.

The Wolf here puts in an appearance, and disperses his pursuers, when a change is made to scene six, Grand Hall in the Castle. By the aid of Fire-fly, the Dame, Marmion, and Billy find their way into the castle disguised as jugglers, and take part in the performances given by the Baron in honour of Bo-Peep, who is to be, unwillingly, made a Baroness. After a pretty Watteau *fete*, revels, and a clever entertainment by M. Zidney, equilibrist, Marmion performs the rope-trick, assisted by Billy, and the Baron is made their prisoner, Bo-Peep escaping with her lover Marmion.

The next is scene seven, Exterior of the Dame's Cottage. The Fox is at last in the clutches of the Beadle. Scene eight is the Interior of the Cottage, where the Dame is found preparing for repose; she finds it in the Wolf's embrace, and is "gobbled up". By way of dessert, the Wolf awaits the arrival of Rosa, who enters. She is about to be devoured when Marmion enters, followed by forty juvenile policemen, and the Wolf is slain.

Scene eight is the Exterior of the Cottage, which is selected as the place in which Benevolentine makes everybody happy, and changes the scene to the transformation, the Dwelling of the Winter Fairies (Mr Charles Brew), which, if not equal to many of that gentleman's previous productions here, is certainly a very novel and beautiful conception, brilliant and harmonious in colour.

The Era, 3/1/1885

1885

> *MADAME NINA CASTELLI, who has been appearing as the Fairy Queen in the pantomime of* Aladdin *at the New Prince of Wales' Theatre, Greenwich, made application to Mr Marsham, the sitting magistrate, at the Greenwich Police-court on Saturday under circumstances she detailed. She said that on Monday evening she was insulted in the theatre, and refused to go on on Tuesday unless an apology were given.*
>
> *Some persons in a box had a number of small bouquets, which they threw at every lady on the stage but herself, her good songs being passed over and flowers thrown to the ballet girls. In the last scene they threw flowers over her head to the chorus girls, and the last four, which were very wet, they threw on her bare arms. Mr Lloyd Clarance, who had charge of the pantomime, picked them up and offered them to her; but she refused them, saying she did not accept flowers after the ballet girls. Subsequently Mr Lloyd Clarance came to her dressing-room and abused her for refusing the flowers. He said "---- you, madam," which she would not put up with from her own husband, let alone from him. She sent a message that unless he apologised she would not appear on Tuesday, and she had not appeared since.*
>
> *On Tuesday one of the chorus was put on in her place and under her name, and she was going to take proceedings for damage to her artistic reputation. She wanted to know if she could compel Mr Lloyd Clarance to pay her for the six weeks' engagement and "the run". Mr Marsham said her remedy could only be in a civil action. He thought she was justified in refusing to appear if she was insulted, but but advised her to explain that she would carry out her engagement if an apology were given. The applicant thanked his worship and retired.*
> *The Era, 31/1/1885*

The Britannia
Daddy Longlegs; or, Harlequin Merrimac and Mother Carey's Chickens

[…] THE first scene represents the haunt of Mother Carey's chickens[11], where an argument is taking place with respect to an enormous egg which has defied all attempts at hatching. A pickaxe is obtained, the egg broken, and Vanderdecken (Mr E Newbound) is discovered within it. Mother Carey (Mr F Beaumont) learns that the object of his visit is to obtain from her the secret of his fatal curse and discover how to rid himself of it. She informs him he must gain the heart and hand of Princess Caramel (Miss Louie Gilbert). Harmony (Miss Frances Talbot), the fairy guardian of the princess's heart, appears and vows to thwart him, and the scene terminates with Vanderdecken's defiance of the good fairy.

Scene the second takes us to the City of Silent Waters, a picturesque, Venice-like set from the brush of Mr Charles Douglass, and here we find preparations being made for the marriage of Caramel with an unknown tourist whose money-bags have won consent to the match from her impecunious father, King Alleyklepto (Mr Fred Carlos). Here we are first introduced to Nutty, otherwise Daddy Longlegs (a part for which Mr G H Chirgwin's elongated limbs admirably suit him), who arrives with the King's washing, in a carriage drawn by a very sleek and handsome donkey (Mr S De Lacey). After a considerable amount of practical fun with this animal, Daddy Longlegs sings a song, "Oh, my Neddy!" to a well-known air by Waldteufel. He is comically attired in black tights, and eccentric "Glengarry", and a jacket which persists in shrinking at short notice into the smallest dimensions, and his appearance alone is sufficient to create the heartiest laughter. The King and his chamberlain, Screwnut (Mr Fred Lay), arrive on the scene, and are followed by Caramel, who objects to the match with the "unknown" – who is attired in a costume which is an ingenious compromise between that of a pantomime demon and of a middle-aged masher – on the grounds of her previous engagement with Prince Merrimac (Miss Millie Howes). This scene is also liberally supplied with musical numbers, and very musical these are, whether choruses to the airs of Miss Bessie Bellwood's[12] most popular effusions or agreeable ditties by individual members of the company. Prince Merrimac now appears, just in time to forbid the banns, and the unknown tourist is discovered by Volanti (Mrs S Lane), a mortal possessed of fairy power, to be none other than the famous Vanderdecken himself. A stormy scene ensues, and Vanderdecken, after paralysing the crowd by his magic power, carries off Caramel in his phantom ship; and a vow is taken (to lively music) on the part of the other principal characters to follow and save her from his clutches.

Then a front scene representing the home of Daddy Longlegs closes in. Here some uproarious practical fun is created by Dame Wosslebird (Mr Frank Hinde), the mother of Daddy, royal laundress by appointment and proprietress of the Wishing Well, drowning in the latter Van Tyko (Mr G B Bigwood), Vanderdecken's boatswain, who comes to collect the taxes and School Board fees from her; and here we have an opportunity of hearing Miss Frances Talbot, as the fairy Harmony, the *dea ex machina* of the plot, sing a pleasing ballad in admirable style. Various other characters enter, and finally Daddy Longlegs is induced by Merrimac and Volanti to join an expedition in search of Caramel. […]

The fourth scene takes us on board the *Sarcy Cat*, a yacht lent for the expedition by a wealthy young gentleman named Midas (Miss Lizzie Howe), of which Merrimac appears by his brilliant and naval uniform appears to be in command. Here we have a rollicking jig by Alleyklepto and Screwnut, who have come aboard as stowaways, having absconded with the revenues of the state; and a midshipmite, little Tommy Topsail by name, obliges with a capital song and dance. Here, of course, are also the Dame and Daddy, and Volanti, and a chorus is sung descriptive of the delights (?) of nautical expeditions. Daddy shoots a Mother Carey's chicken, and a burlesque of the "Ancient Mariner" follows, the story of Vanderdecken being followed in the next incident, that of the delivery and acceptance of the fatal letters, whose reception results in the shipwreck which follows.

When the *Sarcy Cat* has sunk, we see Daddy and his mother afloat on a raft, and this situation permits the introduction of some excellent farcical business on board, an attack by a shark being successfully beaten off, and various articles being fished from the ocean's depths, the last of which is a brandy bottle, which contains a message from below.

This, it appears, has really been sent up by Caramel, who is confined in Vanderdecken's Cave beneath the sea, to which locality we are next introduced. Here Volanti, by the use of a submarine telephone, communicates with Caramel. The raft, with the Dame and Daddy upon it, is seen overhead on the surface of the waters, and it is evident that the message has reached them safely. Daddy and his mother bravely "take a header down below", and appear in Vanderdecken's dominions; and a very pretty idea is the use of a silken clue by which Merrimac, by following its windings, discovers his beloved Caramel.

The next scene closes in upon general rejoicing, the union of the lovers, and a merry chorus, Harmony conveying Caramel to the Valley of Harmony, a brilliant and many-coloured picture for which Mr G Charles is responsible. Here the Grand Ballet of Sylvan Echoes takes place, the well-trained corps of the Britannia disporting themselves in accomplished style, and the activity and grace of the *premieres danseuses*, Miss Kate Floretta and Miss Pauline Rivers, being greatly admired. Here Vanderdecken induces Caramel to accept a bouquet, the fumes of which deprive her of her memory, but do not prevent her from singing in bewitching style a pretty *jodel* song.

The next scene is Sloper's Island, a curious spot where the streams run spirituous liquors, and the trees and rocks are quaintly suggestive of the well-known "Sloperian" hat and umbrella. Here Daddy Longlegs is condemned to be burned to death by Vanderdecken, and this gives the former the opportunity of singing "The Ghost of Benjamin Barnaby Binns[13]", in the chorus of which he is joined with gusto by the other performers. Some clever hits at the slowness of the South Western Railway and the officiousness of the police are introduced at this point, and were very well received by the audience.

The next scene is "The Palace of Music", a gorgeous interior; and here the usual processional displays take place, the *corps de ballet* and the ranks of supers executing their evolutions with commendable precision and care, the *tout ensemble* forming a most effective picture. Here Daddy Longlegs appears in another eccentrically comic costume, and the wedding of Merrimac and Caramel is about to be celebrated, when Vanderdecken appears from the wedding cake, but too late to "stay proceedings", and his discomfiture concludes the action of the story.

Whilst the transformation is preparing the fun is kept merrily going in front by the other members of the company, a stirring patriotic song, and some lively dances and breakdowns pleasantly passing the time till the culminating glory of the evening is disclosed to the eyes of the audience. In this transformation scene, which he has called "The Glorious Fauna of the Indies", Mr W Charles has really surpassed himself. […]

The children were well-drilled, and a performance of popular airs on a peal of bells fixed on their heads evoked loud applause. […]

Drury Lane
Aladdin

[…] WITHOUT taking the reader through all the details of the familiar story as now presented, we may say that we are first introduced to the magician Abanazar's (Mr Herbert Campbell) observatory, where, by potent charms and spells, is welded the magic ring, by the aid of which the magic lamp will be revealed; that we pass on to a very picturesque scene of the City of Pekin, where there is much bustle by reason of the revolt of the populace against the imperial party, and where Aladdin (Miss Grace Huntley) at once leaps into favour by rescuing the Princess Badroulbadour (Miss Kiss Leamar) from the fury of the quaintly-dressed mob. The Emperor's guards are fearfully and wonderfully made – made-up, that is – and are well worthy of attention. We next pass on to the Royal Baths, and are allowed to look on while the lovely Princess takes off her beautiful robes, she and her attendants making up a delightful group, and soon afterwards we are in the Enchanted Cavern with the imprisoned hero, who makes good his escape by the aid of the Slave of the Lamp (Miss Nelly Bennett).

In the next scene we get the grand procession "A Dream of Fair Women", and the grand ballet of "The Riches of Earth", the two spectacles upon which Mr Augustus Harris this year prides himself, and which have occasioned his greatest expenditure. Addressing Aladdin, the Genius of the Lamp exclaims:

I'll show you all the fairest dames who've been
Upon the earth since it was fresh and green;

Blonde and brunette shall pass your eyes before.

To which Aladdin very gallantly replies:

There won't be one to touch Badroulbadour.

When the Genius says "all" he doesn't mean all, but those beauties who have made their names historical. And here they come, their way being appropriately led by Venus borne by Cupids, to remind us that she is the Goddess of Love. Then in quick succession come Semiramis, Queen of Babylon, borne by a Babylonian bull and soothed with music from Rossini's opera; Helen of Troy, attended closely by Paris, whose love she inspired; Cleopatra, dusky herself and heralded by duskier slaves; Theodora, queen of Byzantium, stately and not looking nearly so wicked as she was; Lady Godiva with her beautiful hair down to hide some of those charms she exposed in the interests of the good people of Coventry, seated on a white horse, and without even the suspicion of a Peeping Tom; Fair Rosamond, in her bower; Beatrice, with Dante close by; Isabel of Bavaria, whom the wicked programme printers have set forth as Isabel of Bavana; Diana of Poictiers, a beautiful brunette, whose home for the time being is a resplendent shell; Anne Boleyn toying with a fan, which is shaped like an axe, presumably to remind us that her head was chopped off by that Royal Bluebeard King Henry the Eighth, her train including a number of quaintly-attired Court jesters; the unfortunate Marie Stuart, with Rizzio, unmindful of disaster, playing on his lute; La Belle Gabrielle; Nell Gwynne, who had a very hearty reception because she chats so saucily with the "mashers" of the period, and also because she is described as "of Drury Lane Theatre"; Catherine of Russia, covered with furs to keep away the Drury Lane draughts, and drawn upon an ice – we should say upon a nice – sleigh, making pleasant music with its jingling bells; La Pompadour, with her paint and powder, and her liking for a gavotte; the Duchess of Devonshire, in a hat that made all the ladies present envious; Josephine, attended by pages more handsomely dressed than any of their predecessors; and to complete the list, such heroines of fairy lore as the Sleeping Beauty and the Fair One with the Golden Locks. […]

Of the ballet which follows no adequate description can be given. We look, we admire, and we are bewildered. There is no jewel that is not represented, and as we gaze upon it we are inclined to think that the Drury Lane manager must have found time to visit King Solomon's Mines, of which we have lately been reading, and have brought away their wondrous treasure stores. They fairly fill the vast stage. They are of all sizes and all colours, and yet by a triumph of stage management they are so arranged as to make up a grand harmonious whole. Their brilliance is enhanced by the aid of the electric lights which some of them carry; but resplendent as the whole scene is Mr Harris is not content until, with the assistance of Madame Katti Lanner, he has filled up the picture with the fruits and flowers of the earth, represented by a troop of juvenile dancers, the well-trained pupils of the lady named. […]

From this scene we pass on until in scene twelve we come to something that is worthy of special attention and remark. This is the building of Aladdin's Palace by a small army of British workmen who this time are neither indolent nor given to strikes. Madame Lanner's pupils are again to the fore here, and, disguised as navvies, hod-carriers, bricklayers, plumbers, carpenters, carters commanding beautiful little ponies, stonemasons, &c, they do loyal suit and service to their master, whose name is writ large as "Gusarris, Builder and Decorator", upon the hoarding which at the commencement they set up. When the dinner bell rings they lay down their implements and welcome their wives with their mid-day meals. Each wife has a perambulator, and each perambulator bears a baby, which is forthwith kissed and cuddled. For the British workman in this instance has a soul above a dinner, and he takes advantage of the temporary lull in building operations to enjoy a dance with the "missis". There are more gorgeous scenes than this in the production, as we have shown, but there is none more animated and interesting, and we venture to predict that it will become a favourite with all the good little boys and girls who during the season will be taken to see the pantomime at Drury Lane. The palace being built, there is another magnificent procession of Aladdin's retainers and another ballet, and the eye is once more delighted by a wealth of colour, indicative of much taste and of unsparing expenditure.

The "transformation" is now not far off, and when it is revealed we find that in "Aladdin's Golden Dream" Mr William Beverley has supplied the Drury Lane stage with another gorgeous example of his skill as a scenic artist. […]

But really the only hit in the performance was made by Mr Harry Nicholls, who was genuinely comical as the Widow Twankey, and whose imitation of the dancing of a well-known burlesque actress gave rise to immense enthusiasm and to much merriment. Splendour is all very well in its way, and is very welcome, but it is not everything. We would willingly spare some of it for the sake of an increase of pantomime fun. Happily, since Boxing Night, the increase has appeared, and as the season advances so we may be sure will grow the provocations to laughter. […]

The Pavilion
Jack the Giant Killer

[…] AT more fashionable theatres pantomime fun, in the true acceptation of the term, is mostly relegated to a short harlequinade at the end of the "opening"; but humour – broad, vigorous, and obvious – runs through the whole dozen scenes into which Mr Oswald Allen's production is divided.

The opening scene discloses King Greed (Mr Fred Harrington) – not necessarily of Hungary – instructing Scrunchem-Crunchem (Mr W Heath), the Cornish Anak[14] of our juvenile fancy, to give rein to an abnormal appetite and ravage the earth. He is a terrible fellow in appearance, this giant, but not a "roarer", for he has a gentle voice and a *suaviter in modo* manner that scarcely befits his savage mien. The forces at the disposal of virtue are headed by Fairy Sweetlove (Miss Ada Reeves), who possesses two tiny henchmen, Tinytrotto (Baby Langtry) and Little Toddle Keeno (La Petite Ida Heath).

These determine to destroy the Giant by the aid of Jack (Miss Katie Barry), who is taken by them to a beautiful floral glade (one of the best scenes in the pantomime), treated to a ballet of flowers, and finally equipped with the shoes of swiftness, the sword of sharpness, and the cap of invisibility. Jack's mother (Mr Charles Danby), mindful of her son's creature comforts, packs his carpet bag, and does not omit porous plasters or chest protectors. This worthy person, instead of being a respectable Cornish dame, bears a strong resemblance to a Whitechapel 'Ria, and is the object of much contumely when she takes to getting her living by means of a "baked-tater" can.

The Giant chooses the dominions of King Domino (Mr George English) for his depredations, and when we are introduced to that monarch and his queen the cruelties of the monster are creating great alarm; and Jack is commissioned to slaughter the public pest. He undertakes his task none too soon, for in scene eight, the Giant's Kitchen, he discovers his sweetheart caged, with, as a companion, a certain Floretta Nonebetter (Miss Lilly Heath), a poor flower girl, who is engaged to Prince Charming (Miss Annie Dunbar), a son of King Domino. Here Jack goes through the adventures familiar to childhood, and after his victory, in which he is assisted by Prince Charming and Prince Courtly (Miss Amy Graham), he is fêted in the Grand Palace of Cards, a truly magnificent scene, in which the stage procession of living representatives of all the cards in the pack, and also dominoes, move with well-timed evolutions. Admirable precision marked also the marchings of an army – raised to destroy the Giant in the previous scene.

The last two scenes are occupied with the adventures of Jack with the big brothers of the dead giant, Cormoran (Mr Heller) and Blunderbore (Mr Musgrave), whom he, of course, finally kills, and for his services he is knighted and rewarded with the hand of Bo-Peep (Miss Julia Kent), and the other couples pair off. This is the story as far as we need tell it, and until concluded by the grand transformation its merry development was followed with unfailing attention by the vast audience, who scarcely found time to swallow the light and sold refreshment needed to satisfy the wants of the inner man and woman during the four hours' progress of the entertainment.

The opening scene of the transformation must certainly be the habitat of evil spirits, or else why do we see two immense serpents of the true pantomime breed coiled round huge columns; but further scenic changes bring us to the more canny and more attractive realm of fairy fancy, inhabited by statuesque groups, the splendour of the whole scene being enhanced by the glitter of coloured lights.

In condensing the story we found no occasion to mention Dismallo, the Grand Chamberlain. This individual, however, though little to do with the main purpose of the plot, has everything to do with its divergence into the bypaths of humour, and as represented by Mr Arthur Alexander, Dismallo becomes as funny a pantomime character as we are likely to see during Yuletide. […] He is got up first as the villain of the play with a strong facial resemblance to Mr Irving, whom he burlesques. Later on we see this funny comedian in a dress compounded of that of a Highlander and a Roman warrior, with a spade as a weapon, and as armour a number of tin plates, from which depend forks and spoons; a sackcloth garb and a wondrous check suit with hat to match are further eccentricities of costume; and another dress represents a wooden toy, in which the idea of a dummy was funnily sustained. Mr Alexander of course has a catch phrase, and the continually uttered "I've lost my father" at odd times, in odd places, and to odd people, never failed on Saturday to evince laughter. […]

The Era, 2/1/1886

1886

A FALL FROM THE GALLERY

An accident of an extraordinary character, which was fortunately unattended with any serious results, occurred last Saturday evening at the Theatre Royal, Birmingham. A man named Alfred Manning, aged thirty-two, employed as a packer by Mr Davis, of Macdonald Street, and who resides at four house, nine court, Wrentham Street, went to the gallery of the theatre to witness the performance of the pantomime Robinson Crusoe. *Apparently with the intention of securing a front seat, he made a leap from the third row of seats, towards the front. Miscalculating his distance,*

however, he fell on to the iron rails, and for a moment held on with his hands. He was unable to sustain himself for more than a few seconds, and then fell into the pit below. The fall was fortunately broken by some brasswork which surmounts the front of the upper circle, and in his descent he came into contact with a chandelier projecting from the upper circle. He fell lengthways with considerable force upon the benches in the pit, slightly hurting two or three of the audience, but escaping himself in a miraculous manner, with a severe shaking and a few cuts about the head. A number of people quickly ran to the injured man, who lay in an unconscious condition. A cab was procured, and he was conveyed to the Queen's Hospital, where upon examination he was found to be suffering from no further injuries than a few cuts about the face. He was detained during the night, but on Sunday afternoon he was allowed to go home. The accident occurred a few minutes before seven, and the theatre was nearly full. A five-barred iron railing some time ago was erected above the woodwork in front of the gallery with the object of preventing such an accident.
The Era, 30/1/1886

Crystal Palace
Red Riding Hood

[…] OF course the Wolf (Mr Clarence Hague) is an important character in the story, and the opening scene is in the Wolf's Lair, where the orgies of the Wolf and his cubs are rebuked by the Queen of the Wild Flowers (Miss Lucy Millais). The Wolf answers in operatic fashion with a note of defiance, and the scene changes to Ding-Dong Farm in the village of Hickory-Dickory, where a charmingly idealised picture of rustic life is seen, with a jubilant hunting chorus by graceful little performers in the prettiest costumes. Here also we have idyllic suggestions of the May Queen, and as an amusing contrast a laughable scene between an antiquated Baron and Baroness (Mr George Boyle and Miss Emily Miller). An amusing change from turnip-faced rustics to smart young huntsmen is introduced, and a dance in which tiny little milkmaids, butcher boys, and even chimney sweeps appear, is much applauded.

But now we get to the real business of the story, and pretty Red Riding Hood (Miss Katie Barry) appears, and receives the letter from her grandmama which leads her into the clutches of the awful Wolf. Plenty of fun is made of the letter from Granny, and this is followed by a charming scene between Red Riding Hood and Little Boy Blue (Miss Rose Moncrieff). They part, and the little heroine sets out on her travels, meeting with all sorts of adventures.

There is a wonderful scene of a Spider's Web in the Wood, so artfully constructed, and of such gigantic size, that the Demon Spider, in the person of M. Dezano, crawls down the meshes of the web from the very top of the stage after a fly. So impressed was a charming little maiden sitting near us that she was quite relieved when she saw that the fly came to no harm. But there is a brave fight with the Spider, who is ultimately put to flight.

Then comes a beautiful scene with Dames of the Primrose League, with a host of pretty figures representing various insects and flowers, and no end of sylphs and fairies. Red Riding Hood finds herself in the regions of fairyland, and, naturally, as fairies are always supposed to be dancing, the ballet is introduced in the midst of an exquisitely poetical and romantic scene. The King of the Butterflies (Miss Mabel Coates) is so charmed with Red Riding Hood that he wishes to make her his Queen, but she has to encounter many adventures yet on the prosaic earth. We must not, however, pass over the ballet without warm congratulations to the dancers, special praise being given to the little ladies who represented ladybirds, primroses, violets, and other flowers. The groups were graceful, and the combinations of colour extremely picturesque and fanciful.

Again the heroine is confronted by the Wolf, who uses all his arts to mislead her. But soon the familiar scene, which has so often evoked shouts of juvenile mirth, occurs. In Granny's bedroom pantomime has the fullest scope. The exciting chase of the Wolf, the queer movements of what Mr Wilkie Collins would have called "that terribly strange bed", the daring leaps of the Wolf, the danger of the heroine, and the grotesque fun of the entire scene gained enthusiastic applause, the minds of youthful spectators being greatly relieved when Red Riding Hood is saved from all her perils, and some preliminary scenes usher in the Grand Transformation, which is quite up to the Crystal Palace standard. It is entitled Where the Bee Sucks, and is accompanied most appropriately by Dr Arne's beautiful melody with that title. […]

Queen's Theatre, Manchester
The Babes in the Wood, Bold Robin Hood, Harlequin Herne the Hunter, the Merry Maid Marian, and the Big, Bad Baron

[…] IT is described by the author as a "tragical, comical, pastoral, historical, allegorical, ironical, sardonical, limbsical, whimsical, flimsical, scenical, genical, fantastical, lastical, tiptopical, tropical, quippical, snippical, typical, cynical, djynical, quizzical, physical, farcical, blazical, critical, hitical, moosical, and boozical" pantomime. Unfortunately, the wide scope taken by the librettist in his title has been so cut down through the exigencies of the very large scenic plot prepared by Mr Mansell that the story in its mutilated condition is not very coherent.

The piece opens in the Haunted Home of Herne, the Horned Hunter (Mr T F Nye). The Baroness de Toujours Boozey (Miss Marie Bramah) and her son, Sir Hildebrandt (Mr Bernard Dale), enter into a compact with Herne, who is to aid them by his demon skill. He will compel Maid Marian (Miss Linda Verner), who is in love with Robin Hood (Miss Ethel Castleton), to marry Hildebrandt, and he will assist the Baroness in removing the Babes, who stand between the Baroness's children (a dozen twins) and their inheritance.

In the second scene, the village of Hollyhock – a charming pastoral picture – we get some very picturesque revels and maypole dances, in which a number of daintily attired children take part. Here we are also introduced to the Big Bad Baron (Mr Jonathan Wainwright), a pusillanimous and dissipated character with a partiality for village alehouses and mock-heroic recitations. In fact, he introduces himself right off as the scion of a "proud and thirsty race", and intimates before we have become acquainted with him five minutes that "booze is the thing for the baronial stomach".

The third scene, the Road to the Nursery, introduces us to a young Celtic lady, Miss Bridget Moriarty (Mr F Greville); and in the next we have a school-room full of bustle and merriment, the most uproariously funny feature of the scene being the capital mimicry of two crying dolls by Messrs Archer and White, the two Murderers. We are next transported to Cloudland, and from thence to the Palace, a splendid set, where some graceful dances are contributed to the ballet, specially imported from Paris by Mr Mansell. In scene seven there is a terrific combat between the Ruffians who have abducted the Babes; and in the next – a capital scene representing Sherwood Forest – a grand archery competition supplies the amusement. When Herne the Hunter is apparently baffled, the demon, by an instantaneous change, transports the characters to the scarred and splintered summit of the Brocken, where the Parisian and local ballets dance a weird measure, while the orchestra renders Mendelssohn's "Walpurgis Night" music. After this comes a wonderful scene, representing Old Trafford and the Ship Canal. The river is represented by a huge tank, full of water, on which sail real boats and real steamers. Eventually it is found that Herne has no hold on the Baroness and Sir Hildebrandt, the documents not having been stamped, and the discomfited demon is severely exorcised by Friar Tuck (Mr Charles Medwin). Then comes the Grand Transformation, the Birth of the Butterfly, which is followed by a screaming Harlequinade. [...]
The Era, 1/1/1887

1887

IN the Drury Lane pantomime The Forty Thieves *there is introduced an exceedingly pretty ballet by the little pupils of Madame Katti Lanner. The stage is filled with well-dressed juveniles, who suddenly receive the order to prepare for bed. On the instant they commence to unrobe, and presently are found attired only in their night-dresses. They have danced as they undressed, and now they dance again even while they take their pillows and indulge in that pastime dear to boarding-school pupils, and known as a pillow fight.*

Now it happened that one of the prettiest and one of the smallest of the youngsters was in difficulties directly the order to undress was given. There was an awkward fastening that refused to give way, and so when all her companions were in their night-dresses she was found still as she first came on. She danced all through her difficulties, but these were so evident that sympathy went out towards her from the whole house. This sympathy was increased tenfold when, breaking down at last, the poor little mite began to cry. Her troubles, however, were now speedily brought to an end by friendly hands at the wings, and when she came skipping on again to join in the revels of her companions there was a great roar of applause to give her welcome. That little child's distress had touched a chord of sympathy, and it gave forth no uncertain sound. It was but a small incident, but we venture to say it will be talked of and long remembered by all who were present on Boxing Night.
The Era, 1/1/1887

ON Sunday evening, as Mr Auguste Creamer's Robinson Crusoe *pantomime company were on route from Preston to Burnley, a pig, one of the features of the "comic" scenes, finding the door of the covered truck insecure, jumped out on to the line. His loss was discovered on the arrival of the truck at Burnley. By telegraph means, the railway officials were sent in pursuit of the porker, who was found running along the line unhurt.*
The Era, 19/3/1887

WANTED, Second-hand Inflated Fat-Boy Dress, for Pantomime. Must be in good order. Address, HENRY BLAKE, 12, Parkville Road, Walham Green, London.
The Era, 26/11/1887

The Britannia
King Trickee; or, Harlequin the Demon Beetle, the Sporting Duchess, and the Golden Casket

[…] THE opening scene is the Home of the Beetles, and King Scarabaeus (Mr Mulvy Ouseley) has called the beetles to his aid to secure the ruin of a foundling, Robin Roy (Miss Millie Howes), who has, however, a good friend in the Fairy Queen Floribelle (Miss Myra Massey).

Here a clever mechanical change takes place, and we next see old Roy's farm, where the sports of harvest time are taking place with great spirit, the maypole dance being a principal feature. Robin comes to the farm and joins in the festivity, and so does Trickitrix (Mr G H Chirgwin). Lady St Leger (Mrs S Lane[15]), an aristocratic lover of sport, promises prizes for target shooting, and Tricktrix is beaten by Robin, whereupon the public crier announces that the winner of the prize will be King of Simpleland. The artful Trickitrix at this juncture finds an ally in the Demon Scarabaeus, who lends him a magic bow and arrows, and thus he becomes the winner of the chief prize and the monarch of Simpleland.

There is, of course, a love story interwoven with the main incidents, and May (Miss Katie Cohen), the farmer's daughter, is the heroine. In endeavouring to shield her from the manoeuvres of Trickitrix, Robin has to encounter strange adventures and perils by land and sea. The ocean incidents are the most amusing, and the scenes aboard ship are decidedly novel. The shifty adventurer, Trickitrix, baffles his pursuers, and when brought to bay climbs the funnel of the steamer and leaps into it. He appears to be invulnerable while protected by the demon king, who determines to make him monarch of Simpleland instead of the rightful heir.

But the fairy queen Floribelle has not forgotten him, and at the Valley of Fairy Flowers she assembles her graceful court, and takes counsel how to protect Robin. The hero is presented with with a golden casket containing the secret of his birth, but he is bound under awful penalties not to open the casket until he reaches the court of Simpleland, where he finds that Trickitrix has already secured the throne, and has already installed himself as King Trickee the First.

Now the difficulty is how to depose the usurper, for possession is "nine points of the law". There are festivities going on at court, and amongst other entertainments a grand tournament, at which the crafty King Trickee is challenged to mortal combat by Robin, who has learned that he is the rightful heir; but his claim to the throne cannot be established, because the casket containing the proofs is missing. This, it appears, is in the possession of Trickitrix, who, it will be seen, thoroughly deserves that appellation. But the kind Lady St Leger, who has followed his fortunes throughout, assisted by the good fairy, ever the protectress of pantomime heroes, makes the discovery that Trickitrix is putting up certain effects at an auction, and the golden casket is there recovered.

Upon opening it clear proof is afforded that the foundling Robin has genuine claims to the crown, and, with all difficulties disposed of, there is nothing to be done but to produce the splendid transformation scene, which, we understand, has occupied months in preparation. […] It is called the Apotheosis of Britannia, and the striking figure of Britannia in the centre, surrounded by charming groups of graceful figures, with exquisite floral decorations and beautiful Arabesque embellishments, forms a most effective picture, seen under the changing hues that heighten its rich colour and varied effects. The artist (Mr William Charles) was deservedly complimented by a call to the footlights.

The important character of the usurping monarch King Trickee was played by Mr Chirgwin with all the eccentric drollery he has at command. […] His quaint make-up was remarkable, and the effect of a deep glowing red light on his nose gave the monarch a most sinister expression, besides causing both astonishment and amusement. […]

The principal scenes in the Harlequinade are Shops in Shoe Lane, a scene at the Wild West Show, and a Model Farmyard, furnishing ample scope for the talents of the pantomimists, and for the hilarity of the audience. There is a large selection from the popular ditties of the day, and song, dance, and chorus follow each other without hitch or hindrance for five hours. […]

Sarah Lane, actress and theatre manager

The Surrey
Sindbad and the Little Old Man of the Sea
[...] THE first scene is the Town and Port of Balsora, with a crowd of gaily-dressed figures dancing and carousing. Shears the Tailor (Mr E S Vincent) comes upon the scene, and is soon disputing with the sailors, but the interposition of his strong-minded wife Cogia (Miss Jenny Lee) gets him out of his difficulty, the lady having her own opinions as to which should be master, husband or wife. They sing a lively duet, "I shall have a separation". The Thief (Miss Amy Forrest) and the Tinker (Mr Dan Leno[16]) appear, and also the Soldier (Mr Cyrus Bell), who carries a trombone. Mr Bell causes no little amusement with his magical trombone, which comes to pieces at the slightest touch, but is reconstructed and made musical again with the greatest ease.

After some slight, but amusing, incidents, we have the appearance of the Little Old Man of the Sea, who is fished up by the hero, when he "gets a bite", little imagines that he will haul up a strange-looking jar instead of a fish. But there is a queer fish inside, for Mr George Conquest as the Little Old Man of the Sea emerges from the jar, and, in spite of his ungainly appearance, he commences to make love to the fair Amine (Miss Lydia Reynolds). When this is resented, the Old Man disappears with a suddenness that astonishes all. Waving a cloak round him, he flies, and when they attempt to seize him he is gone. The cloak is the only proof left that he has been there. This "mysterious disappearance" was managed with the utmost skill.

The fair Amine is next carried off to the Harem of the Sultan, but Sindbad follows, and there is a beautiful panorama of the Voyage from the Port to the Sea. The scenes on the deck of the ship are very amusing, but mischief is coming in the shape of the Little Old Man, who, aided by the Tinker, scuttles the ship. There are splendid effects in the wreck scene when the ship comes into collision with a whale. The monster spouts up into the air in the most realistic manner.

The Old Man of the Sea is next seen in a rocky cave, Mr Conquest again displaying singular skill in his appearance as the Rock Fiend, one of his most remarkable changes. Having broken the pledge by indulging in "firewater", he has been condemned by the Gnome (Miss Cissy Farrell) to be imprisoned in the rock for two hundred years; but he is released by a fairy opposed to the Gnome. Prince Amin is entrusted with his release, and henceforth the Old Man is to be his slave.

After his release the Old Man is sent to secure a magic diamond in the Palace of the Sultan. Meeting with Sindbad, that hero gives him some rum, and Mr Conquest then performs a scene similar to that in the famous drama *Drink*. It is far more than a caricature, for the actor displays very remarkable powers in this grotesque scene of realism, in which he touches on topics of the day, political and social, in the most vigorous manner, and gains enthusiastic applause for the striking ability he displays.

The phantom fight for the possession of the magic diamond is another of the effects which would alone be sufficient to attract crowds to the Surrey. The leaps from the traps to the roof and the daring and original conception of the whole scene cannot be too highly commended. It is called the Reptiles' Haunt, and hosts of grim creatures are coiled about in all directions. Sometimes the performers leap into their gaping jaws, and the next moment are vomited forth in a most extraordinary fashion, being either tossed into the air or thrown into the depths of fissures in the rocks.

After this vivid and fantastic fight, which causes quite an excitement amongst the audience, there is another splendid scene in the Hall of Statues. Here the performers are all got up in imitation of sculpturesque figures, and the *poses plastiques* they perform give the spectators the idea of beautiful marble groups arranged in classical studies of a very elegant and artistic kind. Other sensations are introduced in this remarkable scene. Varied hues of brilliant light are thrown upon the figures, and a fountain of real water scatters its spray to the extreme height of the stage.

Soon after this comes the transformation scene, which is as brilliant as could be desired. It is called Mamounie's Home in the Coraline Caves. It is beautiful and novel, and much admired, as it deserved to be. [...]
The Era, 31/12/1887

AT the Star Theatre, Wolverhampton, on Boxing Night, a crowded audience has assembled to witness the pantomime The House That Jack Built. *Miss Sappho as the hero Jack was doing a skipping-rope dance with a rope that had been saturated with inflammable material, and then ignited, when some sparks fell upon her bare arm, and very naturally she dropped the rope, which was at once covered by Mr H C Hazlewood with a blanket. This trifling incident has furnished some of the local reporters with the sensational head-line "An Actress on Fire".*
The Era, 31/12/1887

1888

THERE was the usual "scene" at the Theatre Royal, Nottingham, on Saturday night, with the close of the run of the pantomime, "the boys" making matters exceedingly lively throughout the performance. Miss Violet Evelyn, the representative of Will Scarlet, met with some undeserved hostility, because, not quite grasping the situation, she seemed not to appreciate the compliment intended when to her were thrown the colours of the Notts and Forest

> *Football Clubs; but explanations have ensued, and the lady and the footballers are now on the best of terms. Miss Evelyn says – "I did not know what the flag meant, being quite unacquainted with the colours of the local clubs; and, besides, the stage-manager, to prevent serious accidents, had told us not to pick up anything until the scene was over, as two of the children had been badly hurt with coppers, and one of the ladies stunned by a potato being thrown on the stage. Directly it was explained to me what the flag meant, I wore it on my dress; which, however, I am afraid the "boys" did not see, or they would never have hissed me."*
> **The Era, 3/3/1888**

Crystal Palace
Cinderella

[…] THE first scene introduced us to Father Time (Mr Theodore Reuss), who holds a Council of the Seasons, and confers with Tragedy, Comedy, and the Spirit of Pantomime, the last-named bringing in our old friends Mother Goose, Mother Shipton, Mother Hubbard, Mother Carey, Dame Trot, and the Old Woman who Lived in a Shoe. They are all "at sea", but the Fairy Godmother (Miss Emma D'Auban) settles the question of the subject of the pantomime by suggesting Cinderella, which is unanimously voted to be "the very thing".

Then we get to work in a picturesque wood, where the prettiest of villagers are engaged in gathering sticks and picking blackberries and nuts. Cinderella (Miss Edith Bruce) rescues the Fairy Godmother from insult, and when, on a mossy bank, she falls asleep, the fairy resolves to recompense her for her kindness by finding for her a husband in the person of the handsome and dashing Prince Felix (Miss Susie Vaughan), but first gives animation to the leaves of the forest, and sets going a grand ballet d'action with all the dancers in dresses "carried out from special designs after nature". It is, indeed, a lovely ballet, the most enchanting picture being the dance of the wood-pigeons, brought from their nest to hop about in a way that reflects the highest credit on Mr John D'Auban, to whose able direction the hopping has been confided.

The nest which the wood-pigeons built in the spring
Had two little eggs in it, speckled with grey,
And two little pigeons, all fluffy of wing,
From out of the egg-shells come peeping one day.

Through summer they grow, and when autumn comes round,
These two little birds are as plump as can be;
The leaves of the forest all fall on the ground,
And a wicked old fox thinks they'd serve for his tea.

But schemes that are cunning will frequently fail;
One morning the fox, as he joyfully jogs,
Is caught by the huntsmen, who cut off his tail,
And the pigeons still thrive while he goes to the dogs.

The huntsmen made a gallant show, and were, of course, headed by the Prince. The little people clapped vigorously at sight of the real horses and real hounds, and they were joined by their elders when the scene was completed.

In the next scene we make the acquaintance of the Baron Pumpolino (Mr Clarence J Hague) and Cinderella's half-sisters, Clorinda (Mr Edward Righton) and Thisbe (Miss Amy Liddon); and there come the expected invitations to the ball, causing considerable anxiety as to her hair on the part of Thisbe, who, having submitted her head to a patent "restorer", starts all the company in chorus with "It's another colour now".

In the kitchen scene, where we looked for some bustle and fun, the story was closely followed, the pumpkin, the mice, the lizards, and the rat – wonderful properties these – being transformed into carriage, brilliant with electric lights, horsemen, footmen in gorgeous liveries, and coachman for the once-neglected, but now highly-favoured, Cinderella, who herself becomes suddenly arrayed in costly garments. The boudoir business for her adornment, with the magical production of a swarm of little jewellers, bearing pearls, and of prettily-dressed waiting-maids, bearing fans and flowers and powder-puffs, is sure to be admired and long remembered.

In the sixth scene, illustrating the adventures of Thisbe, Clorinda, and Baron Pumpolino on their way to the ball, there is a little welcome fun, and then in the *bal masqué* within the Prince's palace we get the great scene of the pantomime. At the back of the stage is a solidly built-up gallery, approached by a handsome staircase, and all brilliantly illuminated. Soon the whole scene is filled by a richly-dressed throng, especial attention being demanded by those who come in eccentric costume – Punches, "white witches", Judies, follies, and elderly dwarf nurses dancing in their arms elderly and ugly babies. […]

Drury Lane
Babes in the Wood, and Robin Hood and His Merry Men, and Harlequin Who Killed Cock Robin?
[…] THE "Babes" are first in the title, but they are last in introduction. The curtain rises on a beautiful moonlit glen, where Robin Hood (Miss Harriett Vernon) and his merry men discuss musically the question of the death of "poor Cock Robin", and get from the sparrow and fly and fish and dove the sweetest of answers through the boys of Mr Stedman's well-trained choir. Then at once we pass to the Palace of Games, and get a grand procession and ballet of toys. This is one of the great scenes of the production, and with the other, which comes towards the end, and to which we shall come in due course, is bound to attract all lovers of pantomime fun and pantomime ingenuity. There are Dutch dolls endowed with life, but having all the Dutch doll's woodenness. There are those curiously shaped trees which we remember so well came out of our toy boxes when we played and quarrelled in the nursery or the back kitchen, and there were the toy soldiers, like those with which some of us frightened our anxious mamas in our eagerness to lick the paint off. There were kites and cricket-bats, and all the cards of all the suits, and shuttlecocks; chessmen hobnobbed with tennis players; baby dolls fraternised with big ones, and when the whole crowd, with its wondrous variety of colour, was set in motion the effect was truly remarkable, and old and young among the spectators were disposed to clap their hands in honour of Madame Katti Lanner, who was honoured with a call to the front. […]

Now we approach the legend of "The Babes", and, introduced to a meanly-furnished garret, make the acquaintance of the wicked uncle (Mr Victor Stevens), his wicked wife (Mr Dan Leno), his wicked factotum Jeames (Mr Walter Andrews), and his wicked dog (Mr Charles Lauri Jr), which is not a pug, but a poodle, and a very good poodle too. The impecuniosity of the Baron is indicated by the paucity of the midday meal. Thus, perhaps, there is some excuse for the merry jig which follows the announcement of the death of the Baron's brother and for the sudden resolve to put the brats that stand between him and fortune out of the way.

We do not see these "brats", Cissy (Mr Harry Nicholls) and Bertie (Mr Herbert Campbell) until in the fifth scene we obtain entrance to their nursery, where we find them objecting very much to be washed, and generally vexing the soul of Maid Marian (Miss Florence Dysart), who, for the first time in her career, we believe, has them in charge, and would like to be off to sweet communion in Sherwood Forest with her lover, who is none other than the bold Robin Hood.

She presently takes them for an airing in that direction, and contrives while love-making to lose them. No sooner are they lost than they are found – found by their wicked "nunky-punky" and their equally wicked "aunty-parnty", by whom they are handed over to the tender mercies of the two robbers (the Griffiths Brothers), who promise to tell them pretty stories on the way through the forest.

Here commences a remarkable panorama revealing many picturesque beauties, and reflecting the highest credit on Herr Kautsky, whose artistic skill and ingenuity provided it. Before going far the babes and the robbers come upon the G.O.M.[17], otherwise the Grand Old Woodpecker, chopping wood, but quite ready to explain his Irish policy. Happily, there is no time for this, and we go on to the deepest recesses of the forest, where the gnarled oaks and the twisted beeches not only wave their long arms in the wind, but wag their heads and wink their eyes, while the owls blink and the squirrels hop, and a human serpent in the person of M. Dezano twists and turns and indulges in contortions that are nothing short of marvellous.

The robbers quarrel and fight; the babes sleep and are covered in leafy blankets, and then suddenly we are taken to the Paradise of Birds, where is furnished that other great scene to which we have alluded – a scene that in beauty and richness surpasses all that even Mr Augustus Harris has done. The picture fairly baffles description. With the eyes bewildered and the senses enchanted by all the brilliancy and all the beauty that are here the keenest observer begins to scorn detail and to take delight in one grand, harmonious whole. The ostriches, the parrots, the cockatoos, the lovebirds, the jays, the canaries, the wood pigeons, the birds of Paradise with a hundred other varieties flitting hither and thither, a moving mass of loveliness kept in the most complete order, the spectacle beggars the pen, and makes poor, indeed, any attempt to do it justice. […]

After this nobody cares much how the babes get on, but it may be mentioned here that before the Ballet of the Birds is over Miss Cissy has put in an appearance as a *premiere danseuse*, and Master Bertie, like the Sparrow "with his bow and arrow", has figured as the naughty Cupid. They, of course, put the wicked uncle to confusion in the end, and are made thoroughly happy when the time has arrived for the full development of the transformation scene, designed and painted by Mr Emden, and called "Hail! Smiling Morn". It is a most artistic piece of work, and at the close was hailed with cheers that were eloquent of appreciation. […]

A bedroom scene [in the Harlequinade], with a shadowy illustration of "A Clown's Dream", will please the youngsters, who will also be compelled to laugh over the nefarious practices carried on at a fishmonger's and a pawnbroker's, and at other antics that are played before the Clown (Mr Harry Payne) and his companions, being dropped out of bed into a boat on the open sea, are picked up by a balloon, and, saying "Good-night", are carried up into the clouds. […]

Harry Nicholls and Herbert Campbell

The Surrey
The Forty Thieves and Their Wonderful Cave; or, Ali the Woodman and Morgiana the Slave
[…] THE well-known Arabian Nights story is selected for this year's pantomime, in the first scene, the Library of Fiction, by the Spirit of Pantomime, who chooses the tale from a book, from between the leaves of which comes the fairy Sesame (Miss Cissy Farrell).

This scene changes promptly to the Bazaar in Bagdad, with its groups of populace "discovered", a very effective picture. And here let us say that the dances, marches, and choruses arranged by Mr Frank Sims were decidedly good. There was quite a Savoyard accuracy about the drilling of the chorus of ladies, who marched, sang, and gesticulated quite intelligently. After some conversation between Zorah, Ali Baba's daughter, and Hawkshaw, a detective, which contains allusions to the Whitechapel murders which are rather ghastly and should at once be eliminated, Hassim (Miss Jessie Preston) enters, and joins with the pair in a trio, "A young man taken in and done for". Cassim (Mr Johnny Hansom) comes on in a befuddled condition, having been "indulging" overnight, and sings a song, and then enters Morgiana, whose ballad beginning "Just a little sunshine" is well sung and keenly appreciated. The first hearty laugh of the pantomime is created by the appearance of Cogia. The spectacle of Mr George Conquest's portly figure attired in the garb of a respectable lower middle-class female, with a high forehead resembling a pink bladder of lard, was very laughter-provoking, and his song "When you come to think of it" only needs some new words to make it go even better than it did on Monday, when it was twice encored. Abdalla (Miss C Moxon), attired in a pretty and original costume of pinky-orange and dark crimson, enters, and is followed by Hassarac (Mr E S Vincent), a very truculent-looking individual indeed. Here is introduced a clever concerted piece, in which three bands of thieves enter successively, and there is some well arranged business in connection with the Thieves' Chorus, which soon follows.

When the robbers have departed, Ali (Mr H M Edmunds), Mustapha the Cobbler (Mr James Albert), and Sammi (Mr Willie Albert), Ali's shop-boy, drive in on a donkey-barrow about twenty feet in length. Pantomime-goers will only need a hint to understand how much laughter is evoked by the elevation of the "moke" (Mr Harry Ewins) in mid-air, when the vehicle is tilted up, and by his entire collapse and suppression when the shafts descend to *terra firma*.

The next scene, the Interior of Ali Baba's General Shop, is given over entirely to the wildest popular fun. There is real humour in the disputes which take place between Ali and Cogia in their difficulties in shop-keeping, and in the successive entries and exits of a serious and solitary customer, who on each occasion receiving accidentally in his face some of the articles which "fly about" during the discussions, remarks calmly, "I'll call again when you're not so busy". […]

The cloth, scene four, the Road to the Forest, is capitally painted; and here there is too much of what actors call "cackle" in the book, relieved, it is true, by several songs and by the humour of Mr Vincent's Hassarac. The next "point" in the pantomime is an original duet between Abdalla and Morgiana, "Fare you well my deary", which goes exceedingly well. The fifth scene shows us a forest, and is painted with admirable breadth and boldness; and the entry of the "forty", headed by Abdalla and Hasserac, got up in distinct resemblance to a certain unpopular Royal Duke, with small tricycle and umbrella, is very brilliant.

The change from the forest to the interior of the cave is strikingly effective; and the stage picture of the cavern, with its real water rippling very naturally over stones and crags, and its overarching rocky roof, is thoroughly artistic. In this cave scene are introduced a number of children attired as convicts, who work as such, sing, and go through certain evolutions. This item is a mistake, and should be "cut" remorselessly. It was soundly hissed on Monday, and not even the really wonderful step-dancing of the boy who played Choker could save the scene from condemnation. [...]

In the Gardens of Ali Baba's Palace, illuminated by hundreds of coloured lamps, the erstwhile wood-cutter and his family appear in fine attire, and there is a grand ballet, in which a pack of cards is represented by girls in appropriate dresses carrying cards on poles. The colour in this scene is rich and striking. A game is also played with dominoes carried by semi-concealed boys, and the spectacle on which the curtain descends is gorgeous in the extreme. [...]
The Era, 29/12/1888

1889

ON Tuesday last, at the Darlington Borough Police-court, a youth named Charles Harkless, belonging to Sunderland, was charged with stealing a gold watch and chain, the property of John King. The facts of the case were extraordinary, as it appeared from the evidence that Harkless, who is only sixteen and the son of well-to-do parents, got into his present unenviable plight owing to an infatuation for ladies of the ballet. In February last Messrs Milton-Rays' pantomime *Forty Thieves* appeared at the Theatre Royal, in which the lady of the young gentleman's heart was employed. He took lodgings in the town, representing himself as holding the exalted position of baggage master to the company, and towards the end of the week, in order to keep his inamorata in chocolate bon-bons, he appropriated the goods and chattels of a fellow lodger. Prisoner's company was shortly afterwards in particular request by the minions of the law, but he was not to be found until last week, when he was discovered wandering about Bristol in a most pitiable and distressed condition. The Bench took into consideration the prisoner's youth and the pleadings of his parents, who were prepared to forget and forgive, and let him off with a fine of £5 and costs.
The Era, 25/5/1889

Drury Lane
Jack and the Beanstalk; or, Harlequin and the Midwinter Night's Dream

[...] THE pantomime opens in Oberon's Bower in Fairyland, a lovely scene introducing a charming ballet and chorus. Oberon (Miss Agnes Hewitt) and Titania (Miss Marie Faudelle) have a "little difference" as to the disposing of the fair Princess Diamond Duckz (Miss Maggie Duggan), whose papa and mamma, King Henry (Mr Harry Nicholls) and Queen Fanny (Mr Herbert Campbell), discover to their horror that she loves Jack (Miss Harriett Vernon), who is only a milkman, the maiden being "yearned for" by Gorgibuster the Giant (Mr George Conquest Jr). Titania pleads for love matches. Oberon upholds the rights and privileges of "caste", hence comes the complication soon to be solved by the Giant himself, for, visiting the palace of his fair one's papa, he carries her off, and then follows the struggle of Jack to recover his sweetheart. There is the scene with the cow, and the sale for a bag of magic beans, Jack's adventures among the gods and goddesses of Olympus, and his eventual rescue of the princess. [...]

There are three grand scenes in *Jack and the Beanstalk*, either of which would in bygone days have made the fortunes of a manager. But Mr Harris was determined to puzzle his patrons. He gave them an almost unlimited choice, and they hardly knew which they liked best.

There was the old English market-place where Jack brings his cow to be sold. What a beautiful scene that was with the whole of the stage occupied by animated groups of figures; not dull automatons, but lively personages every one of them and dressed in the daintiest manner. There were dances and choruses of the last century, holiday makers in costumes as rich and tasteful as costly material and elegant designs could make them, and the movement and gaiety of the scene could not be praised too highly.

Then the brilliant Shakespeare procession. What a feast there was for admirers of the national poet. Many of his plays were represented by appropriate and picturesque scenes glowing with colour and harmony of effect, and frequently rendered by the performers with exquisite taste. Scenes from *Hamlet, Macbeth, Lear, As You Like It, Much Ado About Nothing, The Tempest, Romeo and Juliet, Othello,* and many more were beautifully illustrated. This was the scene in the Giant's Library, where piles of gigantic volumes representing the genius and learning of past centuries are arranged so as to form a flight of gigantic steps, down which, to the echoes of a brilliant festival march, come the representative figures of the various plays, pausing a moment before the footlights to give with the requisite action some principal scene of the play. The groups had all been arranged by Mr Harris himself, and the costumes could not have been more perfect in design or costlier in material.

But this is not the last of the Drury Lane spectacular triumphs. As a feast for the eye, and a most wonderful realisation of the splendour and grace of Greek mythology, nothing like the festival of the gods and goddesses of Olympus has ever been seen on any stage. The mythical figures of the Greek poets stand before us in classic garb, and in costumes in which the utmost artistic beauty has been displayed. The loveliest designs are contrasted, and the most exquisite groups include Jupiter, Venus, Mars, Minerva, Hebe, Cupid, Mercury, Pluto, Neptune, &c. […]

Mr Harry Nicholls, besides supplying the book, exerts himself as the comic King. Very funny business it is, indeed, when His Majesty comes home with the milk and cannot find the keyhole. […] Mr Dan Leno has a most amusing character as Mrs Simpson, Jack's Mother, and his song so often disturbed by amorous cats was diverting. Mr Dan Leno's dances must be seen to be believed in. They are electrical. […] What tremendous fun there was in the Dairy Scene with the Brothers Griffiths as the Cow and Cowkeeper! Never was seen such an Alderney as that before. Children shrieked with delight, and grave elderly persons shook their sides to see such fun. […]

The Surrey
Dick Whittington and His Cat; or, the Demon Rat, the Merchant's Daughter, and the Charity Brat

[…] THE libretto is no worse than most effusions of its kind, but the day of versified and pun-studded burlesque is past; and brevity is the best virtue of a modern pantomime "book". There was on Thursday evening far too much of that kind of wit which was gently satirised by Miss Moxon, who, after giving the Cat a tart, and remarking, in the dialogue of Dick Whittington, "I think for a *week* 'twould keep a fellow *strong*," emphasised the indifference of the audience to the jest by saying, "*Week*! *Strong*! You see, pussy? A joke."

But if the patrons of the Surrey were a little blind to the literary merits of the "book", they awarded by a reception of intense cordiality the practical fun of the low comedians; indeed, one gentleman behind us in the pit audibly expressed his fear that the antics and oddities of Mr H M Edmunds would cause him (the spectator) some physical detriment as a result of over-hilarity. Mr Edmunds represents Idle Jack, a nondescript character who is attired, somewhat strangely for a London 'prentice, in a short, modern covert jacket and hat.

Mr H M Edmunds, besides taking advantage of every suggestion and opportunity which occurs in the course of the performance to introduce "screaming" fun, boldly inserts a sketch of his own, in which he is supposed, in melodramatic pantomime, to depict the various incidents in the life of a sailor. In doing this, he comes to loggerheads with the conductor of the orchestra on the question of "incidental music", and finally the director joins with two assistants in the wings in revolver practice at the unfortunate seaman, who, tearing off his waistcoat, reveals that he is bleeding copiously from a number of wounds, and falls, in comic death throes, on the stage.

Not inferior in humorous ability to Mr H M Edmunds is Mr Walter Groves, whose make-up and acting as Greaseilda, an elderly and unprepossessing female of the shabby-genteel order, are exquisite in their peculiar way. Far from creating laughter by a display of female hosiery, Mr Groves makes Greaseilda's intense, if somewhat inconsistent, reverence for propriety the funniest part of his performance. Then there are the Alberts, James and Willie, the first of whom makes extremely amusing the part of the inevitable comic constable, whilst the second, besides being an agile and absurdly "bob-tailed" cat, plays a Scotch air on sleigh-bells hung on his limbs and neck, and fastened to his head and upon his tail. […]

A brief sketch of the spectacular effects of the pantomime must here suffice. The second scene, East Chepe in the Olden Time, is an elaborate and artistic set; and the view from Highgate Hill (scene four) created an undeniable call, which had to be answered by the smiling appearance of Mr George Conquest. While Dick sleeps, he is supposed to be treated by the fairies to a dream of delight, in which he fancies himself in a pleasaunce inhabited by elves representing butterflies and insects, and carrying garlands of beautiful flowers. In the London Dock scene, a "practicable" vessel sails from the quay, and the eighth scene, representing a tropical forest, reflects, as does all the scenery, great credit upon Messrs J Soames, N Hinchey, and their assistants.
The Era, 28/12/1889

NOTES
1 – Sixenait: Six shillings and eightpence was a lawyer's consulting fee at the time.
2 – Katti Lanner (1829-1908): An Austrian-born ballerina and choreographer.
3 – Ada Blanche (1862-1953): A star of burlesque and pantomime. Her career lasted into the Edwardian era, when she enjoyed great success in Lionel Monckton's musical comedy *The Arcadians*.
4 – The plot of *The Corsican Brothers* by Dion Boucicault, premiered in 1852 and based on a novella by Alexandre Dumas *père*, revolves around conjoined twins who are separated at birth but grow up sharing a mystical bond. The play was still being performed well into the twentieth century.

5 – Gilbert Hastings MacDermott (1845-1901): A music hall star best remembered for the song *We Don't Want to Fight But by Jingo If We Do*.
6 – Vesta Tilley (1864-1952): A legendary male impersonator and pantomime principal boy. Her most famous song was probably *Burlington Bertie*.
7 – George Chirgwin (1854-1922): A singer and comedian who varied the usual blackface minstrel makeup by painting a white diamond over one eye. He was known as the White-Eyed Kaffir.
8 – Georgina Weldon (1837-1914): A pioneer of women's rights, notorious litigant – she was known as "the Portia of the law courts" – and campaigner against the Lunacy Laws.
9 – Kate Vaughan (1852-1903): A dancer and actress famous for her performance of the "skirt dance", a type of can-can in which the dancer wears a dress with long voluminous skirts.
10 – Lottie Collins (1865-1910): A dancer and singer, best remembered for her songs *Ta-ra-ra Boom-de-ay!* and *Daddy Wouldn't Buy Me a Bow-wow*.
11 – A nickname for the Storm (or Stormy) Petrel, a small seabird believed by sailors to foretell or somehow cause rough weather.
12 – Bessie Bellwood (1856-1896): A music hall star noted for her performance of "coster" songs such as *What Cheer Ria*.
13 – Probably a reference to the music hall song *The Ghost of Benjamin Binns*, the chorus of which begins "I'm the ghost of John James Christopher Benjamin Binns".
14 – In the Hebrew Bible Anak is the ancestor of the Anakim, a race of giants.
15 – Sarah Lane (c1822-1899): An actress, playwright and manager of the Britannia Theatre in Hoxton. She was related to the Lupino acting family, one of whose members was the Anglo-American actress and film director Ida Lupino.
16 – Dan Leno (1860-1904), born George Wild Galvin: A clog dancer, music hall star and legendary pantomime dame.
17 – "Grand Old Man", the nickname of statesman William Ewart Gladstone (1809-1898).

10
The 1890s
Three Evil Fairies From Liverpool

1890

AT the Hastings Pier Pavilion, during the progress of the pantomime Jack and the Beanstalk *on Tuesday, a curious accident occurred. About fifteen of the ladies of the ballet, dressed as peasants, had formed a ring by joining hands, and were engaged in dancing round and round at a rapid rate, when suddenly one of the dancers, quitting her hold of her companions' hands, was hurled outwards by the centrifugal momentum that she had acquired with such force as to snap asunder the guard protecting the footlights. She fell across the back of a chair, on which an astonished pianist was sitting in the orchestra, and finally was found reclining at the conductor's feet. Though a little surprised and shaken, the young lady, Miss Bessie Barham, took her place on the stage again later in the evening.*
The Era, 18/1/1890

MR JAMES M CHUTE, who, we are pleased to say, is now quite recovered from his late severe illness, gave a tea on Saturday last, between the two performances, at the Prince's Theatre, Bristol, to the thirty-two children who appear in the pantomime. The little ones seemed heartily to enjoy the good things provided, and one sturdy little chap, in answer to a question put to him by a member of the company, remarked, "I never had so much to eat in my life; I've been sick twice."
The Era, 22/2/1890

THE demon of discord played an important part in the pantomime of Aladdin *at the Theatre Royal, Birmingham, on Saturday night. It is a matter of common gossip that it has for weeks past been lurking in out of the way corners behind the scenes, but until Thursday, 20th ult – the occasion of Miss Jenny Hill's benefit – it was not allowed to present itself to the public. On that night the pantomime was abruptly terminated because of Miss Shirley's absence from the stage. On Friday night the performance passed off quietly, and to all outward appearance the the demon had been ruthlessly exorcised.*

It was not so. On Saturday it again put in an appearance, and the large audience which had assembled to wish Aladdin *farewell was treated to an exhibition of temper. When the second scene of the pantomime was reached, it seemed as if the artists were bent on infusing additional mirth and merriment into the performance by introducing funny and unexpected "business". Wigs were exchanged and various "make-ups" were indulged in, and the ludicrous effect produced by these innovations were heartily appreciated by the large audience. The performance, brisk, bright, and funnier than ever, ran with exceeding smoothness until about half-past nine. It then became evident from several ill-natured "gags" introduced by one or two of the artists that some difference of opinion had taken place behind the scenes.*

The announcement made by advertisement on Saturday that Miss Madeline Shirley had been adjudged the winner of the prize for the most talented lady in the pantomime, presented by the proprietor of a weekly journal, was the subject of much unpleasant comment by the artists while on the stage. Those of the spectators, and they were few, who understood what was meant evidently did not appreciate the introduction of personalities, and every now and then hisses from the audience betokened how strong was its disapproval of them.

In the sixth scene Mr Rock, the Abanzar of the cast, and Mr Rich, the Benzine, presented Miss Shirley, in complimentary terms, with a small birthday cake. At the sides of the stage the ballet ladies and choristers had ranged themselves, and, contrary to every known stage custom, indulged in hand-clapping and cheering, a fact which showed strongly how matters stood. After the presentation Miss Shirley sang "The song that reached my heart" with excellent effect, and was honoured with three recalls. She repeated the last verse twice, and an excited admirer threw to the fair singer a handsome bouquet. By accident it fell on the footlights. In a second the paper surrounding the flowers was alight. Miss Shirley, with much presence of mind, promptly rescued the bouquet. She extinguished the flame with her hand and continued the song. But just before concluding she was made aware by the presence of extreme heat that the paper attached to the bouquet was still smouldering, and with a sudden movement she tore the paper off and trampled it on the stage. Of course, the incident heightened the excitement prevailing amongst the audience.

The enthusiasm which had been aroused by Miss Shirley evidently reached the hearts of some of the other artistes. The next scene – Aladdin's Palace – was characterised by disorderly confusion. While Miss Hill and Miss Shirley were on the stage a bun was thrown from the dress circle and fell at the feet of the artistes. This was evidently intended as a satire upon the "cake" incident of the preceding scene, but, if so, it failed in its object. Miss Shirley left the stage almost before the presence of the bun could be remarked, and Miss Hill was left to deal with it. This she did in indiscreet fashion. Miss Hill proceeded with her song, "Bai Jove". In answer to a recall, she walked to the front of the stage and requested to be allowed to make a few remarks, in consequence of "a malicious and slanderous statement which had been in circulation behind the scenes". There were cries of "No" and "Yes" from the audience, and Miss Hill, who was labouring under exceptional excitement, proceeded to deliver herself of a speech. She had, she averred, been accused of securing some person to present Miss Shirley with an explosive bouquet, for the purpose of injuring that lady. It was a wicked and dastardly untruth. She had been before the public for twenty-eight years, and "was it to be expected that from her high pedestal she would stoop to do a degrading and unwomanly act?" Of course the spectators who had witnessed the accident to the bouquet which had been presented to Miss Shirley were aware that Miss Hill, by no stretch of the imagination, could be charged with having thrown the bouquet, which, of course, everyone knew was not filled with explosive material. Cries of "Go on with the pantomime" became general, and then, as Miss Hill persisted in continuing her harangue, complaining bitterly of the manner in which the ballet ladies and choristers had assembled at the "wings" and applauded Miss Shirley, a storm of hisses burst forth from the audience.

Just then Miss Shirley appeared on the stage. She managed to say in tremulous tones that Miss Hill was making a great mistake, and added, "You have made a terrible error, Miss Hill, in mentioning such a thing before the public." Miss Hill retorted that Mrs Keene and Miss Jongmans had told her that a bouquet had been thrown to Miss Shirley which had exploded in her hand and nearly set her on fire. The audience laughed loudly at this. Miss Shirley – I think the people saw what happened. Miss Hill – You and I have never had any quarrels. Miss Shirley – No. Miss Hill then offered her hand to Miss Shirley, and together they left the stage amid the laughter of the audience.

In the Eiffel Tower scene Miss Hill appeared in her "'Arry" costume, but instead of singing that well-known song she rushed suddenly from the stage. She appeared again with tear-dimmed eyes in the "tag" scene, where Miss Shirley, as Aladdin's bride, ought to grasp Miss Hill's arms. Miss Hill refused to allow her to do so, and with an impetuous shake of the head again left the stage, and the other artistes had to bring the pantomime to a close. Some slight mark of sympathy with Miss Shirley was given by a crowd of people who assembled at the stage door, and who followed the cab in which she was seated as it drove to the hotel, at one of the windows of which building Miss Shirley was compelled to appear to bow her acknowledgments to the few hundred people who had assembled below.
The Era, 1/3/1890

Drury Lane
Beauty and the Beast
[…] THE simple old story of "Beauty and the Beast" has, of course, undergone fresh developments for pantomime purposes, but while there are introduced many things that may be accounted "passing strange", the main thread, which naturally has most interest for juvenile visitors, is never too much obscured.

Beauty's (Miss Belle Bilton[1]) lover is this time named King Courage (Miss Vesta Tilley), and she wins his heart at the grand ball to which she has *not* been invited. The course of their true love would run smoothly enough if left to the direction of the Fairy Rosebud (Miss Florence Paltzer) and the handsome King of Diamonds (Miss Sibyl Grey), who have set themselves the task of watching over their interests, but as the history of fairyland must not be too much perverted, evil influences are allowed to prevail for a time, and thus to cause more general rejoicing when happiness is secured at the end. The evil genius this time is Old Bogie (Mr George Temple), the original and only genuine Bogie Man, who just now is being pressed into pantomime service in all directions. He has some powerfully mischievous promoters of his nefarious schemes in his familiars, bearing the unprepossessing names of Envy, Hatred, Malice, Slander, and Lying (the Original Leopold Troupe), whose very appearance, seeing that it is suggestive of the charnel house, is horrible and forbidding. They and their master begin their plotting very early in the piece, and their demoniacal devices are crowned with success before the ball alluded to is well over. Old Bogie has been simply disgusted by His Majesty's good deeds. If only he will devote his time to bad ones he shall have "pomp, riches, glory, wealth, a beauteous wife". Refusing – and, of course, he does refuse – the magic spell is set in motion, and the handsome monarch beloved of Beauty becomes the hideous Beast (Mr John D'Auban).

It is in this ball room scene that we get the first grand display of the pantomime. The whole depth of the stage is requisitioned. In the centre, the plashing of a fountain makes sweet music; on the right is a balcony filled with courtiers; at the back are noble statues; from the masked heads of the attendants ranged on either side spring candelabra, and from the pillar-supported ceiling depend magnificent chandeliers brilliant with the electric light. This spacious apartment is presently filled with the King's handsomely attired guests, and the pleasure of the spectators is manifested by prolonged applause.

Outside the Royal Palace the Beast is cursed by the Bogie, and in the curse may be found a sample of what in the way of text has been served up by the authors of this year's pantomime. Here it is:

May every bed you lie on seem of thorns!
May all your boots and shoes torment your corns!
May all your weather seem like bleakest March!
Your shirts and collars be devoid of starch!
Dressing in haste, may every button fly!
And may you crumple every evening tie!
May you, too, wed a shrew who'll nag and jaw!
May you be never free from ma-in-law!
And, last of all, but by no means the least,
For ever and a day remain a Beast.

The fairy Rosebud has something to say to this. The youthful King shall regain his proper form when unseen of mortal eye, and the spell that has been cast upon him shall be removed eventually by the good old-fashioned power of love.

Now Beauty's father, whose name is Lombarde Streete, sets out on a journey to France in order to restore his downfallen fortunes, and the fun begins in earnest, for Beauty and Beauty's sisters, Mary Anne and Sarah Jane, are to accompany him to the docks, and while the latter select as means of locomotion a tandem tricycle, Beauty prefers to drive a tandem of another sort with a couple of most remarkable "Jerusalem ponies[2]" for steeds. Papa mounts a safety bicycle of primitive pattern, and the mishaps that occur on the road are of the most laughable description. The journey is illustrated by a beautiful moving panorama reflecting great credit on the skill of the scenic artists.

The fun becomes more fast and more furious at the docks, for Old Bogie's assistants disguise themselves as sailors and are engaged to man the ship, and Beauty's "mokes" have to be got on board by means of a crane, the very sight of which brings one of them to his knees to pray to heaven for safe deliverance. A donkey praying, it will be admitted, is a donkey built on extraordinary lines, and it will hardly need to be said that those who looked on roared lustily at the sight. Beauty's sisters prefer their extravagant requests for presents on Papa's return. Beauty asks only for a rose. Now more exquisite fooling in the palace and then still more between decks "on board the lugger" that bears Beauty's father, most distressed among the passengers being the quadrupeds with the long ears, who, having with "oof" secured tickets for sleeping berths, are prepared to insist on their rights, and to enforce them, if needs be, with their "oof" with an aspirate in front.

The wreck of the vessel brings the voyagers presently to the Beast's Rose Garden, and Beauty's Papa obeys her behest, incurring all sorts of pains and penalties, and escaping from the same only on promise to send his youngest daughter as hostage.

Now pass we on to the Grand Hall in the Beast's Palace, where the King awaits loved Beauty's arrival. And here we get the great spectacular display always looked for in a pantomime produced by Mr Augustus Harris. The hall itself is built on lines of loveliness. The ceiling is gay with garlands, and when we look on the grand staircase we know that we may expect a procession that will be of wondrous brilliancy. Here come Amazons in glittering armour, and our attention is at once arrested by the artistic beauty and richness of the cloaks they wear. Here come damsels from whose shoulders spring gorgeous fans. Then a bevy of juveniles quaintly clad and a troupe of Indian dancers with cymbals and glittering scimitars and snake dancers practising their curious calling. The stage is crowded now, and as the evolutions proceed there is presented a picture of grandeur most enchanting. Well may Beauty exclaim on her arrival, "Splendour on all sides meets my wond'ring eyes."

The end is not far off now. Beauty's consent to wed the Beast restores King Courage to his proper form, and that there is soon to be a wedding, and a magnificent wedding breakfast, we are assured by the grand procession of viands with knives and forks and spoons and plates and fish and flesh and fowl and plum puddings and fruits and ices and Beauty's wedding cake, that is sure to make water the mouths of all the juveniles who during the holidays are taken to see the Drury Lane pantomime. With the luxury, though, there is a lesson in a very suggestive box of pills that brings up the rear. The wedding cake makes up the transformation scene, and although on Boxing Night there was a little delay in the serving, its complete development convinced everybody that it was as good as the most exigent could desire.

Beauty was very properly looked for in Beauty's representative, and it was found in the person of Miss Belle Bilton (Lady Dunlo), of whom it may be written that if she did not display any special aptitude for her part she at least acted throughout with grace and refinement and strove to deserve the beautiful basket of flowers handed to her across the footlights in one of the scenes. The most liberal contributors of fun – and, after all, fun is the most essential factor in a successful pantomime – were Messrs Herbert Campbell and Harry Nicholls and the Brothers Griffiths. The gentlemen first named represented respectively Beauty's sisters Sarah Jane and Mary Ann. Their appearance alone was provocative of great laughter, which got to a general and gigantic roar in the scene where the massive ladies were discovered mounted on their tandem tricycles. […] The Brothers Griffiths represented the "mokes", and a more comical pair of donkeys has never been known. From their teeth to their tails, from their ears to their hoofs, they were fruitful of laughter. The way in which they wouldn't be harnessed, their woe-begone submission to being hoisted on shipboard, their turbulence under the influence of *mal de mer* raised screams of delight, and they were voted quite splendid successors of the far-famed donkey whose name was "Blondin". Mr Dan Leno, who impersonated Beauty's father, was, most certainly, "lively on", and we doubt not was also "lively off", for he always came up, if not smiling, yet full of drollery and prepared in speech, song, dance, or "business" to add to the fun and to increase the merriment. Those who saw this Lombarde Street, Esquire, in his tortuous movements on being conducted from the palace by Private Block, of His Majesty's forces, after a too liberal allowance of the wine cup, are not likely soon to forget him. […]

Belle Bilton

The Britannia
The Spider and the Fly; or, King Jokose of Goforem Castle
[…] THE idea of "The Spider and the Fly" has been freely handled by Mr J Addison, so as to admit of the introduction of a large amount of interpolated matter. Of course, there is a demon, personified by the poisonous spider Tarantula (Mr George Lupino Jr), and equally, of course, that demon's desires are conceived but to be thwarted by the good fairy Firefly (Miss Myra Massey). In the second scene, which represents a tropical forest, King Jokose (Mr Fred Cairns), his queen, Margarine (Mrs S Lane), and their suite, come a-hunting, after a pretty lantern ballet has been danced in the wood. Here a hunting song is harmoniously sung by the Paragon Quartette, attired in "tops" and "pink", and Fidelio (Miss Lizzie Chipchase), a young woodman, meets his sweetheart, the Princess Bluebelle (Miss Amy Lister). After the royal picnic, Tarantula succeeds in capturing Bluebelle, and takes her off in his magic net. Into the Council Chamber of King Jokose in the next scene are brought Fidelio and his sister Damaris (Miss Edith French), accused of assisting Tarantula in his abduction. They prove their innocence, and Fidelio heads a rescue party to hunt the demon to his lair.

The next stage picture, the Floral Hall in the Palace of the Queen, is gorgeously elaborate. In the centre is a moulded pavilion with handsome columns, and baskets of beautiful flowers hang from the roof. Here great amusement is created by Tarantula's transformation of his enemies. The Count Crikerico (Mr Harry Lupino) becomes a poodle, Prince Okokolo (Mr William Gardiner) a "woman of the people", King Jokose a coster, and Tarantula himself assumes the form of a parrot.

After a ballet of Court belles, and *pas seuls* by Mlles Kate Floretta and Florence Valeria – in which the dancers prove how much more graceful in the dance are long skirts than the abbreviated muslin kilts so much in vogue – we move on to a dreary swamp, and thence to the Home of the Demon Spider. A built-up house at the back gives opportunity for a spirited chase and rally, and here the Lupinos display their peculiar talents to great advantage. One of the brothers plays on a violoncello, whilst the other, in canine costume, watches him from the top of the house, whence he takes a leap of some fifteen feet on to the stage. An amusing scene follows, in which Mr Harry Lupino's admirable imitation of the tricks and movements of a dog creates loud laughter. The inevitable "Bogie Man" song comes in here, and from this point until the end of the pantomime there is a constant succession of lively songs, dances, and business.

Scene eight, Goforem Castle, is an elaborately constructed piece of stage architecture, with drawbridge and battlements complete. The storming of this stronghold by a party armed with a siege gun which sends showers of turnips and other harmless missiles upwards is vastly laughable.

In the Stalactite Grotto an ingenious imitation of the "wooden-headed family" of the music halls by living members of the cast is introduced, and its effect might be even increased by closer imitation of the voices given by the ventriloquist to his puppets. As it is, the item is one of the funniest in the pantomime.

The cloth then rises upon the transformation scene. Baffled in the attempt to adequately enumerate its manifold glories, we may briefly state that the general effect is created by a number of female figures, each surrounded by radiating fans of gold filigree, the whole scene being bathed in light and colour. [...]
The Era, 3/1/1891

1891

IMPERSONATING AN ACTRESS
AT the Worcester City Police Court, on Wednesday, Mary Elizabeth Eastman, aged sixteen, described as a servant, of 54, Wood Lane, Treetop, near Rotherham, was charged with stealing a black dress and a small silver brooch, value 18s, the property of John Hill, at Little Southfield Street, Worcester, on January 30th. The Chief Constable stated that the case was a curious one. The prisoner went in the first place to Mr Gomersal, the lessee of the Theatre Royal, and told him that she was a daughter of Mr T C King, the tragedian, a former lessee of the theatre. Mr Gomersal did not comply with her request to engage her for the pantomime, and she then went to the house of the prosecutrix, who took in lodgers, and said that she was Miss Maude Stafford, the actress, who was then playing in the pantomime of Red Riding Hood, *at the theatre. She took a bedroom and sitting-room at Mrs Hill's at the rate of 7s 6d a week, and, to keep up the fiction, she used to stay out at night during the time the performance was on at the theatre. Prisoner bore no resemblance to Miss Stafford. Prosecutrix did not receive payment from the prisoner, and on making inquiries found that she was not Miss Maude Stafford. She then told prisoner that she had discovered her deception, and that she must leave the house. Prisoner left, and prosecutrix missed the articles which formed the subject of the charge. The prisoner had also deceived her mother by telling her that she was engaged to a Gerald Lloyd, who had died and was to be buried at Worcester. Her mother went to Worcester, and the prisoner left her by some pretence at the station, and did not return, but took with her some things, which she pawned. She was arrested in the gallery of the theatre on Tuesday night.*

Mrs Hill, the prosecutrix, proved the first part of this statement, and added that when she told prisoner she had discovered that she was not Miss Maude Stafford, the actress, prisoner declared that she was, and said she would fetch Mrs Gomersal.

Prisoner's mother, Mrs Mary Howell, appeared, and said the prisoner was sixteen years of age. In September last she left home, and went into service at Armley, near Leeds. In about a month she was told that her daughter was not at Armley, but was at Rotherham with a theatrical company (Arthur Lloyd's company), and witness went to Rotherham and took her daughter home. Whilst at home her daughter represented that she received letters from Arthur Lloyd's brother (Gerald Lloyd), and she showed witness letters which she believed to come from that gentleman, but, as she was "no scholar," she could not tell. The letters purported to tell the prisoner that she was to go to Worcester to join the company, but witness now believed that they were written by the prisoner herself. She still believed, however, that her daughter had been with the company. She afterwards received a letter from her daughter saying that Gerald Lloyd was dead and was to be buried at Worcester, where the letter was written from. Witness found that this was untrue. The prisoner said she and Gerald Lloyd were to be married at Easter. When a child the prisoner fell from the table and hurt her head, and a doctor had said that her brain was affected. Witness had had a great deal of trouble with her.

Prisoner, in reply to the charge, said she did not know what possessed her to take the dress, which she pawned for 2s. She must have been out of her mind, and she knew that she had a weak brain.

The mother was at first reluctant to take the prisoner back home, saying that she would "get up to some more wickedness;" but, after some persuasion from the magistrates, she consented to do so, and she and prisoner were bound over in £5 for the prisoner to come up if called upon. **The Era, 7/3/1891**

> MR TONY BENSON, of Elliott and Benson, died suddenly in an epileptic fit at Halifax on Wednesday last. Our Barnsley correspondent says it is rather a remarkable coincidence that poor Benson had a mock funeral at Bradford, on Feb 16th. The Theatre Royal and Prince's Theatre pantomime companies had a football match for the benefit of the local charities. During the match Benson, for a joke, pretended to be killed. His remains were paraded round the ground, a pit was dug, and a mock burial took place with musical honours. A splendid wreath was placed at his head, with a bottle of spirits and some cake. Needless to say, the corpse came round, devoured the cake, emptied the bottle, and appeared at night on the Royal stage with the wreath around his neck.
> *The Era, 4/4/1891*

> TO LET, Best Novelty in England, for the Christmas Pantomime, the Trained STAGS and HOUNDS in the great scene of the "Stag Hunt", the same beautiful Stags and Hounds that was the great attraction of Olympia, London. These animals are most docile, and will Leap Gates across the Stage 7ft high, and over Water Jumps 9ft Wide. The scene is the most novel and exciting, and can be fitted in any Pantomime. At the end of the Hunt the Stags and Hounds clear the Water Jump, a Canvas Tank to hold about Twenty Buckets of Water. The Comic Man, Woman and Fat Policeman get drowned, while the Clown and Pantaloon save their lives. Reference, Crystal Palace Theatre, Birmingham Theatre, &c. Splendid and Magnificent Posters and Cuts – these alone a great attraction. The Stag Hunt, as performed by these Trained Stags and Hounds, would make a splendid Novelty for a Touring Company, to write a Drama (Sporting), to finish with the Stag Hunt. On arrival in each town, to parade in their van, followed by the Hounds, Huntsmen blowing their Horns, &c. The Stags and Hounds travel in one van together. Address, F GINNETT, Circus, Brighton.
> *The Era, 21/11/1891*

Theatre Royal, Bradford
Red Riding Hood

[…] SCENE one introduces us to the Wolf's Lair, where Baron Badlot (Mr Frank Manning) is detailing his vile intentions regarding Red Riding Hood (Miss Sara Dudley). He secures the aid of Lupus, the Wolf (Mr Colin Coop), Johnny Stout (Mr J W Hall), Jack Sprat (Mr Fred Selby), and Wormwood (Mr Henry Wardroper) to assist him in his designs, and in the midst of their plotting Fairy Glowworm (Miss Alma Steele) appears, and quickly tells them of her intention to upset their plans by herself protecting Red Riding Hood.

It is thus "war to the knife", and a change takes place to scene two, Manningham Park, in Bradford. It is a band promenade; there is a ballet of park strollers, with a chorus of novelette readers, football players, mill hands, and the inevitable mashers. During the progress of this animated local scene, Red Riding Hood appears, and she is at once taken possession of by her lover, Little Boy Blue (Miss Millie Marion), and shortly afterwards she is crowned Queen of the May. Lupus and the Baron enter, and prove a barrier to further festivities, and these two, along with Stout, Sprat, and Wormwood, hold a council of war, when a decision is made to carry off Red Riding Hood. Boy Blue, however, aided by the Baron's tenants, rescues the heroine, and the villains decamp.

Scene three, the Wash House, is occupied by Red Riding Hood's Granny, Dame Trot (Mr Tom Costello), who is a tenant of the bad Baron. Granny is selected as an object of revenge by the Baron and his associates; Dame Trot alone possesses the secret of Red Riding Hood's noble birth, and this the Baron suspects, and, in order to make the old lady divulge the secret, he tries gentle persuasion, which avails him nothing, and, foiled, he presses for the rent, which is overdue. Granny is driven to desperation, and she defiantly tells him that blue blood has tainted Red Riding Hood, and that she is the only child of his elder brother. Dame Trot produces the deeds in proof of her assertion, and for the possession of these documents a struggle ensues. The Baron and his miscreants are overpowering Granny, when Boy Blue turns up in the nick of time and overthrows the Baron. Granny, however, receives notice to quit, which she does. Boy Blue, however, defends her.

Then we find ourselves at scene four, The Strid, Bolton Woods. Here there are more festivities, but the news of Granny's ill-treatment unfits Red Riding Hood, and she does not participate. She declares herself "an unhappy Queen of May", and goes in search of healing herbs for Granny to Glow-worm Glen, at the suggestion of Wormwood, whom she encounters.

The glen being a favourite resort of the Wolf, endangers the little maid, but Boy Blue is on the alert. He has heard of Wormwood's treachery, and a hue and cry is raised, taking us to scene five, Bolton Abbey, where there is a Watteau ballet, and chorus of Jolly Little Monks. Little Bo-Peep (Miss Birdie Brightling) is here discovered with her flock of real sheep. The Baron and his friends are searching for Red Riding Hood, whom they fail to find. She is, however, found by Lupus, who makes overtures to her, and, being rejected, he is about to seize her, when Fairy Glowworm intercedes. Lupus, foiled, declares "the Dragon (Mr J H Roberts) shall have her"; but the good fairy enlists the services of St George of England (Miss Edith Cole), and we witness the historic combat.

We are then carried to Shipley Glen (scene six). It is holiday time, but Dame Trot, who comes upon the scene, is too much occupied with the probable fate of Red Riding Hood to participate in the revels. The conspirators put in an appearance, and they are overheard conspiring to "settle" Granny, when a change takes place to the Exterior of Dame Trot's Cottage (scene seven), followed quickly by another transformation to the Interior of the Cottage (scene eight), of which the old dame has somehow again become the tenant. It is not for long, though, for the conspirators (as they imagine) finally put her out of the way, and Lupus, being now in uninterrupted possession of the cottage, takes Granny's place in the bed. Red Riding Hood arrives.

With a growl Lupus leaps from the bed, and is about to destroy the maid, when once more Boy Blue saves her, and change is made to scene nine – The Square and Bradford Town Hall – where preparations for the wedding of Boy Blue and Red Riding Hood are in progress. The Baron is now fairly done for and divested of his wealth, and St George gets Bo-Peep as a reward for his valiant conduct.

Scene ten is the Land of Toys, where a marvellous Toy Ballet is witnessed. Scene eleven is the Interior of a Local Music Hall. The bad characters are punished, justice is meted out to the good people, and all ends happily with the transformation scene – A Dream of St George and His Palatial Halls – a very novel and dazzling sight, in which the glitter of armour is very beautiful. [...]

Drury Lane
Humpty-Dumpty; or, Harlequin Yellow Dwarf and the Fair One with the Golden Locks
[...] WITH the most commendable punctuality the proceedings were commenced, and when the musical director, Mr John Crook, facing the mighty audience, lifted his baton, there was not a vacant seat in the house; a multitude to faces brightened, and just a few thousand throats were cleared for indulgence in the choruses that were sure to come. At it they went with wonderful gusto for their own amusement and for the diversion of stalls and dress circle and private boxes and royalty too, for even thus early the Royal box was occupied by the Prince and Princess of Wales, the young princesses, the Duke of Clarence, and the Duke and Duchess of Fife. Stentorian lungs roared "Hi-tiddley-hi-ti", "Get your hair cut" was shouted by those above to those below, who answered only "Wink the other eye", while both joined forces to extol the fascinations of the "Pretty little mermaids at the bottom of the sea", and to "Knock 'em in the Old Kent Road".

All that history has left of Humpty-Dumpty for the edification of the nursery is the record that, having sat on a wall, where probably he was a trespasser, he had a great fall – whether through loss of his own equilibrium or through the malice of another we are not told – and that, having been badly broken, all the King's horses and all the King's men failed in their endeavours to put Humpty-Dumpty together again. Mr Harry Nicholls and Sir Augustus Harris have proved more expert. They have put Humpty-Dumpty (Little Tich[3]) together in splendid fashion and have made him the determined rival of young Dulcimar (Miss Fanny Leslie), King of the Gold Mines, for the hand of the Princess Allfair (Miss Marie Lloyd[4]), daughter of the King and Queen of Hearts (Mr Herbert Campbell and Mr Dan Leno). The Princess at first sternly refuses to have anything to do with Dulcimar, whom she most cordially detests; but a cup of magic tea puts her desperately in love with him and she weds him forthwith, only, however, to be captured even on her bridal day by the resolute Humpty-Dumpty, who carries her, evidently by the underground railway, to a very terrible place, called Steel Castle, whence presently she is rescued by Dulcimar and his wooden-headed soldiers, who afford her the chance of enjoying the Dream of Bliss, the chaste and beautiful transformation, designed by Herr Kautsky, who, in the provision of stage pictures, has been associated with Messrs Cancy, Harker, and Perkins.

There are four special features by which the Drury Lane pantomime of Christmas 1891 will be remembered. The first of these is the scene called the Dolls' At Home, the second is the grand ballet in the scene of the Orange Grove, the third is The Procession of Nations in honour of King Dulcimar and Princess Allfair, and the fourth is the introduction in the person of "Little Tich" of the drollest dwarf ever seen on the Drury Lane stage.

The Dolls' At Home may be said, in the matter of quaintness and the delight of the juvenile audience, to "take the cake". The procession is a scene of indescribable loveliness suggesting the most extravagant outlay, while in the provision of fun Little Tich undoubtedly is most to the fore. Let us deal with the dolls. They are summoned to her father's palace by the Princess Allfair, and very readily they obey – that is, as readily as they can, for many of them are stiff in the joints and altogether wooden in their movements. They are of all sorts and sizes, and it may be added of all nationalities. There are male dolls and female dolls, black dolls, white dolls, dolls that are pale, and dolls that have the customary Lowther Arcadian colour in their cheeks; stiff-legged dolls and dolls that are as elastic as the india-rubber of which they appear to be made; dolls with curly hair and dolls with no hair at all, except such hair as is represented by paint; dolls dressed and dolls undressed; English clown dolls and French punchinellos gorgeous in black and yellow satin, and doll Pierrots; and, most imposing of all, a gathering of giant baby dolls in long – about twelve feet long – garments and becoming hoods, from which escape their flaxen curls and great big blue eyes that stare the spectators out of countenance. Never was known such a remarkable doll collection. At rest they make a wonderful show, but when they begin to dance the effect is altogether beyond description. [...]

The scene of the Orange Grove is sure to be voted enchantingly effective by reason of the floral divertissement, with its startling electric effects. The dancers carry lily or arum boughs in their hands, and similar flowers decorate their dresses. While they dance the foliage over their heads is suddenly brilliantly illuminated, and in an instant each lily on their costume is converted into an electric lamp. A prettier or more startling spectacle could not be conceived, and acclamation loud and long is fairly compelled.

The Procession of Nations is eloquent of wealth expended and of exquisite taste employed. Surely Royal bride never before had so gorgeous an assembly to do honour to her nuptials, and in the way of costumes Mr Percy Anderson, the designer, may be credited with a triumph. In turn, India, Arabia, Dalmatia, Tartary, Cochin-China, Persia, Egypt, Lapland, Japan, Montenegro, Portugal, China, Timbuctoo, Italy, Greece, Holland, Germany, Austria, Russia, Turkey, America, Spain, France, and England have their representatives marching forward towards the throne occupied by the King and Queen of Hearts, and one hardly knows what to admire most, the ambassadors or their train-bearers all resplendently robed. As truthful chroniclers we are bound to tell that Germany and Russia aroused some little hostility; that America was cheered; and that pit and gallery reserved the loudest applause for their noble selves as represented by England. [...]

"Little Tich", whom we have placed fourth in our list of specialities, was easily first in favour among the artistes engaged. It may be possible to give a correct portrait of this funny little man in words, but we long ago in our experiences of him at the music halls abandoned the task as hopeless. He has a funny little body, funny little legs, a funny little face, and a funny big smile that stretches right away from the footlights to the topmost gallery, and on Saturday night this Yellow Dwarf – for into the Yellow Dwarf Humpty-Dumpty develops – kept the house in a roar, now in nautical costume, now in sporting garb, now in a Scotch rig-out, and now – most comical of all – as a ballet girl with a *pas seul* that would send a hypochondriac into fits of merriment. [...]

Mr Dan Leno worked very hard indeed from start to finish, and was responsible for much hilarity. A sly bit of humour was brought into scene eight. The Queen has received her distinguished guests, representative of all the nations under the sun, and has shaken hands with each in turn. The reception over, Her Majesty brings in soap and water, and proceeds to wash her hands. The spectators took the hint at once, and there was a general roar. [...]

Miss Marie Lloyd was the Princess Allfair, and with her song "Whacky, whacky, whack", and with much "kicking up behind and before" seemed to give immense satisfaction to the gods, who cheered her to the echo.

Miss Mabel Love put in some pretty skirt dancing in the scene of the Orange Grove, and, again, during the development of the transformation, her graceful movements being followed with delight and commanding many compliments; and a very young lady who danced in the scene of the Kitchen Garden, where the plum puddings grow and the sucking-pigs are nurtured in cucumber frames, is entitled to high praise, and to have her name in the programme. [...]

Marie Lloyd

Little Tich

The Surrey
The Fair One with the Golden Locks; or, Prince Charming, the Giant, and the Long-Lost Ring
[…] THE action, such as it is, opens in the Cave of Mother Earth (Mr Arthur Hall), where the elements are consulted as to the interests of Prince Charming (Miss Lily Laurel), who is the suitor for the hand of the blonde and beautiful Florinda (Miss Laura Dyson), the daughter of King Henpecked the 1000th (Mr H Fortescue). The king's second wife has a daughter named Troutina (Mr Frank Danby), and proposes to unite the Prince to this young lady, whose appearance is more quaint than prepossessing. Poor Florinda is shut up by the Queen in the tower of a castle, and is compelled to weave and make a dress of silk. This she does with the aid of the fairies. Prince Charming has also his task to accomplish before Florinda can be his. He has to overcome a great giant, Quake (Mr George Conquest Jr), and rescue his lady-love from the custody of the King of Fire.

But if the story of the Surrey pantomime this year be slight, its embellishment is lavishly splendid and finely picturesque. Nor is the necessary element of the grotesque absent. It is long since a better property has been seen on the Surrey stage than the representation of the Giant in *The Fair One with the Golden Locks*. The first we see of this monster is the lower part of his legs as he passes through the forest in which Prince Charming and his companions find themselves. Though we are shown little more than the Giant's feet and calves, they occupy almost the height of the proscenium opening. In order to cut off the monster's head the Prince and his party ascend the trees of the forest, finally arriving where the Giant's arms are waving in front of his enormous head. This gigantic construction is calculated to give juveniles food for Christmas dreams. The eyes open and shut, and the hideous mouth, full of irregular teeth, has a most bloodthirsty grin. Once seen, this Giant is not likely to be forgotten, and the head is certainly a triumph of imitation.

A great contrast to this effective piece of ugliness is the evolutions gone through by files of ladies dressed as Hussars, Lancers, Life Guards, and Highlanders. Their uniforms are dazzling in their colour and brightness, and their wearers perform their drill with marvellous accuracy and smartness.

A clever effect is created in the scene in the Caves of the Dragons of Fire by the sudden spouting up of numerous jets of water in front of gas illuminations of graceful pattern. The scene itself, with the great dragons belching jets of flame, is powerfully fantastic; and the groupings of the ballet when the fiends of fire are attacked by firemen in bright helmets, wielding bright axes, are admirable. […]

The transformation, which is called the Triumph of the Crystal Fays, is unpretentious but exquisitely pretty. Forget-me-nots and other flowers, opening, reveal groups of fairies, whose cut-glass wings sparkle brilliantly in the lime-light. […]
The Era, 2/1/1892

1892

SHOCKING THEATRICAL DISASTER
A SERIOUS disaster occurred at Gateshead on Saturday evening, when, at the Theatre Royal, a panic resulted in the death of ten people. Mr Turner and Mr Bacon, lessees of the Gateshead Theatre Royal, had on Christmas Eve produced their third pantomime, on the subject of Aladdin. *On the night of Boxing Day a holiday audience, numbering twelve hundred, assembled, filling the spacious gallery and pit to overflowing, whilst the other parts of the house were numerously occupied. The theatre has two tiers, the lower being divided into circle and side balcony seats, the higher being the gallery, wherein accommodation is provided for seven or eight hundred spectators. The whole of the ground floor is devoted to the pit.*

As the performance progressed on Saturday the greatest good humour prevailed in the house, and it was on the opening of the last scene – the Great Wall of China – that the incident occurred which was fraught with such terrible consequences. In the lower circle on the left-hand side facing the stage a woman, who was attended by her husband, dropped either a scarf-pin or a florin on the floor. Without thinking that any danger might be caused by the act, the man struck a match and looked for the missing article. By this means a piece of paper on the floor caught fire, and the paper and sawdust smouldering together caused a flame which, though slight, was sufficient to alarm the woman, who called out "Fire, fire." A hand was put across her mouth to prevent a repetition of the words; but, as a volume of smoke was now curling upwards, the alarm spread at once, and the audience started to its feet and made straightway for the exits from the stage.

Mr Turner and his company, realising at once the dreadful nature of the rush, and also the smallness of the fire, called on the audience to keep their places or go out in order. Their appeals were, however, unheeded, and as some of the pit occupants went back to the ordinary exits, crowds tore down the orchestra partition and, clambering to the stage, swarmed out at the narrow private staircase. From the lower circle the people got out safely, but numbers preferred to lower themselves or jump to the pit; whilst from the gallery at the edge nearest the stage the more venturesome jumped direct to the stage. In the meantime, the bulk of the gallery audience made its way to the one exit, the door of which was bolted. Foster, the check-taker in charge, managed eventually to draw the bolt, thus releasing the door; but the act cost him his life, for before he could leave the place the weight of the surging crowd forced him down three stairs to a landing on the way to the main staircase. In their haste to leave the theatre, those who pressed onwards stumbled down the three stairs, and were fallen upon by the mass behind, and the means of egress thus became greatly impeded, though hundreds found their way down to the street without injury.

When the people ceased to pour down the stairs it was assumed by the excited populace in the streets surrounding the Theatre Royal that all had emerged; but as Thomas Butler and James Gordon were ascending the gallery stairs they were terrified to find a heap of living and dead people five deep, whilst, behind them, there still struggled those who had not been able to proceed further. With assistance they pulled out men, lads, women, and girls, most of them suffering from shock, whilst others were more dead than alive, and did not long survive when carried out to the neighbouring houses. A door at the top of the gallery stairs was then opened, and numbers passed through in safety, and windows were broken to admit fresh air. One little lad was held back just as he was on the point of jumping down to the hard surface of Nelson Square from a height of about 70ft.

Inside the theatre, other parts of the house were cleared in good time, and when it was discovered that there was a stoppage at the gallery door, long benches were raised from the pit to the gallery balcony, and down these a great number of people reached the floor in safety, thence making their way to the street, where the news of a panic spreading quickly attracted an enormous crowd, which increased as the victims were carried out to the surrounding houses for medical treatment. It was about half-past ten o'clock when the catastrophe took place, and in a few minutes the fire had been extinguished with the aid of a few buckets of water. Before eleven o'clock death had ensued in several cases, and by midnight there had been ten deaths, whilst at the Newcastle Royal Infirmary several patients were admitted suffering from shock and bruises. Nine of the dead bodies were removed to the Temperance Hall.

On Monday an inquest was opened by Mr Coroner Graham, who remarked upon the necessity of people leaving places of amusement in a quiet and orderly manner when fear of danger arose. The jury had sufficient evidence placed before them to show that the fire had been a very trifling affair comparatively, and one which could have easily and speedily been extinguished without inconvenience to anyone in the building except those in the immediate vicinity. The inquiry was adjourned.

Our correspondent, who was in the theatre, confirms the statement made by Mr Turner, who says: "There was really no fire at all; a little water soon quenched what there was, and when the seats were torn up on Monday morning we found that they were only scorched underneath, and the paper on the wall was not even burnt off." To Mr Turner and Mr Bacon, who retained their self-possession throughout, and did all that men could possibly do to prevent the panic, the greatest praise is due, and sympathy is expressed for them on every hand. The theatre remained closed on Monday and Tuesday, and reopened on Wednesday with the pantomime, when the entire proceeds were handed over to the widow of the deceased check-taker, Thomas Foster, who leaves a family of four children. The lessees also gave another benefit performance for the parents of the children who were killed. [...]

The members of the company all escaped unhurt, but several of them had not time to change their stage dresses for ordinary attire. Immediately on the panic becoming known a number of roughs broke into the theatre and fairly ransacked the dressing-rooms, taking with them most of the artists' clothes, and anything they could lay their hands on. This dastardly outrage has created great indignation in the town.
The Era, 2/1/1892

AT the Marylebone Police Court, on Tuesday, John Brown, of Carlisle Street, Marylebone, was charged on remand with stealing by a trick sixpence from Lina Fuller, of Chichester Road, Kilburn.

The prosecutrix and a cousin went to the Marylebone Theatre to see the pantomime on Boxing Night. Seeing an announcement that early admission could be obtained by payment of an extra fee at the stage-door in Little Church Street, they went in the direction indicated. They came across the prisoner and another man who were standing at an open door, and not knowing the locality well they supposed that was the stage door. The men asked if they wanted the early admission door, and they replied that they did. The men then charged them sixpence, wrote something on a piece of paper, and directed them into the basement of the house. They followed the instructions and soon found themselves in the kitchen of a common lodging-house. The room was full of men who were smoking and talking, and when the young women asked if that was the way into the theatre the men laughed heartily and showed a disposition to play a practical joke, but the women quickly retreated and gave the prisoner into custody, the other man escaping.

The prisoner, in reply to the charge, said he was drunk at the time. He had no intention of taking the money. There were thirty or forty men in the kitchen. He gave the prosecutrix 5½d out of his own pocket because she seemed upset.

Mr Montagu Williams – You were sober enough to commit a rather clever fraud on these young women.

The Prisoner – I was drunk. Drink got into my head. I've been in an asylum.

The Magistrate – Yes, and I understand you have been in an another asylum of a different sort.

> *The Prisoner – I've been in Colney Hatch, and my mind has been a little out of order.*
> *The Magistrate – So I should think. Three months' imprisonment.*
> **The Era, 9/1/1892**

MR J W HALL, the representative of Johnny Stout in the pantomime at Halifax, has been telling a local interviewer that during his career he had met some queer characters. "I was taking a benefit at Wigan one Friday," said he, "and was delivering my hand bills to a host of colliers who were just leaving the pit, when one of them came up to me and asked 'Ar't' ta him as sings "Silly Tommy?' I said I was, and he then said, 'Well, I'm coming deawn ta neet, an' if tha does na sing it I shall put mi clog in thi ribs.' Of course I sang it."

ON the 4*th* inst, *during the performance of* Dick Whittington *at the Prince of Wales's Theatre, Birmingham, the audience was somewhat startled by a man rising in the stalls of the theatre, and producing a revolver, at the same time shouting to Mr O'Gorman, of Messrs Tennyson and O'Gorman, who occupied the stage with Miss Louise Henschell, the Princess of the cast, that he would shoot him. Miss Henschell fainted, and Mr O'Gorman hurriedly left the stage, and refused to return until the individual who had threatened him had been ejected. As it was discovered the revolver was not loaded, no proceedings were taken by the police.*
The Era, 12/3/1892

Morton's, Greenwich
Sinbad the Sailor

[…] WHEN the curtain rises we have the time-honoured opening in which Amphibio (Mr Robert Fairbanks) and his merry band threaten to deal out vengeance to all and sundry. Sinbad (Miss Kate Hedderwick), as a matter of course, is included; he has been, and is, a great deal too good, and, according to the Amphibio creed, he must die. However, when these worthies are hatching a very pretty plot, Coralina, Queen of the Gems (Miss Phyllis de Mowbray), appears, and, to use the classic phrase, "spoils their little game".

After a wordy warfare between the kind-hearted fairy and the bold, bad, inhabitants of the ocean, in which the Grand Old Windbag, Home Rule, the House of Lords, and kindred political subjects are touched upon, we are introduced to the second scene. And now the fun commences. Captain Grimgriffin (Mr Walter Walton) enters, followed by his "pal", Dick Dirtyweather (Mr Ernest Lester). The former Johnnie, it appears, is in love with with petite, pretty Polly Primrose (Miss Florence Burns); but, as she has given her young and (presumably) tender heart to Sinbad, the protestations of affection from the unattractive and uncouth "capting" are not much to the young damsel's liking. This nautical personage tries to mash the aforesaid Polly, but the timely arrival of the well-favoured youth compels him to take a back seat. Sinbad elects to go to "furrin parts" with Grimgriffin and his crew. Before embarking, Sammy Softside (Mr Thomas J Morton) appears on the scene. The chirpy Sammy, we understand, has been having a few words with "his missus", and he, too, is most eager to emigrate, and so avoid another meeting with his very Irish, very muscular, Bridget (Mr Harry T Vale). However, his better – to say nothing of his bigger – half is on the track, with the result that this frolicsome lady ships with the rest on board the *Dancing Dolphin*. During this scene we have a transformation dance by Miss Merrie Rosie – admirably done, by the way.

We now discover the festive crowd in the saloon of the above-name craft. Sammy has an awful attack of *mal de mer*, and wishes himself back again at the dough-punching establishment. The business can easily be overdone, but this clever young comedian was funny, without a trace of vulgarity. His whistle and wheeze caught on famously. The partner o' his joys and sorrows is also in a sad plight owing to the unruly sea. Polly meanwhile also joins, disguised as a cabin boy, with the avowed intention of "keeping an eye" on the somewhat amorous Sinbad.

The old hulk springs a leak, and the crowd fancy they are bound for Davy Jones's locker, but they get away safely from the wreck and find themselves landed on the Island of Heniwhere. Their plight truly is a sorry one, and the arrival of some very dusky natives does not improve matters. King Kockaleekee (Mr C W Spencer) also thinks it's a favourable opportunity of putting in an appearance, accompanied by his daughter, Princess Popsee-Wopsee (Miss Edith Wynter). Grimgriffin addresses his Majesty in the following touching words: "We are shipwrecked mariners, as I'm a sinner." This evidently pleases the copper-visaged King, who replies, "I'll have the fattest one for Sunday's dinner." Sinbad improves the shining hour by mashing the princess. Her irate father orders the immediate execution of our too amorous hero, but stays his hand on the condition that Sinbad shall seek and find the "wondrous talisman" to be discovered somewhere in the Diamond Valley.

The youth, accompanied by his trusty henchman, Softside, eventually annexes the said talisman; the King is appeased, especially when he gets sharing terms in the wealth discovered; Sinbad marries the girl of his heart, the evil spirits are put to rout, and everything ends happily in true pantomime fashion. [...]

The Britannia
The Man in the Moon

IN the first scene, a Fairy Glade, Venus (Miss Alma Brunton) summons North Star (Miss Harriet Davis) and other occupants of the heavenly sphere, and informs them of the love of Lumin, the "Man in the Moon" (Mr George Lupino Jr), for Fair Winifred (Miss Amy Lyster), who is engaged to one Dick Dareall (Miss Rose Hamilton). Mars (Mr Edward Leigh) is summoned, and a discussion takes place as to the best means of defeating Lumin's purpose. The second scene is the Village of Verinear, where Lumin appears to the maiden in the guise of a troubadour, and gains her consent to accompany him to the moon. In scene three, Captain Dewdrop's Cottage, the Captain (Mr Sam Jesson) declares his intention to protect Winifred from Lumin by marrying her to the Baron Bouncer (Mr Fred Carlos), an elderly idiot. The latter is overjoyed, and invites all to the wedding fete. In the Baron's Banquet Hall a grand ball takes place. Mars comes to Dick's assistance, informs him of Lumin's plot, and gives him a magic sword, with which he encounters the Demon, who is in the act of escaping with Winifred. Lumin, however, deprives Dick of the sword, and departs with it and Winifred to the moon. The alarmed mortals repair to scene five, the Green Witch Conservatory, where they mark what takes place in the moon, to which they ascend in a balloon. The Baron and Holdfast (Mr Harry Pleon) plan to escape to the moon alone. Lumin arrives eager to prevent the start, and Dick, discovering him, rouses the crew of the Royal Ironclad, and a chase ensues. Lumin raises a storm to destroy the vessel, but too late to prevent Venus coming to its assistance. The Baron and Holdfast make off in the balloon, leaving the others to proceed as best they can.

Venus, however, supplies the means, so all arrive safely at the Mountains of the Moon, where Lumin endeavours to get Winifred's consent to a union with him. Dick and his friends enter, but at Lumin's command the Moon Syrens charm the travellers to sleep. If they are not roused within the hour from this mysterious slumber, they must thus remain for ever. But Venus averts such a further calamity. Lumin, enraged, makes a further attempt to carry Winifred away with him to earth, but Venus coming between them causes an eclipse, and Lumin is defeated. […]

The scenery by Mr W C and C Douglass, assisted by Mr W Jones, is splendid, roars of applause being evoked by the dazzling and gorgeous Banquet Hall, with its numerous pink-shaded lamps and glittering appointments. The introduction of the immense solidly built steamer in the sixth scene should also be mentioned, and the transformation, with its fairy lakes and floating lilies, and its Juno's car, drawn by swans, is as artistic as it is elaborate.

The Surrey
Puss in Boots

[…] WE are first taken underneath a mill to listen to a little plotting. If we are not particularly interested in this, Felina, the Queen of the Pussies (Miss Cissy Farrell), is, and there is plenty to engage the general attention, for there are any number of rats – all very fine and large – and there is not one whose tail is not at least five yards long. The mill itself is a very pretty set, and here the fun begins with the singing by Billy Buttons (Mr James Norris) and the pert Pertina (Miss Delmont) of a medley that makes use of the titles and tunes of all the popular ditties of the day, a clever concoction, cleverly treated by Mr James Norris and Miss Delmont. And here, too, we are introduced to the Widow Oatmeal (Mr George Conquest Jr), fat, fair, and forty, and on the look out for a rich husband able to support her and her boy Jack (Miss Lilian Bishop). And here, too, come the limbs of the law known in society – respectable society, it may be hoped – as Red Tape (Mr Evans) and Copy o' Writ (Mr Jee), who drive up in a very primitive type of vehicle, belabour the natives, and then sit down to get some very sweet harmony from a couple of mandolines. The widow makes up to and "make up" for Glumpo, the Marquis of Carabas (Mr Charles Seel), and Flourina (Miss Laura Dyson), the miller's daughter, wanting money, listens to the attentions of Auriferous, the Demon King of the Gold Mines (Mr Frank Lister), who recommends a visit to the Devil's Glen, where everything she touches will turn to gold. Flourina, however, is not green enough to be caught by this lure until she finds that her lover Prince Prettypet (Miss Millie Beckett) is also impecunious, when having joined in a very pretty duet and dance she suggests that they might do worse than visit the place mentioned. The King (Mr George Spry) and his gorgeously arrayed attendants here come on to fill up a very effective picture, the appearance and eccentric ways of his Majesty and of Grindoff (Mr Dan Crawley), the miller, not to speak of a wonderful cat (Mr Fred Conquest) and a wonderful dog (Master Arthur), creating great laughter.

It is a very quick journey that takes us to the Devil's Glen, where attention is at once arrested by the serpent that the Demon King keeps on the premises to frighten away intruders. He is indeed a monster, and out of his head comes the famous Dezano to astound all beholders by his tricks of contortion.

It is in a pretty wood and by a pretty lake that Puss gets into his boots, and becomes endowed with speech through the good offices of Felina, and it is here that Mr George Spry (King Muffenough) – and Miss Austin (Princess Brillantine) – make a big hit with their quaint Negro duet, "Just push dem clouds away", with quaint dance to follow.

Flourina being put in prison is ordered to be kept there until she can turn straw into gold; but, being possessed of the talisman found in the Devil's Glen, makes light of the difficulty, and actually builds up a magnificent Golden Palace, which, with the massing and marching of the Gold and Silver Guards therein, may be pronounced one of the most gorgeous and successful features of the pantomime. A very bright and merry entertainment is introduced by the Floridor troupe, who shake sweet bell music from the boughs of trees, and with their knockabout business and eccentric dancing and xylophone playing cause great merriment and command enthusiastic applause.

Auriferous now lays claim to Flourina, and carries her off with the Princess Brillantine to his castle. Jack and the Prince of course set out at once to their rescue, and call by the way at the House that Jack Built, that undergoes some remarkable developments, growing and growing, while the malt and the rat that ate the malt, and the cat that killed the rat, and the dog that worried the cat, and the cow that tossed the dog, and the maiden all forlorn, and the man all ragged and torn, and the priest all shaven and shorn, and the cock that crowed in the morn grow too, until from being Liliputians they assume Brobdignagian proportions. This is a capital scene that is sure to delight the juvenile visitors, as, too, will the presence of the Ogre at table, with his ultimate defeat by Puss, making way for the revelation of the multifarious beauties of the transformation scene, called the Home of Coralina, an artistic triumph for Mr Soames.

Mr George Spry as King Muffenough undoubtedly carries off the largest share of the honours in the representation. He never spares himself, but works hard and well from first to last, and bring much humorous ability to bear on his part. In one scene he has a song called "Father's Overcoat", and a recitation that secures him not only the laughter and applause of his audience, but quite a shower of carrots, cabbages, and other pantomime properties from his companions on the stage, but from the musicians immediately in front of it. [...]

Drury Lane
Little Bo-Peep, Little Red Riding Hood, and Hop o' My Thumb
[...] SIR AUGUSTUS HARRIS has at the outset boldly discarded tradition. The pantomime begins in no magician's cave, is evolved out of no smoking cauldron, while good and evil spirits enlist themselves in the cause of the hero or the villain of the piece; but commences in the hut of Daddy Thumb, a woodman of attenuated frame and bibulous aspect, who, in his shabby frock coat and battered hat, bears a striking resemblance to Mr Dan Leno. Daddy has a Goody, a fat and imposing dame, Mr Herbert Campbell to wit, and the pair are over-burdened by seven children – Hop o' My Thumb, represented by Little Tich; and the rest by Messrs Griffiths, Walton, Tom Terriss, Bennett, and Martell, Miss Retta Walton, and Miss Hettie Bennett. The humours of this household are boisterous in the extreme. Imagine the absurdity of Little Tich in process of being bathed and put to bed by Mr Herbert Campbell! The tableau needs no explanatory remark. "He won't be happy till he gets it," yelled the gallery boys in delighted recognition. Hop o' My Thumb is cynical and precocious. He vigorously discards his baby bottle and asks for a brandy and soda. In fact, he is the most up-to-date infant ever seen.

The next scene is in Arcadia, and very arcadian it is. Mr Perkins has painted a lovely landscape, bathed in warm sunlight, and hither troop Watteau shepherds and shepherdesses, with their pipes and panniers, their crooks and posies, till the stage looks like a little world of Dresden china brought to life and imbued with exquisite grace by Mr John D'Auban, a pretty embodiment of "tea-cup times, of hoop and hood, or when the patch was worn". Here we are introduced to such old friends as Tom Tucker, Jack Horner, Miss Muffit, Margery Daw, Tom the Piper's Son, all impersonated by the prettiest of pretty girls, also to a certain Dame Mary Quite Contrary, an angling spinster who admits that "she hasn't been kissed for years", and who quickly makes the running for a gay village squire of dubious habits and dubious age. Dame Mary has an admirable representative in Mr Arthur Williams, and the Squire in Mr William Morgan. The dashing Boy Blue, Miss Ada Blanche, who is a principal boy worthy of the traditions of Drury Lane; demure Bo-Peep, in her grey Quaker gown; Prince Popperty, played by comely Miss Madge Lucas; and Little Red Riding Hood join in the fun, and then we come to the masque of sports.

There never was such an effective array of stage properties – so admirably realistic and so picturesque. A troop of sportsmen in Highland tweeds pop at imaginary game, gigantic boxing gloves pummel each other lustily, a group of pretty girls trip across the stage with punt poles slipping through their fingers in the most approved style for showing buxom bosoms and well shaped arms, skaters glide by, jockeys win and lose fanciful races, huntsmen in pink mingle with Dianas in smart riding habits, tennis players with their racquets talk with yachtsmen in bright blue, great cricket bats stalk solemnly across the stage, large footballs move in a mysterious way, billiard balls wink insidiously with "quaint enamelled eyes", cyclists vie with skaters, fishermen mingle with fencers – the whole arsenal of British sport is there, reproduced with extraordinary effect and vraisemblance. There is nothing appeals to your Britisher like sport, and the audience was demonstrative in its delight, although there were cockney critics who mixed the implements of lacrosse with those of polo, and called golf sticks punting poles in confidential explanation.

We make the acquaintance of the Wolf family at the Spotted Sun, where the elder Wolf had obviously been drinking. The Wolfs, who are actually the Brother Griffiths, give a suggestion of burlesque kangaroo box, and then comes a most ingenious effect – the moving forest – in which Hop o' My Thumb and his brothers get lost; their irresponsible parents having hit upon this method of getting rid of their family.

Mr Kautsky's beautifully painted trees give a curious idea of motion. Then, from the recesses of this forest issue countless wood nymphs, bearing in their hands tremulous sprays of electric light, with five or six glow-lights at the end of each spray. As they dance on the darkened stage their undulating lights group and divide in kaleidoscopic illumination with exquisite effect. Probably the electric light – that now-popular adjunct of stage illumination – has never been used so ingeniously and so admirably arranged.

The Ogre's Kitchen affords opportunity for a good deal of conventional business. It is a cleverly arranged scene, grotesque heads of carved woodwork peering and blinking from its recesses. The Giant and Giantess are respectively played by Mr H M Clifford and Mr E S Gofton, two well-known "heavy" actors, who are capitally made up. They sing a duet of the Darby and Joan type, set to an old English air, and make love with elephantine finesse that is extremely funny. But the scene reaches its climax of merriment when Mr Dan Leno and Mr Herbert Campbell are strung up to roast before a great cooking fire. Their antics and grimaces, their philosophic remarks on the horrors of their situation, are followed with shrieks of laughter. It is of its kind one of the most comical incidents ever seen on the stage. An exquisitely beautiful "Slumber Song" is sung by invisible voices as the Giant's baby family and Hop o' My Thumb, with his brothers, are put to bed. The pity is that the beauty of this musical effect is marred by the loudly expressed amusement of the audience at the fun in progress before the curtain. Mr John Crook, by-the-by, is responsible for the music.

A little scene in the Prince's corridor permits Miss Ada Blanche to sing – and very acceptably – an old favourite, "How he carries on". This is one of the few songs reproduced in its entirety. Of course, the whole library of contemporary favourites is laid under contribution; but the authors of the pantomime have culled here a verse and there a refrain, paraphrased it, and fitted it to the exigencies of the story. One cannot get away from the impression that there is a dearth of really good comic songs for the moment. [...]

Now we come to what we suppose will go down to stage history as the great scene of a great pantomime. Some commentator on stage effects was remarking, the other day, how seldom glass had been used in dramatic productions. He will now be able to add a notable example to the list. The palace in the Drury Lane pantomime is a noble structure of mirrors raised tier on tier, that transform the vast stage, apparently, into illimitable space. Hither come troops and troops of gorgeously apparelled courtiers and attendants. Then there is an inroad of many serpentine dancers, their flowing draperies in exquisite gradations of art tints. It has been reserved for Sir Augustus Harris to reveal the potentialities of this popular dance. As the pretty girls begin their mazy movements they are reproduced in the mirrors all around them, till there appear to be myriads of dancers "away, away to the *ewigkeit*[5]". It is like Jacob's ladder "up to date". There they pass and repass, swirling and undulating, till the eye wearies before this perpetual motion of grace and beauty. But something more wonderful is to come. At the back of the stage is an imposing staircase, down which there approaches a procession of nursery rhymes and fairy tales. One after another they come, each with its court, telling its tale. We cannot detail them, for there are thirty-nine, and each is really a miniature show in itself, complete, and, we doubt not, as accurate as possible in every detail. It is a gorgeous pageant, a splendid masque of fable and folklore, a liberal education in the art of the stage and the archaeology of the nursery, which, to be sure, is archaeology in its most fascinating form. When the curtain fell upon this stupendous scene there was a great outburst of enthusiasm. [...]

After this scene we get an interval that allows Mr Dan Leno to sing a characteristic song – a good-humoured satire on the unemployed agitation. Mr Leno, in the character of a mob orator, harangues a select audience of loafers, who, after his vocal efforts, smother him with refuse. Then Little Tich gives a most grotesque imitation of a serpentine dance. He smirks at the audience, and ogles the limelight man. He twists his skirts about, loses hold of them, and, in a state of great confusion, finds them again. He whirls himself into an inextricable mess, falls about the stage, then, by way of showing that he can really dance, obliges with a step or two, and makes an outrageous exit. It is an excruciating bit of burlesque.

Shortly we get the traditional incident of Red Riding Hood's visit to her grandmother's cottage, and then the pantomime loses itself in the final splendour of the transformation, which typifies the Language of Flowers with a degree of splendour that defies description. We are afraid if the the children who visit the Drury Lane pantomime have a word to say by way of complaint, it will be that Sir Augustus Harris has dealt so liberally with them in the "opening" that the harlequinade is not reached until too late an hour. It is too good to be missed by suburban visitors bent on catching early trains. [...]
The Era, 31/12/1892

> ONE of the Brothers Griffiths has been the victim of a rather serious accident during the week. The brothers represent the wolves in the pantomime at Drury Lane, and prepare to eat up Little Red Riding Hood by a little exercise in the

bed-room scene, going through a very agile and amusing performance upon the horizontal bar at the back of grandmother's bedstead. On the occasion referred to the supports of this bar gave way, and the performer fell heavily on the stage, bringing the bar down with him, on to his face, smashing his nose and injuring one of his eyes. Surgical aid was, of course, found necessary, but the injured artist has pluckily continued his part.
The Era, 31/12/1892

1893

THE multitudinous beauties of the pantomime Little Bo-Peep *have served to maintain its deserved popularity to the very last nights of its career, but with the coming of these last nights and days – for the matinées are still well supported – Sir Augustus Harris has added to the number, and in the "Rainbow Dance" had introduced an effect that is as novel as it is pleasing. About twenty of the principal members of corps de ballet arranged in white voluminous skirts, made additionally extensive by a contrivance carried by the wearers, go through the serpentine dance under quite new conditions, for as they dance they are occasionally almost lost to view in clouds of steam, upon which coloured lights are made to play with most curious and charming results. The dance has been hailed with shouts of approval and delight by all whose good fortune it has been to see it at Drury Lane.*
The Era, 18/3/1893

Stratford Theatre Royal
Robinson Crusoe

[…] THE supernatural element is conspicuous by its absence in the opening scene, which is not of the usual gloomy character. It is the riverside at Greenwich, where Will Atkins (Mr Horace Barri) and a press-gang are discovered as the curtain rises. Young Robinson Crusoe (Miss Norrie Brandon) is seized by the press-gang and taken away, after he has sworn to be faithful to his sweetheart, Polly Peachblossom (Miss Katie Fredericks), to whom Atkins also pays court. After a visit to Mrs Crusoe's (Mr A E Good) emporium, we find ourselves assisting in the festivities on board the *Stormy Petrel*, the sailors joining in a jovial chorus. Here we again meet the hero and heroine, Will Atkins, Mrs Crusoe, and other characters who have to do with the story, although some of them were unknown to Daniel Defoe. The *Stormy Petrel* is wrecked upon some hidden reefs, the going-to-pieces of the vessel being shown by a cleverly worked mechanical change. Scene the fourth is the Coral Cave Beneath the Wave, where Marina, the Ocean Queen (Miss Flo Villar), welcomes Crusoe to her glittering home. A pretty ballet of sea nymphs takes place, Miss Bertha Belasco appearing as principal dancer. Crusoe climbs a rock, and finds himself upon an island. He makes the acquaintance of Good Friday and Bad Saturday (the Eyremond Trio, one of of whom also plays 'Mungo'), and the next scene reveals Crusoe's Hut. In a Ravine in the Island another ballet takes place, followed by a capital variety entertainment. In this Miss Katie Fredericks, who is the charming representative of Polly, gives a graceful dance, photographs of Lord Salisbury, Lord Beaconsfield, her Majesty, the Duke and Duchess of York, and Mr Gladstone being thrown by the limelight upon her white garments. […] After this the story quickly comes to a conclusion, Robinson discovering that King Kokernut (Mr Crusoe) is no other than his own father, who has long been absent from his native land, while villainy in the person of Will Atkins suffers ignominious defeat. The transformation scene, Crusoe's Dream of Wealth, painted by Mr Arthur Hilyard and assistants, is an admirable piece of work. [...]
The Era, 30/12/1893

1894

A VERY sad event occurred during the performance of the pantomime Dick Whittington and His Cat *at the Elephant and Castle Theatre on Boxing Night. Miss Kitty Tyrrell (Mrs Harry Ewins), who was taking the part of the Rat, after having appeared in the second scene, Fitzwarren's Kitchen, retired to the wings to await her re-entrance. She then complained of feeling faint, but a few minutes afterwards again went on the stage, took part in a dialogue in which she had to say "In due course his road to fortune he'll pave o'er my corse," and then made another exit to the wings. Here she was seen to stagger and reel, and was carried by her husband Mr Harry Ewins, who was taking part in the pantomime, and was also the clown in the harlequinade, to her dressing room. Restoratives were procured, but death appears to have been almost instantaneous. The audience were not made aware of what had taken place, and a substitute was found for the deceased lady. At the inquest, which was held at the Newington Coroner's Court on Friday afternoon, a verdict of Death from Syncope was returned.*
The Era, 29/12/1894

Drury Lane
Dick Whittington

[…] ART has influenced enterprise and expenditure, and splendour has been controlled by taste and harmony. There is also evident a determination to break away from established rules, and to vary the monotony of the ordinary pantomime arrangement.

For instance, instead of the usual "cave of gloom" at the commencement, the curtain rises on the camp at Aldershot, the Surrey hills and white tents forming a background for the groups of white cats, dressed in the kilted uniforms of one of our Highland regiments. These feline warriors are well drilled, and go through a number of complicated manoeuvres with dragoon tabbies mounted upon dun-coloured bulldogs – the latter being "properties".

After this excellent start, and adjournment is made to the interior of Fitzwarren's Emporium. Fitzwarren (Mr Spry) is a "universal provider", and included in his stock are "elephants' eggs", a consignment of "raging Gorgonzola" cheese, and a number of miscellaneous and indispensable articles. The piles of merchandise and groves of drapery make capital sporting ground for the Cat (the Griffiths Brothers, one of whom plays the Mate), who is constantly getting into people's way, and is irritated into making a savage attack on the mate of the *Seagull*, who comes in to make a purchase. Idle Jack (Mr Dan Leno) appears from a shelf, where he has been sleeping; Dick (Miss Ada Blanche) and Alice (Miss Marie Montrose) make love; and the idle one and the cook Eliza (Mr Herbert Campbell) conspire to accuse the hero of robbing the till.

The trick is played successfully, and Dick departs in disgrace, arriving at Highgate Hill, and sinking to sleep on a convenient mound by a milestone. The wild flower ballet which is here introduced is delicately beautiful. Poppies, cornflowers, lilies of the valley, and bluebells are borne by fairies suitably attired. The art of the designer has been shown by the artistic manner in which the natural hues of the blossoms have been toned down and idealised with due regard for general effect. The dresses of the fairies are exquisite, some chrome and lemon yellows being introduced with delicious results. This ballet is one of the best things in the pantomime, and its quiet and unobtrusive beauty deserves our most cordial recognition.

The little scene in which Whittington, half asleep, replies to the questions of a party of harvesters by a prediction of his future greatness is rather dramatic; and in the scene which follows – the London Docks – the ships are painted with great care and finish. Very elaborate in its building up is the Deck of the *Seagull*. The poop of the vessel is constructed solidly enough to sustain the weight of a large body of soldiers in richly ornamented medieval costumes. A gigantic junk comes alongside, and the Seagull is boarded by a party of Japs, who achieve a victory, in spite of the discharges of immense soda-water bottles used as artillery.

Next we get to the Emperor of China's Private Apartment, where the plague of rats rages, dozens of the vermin running up the pillars which support the building. The apartment, with its colossal Chinese figures and gigantic dragon throne, is an imposing piece of stage architecture. Puss overcomes a rat in single combat, and the oft-related story of Dick's good fortune is retold.

The culminating point of the pantomime is the Feast of Lanterns in the next scene. To describe the spectacle in detail would be as difficult as the result would be prolix; but the picture formed at the conclusion may be broadly indicated. There is an ornamental bridge at the back, on which is posted Miss Lila Clay's orchestra. At the corners of the staircases leading down from this bridge are two immense pea-green monsters, of forms familiar to collectors of blue china. Ranged in a semi-circle are "dummy" mandarins, with heads nodding solemnly, and there is also a contingent of Japanese dolls. These details are almost lost in the great masses of harmonised and contrasted colour, in which delicate chromes and blues are gently conspicuous amidst other hues and tints innumerable. Festoons of shaded electric lamps are held aloft by the ballet in the middle distance, and others hang from the "sky-borders" of almond-blossomed foliage. When regiment after regiment of "extra ladies" in lovely attire have moved into their positions, and the band on the stage and in the orchestra have joined in melodious strains, ecstasy reaches its zenith. On Wednesday Sir Augustus Harris was twice summoned at this point of the production to receive the applause so well deserved by his liberality and enterprise.

A comic scene, in which Idle Jack and Fitzwarren become tipsy, and the houses and lamp posts of Old Cheapside wobble sympathetically, is effective and well managed; and there is a memory of melodrama about the Highgate Church scene, where Jack is on the verge of wedding Alice, who sacrifices herself to save her father from ruin. Dick returns, enriched by his rat-killing contract, and plays Claude Melmotte with the idle one's pretensions.

This, and the enforced matrimony of Jack with the stalwart cook, allow time for the arrangement of the elaborate Lord Mayor's Show in the next scene. The blare of bands, the sheen of silver and gold, the glitter and glow of various costumes, and the ponderous panoply of horses in armour, and of those which drag in certain stately triumphal cars, make this scene almost overpowering in its radiance and richness. Only part of the transformation scene was shown on Wednesday, but that part was very pretty indeed.

The Brothers Griffiths have been judiciously entrusted with the parts of clown and policeman in the harlequinade, and well and energetically do they lead the revels which are held outside the Floral Hall and inside the auction room at Covent Garden. […]

Mr Dan Leno is intensely droll as Idle Jack, and will, no doubt, work up the dialogue and business of the part to a high pitch of diversion. As it is, he is irresistible in his lean, grim absurdity; and his jests and gags, delivered in his old intense, eccentric way, create roars of laughter. His appearance in the garb of the middle ages is in itself laughter-provoking, and his singing of certain humorous songs brings down the house.

With him works Mr Herbert Campbell, who looms large and solid as Eliza the Cook, and plays the part with a sedateness and decorum which are admirable. The femininity of the imaginary personage is well preserved, and Mr Campbell's performance loses nothing by the self-restraint of the artist's method. His song about the Empire promenade, "So and so, and such and such", composed by Mr Tabrar, was one of the hits of the evening.

Mr Spry, well made-up, is both characteristic and amusing as Fitzwarren, and introduces some queer tricks, the sudden squirting of water from his garments creating surprise and astonishment. [...]

Dan Leno as Idle Jack

Prince's Theatre, Manchester
Little Red Riding Hood

MR T W CHARLES'S seventh Manchester pantomime *Little Red Riding Hood* promises to be as great a success as any of its predecessors. The version of the well-known story is written and designed by Mr Wilton Jones and Mr Charles himself, and the authors make it a tale of the Good Fairy of Thirlmere and the Genius of the Ship Canal, suggesting events of surpassing interest to Manchester and the district.

The story is opened at Apple Tree Farm by a chorus and dance, the occasion being an apple harvest festival. Farmer Hubbard, the son of Mother Hubbard, and the father of Red Riding Hood, is present, and addresses the workers in a humorous address. Mother Hubbard has her say, and then we are introduced to Red Riding Hood, the village beauty; to the impecunious Baron, who has three marriageable daughters; to Slyfox, the village poacher, who is an ally of the Wolf; and to Jockey Jim, the farmer's son, who is in love with one of the Baron's daughters. The Baron explains that his castles, horses, lands, and farm belong to Red Riding Hood, and this accounts for the subsequent events in the story. Squire Harkaway meets and falls in love with Red Riding Hood. It is evident that the part of Jockey Jim is written for Little Tich, who, with delightful humour and drollery keeps up the idea of being the "big brother" of the heroine.

Tumbledown Hall, the Baron's home, introduces us to the characters of the Baron's three remarkable daughters, "more than common tall", represented by the Sisters Levey, who with song and dance contribute their share to the liveliness of the pantomime.

Some amusing business takes place in a Woodland Pass near Thirlmere, and then is reached the Silvern Rise of Thirlmere, one of the most notable scenes, and Mr K J McLennan, the scenic artist, is to be congratulated on this triumph of scenic art. […] Several pretty spectacles take place here, including a musical ballet of flowers, a ballet of wood-cutters and fern gatherers, a dance of wolves, poodles, rabbits, and frogs, followed by the chase of the Wolf and the appearance of the Thirlmere Fairies. The three evil fairies, Jealoustina, Enviesta, and Malicia, from Liverpool, sneer at the Ship Canal, and contrive schemes which fail, and they quit the scene crestfallen,

The familiar scenes of the tale are set forth in subsequent scenes, including one at the Imperial Institute, a brilliant scene, in which there is an imposing spectacle of a procession of representatives of our various colonies. […]

Little Tich as Jockey Jim is a host in himself, and his appearance as a Chinese general was intensely amusing with his comic methods and the humour of his songs. His love-making to one of the Baron's daughters and his mistaking one for the other are very diverting, as are the sprightly doings of the Sisters Levey. [...]
The Era, 29/12/1894

1895

IN the presence of a crowded audience the Grand pantomime was played for the last time on Saturday, and the occasion was made a pretext for some unexpected and unrehearsed effects. A number of young men, supposed to be medical students, secured nearly all the seats in the stalls, and proceeded to make things lively by taking up the choruses and delivering volleys of flower "button-holes" to their favourite performers. While the scene in which the shipwrecked comedians sit down to eat the "property" kipper was being played, they sent on the stage a perfect storm of red herrings. Later, when Mr Harry Randall was singing his amusing parody of "Baby," a shower of dolls – baby dolls – came from these hilarious gentlemen, and further on bouquets of vegetables for the comedians, and pretty flowers for the ladies. When, however, a disposition to supply oranges and lemons set in, the management stepped in with a warning, and for the rest of the evening these choice spirits contented themselves with roaring choruses and demonstratively applauding.
The Era, 2/3/1895

Theatre Royal, Birmingham
Santa Claus

[…] IN the Apple Tree Close and the Hall Library (two very fine cloths from the brush of Mr Henry Emden) we make acquaintance with the henpecked old uncle, Sir Jasper Grimshaw (Mr J W Handley) and his comelier and younger spouse Lady Gay (Miss Emily Spiller). They are plunged into grief of the usual pantomime sort by the elopement of their daughter Marian (Robin Hood's immortal maid), and the presence of the babes – their little nephew and niece Eric and Rosamond (Miss Marie Wright and Miss Rosie Leyton) – is but sorry compensation. The Baronet is impecunious, of course, and his leisure is employed partly in gaining the affections of the childrens' governess Evadne (Mr Hal Forde) – a capital satire on Madame Sarah Grand's heroine – and partly in devising means of acquiring the fortune with which the orphaned and "Heavenly Twins" are endowed.

It is the discomfiture of the foppish and elderly Sheriff of Nottingham (Mr G Paulton) that we witness at the beginning of part one, for that despised admirer of Maid Marian (Miss Grace Leslie) is high in favour with her designing parents, and the intended bride is carried off a willing captive, almost from the altar steps, by the wily Robin (Miss Sophie Harriss) and his merry men.

The Night Nursery is a capital field for some nocturnal antics to the annoyance of the domestic Minerva Miss Evadne Newfangle, and then the first snore of the children is the signal for the descent of Santa Claus (Mr William Lugg) down the spacious nursery chimney attended by his train of sprightly elves. The stockings, which have been hung up with anticipation, are soon filled to repletion with toys and and confections, and even the pillow-case, which Tatters, the pet dog, has hung up (this part, by the way, is capitally played by Mr O E Lennon) is not neglected.

Soon the children are transported, as with Aladdin's carpet, to the Temple of Knowledge, where didactic science is made to furnish an alphabetic series of tableaux, which are as pleasing as they are original. As each representative of a letter appears (with or without escort, and always in surprisingly apt and various fashion, to the strains of suitable airs) the assembly upon the boards swells until centre, rear, and wings are crowded with a bright and vivid crowd of gaily-caparisoned performers. Every taste is suited – the patriotic, the practical, the fanciful, the juvenile; and one particular tableau (E for electricity) we only select for special mention out of a host of instances equally suitable for reference, because of the ingenuity and appropriateness with which the lightning science is illustrated by a blaze of well-controlled and startling lights. A powerful chorus affords a fitting climax to this feast of fancy, and the act-drop falls amid a wild outburst of applause.

The capture of Sir Jasper and his wife affords some high diversion at the beginning of part two until they are rescued by Robin and his suite, Friar Tuck, Little John, Will Scarlet, Allan-a-Dale, and the rest. But the villains who have waylaid the aristocratic pair are soon released amid the excitement which attends the entry of King Richard (Mr

Charles Thorburn), and that historic worthy holds court upon the sward under the shade of a mighty elm, and in view of a prospect which is one of the most enchanting which the artist, Mr Hawes Craven, has ever set on canvas. Robin wins the royal admiration by his deftness with the bow, and the ban of outlawry is removed.

A change of scene finds the Baronet plotting with his late captors, Rufus and Uriah (Mr Francis Hawley and Mr Reginald Roberts), for the dispatching of his wards, and a blood-curdling trio ensues which, for melodramatic mirth, would be hard to beat. The Babes are decoyed, and the faithful Tatters dies in their defence, to resurrect in the usual convenient way when the end comes. But this is agreeably delayed for a magnificent ballet amid the forest, in which robins and friendly insects, woodland nymphs and goblins conspire to make up a dancing maze of rich variety. The centre of this Terpsichorean rite are Moonbeam, Lullaby, Nightmare, and the Fly, characters which admirably serve to exhibit the agility, grace, and originality of movement in Mlles Ida Bailey, Sismondi, and Pardue, and Mr Frank Sims.

A brief return to Grimsacre shows the remorse of the designing Baronet, and his delight at the safe return of his wards under the care of Queen Mab (Miss Amy Farrell) and Santa Claus. Then these two friendly geniuses lend their escort to the children and their sympathetic audience through a richly variegated and picturesque transformation scene entitled Dreamland, Poppyland, Snowland, and Loveland. Flowers and all the ornaments of earth's carpet, as well as the exhaustless wealth of ocean, make up an accumulation of spectacular beauties which surprise the beholder, even after long knowledge of the finest work Mr Harry Emden has executed.

Drury Lane
Cinderella
[…] THE first scene shows us an imaginary realm inhabited by childrens' toys. Across the stage runs a mammoth reproduction of the primitive railway trains of our youth. It comes to a halt, and various toys, some considerably damaged, alight, gentlemen of the wooden-jacketed and stiff-jointed sort familiar to our memories in connection with Noah's ark leading off lady dolls, bladder-headed effigies of Mrs Chant[6]. Here several dances by juveniles are introduced.

From "Toyland" we pass to the Baron's Kitchen, where the impecuniosity of the owner is accentuated by the visit of two bailiff's officers, who are made at home by the distressed family, and accompany their fortunes to the end of the pantomime.

The next important scene represents a wood in autumn. Some costers come to picnic in a glade, but are ejected by gamekeepers; and then a hunting party with real hounds and real horses arrives, and starts in pursuit of a fox which has previously shown himself for a few moments to bite the leg of the Prince's tutor. A snowstorm comes on; and the colours of the scene change from warm browns and yellows to dusky greys and whites. Here, in the snow, the Prince (Miss Ada Blanche) and Cinderella (Miss Isa Bowman[7]) meet and make love.

The Baron (Mr Herbert Campbell) and Baroness (Mr Dan Leno) give a party at which many amusing incidents take place, and many funny items of entertainment are introduced. Cinderella is left behind, in the customary manner, after the departure of the rest of the family for the Prince's ball, and the usual transformation is made by the Fairy Godmother (Miss Lily Harold). The scene changes to Fairyland, a lovely landscape at the back of which a gigantic wheel revolves covered with many-coloured lights. This wheel, styled on the programme "the Electrical Marvel of the World", is invented by M E Champion, and constructed by a Paris firm of electricians. Daintily-dressed grooms lead on diminutive ponies for Cinderella's chariot; but their services are not required, for the vehicle is on the new "auto-motor" principle, and moves without any visible propelling power. It is designed on very effective lines, and is covered with electrical lamps.

There is a funny scene before the gates of the Palace, where the Baron and Baroness arrive in a real "growler", drawn by a real spotted horse; and then the scene of The Grand Hall bursts upon the view. The multiplicity of costumes, including military uniforms, dresses of various periods, and the yellow and amber robes of the ballet is bewildering. The great stage of Drury Lane is crowded with shapely figures, clad in lovely attire, and grouped in effective masses. Cinderella arrives in a dazzling *costume de bal,* and is affectionately received by the Prince, while her cruel parents and unkind sisters are ignominiously ejected.

After a couple of minor scenes we come to the great transformation, which is really a ballet in itself. It is impossible by any description to give a correct idea of the exquisite beauty of the combination of form and colour in this scene. We may give a general notion of its excellence by saying that delicate tints are employed in preference to primary colours, and agreeable use is made of the tender outlines and feathery forms of birds' wings in the costumes of some of the fairies, the idea of flight being harmoniously carried out by the introduction of the Grigolatis[8], who float and soar in mid-air bearing a garland of golden leaves. When the climax of beauty and brilliancy has been reached, the Prince leads on his bride, two flying fairies holding aloft electric emblems, a heart and an anchor, and "1895" blazes in diamond-like letters from the centre of the stage. This scene certainly beats anything that has ever been seen at Old Drury. Its beauty is simply entrancing, and the warmest praise is deserved by, and should be freely accorded to, the designer of the costumes, M. Comelli, who must be credited with a large share of the signal and stupendous success achieved by this splendid spectacle. [...]

The funny business in *Cinderella* has the advantage of being all in the comedy vein, and never was laughter in an annual evoked more freely and more legitimately than by the efforts of Mr Herbert Campbell and Mr Dan Leno. Mr Campbell looks the sturdy, stolid bourgeois Briton to the life, and the passive resistance he offers to the attacks of his waspish little spouse is most diverting. His acting in the scene in which the baronial pair, by a mistake about tickets, are prevented from following their daughters into the Prince's Palace, is immensely droll; and, throughout, Mr Campbell sustains his role with grim comicality. His burlesque ballad "It is not true" and his attacks in song on the impostures of certain Strand barbers whose misdeeds are yet fresh in public memory, evoke uproarious encores.

As for Mr Dan Leno, he is simply irresistible as the Baroness. His performance is not a caricature, but a genuine, if highly eccentric, impersonation. He works up the role with many little delicate and effective touches of gesture and facial play, and his dances are things to be remembered. Few that have seen it are likely to forget the spectacle of the Baroness's Entry to the Ballroom, mincing and bowing superbly to the assembled guests. Mr Leno's songs are encored, especially the mock-sentimental effusion "It might have been". He may be credited with a performance instinct with genuine comedy and quaint originality.

Isa Bowman in her most famous role – Alice in Wonderland

The Lyceum
Robinson Crusoe

[...] IT is all very well for glib theorists to demand originality from our purveyors of pantomime. Experience is all against them. Little folk are shy of strangers still – they love old friends; and who more dearly than that picturesque hero of romance, Robinson Crusoe? He proved to be an old friend with a new coat at the Lyceum on Thursday afternoon. Miss Alice Brookes, the Crusoe of Mr Barrett's pantomime, discards the white fur of tradition, and wears a costume of brownish fur instead. She makes no more daring a departure than this. The pantomime is to be played only in the afternoons. It is accordingly rather short, and only includes one "big" scene. But if it be short, it is sweet, and admirably symmetrical.

What a happy thought it was to abolish the shipboard scene, so exquisitely emetic, and to tell in a series of dream pictures the story of Crusoe's voyage. Polly Hopkins (Miss Grace Lake), whose lover has been torn from her arms by the press gang, worn out by exciting incident, falls asleep in the old inn kitchen. In her dream she sees, and we also see, the ship that bears our young adventurer riding gaily upon the wave, then battling with the storm, then broken and discarded, Crusoe, aboard a raft, alone surviving. Little Miss Geraldine Somerset plays the part of Chorus to Polly's dream. Miss Somerset is the Spirit of Adventure that instigates and watches over Crusoe; nor could he wish for a sweeter little cherub. Miss Somerset dances with exquisite grace, and her lines are delivered admirably – no effort, no horrible infant falsetto, but even, dulcet tones audible throughout the theatre. [...]

Once more Mr Victor Stevens is found by the side of his long-time chief. Mr Stevens is entrusted with the role of Mrs Crusoe, whose sharp tongue finds much to satirise in her surroundings. She is particularly severe on the Trilby craze[9]; and, with the aid of Mr Fred Emney (Will Atkins) in a duet, describes the length that it has gone. The audience recognised the joke immediately. But Dame Crusoe cannot escape the all-pervading influence, and when a second time we meet her, on the Island of Juan Fernandez, whither she has come in search of the errant Robinson, she is wearing Trilby's short skirts and old military coat. Subsequently, we see the old lady in ball costume; and a very dreadful sight it is. Mr Stevens makes a third toilet, that of a dancing girl. The comedian very soon got on good terms with his audience, and his Dame Crusoe will, no doubt, be a very popular feature of the pantomime.

Man Friday loses none of his importance in the Lyceum version of Robinson Crusoe. This is Mr Charles Lauri's part, and thoroughly he enters into the spirit thereof. When we first encounter him the poor wretch is spitted for a roast; abject terror is depicted in every feature, and is not instantly removed when Crusoe rescues him. But soon Friday is attached to the white man with a dog-like devotion. Mr Lauri does not play the part in dumb show. He talks a queer gibberish, more and more freely interlarded with English words. An animal sketch is introduced with great ingenuity. Friday, hard pressed by his savage pursuers, seizes the skin of a monkey that Crusoe has shot, hastily draws it over him, and performs the maddest, most amusing, and, to his savage pursuers, most mystifying of antics. A pantomime in which Mr Lauri did not introduce one of his quaint studies from the Zoo would be a strange concoction indeed.

But when Robinson Crusoe comes to be quietly reviewed, at a later stage in its history, it may prove that the most remarkable impression was made by Mr Fred Storey, who plays King Hullaballoo, of the Caribee Islands. His Majesty is not a Christy Minstrel monarch, but a very weird and dreadful savage. The "make-up" is wonderful – a long, low, forehead; deeply seated, crafty eyes; white, scanty hair, high cheekbones; a shifty, cruel expression. Now and then Mr Storey breaks into one of his characteristic, inimitable dances. But, for the most part, he plays King Hullaballoo with as much care and dramatic intensity as though he were playing King Lear – which, of course, has been the method of the greatest burlesque actors. Mr Storey's death scene introduces another, and in fact the most effective, travesty of Trilby. When the old rascal has received his death blow from Robinson Crusoe, a table is brought in across which he flings himself, to die after the manner of Mr Tree.

Mr Wilhelm, the designer of the dresses, has devoted himself particularly to one great scene – the festivities in honour of King Hullaballoo's marriage, which does not come off, with Polly Hopkins. Troop after troop of savages file in, till the stage is crowded with quaintly devised and brilliantly fashioned costumes. The colour effects produced are most remarkable; and there is not a single dress or property that will not repay minute inspection – they are so fantastic and ingenious. From this scene the pantomime rapidly proceeds towards the end. Mr Wilhelm's pageant has this particular recommendation, that it is an incident proper to the story.

The transformation, too, is as suitable as it is charming. It is entitled A Souvenir of the Sea; and, beginning with a representation of Neptune riding the deep on his chariot, goes "deeper and deeper still", till it reaches the richly laden bed of ocean – an exquisitely beautiful conceit that has the rare merit of being agreeable to the story. This, with the other scenery employed, is the work of Mr Henry Emden. [...]

The Era, 28/12/1895

1896

A VERY extraordinary instance of animal instinct occurred at the Theatre Royal, Middlesbrough, on Tuesday last during the Palace scene of Louis La Rondelle's pantomime, Babes in the Wood. *Mr John G Brett introduces a miniature circus with ponies, baboon, and a donkey. Whilst putting the baboon through its paces the trainer noticed how eagerly it sought the footlights and scanned the first row of the stalls. A seafaring man, who was evidently the object of interest to the baboon, uttered a peculiarly distinctive cry, when instantly the baboon sprang across the footlights into his arms. An immediate inquiry on the part of Mr Henry Tweedie, the acting-manager, elicited the extraordinary fact that the seaman had originally brought the baboon from its native land, but that was several years ago.*
The Era, 11/1/1896

LAST nights of pantomimes in the provinces are often marked by an unchecked rowdyism which we trust will not be extended into the metropolis. On Saturday evening, during the final performance of Robinson Crusoe *at the Prince of Wales's, Liverpool, the audience became very disorderly, and commenced throwing things on the stage, such as sweetmeats, toys, and biscuits. At length one young blackguard threw a lump of confectionery that hit Mr Fred Williams, the popular Mrs Crusoe, on the face and cut him. The comedian uttered a well-timed rebuke, and something like order was restored on the removal of one of the offenders from the theatre. Mr Williams has suffered no ill effects from the contretemps, and will commence his engagements in town on Monday at Collins's.*
The Era, 21/3/1896

Grand Theatre, Cardiff
Sinbad the Sailor
FOR several days past the public of our busy little town has been somewhat surprised, and to an extent alarmed, at the parading of their streets by a herd of richly-caparisoned camels and dromedaries, mounted by veritable Arab Sheikhs, and a host of other bipeds and quadrupeds suggestive of the Orient, sometimes preceded by a smart tandem equipage driven by an expert "whip". This unusual innovation we soon learnt was an advertisement for Mr Sounes's Christmas annual *Sinbad the Sailor*, which was produced under the direction of that experienced pioneer of modern pantomime, Mr Ormsby Trench, of the Reading circuit, on the 24th *ult*.

The story is ingeniously worked out by the author in twelve scenes. From the Port of Balsora the hero Sinbad (Miss Georgie Wright) takes leave of his companions on the *Argosy*, accompanied by Muchbad and Morebad, well represented by the Brothers Connolly, Captain Wreckeross (Mr B Monti, of Spry and Monti fame), and the crew. Miss Freda Spry also trips on as the Lieutenant, assuming quite a naval air. Mrs Sinbad (Mr James Stevenson) is also to the fore here, and some genuine fun is elicited in her grief over her nomadic son. The embarkation follows, carrying us to scene two, Under the Sea – a gem of scenic art. Here the usual demon business takes place, and we first hear the stentorian voice of Tornado (Mr Carl Benson) and the cultivated contralto of Miss Hettie Mavini, the Fairy Queen. Then we proceed to the main deck of the *Argosy*, and a chorus is again indulged in by a number of well-blended voices. Now we get the storm, and finally the wreck. Tornado is again *en evidence*, and the audience is led to his domain. Scene six is the Shooting-box of King Koffdroppe (Mr Arthur Verne, of the celebrated Canadian Trio), who provides of his store for the distressed crew, and warbles the taking ditty, "Round the Corner".

In the final scene of the first act, the Camp of His Majesty, many of the most attractive items of the production are introduced. Here the King and suite make an entry in procession, utilising nearly the whole of the stupendous company, supplemented by a herd of camels and other livestock. Truly, this is a pageant eclipsing anything we have yet seen on the Cardiff stage. Occasion is given to introduce Miss Georgie Wright in a charmingly written coon song and dance, and quite an ovation greets the performance. Prior to the fall of the act drop, Miss Rita Edwards, a Welsh girl, appears in the tall hat and flannel costume, and gives with stirring effect a song in the national language.

Act two conveys us to the Diamond Valley, another *chef d'oeuvre* of the artist's brush, the cascade of real water at the rear of the stage, illuminated by lights of every hue, lending a delightful effect to the scene, with pelicans, storks, and other water-fowl in profusion. Sinbad, anxious to be the possessor of the great Koh-i-noor, which is the value set on the hand of the Princess, invokes the assistance of the Old Man of the Sea (Little Luna). The Roc Bird, a mammoth property, secures Sinbad in his talons, and takes him aloft.

We are soon on the road again to the Palace (with the diamond well secured), and a fitting finale is found in the revels of Sinbad. The transformation is a suggestion of Nansen and the North Pole. [...]

The Standard
Mother Goose
[...] MOTHER GOOSE, indeed, is full of burlesque types, and it is evident that the story is, after all, but an amusing skit of melodrama. Have we not the avaricious and villainous squire – a grinding landlord of the good old Coburg type – the virtuous maiden, the unscrupulous bailiff, and the poor but honest peasant? True, these old familiar friends are cleverly caricatured by the cast, and the Shoreditchers, who love melodrama with all their hearts, laugh at it all, without for one moment recognising the satire at the expense of their favourite form of amusement.

Mother Goose (Mr E S Vincent) has a reputation for witchcraft, and, determined that she shall not be maligned for nothing, she makes a compact with Mephistopheles. "Give me revenge," cries she. 'Tis done, and after she has assigned herself body and soul to the powers of darkness a change comes over her fortunes. From being a baked potato merchant she becomes possessed of limitless capital by being presented with the Goose that lays the golden eggs (Mr Ted Bernard) – a very handy bird indeed to have about the house. The weather not being to my Lady Goose's liking, she changes it from winter to summer, and we see the village of Hey-Down-Derry, where she keeps the *Cyclist's Rest*, under winter snows and bathed in summer sunshine. The famous ride through Cloudland and the visit of Mother Goose to the Moon is exhibited by means of a panorama, which unfortunately could not be worked at the opening performance.

The story moves briskly through pretty village scenery, forest glades, and gorgeous interiors, all the work of Mr George Tweddell, who had done his work with considerable taste and a proper regard for chaste stage effects. In the Palace of the Golden Eggs, where Mother Goose and Squire Bugle (Mr George H Asquin) cease from plotting and join hands in matrimony with the other principals, he has surpassed himself, and "The Seasons" is a pretty transformation with its fanciful flora and fairy forms under various coloured lights. We anticipate that crowds of happy Shoreditch children will find a feast of delight in its beauties.

They will laugh consumedly, too, at the broad fun and diverting business of the schoolroom in scene seven. Here the company is left to its own devices, and we may be quite sure that the drolleries of Mother Goose and her pupils will increase as time goes on.

In scene eight, the Border of the Forest (sunset), we are treated to a fairy ballet, headed by Mr Ernest Jerome (who plays Mephistopheles) as the Spider and Miss Hettie Lane as the Fly. Both are exceedingly clever, and are gracefully active in a series of skilful Terpsichorean evolutions. Scene twelve is animated by dances, varieties, burlesque, and whimsicalities; and popular songs and choruses – all invariably recognised and taken up with holiday heartiness on Boxing Day – are introduced with as much frequency as possible, not only in this scene but in every one of the others. [...]

Miss Nellie Marler is a capital Sally – a slavey – a similarly conceived character to Oriana in *The Star of India*. Like Oriana, Sally is a novelette-reading slut, and Miss Marler's command of low comedy makes the part a very amusing one. Her apostrophe to her lover, Simple Simon (Mr Harry Elliston), "I should like to be a real play hactress", is the cue for a burlesque scene which is already one of the hits of the pantomime. [...]

Prince's Theatre, Bradford
The Babes in the Wood

[...] SCENE one, the Demon Incubator, is a novelty in openings. White Wings (Mlle De Rose), Queen of the Birds, and Kochinchinar (Mr Rex Kyber), the "fowl" fiend, disagree on the subject for a pantomime. Her Majesty decides, and vows to protect the Babes, and the wicked rooster swears vengeance.

This takes us to scene two, the Village Green, where a hiring fair of the olden time is held. There is also an entertainment by the children, and general May Day rejoicings, amidst which Buttercup (Miss Mabel Frampton) makes her appearance, surrounded by Farm Labourers, &c. Chawles, the Baron's footman (Mr Louis Nanton), and Adolphus the valet (Mr Edward Naylor) are unsuccessful suitors for her hand. The Baron (Mr John Osborne) enters, and after an original song, in which all his wickedness is made known, he encounters Kochinchinar, who introduces to him two Ruffians, who are acting as showmen – viz, Billy (Mr Fred Arthur) and Jim (Mr James Charters). A compact is entered into for the murder of the Babes, Charlie (Miss Madeline Majilton) and Cissie (Miss Jenny Clare). Sports proceed, and courtiers enter – *viz*, Earl Ralph (Miss Ray Wynne), Sir Victor (Miss Mabel Wynne), and Prince George (Miss Edith Wynne). Rosebud enters as Queen of the May, and the Prince, who is smitten with her charms, learns from her the story of the bad Baron and the innocent Babes.

The Prince vows to protect the children, and this takes us to scene three, The Children's Playroom, where Dame Judy (Mr Dan Crawley) relates her troubles. The Baron tells the children to prepare for departure, on the pretence of their visiting an aunt. We are now at scene four, The Baron's Stables, where preparations are made for the start. The Baron here makes love to Liza (Miss Louie Appleby), but he is repulsed, taking us to scene five, Shipley Glen, where a picnic is being held.

The two Ruffians, Billy and Jim, enter, dragging in the Babes. Billy is intent on carrying out the contract, and so earning the reward; Jim is for restoring the Babes. They fight, and the children escape; they are followed by Buttercup and Violet (Miss Blanche Frampton), and the scene changes to The Glade in Winter, where the weary Babes sleep, protected by a bear, and rescued from further harm by the Prince, who finds them, the two Ruffians coming in for a lot of punishment.

The Station is the next scene, and, after much rejoicing at the recovery of the Babes, the scene again changes to Morecambe Bay, where there is a naval hornpipe, a naval trio by the three Sisters Wynne, and a nautical ballet by the Sisters Wood and Frampton. Billy and Jim, disguised as fishermen, encounter the Baron, to whom they unfold the tale of the escape of the children, and a second plot is entered into for their destruction, whereby the cruel uncle may inherit the castle and estates. Some funny business follows, and a change is made to scene nine, the Seashore, where Kochinchinar bemoans the defeat of his scheme for the children's destruction in song. An Inebriated Thoroughfare is the following scene, where the Baron, the worse for liquor, has a bad dream, and he awakes stricken with remorse.

Scene eleven is the Golden Palace, in which there are military evolutions by children clad in armour. The Moulin Rouge quadrille is danced, and in a pageant Queen Victoria is impersonated as she appeared in 1837 and as she appears in 1896. Prince George sings a patriotic song, and a change is made to scene twelve, the Demon's Haunt, where Kochinchinar takes his revenge by effecting a transformation of the principal characters of the story into a harlequinade, which old and time-honoured custom is followed by the very pretty transformation scene. [...]

The Era, 2/1/1897

1897

A NOVEL form of advertising has been adopted by that astute resident-manager, Mr F C Sutcliffe, of the Tyne Theatre, Newcastle-upon-Tyne. In one of the large establishments of Grainger Street, in that city, he has on view an excellent wax model of the heroine of Messrs Howard and Wyndham's thirteenth pantomime of Sleeping Beauty; or, the Mystic

> Yellow Dwarf. *The figure on view is a full life-sized wax model of the Beauty Allfair, as she appears in the fourth scene. By a mechanical effect the figure is made to appear to breathe in a most natural manner, and is attracting much notice.*
> *The Era, 9/1/1897*

> MR REGGIE P RUTTER met with an unfortunate mishap at the matinée performance of Sinbad the Sailor *at the Metropole Theatre, Gateshead, last Saturday. In the Diamond Cave scene, Mr Rutter, the Tinbad of the pantomime, makes an entrance on a machine which is supposed to represent a motor-car. At the same time, Sinbad – Miss Hetty Peel – soars aloft in the clutches of the great eagle; but, on this occasion, the machine came in contact with the outspread wings of the property bird, and the motor-car, on which Mr Rutter occupied a somewhat elevated seat, was upset, and the occupant was thrown with considerable violence on the stage. The audience were naturally alarmed at the occurrence, but were quickly reassured when it was found that Mr Rutter had happily escaped with a few bruises and a wrench to one of his ankles, which, however, did not incapacitate him from continuing to play his part.*
> *The Era, 23/1/1897*

The Britannia
Will o' the Wisp

[…] WILL O' THE WISP (Mr George Lupino), the principal character, is summoned to the aid of Davy Jones (Mr J Dunlop), the old man of the sea (whose power, by the way, is limited to the sea), in order to bring to land a fairy nautilus, believed to contain the key to a treasure vault of which the ancient Mr Jones desires possession. For the sake of the booty Will consents to rebel against his mistress Albania (Miss Florence Stokes), the fairy queen, who punishes her subordinate by rendering him dumb. Comicality soon asserts itself with the arrival of the Baron Allcoodo (Mr James Albert), his secretary Peter Pushpen (Mr H M Edmunds), and the Baron's sister Spinsterina (Miss Polly Albert), on a fishing expedition. They discover the nautilus, and while speculating as to its origin the Fairy Queen arrives to tell them that it is laden with with a casket of precious contents. She takes from the box a key and unlocks a vault in which lie a sleeping youth and maiden, who wake to ask where they are. Albania proceeds to tell their history. They are Fairway (Miss Violet Durkin) and Brighteyes (Miss Marie Brian), children of an exiled king, who to save them sent them, with their mother, adrift on the sea. The Queen perished, but the Fairy rescued the children, whom she preserved, sleeping, in a vault for fifteen years. Fairway is now advised by the Fairy to seek his father, and the Baron offers his yacht for the purpose.

In scene two, 'Tween Decks on the Baron's yacht *Saucy Shrimp*, Will o' the Wisp and Davy Jones vow vengeance on Albania, and determine to destroy the ship. Scene three shows the wreck of the *Saucy Shrimp*, and eventually the characters reach the beach of Tom Tiddler's Island, an inhospitable region apparently, from which the travellers manage to escape to the interior of the island. Here they are again overtaken by the Indians. The King, Kumandsee (Mr Harry Royce), is, however, a white man, and is delighted to find that the captives are English. He bids them welcome, but informs Peter Pushpen that, in accordance with savage custom, he must be married to Spinsterina, and they are united by a native ceremony. Fairway discovers that the King is none other than the father he sought, and the King celebrates the occasion by a grand banquet. Will o' the Wisp, who had been watching the proceedings in the guise of an Indian god, descends from his pedestal, but is confronted by Albania, who denounces him to the Prince and his friends as the destroyer of the Baron's ship. We are then treated to a flying ballet. When next we see our friends they have returned to England, and arrived at scene six, Room in the Baronial Hall, where Pushpen is endeavouring to flee from his wife, in which he is aided by the Baron. When the King and his party arrive they are surprised to see Sylvia (Miss Topsy Sinden) supporting the now-penitent Will, and learn from her that he has been attacked while guarding the King's treasure. As he seems to have something of importance to communicate Albania allows him speech for one day. He then tells them that the royal gems have been stolen, and by Davy Jones. The Fairy bids him seek out the treasure, and promises the thief that if he succeeds he shall obtain his speech permanently. She then presents him with a magic whistle, and he departs on his quest, while the rest repair to scene seven, a Roadside Inn, where they intend to dine. Here all enjoy themselves, especially Sylvia and Fairway, who are formally betrothed, and the party are invited to a Jubilee fête at the palace. Meanwhile Will has arrived at scene eight, Davy Jones's Locker, where he surprises Davy counting the treasure, but Davy calls his marine guard, who makes Will captive. Will manages to blow the whistle, which brings his friends, and Davy Jones, fearful of the number of his opponents, yields the treasure, secreting, however, the largest diamond in his tunic. In scene nine, Grand Pavilion in the Palace Grounds, a glittering palace with wonderful columns, great rejoicings take place at the King's Jubilee, which is celebrated by the distribution of orders. The restored jewels are produced to deck the bride-elect, but the loss of the great diamond has yet to be made good. Albania reminds Will that his task is not yet complete, and that he has only five minutes of speech unless he finds the diamond. Will declares he will find it, and loses his speech as the clock strikes. He departs on his search; he arrives at scene ten, Rocks on the Sea Shore, and, finding Davy Jones asleep, takes the diamond from his tunic. The Baron and suite disturb the slumbers of the demon, who accuses them of stealing the diamond. They satisfy him that they have not taken it; he induces Pushpen and Calves, the Baron's footman (Mr Willie Albery), by a bribe, to conspire with him to recover the gem from Will, and the conspirators depart on their evil quest. Meanwhile Will has reached scene eleven, The Home of Will o' the Wisp, where he gives the gem to Albania, who, in return, bestows the speech he covets. Davy Jones, Pushpen, and Calves now appear, and demand the diamond from Will, who allows them to think it is still in his possession. A struggle takes place, and a grand mechanical trap scene, invented by Mr George Lupino, exposes the trick played upon them. For his conspiracy Pushpen is tried in scene twelve, the King's Council Chamber. Will o' the Wisp receives a well-merited forgiveness, and is taken once more into the service of his Queen; and the King abdicating in his son's favour, all ends in mirth and rejoicing, preparatory to scene thirteen, the grand transformation, a development of naiads in gigantic ocean shells, which open and disclose coloured electric lights, a scene that is as costly as it is tasteful and splendid. [...]

New Theatre, Kingston
Beauty and the Beast

[...] THE first scene is the port and harbour of "the historic and ancient borough of Nowerinparticular", disclosing the residence of Alderman FitzTurtle on the right and the Widow Alferbeater's school on the left. Here some children sing a chorus and nursery rhymes, and join in a dance. The Widow (Mr Selby Howard) is joined by Penelope (Miss Helen Maitland) and Gwendoline (Miss Lily Murry), daughters of the Alderman. The young ladies sing a duet, and then accost Beauty (Miss Mona West) as she is proceeding on her way to school, whom they revile and leave in tears. The Alderman (Mr Newman Maurice) enters and sings a "sentimental" song to the air of "Sally in our Alley", which is encored. Then the Prince Roseate (Miss Rose Moncrieff), travelling *incog*, arrives at the fort, sings a song, dances a hornpipe, and departs with his companions, Valentine (Miss Doris Beresford) and Benedict (Miss Dot Harvey). Whilst they are gone two ancient mariners, Tom Bowlin (Mr Harry Garnham) and Ben Barnacle (Mr George Nash), indulge in some knockabout business which causes merriment. The door of the school opens, and Beauty, in great distress, is forcibly expelled. The Prince meets her, vows an ardent passion for her, and they join in a duet, followed by a dance.

The second scene is a Woodland Glade, to which all the principals have come to enjoy a picnic. Whilst so employed a hideous snake makes its appearance, and is immediately slain by the Prince. The forest is instantly plunged into darkness, and the demon Reptilio (Mr Frank Lincoln) enters and changes the Prince into a beast of the gorilla type. The good fairy Dewdrop (Miss Cybel Wynne), however, assures him that when he shall feel a lovely maiden's kiss he shall again assume his original form, and the scene closes with a fantastic dance by gnomes, and a Will o' the Wisp dance by children carrying miniature electric lamps in each hand.

The third scene is the Interior of the Residence of the Alderman, who is preparing to cross the seas. He indulges in a mock love-scene with the Widow, which causes great laugher, and she and he sing a topical duet. The demon makes his appearance in the disguise of a pilot, and, getting engaged in that capacity, accompanies the party.

The fourth scene is a Garden of Roses, in which some pretty effects are produced by a dance of rose maidens and butterflies. The Alderman, who has had the misfortune to be shipwrecked here, wanders about disconsolately until he sees a beautiful rose, which he instantly plucks. The beast confronts him, pronounces that he must die for the theft, and is about to carry the threat into execution when Beauty appears and pleads for her father's life. The Beast relents, but in doing so seals his own fate, and he staggers and falls and is about to die when Beauty, full of compassion, caresses and kisses his hand. The spell is broken, and the Prince in his former shape stands before her. The scene closes with a grand transformation, The Fairy Wedding Cake.

The harlequinade is in two scenes, A Well Known Corner of Kingston, showing the Parish Church, and At Kempton Park; the performance, which lasts a little over three hours, ending with the tableaux Britannia Surveying Her Mighty Empire. [...]

Alexandra Theatre, Sheffield
Dick Whittington and His Cat

[...] AFTER a spirited overture, which introduces the popular melodies of the day, the curtain rises on a fine and realistic set scene, representing the interior of one of Sheffield's famous rolling mills. We see men busy at the glaring furnace, the steam hammer is at work, and not a detail is neglected in the effort made to give a truthful representation of the way Sheffield armour plates are manufactured. The works, which are under the care of Industry and Enterprise, are haunted by King Rat (Mr J H Booth) and his host of demon rodents, and a spirited dialogue takes place between these personages, followed by the timely entrance of the Good Fairy Bluebell (Miss Beatrice Felsted), who announces her intention to befriend Dick and to frustrate King Rat's knavish tricks.

After singing a version of "Big Ben struck one", fairies, demons, and rats vanish, and in an instant the nineteenth-century forge with its heat, grime, and ruddy glow, has disappeared, and our eyes are gladdened by a sight of Cheapside in Ye Olden Tyme. This is a beautiful scene, and the medieval houses in the foreground are exquisitely drawn. The perspective is also excellently managed, and the colouring is superb. The scene seems so truthful a presentment of what old London would look like six or seven hundred years ago that it is almost a pity that Mr Maugham, taking advantage of the license of pantomime, thought fit to introduce in his background the comparatively modern dome of Wren's St Paul's. Of course, this is merely a matter of taste, and it does not detract from the artistic excellence of the picture. It is early morning, and on troop merry bands of children, representing tailors, cooks, draymen, &c, who sing characteristic choruses. Then follows an old English dance by a crowd of comely and gaily-dressed young women, and with the entrance of old Alderman Fitzwarren (Mr Joe Bracewell), the good craft Whittington gets well under way.

A bright interior is scene three, Fitzwarren's Shop, and after the fun, frolic, and songs incidental to this part of the story, we are transported to Highgate Hill. [...] To this charming spot comes Dick Whittington (Miss Ella Dean), and, tired and footsore, he sinks to rest by the side of the traditional mile-stone, his faithful cat Tommy (Mr Freddie Farren) keeping guard. The Fairy Bluebell appears, and in a vision reveals to Dick his future proud position, and the distant bells of Bow ring out their inspiring message. Cheered and happy, Dick starts back for London with his good cat for company.

After a beautiful ballet, illustrating the quaint costumes of the early part of Queen Victoria's reign, the action is continued in scene five, the Docks, with a view of what Old Father Thames might have been like many, many years ago. The hero ships as "A.B.", under the command of handsome Captain Mainbrace (Miss Amy Rogerson), whose easy method of dealing with the forecastle hands would certainly surprise a skipper typical of the mercantile marine. The events that take place on board the main deck of the *Diamond Jubilee* would startle the most phlegmatic old shell-back afloat, and the doings of the two comical sailors, Ben Bobstay (Mr Frank Lorenzi) and Bob Halliard (Mr Will Lorenzi), would make the most sour-faced Puritan hold his sides with uncontrollable laughter. To see these gallant tars do feats of gallantry and daring, when the good ship is attacked by pirates, is a pantomime in itself.

The vessel is wrecked, and the voyagers, in various conditions of *deshabille*, find themselves on the coast of Morocco. The salt water has not dashed their spirits, however, and they dance and sing in merry fashion. The Emperor of Morocco (Mr J W Hughes) invites the adventurers to his palace, a gorgeous and dazzling set, with revolving pillars of stained glass, illuminated with hundreds of electric lights. The demon rat here appears, and with the help of the Fairy Bluebell Dick's cat worsts him, and he beats a hasty retreat, leaving Dick to be rewarded by the Emperor with untold gold for ridding his dominions from the scourge of the rat tribe.

The monarch and his only daughter decide to visit England, and after passing through ancient Fleet Street, we arrive with the leading characters outside the Guildhall, and behold Dick's entry into civic life as London's honoured Lord Mayor.

In scene eleven, a well-painted view of the Exterior of the Alexandra Theatre, the various characters speak their "tags", and the long succession of scenic glories is brought to a gorgeous and fitting climax by the transformation scene, a beautiful piece of work, poetically entitled "The Ascent of Aurora; or, Moonlight and Sunlight". [...]

Drury Lane
Babes in the Wood
[...] AT the very outset there is a bold bid for the suffrages of the children – accorded with shouts of delighted laughter. The scene is a dormitory, an avenue of dimly draped beds, to whose occupants the nurses sing:

Baby, close your pretty eyes,
Dreams will waft you to the skies.
Fairies o'er you watch are keeping,
Little buds should early close –
Rest in innocent repose.

Which is very well as far as it goes – the Demon Indigestion, a weird creature, admirably represented by Mr Charles Angelo, with whom, as the lawyers say, is Mr Alfred Balfour as the Spirit of Castigation, is of a mind to play old gooseberry with the repose of the sleepers. He inflicts on them a horrid nightmare which delights the urchins sitting in the happy immunity of the stalls, but produces an uproar in the nursery. But Miss Kate Graves as the charming Spirit of Youth comes to the assistance of the afflicted babes and solaces them with the contemplation of Drury Lane pantomime.

Mr Sturgess has evolved a new baron – a sporting "wrong 'un" of the most pronounced type. Oily of tongue, airy of deportment, Mr John A Warden as the Baron Banbury gives a most entertaining picture of a decayed aristocrat now sticking at naught to fill his pockets. He runs a turf commission agency, which is besieged by infuriated clients, when news comes of his brother's death and bequest of "precious treasures". The Baron pops round the corner to celebrate his good luck; meanwhile the precious treasure is deposited at the turf commission agency in the persons of an orphan brother and sister – Reggie, quaintly impersonated by Mr Dan Leno, who looks as though he had stepped from a bab ballad[10], and Chrissie, a toddlekins in whom we recognise Mr Herbert Campbell. The "babes" make themselves quite at home in the turf commission agency. They smash the Baron's typewriter, play havoc with his tape machine, and give a ruinous aspect to his prices current.

Distraught by this visitation the Baron bethinks himself of Miss Gertie Girton, who should be the Baroness if all had their due, but in the meantime is solacing herself by the education of youth. To her academy Reggie and Chrissie are remitted. To the tune of "Darling Mabel" one hears:

REG: Darling Nunkey!
BARON: Saucy monkey!
CHRISSIE: Why must you speed away?
BARON: Here you'll live and learn, love;
Soon I will return, love;
GERTIE: I will tend you,
Wash and mend you,
You must with me go,
BARON: And for these scholastic blessings,
I'll for ever owe.

In such ingenious fashion have Mr Glover and Mr Sturgess annexed and utilised the popular ditties of the day.

At Miss Girton's school the babes pursue their career of mirth-provoking mischief. How Mr Leno will elaborate this "business" in the course of time! Incidental to the prize distribution festivities, Reggie and Chrissie give a costume selection from *Hamlet*, the peaky figure of Master Reggie as the melancholy Dane being truly grotesque. Miss Gertie Girton is not the traditional dame of pantomime. The part is entrusted to Miss Alice Barnett, so long of the Savoy, and very well she plays it.

At Miss Girton's select academy let us leave the Babes, to pick up the love story of the principal boy and girl. Miss Ada Blanche is the vivacious Prince Paragon, the ruler of the nation. He (or she) sings:

A military chappy I am,
And you should see how snappy I am,
When they say my last costume fits too tight,
And I'm rude to my grandmotherly relation.
Don't yer know? Don't yer know? Ah, don't yer know?
She laughs at me – I never like that.
An autocratic aristocrat
Is a man that always must be in the right.
And then, you know, I paint as well as draw,
I am my country's law.
Comic pictures I object to.
Such a clever chap I never saw,
I my country govern and protect too.

...With much more extremely personal to a certain Kaiser[11]. Prince Paragon has exhausted every pleasure, and longs for a new sensation. Oddly enough, he has never tried falling in love, so when he meets the Baron's daughter it is a case immediately. Miss Blanche's pleasant person, inexhaustible vitality, clear elocution, and effective singing voice are once more invaluable to the pantomime, while a very demure and charming Marian is forthcoming in Miss Violet Robinson. The pair do their courting to the haunting refrain of "Little Dolly Daydream".

All the characters are suddenly assembled at an old-fashioned country fair – Codlin yells against Short, the roundabouts shriek horribly, and Miss Gertie Girton, having, as she explains, had her reverses, figures as a fat woman in a freak museum. Miss Alice Barnett lends herself loyally to this exercise in physical humour. Her time is at hand for a more artistic display. Mr Glover and Mr Sturgess have collaborated, with the happiest result, in a parody of the ornithological allegory now so popular. In this case it is about a confiding cockroach and a deceptive jellyfish, who procured his victim to be fried:

And he said with a mut – mut – mutter
As he turned in the but – but – butter,
If that fish I should meet
In a spirit land street,
I shall simply cut – cut – cutter.

Miss Alice Barnett's ponderous revolutions in the Letty Lindian[12] manner are too funny for description. At the fair Baron Banbury, thoroughly weary of the incubus of the twins and eager to finger their fortune, suborns two quaint villains (played by the American knockabout artists Griffin and Dubois, who have a gift of comedy rare in acrobats) to put away poor Reggie and Chrissie.

Their wanderings in the woodland are indicated by a panorama of exquisite beauty, from the studio of the Austrian artist Kautsky. Deeper and deeper we are taken into a wood peopled by weird creatures that walk on their heads, giants, dancing frogs (the agile D'Aubans), and such likes. The masks used in these scenes are perfectly wonderful. At last the panorama ends in a sunlit glade, wherein blossom countless orchids. As the audience appreciated the beauty and splendour of this scene shout after shout of applause went up. Such a feast of colour, such ingenuity of fashion – never surely did girls look so much like flowers before. The skilful use of electric light added to the effectiveness of the display, and then the Grigolati Troupe performed their marvellous and graceful dance. At this juncture there is an interval in the pantomime – very grateful to the spectator longing to exchange with his neighbour superlatives of admiration.

When the pantomime resumed it was found to take a very racy turn. Fast life has brought poor Prince Paragon to the verge of ruin. The Baron is disposed to thrust him into the torrent, and is his constant companion at gambling clubs and suchlike resorts. A race meeting is near at hand that is to settle the Prince's fate – the Baron is of a mind to "mak sicher"[13] by the nefarious means of which he has had such a varied experience. But he has to reckon with the Babes, who were not killed, but, having grown to man's and woman's estate in seclusion, are now under deep suspicion of living by their wits. The humours of life in a "mansion" are graphically depicted; and then we see the resuscitation of the Prince's fortune, and the complete discomfiture of the Baron, by the most comical horse race ever seen.

There is another "big" scene, in absolute contrast to the display of orchids – Prince Paragon's Coming-of-Age and Coronation. This is an idealised military pageant, as excellent in its way, but less novel. All the ladies are armed with fans of different hue, with the aid of which some fine colour effects are produced. A pleasant ballet, arranged by Mr D'Auban, is done; and so the pantomime reaches its end. There is, of course, a harlequinade, with Mr Whimsical Walker as Clown, Mr Tom Cusden as Harlequin, Miss Clarke as Columbine, Mr Waller as Pantaloon, and Mr G Aubrey as Policeman. [...]
The Era, 1/1/1898

Dan Leno and Herbert Campbell as the Babes in the Wood

1898

> ON Monday evening, during the second palace scene in the pantomime *Aladdin at the Elephant and Castle Theatre*, the attention of the audience was riveted on the plumed headdress of Miss Fanny Erris, the talented young lady who so dashingly sustains the part of Pekoe, the Vizier's son. For a moment the spectators imagined they were witnessing an electric effect, but almost instantly flames shot a foot or more upwards, and it was seen that the plumes were on fire. A chorus lady standing behind snatched at the plumes and extinguished the flames. Miss Erris was standing beside the highly inflammable wings and cut cloths, and there can be no doubt that the coolness and promptitude displayed by

both ladies were the means of averting a serious accident. Miss Erris evinced no alarm, and continued to speak her lines. It appears that in entering the scene the plumes passed between the wire guards of a gas bracket in the wings. The affair was over so quickly that the audience had scarce time to become alarmed, and none left their seats.
The Era, 1/1/1898

MISS MARIE LOFTUS *was the complainant in a case heard at Manchester on the 14th inst, the defendant being a cab proprietor named George Beaumont, whom she charged with using abusive language to her. A second summons charged Beaumont with assaulting Miss Loftus's maid, and a cross-summons was taken out by Beaumont against Mr Ben Brown, Miss Loftus's husband, for assault. Miss Loftus is the principal boy in the pantomime,* Jack and Jill, *now running at the Palace of Varieties, Manchester, and the circumstances which led to the issue of the summons arose through a mistake made by Beaumont on driving her home on New Year's Day after the pantomime. Beaumont had a contract to drive two sisters home to Brunswick Street from the Palace every night. On New Year's Day he drove up to the stage door. The attendant put Miss Loftus and her maid into the cab, and the driver went to Brunswick Street. They protested, explaining that they had told him Grafton Street, whereupon he became abusive, and pulled the maid out of the cab. Then he drove to the mews. Afterwards Mr Brown went to the mews and tweaked his nose. Beaumont was fined 10s and costs for using abusive language, and 40s and costs for the assault on Miss Bullen (Miss Loftus's maid), and Mr Brown was fined 21s and costs for assaulting Beaumont.*
The Era, 22/1/1898

AN amusing incident occurred in Manchester last Monday afternoon. Mr George Robey[14], who is appearing as Idle Jack in the pantomime of Dick Whittington *at the Comedy Theatre, has been in the habit of riding from his apartments to the theatre every day either on the back of a young elephant or on a bicycle. On Monday, shortly after 2 o'clock, the animal's keeper, on returning from the theatre, called at the "Oxford Grill" for refreshment. The quadruped coolly followed its keeper into the corridor of the inn, where it was supplied with a pint of ale and two pork pies, which it evidently relished, for it bellowed and thrust forward its trunk, but as no more refreshments were forthcoming the animal was requested to withdraw. But here a difficulty presented itself; the beast could not turn round in the passage in consequence of the inadequate space, and it steadfastly declined to go out backwards, as the outer doorstep was evidently more than the elephant would venture upon. No amount of persuasion proved effective, and a few planks had to be secured and a bridge made from the top step to the pavement. By this means the animal was got out, without the temporary bridge being broken by the weight.*
The Era, 26/3/1898

ON Easter Monday the Theatre Royal, Maidenhead, was crowded, and all went well until the Drama Streets of London *finished and* Aladdin *was well on its way. Then some foolish person raised a false alarm of "Fire!" and the audience rose en masse. Actors and actresses in all descriptions of dress and undress came on the stage and shouted that it was all right, and Mr J B Jackson, the manager, begged of the people to keep their seats, assuring them that there was no danger. Meanwhile hundreds had forced their way out, while many ladies were half-led, half-carried away in a fainting condition. But the rush on the left section of the gallery had proved too great a strain, and with a tremendous crash it gave way, carrying with it about 200 people. The shrieks were appalling; men from all parts of the building, including actors from the stage, went to the help of the people who were entangled in the broken woodwork, and to the intense relief of all it was found that no one had received any serious injury. The marvel was how such a crowd could be precipitated to the ground without many broken limbs, and the only explanation is that all were on their feet when the crash came, and that after the first sway the whole structure settled down straight, simply dropping the people to the floor. Mr Ryder announced from the stage, "Thank God, no one is hurt," and asked the people to disperse quietly. Temporary arrangements have been made for seating the gallery people, and the performances are given as usual. Miss Evelyn has offered a £10 reward for information as to the person who raised the false alarm.*
The Era, 16/4/1898

Prince's Theatre, Bristol
Sinbad the Sailor
[…] THE synopsis of scenery is as follows: the Port of Balsora, a splendidly arranged set with shops and houses in the foreground, shipping in the middle distance, while at the back are seen the Bay of Balsora and the domes and minarets of the city. The brilliancy of the picture is greatly enhanced by the introduction of a charming Oriental ballet, which is capitally danced by a number of cymbal girls in tasteful and appropriate costumes. Miss Blanche Vaudon, the principal dancer, here executes a *pas seul* in artistic and graceful style. The Roc's Retreat precedes the Deck of the *Saucy Puss-Puss* – introducing some clever juggling by Mr Walter Bellonini – followed by effective tableaux, showing Sinbad (Miss Lelia Roze) clinging to the mast. Mrs Sinbad (Mr Walter Sealby) and Binbad (Mr H C Barry) tempest-tossed,

and Sinbad saved, the Spirit of Adventure (Miss Isabel Dillon) appearing in a Nautilus drawn by silver dolphins. After the Island Shore is seen the Orange Grove, an elaborate set, perhaps equal to anything seen at the Prince's. The green of the leaves of the orange trees is relieved by a profusion of white blossoms, among which may be observed the orange-coloured fruit. At the back is a fountain of real water, and as each orange contains an electric light, which is switched on at the conclusion of the scene, the effect is superb. In this scene occurs Sinbad's adventure with the dragon, which is capitally arranged, the dragon being quite a work of art, its jaws flashing forth fire, while its eyes glitter with electric light. When Sindbad succeeds in cutting off the dragon's head with his magic sword the long, sinuous body is seen to consist of ballet ladies, who, throwing aside their long green cloaks forming the scales, suddenly appear in handsome costumes. The death of the dragon is followed by the very pretty Orange and Lemon ballet, the dancers carrying garlands of the fruit, their costumes harmonising with the general surroundings. Miss Blanche Vaudon again displays her ability in a graceful solo dance, and the grand electric tableau concludes the first part of the performance.

In Cool Grot is a substantially built-up set of Balsora Gaol, showing the interior of the cells. A Mountain Path is chiefly notable for Sinbad's adventure with the Old Man of the Sea (Mr Frank Lister). In the Valley of Diamonds the Old Man of the Sea is vanquished, and the Giant Roc ascends with Sinbad. Hall of the Palace is a very fine front cloth, in Mr Coleman's best style, showing an elaborate Oriental interior, perfect in perspective, and containing a mass of decoration and detail rarely seen upon a front cloth. The Palace of Gold is the last scene. This is a magnificent built-up set, with Moorish arches and superb decorations, which when lit up with the electric light forms a picture perfect in all respects and chaste in design. Here is a display of glittering gems on the costumes of the ladies of the ballet, and Miss Blanche Vaudon executes a clever tambourine dance, the curtain descending upon an electric tableau of dazzling splendour. […]

The Surrey
Jack and Jill
[…] THE opening is of the good old-fashioned kind, the first scene representing Falsehood's Lair. The demon (Mr Fred Conquest) joins his myrmidons Sham and Deceit, and tells them how the King o' Diamond's son Jack (Miss Marie Tyler) was kidnapped when a youngster. Old Dame Durden has reared him as her own son, and his father has offered a large reward to anyone who will give a clue that will lead to the boy's discovery. Falsehood proposes to pass off his pal, the Jack o' Clubs, as the missing young prince, but the conference is interrupted by the entrance of the Fairy Truth (Miss Cissy Percival), the steadfast friend of Jack and Jill. It appears that at the bottom of the well lies a magic gem, a diamond which will reveal to its possessor the absolute truth, and it is the object of Falsehood to prevent anyone finding the magic stone. Into the complications of the plot it is needless to enter at length. Suffice it to say that the Fairy is as good as her word, and exerts her powerful influence on behalf of the hero and heroine of the story.

Jack, however, finds it no easy task to obtain possession of the coveted jewel, for the malicious sprite Falsehood is a dangerous foe, and places innumerable obstructions in the hero's path. His way lies through a vegetable forest, a most unpleasant and uncanny place, in which appear animated carrots, turnips, cabbages, &c, to say nothing of monster fruits and other horrors. But Jack, knowing that he has a good cause and a powerful friend, is not easily daunted, and by pluck and perseverance overcomes the many difficulties he has to encounter ere he obtains possession of the diamond. By its changes of colour King Cardo (Mr Ernest Ball) is convinced that Jack is the long-missing heir to the throne. Jill (Miss Ina Rene) has rivals for her hand in the Jack o' Clubs (Mr Arthur Conquest) and the Jack o' Spades (Mr Nat Clifford), comic villains, who are very jealous of each other and of the hero, but who, of course, stand no chance whatsoever of wedding the heroine.

One of the most striking and effective scenes of the pantomime in the Interior of the Palace of King Cardo, where every card in the pack is represented. The blending of colours is very harmonious, the warm red tints imparting a cheery aspect to the whole scene. Here, too, is played a game of nap by living cards. This was too long drawn out at the first performance, but by this time a much brisker game is no doubt played. It is, at all events, an interesting novelty.

In scene thirteen, the Bottom of the Well, Mr Conquest introduces some striking electrical effects. The stage is darkened, and from the gloomy background appear glittering forms, which ascend and descend, cross and recross the stage, and then darkness swallows them up for a time. These aerial manoeuvres have in past years been a feature of the Surrey pantomime, and the business is worked with greater ingenuity than ever. […]

Princess of Wales's
Cinderella
[…] A PRETTY chorus of welcome is extended by her dainty subjects to Flora, Queen of the Fairies (Miss M Osland), who states her desire to befriend Cinderella, various flowers indicating in recitative the virtues they will bestow on the maiden. The demon Aconite (Mr Colquhoun Manifold) intrudes on their revels. His power is assumed after midnight, and his mission is to dispel the fairy influence.

With a chorus of defiance the scene changes to Where the Wild Flowers Grow, gay with huntsmen and villagers in holiday attire, with an effective ballet that is enthusiastically applauded. Here we make the acquaintance of Prince Perfect (Miss Sophie Harriss), who, after singing a hunting song, determines to change places with his valet, Dandini (Miss Marie Campbell), in order to win a wife who will esteem him for himself and not for his rank. Soon laughter is aroused by Grabber, a man-in-possession at the house of Baron Golosh, whose daughters, Thisbe and Zora (the Darnley Brothers), presently arrive and compare their work as poet and painter respectively. There is more fun made out of a difference of opinion, and a duet about "Robin Hood", by the Sisters, ends with an eccentric dance that is encored. Cinderella (Miss Lily Morris) enters and laments her lot, and while she sleeps Prince Perfect arrives attired as a valet and promptly falls in love with the maiden. The Prince awakens her with a kiss, and a pretty duet, "Smile on me, darling", is given. Baron Golosh (Mr Tom Craven) then makes his appearance. He delivers a funny speech, and the merriment grows apace when Thisbe and Zora are introduced to Dandini in the guise of the Prince. Dandini invites the Baron and his daughters to a ball at the Castle, and the scene ends with a spirited finale.

In the Baron's Study (scene three), Mr George Mozart as the page Twitters gives his clever and droll impersonations on the clarionet, and the Baron sings "Getting a bit here and there", and more mirth is evoked from the pranks of the broker's man, the Baron and his daughters, and Twitters.

Scene four reveals the Baron's Kitchen, where Cinderella is awakened by an invisible chorus. She sings of her pleasant dreams and confides her troubles to the kitchen cat (Mr F Whittaker), with whom she goes through a quaint dance that is loudly applauded. After a duet and dance with Twitters, the Prince arrives, but his love-making with Cinderella is interrupted by the Baron, who orders him out of the house. Left alone, Cinderella is visited by the fairy godmother, and then we see the lizard, pumpkin, &c, that are to form Cinderella's equipage when by the magic aid of Flora she goes to the Prince's ball. Aconite enters with flaming torch to work his evil designs and to sing "Shine out, O light", using his fine voice to admirable purpose.

In scene five, the Boudoir of the Fairies – an exquisite set, which secured for the artist, Mr W F Robson, a round of applause – there is a procession and a charming ballet of fans, shoes, and the appurtenances of a boudoir, and when Flora has sung "Queen of the Earth", Cinderella enters in her carriage, which is a brilliant blaze of gold and electric light, drawn by four black Shetland ponies, and which was greeted on Monday with hearty and long-sustained applause.

The second division of the pantomime opens in the Palace Grounds, with the word "Welcome" outlined in a festoon of flowers, another excellent scene due to Mr Robson's marvellous skill. Dandini and a dozen coloured ladies and gentlemen go through a grotesque cake walk, and Thisbe and Zora sing a clever topical duet of "England" that is many times encored. Mr George Mozart here gives his burlesque melodrama, which arouses roars of laughter, and the Baron and his daughters indulge in a droll trio and dance.

The Prince in scene two, a Grand Corridor, sings "I love her so", and Thisbe and Zora are heard as Christy Minstrels in a cleverly-arranged duet, "Ohio". Scene three, the Ballroom, a handsome setting by Mr Stafford Hall, is notable for an excellent chorus and ballet and for some capital dancing by the Diamond Troupe. Here "The little Anglo-Saxon every time" is splendidly sung by Aconite, who comes disguised to the ball. Prince Perfect resumes his identity, adopting a very pretty dress for the purpose, and Cinderella is announced as the Princess Incognito. A vocal minuet is performed, and as the clock strikes the midnight hour Cinderella is seen rushing from the room, while the glass slipper lies glittering on the floor.

The guests meet again in the Reception Room of the Palace, where the business of trying on the shoe is gone through, Cinderella, of course, being proved to be the owner, the Prince joining her in a duet of delight, with an animated chorus to accompany. [...]

Drury Lane
The Forty Thieves

[...] IN every Ali Baba pantomime there must be much the same scenario – at least, as long as the story is adhered to. Realising this, and eager to attain novelty, Messrs Sturgess and Collins have deviated from the "Arabian Nights" outline, and have taken their characters to England. Ali Baba (Mr Johnny Danvers[15]), after plundering the cave, comes to London and takes a fashionable flat. The business of the marking of the doors takes place here, and the boiling down of the robbers is done in the courtyard of the Red Lion Inn, instead of in Persia. Abdallah (Mr Dan Leno), urged by the fair Zuleika (Mr Herbert Campbell) to "break into some big building", makes burglarious entry into Newgate Prison, and there meets Ali Baba, the pair sitting down to dinner with the Governor, and dancing a modified can-can afterwards.

So much for the narrative, which, after all, is secondary in importance compared to the grand spectacular scenes, of which there may be said to be three in the pantomime. For years the public taste in the matter of spectacle has tended more and more to delicacy, and less to mere glitter and glare. The public have long been educated up to admiring half-tones and tints in place of the primary colours, green and crimson tinsel, and red light of long ago. This refinement of taste has been judiciously catered for by Mr Collins, who, in the seventh scene of his pantomime, has presented his patrons with one of the loveliest spectacles ever seen upon any stage. Like Cleopatra's personal appearance, it "beggars description". Imagine the vast area framed by the grand proscenium of Drury Lane, crossed from back to front by a flight of glass steps. Over these falls, spurts, splashes, and foams a cataract of real water, in which reflected lights dance and dazzle. Each side of the waterfall is hedged with elaborate scroll work, and the rest of the stage is occupied with steps and stairs on a steep slope. Down this comes detachment after detachment of fair women symbolising the different types of porcelain. The collector can recognise in the daintily suggested china all the familiar friends of his cabinet. The tender greys, lilacs, and whites of one class are contrasted with the rich reds of another, and the deep blues of a third. Even those who are not experts in bric-a-brac may appreciate the exquisite beauty of the hues, the refined and intricate ornamentation, and the delicious harmony of the colour masses. In the centre, at the foot of the waterfall, a canary-coloured contingent does a pretty dance; while the numbers of the armies of auxiliaries on the stairs and steps are reinforced by every-arriving additions. To "crown the edifice", the Grigolatis rise, fall, and float in air smoothly, easily, and without visible means of sustentation. Words are feebly employed in expressing the artistic excellence of this triumph of the arts of the scenic artist, the costume designer, the costumier, and the stage manager.

Another "great scene" is more brilliant, more dazzling than this one. In Love's Golden Gates the result is obtained by the assembly of hundreds of auxiliaries in spangled and sparkling costumes beneath the rays of different coloured lights. In this way some very beautiful effects, reminding us of the colours in a prism, are created. But it is not only in the mass that beauty is here to be found. Each dress must have cost a large amount of skilled labour. The draperies which flow from the shoulders of the fair auxiliaries are adorned with handsome designs "applied" with great care and finish. The coloured rays are flashed back to the eye by the reflections from a thousand morsels of glass, of polished and gilded metal; and, to give the great stage picture a foreground, the principal personages in the pantomime appear in gorgeous dresses.

The third elaborate scene is laid in the Zoological Gardens. It would be hard to overpraise either the way in which the animals are represented or the well-modelled masks, by the aid of which intelligent supernumeraries represent celebrities of the hour. The idea is worked out with remarkable care and finish. Too often the likenesses of pantomime masks are feeble; but, in this case, the portraitures are faithful and accurate. A great deal of fun is created by the remarks made by the principals to the representatives of the notabilities of the day; and, at the end of the scene, the American Eagle fraternises with the British Lion amidst the waving of dozens of Union Jacks.

With such artists as Mr Collins has secured, the acting of the pantomime was certain to be excellent. Mr Dan Leno gave full liberty to his eccentric exuberance as Abdullah. His first appearance on an orange-tawny steed, in burlesque of Mr Beerbohm Tree's entry as D'Artagnan in *The Musketeers*, brought down the house immediately. His costume, with a cloak made of an "Early Victorian" tablecloth, was extravagantly droll, and throughout his flow of jest and gag was copious and diverting. It was rare fun to see him as the president of the Forty Thieves Company, Limited, taking the chair at a burlesque board meeting and presenting the shareholders with a "bogus" balance-sheet. The satire was received with roars of laughter. His mock operatic solos, his odd and active dancing, and all his multifarious quips and japes evoked laughter loud and long. Mr Herbert Campbell as the Fair Zuleika looked irresistibly absurd in Turkish female costume, and his performance was a worthy companion picture to Mr Leno's Captain of the Forty. […]

Grand Theatre, Islington
The Babes in the Wood; or, Harlequin Maid Marian and Bold Robin Hood
[…] THE pantomime commences with a very pretty scene in Babyland, where Natura, the Good Fairy (Miss Gertrude Aylward), and a certain Scarlet Witch (Mr J M Jones) have the usual preliminary argument; in which also Maligna (Miss Ada Homer), a malevolent spirit, and Cock Robin (Miss Gladys Harris), king of all the redbreasts, takes part. The two robbers appear as "blind" beggars in the third scene; and in the Baron's sanctum, where a guard of shapely silver-clad warriors is drawn up, Weary Will and Tired Tim (the Passmore Brothers) agree to murder the Babes (Miss Marie Harris and Miss Dorrie Harris), who are carried away by them struggling and kicking. The bold bad Baron Mugwump (Mr Frank Danby) is watched by an imitation of Sherlock Holmes, called Bertie the Nark (Mr Harry Randall), who is always finding clues and assuming disguises. To the forest with the Babes go the Robbers; and have the usual quarrel and combat, the first part of the pantomime ending with a very pretty snow ballet, which will be perfectly pleasing when the dancers have learnt to avoid the net which gives atmospheric effect to the picture.

The Babes escape and become two little vagabonds, and the story proceeds on the usual lines till the introduction of a delightful and carefully studied spectacle, showing the uniforms of the British army from an early date. This is not only beautiful and picturesque, there is a real interest to be found in observing the development of our military tailoring in the course of years. The procession went without a hitch on Monday, and each of the modern crack regiments as it appeared had a hearty round of applause. Dazzlingly brilliant is the grand ballet of Jewels in the tenth scene, the stage being filled with symmetrically shaped ladies wearing costumes composed of all the most valuable precious stones, a most coruscating display. The denouement is done by the Baron being brought to see a *tableau vivant* representing the murder of the Babes, a burlesque of the play scene in *Hamlet* proving very funny. Mr G R Hemsley's transformation represents the seven ages of man, the theme being treated with artistic skill and fine taste; and the performance concludes with a harlequinade, in which the scenes are 'Cuba in England' and 'Merrie Islington'. […]

The "leader of the revels" at the Grand Theatre on Monday afternoon was Mr Harry Randall, and we may say at once that we never saw this popular songster and comedian to greater advantage. His bold, emphatic method was exactly suited to the requirements of the position, and his performance as Bertie the Nark inspired the whole production with briskness and vigour. As the burlesque detective Mr Randall was irresistible. His appearance in various disguises was screamingly funny, but even funnier than his "make-ups" was the droll business which he introduced in each instance. His dance in the Highland kilt brought down the house, and it was impossible not to laugh at the spectacle of Mr Randall – lying on his stomach in a leafy glade, in the costume of a sportsman, with his brown gaiters waving nervously in the air – shooting at a rabbit and "bringing down" a tin of potted rodent. [...]
The Era, 31/12/1898

1899

Garrick
Puss in Boots
[…] SURPRISING as a spectacle, *Puss in Boots* certainly is not; but it has the much-to-be-desired qualities of daintiness and prettiness with many touches of sentiment. The scenes are mostly of a rustic type, and the tangled greenery of English landscape is found sufficiently attractive by the scenic artists, Messrs C Tritschler, W R Coleman, E Howard, and W Howath, who have given us of their best. In Mr Tritschler's later sets, however – the Silver Hall of the Ogre and the Garden of Flowers – the developments are of the fanciful nature that one looks for in pantomime, and the brightness and brilliance of both scenes are due to the effective blending of colours, irradiated by the glowing incandescence of a number of coloured lights. Of ballet in its transcendental phase we get little, but there are many captivating dances by villagers clad in sober browns and subdued reds, a *minuet de la coeur*, a characteristic *pas seul* by Miss Susie Raymonde, who represents the Spirit of Terpsichore, and an effective and spirited dance by Amazons, whose blue skirts are so arranged as to exhibit the Union Jack.

The plot is simply and directly told. Soon after the opening we assist at the endowment of the wonderful booted feline with speech. He is, indeed, the Talleyrand of cats, and his perspicuity, audacity, and shrewdness should endear him to every juvenile in London, to whom Mr Wood's pantomime especially appeals. It is essentially an entertainment for the kiddies, and there is less, therefore, of the laboured efforts at dragging in topical references in a duet, and more of those humorous tricks which are especially cherished by childish imaginations. First favourite in the Garrick production will be Mr Charles Lauri, who, as we all know, reigns king in the world of animal impersonators. His Slyboots at once took the fancy of the house on Tuesday afternoon, and the youngsters roared in delight when Slyboots returned from a poaching expedition with a bird in his mouth. They admired, too, the natural way he sat down and did his toilet; and if one might object to this remarkable cat's methods on moral grounds, yet nothing could be more engaging than his continued activity or his happy method of compassing apparently insurmountable difficulties.

Miss Letty Lind cannot be other than delightful, and her Princess Ivy at once takes us captive by its simplicity and charm. Of course, Miss Lind dances, and that statement brings us to the consideration of her doll dance with Mr Edward Lauri as a sort of Fuzzy-wuzzy doll. […] Mr George Grey as King Grabbus, Mr Robb Harwood as Baron Rumphiz, and Mr George Miller as Dame Shortly, share the humours of a most entertaining burlesque of *King John*, in which Mr Beerbohm Tree and Mr Wilson Barrett's style are whimsically parodied.

Mr Walter Bellonini, one of the best of our jugglers, is effectively introduced into the opening as Fritz, the waiter, and astonishes his customers by the facility with which he keeps going a hat, an umbrella, and a cigar. He does many other tricks that are equally unexpected and surprising, and also makes his mark in the Palace scene by his special act, which includes some very clever hat spinning. [...]

The Surrey
Goody Two-Shoes
[…] IT only needs compression, and *Goody Two-Shoes* will rank among the best of Mr Conquest's efforts, and that is surely praise enough. The story upon which is embroidered all these hours' amusement? Well, Goody Two-Shoes (Miss Amy Dyson) is the real heiress to the kingdom of Funniopolis, and she is to all appearances but a sweet peasant maid, beloved of Johnny Horner (Miss Jenny Belomore) – as gallant a lad as ever was – so it is only fitting that the Fairy Butterfly (Miss Cissy Percival) should befriend her, and it is only likewise that King Moth (Mr Fred Conquest) should plot against her happiness, and so the good fairy gives her a pair of shoes that will ensure the love of every one she encounters – such are their magic qualities. This, naturally, does not fit in with the ideas of his Moth Majesty, so

the time-honoured conflict between the good and evil spirits goes on in the sweet old way, with a little mortal assistance thrown in.

Leaving a Ferny Forest by Mellow Moonlight behind, we find ourselves at the Port of Funniopolis, with its crowd of fruit sellers and other picturesque personages, and on dash the Tonnere Troupe to regale us with a fascinating Spanish dance, to the click of the castanets and the melodious melody of the "Toreador Waltz". Then enter Betsinda (Mr George Conquest Jr), a portly and amorous dame, the gallant Johnny Horner, the Princess Rosilda (Miss Isabel Oliver), Hamletto (Mr Arthur Conquest), a minor villain, the traditional pantomime King Grumpo the Oneth (Mr Fred Carlton), Dicky Desperado (Mr Fred Zola), and the other characters, and having made their acquaintance things rapidly and comically move forward to the Palace Gardens and an Ante-room in the Palace and on the Sad Sea Shore – all the while much fun – to the State Ball in the Palace, and here we get the congress of nations and the butterflies' ball, both of these rich and well-managed spectacles. Opportunity is here taken to include several specialities, among whom the Tonnere Troupe again score, this time with some very fetching Parisian dancing, and a marvellous youngster called Baby White gives a coon song and dance with all the confidence of maturity, and gains a most enthusiastic reception. Then Zarno and Arno give a really wonderful acrobatic performance, and we get on to the Old Mill, and here the Brothers Conquest maintain the best traditions of the family with some really marvellous trap work. Here King Moth contrives to steal the magic shoes, after they have passed through many hands and caused many complications, and so we go on to the Interior of the Volcano, with its ballet of fairy flying flames, a wonderfully contrived piece of work, with its lurid fires casting weird lights around and the fairies apparently floating in space. The next scene is the Mouth of the Volcano again, and here Cleopatra gives her wonderful serpent-charming show. Then we shift to the Gardens of the Palace, where everything is cleared up, and the charming Goody and the gallant Jack are set fair in the way to be "happy ever after", vice meeting with its fitting pantomime punishment.

Next we have a curtain, on which is painted a very heroic figure of Britannia, from the brush of Mr Howden, and Miss Kate Olga Vernon comes on to recite Kipling's poem[16] to thunders of applause, and so on to the transformation scene, the Electrical Butterflies' Haunt, a picture of ravishing colour and wonderful employment of electric light that once again places Mr Conquest in the front rank of pantomime producers. […]

West London Theatre
Jack of Hearts

[…] THE pantomime opens in the Village of Dingley Dell, where, after the opening chorus, we are introduced to a bevy of village maidens, dancing with their rustic partners. Simple Sammy (Mr J Pingree) and Chasemegurls (Mr F Damary), in the fullness of their hearts, give the poor old Dame, Martha Winterbloom (Mr Prince Miller), rather a rough five minutes, but she is rescued by the hero of the story, Jack (Miss Dolly Tree), who is supposed to be her son. Pomposio (Miss Lucy Tree) then enters and reads a proclamation. The crowd retire, and after a song the herald follows suit. Lottie Lollipop (Miss Marian Armitage) and Susie Shy (Miss Alice Sinclair) then appear upon the scene, and sing a pretty Dairy-maids' duet. After a little argument with the Knave (Mr T P Percival), they leave him to his reflections, and the King of Hearts (Mr Oliver Rogers), the Queen of Hearts (Mr H G Brandon), and Amabel (Miss Bibby Tree) are next seen at the head of a procession. The villagers gather round, and the King treats them to a short speech, when suddenly cries for help are heard, and the Queen recollects that the King's niece, Princess Florina (Miss Portia Tree), stayed behind to pick some wild flowers, and discovers to her horror that the maiden is being attacked by a bull. Jack goes to the rescue, and brings Florina to the Queen safe and sound. Jack, madly in love at first sight, asks for Florina's hand. The King, being angry at such boldness, has him placed in the stocks, and retires with his Court to the palace. Poor Jack is left alone, but the fairy Luna (Miss Flo Barnes) enters, and sets him free. She also tells him that he is of royal descent, and was changed at birth by the mother of the Knave of Hearts, the latter, who is the villain of the piece, having usurped his rights. Jack, left to himself, sings a ditty, and goes off rejoicing. The Knave, who has been listening, then enters, and vows vengeance, for he also loves the fair Florina.

After a bustling scene in the Corridor of the Palace, the King is discovered in his Counting-House, and the Queen obliges with a song. The Knave continues to persecute the Princess, and she succeeds in driving him away. She is in trouble because Jack is missing, but Tinseletta (Miss Dorothy Carmen) promises to assist Florina to find him. Martha obtains an audience with the King, but he refuses to release Jack.

At the gracious invitation of the Queen, who is proud of her skill as a cook, everybody is invited to the Royal Kitchen to see her make the famous tarts. This condescension on the part of her Majesty is duly appreciated, but the Knave, at his wicked tricks again, puts a magic potion in the jam, and sends the Princess to sleep for seven years. Luna appears and informs the Queen that the only way to remove the spell is for a youth, good and true, to go to the Palace of Truth and fetch some water from the magic well. This Florina must drink, and she will awaken. Desolatus (Mr Fred D'Albert) appears, accompanied by his imps, and they indulge in some startling demon gambols.

Jack is allowed to journey to the Palace of Truth, passing through a dismal swamp on the way. He succeeds in his mission, and on his return awakens the sleeping princess. He also produces the proof of his royal birth, these having been handed to him by the fairy Luna. A *bal masque* is given, at which the betrothal of Jack and the Princess is celebrated, but the Knave and Desolatus appear disguised and carry off Florina to an enchanted castle. Jack and his gallant Knights attack the castle and carry it by a grand assault. The Knave of Hearts is defeated, and the Princess rescued. The former is captured and sentenced to death, but Luna appears and asks his pardon, which is granted. The lovers are united, and happiness reigns supreme. […]

Drury Lane
Jack and the Beanstalk

[…] IN the first scene, at the roots of the magic beanstalk, the usual dispute takes place between the good and evil agencies, and we are soon shown Dame Trot's Dairy. The Dame is in difficulties, and, proceeding with her fat boy, Bobbie, to market, meets King Rattatat, an affable monarch, who associates freely with his subjects, and, taking a fancy to the Dame, purchases for her various presents. A very beautiful and elaborate ballet of fowls takes place here. The costumes are marvellously made, the different breeds being carefully distinguished, and the feathered disguises being admirably worked out. Another ingenious and artistic ballet is one in which some vegetables are represented with quaint fidelity and no little humour, while others are idealised in most delicately fantastical style. Broad fun is created by the troublesome tricks of a cat in Dame Trot's attic; and there are amusing doings on the roof of her house, when King Rattatat, coming to visit the Dame, hastily moves from the top of a chimney pot on which he has seated himself, the soot in the chimney having caught fire, covering the party in a shower of "blacks".

At last we arrive at the concluding scene of the first part, called the Land of Harmony. Music is the "motive" of this splendid spectacle, which, like similar achievements at Drury Lane, is indescribably beautiful. A rough idea may be given of the ensemble by saying that at the back is a colossal harp, while there are suggestions of similar instruments in the wings. When the climax is reached the stage is filled with symbolisations of the different departments of music, suggestions of Wagner being made by a bevy of knights in swan helmets, while fair "instrumentalists" place to their lips the double trumpet of the ancients. Real harpists and mandolinists perform upon the stage, and the combinations of form, colour, and sound when the orchestra swells out into a crescendic blare is overpowering in its appeal to the various senses.

In the second part of the pantomime Jack's adventures in Giant-land are dealt with, and the way in which the Brobdignagian people are represented must be unreservedly praised. Never, surely, were seen giants so tall, so easy and natural in their movements, and so entirely free from any suspicion of "grogginess" at the knees. The Giant is shown falling and lying gigantic on "many a rood of ground", his chest heaving as he breathes his last. From his breast pockets emerge contingents representing the various arms of the service now occupied in South Africa, including a troupe of miniature colonials on Shetland ponies. The final tableau represents the end of the century, and various inventions of the period are noted and symbolised. At the back, flanked by a pair of open-mouthed lions, sits the Queen on her throne, whilst the Grigolatis, attired as angels, hover over the royal head.

Mr Dan Leno is a comedian whose "vogue" only grows greater with years of popularity. We look upon his Dame Trot as it was presented on the first night of *Jack and the Beanstalk* at Drury Lane on Tuesday as a sample of what the part will be when this accomplished droll has worked it up. His "specialities" were amongst the most amusing things in the entertainment. He had a burlesque of a French *chanson* singer's methods, which was intensely humorous, and there was the scene above referred to, in which the Dame, while telling her son a story, was teased and troubled by their cat. This promises, when well thought out and increased, to be extremely diverting. A brisk bit of business was done by Mr Leno in the twelfth scene, where he darted to and fro between a couple of rooms, in each of which a wedding breakfast was prepared for the Dame by the King and his minion Pitapat, to whom she had separately betrothed herself. At present there is plenty of room in the performance for the further development of Mr Leno's eccentricity, and the same may be said of Mr Herbert Campbell's Bobbie, which has obvious laughter provoking possibilities. The sooner he and Mr Leno are provided with several good songs the better for the pleasure of the audience who will be attracted to Drury Lane by the great reputation of the house, and by the certainty of witnessing the splendid spectacles invariably supplied there.

Mr Johnny Danvers's quaint and original method was well suited to the character of King Rattatat, and he sustained it with dry humour that was very effective. Mr William Morgan spoke his lines as the Demon Worm with resonant distinctness, and Messrs Queen and LeBrun supplied a clever caricature of vaccine idiosyncrasy as the Cow. […] Madame Grigolati as the Spirit of Spring made a startling aerial swoop over the heads of the audience in the stalls – an exploit quite unexpected and very ingeniously and artfully arranged. [...]

The Era, 30/12/1899

Dan Leno, Johnny Danvers and Herbert Campbell

NOTES

1 – Belle Bilton (1867-1906): A music hall singer best remembered for her scandalous marriage to Viscount Dunlo, eldest son of the fourth Earl of Clancarty. On her father-in-law's death in 1901 Belle became the Countess of Clancarty, but died of cancer five years later at the age of 39.
2 – Donkeys.
3 – Little Tich (1867-1928), born Harry Relph: A dancer and music hall comedian particularly noted for his "big boot dance" in which he stood on tiptoe in boots 28 inches long. He was 4' 6'' tall and had six fingers on each hand.
4 – Marie Lloyd (1870-1922), born Matilda Wood: A singer and comedienne known as the Queen of the Music Hall. Her best-remembered song is probably *My Old Man Said Follow the Van*.
5 – Ewigkeit: Eternity.
6 – Laura Ormiston Chant (1848-1923): A social reformer and temperance advocate who was strongly opposed to what she regarded as the immorality of music hall entertainment.
7 – Isa Bowman (1874-1958): A child actress and friend of Lewis Carroll.

8 – The Grigolatis Troupe specialised in aerial ballet, wearing corsets attached to steel wires wrapped in silk to reduce reflection from the stage lights and produce the illusion of flying.

9 – George du Maurier's 1894 novel *Trilby*, the story of an artists' model transformed by the evil hypnotist Svengali into a famous singer, was blamed for encouraging young women readers to adopt a bohemian lifestyle.

10 – W S Gilbert's *The Bab Ballads*, first published in 1869, is a collection of comic poems illustrated by the author.

11 – Kaiser Wilhelm II (1859-1941): Grandson of Queen Victoria and the last emperor of Germany.

12 – Letty Lind (1861-1923): An actress and singer, she was also famous as an exponent of the "skirt dance", in which the performer used her arms to manipulate voluminous skirts whilst performing movements derived from traditional step-dancing.

13 – Perhaps from the German "sicher mach", "make sure".

14 – George Robey (1869-1954), real name was George Edward Wade: A leading music hall star and pantomime dame known as "the Prime Minister of Mirth".

15 – Johnny Danvers: The uncle of Dan Leno.

16 – Copies of Kipling's *The Absent-Minded Beggar*, later set to music by Sir Arthur Sullivan, raised over £250,000 for British soldiers fighting in the Second Boer War and their dependents.

11
The 1900s
Frying Pans For Racquets and Potatoes For Balls

1900

AT the New Theatre Royal, Croydon, on Thursday evening, an accident occurred owing to some of the scenery giving way, several of the ladies representing fairies in the Palace scene in Aladdin *falling from a considerable height on to the stage. Some of the principals fainted and five of the fairies were sent in cabs to Croydon Hospital to be treated for sprains and bruises, two being seriously injured.*
The Era, 20/1/1900

MISS MILLIE HYLTON, the popular principal boy of Goody Two Shoes, *at the Grand Theatre, Leeds, met, we are sorry to hear, with a painful accident on Wednesday night last. In the Court scene Mr Thompson and other members of the company pretend to play croquet, and meanwhile Miss Hylton stands near. Mr Thompson had in his hand a heavy property mallet, and while in the act of raising it to "drive" an imaginary ball he accidentally struck Miss Hylton on the right side of her head. The blow rendered her unconscious, and she had to be carried from the stage. A surgeon who was quickly in attendance found that she had sustained a severe cut on the right ear. She was conveyed home, and has since been confined to her room. She will resume her part in* Goody Two Shoes *as soon as her medical attendant will allow her, and in the meantime it is in the capable hands of Miss Norah Cecil.*
The Era, 10/2/1900

WANTED, Rubber Sheet, also Fat Policeman's Dress, for Water Pantomime. Good Condition. Lowest Price. PONGORILA, 3, Market Street, Coleshill Street, Birmingham.
The Era, 7/7/1900

WHEN Mr H E Moss announced that Cinderella's slipper was to cost over £100, much speculation was aroused as to the cost of the whole production at the London Hippodrome. Here are some interesting items: – Cinderella's coach, which is built of glass, covered with myriads of tiny electric lights, will be worthy of a place in the British Museum. As a novelty from a spectacular point, nothing has been seen like it; as a valuable property, it would tax the exchequer of a millionaire to purchase such another. It is shaped exactly like the Lord Mayor's State carriage, and will be drawn by six black ponies, caparisoned in red morocco and gilt harness, and attended by twelve flunkeys and outriders in costumes costing £63 each. The coach itself has cost £1,000. The whole of the arena will be turned into a gigantic ball-room, and Mr Moss promises the most remarkable electrical effects that have ever been conceived. Altogether 400 persons will appear in Cinderella.
The Era, 15/12/1900

The Surrey
Little Miss Muffit
ROUND the very short nursery story of "Little Miss Muffit", and the rhyme of "The Maid and the Magpie", Messrs George Conquest and Henry Spry, pantomime authors of unique experience, have woven a fanciful texture of fairy lore and given to the Surrey-siders a rare and glowing spectacle, with all the best features of old-fashioned pantomime introduced.

The opening is divided into twelve scenes, and the plot turns on the loss and subsequent recovery of a magic spoon. Jack (Miss Jeannie Richards), the hero, who wears a magic cap, is the son of Mrs Winkle (Mr Bob Hutt), a lady who sets considerable value upon herself. She is blessed naturally with all the patriotic sentiment that is so dear to audiences "across the bridge", but has likewise a keen sense of fun. It is quite in accordance with the fitness of things that Jack should return from South Africa, the event being signalised by the advent of a number of Tommies in khaki. Early in the extravaganza we are introduced to the Golden Goblin (Mr Fred Conquest), a creature of the tarantula type, chief of the forces of malignancy, who frightens the gentle heroine by coming down the chimney. It is quite evident that he has learnt something of the crafty commercial code of the Celestials by his device of disguising himself as a pedlar, in order to carry out his fell purpose of annexing the magic spoon. Little Miss Muffit (Miss Lottie Sargent) – artful minx that she is – sells him nickel instead of the real article. Mrs Winkle finds out that Miss Muffit has sold the spoon, and charges her with stealing it. Midas (Mr B S Monti) – not our old friend the classic King of Phrygia, but an individual of more broad-minded tendencies – tells the assembled crowd that he is a JP, and will try the heroine in the morning at the Court of Injustice.

In this scene the comic trial of Miss Muffit occurs, and against her the Golden Goblin, still disguised as the Hebraic vendor of unconsidered trifles, gives evidence. But the course of pantomime justice never does run smooth, and the deliberations of the Court are continually interrupted by knockabout fun and some clever trap business. Little Miss Muffit's fate is never in doubt, and the opening winds up with a happy ending and a jubilant chorus.

There are many fine scenes, and all the beauty of electric lighting and admirable colouring seem to have been lavished on the Palace of Midas, where, of course, golden tints prevail. The programme calls the set a "gorgeous electric roof garden", and the phrase truly describes it. Herein we are treated to comic bicycle revels by the Brothers Crank, who do some really clever work, and to a pretty and ingenious serpentine dance on the rolling globe by Miss Lily Rouletta. In the Palace of Midas, too, we meet such guests as President Kruger, Bobs[1], Baden-Powell, De Wet[2] (who easily escapes), French, Sir George White, Kitchener, and Sir Redvers Buller, and are treated to a procession of Colonial representatives, who typify the Imperial spirit that has grown by leaps and bounds during the last year of the century.

But the genius of Mr George Conquest as an inventor and producer of original effects in pantomime is seen at its very best in scene ten, the Bottomless Pool, a fanciful dream of fays and water nymphs, who float gracefully above the real rushes and real water, realising in a delightful way the most fantastic dreams of childhood. This scene is bound to be much talked about, and justifies the reputation of the Surrey as a popular house for Christmas fare of the best kind. [...]

Drury Lane
Sleeping Beauty and the Beast
[…] THE two tales are connected in this way: when Prince Caramel has waked Sleeping Beauty with a kiss, the witch Malevolentia plays her second and last card. She changes the Prince into a hideous monster, who can only be restored to his human and handsome shape by a kiss from a maiden fair. One good turn, we know, deserves another; and, as Beauty has been restored to animation by the Prince's embrace, what more poetically just than that she should return the compliment when he is also under the witch's spell?

So much for the general idea of the book on which a clever corps of scenic artists has been let loose to invent, to embroider, and to embellish. Instead of opening his pantomime in the conventional gloom, with "lights down" in the auditorium and the throaty mumblings of the demon droning through the shades, Mr Collins cheers us up at once by introducing us to Fairyland. This scene, which is by Mr R Caney, is, of course, but a foretaste of the glories to follow; but it is nevertheless very dainty and fanciful indeed. Mr Julian Hicks then comes in with a contrast – a burlesque of a Continental hydropathic establishment, where there is opportunity for plenty of funny business with the King and Queen of the cast (Mr Herbert Campbell and Mr Dan Leno), who are carried in concealed in the sedan chairs with which all visitors to Aix-le-Bains are familiar. Next we are shown the haunted vaults of the castle, where by some "cantrip[3] sleight" connected with electricity, grinning faces of fire appear on the ends of the barrels and on the walls. The fatal spinning wheel has to be introduced, and it is magically presented by the witch's attendant. In a gorgeous and gilded scene showing the Royal Aviary, we see Beauty (Miss Madge Lessing) approach the dangerous period of her seventeenth birthday. The doors are barred, but what can bolts and locks do against witchcraft? Away goes the aviary, birds, and perches, and all; and, attended by a party of witches, Malevolentia (Miss Alice Aynsley Cook) invites Beauty to seat herself at the golden spinning wheel, which the witch has brought as a birthday present. Thus does the Princess prick her hand and fall into a trance. A hundred years elapse in as many seconds; and, through the tangled forest, comes Prince Caramel (Miss Elaine Ravesburg), who has heard of the legend of the Sleeping Court, and vows to brave all dangers to restore the Princess to life. Despite the opposition which he meets with from an ugly crew of witches and warlocks, he makes his way to the Castle, kisses the Sleeping Beauty, and breaks the spell.

Here comes in Mr Henry Emden's opportunity; and he takes advantage of it by giving us one of the loveliest possible backgrounds for an exquisite ballet, representing the Dream of the Year. The seasons, and even the months, are symbolised by detachments of superbly-attired dancers; and, in the background, appear pictures of English landscape at different times of the year. Then, on the ground supplied by the tenderer tints, are thrown flecks of intense black when the Grigolatis, in swallow costumes, rise and fall in the air. As the whites and greys of winter replace the rich autumnal hues, vivid scarlets and vermilions harmonise with the glowing crimson of the holly berries. The exquisite art of this spectacle – or, rather, series of spectacles – could scarcely be surpassed.

The second part of the pantomime commences less satisfactorily. In the cutting to which the book will necessarily be subjected, it would be well if all the satire on the French nation and Government were eliminated. It elicits little sympathy, and such "smacks" certainly do not make for international amity. It is more important to pass at once to the Enchanted Crystal Garden in the Palace of the Beast. The illuminated fountains, which were promised to create such a great sensation, did not "play" on Wednesday, and something went wrong, too, with Salviati's palace of glass, but now all defects have been removed, and the splendours of these two scenes are surprising.

The transformation depicts Beauty's Wedding Gifts, prominent amongst them being a colossal diamond tiara and pearl necklace. Features of the scene are the descent of a picture disclosing a number of water-lilies, and the opening of enormous globular plants of gold. The scene, when all its beauties have burst upon the view, is dazzlingly beautiful.

The acting and singing on Wednesday were as excellent and admirable as the spectacle. We have seldom seen Mr Dan Leno better on a first night than he was at the "Lane" on Wednesday; and this may have been attributed to the fact of the pantomime having been remarkably well rehearsed. Mr Leno as Queen Ravia supplied another of those calmly quaint impersonations of eccentric females of uncertain age which we always expect from this inimitable comedian. A great deal of cleverly-contrived fun is introduced by him and Mr Herbert Campbell as King Screwdolph. They come on in a motor-car – which eventually "bursts up" – and burgle the National Museum, where the regalia is supposed to be kept. They are imprisoned in the Courtyard of the Palace of Justice, and harangue the raging mob from the top of a wall; and they play an utterly absurd game of golf. It may easily be imagined how such business as this is worked up by these two clever artistes, whose songs are entirely amusing and up to date. [...]

Kingston Theatre, Kingston-upon-Thames
Cinderella

[...] THE first scene is a Woodland Glade, where Prince Glorio (Miss May Dark) is found pursuing the sport of falconry, and it is here that he first meets with Cinderella (Miss Eliza Earle), to whom the fairy Benevolentia (Miss Marion Lind) appears in a dream. In this scene there is a very pretty *pas de parapluies* by six "young sparks" and their lady loves. The next scene, the Kitchen of Baron Steakandchips (Mr Harold Carson), affords an opportunity for a good deal of highly diverting low-comedy work. We are shown Ballahooley's Emporium, whither comes Cinderella to find something wherewith to deck herself for the ball. But her crooked sixpence, given to her by the kind fairy, she parts with to an old woman, who afterwards turns out to be the fairy herself, and in return for the kindness is transported to the establishment of a Madame Vanité (Miss Jessie Burgwitz), called "The Pink of Perfection", where all that the heart of maid can desire may be had in abundance. This scene, which is all in pink, is a very fine piece of stage painting. The first part ends with the departure of Cinderella for the ball in a grand electrically lit carriage, drawn by two diminutive ponies.

The Grand Entrance to the Palace, with which the second part opens, is also a very fine stage piece. Here Dandini (Miss Emmeline Orford) sings with great effect a patriotic song entitled "The little bit of cloth I love". An interesting feature is the arrival of a number of guests representing characters in well-known plays, each of which is impersonated by a little girl. Here also Ballahooley (Mr George Nash) sings Herbert Shelley's "Regimental Belle", the drilling of six young ladies dressed in khaki uniforms being excellent. After the flight of Cinderella the scene changes to the Prince's Audience Chamber, where the fitting of the slipper takes place, and the owner of it is discovered, the pantomime ending with the magical disappearance of the Royal Palace and the revelation of the fairy's betrothal gift, a grand diamond tiara, brilliantly outlined with with electric lamps. [...]
The Era, 29/12/1900

1901

MISS WINIFRED HARR, who is playing Dick Whittington in the pantomime at the Coronet, Notting Hill, received a letter on her arrival at the theatre on the evening of the 3rd inst, the writer of which threatened to kill her on the following day, and to similarly treat all the leading actresses in London. The letter was signed "Jack the Ripper", the writing being crude and juvenile. Miss Hare attaches no importance to the epistle.
The Era, 19/1/1901

ONE of the decorations in the Palace scene in the pantomime of Cinderella *at the Pavilion Theatre, Mile End, is a festoon of artificial flowers which stretches from side to side of the stage. The scene opens with a duet between Korodian, the Evil Spirit (Mr Arthur Laurence) and Fairy Lightheart (Miss Kate Cohen), and while this was being sung on Thursday night the centre portion of the festoon was seen to be on fire. With admirable presence of mind the two occupants of the stage continued their duet as if nothing out of the way had happened; the festoon was at once*

lowered, and several of the stage hands, rushing on, speedily put out the fire. Some of the sparks having alighted on the border above, that was also lowered, and all further risk of the flames spreading was thus prevented. The audience behaved excellently, showing no signs of panic, and the incident, alarming though it was, only interrupted for a few moments the enjoyment of those present.
The Era, 2/2/1901

MUCH to the regret of the kiddies Charles Lauri is not to play in town this Christmas. His services have been secured for the Grand Theatre, Leeds, where will be produced a pantomime version of the story of Robin Hood. *The "Garrick of animal mimes" will play the part of a poodle to a band of outlaws, and there will be several novel scenes, including that of a dogs' home. It was at the Lyceum a few years ago that the popular Charles played a collie, whose death caused so much sorrow amongst the little ones that they petitioned for the animal's recovery, and in obedience to their request he survived his heroic struggle against the forces of pantomime evil.*
The Era, 7/12/1901

Tyne Theatre, Newcastle-on-Tyne
Little Red Riding Hood

[…] THE first scene represents the Lair of the Wehr-wolf (T E Ryan), and forms a fitting background for the appearance of Maledictus (Miss Dorothy Cameron), the Wehr-Wolf (Mr Harry Lupino) and attendant demons. We are quickly transported to a corn field, a truly charming pastoral picture by T E Ryan, the golden grain contrasting well with the green of the fields and foliage. Here we are introduced to the greater number of the characters, to wit, Prince Jasper (Miss Lilian Dickinson), Lady Dorothy (Miss Nell Gwynne), May (Miss Nelly Hardinge), Jack (Miss Leo Grieve), Squire Bantam (Mr Will Johnson), Simon (Mr George Mozart), Dame Margery (Mr Dan Crawley), Sniffle and Snaffle (the Griffiths Brothers), the Permane Brothers as two French valets, and Rats (Master Harry Lane), nearly all of whom appear with song or dance or both, and are soon on the best of terms with the audience. An umbrella dance by the Coppi Troupe of dancers with rain and rainbow effects is distinctly novel and admirably executed. In this scene we are given a foretaste of the great trouble and care which has undoubtedly been bestowed on the dressing of the production throughout. The villagers are daintily attired, and in the harvest home procession with which the scene closes the groupings and colours are all in the best of taste. Scene three depicts the Squire's stables (T F Dunn). The Squire would seem to be an impecunious owner of a racehorse, which has just died, and some entertaining fun is forthcoming from the Squire's grooms, the Brothers Griffiths, in their efforts to improvise a substitute. An idyllic scene is disclosed to view when the curtain rises on the fourth scene, a glade in the woods (T E Ryan), where a rustic bridge across a stream occupies the centre of the stage, surrounded by leafy trees, with a waterfall in the distance. The delightful picture is complete when Red Riding Hood, in the person of Miss Phyllis Beadon, attired in the traditional costume of the part, makes her appearance across the bridge. Scene the fifth is a a representation of the Blackberry Brake, by T E Ryan, and thence a transition takes place to another example of this scenic artist's clever work in Little Red Riding Hood's Dream, a veritable triumph of harmonious colouring. The Grasshoppers' Feast and the Butterflies' Ball form the subject of the dream, and a more gorgeous spectacle has seldom, if ever, been seen on the "Tyne" stage. The costumier's art is here revealed in its highest form, as butterflies and insects of all descriptions make their appearance and crowd the stage with a mass of glowing colour, endless in its variety and brilliant in the extreme. A monster butterfly in crystal is lowered from above, and when electrically illuminated the magnificent tableau is complete, and the curtain descends on the first portion of the pantomime.

The Squire's Garden (T E Ryan) forms the opening scene after the interval, and some quaint costumes are here worn by the participators in the garden party, while a comic auction supplies diversion in scene eight, the Squire's Library, by T F Dunn. The same artist is responsible for the succeeding scene, the Cottage in the Wood, one of the prettiest stage pictures of the pantomime. A grand pageant, Our United Kingdom (T E Ryan), brings the pantomime to a close. The pomp and splendour of this picture increase with every moment, until finally Britannia is disclosed seated upon a globe of crystal at the extreme back of the stage, and the curtain falls upon a further triumph of spectacular display.

The company engaged is a good one all round. Mr George Mozart at once established himself as a warm favourite. He is by no means so "simple" as his initial appearance in bucolic attire as Simon would suggest, and a pleasant wit stands him in good stead throughout the evening. The business in which he portrays with much humour and truth various style of walking prove him to have the imitative faculty strongly developed, while his further business with the kettledrum, and his sketch illustrative of the course of true love, in which he plays the clarionet and utilises for his purpose the opening bars of well-known songs, are all productive of much mirth and enjoyment. […] A most excellent animal impersonator in Mr Harry Lupino undertakes the part of the Wolf, and his dances, in some of which he is assisted by Master Harry Lane, the Squire's puppy, are characterised by much agility. The Griffiths Brothers are responsible for some of the heartiest laughter heard during the performances. In their roles as Sniffle and Snaffle they seize every convenient opportunity for the introduction of excruciatingly funny business, notably their lion-taming and wrestling acts, which, although not absolutely new, still go as well as ever. […]

Drury Lane
Blue Beard

[…] INSTEAD of the usual demon cave opening, we have a Dutch landscape, whose glooms and shadows form an effective contrast to the brilliancy of the spectacle which follows in the Slave Market. With an Oriental seascape in the background, a vast crowd of soldiers, citizens, and slaves is marshalled; and here Fatima (Miss Julia Franks) enters on a large elephant, a marvel of property-making. In the next scene, on board a liner, a panorama gives the effect of the vessel's progress; and then bursts on the bewildered spectator the vision of the Land of Ferns, a lovely glade where frogs, parraquets, cockatoos, and other creatures form a picture of the most attractive and agreeable character. This scene alone would make the fortune of an ordinary annual; but it is nothing to what follows, when, after sets representing Blue Beard's Castle and the Chamber of Curiosities have been admired, a superb Fan Ballet concludes the second part of the pantomime. No description could do justice to this marvellous spectacle. An immense fan shuts off the back of the stage, and the ribs at the centre are removed to allow of the successive entrances of fair contingents carrying the fans of every nation, from the frivolous French to the simple South Sea Islanders. The colour and radiance of this scene are inexpressible in words; it must be seen to be appreciated. The great triumph of the third part is the set in which a tall winding staircase occupies the "middle distance", illuminated by hundreds of electric lamps. There is, of course, the usual magnificent tableau at the conclusion, in which the Grigolati troupe rest on tiptoe on the points of crystal stars, illuminated from within and revolving rapidly. […]

Much was expected of Mr Dan Leno, who has to "live up" to his famous performance before the King; and more than had been hoped for is supplied by this exquisitely eccentric comedian, whose Sister Anne is certainly one of the funniest things ever seen in pantomime. The part is ingeniously contrived to supply Mr Leno with opportunities. Sister Ann, in this version, is bought by Blue Beard as an "odd lot" when purchasing his wives of the mercenary Mustapha (Mr Fred Emney[4]); and all through the piece she forces her undesired endearments on her husband, the burlesque of sentimentality being irresistable. No one who sees Mr Leno, in a "check" gown of the most modern cut, reclining in sinuous attitudes by the side of Blue Beard while they discuss the intricacies of Bradshaw[5], can help being amused; and as for "Dan's" coon song with chorus, it simply sends the house into screams of delighted laughter. Mr Leno is a good dancer, and has all the tricks of the trade at his fingers' – or rather his toes' – ends; and his caricature of the corybantic efforts of the up-to-date "coon" singer is supremely ludicrous and most cleverly reminiscent of the original. Then he has a skit on the "cigar scene" in *Sherlock Holmes*[6]. This is done in the prison set in the second act, where Mr Leno and Mr Herbert Campbell – whom it is difficult to disassociate from his partner in drollery – play an extravagantly funny game at ping-pong, using frying-pans for racquets and potatoes for balls. These are the salient points of Mr Dan Leno's performance as Sister Anne, and he will, we believe, work up the burlesque of the Play scene in *Hamlet* into something even more fully diverting than at present. As it is, the spectacle of Sister Anne wrapping herself up in a bearskin rug, and waiting for the cry of "Lights!" to come from her conscience-stricken spouse, is sufficiently funny to create laughter long and loud.

Mr Herbert Campbell's bluff and burly style is exactly suited to the character of the callous Blue Beard, and his appearance, especially in a German costume of the Middle Ages, is deliciously quaint and comical. He forms a very striking and prominent feature of the production, and only wants one or two really remarkable songs to complete his triumph.

We must bracket with Messrs Leno and Campbell Messrs Queen and Lebrun, who play a baby elephant, called "Trunko" on the programme, but addressed by Sister Anne, more lovingly, as "Doodah". There is meaning is every wag of Doodah's tail, and in every wave of his trunk, and in every wink of his eye. It is impossible to help laughing at the difficulties and embarrassments of Doodah's mistress, and at the absurd antics of the eccentric animal. […]

There are two scenes in the merry harlequinade – On the Pier and the Barrack Yard, both painted by E Nicholls. The first of these only was given on Thursday; and if the second is as amusing the harlequinade at Drury Lane this year will be a thing to wait for. The Pantaloon and the Clown take possession of a coffee-stall, and are greatly troubled by the dishonesty and vagaries of their customers. Finally, a tall, thin, and starved-looking vocalist takes up a position on the pier, and begins to warble "Queen of My Heart". Nothing will remove this obstinately persevering singer. The Clown (Mr Whimsical Walker[7]) and the Pantaloon (Mr Charles Ross) belabour him vigorously with boards, but all in vain. He is there, and there he remains till the fall of the curtain, still chanting Alfred Cellier's serenade. […]

The Era, 28/12/1901

Dan Leno as Sister Ann

> IT is marvellous that in such a vast and complicated production as that of Blue Beard at Drury Lane Theatre so few mishaps should occur, and those of such an unimportant nature as only to add to the general hilarity and enjoyment. On Thursday night Mr Fred Zola, in his energetic slapping of his own face, knocked his false nose off into the wings; and Queen and Le Brun, in doing a tumble inside the skin of the baby elephant, lost connection, and one of the performers was distinctly seen grappling in his shirt sleeves to regain hold of his companion. The first incident was scarcely noticed, and the second evoked a sympathetic and encouraging round of applause from the good-natured audience.
> *The Era, 28/12/1901*

Woolwich Soldiers' Theatre
Little Tom-Tit
[…] THE plot of *Little Tom-Tit* is sufficiently simple, as delineated by Mr John Addison. Two fairies, Heartsease and Primrose, were chatting together after sunset about the mortals whom they loved, and how they might help them to be happy, when suddenly they heard a sound as of a child crying, and looking about soon found a bonny baby boy lying in a bird's nest and weeping bitterly. Just as Primrose was going to take it in her arms Nettlesting, a wicked magician, appeared, and angrily commanded them to let the child alone. After further parleying, the wizard derides the fairies' claim to endow the infant with their own ethereal power, and reminds them that the secret of its birth remains with him, and that he witholds it from them. The fairies, of course, resolve to protect the baby and place it in the care of a worthy armourer, who, one night, finds it on the threshold of his house with a bag of guineas beside it, and a letter telling him that if he cared for the child, whom he was to call Tom-Tit, it would grow up to be a wonderful blessing to him.

The story is subsequently concerned with the working out of the promise of the letter. The hero becomes a gallant youth, and in the course of his adventures bravely attempts to rescue a captive maiden from the clutches of the cruel Baron Felintent. The Fairy Heartsease comes to his aid, and Tom, who is, of course, in love with the unfortunate maiden, the Princess Floraletta, attacks the Baron in his castle, smites him with his sword, and carries off his inamorata. Further troubles, however, are in store for the hero. The truculent Baron appears at the village sports, at which Tom and the Princess are present, seizes the letter, and carries her off. The climax is reached in Tom and his friends besieging the Baron's Castle, which they take by storm, and, amidst fire and thunder, Floraletta is restored to her lover's arms, and the Baron and Nettlesting, and all the powers of evil, are overthrown.

The unravelling of the plot affords considerable scope for the display of pantomime effect and exciting scenes. All ends happily, of course. Tom, it is discovered, is really the son of a Baron, whose steward Felintent used to be. When the child's father died the bad steward plotted to destroy the infant. Nettlesting took the latter and placed it in a bird's nest, where the two fairies had found it. His gentle birth being proved by demonstration, Tom is in a position to marry the Princess, and all ends merrily amid frolic and festivity in Floraletta's Palace. [...]

Dame Steelhard, wife of the armourer, by whom Tom is taught his trade, is a prominent factor in the plot, and is represented by a lady, Miss Nellie Wallace[8], who may be described as Dan Leno and Louie Frear rolled into one. Indeed, it would have been hard to find a male exponent who would have done ampler justice to the humour of the part. [...]

The scenery, as we have already indicated, in remarkably artistic, and the management have spared neither pains nor expense in the matter of dresses, of which some 350 varieties are presented in the course of the twelve scenes. The siege of the Baron's Castle is a very humorous affair, in which combatants, dressed half in Highland costumes and half in khaki, are engaged. A Maxim gun goes off like a policeman's rattle, and amid a scene of wild and fantastic fun the Castle is stormed and eventually blown up. In a scene representing a charming woodland glade, there is a capital display of old English sports, carried out by skilled executants, and there is a procession in old time costumes, which makes an effective show. A striking feature of the pantomime is the wonderful performance by ten flying ladies who perform all kinds of feats in mid-air. The ballet mistress, Blanche Mai, who directs this talented band of performers, executes a wonderful feat, and ascends in a mushroom-shaped contrivance to a considerable height, and then dives head first through to the stage. Other lady fliers, dressed as butterflies, ascend from the stage, high over the auditorium, midway to the dress circle, and scatter flowers amongst the audience, then join hands, turn round, and fly back to the stage. [...]
The Era, 28/12/1901

1902

THE Marquis of Anglesey[9] *did a butterfly dance in his pantomime of* Aladdin, *which has been running at the "Gaiety Theatre, Anglesey Castle", under the direction of his lordship. The Marquis, who plays the Vizier, is richly adorned with brilliants. Miss Mavis Hope and Miss Julia Kent are in the cast.*
The Era, 11/1/1902

Lord Henry Paget, 5th Marquis of Anglesey, in pantomime costume

> **SOUVENIRS AT THE CAMDEN**
> The London staff of the British Goldsmiths' Company paid their annual visit to the Camden Theatre last Tuesday, and greatly enjoyed the successful pantomime of Dick Whittington. A tasteful souvenir was presented by the company to each member of the audience in the shape of a pendant medallion portrait of the late Queen Victoria mounted in a 9-carat gold rim. At the beginning of the second part of the pantomime, in answer to a continued and enthusiastic call, Mr E G Saunders came forward and said – "Ladies and gentlemen, I wish to thank you for your visit tonight, and also, on behalf of a large part of the audience, for the very handsome souvenir presented by your company to every visitor to the theatre this evening. I have had a large experience of theatrical souvenirs, but never have I seen such a magnificent one given away in any London playhouse. I can remember Mr Penley's gift of silver match-boxes, and Mr G Edwardes' presenting a complete musical score. I also remember one of the papers forecasting that the next thing would be a piano for every playgoer. I had the pleasure of meeting Mr Tree tonight, and showing him our souvenir, and he was simply amazed at its value. I think you will agree with me that he has himself given some very fine souvenirs at Her Majesty's. I only hope that the next time the British Goldsmiths wish to patronise a pantomime they will select the Camden again. It has always been my ambition to make this theatre second to none in North London, and I hope always to maintain its present high standard. I think I cannot do better now than call for three hearty cheers for the British Goldsmiths' Company."
>
> OFFERINGS in the shape of fruit and vegetables of all descriptions are a favourite method with an audience on special occasions to show its appreciation of popular pantomime comedians, but when these take the form of oranges, turnips, &c, hurled with considerable force from pit and gallery, the humour of the proceeding is not very apparent. On Tuesday night at the Palace Theatre, Newcastle, during a benefit performance to Little Ganty, the audience was most demonstrative, and a turnip which was thrown from the gallery struck Mr Harry Evans, a popular member of Mr Pitt Hardacre's company, on the abdomen with such force that he was laid prostrate, and had to be carried from the stage. It is feared that he has ruptured a blood vessel, and on Wednesday he was unable to appear.
> *The Era, 1/2/1902*

The Britannia
King Krooked

[…] THE action opens in the Public Square, Rum Tum (scene one), with the entrance of Prince Lucky (Miss Lily Sharplin), Margery Daw (Miss Marie Brian), a country girl with whom Lucky has flirted, and who is now following him disguised as his valet; the Count de Pimple (Mr Harry Pleon), an impecunious nobleman on his travels, and his attendant, Dumdum (Mr Barry Lupino). Pimple immediately claims acquaintance with King Funnian the Fifth (Mr Ernest Heathcote) on his arriving with his two gushing daughters, the Princesses Lily (Mr James Dunlop) and Dulcie (Mr Fred Lawrence), attended by the Lord High Everything, Goldstick (Mr Fred Hone), and the secret police, Pinch and Push (Messrs Pete and Juno), to preside at the drawing of the Royal lottery. The hero at this point arrives in the form of Prince Paragon (Miss Kittee Rayburn), and here, following the orthodox rule, he meets the heroine, the King's youngest daughter, Princess Beauty (Miss Gipsy Woolf), visiting the city against her father's wish.

Disturbed by the return of the Royal party, Beauty hurriedly departs, but is met by the evil spirit, Malignant (Mr Edward Leigh), who in revenge for a fancied slight at her father's hands, induces her to accompany him to The Depths of the Crater (scene two), and to release from the solid rock in which he has been entombed as the punishment for his own misdeeds, the monster, King Krooked (Mr George Lupino). The task accomplished, Krooked, fascinated by Beauty's charms, forces his unwelcome attentions on her, but Paragon, who is naturally at hand, intervenes, and bears Beauty away, leaving Krooked vowing vengeance.

News of the Prince's arrival reaching King Funnian in The Royal Dressing Room (scene three), he decides to give a ball, which accordingly takes place in The Grand Hall of the Palace (scene four|), where Lily and Dulcie make determined efforts to secure partners, and Dumdum finds a sweetheart in the Royal slavey, Cinders (Miss Eva Hope Pleon). Paragon and Beauty meet again, but their joy is of short duration. Malignant and Krooked appear upon the scene, and Krooked makes a claim for Beauty's hand, but, being refused, carries her off, leaving Paragon in despair.

Beauty's whereabouts, however, are discovered by Dumdum in The Royal Museum (scene five), whither Krooked comes to obtain, with Malignant's aid, a magic ring, which has the power to rid him of his distorted form. Dumdum conveys the information to Paragon, who determines to proceed to Beauty's rescue, but finds an unexpected rival in Pimple, and a desperate chariot race then ensues, in which Paragon emulates Ben-Hur and is victorious, but to no purpose.

Dumdum being discovered preparing Beauty for the attack to be made on King Krooked's Castle (scene six), is transformed into an ape by Krooked, who then escapes with Beauty, leaving the castle to fall an empty prize into the attacking party's hands.

The Royal party returns, foiled in their plans, to The Village Avenue (scene seven), but Fortune finds the lovers a friend in the Fairy Queen Crystal (Miss Ivy Dawn), who reveals herself to Beauty in The Haunt of the Fairies (scene eight), where the magic sword is prepared for Paragon, and a grand flying ballet takes place, introducing Mlle Jennie Mills in her famous Danse Lumeneuse; the scene terminating with a wonderful change from The Land of Virgin Ice to The Regions of Eternal Fire, with a volcanic eruption and flow of golden lava.

Lily and Dulcie resort to a new method of obtaining lovers in The Royal Menagerie (scene nine), where also Margery reveals her sex and wins Lucky's love; and Paragon liberates Dumdum in his monkey form from the cage in which he has been bound, earning thereby his eternal gratitude and Crystal's favour, and penetrating, guided by the monkey, to Krooked's retreat, The Ruined Abbey (scene ten). Beauty is rescued, and a wonderful trap scene and phantom fight takes place, which ends in Dumdum's restoration to his human form and the destruction of Krooked.

King Funnian makes a last attempt to obtain funds by cashing a forged note in The New Bank (scene eleven), but escapes punishment; and with Lily and Dulcie finding prospective husbands at last in Pimple and Goldstick, and complete happiness assured to Paragon and Beauty, the story reaches a fitting conclusion in the grand transformation (scene twelve), entitled The Treasures of the Sea, painted by Mr Davies Massey. […]

Drury Lane
Mother Goose

[…] THE first stage picture is the Ruined Belfry. Here the Demon (Mr Alec Davidson) causes to be hatched from immense eggs all manners of evils, and sends them forth to annoy and injure the world. The set, Mother Goose's Cottage, is a pretty rural bit; and here Mother Goose (Mr Dan Leno) enters in a donkey cart, which is overturned by a motor-car. The altercation which follows is spirited, and suggests the energetic and eccentric nature of the "heroine" of the pantomime. More troubles are in store for her. Her landlord, the local mayor (Mr Fred Emney), calls for his rent; and, the cash not being forthcoming, distrains with the aid of a posse of policemen, the whole of the "Mother's" furniture being carried out and placed in the road. While Mother Goose and her children, Jack and Gill, are camping out amongst the ruins, a loud quacking is heard, and it is discovered that a curious goose who has paid Mother Goose a visit has laid a golden egg. This relieves the lady from her difficulties, and opens vistas of great wealth as long as the bird continues to "lay". We next find her and her family – including a pretty general servant named Gretchen – in a hall of gold, in which the precious metal is "everywhere". The blunders and absurdities of the elderly parvenu are very amusing; but eventually the Demon enters, and, denouncing the vulgar display around him, invites all to his tasteful Palace of Fantasy, where a brilliant ballet concludes the first part of the pantomime.

The second commences with an excruciatingly droll caricature of a fox-hunting "meet", with muzzled hounds and other wild absurdities. Mother Goose's only desire now is to be beautiful; and she learns that to become so she has but to bathe thrice in a certain Magic Pool in the mountains. Thither she repairs, and the desired alteration in her appearance is effected. She becomes young and comely, but finds the result disappointing, and in the last "part" goes to the Wishing Gate and begs for her pristine plainness to be restored. Her prayer is granted; but the Magic Goose disappears, and all the principals go to Gooseland in search of it. The country of King Goose is elaborately represented, the "goosey" population being shown engaged in various occupations, including "mixed bathing". Here Mother Goose recovers the magic bird, and her former prosperity is restored to her, her daughter Jill marrying a certain Colin, while her son Jack pairs off with Gretchen.

Then comes the grand transformation scene, and the pantomime concludes with a delightful harlequinade, full of the riotous fun and frolic which tradition has assigned to this class of entertainment. […]

As usual, it is hopeless to endeavour to give any idea, in mere printed words, of the brilliancy of the ballets and stage pictures in the Drury Lane pantomime. Comelli's designs for the costumes are simply exquisite. One lovely colour effect succeeds another, one bevy of beautifully dressed dancers is followed by a second "crowd", until the eye is bewildered by the *embarrass* of artistic richness. Among the "points" of the pantomime, however, may be reckoned a dance in long skirts, which, with their *lingerie*, are held up and very gracefully handled by their fair wearers, and a magnificent set of costumes, which are embroidered in peacock's feather patterns – a detail which shows, at least, that Mr Collins is superior to ordinary theatrical superstitions. There is also a troupe of dashing female trumpeters, who actually play on the shining instruments they carry. […]

Mr Dan Leno is always irresistible as an elderly female in humble life. His insight into the manners and customs of the feminine working-class is marvellous, and his knowledge of their vocabulary is extensive and peculiar. Mr Leno is delightful as the elderly, careworn Mother Goose. The difficulties of the poor woman are made screamingly funny; and whether she is arguing with the landlord about the rent, abusing a couple of motor-carists, or flaunting in gay attire and regretting that she has so many beautiful things underneath that she can't show, this Mother Goose is laughter-provoking in the extreme. The burlesque of beauty after Mr Leno has bathed in the Wishing Well and has become lovely in face and feature, is most amusing, and the song sung by Mr Leno, which we suppose is called "The wasp and the hard-boiled egg", makes the audience laugh almost to hysteria. The whole house rings, too, with shouts of merriment when Mother Goose, in riding habit and hat, puts a spotted "property" horse through some of the best-known performances of the circus-ring. Whenever Mr Leno is on the stage the house is richly amused, and it is safe to say that by the time he has got in all his "gags" the pantomime will be doubly diverting.

Miss Marie George as Gretchen undoubtedly won some of the highest honours of the production. Miss George is dainty and "cute" in a remarkable degree, and in her Dutch headdress and short skirts looks very quaint and winning. Her song "I don't want to be a lady" is encored again and again; her dancing is full of agility and vivacious grace; and her facial expression is very amusing and eloquent indeed. As the servant, who is "one of the family", Miss George made one of the greatest successes of the evening.

There was something so comical in the very appearance of Mr Herbert Campbell in the garb of a fat boy of the early eighties, that to see him was to smile. He made the most of the part, and his dry jokes were received with hearty cachinations. Mr Campbell has not, in this pantomime, any of those strikingly successful songs with which he usually embellishes his Christmas creations; but doubtless, later on, he will introduce a ditty which will "take the town". [...]
The Era, 3/1/1903

Dan Leno as Mother Goose by Tom Browne

1903

A STRIKING NOVELTY *is being used by the London Hippodrome to advertise the very successful pantomime* Dick Whittington. *A number of men parade the streets nightly wearing tall silk hats. At a given signal, by some unseen means, the crowns of the hats lift up and display a brightly illuminated advertisement. This unique novelty arouses great interest, and at the same time causes considerable amusement to the large numbers of playgoers and others by whom it is seen.*
The Era, 24/1/1903

MR FRED FARREN *is the Louis Wain of the stage. His performance of Dick Whittington's Cat, at the Hippodrome, is the perfection of detail in "business" and makeup. The former has been studied by Mr Farren from real animals, and the latter, from the pneumatic tail to the skilfully painted eyelids, is one of the best ever seen. His catskin is all made of hair on a silk foundation, and hardly weighs two pounds. Mr Farren – no connection of the famous Farren family of actors – has been on the stage for seventeen years, having made his debut in the part of a frog at Drury Lane. After that he went on tour, playing a waif in* Human Nature *for five years, with an annual "holiday" at Christmas in pantomime.*
The Era, 31/1/1903

MISS FLORENCE LAURI, who plays the title-role so daintily in Cinderella *at the Theatre Royal, Plymouth, has been presented by the officers of the 1st Warwickshire Regiment with a magnificent full-sized floral model of a Maxim gun. This time last year the Warwicks were stationed at a place in South Africa where Miss Lauri was performing.*
The Era, 7/2/1903

A LEEDS theatrical landlady was the plaintiff, on the 20th inst, at the Leeds County Court in a case in which £8 15s was claimed for five weeks' rent of apartments from Harry Tate, lately appearing in the pantomime of Aladdin, *at the local Theatre Royal. He resisted the claim partly because, as he alleged, he had ordered soles for breakfast, when a cod "a yard and a quarter long" was served, so that it might do for breakfast, dinner, and supper. It was also pleaded that a rice pudding, which had been partly eaten by the plaintiff's family, was served in a small bucket, that the furniture of the rooms had been substituted by articles of an inferior nature, and, further, that the house was draughty. The plaintiff gave a general denial to the defendant's allegations, and his Honour Judge Greenhow gave judgement in her favour, holding that there was not sufficient ground for relinquishing the apartments.*
The Era, 28/2/1903

*HOW theatrical things change! Walking down the Strand this week we met a line of sandwich-men carrying boards with the inscription "*Humpty-Dumpty, *produced at Drury Lane this Christmas. Booking-office now open." What would the playgoers of the last generation have thought of taking seats for a Christmas pantomime early in October?*
The Era, 17/10/1903

Royal County Theatre, Kingston-upon-Thames
Goody Two Shoes

[…] THOUGH entitled *Goody Two Shoes*, Mr Peter Davey hit upon the happy idea of intermingling with the story the romantic legend of Lady Godiva, and the result is a bright, tuneful, and mirthful pantomime, with a consecutive story full of interest. And the great feature of all the Kingston pantomimes, namely, the frequent appearance in it of a crowd of happy children, has been well attended to this year, a score of these little ones taking part in a number of choruses and pretty dances.

The first scene in the pantomime is Dame Durden's Moral Tea Shop in Coventry. The dame (Mr J G Taylor Jr) is an elderly lady whose husband had deserted her shortly after marriage, and who finds a difficulty in keeping the wolf from the door. Her tea shop is much resorted to by the young apprentices of Coventry and the maidens of the town, who enjoy themselves a good deal with singing and dancing. Goody (Miss Lilian Hubbard), with only one shoe, seeks refuge in the tea shop from a crowd of children, but the dame turns her away. Crispin (Miss Mary Thorne), the best of all the apprentices, takes pity on the little girl, and vows not only to make her a pair of charming shoes, but to protect her as well. An unexpected visitor to the tea shop is the powerful Earl of Godiva (Mr George Mudie). He is the dame's missing husband, though she does not know it, and is masquerading as the Earl, who died abroad whilst the pseudo-Earl was acting as his valet. Godiva demands the rent of the tea shop. The dame has not got it, and it is only on condition that she finds Goody and gets her to wait on him in the tea shop that he consents to be lenient. Goody is accordingly brought back and installed as a tea-girl, with the result that customers flock to the shop in shoals. The next scene shows the Baronial Hall at Godiva Castle, where there is a mock trial of various persons for various offences. Amongst them is Crispin, whom Godiva sentences to be flogged, and when Goody pleads for him her prayer is granted on condition she consents

*To ride on horseback through this ancient town
Enrobed in neither kirtle, cloak, nor gown.*

Goody, with great reluctance, consents. The third and last scene of the first part depicts the Market Place of Old Coventry, and we see the passing of Goody, riding a white palfrey through the town. Crispin eventually proves that Earl Godiva is an imposter, and that he himself is the rightful heir. [...]

The Camden
The Forty Thieves

[…] MR JOHNNIE SCHOFIELD, the Ali Baba, has for his "specialities" a peculiar husky voice and the depiction of nervous and irritated imbecility. These assets are fully realised in the motor-car "skit" which he introduces in the second part of the pantomime. The scene is elaborately arranged, minor characters being introduced. The representatives of all these do their work very neatly, the result being most amusing and, so to speak, realistic. First we see Ali Baba, in full motoring costume and accompanied by a *chauffeur*, seated in his car. To an unseen friend, standing "off", he jauntily explains that he has only eighty miles to travel, and that he expects to do the distance in half an hour. Asked if he understands the details of the machine, he gaily boasts that he "knows every cog of it by heart", and if there is anything the matter can tell where it is "by the smell". After travelling a few yards the car stops dead. Ali instantly dismounts, and proceeds to put matters right. He gets more and more irritable as he proceeds, engaging in heated discussion with his *chauffeur* – whom he alludes to as a *chefonnier* – and eagerly consulting a work on motor machinery. An imperturbable boy "loafs" near, driving the motorist almost to frenzy by his remarks and interferences, and giving him a cigarette which explodes like a squib when lighted. Finally, when Ali Baba is on the verge of idiocy, the climax of his trouble is reached, for a stern and solemn country policeman enters, and takes down Ali's name and address in view of a summons for "exceeding the speed limit". The car blows up and the sketch – which kept the audience in roars and screams of laughter during its performance and was rewarded with a hearty round of applause – comes to an end.

Royal Theatre, Newcastle-on-Tyne
Santa Claus, Junior

[…] THE Workshop of Santa Claus (Mr J O Stewart) forms the opening scene, and we find that venerable gentleman, in view of advancing years, desirous of discovering a successor to undertake his arduous, but kindly, mission; and the choice falls on his young hopeful, Santa Claus, junior (Miss Madge Vincent), who, accompanied by Jack Frost (Miss Blanche St Leger), is sent to earth to gain some knowledge of the world and its inhabitants, and thus enable him to discriminate in the distribution of the unlimited gifts at his disposal.

At the Treaty Port of Yokohama, then, Santa Claus, Junior, commences his wanderings on Christmas Day, and here he falls in love with Mimosa (Miss Lucie Caine), a Japanese flower-seller, but who in reality is an English girl, who has been stolen from her home when a child by the rascally Hang High (Mr George F Black). Kow Chow (Mr W H Rawlins), the Governor of Yokohama, claims Mimosa for his bride, but she escapes with young Santa Claus. They are pursued by Kow Chow, together with his servant, Wim-Wom (Mr Horace Mills), and O Mama Wan (Mr J J Dallas), nurse to See-Mee (Miss Fanny Dango), the Governor's niece, and other characters, among whom is Timothy Combes (Mr Walter Groves), an English detective, sent out to discover the whereabouts of the missing English girl, and such is the extent of their wanderings that we find ourselves at such far-distant points as the Rialto at Venice, a Burmese desert, and Lorenzo Marquiz, until finally we reach the Realms of Santa Claus himself, where the quest is concluded, and the Wedding of Santa Claus with Mimosa is celebrated with fitting pomp and ceremony.

From this description it will be seen to what an illimitable extent the production lends itself to a varied spectacular display, and the opportunity has been taken advantage of with magnificent results. The treaty port of Yokohama is a cleverly designed set, and the picture of the Japanese port basking in the Eastern sun, and peopled with its crowds of inhabitants in all manner of quaint and tasteful garb, could not well be surpassed for picturesque effect. In the Glade of a Million Blossoms we have a fairy scene in which the title is realised to the full, and here takes place a ballet of roses, wherein the dresses worn by the dancers are remarkable for their elegance and originality of design, and the tableau when fully developed created much enthusiasm. Later on, there is a further variety in the dresses when we are transported to Venice, but again these are characterised by the same good taste and discrimination which makes the production throughout, and the Carnival ballet forms a joyous conclusion to the scene. The climax, however, is attained in the stage picture of The Realms of Santa Claus, with its built-up staircase extending away in the distance, and here the denizens of this mysterious abode, sumptuously clad in gleaming white, and bearing symbols and devices of all descriptions, crowd the stage in artistic array until the curtain is finally brought down with tremendous *éclat*, the whole series of processions and ballets constituting a perfect paradise of picturesque pageantry. […]

Drury Lane
Humpty Dumpty

[…] GREAT self-congratulations on the part of the audience were caused by the fact that they were not deprived of their Dan Leno. That popular comedian has become almost as strong a tradition as the Drury Lane annual; and the fears that he might not be well enough to appear, and the delight of his recovery, added intensely to the fervour of his welcome. Mr J Hickory Wood and Mr Arthur Collins have compiled a "go-as-you-please" libretto which gives full freedom to "introductions" and complete scope to the scenic artists.

King Sollum (Mr Herbert Campbell) and Queen Spritely (Mr Dan Leno) are a royal couple who live under the dread of deposition; for it is oracularly stated that when a celebrated egg which stands on a wall outside their Palace shall fall, the King will "find a daughter and lose a crown". The as yet undiscovered child is named Blossom (Miss Marie George), and she is courted by Humpty Dumpty (Miss Louise Willis) and Rudolph (Miss Ruth Lytton). Then a certain magic ring comes into the story, and it is "sent" by Humpty Dumpty to the bottom of the sea. The principal characters go in search of the ring, appearing eventually in a wrecked and dishevelled condition. The ring is found, Blossom is untied to her parents and married to Rudolph, and all ends well.

The scenario is arranged – as all practical pantomime "books" should be – to admit of several "big" spectacular scenes. The first of these, painted by R C McCleary, is The Fairy Forest, and here the costumes are very pretty indeed, a notable feature being the harps borne by some of the coryphées, whilst others are attired in fanciful dresses "founded" on the tail-feathers of the curious lyre-bird. The Grigolati Troupe, an indispensable attraction in a Drury Lane pantomime, are much in evidence here; and in the final tableaux they are shown resting in mid-air upon large wreaths of yellow blossoms. The scene in the Royal Kitchen is remarkable for its elaborate realism, oxen roasting whole above some very deceptive flames. The most delightful spectacle in the pantomime, however, is Mr Henry Emden's City of Coral, shown at the end of the second part. The costumes of the ballet in this scene do immense credit to the invention of Comelli, who is responsible for all the dresses in the annual. The transformation scene by Mr Bruce Smith symbolises the Four Seasons of Wedlock, and is a most agreeable combination of colours and forms. The ballets, which have been planned and arranged by Carlo Coppi and John D'Auban, are marvels of intricacies and effects, and how the hundreds of dancers, sometimes bearing encumbrances in the shapes of harps, branches, and other impediments, manage to keep clear of each other is a miracle which can only be explained by the careful and assiduous training which they have received. […]

With three such comedians in the cast as Mr Dan Leno, Mr Herbert Campbell, and Mr Harry Randall, *Humpty Dumpty* is assured of the plentiful supply of the comic element. Mr Leno's Queen Spritely is a mincing, "young-old" lady, with an almost apologetic air – somewhat resembling the Parisian caricatures of the "Mees Anglaise". One of the most amusing things in the pantomime is the interview between Mr Leno and Mr Randall as mistress and cook. The Queen comes down into the Kitchen – "my kitchen", as Little Mary calls it – and cross-examines her domestic on her immense outlay in the way of onions and lard. The Cook is highly indignant at being suspected of extravagance; and has, indeed, "an answer to everything". The dialogue between the pair is very diverting indeed, Little Mary's explanations evoking peal after peal of laughter. Mr Leno is also extremely funny in a burlesque game of bridge. The trio of comedians work so constantly together that it is impossible to separate them in discussing their performances. For instance, Mr Leno and Mr Randall "share and share alike" in a scene in which the pair, sitting under a magic tree, find a fruit drop on their heads each time that one of them tells a "tarradiddle". Mr Randall, however, has the stage all to himself for his famous lecture on "Man", which goes as well as ever, and is evidently quite a novelty to most of the patrons of Drury Lane. Mr Herbert Campbell, who makes a most burly and benign monarch – a sort of genial "Farmer George" – gives robust effect to a flamboyant song about "Good Old Joe!" which raises to a high pitch the patriotic sympathies of the audience. [...]
The Era, 2/1/1904

1904

TWO thousand poor children under the age of fourteen years were the guests of the Playgoers' Club at the Grand Theatre, Islington, on Saturday afternoon last, when they witnessed the pantomime of Blue Beard. *Each child received a bag containing a meat pie, piece of cake, an orange, and a packet of sweets, with the message, "The Playgoers' Club wishes you a happy afternoon."*
The Era, 13/2/1904

MISS FLORENCE BATES AND MISS LOTTIE BATES, sisters, who had been performing in the pantomime of Sinbad the Sailor *at a Birkenhead theatre, were returning to their apartments about midnight on the 19th inst when, on approaching the house, they were confronted by a Mr Gilbert, Justice of the Peace for Essex, who pointed a revolver at them and fired two shots. Miss Lottie Bates escaped injury, but her sister was shot in the wrist, and the second bullet, grazing her, struck a youth named Roberts in the back. A man who had previously noticed Gilbert walking up and down the street approached him, whereupon Gilbert thrust the revolver into his mouth and fired. He fell to the ground, and subsequent examination showed that death must have been instantaneous. Some time ago Gilbert became engaged to Miss Florence Bates. He purchased a public house in London and presented it to her on condition that she left the stage, but eventually she broke off the engagement. In June last Gilbert was charged at Worship Street Police Court with threatening to murder Miss Bates, and was bound over to keep the peace for six months. Latterly he had been following her about the provinces. Miss Bates's wound was dressed at the hospital.*
The Era, 27/2/1904

THE Marquis of Anglesey met his creditors by deputy at the Institute of Chartered Accountants in Moorgate Street on Thursday. His liabilities exceeded £544,000. In Aladdin, *which he produced in the February of 1902, he wore a pink satin doublet and cloak and pink and white tights. Bows of diamonds, big turquoises, emeralds, rubies, and glittering chains of gems were fastened to his doublet, and his helmet was decked with pendant pearls. In the December of the same year, in* Little Red Riding Hood, *in which he represented Bonnie Boy Blue, he glittered with diamonds from head to foot. Last winter he went on tour with* An Ideal Husband, *he enacting Lord Goring. He has also appeared in* A

Runaway Boy, A Royal Divorce, *and* The Marriage of Kitty. *The Marquis can truly state that his productions were "costumed regardless of expense."*
The Era, 4/6/1904

DEATH OF DAN LENO
"A fellow of infinite jest, of most excellent fancy!" Such, indeed, was the late Dan Leno, whose unexpected death on Monday morning will be deeply mourned not only by his brothers and sisters of the music hall profession but by thousands of laughter-lovers who have enjoyed to the full his simple expedients for creating wholesome fun, his timely quip, and his rare fund of eccentricity. The immediate cause of death was heart failure, although for eighteen months the famous jester had suffered from a form of mental disease known to medical experts as general paralysis of the brain. Since his return to the London Pavilion it was painfully apparent to his friends that he was no longer the Leno of former years. Mental concentration was impossible, and it is certain now that the malady, of which the course had been arrested in a most remarkable way, was again making itself felt. On Thursday, the 20th ult, Mr Leno made his last appearance in public at the London Pavilion, and danced with the vigour that invariably characterised his efforts in the days when he claimed championship honours as a step-dancer. He was taken home to his residence, Springfield, Clapham Park, and nursed night and day. He had been confined to his bed for about ten days in charge of two attendants, but his death was not anticipated. He lapsed into semi-consciousness on Sunday, and was unable to recognise his relatives. His attendant on Monday morning noticed a serious change, and at once summoned Dr Vallery and the members of the family. Surrounded by them, he passed away in his wife's arms. Poor Dan Leno! Which one heard on every side when it was known more than a twelvemonth ago that he was suffering from dementia, will be repeated now, for there can be few comedians and few men living who made more unknown friends on the other side of the footlights.
The Era, 5/11/1904

FUNERAL OF DAN LENO
ONLY a few days ago was borne to the grave, at a ripe old age, the veteran who was known far and wide as the "father of the halls", the late Charles Morton. And now the famous little comedian, who was justly proud of the title of "the King's jester", has been laid to rest, at an age when most members of his profession are regarded as still in their prime. The deep regret expressed at the passing away of one who added so much to the innocent gaiety of the patrons of both theatre and music hall has been universal; and that the funeral of Dan Leno on Tuesday should have evoked remarkable demonstrations of the widespread popularity of the deceased comedian was only to be expected. It was a bright, cheerful morning; but as mid-day approached heavy clouds gathered, threatening rain, and a cold wind blew across Clapham Common. Along the main road one perceived a stream of people all hurrying along in the direction of the residence of the deceased comedian. Just at the point where the funeral cortège had to cross the Balham High Road a vast crowd had gathered, and the traffic was entirely suspended while the procession wound its way to the Church of the Ascension, where the first part of the service was conducted. Even the LCC tram cars, which were packed inside and out, were compelled to stop running for the time being. The funeral procession was timed to leave Mr Leno's residence, Springfield, Atkins Road, Clapham Common, at half-past twelve, but for more than a couple of hours previously people began to assemble in the neighbourhood of the house, and, under the control of the police, lined the footpaths which led in the direction of the Church of the Ascension. The body of the late comedian, enclosed in a coffin of solid oak, had been placed in the large drawing-room. The brass plate bore the following inscription:

George Galvin
(Dan Leno)
Who entered into rest Oct 31, 1904
Aged 43

The Era, 12/11/1904

NOTES
1 – "Bobs": The nickname of Field Marshal Frederick Sleigh Roberts (1832-1914), commander of British forces in the Second Anglo-Boer War.
2 – Christiaan Rudolf de Wet (1854-1922): A Boer commander in the second Anglo-Boer War.
3 – A witch's magical spell or trick.
4 – Fred Emney (1865-1917): A star of music hall, musical comedy and pantomime. His son, also named Fred Emney, was a familiar face in British films and on television.

5 – *Bradshaw's Guide* was a compendium of railway timetables.
6 – From *The Era* of 17th August 1901: "For the past two years the drama *Sherlock Holmes* has proved a great success in America. In one scene Mr Gillette as Holmes has to save a young woman from a gang of bullies. He knocks over the lamp, and plants his cigar, the light of which has been guiding the ruffians to their expected prey, in a corner of the room, while he and the lady escape into the Ratcliffe Highway."
7 – Whimsical Walker (1851-1934): A circus clown and pantomime star.
8 – Nellie Wallace (1870-1948): One of the greatest music hall stars, she was known as "The Essence of Eccentricity" and "The Female Dan Leno". She was one of the few women to play the Dame in pantomime.
9 – Lord Henry Cecil Paget, 5th Marquis of Anglesey (1875-1905): An amateur actor and dancer who was declared bankrupt a year before his death, having accumulated debts of £544,000 – the equivalent of approximately sixty million pounds in today's money.

INDEX

A APPLE PIE; or, Harlequin Alphabet (Surrey, 1829): 35
A FROG HE WOULD A-WOOING GO; or, Harlequin, Sleeping Beauty, and the Demons of the Mystic Pool (Elephant and Castle, 1884): 167
ALADDIN (New Prince of Wales' Theatre, Greenwich, 1884): 169
ALADDIN (Drury Lane, 1885): 170
ALADDIN (Theatre Royal, Birmingham, 1889): 183
ALADDIN (Theatre Royal, Gateshead, 1891): 191
ALADDIN (New Theatre, Croydon, 1899): 220
ALADDIN (Theatre Royal, Leeds, 1902): 230
ALADDIN AND THE WONDERFUL LAMP; or, Harlequin and the Forty Thieves and the Flying Horses of Lambeth (Astleys' Amphitheatre, 1874): 129
ANNE BOLEYN; or, Harlequin King Harry and the Miller of the River Dee (City of London, 1856): 108

BABES IN THE WOOD (Theatre Royal, Middlesborough, 1895): 203
BABES IN THE WOOD (Drury Lane, 1897): 208
BABES IN THE WOOD, AND ROBIN HOOD AND HIS MERRY MEN, AND HARLEQUIN WHO KILLED COCK ROBIN? (Surrey, 1888): 178
THE BABES IN THE WOOD (Prince's Theatre, Bradford, 1896): 205
THE BABES IN THE WOOD, BOLD ROBIN HOOD, HARLEQUIN HERNE THE HUNTER, THE MERRY MAID MARIAN, AND THE BIG, BAD, BARON (Queen's Theatre, Manchester, 1886): 173
THE BABES IN THE WOOD; or, Harlequin Maid Marian and Bold Robin Hood (Grand Theatre, Islington, 1898): 214
THE BABES IN THE WOOD; or, Harlequin Robin Hood and his Merry Men (Covent Garden, 1867): 103
BEAUTY AND THE BEAST (Marylebone, 1884): 167
BEAUTY AND THE BEAST (New Theatre, Kingston, 1897): 207
BEAUTY AND THE BEAST (Drury Lane, 1899): 221
BIRDS, BEASTS, AND FISHES; or, Harlequin Natural History (City of London, 1854): 73
BLUE BEARD (Pavilion, 1840): 51
BLUE BEARD (Drury Lane, 1879): 143
BLUE BEARD (Drury Lane, 1901): 224, 225
BLUE BEARD (Grand Theatre, Islington, 1903): 232
BLUFF KING HAL; or, Herne the Hunter and the Miller's Daughter of the River Dee (Victoria, 1868): 108
THE BUTTERFLY'S BALL AND THE GRASSHOPPER'S FEAST; or, Harlequin and the Genius of Spring (Haymarket, 1855): 78

THE CASTLE OF OTRANTO; or, Harlequin and the Giant Helmet (Covent Garden, 1840): 48
CASTLES IN THE AIR; or, Columbine Cowslip (Aquatic Theatre, Sadler's Wells, 1809): 14
THE CHILDREN IN THE WOOD (Theatre Royal, Manchester, 1871): 118
THE CHILDREN IN THE WOOD; or, Harlequin Queen Mab and the World of Dreams (Drury Lane, 1872): 122
CINDERELLA (Temple Opera House, Bolton, 1881): 156
CINDERELLA (Drury Lane, 1883): 165, 166
CINDERELLA (Crystal Palace, 1888): 177
CINDERELLA (Drury Lane, 1895): 201
CINDERELLA (Princess of Wales's, 1898): 212
CINDERELLA (Pavilion, 1900): 222
CINDERELLA (Kingston Theatre, Kingston-upon-Thames, 1900): 222
CINDERELLA (London Hippodrome, 1900): 220
CINDERELLA (Theatre Royal, Plymouth, 1902): 230
CINDERELLA; or, Harlequin and the Fairy Slipper (Drury Lane, 1878): 139

DADDY LONGLEGS; or, Harlequin Merrimac and Mother Carey's Chickens (Britannia, 1884): 169
DICK WHITTINGTON (Prince of Wales Theatre, Birmingham, 1891): 193

DICK WHITTINGTON (Drury Lane, 1894): 198
DICK WHITTINGTON (Coronet Theatre, Notting Hill, 1899): 222
DICK WHITTINGTON (Camden Theatre, 1901): 227
DICK WHITTINGTON (London Hippodrome, 1902): 229
DICK WHITTINGTON AND HIS CAT (Elephant and Castle Theatre, 1894): 197
DICK WHITTINGTON AND HIS CAT (Alexandra Theatre, Sheffield, 1897): 207
DICK WHITTINGTON AND HIS CAT; or, the Demon Rat, the Merchant's Daughter, and the Charity Brat (Surrey, 1889): 181
DICK WHITTINGTON AND HIS TREASURE OF A CAT (Theatre Royal, Manchester, 1870): 113
DICK WHITTINGTON AND HIS WONDERFUL CAT; or, Harlequin Humpty Dumpty and the House of Content in the Realms of Happiness (Pavilion, 1863): 97
DING-DONG-BELL, PUSSY'S IN THE WELL; or, Harlequin Who Killed Cock Robin? (Marylebone, 1866): 101
THE DRAGON OF WANTLEY; or, Harlequin Knight, and the Fire King of the Burning Isle (Birmingham Theatre, 1844): 54

THE ENCHANTED DOVE; or, the Princess, the Poodle, and the Sorceress (Britannia, 1881): 152
THE ENCHANTED PRINCE; or, Harlequin Beauty and the Bears (Standard, 1877): 136
EGYPT 3,000 YEARS AGO; or, Queen Cleopatra – a Dream in the Crystal Palace (Britannia, 1854): 74
EYES, NOSE, AND MOUTH; or, Harlequin Prince Perfect and the Birth of Beauty (Marylebone, 1847): 55

THE FAIR ONE WITH THE GOLDEN LOCKS (Theatre Royal, Manchester, 1866): 102
THE FAIR ONE WITH THE GOLDEN LOCKS; or, Prince Charming, the Giant, and the Long-lost Ring (Surrey, 1891): 191
FAW, FEE, FO, FUM; or, Harlequin Jack the Giant Killer (Drury Lane, 1867): 104
THE FORTY THIEVES (Drury Lane, 1876): 134
THE FORTY THIEVES (Drury Lane, 1898): 213
THE FORTY THIEVES (Camden, 1903): 230
THE FORTY THIEVES AND THE COURT BARBER; or, Harlequin and the Five Tiny Pigs, the Sad Little Prigs, and the Fairies of the Laburnum Lake (Surrey, 1874): 127
THE FORTY THIEVES AND THEIR WONDERFUL CAVE; or, Ali the Woodman and Morgiana the Slave (Surrey, 1888): 179

GISELLE; or, the Phantom Night Dancers (Victoria, 1863): 99
THE GOLDEN BRANCH (Royal Lyceum, 1847): 56
GOODY TWO SHOES (Surrey, 1899): 215
GOODY TWO SHOES (Grand Theatre, Leeds, 1899): 220
GOODY TWO SHOES (Royal County Theatre, Kingston-upon-Thames, 1903): 230
GOOSEY GOOSEY GANDER; or, Harlequin and the Fairy of My Lady's Chamber, Pavilion, 1832): 37
GULLIVER'S TRAVELS; or, Harlequin Billy Taylor and the Good Spirit of Energy (Prince's Theatre, Manchester, 1867): 105
GULLIVER'S TRAVELS THROUGH LILLIPUT, HORSE ISLAND, AND BROBDIGNAG; or, Harlequin Britannia (Astley's, 1854): 72
GUY FAUX; or, the Amazon Queen and Her Sea-girt Isles (Royal Grecian, 1858): 85
GUY OF WARWICK; or, Harlequin and the Dun Cow (Covent Garden, 1841): 51

HARLEQUIN AND ASMODEUS; or, Cupid on Crutches (Covent Garden, 1811): 16
HARLEQUIN AND BLUE BEARD, THE GREAT BASHAW; or, the Good Fairy Triumphant over the Demon of Discord (Princess's, 1854): 76
HARLEQUIN AND COCK ROBIN; or, the Babes in the Wood (Drury Lane, 1827): 30
HARLEQUIN AND COCK ROBIN; or, Vulcan and Venus (Covent Garden, 1829): 34
HARLEQUIN AND FANCY; or, the Poet's Last Shilling (Drury Lane, 1815): 20
HARLEQUIN AND FRIAR BACON; or, the Brazen Head (Covent Garden, 1820): 25
HARLEQUIN AND HUMPO (Drury Lane, 1812): 18
HARLEQUIN AND LITTLE KING PIPPIN; or, the Golden Crown and Goblin of the Apple (Surrey, 1834): 39
HARLEQUIN AND LITTLE RED RIDING HOOD; or, the Wizard and the Wolf (Covent Garden, 1828): 32
HARLEQUIN AND LITTLE TOMMY TUCKER; or, the Little Old Woman Who Lived in a Shoe and had so Many Children She Didn't Know What to do (Princess's, 1863): 96
HARLEQUIN AND MARGERY DAW; or, the Saucy Slut and the See-saw (Adelphi, 1832): 38

HARLEQUIN AND MOTHER BUNCH; or, the Yellow Dwarf (Covent Garden, 1821): 25
HARLEQUIN AND MOTHER GOOSE; or, the Golden Egg (Covent Garden, 1806): 13
HARLEQUIN AND OLD COCKER (Olympic, 1842): 54
HARLEQUIN AND OLD FATHER ÆSOP; or, Little Cock Robin and the Children in the Wood (Sadler's Wells, 1839): 45
HARLEQUIN AND OLD IZAAC WALTON; or, Tom Moore of Fleet-street, the Silver Trout, and the Seven Sisters of Tottenham (Sadler's Wells, 1858): 84
HARLEQUIN AND PADMANOBA; or, the Golden Fish (Covent Garden, 1811): 17
HARLEQUIN AND POOR RICHARD; or, Old Father Time and the Almanac Maker (Sadler's Wells, 1840): 50
HARLEQUIN AND POOR ROBIN; or, the House that Jack Built (Covent Garden, 1823): 29
HARLEQUIN AND PUSS IN BOOTS; or, All the World and His Wife, and the Ogre of Rats' Castle (Sadler's Wells, 1855): 79
HARLEQUIN AND THE DANDY CLUB; or, 1818 (Drury Lane, 1818): 22
HARLEQUIN AND THE ELFIN ARROW; or, the Basket-maker and His Brothers (Queen's, 1831): 38
HARLEQUIN KING PIPPIN; or, the Enchanted Chicken (Victoria, 1859): 89
HARLEQUIN AND THE ENCHANTED FISH; or, the Geni of the Brazen Bottle (Adelphi, 1840): 49
HARLEQUIN AND THE FLYING CHEST; or, Malek and the Princess Shirine (Drury Lane, 1823): 27
HARLEQUIN AND THE MAGIC MARROW-BONE; or, Taffy was a Welshman (Adelphi, 1828): 33
HARLEQUIN AND THE MAGIC TEAPOT; or, Chi-Ki Ski-Hi, King of the Golden Pagodas (Standard, 1849): 59
HARLEQUIN AND THE OGRESS; or, the Sleeping Beauty of the Wood (Covent Garden, 1822): 26
HARLEQUIN AND THE RED DWARF; or, the Adamant Rock (Globe, 1812): 18
HARLEQUIN AND THE SWANS; or, the Bath of Beauty (Covent Garden, 1813): 19
HARLEQUIN AND THE SYLPH OF THE OAK (Covent Garden, 1816): 21
HARLEQUIN AND THE THREE BEARS; or, Little Silverhair and the Fairies (Haymarket, 1853): 69
HARLEQUIN AND TOM THUMB; or, the Seven League Boots (Drury Lane, 1831): 37
HARLEQUIN AND WILLIAM TELL; or, the Genius of the Ribstone Pippin (Drury Lane, 1842): 52
HARLEQUIN BLACK BEARD; or, Dame Trot and Her Comical Cat (City of London, 1863): 98
HARLEQUIN BUTTERCUPS AND DAISIES; or, Great A, Little A, Bouncing B, and the Cat's in the Cupboard and She Can't See (Standard, 1850): 62
HARLEQUIN CHARITY BRAT; or, the Magic Christmas Piece (Royal Grecian Saloon, 1854): 70
HARLEQUIN CHERRY AND FAIR STAR; or, the Green Bird, the Dancing Waters, and the Singing Silver Tree (Princess's, 1852): 67
HARLEQUIN GUY FAWKES (Covent Garden, 1835): 41
HARLEQUIN HORNER; or, the Christmas Pie (Drury Lane, 1816): 20
HARLEQUIN JACK-A-LANTERN; or, the Witch of the Dropping Well (Drury Lane, 1837): 43
HARLEQUIN JACK SHEPPARD; or, the Blossom of Tyburn Tree (Drury Lane, 1839): 44
HARLEQUIN KING PIPPIN; or, the Enchanted Chicken (Victoria, 1859): 89
HARLEQUIN LORD LOVEL; or, Lady Nancy Bell and the Fairies of the Silver Oak (Surrey, 1848): 58
HARLEQUIN MOTHER RED-CAP; or, Merlin and the Fairy Snowdrop (Adelphi, 1839): 45
HARLEQUIN MUNCHAUSEN; or, the Fountain of Love (Covent Garden, 1818): 23
HARLEQUIN PAT AND HARLEQUIN BAT; or, the Giant's Causeway (Covent Garden, 1830): 36
HARLEQUIN, PRINCE ROVER, AND THE PRINCESS TRICKSEY-WICKSEY (Prince of Wales Theatre, Birmingham, 1875): 132
HARLEQUIN RIC RAC, THE GIANT OF THE MOUNTAINS, AND THE GOBLIN GIFT AND THE KINGDOMS THREE; or, the Good Fairy and the Pretty Princess (Grecian, 1867): 103
HARLEQUIN ROKOKO, THE ROCK FIEND: or, Kingdoms Three, the Toad and the Tree (Grecian, 1879): 142
HARLEQUIN SILVER SIXPENCE AND THE GIANT PENNYPIECE (Adelphi, 1837): 42
HARLEQUIN SING A SONG OF SIXPENCE; or, Pocket Full of Rye, Four and Twenty Blackbirds Baked in a Pie (City of London, 1862): 94
HARLEQUIN SPIT-SPITZE, THE SPIDER CRAB; or, the Sprite of Spitzbergen (Grecian, 1875): 130
HARLEQUIN ST GEORGE AND THE DRAGON; or, Old Father Time and the Seven Champions of Christendom (Surrey, 1869): 112
HARLEQUIN WHITE CAT; or, the Princess Blancheflower and Her Fairy Godmothers (Princess's, 1857): 83
HARLEQUIN YELLOW DWARF; or, the King of the Gold Mines (Alexandra Palace, 1875): 131
HARLEQUIN'S VISION; or, the Feast of the Statue (Drury Lane, 1817): 21
HEY DIDDLE DIDDLE; or, Harlequin King Nonsense and the Seven Ages of Man (Drury Lane, 1855): 77

HOP O' MY THUMB; or, Harlequin No-Body, Some-Body, Busy-Body, and the Wicked Ogre with the Seven League Boots (Surrey, 1880): 147
THE HOUSE THAT JACK BUILT (Star Theatre, Wolverhampton, 1887): 176
HUMPTY DUMPTY (Drury Lane, 1903): 231
HUMPTY-DUMPTY; or, Harlequin Yellow Dwarf and the Fair One With the Golden Locks (Drury Lane, 1891): 189

JACK AND JILL (Surrey, 1898): 212
JACK AND JILL AND THE SLEEPING BEAUTY; or, Harlequin Humpty Dumpty (Surrey, 1868): 106
JACK AND JILL; or, Harlequin and the Four Leaved Shamrock (Pavilion, 1854): 74
JACK AND JILL; or, Harlequin King Mustard and the Four-and-Twenty Blackbirds Baked in a Pie (Drury Lane, 1854): 70
JACK AND JILL; or, the House that Jack Built After the Water was Spilt (Surrey, 1883): 165
JACK AND THE BEANSTALK (Drury Lane, 1899): 217
JACK AND THE BEANSTALK (Hastings Pier Pavilion, 1889): 183
JACK AND THE BEANSTALK, AND SEE-SAW MARGERY DAW; or, Harlequin Man in the Moon and the Love Birds of Fairyland (Surrey, 1873): 126
JACK AND THE BEANSTALK; or, Harlequin and the Midwinter Night's Dream (Drury Lane, 1889): 180
JACK AND THE BEAN STALK; or, Harlequin and the Ogre (Drury Lane, 1819): 23
JACK AND THE BEANSTALK; or, Harlequin and the Seven Champions as We've Christened 'em (Covent Garden, 1878): 140
JACK AND THE BEANSTALK; or, Harlequin Leap-year and the Merry Pranks of the Good Little People (Drury Lane, 1859): 86
JACK FROST; or, Goody Hearty (Drury Lane, 1838): 43
JACK IN THE BOX; or, Harlequin and the Princess of the Hidden Island (Drury Lane, 1829): 33
JACK OF HEARTS (West London Theatre, 1899): 216
JACK THE GIANT KILLER (Pavilion, 1885): 172
JACK THE GIANT KILLER (Gaiety, 1878): 138
JACK THE GIANT KILLER; or, Harlequin King Arthur and the Knights of the Round Table (Princess's, 1859): 86

KING FLAME AND QUEEN PEARLYDROP; or, Harlequin Simple Simon (City of London, 1865): 100
THE KING OF THE CARBUNCLES; or, Harlequin Prince Peerless and the Enchanted Beauty of the Diamond Castle (Queen's, 1852): 65
THE KING OF THE GOLDEN SEAS; or, Harlequin Bluecap and the Four Kingdoms, Animal, Vegetable and Mineral (Surrey, 1851): 63
KING SILLYNINNY, WHO SOLD HIS WIFE FOR HALF A GUINEA; or, Harlequin and the Enchanted Princess (Pavilion, 1862): 93
KING KROOKED (Britannia, 1902): 227
KING TRICKEE; or, Harlequin the Demon Beetle, the Sporting Duchess, and the Golden Casket (Britannia, 1887): 174
KNIFE, FORK, AND SPOON; or, Harlequin's Breakfast, Dinner, Tea, and Supper (City of London, 1850): 61

LADY BIRD; or, Harlequin Lord Dundreary (Astley's, 1862): 93
LADY GODIVA; or, St George and the Dragon (Astley's, 1871): 117
THE LAND OF LIGHT; or, Harlequin Gas and the Four Elements, Earth, Air, Fire, and Water (Victoria, 1848): 58
LITTLE BO-PEEP, LITTLE RED RIDING HOOD, AND HOP O' MY THUMB (Drury Lane, 1892): 195
LITTLE BO-PEEP; or, Harlequin and the Girl who Lost her Sheep (Haymarket, 1854): 75
THE LITTLE BOY BLUE; or, the King of the Gold Mine (Pavilion, 1842): 53
LITTLE GOODY TWO SHOES; or, Harlequin and Cock Robin (Drury Lane, 1862): 94
LITTLE MISS MUFFIT (Surrey, 1900): 220
LITTLE PUSS IN BOOTS; or, Harlequin the Cruel Ogre and the Miller's Son (Princess's, 1873): 125
LITTLE RED RIDING HOOD (Theatre Royal, 1867): 106
LITTLE RED RIDING HOOD (Covent Garden, 1873): 127
LITTLE RED RIDING HOOD (Prince's Theatre, Manchester, 1894): 199
LITTLE RED RIDING HOOD (Tyne Theatre, Newcastle-upon-Tyne, 1901): 223
LITTLE RED RIDING HOOD AND HER SISTER BO-PEEP (Theatre Royal, Bradford, 1884): 168
LITTLE RED RIDING HOOD; or, Harlequin Boy Blue, Miss Muffit, the Wolf, and the Bears (Standard, 1882): 158
LITTLE TOM-TIT (Soldiers' Theatre, Woolwich, 1901): 225

THE MAID AND THE MAGPIE (Princess's, 1855): 79

THE MAN IN THE MOON (Britannia, 1892): 194
THE MAN IN THE MOON; or, Harlequin Dog Star (Drury Lane, 1826): 30
THE MAN IN THE MOON; or, the World of Waggery (Strand, 1847): 56
MAY AND DECEMBER; or, Harlequin June and His Magic Tune (Theatre Royal, Halifax, 1858): 85
A MERRY CHRISTMAS; or, Harlequin King Candle and Princess Prettydear, of Taper Land (Standard, 1855): 80
THE MERRY DEVIL OF EDMONTON; or, the Great Bed of Ware (Covent Garden, 1839): 44
MOTHER BUNCH (Marylebone, 1842): 53
MOTHER BUNCH AND THE MAN WITH THE HUNCH; or, the Reeds, the Weeds, the Priest, the Swell, the Gipsy Girl and the Big Dumb Bell (Surrey, 1881): 153
MOTHER GOOSE (Standard, 1896): 204
MOTHER GOOSE (Drury Lane, 1902): 228
MOTHER GOOSE; or, the Queen of Hearts and the Wonderful Tarts (Surrey, 1862): 95
MY SON JACK; or, Harlequin Mother Goose and the Gaping, Wide-mouthed, Waddling Frog (Surrey, 1870): 115

NELL GWYNN; or, Harlequin and the Merrie Monarch and the Orange Girl (Adelphi, 1852): 66
NIX, THE DEMON DWARF; or, Harlequin, the Seven Charmed Bullets, the Fairy, the Fiend, and the Will-o'-the-Wisp (Grecian, 1872): 124

THE OCEAN QUEEN, AND THE KING OF THE RUBY CASTLE (Garrick, 1840): 50
OLD FATHER TIME; or, Harlequin and the Four Seasons (Princess's, 1847): 55
OLD MOTHER HUBBARD AND HER DOG; or, Harlequin and Tales of the Nursery (Covent Garden, 1833): 39
ORANGES AND LEMONS; or, Harlequin and the Bells of St Clement's (Adelphi, 1834): 40

PETER PIPER; or, Harlequin and the Golden Peck of Pepper (Queen's, 1839): 46
PLUM PUDDING AND ROAST BEEF; or, Harlequin Nine Pins and the Card King of the Island of Games (Royal Standard, 1853): 68
THE PRINCE OF THE PEACEFUL ISLANDS; or, Harlequin, the Magic Pearl, the Centaur, and the Fairy Amazon (Sadler's Wells, 1863): 96
PRINCE RIQUET WITH THE TUFT; or, Harlequin and Mother Shipton (Princess's, 1862): 95
PUNCH AND JUDY; or, Harlequin Prince Valiant, Shallabalah; or, the Good Little Fairy of the Wood (Grecian, 1864): 100
PUSS IN BOOTS (Covent Garden, 1877): 137
PUSS IN BOOTS (Garrick, 1899): 215
PUSS IN BOOTS, THE OGRE, THE MILLER, AND KING OF THE RATS; or, the Pretty Princess and Queen of Cats (Surrey, 1882): 161

QUEEN ANNE'S FARTHING AND THE THREE KINGDOMS OF COPPER, SILVER, AND GOLD; or, Harlequin Old King Counterfeit and the Good Fairy of the Royal Mint (Standard, 1858): 85
QUEEN DODO; or, Harlequin Babilo and the Three Wonders (Britannia, 1883): 163
QUEEN LADYBIRD AND HER CHILDREN; or, Harlequin and the House on Fire (Haymarket, 1860): 89

RED RIDING HOOD (Crystal Palace, 1886): 173
RED RIDING HOOD (Theatre Royal, Bradford, 1891): 188
ROBIN HOOD (Lyceum, Sunderland, 1865): 101
ROBIN HOOD (Theatre Royal, Nottingham, 1887): 176
ROBINSON CRUSOE (Covent Garden, 1876): 133
ROBINSON CRUSOE (Stratford Theatre Royal, 1873): 197
ROBINSON CRUSOE (Drury Lane, 1881): 155
ROBINSON CRUSOE (Theatre Royal, York, 1882): 157
ROBINSON CRUSOE (Plymouth Theatre, 1882): 163
ROBINSON CRUSOE (Theatre Royal, Birmingham, 1885): 172
ROBINSON CRUSOE (Lyceum, 1895): 202
ROBINSON CRUSOE (Prince of Wales', Liverpool, 1895): 203
ROBINSON CRUSOE; or, Harlequin and his Man Friday, and the Magic Pearl (Grecian, 1863): 97

SANTA CLAUS (Theatre Royal, Birmingham, 1895): 200
SANTA CLAUS, JUNIOR (Royal Theatre, Newcastle-on-Tyne, 1903): 231
SINBAD THE SAILOR (Her Majesty's Opera House, Aberdeen, 1876): 135
SINBAD THE SAILOR (Metropole Theatre, Gateshead, 1896): 206

SINBAD THE SAILOR (Prince's Theatre, Bristol, 1898): 211
SINDBAD AND THE LITTLE OLD MAN OF THE SEA (Surrey, 1887): 176
SINDBAD THE SAILOR (Covent Garden, 1879): 145
SINDBAD THE SAILOR (Drury Lane, 1882): 160
SINDBAD THE SAILOR (Grand Theatre, Cardiff, 1896): 204
SINDBAD THE SAILOR; or, the Great Roc of the Diamond Valley and the Seven Wonders of the World (Drury Lane, 1863): 98
THE SINGING MOUSE; or, the Giant, the Talking Cat, and Amazonian Queen (Marylebone, 1843): 54
SIR JOHN BARLEYCORN; or, Harlequin Champagne and the Fairies of the Hop and the Vine (Marylebone, 1851): 64
SLEEPING BEAUTY (Holte Theatre, Birmingham, 1878): 147
SLEEPING BEAUTY; or, the Mystic Yellow Dwarf (Tyne Theatre, Newcastle-upon-Tyne, 1896): 205
SLEEPING BEAUTY AND THE BEAST (Drury Lane, 1900): 221
THE SLEEPING BEAUTY; or, Harlequin and the Spiteful Fairy (Covent Garden, 1870): 114
THE SLEEPING BEAUTY IN THE WOOD; or, Harlequin and the Spiteful Fairy (Haymarket, 1857): 82
SNIP-SNAP-SNORUM; or, Harlequin Birds, Beasts, and Fishes (Grecian, 1874): 128
THE SPIDER AND THE FLY; or, King Jokose of Goforem Castle (Britannia, 1890): 186

TOM THUMB THE GREAT; or, Harlequin King Arthur and the Knights of the Round Table (Drury Lane, 1871): 119

UNDINE, THE SPIRIT OF WATER; or, Harlequin Teetotum and the Chinese Cup and Sorcerer (Marylebone, 1852): 65

VALENTINE AND ORSON; or, Harlequin and the Magic Shield (Covent Garden, 1880): 150

THE WHITE CAT (Lyceum, 1811): 17
THE WHITE CAT (Drury Lane, 1877): 136
WHITTINGTON AND HIS CAT (Theatre Royal, Bradford, 1870): 116
WHITTINGTON AND HIS CAT (Theatre, Southport, 1883): 166
WHITTINGTON AND HIS CAT; or, Harlequin King Kollywobbol (Princess's, 1861): 91
WHITTINGTON AND HIS CAT; or, Harlequin Lord Mayor of London (Drury Lane, 1835): 40
WILL O' THE WISP (Britannia, 1897), 206
THE WORLD OF WONDERS; or, Harlequin Caxton and the Origin of Printing (Victoria, 1847): 56

THE YELLOW DWARF; or, Harlequin Cupid, and the King of the Gold Mines (Covent Garden, 1869): 108

YE BELLE ALLIANCE; or, Harlequin Good Humour and Ye Field of the Cloth of Gold (Covent Garden, 1855): 79
YE SIEGE OF LEVERPOLE; or, Harlequin and Prince Rupert and Ye Fayre Mayde of Toxteth (Royal Park Theatre, Liverpool, 1852): 68

ZIG-ZAG THE CROOKED; or, Harlequin, the White Cat, the King, and the Pretty Princess (Grecian, 1871): 118

ABOUT THE AUTHOR

Julia D Atkinson was born in Bradford, West Yorkshire, in 1960. She was formerly a critic for the British Theatre Guide. Her ground-breaking article *A name not just now familiar to ears polite:* The Importance of Being Earnest *and* Lady Windermere's Fan *on tour, 1895-1900*, was published in the July 2015 issue of *The Wildean: A Journal of Oscar Wilde Studies*. She now lives in York.

From the same author in the "*Comic and Curious Clippings From the Legendary Theatrical Paper* The Era" series:

Gigantic Chickens With Fireworks In Their Mouths: 1860-1870
A Complete Somersault Into The Orchestra: 1870-1880
Please Throw Two Carrots At Your Mother: 1880-1890
Fairies In Cabs: 1890-1900
Crocodiles In The Green Room: 1900-1910

That Great Magician: Comic and Curious Shakespearean Snippets

www.ingramcontent.com/pod-product-compliance
Lightning Source LLC
Chambersburg PA
CBHW081107080526
44587CB00021B/3478